Child, Family, School, Community

Socialization and Support

Ninth Edition

Roberta M. Berns
University of California, Irvine
Saddleback College
(Emeritus)

WADSWORTH
CENGAGE Learning™

Australia • Brazil • Japan • Korea • Mexico • Singapore • Spain • United Kingdom • United States

WADSWORTH
CENGAGE Learning™

Child, Family, School, Community: Socialization and Support, Ninth Edition
Roberta M. Berns

Senior Publisher: Linda Schreiber-Ganster
Executive Editor: Mark Kerr
Development Editor: Melissa Kelleher
Assistant Editor: Genevieve Allen
Editorial Assistant: Greta Lindquist
Marketing Manager: Kara Kindstrom
Senior Marketing Communications Manager: Heather L. Baxley
Senior Media Editor: Ashley Cronin
Marketing Coordinator: Klaira Markenzon
Content Project Management: PreMediaGlobal
Creative Director: Rob Hugel
Art Director: Jennifer Wahi
Print Buyer: Rebecca Cross
Rights Acquisitions Account Manager, Text: Roberta Broyer
Rights Acquisitions Account Manager, Image: Dean Dauphinais
Production Service: PreMediaGlobal
Text Designer: PreMediaGlobal
Photo Researcher: PreMediaGlobal
Cover Designer: CMB Design Partners
Cover Image: Getty Images
Compositor: PreMediaGlobal

Library of Congress Control Number: 2011934949

ISBN-13: 978-1-111-83096-0

ISBN-10: 1-111-83096-7

Wadsworth
20 Davis Drive
Belmont, CA 94002
USA

Cengage Learning is a leading provider of customized learning solutions with office locations around the globe, including Singapore, the United Kingdom, Australia, Mexico, Brazil, and Japan. Locate your local office at: **international.cengage.com/region**

Cengage Learning products are represented in Canada by Nelson Education, Ltd.

For your course and learning solutions, visit **www.cengage.com**

Purchase any of our products at your local college store or at our preferred online store **www.cengagebrain.com**

Printed in the United States of America
1 2 3 4 5 6 7 15 14 13 12 11

Brief Contents

Contents

PART 3 What Are the Developmental Consequences of Socialization Processes?

Preface

Purpose

Child, Family, School, Community was first published in 1985. The concept for the book emerged from a consortium of early childhood education professors in California, myself included, at an annual conference of the National Association for the Education of Young Children. The consortium met to share syllabi for the course in child, family, and community relations, required by the state of California for an early childhood teacher's license. There was no textbook.

Our group continued to meet for several years at the annual conference. We shared frustrations about training teachers, about being sensitive to diversity, about developmental appropriateness, about communication with parents, about the impact of societal and technological change, and so on. We concurred that a book was sorely needed to encapsulate all the pertinent information for students. I took on the challenge and have continued to be challenged through each of nine editions.

Most influential in my organization of the material was Dr. Urie Bronfenbrenner's approach to studying human development. He was my child development and family relationships professor at Cornell University, and I had followed his work after graduation and implemented it in my teaching at the community college and the university.

Audience

Child, Family, School, Community is for anyone who deals with children—parents, teachers, and professionals in human services, home economics, public health, psychology, and social work. It is an introductory text for the combination of disciplines that most affect a child's development. It can be used for both lower- and upper-division courses, such as child and community relationships and child socialization. I have used it at the community college level as well as at the university level by varying the type and depth of assignments.

Distinguishing Features

- **New features.** Every chapter in this edition begins with a socialization sketch exemplifying socialization outcomes related to the particular chapter. An Education CourseMate with videos related to each chapter has been added. NAEYC (for early childhood teachers) and NASW (for social workers) standards with links occupy the inside front and back covers. New topics include obesity, social networking, new technologies, more on diversity, and more on bullying.
- **Comprehensive and informative.** *Child, Family, School, Community* (CFSC) integrates the contexts in which a child develops, the relationships of the people in them, and the interactions that take place within and between contexts. Depth of coverage includes relevant classic and contemporary research.
- **Practical.** Because society is changing so rapidly, a major concern of parents, professionals, and politicians is how to socialize children for an unknown future. What skills can we impart? What knowledge should we teach? What traditions

do we keep? The impact of historical events on society is discussed to help us deal with the future. In Practice boxes are provided as well as activities, related readings, and Internet resources.

- **Well organized.** CFSC begins with the bioecological theory of human development (the framework for the book) and child socialization processes (aims, agents, methods, outcomes), then discusses each socialization context in which the child develops, and concludes with child socialization outcomes.
- **Engaging and meaningful.** CFSC provides critical thinking questions, socialization sketches, examples, boxes (In Context, In Practice), figures, tables, photos, activities, and a clear, concise writing style.

Themes and Pedagogy

- **Basic premise.** Children need adults, adults need each other, and we all need a sense of community to optimally live in this world.
- **Relevancy.** I have revised this ninth edition of *Child, Family, School, Community* to update the scientific research as well as to incorporate the changes that have taken place in social, political, and educational policies.
- **Socialization Sketches.** Every chapter is introduced with a socialization sketch, a short biography of a famous icon whose background and contributions relate to the chapter's concepts.
- **Organization based on the bioecological model.** I have organized classic research as well as contemporary studies on children, families, schools, and communities according to the bioecological approach to enable students to understand the many settings and interactions influencing development. The bioecology of human development encompasses the disciplines of biology, psychology, sociology, anthropology, education, and social work as they affect the person in society.
- **Analyses and syntheses.** I have analyzed the socialization influences of the family, nonparental child care, the school, the peer group, the mass media, and the community on children's development and synthesized the processes of dynamic and reciprocal interactions of these agents with the child and with each other, contributing to socialization outcomes—values, attitudes, motives and attributions, self-esteem, self-regulation/behavior, morals, and gender roles.
- **Relating theory to practice.** Whenever one analyzes something, one takes it apart and evaluates its components. Occasionally, in the process, one loses sight of the whole. I have tried to avoid this by including chapter outlines, learning objectives, socialization sketches, open-ended questions in main sections of chapters to engage the reader, examples, boldface glossary terms, and summaries. I have also included In Context and In Practice boxes, videos, and activities in each chapter to enable students to experience the relationship between theory and practice. For further study, related readings and resources are listed.
- **Approach to diversity.** Child development/socialization research on *diverse cultural groups* is organized according to collectivistic and individualistic orientations. Research on *diverse socioeconomic groups* is organized according to the social selection perspective (biological traits influence parental achievement, thereby affecting children's opportunities) and the social causation perspective (contextual influences, family stress or family resources, affect parenting styles and consequent child outcomes). Research on *diverse families* (single, remarried, joint custody, same-sex, biracial, grandparent or kin custody) is discussed in terms of socialization effects on the child.

Ancillaries

- **Instructor's Manual.** An online Instructor's Manual accompanies this book. The manual contains information to assist the instructor in designing the course, including learning objectives, chapter outlines, sample assignments, and additional online resources.
- **TestBank with ExamView.** For assessment support, the updated test bank includes true/false, multiple-choice, matching, short answer, and essay questions for each chapter. Available for download from the instructor website, ExamView® testing software includes the Test Bank in electronic format, enabling you to create customized tests in print or online.
- **Presentation slides.** Preassembled Microsoft® PowerPoint® lecture slides for each chapter cover content from the book.
- **Education CourseMate.** Education CourseMate brings course concepts to life with interactive learning, study, and exam preparation tools that support the printed textbook. CourseMate includes an integrated eBook, quizzes, flashcards, videos, related links, and other resources, and Engagement-Tracker, a first-of-its-kind tool that monitors student engagement in the course. The accompanying instructor website offers access to password-protected resources such as an electronic version of the Instructor's Manual, test bank, and PowerPoint® slides. Students can register an access code or purchase access at CengageBrain.com. Instructors, visit login.cengage.com to create an account or log in.
- **WebTutor on Blackboard and WebCT.** Jump-start your course with customizable, rich, text-specific content within your Course Management System. Whether you want to web-enable your class or put an entire course online, WebTutor™ delivers. WebTutor™ offers a wide array of resources including access to the eBook, videos, quizzes, web links, exercises, and more.

Supportive Socialization Influences

The seeds for this book were sown more than 50 years ago. I was a freshman in the College of Human Ecology at Cornell University, taking a child development course taught by Dr. Urie Bronfenbrenner. Dr. Bronfenbrenner, who died in 2005, was a distinguished professor of psychology, human development, and family studies. His bioecological theory of human development has stimulated much new research on children and families in various settings as well as advocacy of government, business, and educational policies to support families.

Dr. Bronfenbrenner's enthusiasm for children and families, his dynamic lecture style, and his probing questions regarding the current state of human development research, as well as public policy, provided me with an analytic perspective to examine whatever else I read or heard thereafter.

The seeds for this book could not have flowered had it not been for the care their host (the author) received in her growth and development. My family, my teachers, my friends, the neighborhood in which I grew, and my experiences growing up all contributed to this book. Even after I reached adulthood, the seeds for this book are still being nurtured along by others—my husband (Michael), my children (Gregory, my son, and his wife, Kathleen, and Tamara, my daughter), my grandchildren (Helen and Madeline), my friends, my neighbors, my students, and my colleagues.

As flowers grow, to maintain their shape and stimulate new growth they must be pruned and fertilized. I would like to thank my reviewers of all editions and my editors for their valuable input in this process. Specific thanks to the reviewers of this edition: Tamara Karn, Mount San Antonio College; Laurel Anderson, Palomar College; Rachel Bernal, San Jacinto College; Scott Bounds, Houston ISD; Jennifer Briffa, Merritt College; Belinda Hammond, Cuesta College; Donna Kirkwood, University of Houston Clearlake; Amy Strimling, Sacramento City College.

For the fruit of the harvest, this ninth edition, I would like to thank my Developmental Editors, Lisa Mafrici and Melissa Kelleher, for plowing this version with me. Also many thanks to the rest of the book team: Mark Kerr, Executive Editor, Greta Lindquist, Editorial Assistant, Genevieve Allen, Assistant Editor, Ashley Cronin, Senior Media Editor and Lindsay Bethoney, Project Manager.

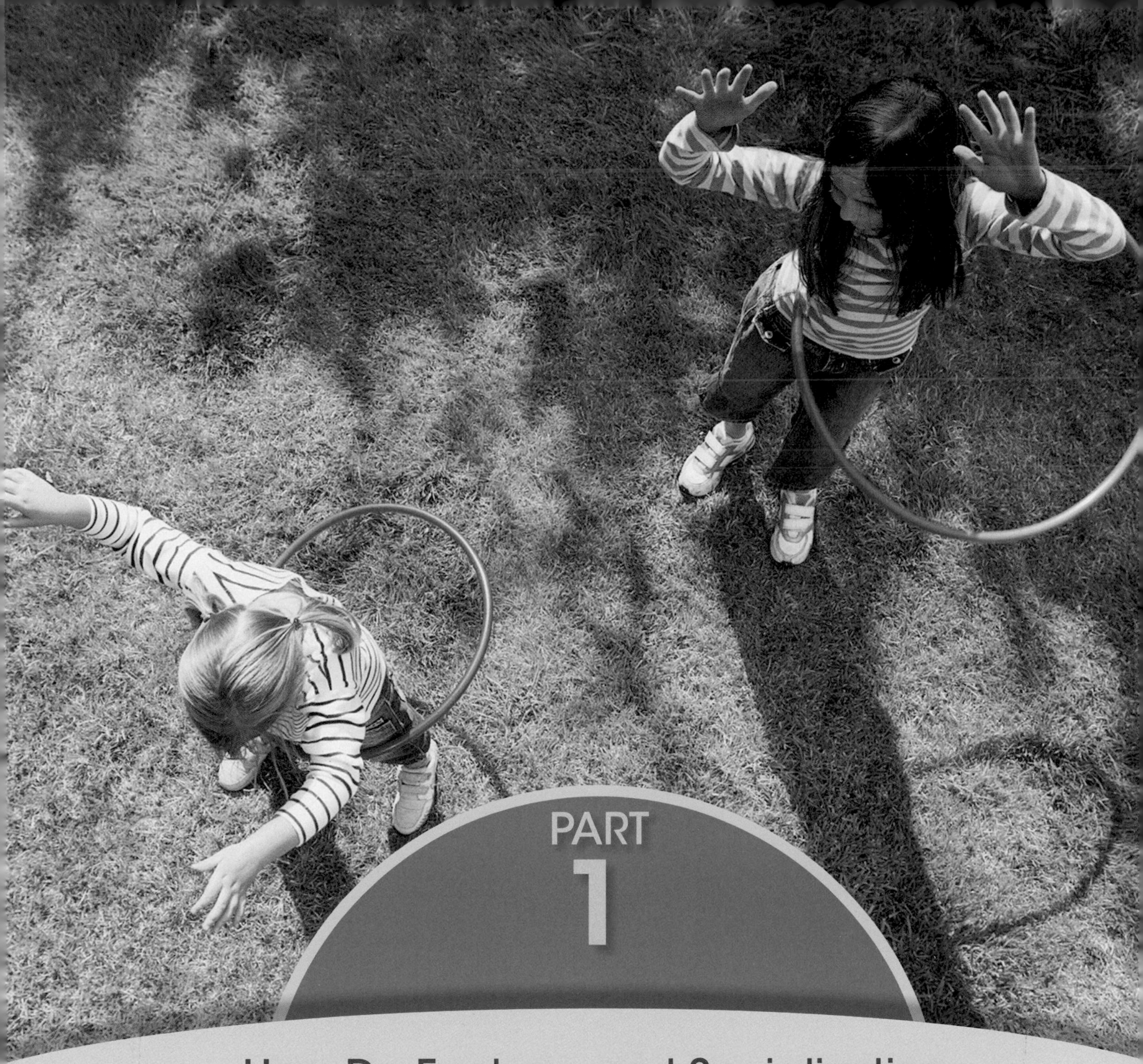

PART 1

How Do Ecology and Socialization Impact Child Development?

Fogstock LLC/Index Stock Imagery/PhotoLibrary

1

Ecology of the Child

The more things change, the more they remain the same.

ALPHONSE KARR

AP Photo/Dima Gavrysh, file

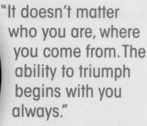

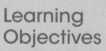

Learning Objectives

After completing this chapter, you will be able to:

1. Define ecology and discuss how it relates to child development.
2. Define socialization and explain how it relates to child development.
3. Describe and illustrate how society's concept of childhood has changed from the Renaissance to the present day.
4. Define a theory and explain the uniqueness of the bioecological theory.
5. Describe how socialization occurs in a bioecological context.
6. Explain how the microsystem, mesosystem, exosystem, and macrosystem interact over time (the chronosystem).
7. Discuss contemporary ecology, naming societal trends affecting children.

SOCIALIZATION SKETCHES

Oprah Winfrey

(b. 1954)

"It doesn't matter who you are, where you come from. The ability to triumph begins with you always."

— OPRAH WINFREY

Oprah's philosophy of socialization is encapsulated in this quote. The Socialization Sketch that follows describes some significant influences on her life.

Family

Oprah Gail Winfrey was born in 1954 on the family farm in Kosciusko, Mississippi. Her father, Vernon Winfrey, who was stationed as a soldier at a local army base, and her mother, Vernita Lee, were both young at the time of Oprah's birth. Her parents never married. Shortly after she was born, her mother moved to Milwaukee, Wisconsin, where she found a job as a housemaid and Oprah was left in the care of her grandmother, Hattie Mae Lee.

As a child, Oprah relied on her imagination to play. On the farm, her only friends were the animals, so she gave them parts in the plays she made and included them in games. On Sundays she and her grandmother would go to church. It was in church that Oprah gave her first recital—she was 3 years old and already knew how to read. She read verses and poems aloud to the congregation. By age 4, she was known around town as "the little speaker." Such early experiences gave her an advantage when she entered school.

When Oprah entered kindergarten, she knew how to write, as well as read. On the first day of school, she wrote, "Dear Miss New, I do not think I belong her [*sic*]." She was moved to the first grade and by the end of the year, she was skipped to the third grade.

At age 6, Oprah was sent to live with her mother and half sister in Milwaukee. They lived in one room of another woman's house. Her mother worked long hours, leaving Oprah with her cousins and neighbors. It was her job to entertain her little sister.

When Oprah was 9, a 19-year-old cousin, who was babysitting, raped her. He swore her to secrecy. During the time she lived in Milwaukee, Oprah was sexually abused by her mother's live-in boyfriend and a once-favorite uncle. She never told anyone, but became rebellious. At age 14, she gave birth to a son, who died in infancy. Unable to handle her, Oprah's mother sent her to live with her father and his wife in Nashville. This proved to be a significant influence on her motivation to achieve.

Vernon Winfrey was a strict disciplinarian. Oprah was given new clothes, a set of rules, a 12:00 curfew, and some tasks. She also had to read and do a book report each week for her father, as well as memorize five new words each day. If she hadn't done her tasks, she would not be given any food. Oprah said, "As strict as he was, he had some concerns about me making the best of my life, and would not accept anything less than what he thought was best" (www.biography.com).

School

Also influential on Oprah's study habits, as well as self-esteem, was her fourth-grade teacher and mentor, Mrs. Duncan. Mrs. Duncan helped her to not be afraid of being smart. She encouraged Oprah to read and often let her stay after school to help grade papers while discussing book choices. Oprah said, "A mentor is someone who allows you to see the higher part of yourself when sometimes it becomes hidden from your own view" (WCVB-TV interview, January 13, 2002).

Oprah attended Nashville East High School where she was well liked by the students and teachers. She took public speaking and drama classes, landing a job in radio while still in high school. This prepared her for a career path in communications.

Oprah's last year in high school was most influential. She had been elected president of the student body and, as such, got to attend The White House Conference of Youth, meeting President Richard Nixon and school representatives from all over the country. That same year, Oprah entered a public speaking contest with a scholarship to Tennessee State University as the grand prize. She won the scholarship and began taking courses toward a degree in Speech Communications and Performing Arts. She continued her work at the radio station, studying at night.

Media

Oprah was chosen to co-anchor the local evening news at the age of 19. Her emotional ad-lib delivery eventually got her transferred to the daytime television talk show venue. After boosting a third-rated local Chicago talk show to first place, the format was expanded and in 1985, was renamed *The Oprah Winfrey Show.* Seen nationally since 1986, *The Oprah Winfrey Show* became the number one talk show. The show emphasized spiritual values, healthy living, and self-help. She also interviewed top names in the entertainment industry. The show received numerous awards and she, herself, received the "Broadcaster of the Year" Award, becoming the youngest person and only the fifth woman ever to receive the honor, bestowed by the International Radio and Television Society.

Community

Motivated by her own memories of being abused as a child, Oprah initiated a campaign to establish a national database of convicted child abusers. She testified before the Senate Judiciary Committee on behalf of the National Child Protection Act. President Clinton signed the "Oprah Bill" into law in1993, establishing a national database available to law enforcement agencies and concerned parties.

Oprah Winfrey was named one of the 100 most influential people of the 20th century by *Time* magazine. Her influence extends from television to the publishing industry through her book club. She is also a benefactor. Her Angel Network gives a $100,000 "Use Your Life Award" to people who are using their lives to improve the lives of others. And finally, she has founded a school for girls in South Africa to build leadership skills, giving back to the community what she gained from the schools and teachers in her life.

- What events or people in your past and present have influenced your ability to thrive?
- What are some things you might do to contribute to the community based on your own experiences and interests?

How does growing up in a changing world affect how children are socialized?

Ecology, Change, and Children

The concept of **ecology** (the science of interrelationships between organisms and their environments) traditionally describes plant or animal environments, but it can be applied to humans. Human ecology involves the biological, psychological, social, and cultural contexts in which a developing person interacts and the consequent processes (for example, perception, learning, behavior) that develop over time (Bronfenbrenner & Morris, 2006).

ecology the science of interrelationships between organisms and their environments

adaptation the modification of an organism or its behavior to make it more fit for existence under the conditions of its environment

demographics statistical characteristics of human populations, such as age, income, and race

economics the production, distribution, and consumption of goods and services

The concept of **adaptation** is the modification of an organism or its behavior to make it more fit for existence under the conditions of the environment. As humans develop, they must continually adapt to change, on a personal, social, and societal level. For example, such forces as **demographics** (statistical characteristics of human populations, such as age, income, and race), **economics** (the production, distribution, and consumption of goods and services), politics, and technology present challenges to human adaptation. The purpose of this book is to examine how growing up in a changing world affects the development of children through socialization. Children are socialized and supported by their families, schools, and communities, in that these significant agents accept responsibility for ensuring children's well-being. These socializing agents nurture children's development, enabling them to become contributing adults.

Kids Today: Are They . . .

media junkies?	bombarded by commercialism?
computer savvy?	virtual-world visitors?
social networkers?	over-scheduled?
coupled to their cell phones?	reward-reliant?
frightened by disaster and violence?	self-absorbed?
confused by choices?	inundated with information?
driven to distraction?	distressed?
seduced by celebrities?	competition-driven?

What is socialization?

Socialization and Child Development

Socialization is the process by which individuals acquire the knowledge, skills, and character traits that enable them to participate as effective members of groups and society (Brim, 1966; Maccoby, 2007).

socialization the process by which individuals acquire the knowledge, skills, and character traits that enable them to participate as effective members of groups and society

- Socialization is what every parent does: "Help your brother button his jacket." "We use tissues, not our sleeves, to wipe our noses."
- Socialization is what every teacher does: "Study your spelling words tonight." "In our country we have the freedom to worship as we choose."
- Socialization is what every religion does: "Honor your father and mother." "Do not steal."
- Socialization is what every culture does via its language, customs, and beliefs.
- Socialization is what every employer does: "Part of your job is to open the store at 8:00 and put the merchandise on the tables." "Your request must be in writing."
- Socialization is what every government does through its laws and system of punishment for violations.
- Socialization is what friends do when they accept or reject you on the basis of whether or not you conform to their values.
- Socialization is what the media do by providing role models of behavior and solutions to common problems.

The concept of socialization, including parenting or child rearing, social development, and education, really goes back in time as far as human life: "Train up a child in the way he should go, and when he is old, he will not depart from it" (Proverbs 22:6). As we shall see, many forces in society contribute to children's development—as do the children themselves. Socialization takes place in the family, school, peer group, and community, as well as via the media. While socialization enables a person to participate in social groups and society, it also enables the very existence of a society and its consequent social order. According to Handel, Cahill, and Elkin (2007, p. 84), socialization occurs:

- over time,
- through interaction with significant others,
- by means of communication,
- in emotionally significant contexts,
- and leads to certain outcomes that are shaped by various social groups.

Socialization as a Unique Human Process

What makes socialization unique to humans?

Most social scientists agree that socialization is unique to human beings. More than 75 years ago George Mead (1934), a social interaction theorist, wrote that it is language that sharply separates humans from other animals. Mead goes on to say that language makes ideas and communication of these ideas possible, and language also makes it possible to replace action with thoughts and then use thoughts to transform behavior. A little boy who breaks his mother's favorite vase and encounters her anger understands her threat the next day when she says, "If you don't hold your glass with both hands, it might fall and break, and then I will be very angry." The child now well understands what *break* and *angry* mean.

Language enables humans to develop the ability to reason and a characteristic pattern of behavior. It is reason and behavior that enable us to internalize the attitudes of others. (*Internalization* is the process by which externally controlled behavior shifts to internally, or self-regulated, behavior.) Children internalize the attitudes of their parents in the form of role-taking. They incorporate parental and significant adult expectations into their behavior, thereby becoming socialized as a "generalized other." They, in turn, have similar expectations of others with whom they interact. These expectations for people to behave appropriately form the foundation for a society.

IN CONTEXT Four-year-old Abby's thought one day was to try out Mom's makeup. In the process, the eye shadow got on her fingers, and she wiped it on her shorts. She then sat down on Mom's bed to look in the mirror, leaving a smudge of blue shadow where her bottom touched. She soon got bored with this activity, wiped her moist, red mouth on Mom's yellow towel, and went outside to play. Fifteen minutes later, tears were streaming down Abby's cheeks, indicating her feeling of remorse for her behavior. Mom pointed to the trail of evidence while scolding her for taking other people's things without permission (not to mention the mess that had to be cleaned).

Abby's thoughts led to behavior that caused her mother to vehemently express her feelings regarding taking other people's things without permission. Her mother's communication of values such as this to Abby will lead to Abby's internalization of self-control. If other children, too, learn to internalize behavioral control (for example, respect each other's property), then a human society is possible.

Socialization as a Reciprocal Dynamic Process

How does the child influence his or her developmental outcomes?

Socialization begins at birth and continues throughout life. It is a *reciprocal* process in that when one individual interacts with another, a response in one usually elicits a response in the other. It is also a *dynamic* process in that interactions change over time, with individuals becoming producers of responses as well as products of them

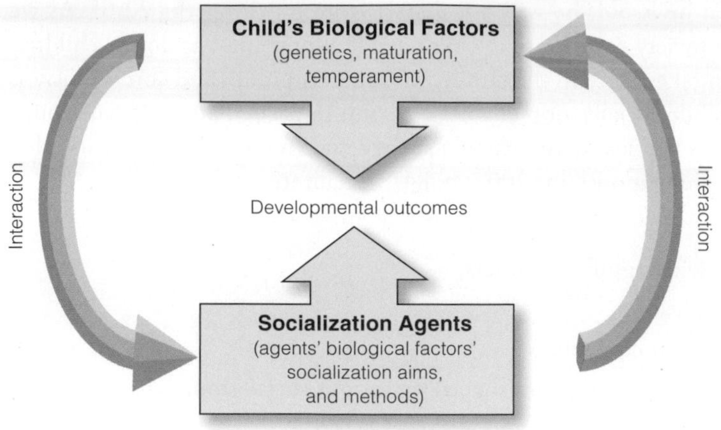

FIGURE 1.1 **How Children Affect Their Own Developmental Outcomes**

(Maccoby, 2007). These reciprocal dynamic processes become more complex throughout development (see Figure 1.1).

Maturation

maturation developmental changes associated with the biological process of aging

Maturation refers to developmental changes associated with the biological process of aging. Newborn humans come into the world with inherited characteristics and with certain needs and abilities that change as they mature. They are given names, which indicate that they are members of society. They are clothed in the manner appropriate to the society into which they are born. In the United States they are diapered, dressed in stretch suits, and kept in cribs. In certain African societies they are swaddled and put on their mothers' backs. The way their parents respond to their cries and their needs, the way their parents communicate expectations, the people with whom their parents allow them to spend time (babysitter, relatives, and so on) all contribute to infants' socialization and consequent development.

As children mature, their needs and abilities elicit changes in parental expectations for behavior. Toddlers may need adult assistance when eating; preschoolers can eat independently using some utensils; school-agers are capable of taking some responsibility in meal preparation (such as making sandwiches, using a microwave, or cleaning utensils).

Throughout development, children play a role in their own socialization. As most parents will tell you, children sometimes instigate how others treat them. You know that if you smile, you are more likely to get a smile back than if you frown. The way you socialize children is often influenced by their reaction to you. For example, I needed only to look sternly at my son or speak in an assertive tone, and he would comply with what was asked of him. My daughter, however, would need to experience consequences (usually several times)—being sent to her room, withdrawal of privileges, having to do extra chores—before she would comply with family rules. Even in college, she had to get numerous parking tickets before she realized paying for them was more painful than getting up earlier to find even a distant parking space from her class and walking. Thus, not only do children actively contribute to interactions, but in so doing, they affect their own developmental outcomes, transforming themselves in the process (my daughter had to work to pay off her tickets) and influencing how others reciprocate (I nagged) (Bugental & Grusec, 2006).

Genes

genotype the total composite of hereditary instructions coded in the genes at the moment of conception

Biology plays a role in the child's contribution to his or her developmental outcomes, beginning with the child's **genotype**, the total composite of hereditary instructions coded in the genes at the moment of conception. According to Plomin and Asbury (2002) as well as Scarr and McCartney (1983), parents not only pass on genes to children but also provide environments, or contexts for development (see Figure 1.2). In other words, there is a correlation between the influence of one's genotype and one's environment on developmental outcomes (Rutter, 2006). Because children inherit genes from their parents, children are "prewired" or predisposed to be affected by the environments their parents provide. This type of genotype–environment interaction is referred to as *passive*. For example, a child born to intelligent parents will, most likely, possess the genes involved in intelligence. The parents, because of their genotypes and their developmental experience, will likely provide intellectually stimulating things and activities in the home. The child's "prewiring" will enable him or her to benefit from such stimulation. As an example, my sister-in-law was raised by her father, an accomplished musician. She tinkered at the piano as soon as she could reach the keys. As a child, she learned to play several musical instruments. Today, she is a music teacher and directs a community band.

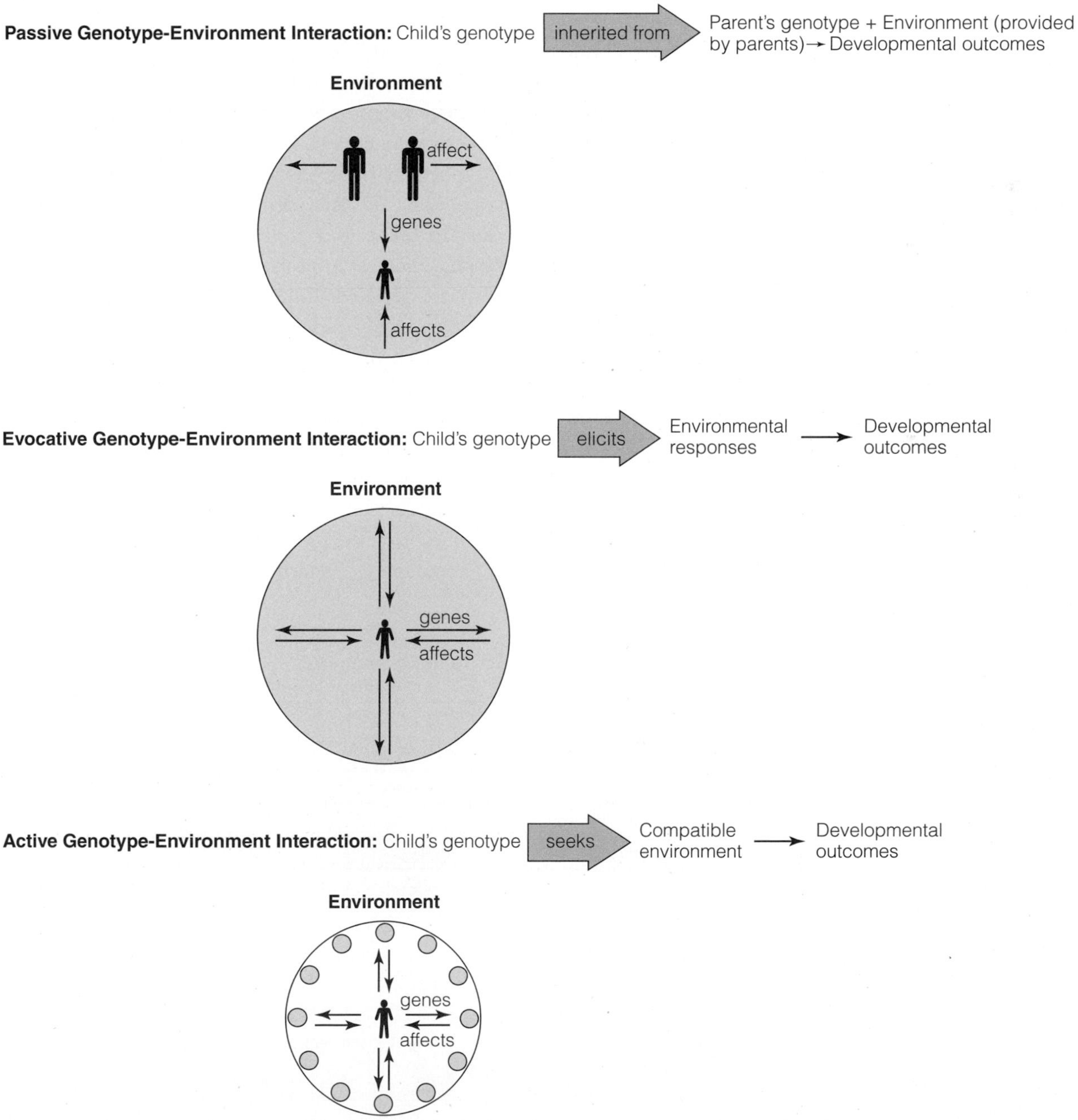

FIGURE 1.2 **Genotype–Environment Interactions**

Another type of genotype–environment interaction is *evocative*, meaning an individual's genotype will tend to evoke, or elicit, certain responses from the environments in which they interact. For example, a happy, sociable child is more likely to engage others in social activities than is a moody, shy child. Consequently, the happy child tends to experience more warm, responsive environments growing up.

Still another type of genotype–environment interaction is *active*, meaning an individual's genotype will tend to motivate that person to seek out environments most compatible with his or her genetic "prewiring." For example, a shy child might prefer solitary activities to group ones, consequently influencing the path of that child's development. My yoga teacher describes herself as an introspective person. As a child she grew up in a beach community in Southern California. Rather than join the extroverted beach culture, she preferred to daydream, making castles in the sand. Her high school activities were dance and gymnastics. Having those skills, she tried the cheerleading squad, but did not feel comfortable in the "rah-rah" role, so years later chose yoga.

Temperament

temperament the innate characteristics that determine an individual's sensitivity to various experiences and responsiveness to patterns of social interaction

Another aspect of one's biological makeup, in addition to genes, is **temperament**—the innate characteristics that determine an individual's sensitivity to various experiences and responsiveness to social interaction. Research supports what parents have known for centuries: Babies are born with different temperaments (Chess & Thomas, 1996; Kagan, 1994; Thomas, Chess, & Birch, 1970; Wachs & Bates, 2001). That is, they respond differently physiologically to various experiences. This is evident soon after birth in the individual differences in activity level, distractibility, adaptability to new situations, mood, and so on (see Figure 1.3). Children's physiological responses fall into three broad temperamental categories: "easy," "slow-to-warm-up," and "difficult."

TeachSource Video Activity

Go to the Education CourseMate website to access the video entitled "0–2 Years: Temperament in Infants and Toddlers" and think about how each of the three types of temperament seen in the video might be exhibited in the behavior of preschoolers, school-agers, and adolescents.

How caregivers respond to their children's temperaments influences the socialization process. If there is a "goodness of fit" between the child's temperament and his or her caregivers, then socialization is likely to proceed smoothly (Chess & Thomas, 1996). For example, if the child does not adapt easily to new situations (is a "slow-to-warm-up" child), and the caregivers understand this and are patient (not pushing the child, yet encouraging him or her to get used to new things slowly), then socialization is likely to be smooth. In a longitudinal (long-term) study on the socialization of conscience, or internal monitor, Kochanska (1995, 1997) found that the use of gentle parenting techniques such as persuasion ("Why don't you ___ because ___"), rather than harsh power assertion

Temperamental Quality	Easy Child	Slow-to-Warm-Up Child	Difficult Child
Rhythmicity	Very regular	Varies	Irregular
Approach/withdrawal	Positive approach	Initial withdrawal	Withdrawal
Adaptability	Very adaptable	Slowly adaptable	Slowly adaptable
Intensity of reaction	Low or mild	Mild	Intense
Quality of mood	Positive	Slightly negative	Negative

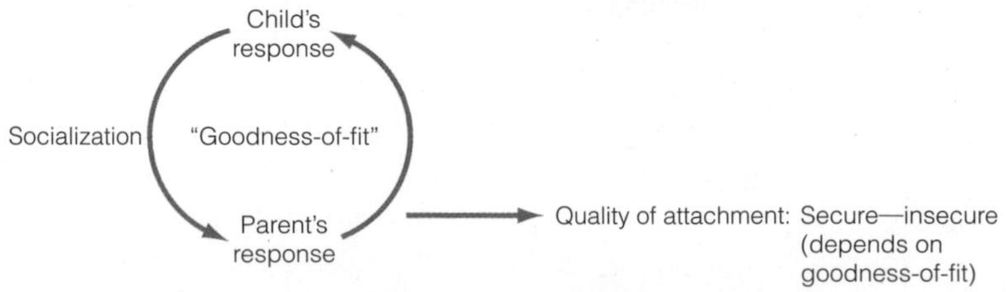

FIGURE 1.3 Temperament and Socialization
Source: Based on Chess & Thomas, 1996.

("Do ___ or else ___"), was more effective in getting timid children to comply, whereas assertive children responded better to harsh power assertion.

If, on the other hand, the fit between the child's temperament and the caregivers' is poor, socialization is likely to be rough. For example, if the child is very active, responds intensely to people and things, and is moody (a "difficult" child), and the caregivers force him or her to sit still, punish him or her for crying or being frightened, and demand a smile much of the time, then socialization may become a battleground of wills. A longitudinal study of more than 1,000 twins and their families showed that genetically influenced antisocial behavior (difficult temperament) was a significant provoker of parental use of harsh discipline (Jaffee et al., 2004). The impact of temperament on parenting styles is discussed in more detail in Chapter 4.

As infants become children, adolescents, and then adults, they interact with more people and have more experiences. In so doing, they acquire skills, knowledge, attitudes, values, motives, habits, beliefs, interests, morals, and ideals. You may learn to read from your first-grade teacher. You may learn to appreciate music from an uncle who takes you to concerts. You may learn about sportsmanship from your coach and about love from the girl or boy down the street.

Thus, from the point of view of society, individuals are socialized to fit into an organized way of life (a *social identity*). And from a personal point of view, socialization enables them to discover themselves—their potentialities for personal growth and fulfillment (a *personal identity*). The environment (including various genotype–environment interactions, discussed earlier) also plays its part in the socialization process. The environment is what the child experiences—the setting, the roles, and the interactions. For example, a child growing up in a large family on a farm has different socialization experiences than does a child growing up in a single-parent family in the city. Over time, children choose and are exposed to many different environments that affect their development (Bronfenbrenner & Morris, 2006). By going to school, children not only gain knowledge; they also find out in what subjects they do best. As members of a peer group, they not only learn to cooperate; they find out whether they are leaders or followers. One child may discover that he or she likes art, another likes dance, still another prefers sports. As these children are enabled to pursue their interests and their abilities are encouraged, they have different socialization experiences.

How does the parent influence the child's developmental outcomes?

Based on earlier studies of socialization processes (Bugental & Grusec, 2006; A. P. Fiske, 1992), Grusec and Davidov (2010) have proposed an integrative framework to examine how parents socialize children. They view socialization as a domain-specific process in that different child situations elicit different parental interactions and require different socialization methods. Developmental outcomes vary according to the domain: Does the child need *protection*? Does the child desire *reciprocity* (play or communication) from the parent? Does the child's behavior warrant adult *control* (guidance or discipline)? Do the child's actions require *guided learning* by an adult? Does the child need to identify with a social group and engage in *group participation*? (See Table 1.1.)

Intentional and Unintentional Socialization

Is all socialization deliberate?

Much socialization is intentional, done on purpose. When an adult tells a 6-year-old to share a toy with a 4-year-old sibling, that is intentional socialization. Or when an adult reminds a 10-year-old to write a thank-you note to Grandma, that too is intentional socialization. Thus, when adults have certain values that they consistently convey explicitly to the child, and when they back these up with approval for compliance and negative consequences for noncompliance, it is referred to as *intentional socialization*.

Much of socialization, however, takes place spontaneously during human interaction, without the deliberate intent to impart knowledge or values. *Unintentional socialization* may be the product of involvement in human interaction or observation of interaction. For example, a 4-year-old approaches two teachers conversing and excitedly says, "Miss

Table 1.1 Domains of Socialization Between Parent and Child

Domain	Nature of Parent–Child Relationship	Required Parental Behavior	Mechanism of Socialization
Protection	Provider–recipient	Alleviate child's distress	Confidence in protection
Reciprocity	Exchange/equality tendency	Comply with child's reasonable requests and influence attempts	Innate to reciprocate
Control	Hierarchal	Use discipline method best suited for achieving parental goal	Acquired self-control
Guided learning	Teacher–student	Match teaching to child's changing level of understanding	Internalization of language and approach used by teacher
Group participation	Joint members of same social group	Enable child to observe and take part in appropriate cultural practices	Firm sense of social identity

Source: Grusec, J. E., & Davidov, M. (2010). Integrating different perspectives on socialization theory and research: A domain-specific approach. *Child Development, 81*(3), p. 694.

Jones, Miss Jones, look!" One teacher says, "Sally, don't interrupt; we're talking." Later that morning Sally and her friend Tanya are busily playing with Legos. Sally is explaining and demonstrating to Tanya how to fit the pieces together. Miss Jones comes over to the block corner and interrupts with, "Girls, please stop what you're doing and come see what Rene has brought to school." It is very likely that the message Sally received from the morning's interactions was that it is not OK for children to interrupt adults, but it is OK for adults to interrupt children.

Sometimes, a socialization goal can be intentional on the part of the parents, but have both intentional and unintentional outcomes on the child. For example, toilet training is usually purposeful and deliberate in Western cultures. Behavior-learning techniques for using the potty involve conditioning children to associate the urge to urinate or defecate with using the potty; reinforcement (praise and juice) is used for effort and success. The problem is that not all children respond as intended, and sometimes the outcome of being "toilet-trained" is short-term because of other events in the child's life. For example, if a new baby enters the family, the toilet-trained child, who has gotten much attention for his or her achievement, may perceive the new baby as getting attention for wetting its diaper. The toilet-trained child may then regress to wetting his or her pants in order to regain attention.

In sum, children take cues, emote, and learn from others' behavior as well as from their verbal statements. This information is all processed (constructed, interpreted, transformed, and recorded) in the brain to influence future behavior and feelings.

How do you socialize children to be prepared for the future?

Socialization, Change, and Challenge

Children are socialized by many people in society—parents, siblings, grandparents, aunts, uncles, cousins, friends, teachers, coaches, religious leaders, and role models in the media. These agents of socialization use many techniques, which will be discussed, to influence children to behave, think, and feel according to what is considered worthy.

Socialization is a very complex process indeed. The more technological and diverse the society, the more children have to learn in order to adapt effectively, the more socializing agents and experiences contribute to the process, and the more time the socialization process takes. As society changes, more and more challenges are posed to the socializing agents because there are more choices to be made. How should the period of childhood be adjusted to accommodate all the opportunities that exist?

When societal change occurs as, for example, rapid technological and scientific advances that result in economic fluctuations, socializing agents are affected. Adults are affected *directly* by the uncertainty that change produces, as well as by the new opportunities and challenges it may present. Economic fluctuations can affect job security and can have a major negative impact on family finances. Family members may have to work longer hours; purchasing power may decrease; the family may have to move. However, sometimes such stresses uncover positive strengths in the family members—for example, spousal emotional support and children's cooperation in assuming more responsibilities for household chores. How adults adapt to societal change *indirectly* affects children. For example, two parents in the workforce usually require child care, and family time becomes the "second shift" (Hochschild, 1989, 1997). Parents learn to adapt by performing several tasks simultaneously. New technology helps (talking on a speakerphone while folding clothes), but the efficiency gained in doing multitasks may contribute to diminished attentiveness to family members.

A parent motivating a child's interest in a sport.

Chrisjo/Big Stock Photo

One result of societal change is seen in the goals of child rearing and education. Many psychologists (Elkind, 1994, 2001) see today's parents as being very concerned with developing their children's intellectual abilities. This concern is evidenced by the growth of preschools and kindergartens with academic programs; the development of infant stimulation programs such as "Mommy and Me" classes; the availability of "how-to" books on teaching your baby to read, do math, and be brighter; the proliferation of computer software for children; and the array of after-school activities. The concern is also evidenced by the pressure on elementary, middle, and high schools to produce competent learners. The No Child Left Behind Act (NCLBA) of 2004 mandates performance standards (achievement levels for each grade), accountability (assessments to measure achievement), and flexibility (tailoring assessments for students with disabilities and children with limited English-speaking proficiency). Opposing the NCLBA are educators who believe curricula should be individualized according to the child's developmental level rather than to government-mandated performance standards. A **developmentally appropriate** curriculum involves understanding children's normal growth patterns and individual differences. It also involves exposing children to active, hands-on, age-appropriate, meaningful experiences. Developmental appropriateness is discussed in more detail in Chapter 4.

developmentally appropriate a curriculum that involves understanding children's normal growth patterns and individual differences

As a consequence of this family and school concern with nourishing the intellect, children are under pressure to become "intellectually independent" and "intellectually successful" at an early age. This is measured by test scores, performance in various activities such as athletics and music, and being accepted by certain prestigious schools (even preschools!). Elkind (2001) cited an example of this push for having superkids. A mother complained to her son's first-grade teacher, "How is he going to get into M.I.T. if you only give him a 'satisfactory'?" Elkind believes such a push for excellence is causing an increase in stress symptoms in children.

IN CONTEXT

Carol's parents were very proud of their daughter. Considered a "gifted" student, she did very well in school while juggling a full schedule that included ice skating, gymnastics, and piano lessons. At age 10, Carol won her elementary school's outstanding student award, placed first in an ice-skating competition, and gave a solo piano recital. At age 13, she was selected as a candidate for admission to a prestigious private girls' high school. Two days before the scheduled entrance exam, Carol took an overdose of sleeping pills.

Why did Carol choose suicide? Other adolescents face varying degrees of pressure and stress, yet develop coping strategies. Was it her family situation? Friends? School? Community? Or a combination of these complex relationships?

Children working in factories was a common sight prior to child labor laws prohibiting such practices.

Lewis Wickes Hine/Bettmann/Corbis

That children are pressured to know more than their parents is really not a new phenomenon; it is part of evolution or societal change. As new knowledge is discovered, it is the children who learn it in school. For example, children in many schools use computers for learning tasks. There is likely to be tension in the parent–child relationship when children can figure things out more efficiently with computers than their parents can with traditional paper-and-pencil methods. As another example, children of immigrants learn to be Americanized in school, whereas their parents may cling to the traditional attitudes and behavior patterns learned in their countries of origin. Thus, societal change can produce family tensions; it can also produce challenges. To reduce tension in the parent–child relationship resulting from an imbalance of knowledge, parents can be challenged to become knowledgeable in the very activities their children are pursuing. For example, parents can share activities; they can provide the opportunity for children to teach them; they can read books, talk to experts, and request adult education courses (for example, on how to use a computer); they can volunteer to help in the classroom in order to learn along with their children. There needs to be a distinction between encouraging and motivating children to succeed and pressuring them with inappropriate expectations. Schools can also be challenged to involve parents more in their children's learning. Parent involvement in school will be discussed in Chapter 6.

What is "childhood"? Is it static or dynamic? How is it different from adulthood?

Change and the Concept of Childhood

One of the challenges brought on by change is the society's concept of childhood. We assume childhood to be a special period of time when we are cared for, taught, and protected because we are not mature enough to do these things for ourselves. Does the period of childhood change—lengthen or shorten—when society changes? Based on studying the artwork of various periods, historian Philippe Aries (1962) concluded that the concept of childhood did change throughout the centuries in that the treatment of children by parents and society improved considerably. In contrast, based on studying 400 diaries and journals from 1500 to 1900, psychologist Linda Pollock (1984) concluded that the concept of childhood, particularly parent–child relations, had not changed very much in that parents had emotional ties with their children and socialized them to adapt to the ways of society during each century. History professor, Steven Mintz (2006), agrees that in that throughout American history, adults have defined how children experienced childhood. However, in the last part of this century, adolescence became a protracted concept and youth began to define its own culture (language, dress, music, and so on). (See Table 1.2.)

Table 1.2 A Brief View of Childhood through History

Time Period	Significant Event	Child Treatment
14th–16th century	Renaissance	Children treated as miniature adults, harsh treatment, expected to work, included in all adult activities (partying, same punishment for crimes)
16th–18th century	Printing press invented	Children treated as uninformed adults, therefore schools were created to teach them
18th–20th century	Industrial Revolution	Children need to be prepared for adulthood in a complex society, compulsory education laws, recognition of children's rights, passage of labor laws
20th–21st century	Information Age	Children viewed as consumers, pressured to compete, to achieve, to be independent and self-reliant

Source: Based on Aries, 1962; Heywood, 2001; Mintz, 2006.

There is a general concern among child development specialists and educators about the loss of childhood (freedom from responsibility). Children today must cope with a world in which both parents work, drugs are readily available, sex is as close as the TV or Internet, and violence is just around the corner (Children's Defense Fund, 2010; Elkind, 1994, 2001). In sum, the age of protection for children has been undermined by societal pressures on parents. What can we do to cope with these consequences of change? Can we meet the challenge?

Socialization and Adaptation

How can socialization help children adapt to change?

Socialization is elaborate; it involves many variable and reciprocal experiences, interactions, and environments that affect children's development. Analyzing some of the variables involved in the socialization process can help people adapt to change. For instance, understanding how the "input"—socialization interactions in various settings and situations—affects the "output" of socialization—values, attitudes, motives and attributions, self-esteem, self-regulation of behavior, morals, and gender roles—may enable us to manipulate that input to induce the desired output (see Table 1.3).

- A simplified example of this kind of manipulation is described in a classic book, *Walden Two*, by B. F. Skinner (1948). *Walden Two* is a utopian community founded on behavioral principles. To learn self-control, young children (age 3 to 4) are given lollipops dipped in sugar at the beginning of the day, to be eaten later, provided that they have not been licked (reinforcement). There are practice sessions in which the children are urged (instruction) to examine their own behavior in the following situations: when the lollipops are concealed, when the children are distracted from thinking about the candy by playing a game, and when the lollipops are in sight. Thus, when the children are given the lollipops again for a real exercise in self-control (learn-by-doing), they have at their disposal some adaptive behaviors to use (put them out of sight or keep busy) to help them avoid the temptation.
- Another example of how input can be used to affect output is Sherif's (1956) classic Robber's Cave experiment, in which manipulation of the environment was used first to bring about antisocial behavior (hostility) via competitive strategies between two groups of young boys, and then to reverse that pattern via cooperative strategies. How was this done? To produce friction, competitive tournaments were held—baseball, tug-of-war, touch football, and so on. Frustration led to name-calling, raids, and aggressive behavior. To eliminate this friction, the counselors rigged a series of crises that forced all the boys to work together in order to solve the problem. Once, the water line was deliberately broken; another time, the camp truck broke down just as it was going to town for food. Thus antisocial behavior gave way to prosocial behavior when a compelling goal for all concerned had to be achieved. (Does this make you think of the television show *Survivor*?) Anti- and prosocial behavior will be discussed in more detail in Chapter 12.

The previous examples are illustrations of *intentional socialization*, in which input affected desired output. In reality, all of us have unique biological characteristics; we come into the world with different "wiring." As a result, we perceive and interact with the world differently, resulting in a range of outputs. A muscular, coordinated child will tend to be attracted to sports, while a frail, timid child will tend to avoid competitive activities. Thus, children play a role in their own socialization (Scarr, 1992), which sometimes makes intentional socialization difficult. In contrast to the scientifically shaped utopian society described in *Walden Two* or the manipulated situation in the Robber's Cave experiment, in reality each human being is exposed to many different environments in which many different interactions and experiences, both intentional and unintentional, take place. Therefore, individuals reflect both their biological characteristics and their socialization experiences (Bugental & Grusec, 2006; Collins et al., 2000). As the child changes, so must the process of socialization. Socialization is not static; it is dynamic, transactional, and bidirectional, or reciprocal (Sameroff, 2009). Ideally, as children develop, control over their behavior gradually shifts from the adult to the child. More specifically, infants and toddlers require much adult direction. Preschoolers are developmentally capable of directing some of their activities and are exhibiting some self-control of their behavior. School-agers can direct most of their activities with adult support and some direction. Adolescents who have been socialized by nurturant adults exhibit much self-control and self-directed behavior, even though they still need some adult guidance.

Table 1.3 Socialization Variables

Examples of Input	Examples of Output
Instruction	Values
Setting standards	Attitudes
Learn-by-doing	Motives and attributions
Feedback	Self-esteem
Reinforcement	Self-regulation of behavior
Punishment	Morals
Group pressure	Gender roles

How do socialization theories, especially the bioecological theory, explain children's developmental outcomes?

The Bioecological Theory of Human Development and Other Theories of Socialization

Recall that "ecology" is the science of interrelationships between organisms and their environments. The term **"bioecological"** refers to the role organisms play in shaping their environments over time. Here we focus on human organisms—their biological, social, and psychological characteristics.

bioecological refers to the role organisms play in shaping their environment over time

> Human beings create environments that shape the course of human development. Their actions influence the multiple physical and cultural tiers of the ecology that shapes them, and this agency makes humans—for better or worse—active producers of their own development. (Bronfenbrenner, 2005, p. xxvii)

A **theory** is an organized set of statements that explains observations, integrates different facts or events, and predicts future outcomes. Theories:

theory an organized set of statements that explains observations, integrates different facts or events, and predicts future outcomes

- provide a framework for interpreting research findings and give direction for future study,
- explain a particular aspect of development, such as genetics,
- describe settings that influence many aspects of the child's development, such as culture, or
- examine the interaction between the child and his or her environment, such as ecology.

The general framework for the whole book is based on developmental psychologist Urie Bronfenbrenner's bioecological model of human development (1979, 1989, 1995, 2005; Bronfenbrenner & Morris, 2006). The model provides the "whole picture" of the developing child, encompassing relevant theories within it. Such theories, including biological, behavior-learning, sociocultural, psychoanalytical, cognitive developmental, information processing, and systems theories, are discussed throughout the book as they apply to particular topics.

The bioecological model of human development represents the evolving character of science because it can accommodate other theories and old research while providing a conceptual scheme to assimilate new research. It is possible to do such integrative and complex studies due to computer technology, which enables multifaceted analyses, and communication technology, which enables collaboration among researchers. While some theories focus on patterns or similarities among individuals to explain human development, Bronfenbrenner (1979, 1989, 2005; Bronfenbrenner & Morris, 2006) has provided a way to explain human variation and adaptation within general patterns. An example of a theory that describes a pattern is that of Piaget (1952). His theory of cognitive development delineates the stages in which children, in general, develop a conceptual understanding of the world based on their maturation and active experiences.

- Infants and toddlers (age 0–2) understand things in terms of their senses and motor activity. They recognize a rattle by its feel, its taste, and its sound.
- Preschoolers (age 3–5) are beginning to understand relationships between people, objects, and events, but in an intuitive or imaginative, rather than logical, way. "My grandma has gray hair; that lady is a grandma because her hair is gray."
- School-agers (age 6–11) can use logic to understand relationships, but only on concrete, or real, people, objects or events. "That animal is a dog because it has four legs, pointy ears, furry hair, and it barks."
- Adolescents (age 12 and beyond) can understand abstract and hypothetical relationships and therefore can solve problems regarding things they haven't experienced directly. "The moon rotates in an orbit around the Earth."

Bronfenbrenner (1993) looks beyond general developmental patterns; he proposes that researchers examine various ecological settings in which the child participates, such as family and child care, to explain individual differences in children's development (in this case, cognitive development). To exemplify, an ecological longitudinal study on the effects of nonparental care ("child care") on children's cognitive development from birth through age 15 has found that toddlers and preschool children, especially those from low-income families, who attend a quality child-care center are more advanced cognitively, demonstrating Piaget's stages of development earlier and scoring higher on school achievement tests than those children who do not (National Institute of Child Health and Human Development, 2005).

The bioecological model represents a composite of bits and pieces of information about human development designed to foster understanding. It is like a mosaic or a graphic design, as in a website comprised of words, colors, figures, or pictures, and so on to convey meaning. The bioecological model of human development comprises information relating to persons, processes, contexts, and outcomes. This book follows such a pattern, discussing (1) the child as a biological organism, (2) socialization processes, (3) significant contexts of development, and (4) socialization outcomes.

Examining Socialization in an Ecological Context

What ecological contexts and interactions influence the process of socialization?

The social context of individual interactions and experiences determines the degree to which individuals can develop their abilities and realize their potentials, according to Bronfenbrenner (1979, 1989, 1995, 2005; Bronfenbrenner & Morris, 2006). His conceptual model (see Figure 1.4) for studying humans in their various social environments—the bioecology of human development—allows for a systematic study of interactions and serves as a guide for future research on the very complicated process of socialization.

According to Bronfenbrenner's bioecological theory, there are four basic structures—(1) the *microsystem*, (2) the *mesosystem*, (3) the *exosystem*, (4) and the *macrosystem*—in which relationships and interactions take place to form patterns that affect human development. Such a conceptual framework enables us to study the child and his or her family, school, and community as dynamic, evolving systems that are influenced by broader social change (the *chronosystem*), as in economics, politics, and technology.

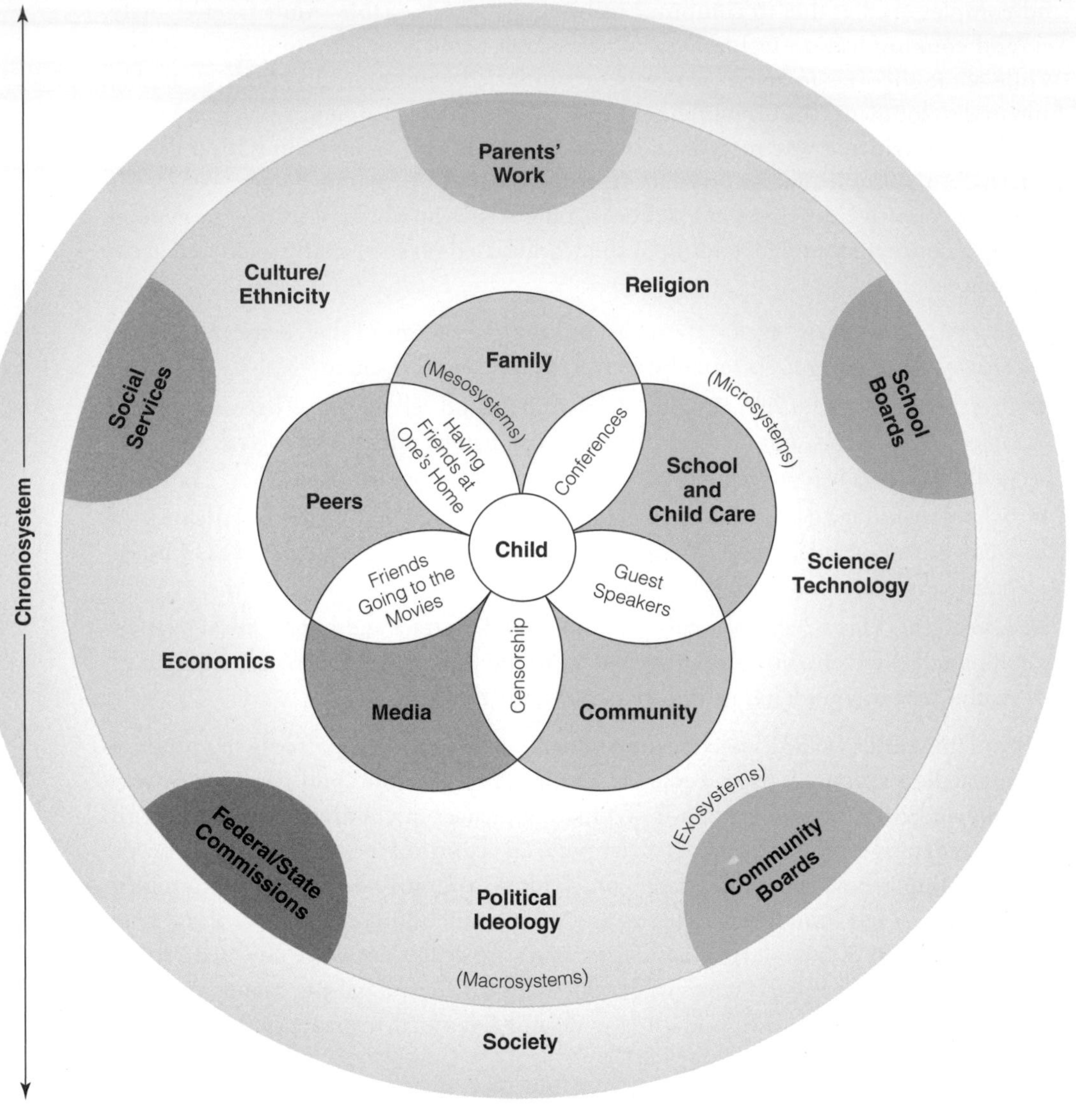

FIGURE 1.4 A Bioecological Model of Human Development
Source: Based on concepts from Bronfenbrenner, 1989.

What are the most significant contexts in which a child interacts?

Microsystems

The first basic structure, the **microsystem** (*micro* meaning small) refers to the activities and relationships with significant others experienced by a developing person in a particular small setting such as family, school, peer group, or community (see Figure 1.5).

microsystem activities and relationships with significant others experienced by a developing person in a particular small setting such as family, school, peer group, or community

Family

The *family* is the setting that provides nurturance, affection, and a variety of opportunities. It is the primary socializer of the child in that it has the most significant impact on the child's development. According to James Garbarino (1992), the child who is not adequately nurtured or loved, such as one who grows up in an abrasive or dysfunctional family, may have developmental problems. Also, children who do not have sufficient opportunities to manipulate objects, to model desirable behaviors, to initiate activity, or to be exposed to a language-rich environment will be at a disadvantage when they reach school. This early disadvantage will persist and even worsen as the child progresses through school unless intervention, such as that provided by some quality child-care programs, can modify the opportunities at home and in school.

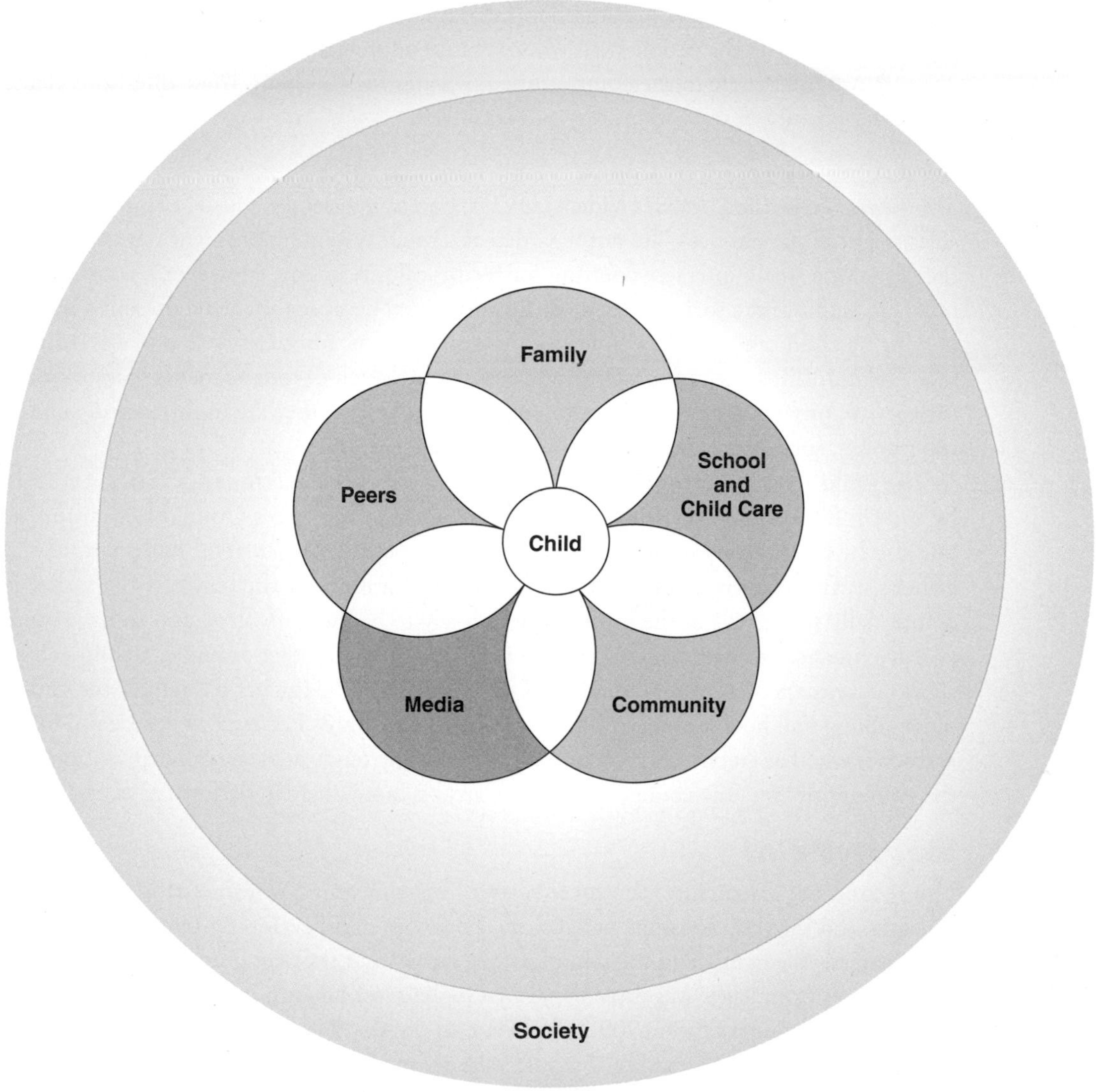

FIGURE 1.5 **Microsystems**

These children are participating in a community event, learning about competition.

TAO Images Limited/PhotoLibrary

School

The *school* is the setting in which children formally learn about their society. The school teaches reading, writing, arithmetic, history, science, and so on. Teachers encourage the development of various skills and behaviors by being role models and by providing motivation for children to succeed in learning.

Peer Group

The *peer group* is the setting in which children are generally unsupervised by adults, thereby gaining experience in independence. In the peer group, children get a sense of who they are and what they can do by comparison with others. Peers provide companionship and support as well as learning experiences in cooperation and role taking.

Community

The *community*, or neighborhood on a smaller scale, is the main setting in which children learn by doing. The facilities available to children determine what real experiences they will have. Is there a library? Are stores and workplaces nearby where children can observe people at work? Are the people with whom children interact in the community similar or diverse? Are the people in the community advocates for children? These questions relate to the significance of the community as a socializer.

Media

The *media*—television, movies, videos, DVDs, books, magazines, music, computers, consoles, and cellular phones—are not regarded as a microsystem by Bronfenbrenner because they are not a small, interactive setting for reciprocal interaction. However, I consider the media as significant a socializer as those just described because the media present a setting in which a child can view the whole world—past, present, future, as well as places, things, roles, relationships, attitudes, values, and behaviors. Much of today's media technology is interactive, providing opportunities to relate socially in that they are multifaceted, such as cell phones, social networking sites, and computerized games.

The child's development is affected in each of the aforementioned settings not only by the child's relationships with others in the family, school, peer group, or community, but also by interactions among members of the particular microsystem. For example, the father's relationship with the mother affects her treatment of the child. If the father is emotionally supportive of the mother, she is likely to be more involved and to have more positive interactions with the child (Cox et al., 1992). For another example, a child's classroom performance varies as a function of whether or not the teacher has taught the child's older sibling and how well that sibling performed (Jussim & Eccles, 1995; Seaver, 1973). A teacher who has taught a high-achieving older sibling tends to have high expectations for the younger sibling. The younger sibling, in turn, is more likely to perform as expected.

How are the child's significant contexts of development linked to one another?

Mesosystems

mesosystem linkages and interrelationships between two or more of a person's microsystems (for example, home and school, school and community)

The second basic structure, the **mesosystem** (*meso* meaning intermediate), consists of linkages and interrelationships between two or more of a developing person's microsystems, such as the family and the school, or the family and the peer group (see Figure 1.6). The concept of linkages was introduced by Guglielmo Marconi, inventor of the wireless telegraph and winner of the 1909 Nobel Prize in physics. He posited the principle of "six degrees of separation," meaning it would take no more than six connections to link any two people in the world. Marconi was referring to telegraph stations, but today social scientists apply the idea to personal linkages. By having subjects send letters to people they knew in the United States, Stanley Milgram (1967) found that two random people were connected by an average chain of six acquaintances.

The impact of mesosystems on the child depends on the number and quality of interrelationships. Bronfenbrenner (1979) uses the example of the child who goes to school alone on the first day. This means that there is only a single link between home and school—the child. Where there is little linkage between home and school "in terms of values, experiences, objects, and behavioral style," there also tends to be little academic achievement for the child. In contrast, where all these links are strong, there is likely to be academic competence. To illustrate, many studies have found a consistent relationship between the joint effects of family and school over time and academic performance (Epstein & Sanders, 2002). When the style of family interaction was similar to the school's, in that both settings encouraged child participation, academic performance was enhanced (Ginsburg & Bronstein, 1993). Thus, the more numerous the qualitative links or interrelationships between the child's microsystems, the more impact they have on socialization. Mesosystems, then, provide support for activities going on in microsystems. For example, when parents invite a child's friends to their home, or when parents encourage their child to join a certain club, team, or youth group, the socialization impact of the peers is enhanced through parental approval.

Another example of mesosystem impact occurs when businesses in the community form partnerships to support schools (Target stores do this), sponsor local events, or give rewards.

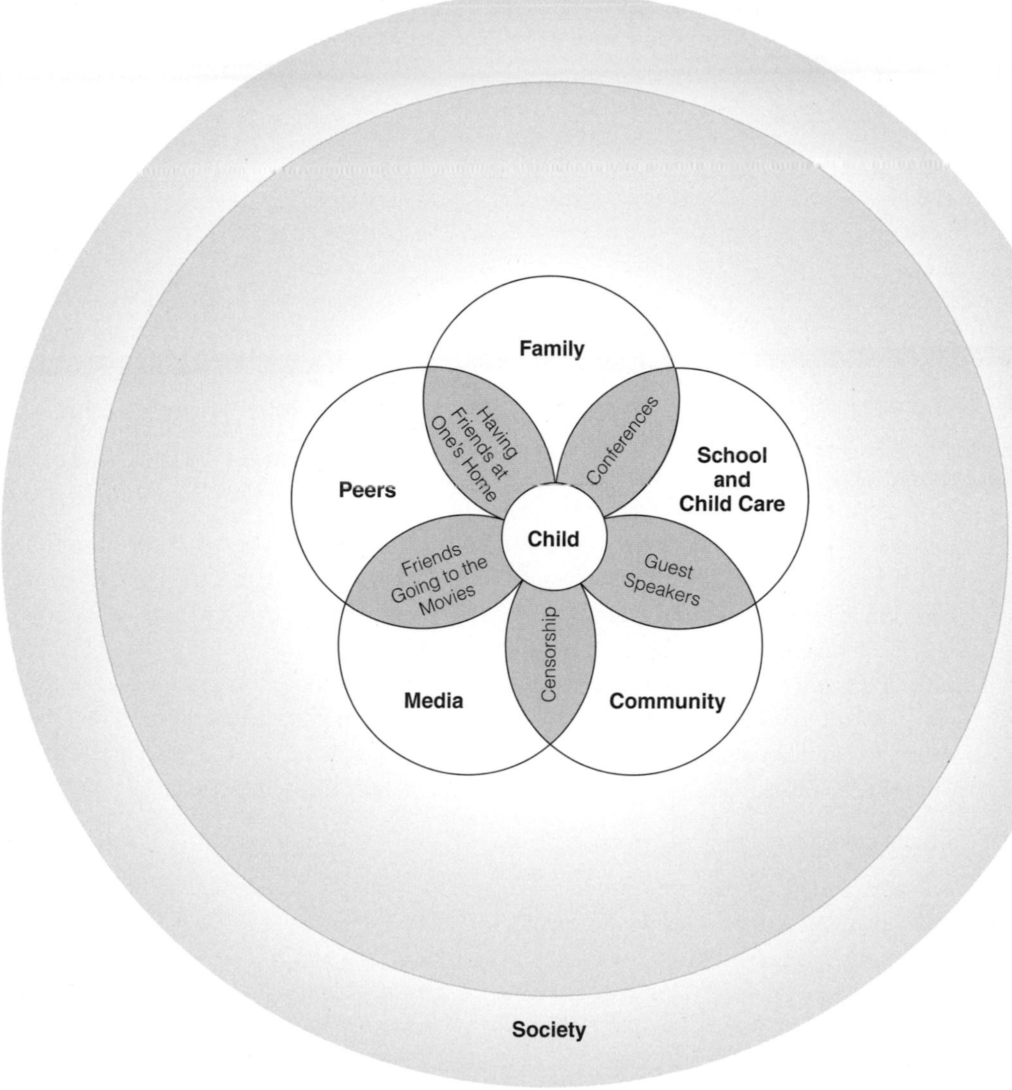

FIGURE 1.6 **Mesosystems**

Exosystems

How do settings in which the child does not participate influence his or her development?

The third basic structure, the **exosystem** (*exo* meaning outside), refers to settings in which children are not active participants, but that affect them in one of their microsystems—for example, parents' jobs, the city council, or parental social support networks (see Figure 1.7). The effects of exosystems on the child are indirect via the microsystems. To illustrate, when parents work in settings that demand conformity rather than self-direction, they reflect this orientation in their parenting styles, tending to be more controlling than democratic. This orientation, in turn, affects the child's socialization. When the city planning commission approves a freeway through a neighborhood or an air traffic pattern over a school, children's socialization is affected because the noise interferes with learning. Studies show that parental employment, income, and setting affect child development outcomes. For example, low-income parents involved in work-based antipoverty programs (ones that provide sufficient family income, child care, health insurance, and support services) have been shown to enhance the school performance and social behavior of their children (Huston et al., 2001). On the other hand, high-income parents living in upwardly mobile suburban communities have been shown to have children who exhibit a relatively high rate of lower-than-expected school performance and negative social behavior (anxiety, depression, and substance abuse) as a reaction to achievement pressure (Luthar & Becker, 2002).

exosystem settings in which children do not actually participate, but which affect them in one of their microsystems (for example, parents' jobs, the school board, the city council)

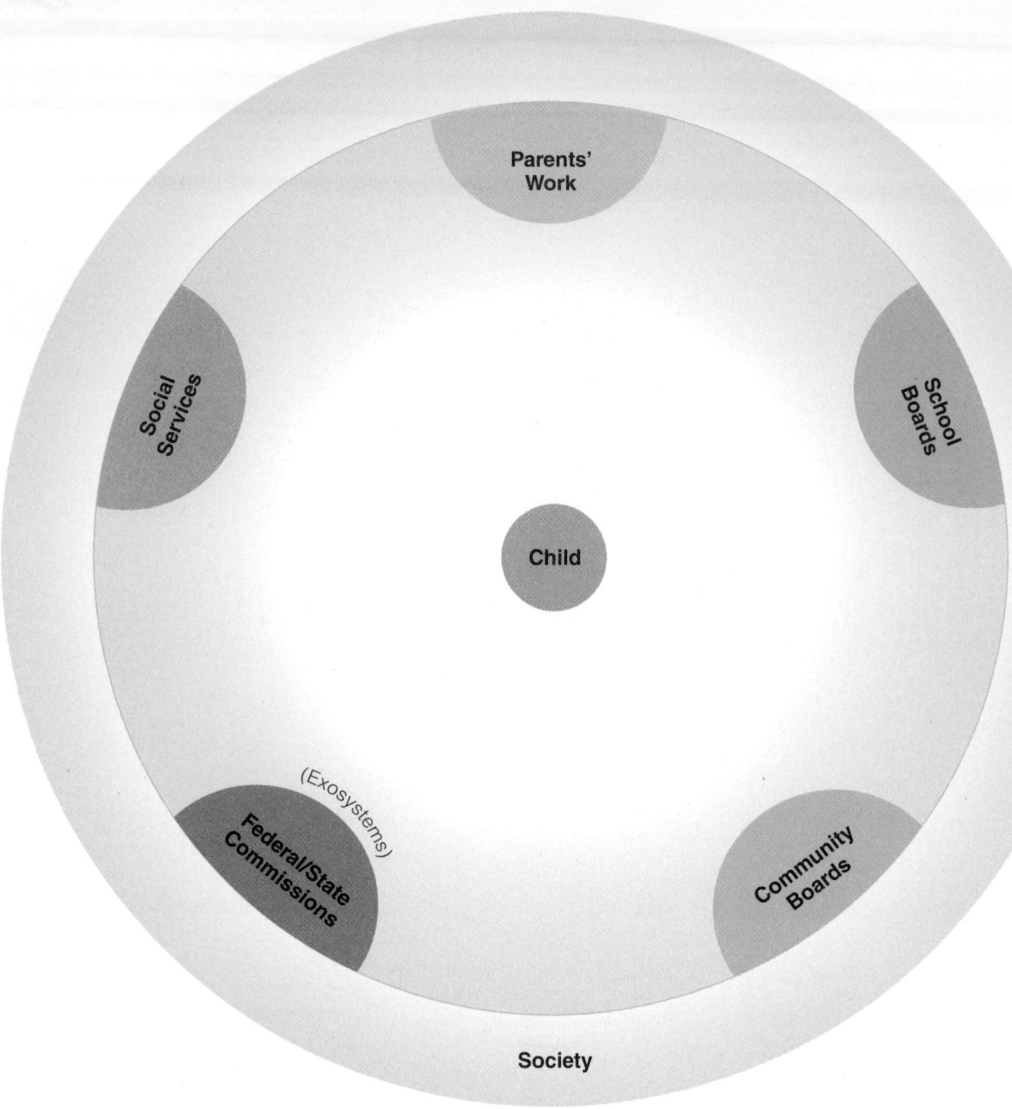

FIGURE 1.7 **Exosystems**

How do characteristics of the larger society influence the child's development?

Macrosystems

The fourth basic structure, the **macrosystem** (*macro* meaning large), consists of the society and subculture to which the developing person belongs, with particular reference to the belief systems, lifestyles, patterns of social interaction, and life changes (see Figure 1.8). Examples of macrosystems include the United States, the middle or lower class, Latino or Asian ancestry, Catholicism or Judaism, and urban or rural areas. Macrosystems are viewed as patterns, or sets of instructions, for exosystems, mesosystems, and microsystems. Democracy is the basic belief system of the United States and so is considered a macrosystem. Democratic ideology affects the world of work, an exosystem—for example, employers cannot discriminate in hiring. Democratic ideology also affects school–family interaction, a mesosystem—for example, schools must inform parents of policies, and parents have the right to question those policies. Finally, democratic ideology affects what is taught in schools, a microsystem—for example, children must learn the principles upon which the United States was founded.

macrosystem the society and subculture to which the developing person belongs, with particular reference to the belief systems, lifestyles, patterns of social interaction, and life changes

ethnicity an ascribed attribute of membership in a group in which members identify themselves by national origin, culture, race, or religion

A person who lives in the United States and subscribes to its basic belief system of democracy, and consequently is influenced by that macrosystem, may also be part of other macrosystems, such as his or her ethnic group and culture. **Ethnicity** refers to an *ascribed* attribute of membership in a group in which members identify themselves by

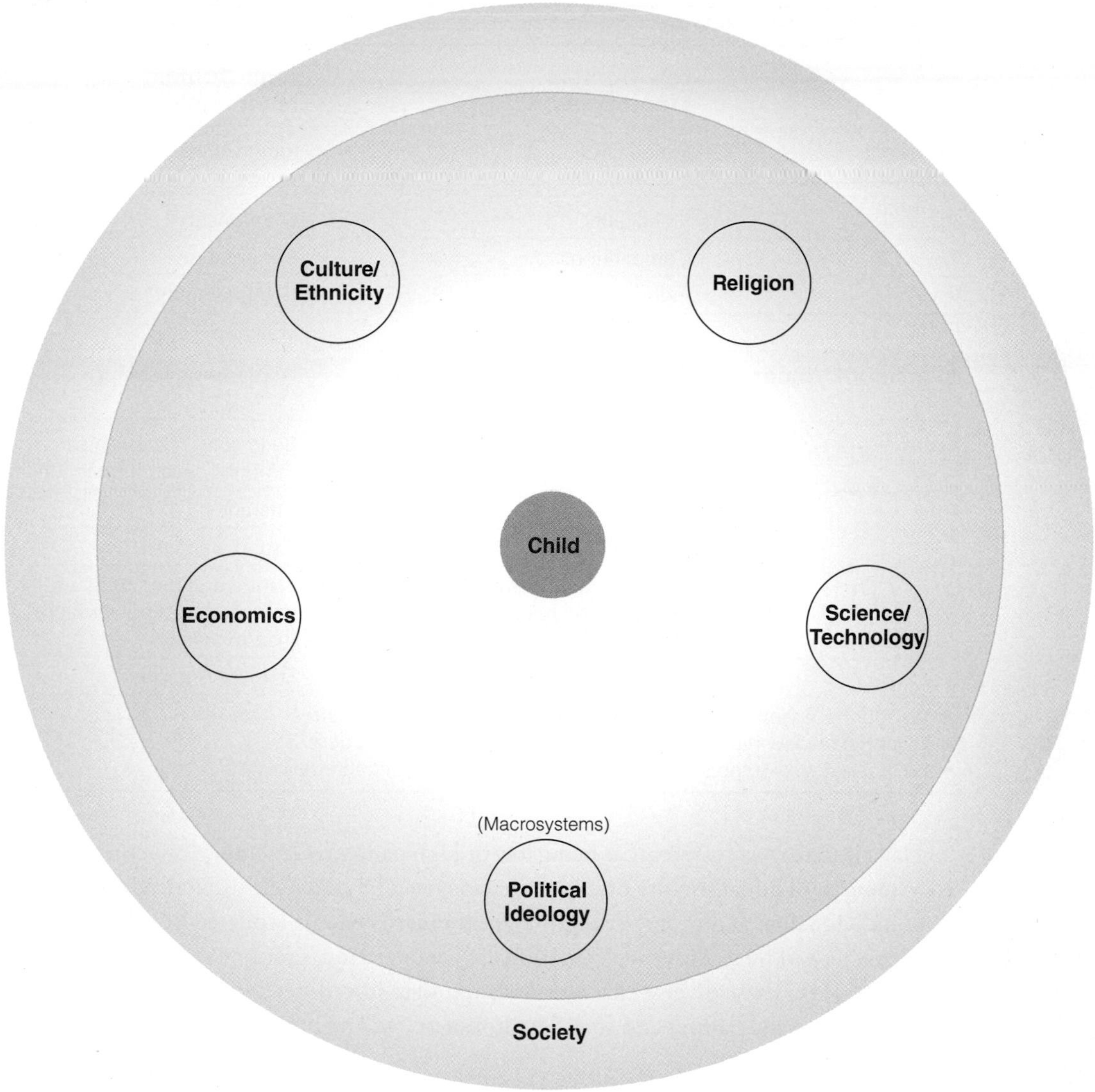

FIGURE 1.8 **Macrosystems**

national origin, culture, race, or religion. Members of an ethnic group share biologically and/or socially inherited characteristics. **Culture** refers to the *acquired*, or learned behavior, including knowledge, beliefs, art, morals, law, customs, and traditions, that is characteristic of the social environment in which an individual grows up. While "ethnicity" and "culture" often overlap because an ethnic group usually has a common culture, Bugental and Grusec (2006) clarify the distinction: "Ethnicity" refers to *ascribed* attributes passed on by one's family (for example, biology and/or social status) and "culture" refers to *acquired* attributes cultivated through learning (for example, language and/or celebrations). Since the United States is becoming increasingly diverse, we need to understand some basic effects of various macrosystems. Examples of how children, families, schools, and communities adapt to cultural contrasts will be discussed throughout the book.

culture the learned, or acquired, behavior, including knowledge, belief, art, morals, law, customs, and traditions, that is characteristic of the social environment in which an individual grows up

Diverse Macrosystems: Low- and High-Context

According to cultural anthropologist Edward T. Hall (1964, 1966, 1976, 1983), people from different macrosystems, or cultures, view the world differently, unaware that there are alternative ways of perceiving, believing, behaving, and judging. Particularly significant are the unconscious assumptions people make about personal space, time, interpersonal relations, and ways of knowing.

Low context

High context

Low-context cultures value cultivating the land, whereas high-context cultures value living in harmony with it.

Jupiter images
Keith Levit Photography/Index Stock Imagery/PhotoLibrary

low-context macrosystem culture generally characterized by rationality, practicality, competition, individuality, and progress

high-context macrosystem culture generally characterized by intuitiveness, emotionality, cooperation, group identity, and tradition

Table 1.4 Worldviews

	Low-Context Macrosystems	High-Context Macrosystems
General Characteristics	Rationality	Intuitiveness
	Practicality	Emotionality
	Competition	Cooperation
	Individuality	Group identity
	Progress	Tradition
Significant Values	Emphasis on concrete evidence and facts	Emphasis on feelings
	Efficient use of time	Build solid relationships through human interaction
	Achievement	Character
	Personal freedom	Group welfare
	Humans can control nature and influence the future	Nature and the future are governed by a power higher than human
	Change is good	Stability is good

- What if these views represented two individuals wanting to marry?
- What if one view represented a teacher's and the other a student's?
- What if one view represented an employer's and the other an employee's?

Hall classifies macrosystems as being low or high context. Generally, **low-context macrosystems** (individualistic-oriented) are characterized by rationality, practicality, competition, individuality, and progress; **high-context macrosystems** (collectivistically oriented) are characterized by intuitiveness, emotionality, cooperation, group identity, and tradition (see Table 1.4). These diverse characteristics translate into differences in communication, relationships to the natural and social environment, and adaptive behavior to survive.

Diverse Patterns of Behavior

The following low- and high-context behavior patterns, presented here as extremes (either-or), occur more often in reality by degrees. Examples of low- and high-context cultures are represented as a continuum in Figure 1.9.

- **Communication.** In a low-context macrosystem, meaning from a communication is gleaned from the verbal message—a spoken explanation, a written letter, or a computer printout. *What* is said is generally more important than *who* said it. Many employees in government, business, or education routinely communicate by phone or memorandum without ever meeting the other individuals involved. On the other hand, in a high-context macrosystem, meaning from a communication is gleaned from the setting in which the communication takes place. In some languages, one can communicate familiarity by whether one uses the formal or informal word for "you." Body language, such as eye-lowering or bowing, can be used to communicate degree of respect.
- **Relationship to Natural and Social Environment.** In a low-context macrosystem, people tend to try to control nature (such as irrigating desert areas) and to have more fragmented social relations—that is, they may behave one way toward friends, another way toward business colleagues, and yet another way toward neighbors. In a high-context macrosystem, people tend to live in harmony with nature and with other humans who are part of their social network. Whereas individuals in low-context macrosystems usually develop an identity based on their personal efforts and achievements, people in high-context macrosystems tend to gain their identity through group associations (lineage, place of work, organizations). Members of low-context

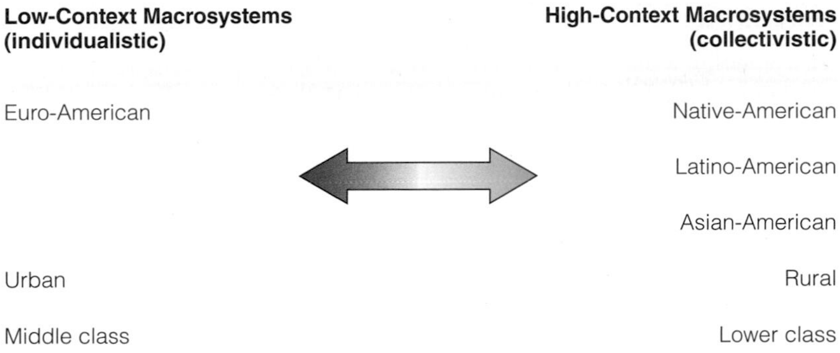

FIGURE 1.9 **Examples of Diversity**

cultures expect personal freedom, openness, and individual choice. Members of high-context cultures are less open to strangers, make distinctions between insiders and outsiders, and are more likely to follow traditional role expectations.

- **Adaptive Behavior to Survive.** Both low- and high-context macrosystems illustrate adaptive behavior to survive, which includes parenting styles. Low-context cultures, valuing progress, provide ways of changing and using new knowledge that can benefit society. Parenting style influences child's independence and creativity. On the other hand, high-context cultures, valuing tradition, provide a strong human support network that helps guard against the alienation of a technological society. Parenting style influences child's interdependence and conformity.

IN CONTEXT On a daylong cruise to see the glaciers in Alaska, I had the opportunity to observe the contrast in parenting styles in a high- and low-context family. The high-context family consisted of a mother and father, a baby (about 10 months old), and a grandmother and grandfather. The baby was continually held and played with by one of the adults. She was kissed and jiggled and spoken to. There were no toys to amuse her. When it was lunchtime, the mother, after distributing to the adults the food she had brought, took some food from her plate, mashed it between her fingers, and put it in the baby's mouth. After lunch the grandmother and grandfather took turns rocking the baby to sleep. The baby never cried the whole day. The care she received fostered a sense of interdependence.

In contrast, the low-context family, consisting of a mother, a father, and a baby (about 15 months old), had brought a sack of toys for the baby to play with while the parents enjoyed the sights through a nearby window. After a while, the baby began to fuss; the father picked him up and brought him to the boat's window, pointing out seals and birds and glaciers. Later, when the baby tired of his toys, the mother held his hands and walked him around the deck. The baby was given crackers and a bottle to soothe him when he cried. The care he received fostered a sense of independence.

Interaction of Ecological Systems over Time: The Chronosystem

What role does time play in how environmental conditions affect the child and how the child affects his or her environments?

The **chronosystem** involves temporal changes in ecological systems, or within individuals, producing new conditions that affect development. For example, significant societal events can produce a variety of effects on children. Accessibility to knives and guns has affected many on-campus security procedures; schools installed metal detectors, hired guards, and initiated "zero-tolerance" policies whereby aggressive students are expelled for one offense. For another example, the physical changes a child experiences during puberty can affect his or her self-esteem, depending on how the child's developing body compares to his or her friends' as well as to the cultural ideal body type.

chronosystem temporal changes in ecological systems or within individuals, producing new conditions that affect development

Impact of Significant Historical Events

To illustrate that changes in a macrosystem can result in changes in exosystems, mesosystems, and microsystems, sociologist Glen Elder (1974, 1979) and his colleagues (Elder & Hareven, 1993; Elder, Van Nguyen, & Casper, 1985; Elder & Shanahan, 2006) conducted a very thorough, longitudinal study of 167 California children born 1920–1929. They compared the life-course development of children whose families had experienced a change in their socioeconomic status during the Great Depression (a period of widespread economic insecurity in the United States) and those who had not. The immediate exosystem effect was loss of a job. This in turn caused emotional distress, which was experienced in the home and affected the children (effect on a microsystem). There were also secondary exosystem effects: In families hit by the Depression, the father lost status in the eyes of the children and the mother gained in importance. The affected father's parenting behavior became more rejecting, especially toward adolescent girls. Children, especially boys, from affected families expressed a stronger identification with the peer group. Children from affected families also participated more in domestic roles and outside jobs, with girls being more likely to do the former and boys the latter.

The fact that longitudinal data were available over a period of more than 60 years gave Elder the opportunity to assess the impact of childhood experience, within and outside the family, on behavior in later life (effects of chronosystem). He found that the long-term consequences of the Depression varied according to the age of the child at the time. Children who were preadolescents when their families suffered economic loss did less well in school, showed less stable and less successful work histories, and exhibited more emotional and social difficulties, even in adulthood, than did those of the same socioeconomic status from families who did not suffer economically. Such adverse effects have been explained (Conger et al., 1994) as due to the impact of economic hardship on the quality of parenting and hence on the psychological well-being of children.

In contrast, those who were teenagers when the Depression hit their families did better in school, were more likely to go to college, had happier marriages, exhibited more successful work careers, and in general were more satisfied with life than youngsters of the same socioeconomic status who were not affected by the Depression. These favorable outcomes were more pronounced for teenagers from middle-socioeconomic-status backgrounds but were also evident among their lower-status counterparts.

Interestingly, adults whose families escaped economic ruin turned out to be less successful, both educationally and vocationally, than those whose families were deprived. Why was this so? According to Elder (1974):

> It seems that a childhood which shelters the young from the hardships of life consequently fails to develop or test adaptive capacities which are called upon in life crises. To engage and manage real-life (though not excessive) problems in childhood and adolescence is to participate in a sort of apprenticeship for adult life. Preparedness has been identified repeatedly as a key factor in the adaptive potential and psychological health of persons in novel situations. (pp. 249–250)

Thus, a major consequence of the Depression was that economic loss changed the relation of children to the family and the adult world by involving them in work that was necessary for the welfare of others. This early involvement contributed to deprived children's socialization for adulthood. Elder hypothesized that the loss of economic security forced the family to mobilize its human resources. Everyone had to take on new responsibilities.

In sum, Elder's study shows how ecological change over time can have varying impacts on a child's socialization depending on other variables, such as the age and gender of the child, the existing family relationships, and the socioeconomic status of the family before the change, thereby illustrating the multiplicity of variables interacting to affect socialization.

Impact of Ongoing Events

Socialization must pass on the cultural heritage to the next generation while also enabling that generation to become competent adults in society. Thus, every socializing agent engages in preparing children for both stability and change. Training for stability, which is implemented by passing on the cultural heritage and the status quo to children, involves making their behavior somewhat predictable and conforming; but paradoxically, preparation for change, enabling children to become competent for a future society, very likely involves disrupting some stable patterns and encouraging new ways of thinking and behaving.

Contemporary Ecology

What are some societal trends affecting children?

Some contemporary societal trends (Naisbitt & Auburdene, 1990; Toffler & Toffler, 2006) affecting the future of families and children are outlined as follows:

- **Biotechnology.** Genetic engineering can potentially cure inherited diseases by substituting normal genes for defective ones; but what about using such techniques to increase intelligence? Will children have "designer" genes? Assisted reproductive techniques (sperm donation, egg donation, in-vitro fertilization, frozen embryos, surrogacy) enable adults who have fertility problems to become parents; but what about medical, legal, and ethical risks regarding the child's welfare? For example, if a male and female contribute sperm and egg for conception to take place in a dish, several resulting embryos are frozen, one or two are implanted in a surrogate who is paid to carry through with the pregnancy, and the biological parents die, what happens to the children—to whom do the babies and embryos belong? What makes one a parent—genes, prenatal environment, postnatal environment?

  Large businesses, especially electronics and computers, rarely provide on-site personalized service for problems with equipment. Instead, you, the consumer, must consult the manual and try to diagnose the problem before calling the manufacturer. How will such business practices affect how children are educated—will they need to be exposed to more "hands-on" problem solving?
- **Reconceptualization of Societal and Individual Responsibilities.** Government, too, is shifting from "paternalistic" policies (a strong authority takes care of less able citizens) to "empowerment" policies (any individual can learn to care for him- or herself). For example, government welfare support is waning while "workfare" is waxing. Government funding of Social Security plans is yielding to private insurance and investment programs. How will children whose parents must become more economically responsible be affected?
- **Information Technology.** The concept of information technology (IT) is broadening to include not only traditional computer hardware and software but also a wide range of communication tools (such as cell phones, smart phones, and scanners), media (such as television, cameras, and recorders), and data. Wireless networks allow users to work, play, and shop any time, any place. For businesses, operations can be streamlined and efficiency increased by enabling workers to make plans, make decisions, and generate sales reports without going to the office. For consumers, mobile commerce offers the ability to shop for tickets, books, or pizza while waiting in line or at the doctor's office. People can also download music, videos, and games on hand-held devices. For parents, children might require less time in day care due to eliminating the work commute and having more flexible time available for family matters.

  IT enables knowledge creation and capitalization (one can get medical information from numerous Internet sources and go to the doctor requesting an advertised

As technology increases, humans compensate by finding new ways to interact, as exemplified by cell phones.

MandyGodbehear/Big Stock Photo

medication rather than allowing the doctor to diagnose and prescribe). How do individuals cope with even more choices, advertising, and distractions? How do you feel when you need information or assistance and a computer answers the phone rather than a live person? What about privacy issues, personal security, and information errors? Will IT foster closer connections among family and friends, or come between them, competing for time and space?

According to social forecaster John Naisbitt (2006), in his book, *Mindset!: Reset Your Thinking and See the Future*, "Technology is a great enabler, but only when in balance with needs and skills and human nature. . . . When a new technology is introduced, make it a rule to ask: What will be enhanced? What will be diminished? What will be replaced? What new opportunities does it present?" (p. 109).

Technology has enabled people to multitask. While multitasking may enhance efficiency and productivity in adults, research (Clay, 2009) shows that it actually slows children's productivity, changes the way they learn, and may reinforce superficial social relationships.

- **Globalism/Nationalism.** Telecommunications and transportation facilitate a global economy. Labor, production, marketing, and consumption can occur in different places in the world. Does such globalism affect standards of production? For example, in 2007, some toys made in China containing unsafe parts were recalled because some children got hurt. Does globalism affect the work families do—job competition, type of job, location of job, skills needed?

  As people throughout the world are exposed to greater homogeneity through travel, media, and telecommunications, they sometimes become more nationalistic, clinging to their religious/ethnic traditions for identity. In *Jihad vs. McWorld* (Barber, 1996), the author defines *McWorld* as the "universe of manufactured needs, mass consumption, and mass infotainment." It is motivated by profits and consumer preferences. *Jihad*, or holy war, is shorthand for the "fundamentalist politics of religious, tribal, and other zealots." It is motivated by faith in a spirit that governs all aspects of life. The terrorist attacks in the United States on September 11, 2001, were an extreme example of the fanatically defended beliefs in spiritual determinism versus self-determination. How has the fear of terrorism changed our lives? We have greater emphasis on national security, exemplified by stricter immigration laws, racial profiling, and government surveillance technology. Are children growing up with attitudes of suspicion and prejudice?

- **Shift in Decision-Making Responsibility.** New advances in science, medicine, education, economics, communications, media, transportation, security, privacy, and ecology require skills to cope with massive amounts of information. Recently an exterminator asked me to decide which of several available pesticides should be used in my house to get rid of ants. Even though I was informed of the varying effectiveness and safety of each, I did not really have the appropriate background knowledge on which to base such a decision; yet the responsibility for consequences was shifted to me.

  Another example is the shift in responsibility for children's learning. The No Child Left Behind Act of 2004 requires that children take standardized achievement tests. Schools and teachers are held accountable for children's learning in that political leaders make decisions regarding funding based on test scores—schools producing low scores are at risk of losing public funding. Does such a system influence teachers to "teach to the test" rather than the child?

- **Information Intermediaries.** One way the business world has capitalized on today's information glut is to offer endorsements (celebrity), enticements (rewards), and services (consulting) to help consumers make decisions. When you buy a book, isn't it easier to choose one from the *New York Times* Best Seller List or Amazon's recommendations than to read the book jackets? Do you choose an airline because of its rewards program or the convenience of its schedules and destinations? Do you need to hire a wedding planner or an investment counselor? Will children learn to look to others for decisions, rather than themselves?

Thus, a challenge resulting from these societal trends is the need to create caring communities in which children can learn to think—to apply, analyze, synthesize, and evaluate information, not just regurgitate facts (Fiske, E.B., 1992) or form opinions based on conformity to a celebrity. The ability to think and use knowledge becomes critical in a world plugged into machines and bombarded with information and choices (Postman, 1992). Because of new technology and new information, children will have to learn to solve problems not previously encountered. They will have to extrapolate from previous experiences. How will we teach them?

In sum, these contemporary societal trends affect how people use available resources—economic, social, and psychological—in their daily lives; their choices ultimately have consequences for children. Next, we examine ecological trends affecting children's well-being.

Effects of Change on the Well-Being of Children

How does the U.S. government address the needs of children?

Every year, the federal government issues a report, *America's Children: Key National Indicators of Well-Being*, showing the overall status of the nation's children. Political leaders use the following indicators (Federal Interagency Forum on Child and Family Statistics [FIFCFS], 2010) to make decisions regarding what services for children will be funded and what new programs need to be developed to address their needs (examples of such services will be discussed in Chapter 10).

- **Family and social environment indicators** document the number of children as a proportion of the population, racial and ethnic composition, number of non–English-speaking children, family structure and children's living arrangements, births to unmarried women, child care, and child maltreatment.
- **Economic circumstance indicators** document poverty and income among children and basic necessities such as housing, food, and health care.
- **Health care indicators** document the physical health and well-being of children, including immunizations and probability of death at various ages, dental care, and number of children with health insurance.
- **Physical environment and safety indicators** document the number of children living in counties with excess concentration of pollutants, children living in communities with substandard water, children with elevated blood lead levels, housing problems, crime, injuries, and death.
- **Behavior indicators** document the number of youths who are engaged in illegal, dangerous, or high-risk behaviors such as smoking, drinking alcohol, using drugs, having sex, or committing violent crimes.
- **Education indicators** document success in educating the nation's children, including preschool, reading, overall achievement, completion of high school, and college attendance.
- **Health indicators** document the number of infants with low birth weight, children with emotional or behavioral difficulties, children who are overweight, and children with asthma.

Bullying in the neighborhood is a reality many children face, impacting their well-being.

MandyGodbehear/Shutterstock.com

Summary

- Ecology involves studying humans in their physical, social, and cultural environments, all of which are affected by societal change.
- Socialization—the process by which individuals acquire the knowledge, skills, and character traits that enable them to participate as effective members of groups and society—enables adaptation to change.
- Socialization, occurring through human interaction, begins at birth and continues throughout life. Biological factors (genetics, maturation, temperament) influence developmental outcomes.
- Socialization is reciprocal, or bidirectional, with children playing a role in their own developmental outcomes.
- Society's concept of childhood has changed over time. The period of protection for children has gone from being shorter during the Renaissance to longer during the Industrial Revolution due to a need for formal schooling.
- The agents of socialization are the family, the school, the peer group, the media, and the community. These agents employ different socialization techniques.
- A theory is an organized set of statements that explains observations, integrates different facts and events, and predicts future outcomes. Theories provide a framework for research.
- The bioecological theory of human development incorporates the child's development in microsystems, mesosystems, exosystems, and macrosystems, with relationships and interactions that take place over time (the chronosystem).
- The microsystem is the immediate small setting where the child is at a particular time.
- The mesosystem consists of the intermediate interrelationships between two or more of a person's microsystems.
- The exosystem refers to outside settings in which children do not actually participate, but that affect them in one of their microsystems.
- The macrosystem refers to the larger society and its ideology in which a child grows up. Macrosystems can be classified as low context or high context, each type having different influences on a person's perspectives on the world.
- Low-context cultures tend to value individualism; high-context cultures tend to value collectivism.
- The chronosystem refers to changes in ecological systems over time well as in individuals producing new conditions that affect development.
- Effects of change in the macrosystem on exosystems, mesosystems, and microsystems are exemplified in Elder's study comparing families who were deprived during the Depression and those who were not. A major influence for children growing up in deprived families was their involvement in the adult world of work necessary for the welfare of others.
- Contemporary ecology involves societal trends affecting children's well-being. These are biotechnology, reconceptualization of societal and individual responsibility, a shift in decision-making responsibility, information technology, and globalism/nationalism.

Activity

PURPOSE To understand the impact of change (chronosystem) on microsystems and mesosystems.

1. Describe one to three changes you observed:
   - in your family as you grew up
   - in your school
   - in your peer group
   - in the media—television, movies, or books
   - in your community
2. Pick one change for each microsystem and discuss:
   - why you think it occurred
   - how it affected you
   - what impact, if any, it had on the other microsystems (mesosystem)

Related Readings

Boocock, S. S. (2005). *Kids in context: The sociological study of children and childhoods.* New York: Rowman & Littlefield.

Bronfenbrenner, U. (1979). *The ecology of human development.* Cambridge, MA: Harvard University Press.

Campbell, J. (2008). *The hero with a thousand faces* (3rd ed.). Novato, CA: New World Library.

Chess, S., & Thomas, A. (1996). *Know your child: An authoritative guide for today's parents.* New York: Jason Aronson.

Garbarino, J. (1995). *Raising children in a socially toxic environment.* San Francisco: Jossey-Bass.

Gardner, H. (2006). *Five minds for the future.* Boston, MA: Harvard Business School Press.

Mintz, S. (2006). *Huck's raft: A history of American childhood.* Cambridge, MA: Belknap/Harvard University Press.

Moen, P., Elder, G. H., Jr., & Luscher, K. (Eds.). (1995). *Examining lives in context: Perspectives on the ecology of human development.* Washington, DC: American Psychological Association.

Naisbitt, J. (2006). *Mindset!: Reset your thinking and see the future.* New York: Harper Collins.

Rutter, M. (2006). *Genes and behavior: Nature-nurture interplay explained.* Hoboken, NJ: Wiley-Blackwell.

Skinner, B. F. (1948). *Walden two.* New York: Macmillan.

Toffler, A., & Toffler, H. (2006). *Revolutionary wealth.* New York: Knopf.

Resources

America's Children—Key National Indicators of Well-Being
http://www.childstats.gov/americaschildren

The Future of Children—translating research into policy
http://www.futureofchildren.org

Department of Health and Human Services—improving the health, safety, and well-being of America
http://www.hhs.gov/children

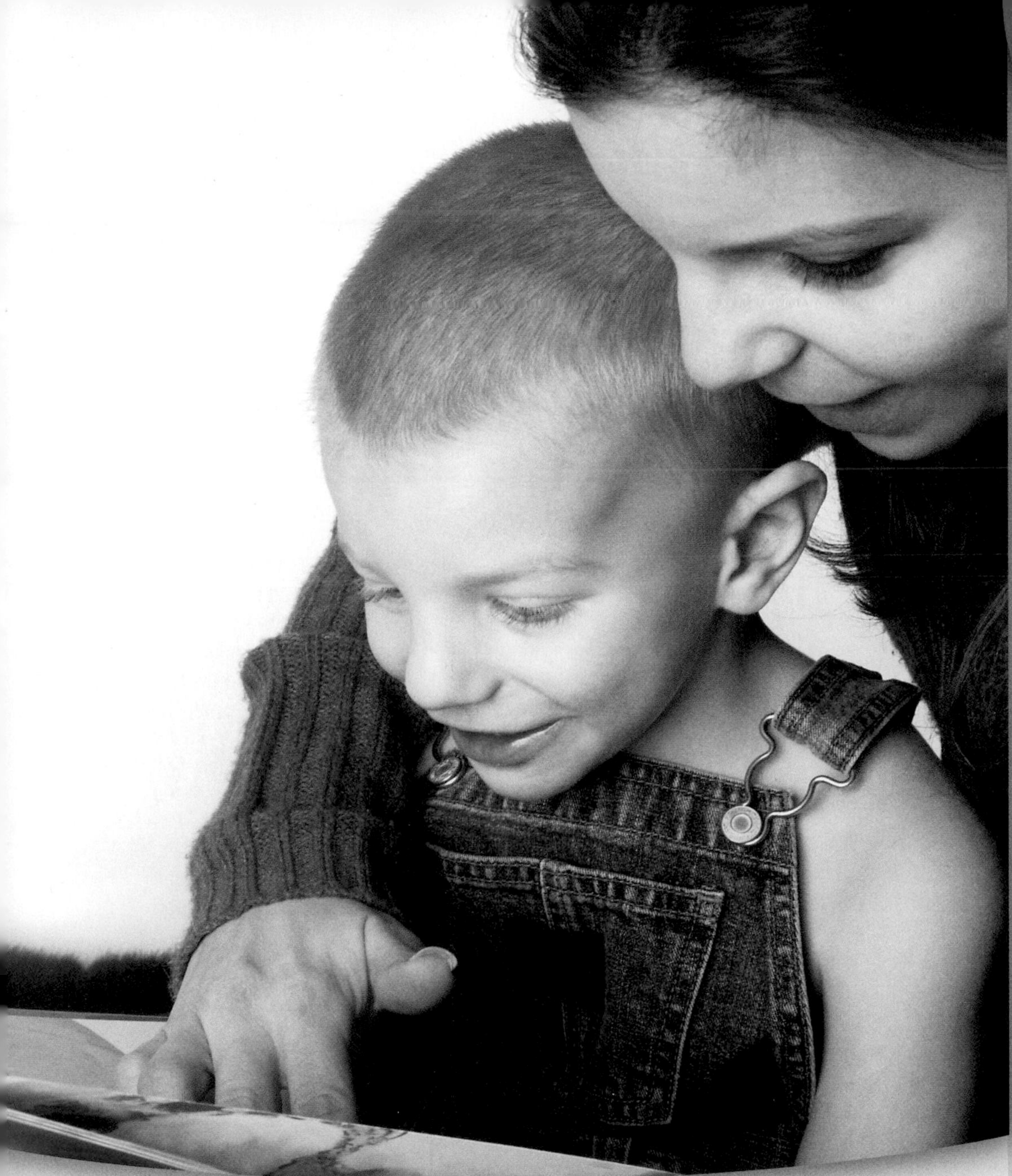

Stephanie Horrocks/iStockPhoto.com

2

Ecology of Socialization

Train up a child in the way he should go; and when he is old, he will not depart from it.

—PROVERBS, 22:6

SOCIALIZATION SKETCHES

Albert Einstein

(1879–1955)

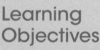

MPI/Archive Photos/Getty Images

"Anyone who has never made a mistake has never tried anything new."

— ALBERT EINSTEIN

This quote from Albert Einstein sets the stage for the socialization agents, methods, and outcomes discussed in this chapter, in particular, the operant method of "learning-by-doing." The socialization sketch describes the significant people and events in Einstein's life that were influential in enabling him to discover new scientific principles.

Albert Einstein received the 1921 Nobel Prize in Physics for his theory of relativity. Other scientific contributions included reconciling laws of mechanics with laws of electromagnetic fields. He also contributed to the theory of radiation and the thermal properties of light, to name a few.

Family

Albert Einstein was born in Germany into a Jewish family. His father, Hermann Einstein, was a salesman and engineer. His mother was Pauline Einstein. When Albert was 1, the family moved to Munich where his father and uncle founded a company that manufactured electrical equipment, providing cabling and lighting to a Munich suburb.

Since his parents were not observant of Jewish religious practices, Albert was sent to a Catholic elementary school. In spite of early speech difficulties, Albert was an excellent student.

When Albert was 5, his father showed him a pocket compass. That something in the empty space was moving the needle fascinated him. At his mother's insistence, Albert began violin lessons at age 6.

Significant Adults

As Albert grew, he liked building models and mechanical devices. He also began to show an aptitude for math. When Albert was 10, a family friend who was a medical student, Max Talmud, introduced him to key science, math, and philosophy texts. From authors such as Kant and Euclid, Albert began to understand deductive reasoning. He learned Euclidean geometry by age 12 and began to investigate calculus.

School

In his early teens Albert attended a prestigious high school. His father intended for him to pursue electrical engineering, but Albert resented the school regimen because it stressed strict rote learning rather than creative thinking.

When Albert was 15, his father's business failed and the Einsteins moved to Italy. Albert was left in Munich to finish high school. During this time he wrote his first scientific work regarding magnetic fields. He withdrew from high school before completion to join his family. He decided to go directly to the Swiss Federal Institute of Technology in Zurich, Switzerland. However, even though he got exceptional scores in math and physics, he failed the entrance exam. It was that year, at age 16, that he first performed his famous thought experiment, visualizing traveling alongside a beam of light.

The Einsteins sent Albert to Aarau, Switzerland, to finish secondary school. Albert studied Maxwell's electromagnetic theory and graduated at age 17. To avoid German military service, with his father's approval, Albert renounced his German citizenship and succeeded in enrolling at the Swiss Federal Institute of Technology in the mathematics program, also gaining Swiss citizenship.

Peers

Following graduation Albert could not find a teaching position. A classmate's father got him a job as assistant examiner at the Swiss Federal Patent Office evaluating applications for electromagnetic devices. While this was not his primary interest, he was able to feed his intellectual curiosity by forming a club with a college friend, who also worked at the patent office. The club's weekly discussions were based on readings in science and philosophy. It was these discussions that motivated Albert's scientific work.

- If you had a disability that impaired your success in certain areas, would you seek out other areas in which to succeed?
- What do you think are the ingredients of, and the influences on, creativity?

Learning Objectives

After completing this chapter, you will be able to:

1. Understand the socialization process.
2. Describe the aims of socialization.
3. Describe the agents of socialization.
4. Discuss methods of socialization by giving examples from the book and from personal experience.
5. Discuss the outcomes of socialization.

Socialization Processes

How do you enable a helpless infant to eventually become a contributing adult?

This chapter explores the process of socialization, including its aims or goals, its agents, their methods, and its outcomes. Figure 2.1 shows an ecological model of the bidirectional interactive systems involved in the process. Because socialization outcomes are affected by many variables (biological, sociocultural, interactional), they will be discussed more specifically in the concluding chapters.

In the past, socialization research focused on the effect of forces *outside* the child (for example, the influence of significant adults on the child's moral development) or forces *inside* the child (for example, the influence of unconscious motives on aggressive behavior). Today, socialization processes have come to be regarded as dynamic and reciprocal—dynamic in that the aims and methods change as does the child; reciprocal in that the child contributes to his or her own developmental outcomes (Laible & Thompson, 2007).

Socialization processes are affected by biological, sociocultural, and interactive factors (Bugental & Grusec, 2006).

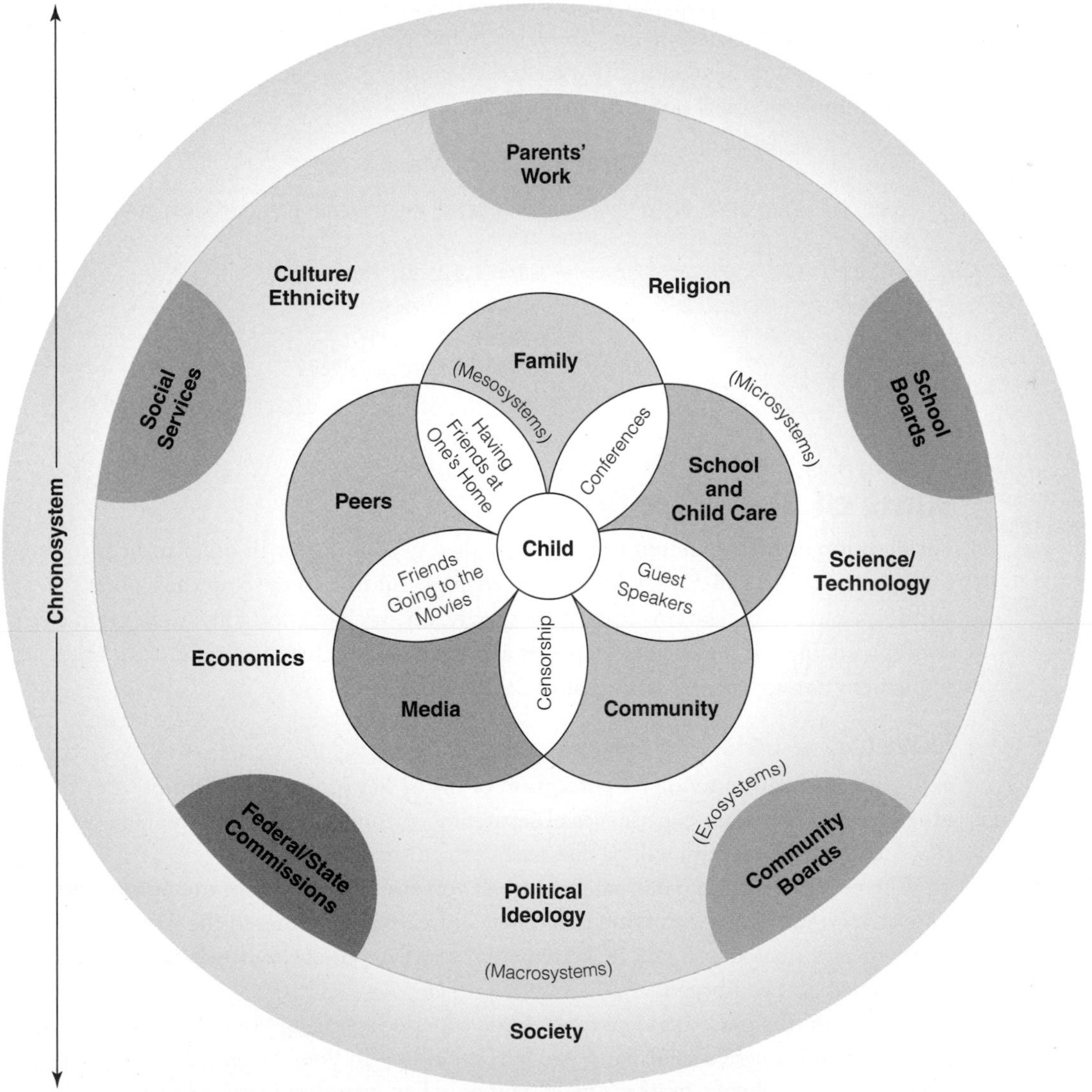

FIGURE 2.1 A Bioecological Model of Human Development

Socialization involves bidirectional interactions between the child and significant others in microsystems, mesosystem links, exosystems, macrosystems, and over time (the chronosystem).

experience-expectant the neural connections that develop under genetic influence, independent of experience, activity, or stimulation

experience-dependent the neural connections that develop in response to experience

- **Biological factors** (genetics, evolution, hormones) are thought to influence basic neural circuitry of the brain during early development. These neural connections, referred to as **experience-expectant**, develop under genetic influence independent of experience, activity, or stimulation (Bruer & Greenough, 2001). For example, our brains are equipped at birth to receive visual, auditory, tactile, and other stimuli from the environment. One-month-old infants can distinguish different speech sounds and prefer to listen to sounds falling within the frequency range of the human voice (Aslin, Jusczyk, & Pisoni, 1998).
- **Sociocultural factors** are also thought to influence the development of brain neural circuitry. These neural connections, referred to as **experience-dependent**, develop in response to experience. This mutual facilitation between the environment and the brain is thought to be significant in learning to adapt (Bruer & Greenough, 2001). For example, a child's language development depends on being spoken to and participating in conversation, beginning with eye contact, then babbling, single words, and finally sentences.
- **Interactive factors**, such as individual life history, include the child's receptivity to socialization. For example, a child with a difficult temperament may react rebelliously to parental demands for compliance (Dodge & Pettit, 2003). For another example, a child exposed to extreme stress, such as maltreatment, war, or natural disaster, may be at risk for developmental problems (Chisholm, 1998); or the child may be resilient in the face of adversity (Rutter & O'Connor, 2004) because of his or her biology or supportive social networks in his or her life.

Parental Script Messages

What comes to mind, like a tape recording, when you think about what your parent(s) said about . . .

Doing work?	Making your own decisions?
Getting an education?	Achieving success?
Using money?	Developing talents?
Being sexual?	Assuming responsibility?

What are society's goals for children?

Aims of Socialization

Socialization enables children to learn what they need to know in order to be integrated into the society in which they live. It also enables children to develop their potentialities and form satisfying relationships. More specifically, socialization aims to develop a self-concept, enable self-regulation, empower achievement, teach appropriate social roles, and implement developmental skills (Laible & Thompson, 2007).

How do you perceive yourself and why?

Develop a Self-Concept

self-concept an individual's perception of his/her identity as distinct from others

self-esteem the value one places on his/her identity

Self-concept is an individual's perception of his or her identity as distinct from that of others. It emerges from experiences of separateness from others. The value one places on that identity, **self-esteem**, will be discussed later in the chapter.

When you were born, your parents named you and may have sent out announcements to relatives and friends signifying that a new individual had entered the world. Although everyone else treated you as a separate being, you were unaware of where your environment ended and you began.

As the months passed and you had some experiences using your senses, you noticed that when you touched your hand you felt something in your fingers and hand, whereas when you touched your mother's hand, you only felt sensation in your fingers.

Gradually, as people met your needs, you realized they existed even when you could not see them. As you developed language, you learned that objects have names and so did you, and each had an independent existence. Language enabled you to describe and compare. Sometime around 15 to 18 months, you put it together and understood that you are you. You could recognize yourself in a mirror. You could assert your wants ("Me do it!"), especially when you perceived that someone else was controlling you.

As you got older, your concept of self—your identity, your understanding of who you are—was influenced by significant others (such as family, teachers, friends, coaches). If your needs were met consistently and you were given opportunities to discover things on your own, you developed a sense of autonomy, or self-regulation and control. If, on the other hand, your needs were not met consistently and you did not get to explore your environment, you developed a sense of doubt. These significant others also acted as a mirror, providing constant feedback on your achievements and failures. And so, in developing a self-concept or identity, you also developed self-esteem.

As you entered adolescence, your self-concept included how you related to others. Being a member of a group was important to your identity. In the later part of adolescence, your self-concept expanded to include how you related to the larger community. Self-concept involves not only "who am I?" but "where am I going?" and "how will I get there?"

Charles Horton Cooley (1909/1964), one of the founders of sociology, observed that through the experiences of interacting with others, children begin to distinguish themselves from others. Children call themselves "I" or "me"—"I hungry," "Me go." As they begin to act independently, they gradually become aware that others are evaluating them, saying "Good boy/girl" or "No, don't do that." Thus, their behavior is being judged according to certain rules and standards. These rules and standards must be learned and understood before the individual is capable of self-evaluation. As children gradually learn these criteria, each develops a self-concept; this concept, which reflects the attitudes of others, is termed the "looking-glass self." Cooley summed up his postulate:

> Each to each a looking glass
> Reflects the other that doth pass.

George Herbert Mead (1934), another important sociological theorist, referred to this gradually maturing way of looking at the self as the "generalized other." When children refer to themselves as "shy" or "hardworking," they have incorporated the standards of others into the description.

Thus, a self-concept develops when the attitudes and expectations of significant others with whom one interacts are incorporated into one's personality, making it possible to regulate one's behavior accordingly. One's perceived competence in self-regulation/control is part of one's self-esteem. Susan Harter (1999; 2006) studied various types of competence involved in self-esteem—behavioral, academic, physical, and social—which will be discussed in Chapter 11.

TeachSource Video Activity

Go to the Education CourseMate website to access the video entitled "5–11 Years: Self-Concept in Middle Childhood." What experiences do you think might have contributed to each child's sense of self?

Psychosocial Influences on the Development of Self

Psychologist Erik Erikson (1963, 1980) has explained the personality development of individuals as the outcome of their interactions in their social environment. He identified eight critical stages of psychosocial development in a human's life that affect the self-concept: *trust versus mistrust*, *autonomy versus shame and doubt*, *initiative versus guilt*, *industry versus inferiority*, *identity versus identity diffusion*, *intimacy versus isolation*, *generativity versus self-absorption*, and *integrity versus despair* (see Figure 2.2). How one copes with these normal challenges at one stage of development affects one's ability to overcome difficulties in the next stages.

Infancy: Trust versus Mistrust (Birth to Age 1)

The first "task" of infants is to develop the "cornerstone of a healthy personality"—a basic sense of trust in themselves and of the people in their environment. The quality and consistency of care the infant receives determines the successful outcome of this stage. A child whose basic needs for nourishment and physical contact are met will develop a sense of

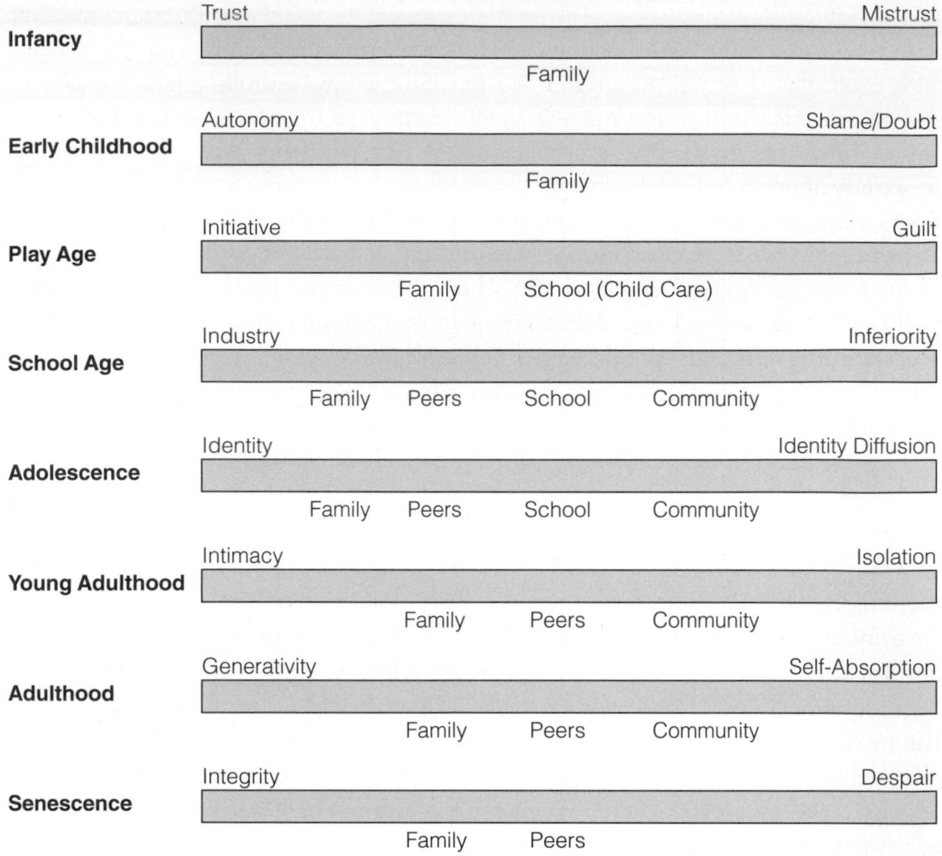

FIGURE 2.2 Erikson's Stages of Psychosocial Development

Note that an individual's development could be described as being at any point on the horizontal dimension lines, rather than at one extreme or the other. The importance of interactions with one's social environment in the development of a self-concept is indicated by the socializing agents that are most significant at various stages.

trust. This sense of trust lays a foundation for positive self-esteem. A child whose care is negligent or inconsistent will develop a sense of mistrust, which may persist throughout life and result in negative self-esteem. Some mistrust, however, is healthy in that it can guard against danger and manipulation.

Contemporary research shows a positive relationship between parental nurturance and self-worth (Cheng & Furnham, 2004; Harter, 1999; Hopkins & Klein, 1994).

Early Childhood: Autonomy versus Shame and Doubt (Age 2 to 3)

Physical and cognitive maturation enables children to behave autonomously—to walk without help, feed themselves, get things off the shelf, assert themselves verbally. If children are allowed to be self-sufficient according to their ability, the outcome of this stage will be a feeling of autonomy. If children are deprived of the opportunity to develop a will, if they are continually being corrected or reprimanded, later they may feel shame when being assertive and self-doubt when being independent. However, some shame is healthy in that it can prevent certain socially unacceptable behaviors such as picking one's nose in public.

Studying of the influence of parental rearing style on self-esteem and self-criticism, Cheng and Furnham (2004) found a significant correlation between maternal rearing style and teenagers' reported self-esteem and self-criticism.

Play Age: Initiative versus Guilt (Age 3 to 5)

Children's increasing ability to communicate and to imagine leads them to initiate many activities. If they are allowed to create their own games and fantasies, to ask questions, to use certain objects (a hammer and wood, for example) with supervision, then the outcome of this stage will be a feeling of initiative. If they are made to feel that they are "bad" for trying new things and "pests" for asking questions, they may carry a sense of guilt throughout life. Probably the reason "Pinocchio" has remained a favorite story is that, like all children, Pinocchio was continually learning which activities he initiated were OK and which were not. Thus, some guilt is healthy in that it can control misbehavior.

In a study of preschoolers and their first years at school (Tudge et al., 2003), a relationship was found between initiating activities and conversation in preschool and academic competence, as reported by teachers, two years later.

School Age: Industry versus Inferiority (Age 6 to Puberty)

During school age, while learning to accept instruction and to win recognition by showing effort and by producing "things," the child is developing the capacity to enjoy work. The outcome of this stage for children who do not receive recognition for their efforts, or who do not experience any success, may be a feeling of incompetence and inferiority. Children who are praised for their efforts will be motivated to achieve, whereas children who are ignored or rebuked may give up and exhibit helplessness. Some feelings of inferiority are healthy, however, in that they can prevent the child from feeling invincible and taking dangerous risks.

A study of 3rd to 5th graders (Skinner & Belmont, 1993) found a relationship between teacher involvement in students' classroom activities and children's motivation to achieve. Specifically, teacher provision of autonomous support and optimal structure led to higher levels of student engagement in schoolwork all year. In turn, student effort led to teachers' increased responses. Based on their findings, the researchers suggest that disengaged students receive teacher responses that further undermine their motivation to achieve (hence, fostering helplessness).

Adolescence: Identity versus Identity Diffusion (Puberty to Age 18+)

With rapid growth and sexual maturity, the young person begins to question people, things, values, and attitudes previously relied on and to struggle through the crises of earlier stages all over again. The developmental task (developmental tasks for all stages are discussed later) during adolescence, then, is to integrate earlier childhood identifications with biological and social changes occurring during this time. The danger in this stage is that while young people are trying out many roles, which is a normal process, they may be unable to choose an identity or make a commitment and so will not know who they are or what they may become (identity diffusion). Because adolescence is a time for exploration, some diffusion is healthy in that it can allow for learning what is suitable and what is not for an individual.

TeachSource Video Activity

Go to the Education CourseMate website to access the video entitled "12–18 years: Self-Concept and Identity Formation in Adolescence." Compared to the video on self-concept in middle-childhood, what similarities and differences do you detect?

This exploration time has been labeled "moratorium" by psychologists (Marcia, 1966). The process of identity formation in a study of a sample of over 1,500 early and middle adolescents from various cultural groups (Crocetti et al., 2007) actually differentiated five statuses in the process of developing an identity: (1) *achievement* (choices explored and commitment made), (2) *foreclosure* (commitment made without exploring choices), (3) *moratorium* (exploring choices in order to make commitments), (4) *searching moratorium* (reevaluating choices and commitments and reexploring choices), and (5) *diffusion* (little choice exploration and no commitments made). These statuses were associated with distinct personality features, such as: high self-esteem in the achievement status, conformity in the foreclosure status, high anxiety in the moratorium as well as in the searching moratorium status, and depression in the diffusion status.

Young Adulthood: Intimacy versus Isolation (Age 18+ to Middle Adulthood)

Individuals who have succeeded in establishing an identity are now able to establish intimacy with themselves and with others, in both friendship and love. The danger here is that those who fear losing their identity in an intimate relationship with another may

A sense of initiative is influenced by having opportunities to produce things.

Cengage Learning

develop a sense of isolation. Some isolation is healthy, however, in that it can enable one to learn about oneself and provide time for individual pursuits.

Researchers (Kacerguis & Adams, 1980) found a relationship between identity development and intimacy. Male (44) and female (44) college students were assessed via measures of identity and intimacy. Those more advanced in identity formation, especially occupational identity (they had made a commitment to a particular field of work), scored higher on intimacy measures.

Adulthood: Generativity versus Self-Absorption (Middle Adulthood to Late Adulthood)

From the development of intimate relationships comes **generativity**, an interest in establishing and guiding the next generation. This interest can be manifested by becoming a parent; by being involved with the development of young people through teaching, religion, Scouts, or other means; or through productivity and creativity in one's work. In this stage, a lack of generativity may result in self-absorption, which may show up as depression, hypochondria, substance abuse, or promiscuity. Yet some self-absorption is healthy in that it can lead to creativity and the development of hobbies.

generativity interest in establishing and guiding the next generation

A sample of educated, midlife women were assessed for generativity at age 43, and again 10 years later. Those who scored high on the measure at age 43 reported a greater investment ten years later in intergenerational roles (for example, daughter and mother), fewer subjective feelings of burden in caring for aging parents, and more knowledge about community resources for elders (Peterson, 2002).

Senescence: Integrity versus Despair (Late Adulthood to Death)

The individual who has achieved an identity, has developed a satisfying intimacy with others, and has adapted to the joys and frustrations of guiding the next generation, reaches the end of life with a certain ego integrity or positive self-esteem—an understanding acceptance of personal responsibility for one's own life (past and present). For those who have not achieved that integrity, this stage may produce despair or extremely negative self-esteem. Despairing individuals tend to be in ill health, to abuse drugs and/or alcohol, or to commit suicide. They may become burdens to their families physically, financially, or psychologically. On the other hand, individuals with a sense of integrity are likely to have friends, to be active (physically and mentally), and to look at life positively even though they know that death is imminent. Probably the only characteristic of despair that could be considered healthy is that which leads to change or greater appreciation of life.

A sample of older women living in a supported accommodation completed an anonymous self-report questionnaire. The results showed that accepting the past was a significant predictor of ego integrity, along with the variables of social support and positive affectivity. On the other hand, those who regretted or blamed things in the past, along with the variables of negative affectivity and physical dependence, were more likely to experience depression and ego-despair (Rylands & Rickwood, 2001).

Enable Self-Regulation

How did you learn to control your feelings and behavior?

Self-regulation involves the ability to control one's impulses, behavior, and/or emotions until an appropriate time, place, or object is available for expression. This can be interpreted as routing our feelings through our brains before acting on them according to the situation. Regulated behavior often involves postponing or modifying immediate gratification for the sake of a future goal. This implies being able to tolerate frustration. For example, you curb your urge to spank a child who has just thrown a plate of food on the floor in a tantrum because you want to set an example of how to deal with frustration. When you are trying to maintain your weight, you postpone satisfying those hunger

self-regulation the ability to control one's impulses, behavior, and/or emotions until an appropriate time, place, or object is available for expression

pangs until mealtime. You postpone sexual intercourse until marriage because of your religious or personal goals. Even though you hate to wake up early, you set your alarm in order to be at work on time because your supervisor depends on you.

Early relationships, especially attachment to parents, play a significant role in the development of emotional regulation (Bridges & Grolnick, 1995) and "emotional intelligence" (Goleman, 1995). As the child progresses from infancy to childhood, emotional and behavioral regulation gradually shifts from external socializing agents to internal, self-induced mechanisms (Eisenberg, 2006). Caregivers provide children with information (body language, facial expressions, verbal instructions and explanations) to help them deal with situations. As children develop cognitively and have more real experiences, they learn how to interpret events and how to express emotions appropriately. They develop strategies for coping with disappointment, frustration, rejection, and anger. Self-regulation/control is related to moral development, an outcome of socialization to be discussed in Chapter 12.

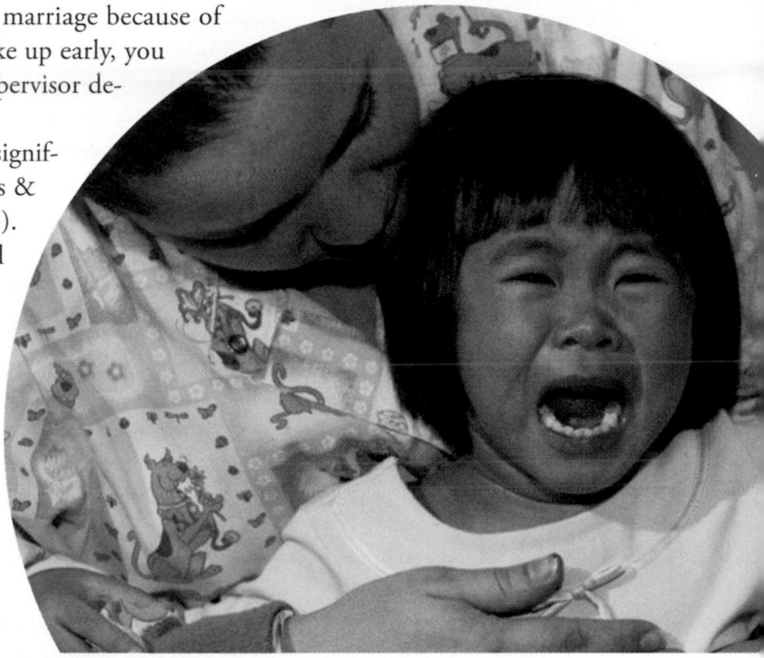

A child having trouble controlling her temper.

Cengage Learning

Empower Achievement

Socialization furnishes goals for what you are going to be when you become an adult—a teacher, a police officer, a business executive. These goals provide the rationale for going to school, getting along with others, following rules, and so on. In other words, socialization gives meaning or purpose to adulthood and to the long process a child has to go through to get there. In order for Pinocchio to become a real boy, he had to go to school as well as learn right from wrong.

How did you decide what you were going to do as an adult?

Significant adults and peers influence one's motivation to succeed. For example, adults who understand child development and provide the appropriate challenge at the "right" time with the "right" amount of support are likely to produce highly competent and motivated children (Wigfield et al., 2006). The motive to achieve and attributions of achievement (explanations for success and failure) are among the socialization outcomes discussed later in the chapter.

Teach Appropriate Social Roles

How do we learn to act according to what is required in different social settings?

In order to be part of a group, one has to have a function that complements the group. For example, in a group of employees, the supervisor's function or role is to lead the employees; in a family group, the parents' role is to nurture the child; in a peer group, the role of friends is to provide emotional support. We have many social roles throughout life, some of which occur simultaneously, and we must assume the appropriate behavior for each at the appropriate time. I am a wife, a parent, a child, a teacher, and a friend—all at the same time. As a wife, I am a confidante; as a parent, I am nurturant; as a child, I am submissive; as a teacher, I am a facilitator; as a friend, I am emotionally supportive.

Gender is a social role, too, in that boys and girls learn gender-appropriate behavior from significant members of their society (McHale, Crouter, & Whiteman, 2003; Ruble, Martin, & Berenbaum, 2006). What is appropriate (Maccoby, 2000) is affected by culture, ethnicity, and religion (macrosystem influences), as well as time (chronosystem influence).

Implement Developmental Skills

How do you meet your own needs while accommodating society's expectations?

Socialization aims to provide social, emotional, and cognitive skills to children so that they can function successfully in society. Social skills may involve learning how to obtain information from other people, use the telephone, or conduct business negotiations.

Emotional skills may involve controlling aggressive impulses, learning to deal with frustration by substituting another goal for one that is blocked, or being able to compensate for mistakes. Cognitive skills may include reading, mathematics, writing, problem solving, geography, history, and science.

Psychologist Robert Havighurst (1972) examined how society's expectations with regard to certain behavioral skills change according to the maturation of the individual (chronosystem influence), using the term *developmental* task to explain this aspect of socialization. According to Havighurst, "a *developmental task* is midway between an individual need and a societal demand." The developmental tasks of life are those things one must learn if one is to get along well in society (macrosystem influence). As we grow, we develop physically, intellectually, and socially. Our physical development will enable us to walk, control our bladders, and use a pencil. Our intellectual development will enable us to learn to read, do arithmetic, and solve problems. Our social development will enable us to cooperate, empathize, and interact with others. And our emotional development will enable us to regulate our impulses and express our feelings. Some examples of developmental tasks categorized according to societal demands for certain behaviors are listed here; how they change for the individual from birth to death can be found on the CourseMate website.

CourseMate

1. Achieving an appropriate dependence/independence pattern
2. Achieving an appropriate giving–receiving pattern of affection
3. Relating to changing social groups
4. Developing a conscience
5. Learning one's "psychosociobiological" role
6. Accepting and adjusting to a changing body
7. Managing a changing body and learning new behavioral patterns
8. Learning to understand and control the physical world
9. Developing an appropriate symbol system and conceptual abilities
10. Relating oneself to the cosmos

As we develop along these dimensions, we face new expectations from significant socializing agents in the surrounding society. We are expected to learn to walk, talk, use the toilet, and dress ourselves. We are expected to read, write, add, and subtract. We are expected to share, develop a conscience, and achieve an appropriate gender role. We are expected to love other people and be responsible for our actions.

developmental tasks a task that lies between an individual need and a societal demand

Thus, developmental tasks arise from societal pressures on individuals according to their development: "If the task is not achieved at the proper time, it will not be achieved well, and failure in this task will cause partial or complete failure in the achievement of other tasks yet to come" (Havighurst, 1972, p. 3). If children do not have experiences in language, such as being spoken to and making sounds during the critical stage of language development (first year), their ability to communicate will be handicapped for the remainder of their lives. A child who is not socialized to develop a conscience may engage in delinquent behavior in adolescence. A child who does not have experiences receiving and giving affection may not succeed in a marriage or family relationship.

In some cultures, infants sleep with their mothers (and sometimes with their fathers, too) to be able to nurse on demand. This occurs until the infant is weaned.

Fuse/Jupiter Images

Developmental Tasks and Cultural Diversity

Developmental tasks differ from society to society, and each group in a society has its own developmental definitions and expectations. For example, a developmental milestone for many American, middle-class infants is to "sleep through the night." This expectation is usually fulfilled by about age 4 to 6 months and is often facilitated by parents' feeding the baby just before they go to sleep and/or playing with the baby and putting him or her to sleep for the night as late as possible. However, in other families where the infant sleeps with the mother and nurses on demand, "sleeping through the night" is not pushed as a developmental milestone—this is more the norm in other cultures around the world. Differences in developmental definitions and expectations may account for some of the

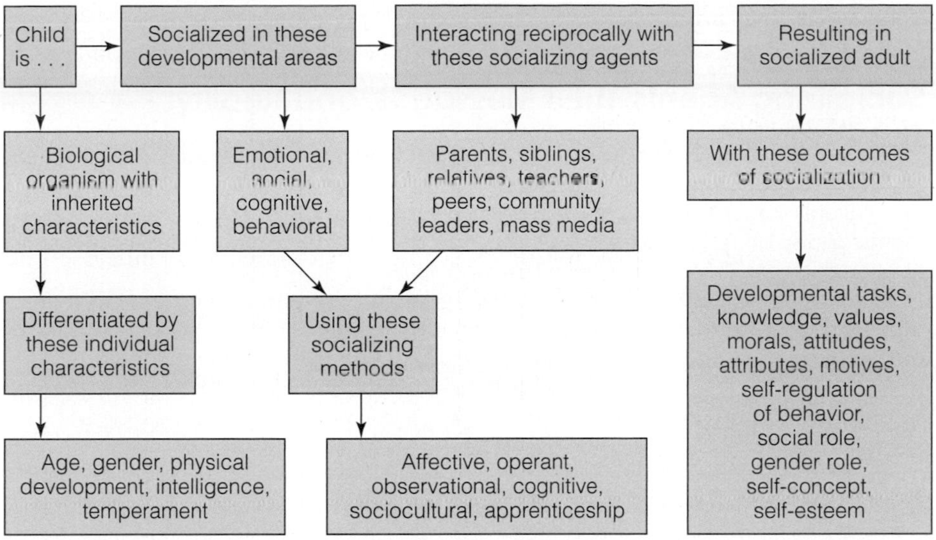

FIGURE 2.3 Socialization Processes and Outcomes

social adjustment problems in school among children from diverse cultural groups. For example, the developmental task for achieving an appropriate dependence/independence pattern may be interpreted differently by various families.

Most middle-class American mothers, as well as American teachers, expect children to be independent of adults by school age in that they can take care of personal needs and learn on their own with some directions. In Japan, however, mothers expect some of their child's dependency needs to be transferred to the teacher when the child goes to school, and Japanese mothers generally remain very involved in their child's learning throughout school. In other cultures, such as Latino and Hawaiian, mothers expect their child's dependency needs to be transferred to older siblings, and interdependence, rather than independence, is encouraged. Thus, children from high-context cultures (such as Japanese, Latino, Hawaiian, and others) may experience conflicts between developmental skills taught by their families and those taught in American schools (Bennett, 2010).

Every individual in a society is the outcome of the process of socialization (along with his or her genetic traits). The success of this outcome in terms of society's expectations will depend on a series of interactions with significant socializing agents—such as parents, teachers, peers, and media—that constitute the community in which this individual lives (Collins et al., 2000). Figure 2.3 illustrates the processes and outcomes of socialization.

Agents of Socialization

Who was significant in shaping you?

The generalized community is made up of many groups that play a part in socializing an individual. These agents of socialization exert their influence in different ways and at different times (Arnett, 2007).

In the early years, the family assumes the primary role of nurturing the child. As the child gets older, the peer group becomes a primary source of support. In primitive societies, training for competency occurs in the family in the form of learning to hunt or build a shelter, whereas in industrial societies it occurs in the school in the form of learning to read, write, compute, and master a wide range of subject matter.

Each agent has its own functions in socialization. Sometimes the agents complement each other; sometimes they contradict each other. The value of getting along with others is usually taught in the family, the school, the religious community, the peer group, and perhaps in the media, with the agents complementing each other. The value of academic achievement, however, may be supported by some families and the school, but scorned by the peer group—an

IN PRACTICE

Socializing Agents, Their Messages, and Reality: The Discrepancy

Typical American children start the day with some instructions and expectations from their parents about finishing breakfast, setting an after-school schedule, cleaning their rooms, and so on. A few additional remarks may be added by older siblings regarding the condition of the bathroom when they went to use it.

At school, one teacher may stress independence and competition, and another may emphasize cooperation and dependence on the group. After school, caregivers may have specific goals and socialization methods. The team or club members may value the best athlete or the one who sells the most raffle tickets, but in the classroom setting the one who gets the best grades or reads the most books may be disliked by peers.

Back at home, the television set sends messages via the various programs. One day a child may watch *Barney and Friends* or another children's entertainment show and feel empathic and altruistic. Another day the child may watch *Spiderman* or another action/drama show and come away feeling powerful and aggressive. Video or computer games provide for the interactive expression of emotions without real adult involvement.

In reality, children receive many demands from socializing agents as well as conflicting messages. As we discussed in Chapter 1, the process of socialization is reciprocal and dynamic, with children playing a role in their own socialization. A child's temperament—the innate characteristics that determine an individual's sensitivity to various experiences and responsiveness to patterns of social interaction—can elicit different reactions in caregivers. For example, a relaxed, happy baby tends to elicit smiles; a tense, crying baby tends to elicit concern or anxiety. As children develop and change, so, too, do others' reactions to them. My son and I have similar temperaments, which made the management of socialization goals and methods easier than for my daughter, whose temperament is different from mine. What role do you think your temperament played in the bidirectionality of socialization interactions in your family?

example of contradiction among the agents of socialization. The media and the peer group may support sexual experimentation, while the family and religious group condemn it.

How did your family influence who you are?

Family

The family is the child's introduction to society and has, therefore, borne the major responsibility for socializing the child. The family into which a child is born places the child in a community and in a society; newborns begin their social lives by acquiring the status and cultural heritage of their families, which in turn influence their opportunities and developmental outcomes (Leyendecker, Harwood, & Comparini, 2005). For example, children in low-income families not only have fewer material things, they also have less opportunity to develop their abilities. Because they perceive that they cannot compete with others of their age who have more things and more opportunities, children from families with low incomes are likely to believe that they have little control over the future and, therefore, try less hard in school, accomplishing less. Characteristics of families and possible outcomes for children will be discussed in Chapter 3.

The family also passes on its socioeconomic status through its ability to afford higher education for its children. Children from middle- and upper-income families are more likely to go to college after high school, whereas children from low-income families are more likely to go to work. And those who have not achieved in high school, perhaps from lack of motivation, have fewer job opportunities. Educational level, then, is a strong determinant of future occupation and income.

The family exposes the child to certain cultural experiences available in the society—perhaps religious instruction, Scouts, music lessons, Little League, or soccer. Parents buy certain toys for their children and arrange certain activities together such as games, outings, and vacations. These depend, to a large extent, on socioeconomic status.

The family functions as a system of interaction, and the way it conducts personal relationships has a very powerful effect on the psychosocial development of children (Grusec & Davidov, 2007). Through various interactions with family members, such as siblings, grandparents, and other relatives, the child develops patterns for establishing relationships with others. These patterns are expressed and further developed in relationships with peers, authority figures, co-workers, and ultimately a spouse and children (Parke & Buriel, 2006).

IN CONTEXT Terry, the oldest of three children, was responsible for helping her mother care for her younger siblings. She often had to play a game with her younger sister while her mother nursed the baby, or she had to watch the baby while her mother drove her sister to preschool. In her relations with her friends, Terry was the one always saying, "Let's play this" or "Let's play that" or "This is the way you're supposed to draw a house (or dog or cat)." In school she was often appointed to be a monitor. As an adult, Terry got a managerial position in her office.

The family into which a child is born is the child's first reference group. A reference group is one whose values, norms, and practices a person adopts and refers to in evaluating his or her own behavior. As part of a family, the child's observations, experiences, and interactions become the "norm" (Handel, Cahill, & Elkin, 2007). For example, there is now evidence that marital conflict and distress are related to children's difficulties with peers (Rubin, Bukowski, & Parker, 2006; Rubin & Thompson, 2003). For another example, it has been found that children of employed mothers from kindergarten age through adulthood have less-restricted views of gender roles (Ellis, 1994). In passing on values, expectations, and practices, families also pass on to children certain behavior patterns toward others. These behavior patterns tend to vary by cultural orientation (Greenfield et al., 2003; Greenfield, Suzuki, & Rothstein-Fisch, 2006). Diverse parenting styles will be discussed in Chapter 4.

Behavior Patterns in Culturally Diverse Families

In Chapter 1, socialization outcomes of different worldviews (low- and high-contexts) were discussed. Here we discuss four dimensions of cultural behavior patterns from diverse families. Their socialization outcomes are significant, especially when they differ from the standards socialized by the school or from those that predominate in the community. These dimensions represent extremes; usually, however, there is individual variation within groups (Trumbull et al., 2001).

Some Examples of Diverse Behavior Patterns According to Heritage

Collectivistic
Individualistic
Japanese
Hawaiian
Mexican
Middle Eastern
Middlle-Class American
Western European

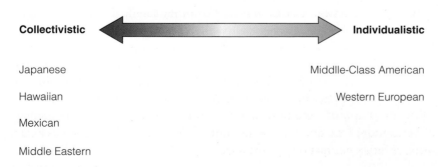

1. **Orientation: Collectivistic ⟷ Individualistic**
At one extreme of this dimension is the cultural value of *collectivism* (orientation toward the group), usually found in low-context cultures and exemplified by many families of Japanese, Hawaiian, Mexican, and Middle Eastern heritage. These groups tend to emphasize affiliation, cooperation, and interpersonal relations. At the other extreme of this dimension is the cultural value of *individualism* (orientation toward the individual), usually found in high-context cultures and exemplified by many families of middle-class American and Western European heritage. They tend to focus more on individual accomplishment, competition, and independence from the group. An individual's orientation on this dimension becomes significant in situations in which he or she has to choose between obligation to family and personal ambition—for example, deciding to remain geographically close to kin rather than relocating to earn more money or prestige. An individual's orientation on this dimension also influences business behavior: risk-taking, or innovation, versus conservatism, or conformity (Hayton, George, & Zahra, 2002). How would you describe your family?
2. **Coping Style: Active ⟷ Passive**
An active coping style is associated with "doing" and "getting things done," a passive coping style with "being" or "becoming." An active coping style also involves a future time orientation, a perception that time moves quickly and that one can control and change the environment. A passive coping style is associated with a belief that all events are determined by fate and are, therefore, inevitable. Some families, influenced by their cultural, religious, and/or economic backgrounds, exhibit a less active coping style than do others (Bennett, 2010). Coping style becomes significant in motivating families to seek social services, such as psychological support, when problems occur (McGoldrick et al., 1996). How would you describe your family?
3. **Attitude toward Authority: Submissive ⟷ Egalitarian**
This dimension can be observed in children: Do they regard their parents and teachers as clear authority figures whom they respect and obey without question, or do they see them as more nearly equal figures with whom they may disagree and question? For example, young children with Latino or Asian backgrounds have generally been found to be more obedient, respectful, and accepting of authority than are children with Euro-American backgrounds (Bennett, 2010). One's attitude toward authority on this dimension becomes significant in such situations as workplaces that reward assertiveness (Hofstede, 1991). How were you socialized regarding this dimension?
4. **Communication Style: Open/Expressive ⟷ Restrained/Private**
Some children tend to be more openly and freely expressive, sharing feelings and thoughts in a wide variety of situations, than are other children. Some children tend to be more direct and open in familiar social interactions than in unfamiliar ones. Still other children tend to be more polite and ritualistic in almost all situations (Bennett, 2003). An individual's communication style on this dimension becomes significant in relating to those whose way of interacting differs. A communication style reflects cultural values that are first learned in the family. For example, some families may believe that for the group to function effectively, its members' personal feelings must be openly expressed so differences of opinion can be compromised. Other families, on the other hand, may believe that for the group to function effectively, its members must refrain from expressing their personal feelings and opinions by keeping them private (Blake, 1994). How has your style of communication been affected by your family's cultural values?

Babies are born into a culture and learn appropriate social roles.

Lana K/Shutterstock.com

According to extensive cross-cultural research done by Kagicibasi (1996), family behavioral patterns and consequent socialization practices can be categorized as *interdependent* (stress on family loyalty, intergenerational dependency, control, and obedience) or *independent* (stress on individual achievement, separateness of generations, egalitarianism, and consensus). A child brought up with interdependent values would *give* his or her parent money if needed; a child brought up with independent values might *lend* the parent money, perhaps even charging interest.

Many immigrants have brought their cultural behavior patterns to the United States. The following is an excerpt from a family analysis done by a college student from a Persian Jewish family in Los Angeles (quoted in Greenfield & Suzuki, 1998, p. 1108).

IN CONTEXT Being a first-generation immigrant I have had to deal with . . . adjusting a collectivistic upbringing to an environment of individualism. . . .

We were brought up in a home where the "we" consciousness was stressed, rather than the "I" consciousness. We were taught that our behavior not only had implications for . . . ourselves but also for the rest of the family; for example, if I stayed out late at night, not only would I be taking the chance of getting robbed, raped, and/or murdered (implications of that experience for me), but also my younger brother and sister who looked up to me would also be jeopardized (implications of my actions for others). . . .

We were also taught to be responsible not only for ourselves, but also responsible for every other family member, thereby sharing the responsibility for both good and bad outcomes and playing a major part in each other's lives. For example, if my brother did bad in school, I was also responsible because as his older sister I was responsible to help him and take care of him and teach him right from wrong. I was, to an extent, as responsible for his actions as he and my parents were.

School and Child Care

Educational Philosophy

How did your school experiences and interactions influence your life?

The school acts as an agent of society in that it is organized to perpetuate that society's knowledge, skills, customs, and beliefs. Yet all education springs from some image of the future. Hence, the transmission of culture, in addition to the expanding knowledge and technology base, makes for difficult choices in curriculum regarding what information is most important. Socializing children for a society of rapid change is a continual challenge: How do you educate for adaptability? Do you teach basic skills or problem solving? Do you emphasize individual or group activities? Do you stress conformity or creativity?

Education professor John Goodlad (2004) studied documents related to the purposes of schooling spanning 300 years of U.S. history. He found four broad categories of goals: academic (reading, writing, arithmetic); vocational (preparation for the world of work); social and civic (preparation to participate in a democracy); and personal (development of individual talent and self-expression). Schooling goals and outcomes will be discussed in Chapter 6.

Classroom Management

The social order of society is communicated to the child largely in the classroom—a setting in which children are evaluated by the teacher's comments, report cards, marks on papers, charts, classmates' judgments, and self-judgments. "Who can help Sally with that problem?" "Who has read the most books?" "Only papers with the best handwriting will be displayed for parents' night." Evaluation contributes to socialization in that the norms and standards of society are learned via the criteria of the evaluation. The self-concept emerges from how well the child meets the expectations of others, the evaluators (Harter, 1999).

The political ideology of society is communicated to the child through textbooks and how subjects are taught. How

Grades are the evaluation method used in this classroom to encourage and reinforce learning.

Tetra images/Getty Images

is the classroom setting organized? Do students compete with one another, participate in discussion, or pursue activities independently? Do they collaborate and help each other on projects?

Socialization outcomes in teacher-centered and learner-centered classrooms are different (Wells, 2001). Teacher- and learner-centered classrooms will be discussed in more detail in Chapter 7. The teacher in the school also contributes to the socialization process by serving as a model for children to imitate. Teachers who are involved in their subject matter tend to have active, curious students who want to learn (Brophy, 1992).

Child Care

As a result of societal changes, child care has become an important socialization agent. The specific effects of care from someone other than a parent are controversial, involving many variables such as a child's temperament, type of care, hours/day in care, age when day care began, and parents' involvement (Vandell et al., 2010). Specifics will be discussed in Chapter 5.

As a child, who was your best friend and why?

Peers

The peer group comprises individuals who are of approximately the same age and social status and who have common interests. Experiences in child-care facilities can expose children to peer relations months after birth. However, reciprocal interactions in the peer group don't usually begin until about age 3, when the child starts to understand the views of others and, therefore, is able to cooperate, share, and take turns. Cognitively, the child is beginning to move away from **egocentrism**, the inability to look at the world from any point of view other than one's own. As the child matures and develops new interests, his or her peer groups change. Some may be based on proximity, such as the children in the neighborhood or the classroom, and others on interest, such as those on the soccer team or in Scouts.

egocentrism the cognitive inability to look at the world from any point of view other than one's own

> The peer group gives children experience in egalitarian types of relationships that are qualitatively different from relationships with authority figures. In peer groups children engage in a process of give-and-take not ordinarily possible in relationships with adults. In the family and school, children necessarily are subordinate to parents and teachers. . . . Peer groups have their own subcultures with their own norms, values, and established patterns of behavior. Children entering a peer group want the companionship, attention, and good will of its members. For having acceptable characteristics and acting in the appropriate or valued manner, the group rewards its members by bestowing attention, approval, or leadership. For being, or behaving, otherwise, the peer group punishes by disdain, ostracism, or other expressions of disapproval. (Handel, Cahill, & Elkin, 2007, p. 184)

Thus, children come to look at themselves from the point of view of the group. The peer group rewards sociability, or getting along, and rejects deviations, such as eccentricity, aggression, and showing off (Kindermann & Gest, 2009). The child learns to obey the "rules of the game" and how to assume the various roles required in the game, such as batter, pitcher, or catcher. The peer group exerts control by refusing to include those who do not conform to its values or rules. Victimization and bullying of the deviant can also occur.

> An example of the power of peer group pressure is the classic children's story by Hans Christian Andersen, *The Emperor's New Clothes*. The emperor, who was very vain about his clothes, bought some cloth that—according to the merchants who sold it—was invisible only to those not worthy of their positions in life. He proudly wore his new outfit made of this unique cloth in a parade before the entire town. No one dared admit to others that the emperor really hadn't any clothes on, for fear of being judged unworthy. It took the astonished cry of an innocent child to make everyone realize the truth.

The peer group functions as a socializing agent in that it provides information about the world and oneself from a perspective other than that of the family (Hartup, 1996; Rubin, Bukowski, & Parker, 2006). It is a source of social comparison. From the peer group, children receive feedback about their abilities. Through interaction with their equals, people find out whether they are better than, the same as, or worse than their friends in sports, dating, grades, and other areas of life. Within the peer group the child can experiment with various roles—leader, follower, clown, troublemaker, or peacemaker—and discover how the others react. There is increasing evidence that experiences with peers affect children's feelings, thoughts, and behavior (Bukowski, Brendgen, & Vitaro, 2007). For example, peer rejection is associated with later antisocial and/or aggressive behavior.

Peers also serve as a support group for the expression of values and attitudes (Hartup, 1996; Schneider, 2000). Members often discuss situations with parents, siblings, and teachers. Beyond that, friends may offer sympathy and/or advice in handling problems. That children spend an increasing amount of time with their peers was illustrated in studies of children ages 2 to 12 (Bukowski, Brendgen, & Vitaro, 2007; Ellis, Rogoff, & Cromer, 1981). It was observed that by age 8, due to school, child care, and after-school activities, children were interacting with other children six times more than with adults. Infinite opportunities to connect to peers (social networking) occur via the Internet and cell phones through e-mail, text messaging, and voice communication. Such technology provides a means for school-agers and adolescents to relate to one another virtually any time and any place, and anonymously if they so choose. The peer group, then, as an agent of socialization exerts a strong influence on children's ideas and behavior, especially those who need social approval and fear rejection. The quality of the parent–child relationship is the most important mediating factor affecting peer group influence (Collins et al., 2000). Peer group influences will be discussed in Chapter 8.

Mass Media

As a child, what was your favorite book or movie and why?

Mass media include newspapers, magazines, books, radio, television, videos, movies, computers, consoles, and other means of communication and information technology that reach large audiences via an impersonal medium between the sender and the receiver. Unlike other agents of socialization, the mass media do not ordinarily involve direct personal interactions; the interactions are of a more technical nature. The mass media must be considered socializing agents, not only because of their prevalence, but because they reveal many aspects of the society and elicit cognitive processes in children that cultivate their understanding of the real world (Comstock & Scharrer, 2007; Kaiser Family Foundation [KFF], 2010). Newspapers report such items as current baseball scores or government policy; magazines illustrate the latest fashions or suggest things to do with free time in the summer; radio stations play popular songs; books discuss issues such as sex and drugs; television gives glimpses of hospitals, courtrooms, and family situations; computers and consoles provide interactive activities, both real and virtual. Television, videos, and movies also show relationships between people in various settings, providing children with images or patterns of how to behave or interact in similar situations.

The interactivity potential of the computer makes it influential in socialization.

Cengage Learning

Television, movies, books, and computers (the Internet) provide information about society. Through them children come to learn about parts of the world they might not otherwise encounter or experience. They are taken under the sea, to outer space, to the jungles, to other times, and to other countries. The media also provide role models—the hero, the villain, the detective, the doctor, the lawyer, the mother, and the father. They reflect social attitudes—beliefs about political issues, such as war or taxes, social issues such as abortion or child abuse, occupations, sex, and minority groups. Media effects can be short-term, such as excitation and simple imitation, or long-term, such as observational learning and emotional desensitization (Dubow, Huesmann, & Greenwood, 2007).

Children, because of their cognitive immaturity, are of special concern regarding media influence (Roberts & Foehr, 2004; Perse, 2001). They process the content they see and hear and transform it into something meaningful to them, which may or may not be accurate or desirable. One concern is that young children may come to think of all people in a group as having the same characteristics as the people in that group as presented on TV or in books, and this may influence their attitudes. For example, in the majority of television shows and movies, the white male is portrayed as dominant, brave, powerful, and competent (Berry & Asamen, 2001; Huston & Wright, 1998; Signorielli, 2007). This is true in books as well (Anderson & Hamilton, 2006). These images are especially influential for children who do not have the real experience to evaluate the attitude portrayed.

Another concern is children's susceptibility to advertising (Calvert, 2008; Huston & Wright, 1998; Kunkel, 2001). Many children demand that parents buy products and toys seen on TV. Children often imitate well-known media characters, especially active, powerful ones. They role-play, they bring the toys to school, and they wear clothing decorated with the media characters. The problem with marketed media-related toys, clothing, and supplies is not only the materialistic and competitive values they foster, but the aggressive acting-out behavior they inspire in children's play (Levin, 1998). Commercialism abounds in children's sports and schools, as well as on TV.

With the introduction of new technology to mass media, such as modems connecting to the Internet and cell phones connecting to friends, children can play a greater role in their own socialization. They can, for example, access any information that is on the Internet (unless access to a site is blocked). They also have more opportunities to interact with media independent of adult mediation, as many households have more than one TV, and cell phones, e-mail, and social networks provide opportunities for instant communication. Various media influences will be discussed in Chapter 9.

What kind of neighborhood(s) did you grow up in?

Community

The term **community** is derived from the Latin word for fellowship. It refers to the affective relationships expected among closely knit groups of people sharing common interests. It also refers to people living in a particular geographical area who are bound together politically and economically. The function of the community, then, is to provide a sense of belonging, friendship, and socialization of children (Etzioni, 1993). A survey by the National League of Cities cited five characteristics that make a city "family-friendly": education (accessible quality school programs), recreation, community safety, citizen involvement, and physical environment (Meyers & Kyle, 1998). Many sociologists and psychologists are concerned with the erosion of community ties as we move toward the future (Putnam, 2000). The factors contributing to this erosion, such as fear of violence, technology, mobility, and "busyness," as well as coping strategies (developing social capital), will be discussed in Chapter 10. "**Social capital**" is a term referring to individual and communal time and energy (human resources) available for such things as social networking, personal recreation, community improvement, civic engagement, and other activities that create social bonds between individuals and groups (CDC, 2009a).

community a group of people sharing fellowship and common interests; a group of people living in the same geographic area who are bound together politically and economically

social capital term referring to individual and communal time and energy (human resources) available for such things as social networking, personal recreation, community improvement, civic engagement, and other activities that create social bonds between individuals and groups

The size, population, and mobility pattern of a community determine the pattern of human interaction. In a town with a small and stable population of a few thousand, most people know each other, in contrast to a larger, more mobile town of many thousands. Small-town interaction involves more intimate details of people's lives than does large-town interaction. In a small town, people see each other in many settings—at the store, at school, at the movies, at church. In a large town, relationships are more fragmented—it is unlikely that one would just by chance see a friend at a restaurant, simply because there are so many restaurants available in a large town. Similarly, a large town provides more activities than does a small town. Thus, one's interactions focus on the community groups to which one belongs—Scouts, Little League, the "Y," and so on.

One function of such community groups is to give children different perspectives on life—to broaden their range of experience and give them new statuses or roles. In this respect, community agencies and organizations contribute to the socialization of children. In Scouting, for example, children learn about various occupational roles through a badge program. The Scout is supervised by a designated community "sponsor"—perhaps by a veterinarian in caring for an animal. A church or temple youth group might participate in a project of visiting people in a home for the elderly on a regular basis. Community libraries open the world of reading to children; museums open the worlds of art, science, and natural history.

This community setting, with sidewalks in front of the homes and a nearby neighborhood school, provides opportunities for children to walk to school together.

Yarinca/iStockphoto.com

Neighborhoods are often stratified by economic status (Leventhal & Brooks-Gunn, 2000). Lower-economic-status families may live in less desirable sections, whereas upper-economic-status families may live in large homes surrounded by green lawns or in apartments with doorkeepers. The location of these neighborhoods in the larger community influences interaction patterns. If children from different neighborhoods attend a particular school, or share community services such as recreation centers and library, all the children have an opportunity to interact with many diverse individuals. On the other hand, if the neighborhoods are segregated, each having its own school and recreational facilities, the children generally interact with those like themselves.

People in the neighborhood, adults and older children, are the ones with whom the young child interacts and "probably stand second only to parents in terms of their power to influence the child's behavior" (Bronfenbrenner, 1979, p. 161; Schorr, 1997). The adults in the neighborhood are role models. They may be carpenters, engineers, entrepreneurs, teachers, or recreation leaders. The older children are models of behavior and interaction. Children often learn games and cues about getting along with certain people from older children: "Mrs. Grady is an old grouch; she won't give your ball back if it goes in her yard." The organization of community practices and routines, such as whether children are involved directly (participate and learn alongside adults) or indirectly (engage in activities planned for them by adults) impact developmental outcomes (Rogoff, 2003). Direct involvement provides experiences in learning by doing; indirect involvement provides experiences in learning by instruction.

A community can offer an *informal social support system*—relatives, friends, neighbors who can be counted on to help in a crisis. For example, when Mrs. Cooper went to the hospital, her mother-in-law came to care for the children and the neighbors took turns cooking meals and doing errands for the family. A community can also have a more *formal social support system*, such as institutionalized child care, Big Brothers/Big Sisters, Meals on Wheels, and Parents Without Partners. These formal support systems may be funded by tax dollars, donations, or membership fees.

Formal support systems in a community usually emerge through the process of advocacy. **Advocacy** means speaking or writing in support of something—for example, setting goals on behalf of children and seeing that politicians or governmental agencies implement them. It is a long and arduous process, however, to go from goals to laws. Thus, if community members want to improve opportunities for their children, they must get involved in politics. Politics begins locally, in one's own community. If community members want their children to have "the right to full opportunity for play and recreation," they can communicate this desire to their city council members and follow through by examining how their local tax dollars are distributed. For example, one city doubled the money previously budgeted for programs such as child care, youth activities, senior citizens' food, and a shelter for victims of domestic violence. Most of the money had been previously allocated to street repair. The most effective community services supporting children and families involve collaboration between informal and formal networks providing empowerment (Epps & Jackson, 2000).

advocacy speaking or writing in support of a person, a group, or a cause

How do we learn the ways of the society in which we live?

Methods of Socialization

Given that socialization is the process by which people learn the ways of society so that they can function effectively within it, we now turn to examine the various methods by which these ways are transmitted to children (see Table 2.1). These socialization methods vary according to culture, family, child, and situation (Bugental, 2000; Laible & Thompson, 2007).

Why do you have to be attached to someone to be socialized?

Affective Methods of Socialization

affective having to do with feelings or emotions

attachment an affectional tie that one person forms to another person, binding them together in space and enduring over time

Affective refers to feelings or emotions, such as love, anger, fear, or disgust. Affective mechanisms include responses to others, feelings about self, feelings about others, and expression of emotions. Affect emerges from person-to-person interaction, which leads to attachment. The socialization of the child, whether intentional or unintentional, is accomplished through person-to-person interaction. When people are attached to one another, they interact often; thus, attachment and interaction are bidirectional, or reciprocal (Laible & Thompson, 2007). Reciprocal parent–child relations are foundations for socialization.

Attachment is an "affectional tie that one person forms to another specific person, binding them together in space and enduring over time" (Ainsworth, 1973, p. 1). Socialization begins with personal attachment (Collins et al., 2000; Handel, Cahill, & Elkin 2007). The human infant is born helpless, requiring care. In the process of caring for the infant, the parents or caregivers hold, play with, and talk to the infant. They respond to the feelings evoked in them by the child. This sensitive, responsive caregiving is the foundation for social interaction, and it is this interaction that contributes to many socialization outcomes for the child (Kuczynski, 2003; Laible & Thompson, 2007).

Infants who are responded to when they cry, who are fed, held, and spoken to, will develop a secure *attachment* and a sense of trust toward the world. On the other hand, infants who receive minimal or inconsistent care will develop an *insecure attachment* and a sense of mistrust (Erikson, 1963). Our first human relationship, then, provides the basis for our later expectations regarding other relationships.

TeachSource Video Activity

Go to the Education CourseMate website to access the video entitled "0–2 yrs. Attachment in Infants & Toddlers." Why is early attachment so influential in later relationships?

Table 2.1 Methods of Socialization

Method	Techniques
Affective (effect emerges from feeling)	Attachment
Operant (effect emerges from acting)	Reinforcement Extinction Punishment Feedback Learning by doing
Observational (effect emerges from imitating)	Modeling
Cognitive (effect emerges from information processing)	Instruction Setting standards Reasoning
Sociocultural (effect emerges from conforming)	Group pressure Tradition Rituals and routines Symbols
Apprenticeship (effect emerges from guided participation)	Structuring Collaborating Transferring

An outcome of attachment, in addition to being a reference for future social interactions, is the feeling of competence. The more securely attached children are to a nurturing adult, the more willing they are to separate to explore the environment; the more insecurely attached they are, the less likely they are to separate and try out new things (Ainsworth, 1973). Preschoolers who as infants were judged to be securely attached at age 1.5 years were observed to be more enthusiastic, sympathetic to others, cooperative, independent, and competent than those who, as infants, displayed insecure attachments (Sroufe et al., 2005). Insecurely attached children have also been found to exhibit disruptive, hostile, or aggressive behavior in preschool (Sroufe, 1996; Waters et al., 1993). This is especially true for boys (Fearan et al., 2010). This behavior may be influenced by the child's temperament; a difficult temperament has been found to contribute to such negative externalizing behavior (Burgess et al., 2003).

Mother–child interaction is the basis for attachment and a sense of trust.

Cengage Learning

Attachment to the primary caregiver is the first of many important emotional relationships with significant others that the child will form in the future. These significant others may include relatives, teachers, friends, and coaches. Because each of these others is unique and because each situation the child encounters with these others is unique, each will contribute in a different way to the child's socialization.

David Elkind (1981b) discusses the importance of attachment in determining how children learn: "In children's early years, adults predigest experience for them much as mothers predigest food to provide milk for their babies" (p. 20). Elkind cites an example of a teacher who always had children around her when she used various art materials. She showed them different ways paper could be folded and how to use a brush, and she joyfully produced new colors when she mixed the paints. The children not only acquired the ability to fold paper, make brush strokes, and mix paint; they also acquired an attitude of appreciation, enjoyment, and respect for art materials.

According to a review of the research by Laible and Thompson (2007), the quality of the early attachment relationship between parent and child moderates the influence of parental emotional communication, rewards and sanctions, parental instructions, and the child's understanding of parental behavior and transmission of values. In sum, a child who is securely attached to a parent is more likely to comply with parental standards than a child who is insecurely attached.

When the child is attached to a caregiver, socialization takes place in many ways. Some of these result from the child's action (an *operant method*); some of them result from the child's imitating (an *observational method*); some of them result from the child's information processing (a *cognitive method*); some of them result from the child's cultural traditions (a *sociocultural method*); and some of them result from guided participation (an *apprenticeship method*). A discussion follows.

Operant Methods of Socialization

What influences whether your behavior will be repeated or modified?

Operant refers to producing an effect. When one's behavior is followed by a favorable outcome (reinforcement), the probability of that behavior occurring again is increased. When one's behavior has no favorable outcome (for example, it does not get attention, it is ignored) or has an unfavorable outcome (punishment), the probability of that behavior occurring again is decreased. Operant methods take into account the participatory role of individuals in their own socialization.

operant producing an effect

Several socialization techniques can be used to increase desired behavior: positive reinforcement, negative reinforcement, and shaping.

reinforcement an object or event that is presented following a behavior and that serves to increase the likelihood that the behavior will occur again

Reinforcement

A **reinforcement** is an object or event that is presented following a behavior and that serves to increase the likelihood that the behavior will occur again. Reinforcement can be positive or negative. **Positive reinforcement** is a reward, or pleasant consequence, given for desired

positive reinforcement a reward, or pleasant consequence, given for desired behavior

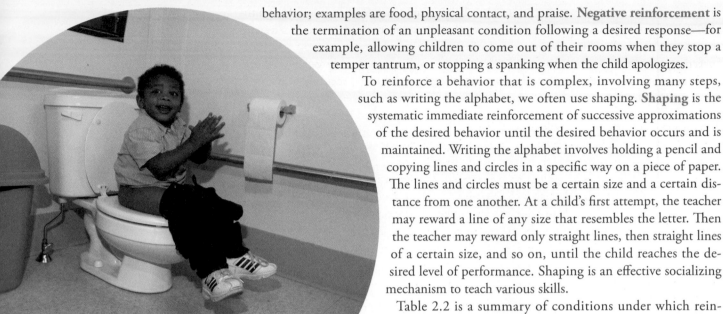

This young child has likely been reinforced for using the potty.

Cengage Learning

negative reinforcement the termination of an unpleasant condition following a desired response

shaping the systematic immediate reinforcement of successive approximations of the desired behavior until the desired behavior occurs and is maintained

behavior; examples are food, physical contact, and praise. **Negative reinforcement** is the termination of an unpleasant condition following a desired response—for example, allowing children to come out of their rooms when they stop a temper tantrum, or stopping a spanking when the child apologizes.

To reinforce a behavior that is complex, involving many steps, such as writing the alphabet, we often use shaping. **Shaping** is the systematic immediate reinforcement of successive approximations of the desired behavior until the desired behavior occurs and is maintained. Writing the alphabet involves holding a pencil and copying lines and circles in a specific way on a piece of paper. The lines and circles must be a certain size and a certain distance from one another. At a child's first attempt, the teacher may reward a line of any size that resembles the letter. Then the teacher may reward only straight lines, then straight lines of a certain size, and so on, until the child reaches the desired level of performance. Shaping is an effective socializing mechanism to teach various skills.

Table 2.2 is a summary of conditions under which reinforcement can be effective as a socializing technique (Martin & Pear, 2010).

Using reinforcement as a socializing technique has several problems, besides having to wait for the desired behavior to occur: (1) Individuals respond differently to reinforcers. For some children, a toy is an effective reinforcer; for others, adult approval is more effective. It is sometimes difficult to find the best one. (2) The child may become bored with the reinforcer, so its effectiveness diminishes. (3) Being human, it is difficult for adults to constantly reward children's desired behavior, even during the initial stages. If parents want to train a child to urinate in the toilet, they must be present as well as ready to put the child on the toilet at certain intervals. They also must wait patiently for the desired behavior to occur. (4) Adults sometimes unintentionally reinforce the very behaviors they want to eliminate. When children who have been toilet trained begin to urinate in their pants again, perhaps because they see their baby brother or sister do it, and the mother says "I thought you were a big boy (girl)," it is highly likely that the undesired behavior

Table 2.2 Conditions for Reinforcement

	Behavior	Example	Comment
Condition (1).	The desired behavior must first be exhibited before it can be reinforced.	In training a child to defecate in the toilet, the caregiver must put the child on the seat and wait for the behavior to occur before reinforcing it.	The main unresolved question accompanying the technique of positive reinforcement is: How do you get children to make the desired response in the first place so that they can be rewarded?
Condition (2).	The desired behavior must be reinforced immediately the first time it occurs.	If you want children to verbalize their requests rather than point to or grunt for desired objects, you must reward them when they say, for instance, "Juice."	Initially, the desired behavior must be reinforced each time it is exhibited. Every time children verbalize their requests, they should get what is asked for. Every time children defecate in the toilet, they should be rewarded.
Condition (3).	When the newly acquired behavior is being performed relatively frequently, reinforcement can then become intermittent. Reward or praise can be given every few times the behavior is performed (or every few days).	"I'm glad you're asking for what you want." "I'm proud you're using the toilet now."	Because the long-range goal is self-reward, subjective reinforcers, such as privileges and praise, should be used in conjunction with objective reinforcers, such as food, toys, or money.

will occur again, because negative attention is better than no attention. (5) Although the goal is for the child to internally regulate his or her behavior, reinforcement is externally regulated and may reduce the motivation for self-control.

Other socialization techniques that can decrease or eliminate undesired behavior include extinction, punishment, feedback, and learning by doing.

Extinction

If reinforcement increases the likelihood that a response will occur again, then removal of the reinforcement should decrease and eventually eliminate, or extinguish, the likelihood of that response. **Extinction** is the gradual disappearance of a learned behavior following the removal of the reinforcement. Basically, it involves ignoring undesirable responses. For example, to extinguish the habit of nail biting, a father decides to ignore his daughter every time she bites her nails instead of nagging her to stop, as he used to do. Thus, he removes the previous reinforcement of attention. When she does not bite her nails for a 10-minute stretch, however, he praises her. Gradually the interval between nail-biting episodes becomes longer and longer, with the father giving praise every half-hour for not nail biting, but still ignoring his daughter when she does bite her nails.

extinction the gradual disappearance of a learned behavior following the removal of the reinforcement

Extinction must be used in conjunction with reinforcement to be effective as a socializing method. Annoying behaviors such as tantrums, dawdling, and tattling respond well, but more complex or deep-seated behaviors such as aggression, stealing, and overeating do not.

Timeout is a type of extinction in which all reinforcement is removed. Usually, the child spends a specified amount of time in his or her room, in a corner, or in any place where behavior can be ignored. A timeout can give a child time and space to better manage emotions and behavior. Reasons for the timeout should be given, so the child can use them for self-control in the future.

Punishment

According to David Ausubel (1957), it is impossible to guide behavior effectively using only positive reinforcement and extinction; children cannot learn what is not approved or tolerated simply by making a reverse generalization from the approval they receive for acceptable behavior. Children must be enabled to process what they are *not* supposed to do, as well as what they *are*. Thus, non-hostile punishment or constructive responses designed to correct misbehavior can have an informative effect.

Punishment consists of physically or psychologically painful stimuli or the temporary withdrawal of pleasant stimuli when undesirable behavior occurs. A physically painful stimulus might be a spanking; a psychologically painful stimulus might be a scolding or harsh criticism causing shame; withdrawal of a pleasant stimulus might be removing a privilege such as TV. Punishment is used as an intervention technique to discourage undesirable behavior. It is probably most valuable when a child's behavior must be stopped quickly for safety reasons. A 2-year-old who runs out into the street is more likely to be stopped from doing it in the future by a quick swat on the rear end than by a reward for staying on the sidewalk. A 2-year-old also cannot really understand the logical reasons for not running into the street. Thus, a more concrete physical reminder may be necessary.

punishment physically or psychologically painful stimuli or the temporary withdrawal of pleasant stimuli when undesirable behavior occurs

Research has found that the quality of the early parent–child attachment relationship moderates the influence of punishment. Specifically, securely attached children were more attentive to parental socialization efforts (reinforcement and punishment) than those who were insecurely attached (Laible & Thompson, 2007).

For punishment to be useful as an effective socializing technique, the following summary applies (Martin & Pear, 2010):

- **Timing.** The closer the punishment is to the behavior, the more effective it will be.
- **Reasoning.** Punishment accompanied by an explanation is more effective than punishment alone. "We do not play in the street because cars might hurt us."

- **Consistency.** If children are consistently punished for repeating a behavior, they are more likely to stop it than if they are sometimes punished, sometimes ignored, and sometimes rewarded. Aggression is an example of a behavior sometimes handled inconsistently. It may be punished at home or at school when the child is caught, yet may be rewarded in the peer group.
- **Attachment to the person doing the punishing.** The more nurturant the relationship between the punisher and the punished, the more effective the punishment will be. A child whose parent denies a privilege for undesired behavior, such as coming home late, is less likely to repeat that behavior than if an acquaintance, such as a babysitter, administers the punishment.

The use of punishment as an effective technique in modifying behavior has been criticized for the following reasons (Martin & Pear, 2010):

- Punishment may stop the undesirable behavior immediately, but by itself it does not indicate appropriate or desired behavior.
- Punishment may merely slow the rate at which the undesirable behavior occurs, rather than eliminate it entirely. Or it may change the form in which the undesirable behavior occurs. People who stop smoking often report they begin eating more. Children who are punished for physical aggression may engage in verbal aggression ("I hate you," "You big doody head").
- Punishment by an adult may have an undesirable modeling effect on the child. Parents who abuse their children are likely to have been abused by their parents.
- The emotional side effects of punishment (fear, embarrassment, shame, low self-esteem, and tenseness) may be psychologically more damaging than the original behavior.

In sum, punishment can function as a socializing technique when used appropriately (Martin & Pear, 2010). It can provide an opportunity to reestablish attachment or affection following emotional release; it can provide vicarious learning by observation of others being punished; it can reduce guilt in that it can provide an opportunity to correct the misbehavior; and, when combined with reasoning, it can enable the internalization of moral standards. Thus, when using punishment, be aware of the negative, as well as the positive, consequences for the child.

For a summary of behavioral consequences, see Table 2.3.

IN CONTEXT When a group of 10-year-old boys wrote on the wall of their camp cabin, their counselor required them to spend the afternoon scrubbing walls instead of going swimming. This type of punishment is referred to as a "logical consequence"—one that is arranged by the parent or another adult and that is logically related to the misbehavior (Dreikurs & Grey, 1968). For a logical consequence to be effective, however, it must make sense to the child. For example, Todd continually left his clothes around his room after repeatedly being told to put them in the hamper. His mother finally said, "Clothes that do not get picked up do not get washed." Todd still did not pick up his clothes. Finally, when Todd wanted to wear his favorite shirt and realized it was not washed because he had not put it in the hamper, the consequence became effective—he picked up his clothes.

Feedback

feedback evaluative information, both positive and negative, about one's behavior

Feedback is evaluative information, both positive and negative, about one's behavior. It is an example of a dynamic, bidirectional relationship between teacher and learner in that the teacher modifies his or her response according to that of the learner.

Feedback responses may include an approving nod, a questioning look, a comment, further instructions, or a reminder. Feedback provides knowledge of results and how to

Table 2.3 Summary of Behavioral Consequences

Type	Definition	Effect
Positive reinforcement	Present a stimulus (give attention)	Increases desirable response
Negative reinforcement	Remove aversive stimulus (stop scolding)	Increases desirable response
Extinction	Remove pleasant stimulus (stop giving attention)	Decreases undesirable response
Punishment	Present aversive stimulus (start scolding)	Decreases undesirable response

improve them, factors shown to be important to learning (Bangert-Drowns et al., 1991; Bransford, Brown, & Cocking, 2000).

A classical example of a feedback experiment involved being apprised of performance accuracy while learning a simple skill (Baker & Young, 1960). The task to be learned was to reproduce on paper the length of a 4-inch piece of wood. The subjects were blindfolded. However, they could feel the piece of wood. One group of subjects was told after each performance whether they were within .20 inch of the correct length. The other group received no feedback. When both groups were tested, the group receiving feedback consistently improved, whereas the group receiving no knowledge of results made no consistent progress. When the feedback was stopped, the first group's accuracy dropped abruptly.

This experiment demonstrated that in order to increase accuracy of performance, individuals must change incorrect responses. In this case, unless the individuals were made fully aware of their incorrect behavior, change was unlikely to occur.

The effects of feedback on performance can be summarized as follows (Good & Brophy, 1986):

- Feedback generally increases motivation.
- Feedback usually improves subsequent performance.
- Generally, the more specific the knowledge of performance, the more rapidly performance improves.
- Feedback given punctually is usually more effective than feedback given long after a task has been completed.
- Noticeable decreases in feedback often result in a marked decline in performance.
- When knowledge of results is not provided, individuals tend to develop substitutes. For example, they may compare their performance to that of peers to determine whether it is better or worse.

Thus, feedback provides children with information on how they are measuring up to standards of behavior and performance: "Susie, your letters need to go on the line. I've circled your best one; make five more just like it." "Jack, that frown on your face is most unpleasant; what is your problem?" "Garth, next time you have a friend over, say 'Thank you for coming.'" "Terry, that outfit looks very good on you."

Learning by Doing

Sometimes socialization occurs through experiencing and interacting. As an ancient Chinese proverb says, "I hear and I forget, I see and I remember, I do and I understand." Psychologist Jean Piaget (1952), known for his developmental theory of cognitive development, states that children learn through their own activity. Likewise, psychologist Jerome Bruner (1981) believes that children learn through discovery. Learning is a slow process of construction and transformation of experience into meaning. Learning to ride

A child learning to do something by doing it.

Cengage Learning

self-efficacy the belief that one can master a situation and produce positive outcomes

a bicycle is an example of learning by doing. It involves experimenting and discovering how to shift your weight while pedaling, holding on, and watching where you are going, all at the same time. Albert Bandura (2000) relates learning by doing to the attribution of **self-efficacy**—the belief that one can master a situation and produce positive effects. For example, children who are encouraged and given opportunities to become competent (as by helping to cook, putting a puzzle together, or creating artwork) tend to be motivated to achieve on other tasks.

Offering developmentally appropriate choices, meaningful activities that create opportunities for children to succeed, enables children to learn by doing because they can experience what works and what doesn't (Schank, 2004). Evidence from studies on children supports the relationship between learning by doing and successful problem solving. For example, in one study (Smith & Dutton, 1979), a group of children was given the opportunity to play with materials involved in a problem. Another group received instruction on how to solve the problem, but was not given the opportunity to play with the materials. The group that played with the materials ended up solving the problem as easily as the children who had received instruction. On a more complex problem, requiring innovative thinking, the group that had the opportunity to play with the materials did better in solving the problem than the group that had received instruction. Thus, as Piaget and Bruner said, experience, or learning by doing, leads to discovering ways to tackle problems.

Interacting with the computer is an example of how learning by doing is effective. The computer and various software programs provide opportunities for experiential learning—problem solving, creativity, simulations, and personal tutoring (Schank, 2004). These opportunities offer support for different learning styles (visual, auditory, kinesthetic, and so on) to enable various users to learn (Papert, 1993). Every time I get new software for my computer, I learn how to use it by doing it—seeing what works and what doesn't; I only refer to the instruction manual when my experience no longer serves me.

When children play, they are learning by doing (Hughes, 2010). They are being socialized in that they are practicing physical, intellectual, and social skills—physical skills such as climbing, jumping, writing, and cutting; intellectual skills such as remembering, reasoning, making decisions, and solving problems; social skills such as communicating, sharing, cooperating, competing, and having empathy. For example, as children experiment with different behaviors and social roles, they are finding out what it feels like to be Mom, or baby brother; they are experiencing what it is like to wash the car, or to play doctor; they are feeling the joy of approval and the despair of disapproval. They are constructing views of the world that will influence future thinking and behavior.

How can you learn complicated behavior by observing it?

Observational Methods of Socialization

Modeling

Modeling is a form of imitative learning that occurs by observing another person (the model) perform a behavior and experience its consequence. It enables us to learn appropriate social behavior, attitudes, and emotions vicariously or secondhand. The models can be parents, siblings, relatives, friends, teachers, coaches, or television characters.

modeling a form of imitative learning that occurs by observing another person (the model) perform a behavior and experience its consequence

IN CONTEXT Six-year-old Serena went on her first boat ride in her uncle's new boat. She watched the waves ripple on the lake as her uncle joyfully demonstrated the power of his boat's new motor to her parents. When they docked, Serena's uncle tied up the boat. The next day Serena could not wait to go for another ride. She besieged her uncle with questions while motoring around the lake, and when they pulled up to the dock, to her uncle's amazement Serena jumped out, grabbed the rope, and tied up the boat.

Serena's behavior, her attitude about boating, and her performance in tying up the boat illustrate socialization through observational learning, or modeling. Modeling is a significant socializing method. As children mature, they acquire a wide range of complex patterns of behavior through identification with admired models and these patterns become part of their repertoire for future interactions.

Modeling (observational learning) involves the ability to abstract information from what is observed, store it in memory, make generalizations and rules about behavior, retrieve the appropriate information, and act it out at the appropriate time. Thus, modeling enables one to develop new ways of behaving in situations not previously experienced. Serena, for example, "knew" how to tie up the boat without having previously tried it or been instructed on how to do it. The probability that children will imitate a model is a function of their (1) attention, (2) level of cognitive development, (3) retention, (4) type of activity being observed, (5) motivation, (6) ability to reproduce the behavior, and (7) repertoire of alternative behaviors (Bandura, 1989, 2001).

Observation and modeling are emphasized as socialization methods in some families, especially those whose cultural heritage is high-context. These methods enable children to participate in chores alongside adults or older siblings according to their developmental abilities. For example, in some African tribes girls as young as age 3 are given their own hoes to work in the gardens with their mothers and older sisters (Whiting & Edwards, 1988). In some New Guinean tribes, after having observed their mothers and helped turn things over on the fire with tongs, 3- to 5-year-old girls are given the responsibility of collecting firewood and starting the fire for cooking; boys of this age, having helped older males cut open fish, are given their own small pocket knives (Rogoff, 2003).

Various factors affect the extent to which children will imitate modeled behavior. A basic criterion is a good relationship between caregiver and child (Forman, Aksan, & Kochanska, 2004). Models who are perceived as similar (physically and/or psychologically) to the observer are likely to be identified with and imitated: "I have yellow hair, just like Mommy." "You have a strong will just like your grandfather." Models who are perceived as nurturant are more likely to be identified with and imitated: "My daddy always brings me presents when he comes back from a trip." "My coach always has time to listen to me." Models who are perceived as powerful or prestigious are more likely to be identified with and imitated (Bandura, Ross, & Ross, 1963): "My grandmother won first prize in the fair for her chocolate cake!" "My teacher is the smartest person in the whole world!"

Children's behavior is also influenced by whether the model with whom they identify is punished or reinforced. It has been demonstrated that children who see a model being punished for aggressive behavior are less likely to imitate that behavior than children who see a model being rewarded or experiencing no consequences (Bandura, 1965).

Television provides an excellent example of a context in which observational learning and consequent modeling take place. There is much evidence that children learn both prosocial and antisocial behavior by watching TV (Comstock & Scharrer, 2007; Perse, 2001; Roberts & Foehr, 2004). For example, conducting a series of studies on the behaviors of preschool children during free play, Friedrich and Stein (1973) found that the group who watched 12 episodes of *Mister Rogers' Neighborhood* (prosocial) over a four-week period persisted longer on tasks, were more likely to obey rules, and were more likely to delay gratification without protest than the group who watched 12 episodes of *Batman* and *Superman* (antisocial) for the same period or the group who watched shows about farms and animals (neutral). For another example, studies of preschool children have shown a relationship between violent television viewing and aggressive behavior during free play at preschool (Levin & Carlsson-Paige, 1995; Singer & Singer, 1980).

The reason that televised behavior, whether prosocial or antisocial, is likely to be modeled is that children observe someone being rewarded for an act. Prosocial behavior on

TV is generally reinforced by the person's getting lots of attention or becoming a hero. Antisocial behavior is generally reinforced on TV by the person's "getting away with it" or obtaining a desired object.

What socialization methods coincide with the ways you process information most effectively?

Cognitive Methods of Socialization

Cognitive methods of socialization focus on how an individual processes information, or abstracts meaning from experiences. Socialization agents use proactive strategies including instruction, setting standards, and reasoning to influence outcomes. Outcomes are also affected, however, by the individual's cognitive representations of the social world (Bugental & Grusec, 2006). For example, a child who is maltreated will interpret proactive strategies differently than a child who has experienced affectional early relationships (controlling versus guidance).

Instruction

Instruction provides knowledge and information and is a useful socializing mechanism. For instruction to be effective, however, the child must be able to understand the language used as well as remember what was said. In other words, instruction must provide specific information at a child's level. "Bring me your shoes" would be appropriate for a 2-year-old. "Get your jacket out of the closet, turn out the pockets, and bring it to me" would not. Even a 2-year-old who knows what a jacket is will probably forget the second part of the instruction ("turn out the pockets") because a child at that age simply cannot remember to do three things at once.

"Instructions" conjures up the image of the manual that comes with the computer. Instructions usually communicate how to do something or solve a problem, but they can also communicate directions or orders for behavior. "Don't sit on the coffee table, sit on the chair."

IN CONTEXT "Greg [age 9], please clean up your room," says Mom.

An hour later, Mom goes into Greg's room and observes that his bedspread is rumpled, books are on his desk, and his model airplanes are strewn among his shoes on the floor of his closet.

Mom yells, "I told you to clean up your room!"

Greg replies, "But I did; I put all my books and toys away."

And that he had.

The problem here is that the instructions are not specific enough for Greg. (If the instructions for getting the computer to work were as vague as Mom's, it would probably be exchanged for another brand.) Mom probably has an image of a clean room that includes an unrumpled bed, books on the bookshelf, and toys on the appropriate closet shelf. Greg's image of a clean room, on the other hand, may simply include space to walk and lie down. Thus, Mom's instructions, to be effective, must say, "Greg, please clean your room—straighten your bedspread, put your books on the bookshelf, and your toys on the shelf in your closet." If Greg were younger—for example, age 4—he might answer, "But I don't know how to straighten my bed." Then Mom would know what parts of the instructions could and could not be followed independently.

Setting Standards

standard a level or grade of excellence regarded as a goal or a measure of adequacy

A **standard** is a level of attainment or a grade of excellence regarded as a goal or a measure of adequacy. When parents set standards for children, they are telling children what they should do: "You are 3 years old now; I want you to dress yourself." "I expect only A's and B's on your report card." Setting standards provides children with advance notice of what is expected or not expected of them, thus helping them become socialized. The laws of a country, driver's license requirements, school achievement tests, and a city's building code are all examples of standards. A contract, or written agreement, specifying goals for learning or behavioral expectations can be a vehicle by which standards are communicated.

Standards are set by many socializing agents. In *Are You There, God? It's Me, Margaret,* a classic book for tweens by Judy Blume (1970), to be a member of the secret sixth-grade club you had to wear a bra, tell when you got your period, and keep a Boy Book (a list of boys you liked). The standards are set in this example by a peer group. Standards are also set by teachers. Some accept only good handwriting and perfect spelling on papers to be graded. Others may set standards regarding content and creativity. Good and Brophy (2007) noted that teachers tend to demand better performances from high-achieving students; for example, they are less likely to accept an inadequate answer from high achievers than from low achievers. Standards are set by coaches: "You will do ten sit-ups every day, get eight hours of sleep a night, and eat a balanced diet." Standards are set by employers regarding job performance. Thus, setting standards is a recurring method of socialization throughout life.

Reasoning

Reasoning is giving explanations or causes for an act. The purpose of giving reasons in the process of socialization is to enable the child to draw conclusions when encountering similar situations, thereby internalizing self-regulatory mechanisms.

reasoning giving explanations or causes for an act

When a teacher says to a preschool child who has just spit on another child, "Keep your spit in your mouth; spitting spreads germs and is rude. How would you like that?" that teacher is using reason to influence the child's behavior.

The problem with giving reasons is that children may not understand the words used (for example, "spreads germs," "is rude"), and often they are not able to generalize a reason to another situation. Because, according to Piaget (1974), children under age 3 are generally egocentric—that is, they lack the cognitive ability to take another's point of view—the child in the previous example may not be able to mentally take the view of the child who has been spit upon and so may not relate to the teacher's reasons.

For reasoning to be effective as a socializing method with children under the age of 3, it must be combined with other techniques such as an emotional reaction. To illustrate, a team of researchers (Radke-Yarrow & Zahn-Waxler, 1986; Radke-Yarrow, Zahn-Waxler, & Chapman, 1983; Zahn-Waxler, Radke-Yarrow, & King, 1979) examined how mothers of 15- and 20-month-old children taught them to be altruistic when another child was in distress. (**Altruism** refers to actions that are intended to aid or benefit another person or group of people without the actor's anticipation of external rewards. Such actions often entail some cost, self-sacrifice, or risk on the part of the actor.) The mothers were trained to observe and report incidents of their children's altruism when others were distressed, such as efforts at reparation when someone was hurt, trying to comfort a victim, offering a toy, or going to find someone else to help. The researchers found that the way the mother interacted with her child when another was in distress was clearly related to her child's degree of altruism. The mothers of highly altruistic children did not simply offer cognitive reasoning of the other's distress; they reacted emotionally, sometimes quite strongly, and stated forcefully that socially responsible behavior was expected, such as "You made Shawna cry; you must never bite."

altruism actions that are intended to help or benefit another person or group of people without the actor's anticipation of external rewards

To use reasoning effectively with young children over age 3, some knowledge of their cognitive development is necessary. Children between age 4 and 7 are moving away from egocentrism and toward **sociocentrism**—the ability to understand and relate to the views and perspectives of others. These children may be able to understand how another person feels or views things, but may not be able to generalize the reason to another situation. At this age, a child's ability to reason is **transductive** (connecting one particular idea to another particular idea based on appearance rather than logic) rather than **inductive**

sociocentrism the ability to understand and relate to the views and perspectives of others

(connecting a particular idea to a more general idea based on similarities) or **deductive** (connecting a general idea to a particular idea based on similarities and differences). The following examples help to illustrate these different types of reasoning:

transductive reasoning reasoning from one particular fact or case to another similar fact or case

inductive reasoning reasoning from particular facts or individual cases to a general conclusion

deductive reasoning reasoning from a general principle to a specific case, or from a premise to a logical conclusion

- ***Transductive reasoning:*** "Kyle has red hair and hits me; therefore all boys with red hair hit."
- ***Inductive reasoning:*** "I can't hit Kyle; therefore, I can't hit any other children."
- ***Deductive reasoning:*** "I can't hit other children; therefore, I can't hit Kyle."

Around age 7, children begin to think less intuitively and more concretely (Piaget, 1952); that is, they can understand reasons if they are associated with real, concrete events, objects, or people. The 7-year-old understands "You must not hit people with blocks because it hurts very much; look how Kyle is crying," because 7-year-olds can see that hitting Kyle with a block caused Kyle to cry. Children who think concretely, however, cannot yet reason in terms of abstract principles; they cannot yet understand "The law punishes people who hit." Since they cannot visualize it, the law is an abstraction of which they have no concept.

Around age 11 or 12, children begin to think less concretely and more abstractly. They are able to perform formal, or logical, operations (such as those involved in science); they are capable of rational thought (Inhelder & Piaget, 1958). They can think in terms of past, present, and future and can deal with hypothetical problems: "If everyone went around hitting everyone else whenever angry, then the world would end up in a war."

Reasoning as a socializing mechanism is most effective when children exhibit the ability to think logically and flexibly. This occurs after age 11 or 12, as the child enters adolescence. At this stage, reasoning ability allows for adaptation to whatever problem is presented, thus enabling adolescents to benefit and learn from concepts imparted to them as young children. Reasoning tends to be used more often as a socializing method in families and cultural groups that value verbal skills, abstract thought, assertiveness, and self-reliance (Peterson, Steinmetz, & Wilson, 2003).

authoritative parenting a style of democratic parenting in which authority is based on competence or expertise

permissive parenting a style of child-centered parenting characterized by a lack of directives or authority

authoritarian parenting a style of parent-centered parenting characterized by unquestioning obedience to authority

Baumrind (1971, 1989) distinguishes parents who are willing to offer reasons behind the directives they issue (**authoritative** parents) from parents who do not offer directives at all, relying on manipulation to obtain compliance (**permissive** parents), and parents who expect the child to accept their word as right and final without any verbal give-and-take (**authoritarian** parents). According to Baumrind, the authoritative approach may best enable children to conform to social standards with minimal jeopardy to "individual autonomy or self-assertiveness." In one study, preschool children from authoritative homes were consistently and significantly more competent than other children (Baumrind, 1989). In another study (Elder, 1963), it was shown that 7th- to 12th-graders were more likely to model themselves after their parents if their parents explained the reasons behind their decisions and restrictions.

Thus, it would seem that even though reasoning as a socializing mechanism is not as effective for young children as it is for adolescents, the continual use of reasoning by parents is habit-forming. Children who are habitually given reasons for directives benefit more and more from reasoning as they mature, becoming increasingly able to rationalize and regulate their own behavior (Hoffman, 2000).

What socialization methods ensure that you conform to your social or cultural group?

Sociocultural Methods of Socialization

As discussed earlier, culture involves learned behavior, including knowledge, beliefs, art, morals, law, customs, and traditions, that is characteristic of the social environment in which an individual grows up. The sociocultural expectations of those around an individual continually influence that individual's behavior and ensure conformity to established precedents (Rogoff, 2003). Some of the socializing techniques by which sociocultural expectations influence behavior are group pressure, tradition, rituals and routines, and symbols.

Group Pressure

Notice the similarity in clothing of the boys, as well as the girls, in this peer group.

Catherine Yeulet/iStockphoto.com

Group pressure is a sociocultural method of socialization because it involves conforming to certain norms. Communities are made up of social groups, including family, neighborhood, religious community, peers, clubs, and school. The groups to which one belongs influence one's behavior. Because humans have a need to affiliate with other humans, and because social approval determines whether or not one is accepted by the group, humans will tend to conform to the group's expectations (group pressure).

In a classic study by Solomon Asch (1958), male subjects were asked to judge the length of lines. In each experimental session, only one of the participants was an actual subject; the others had been previously coached to express certain opinions. Thus, the real subject often faced a situation in which his eyes told him that one line was the longest while the others in the group all said another line was the longest. Several of the subjects consistently yielded to the pressure of the group, even when the group's opinion was clearly erroneous. In later interviews, those who conformed to the majority opinion explained that they thought something was wrong with their eyesight and that the majority were probably correct.

In a similar experiment by other researchers (Hamm & Hoving, 1969), children age 7, 10, and 13 were asked to judge how far a light moved—a perceptually ambiguous task. Before the subjects made their decisions, however, two other children gave their answers. Just as Asch discovered, many of the subjects patterned their answers on the group estimates.

Cross-cultural studies on conformity have shown that individuals from collectivistic cultures exhibit a higher degree of conformity in group pressure situations than do those from individualistic cultures (Bond & Smith, 1996).

Does history repeat itself? Did group pressure compound the obedience to authority displayed by the Nazis in World War II? Did it play a role in the abuse of Iraqi prisoners by U.S. Marines in 2004? Philip Zimbardo (www.zimbardo.com), who conducted the famous Stanford Prison Experiment in 1971 (Haney, Banks, & Zimbardo, 1973), believes individuation and reason can succumb to deindividuation and impulsivity in certain group pressure situations.

Individuals are influenced by group pressure because they desire social identity, they seek social approval, and/or they believe the group's opinions are probably correct (Bugental & Grusec, 2006). The influence of the social group varies according to several factors (Bukowski, Newcomb, & Hartup, 1996):

1. **Attraction to the group.** The more people want to belong to a group, the more likely they will be to conform to group pressure. In elementary school and junior high school, attraction to the group becomes very important. Children of this age may have the same hairstyles, wear the same kind of shoes, and even talk alike.
2. **Acceptance by the group.** The role or status a person has—leader versus follower—in a group affects the degree of influence. A follower is more subject to group pressure than is a leader. One study found that boys who were anxious, dependent, and not sure where they stood in the group were more susceptible to group influence (Harrison, Serafica, & McAdoo, 1984).
3. **Type of group.** The degree of influence a group has depends on the affective relationships among the members. Groups in which the ties are very close, such as family or friends, exert a stronger influence than groups in which the affective ties are more distant, such as Scouts or Little League.

When individuals are influenced by group pressure because they believe the group's opinions are probably correct, it is usually because they lack confidence in their own judgment. For example, if you like a movie and later find out everyone else dislikes it, or if you have a certain political opinion and find out the rest of the group believes differently, you may begin to question your own judgment. Children who lack the experience and knowledge to have faith in their own judgment are more likely to succumb to group pressure, especially if the group is older, because they are more likely to trust the group's opinion.

Certain collectively oriented cultural groups that value a sense of dependence on the group and community emphasize group pressure as a socializing technique to control nonconforming behavior and foster achievement ("What will other people think?"). Other groups that value interdependence emphasize group cohesiveness. Individuals may express opinions, but group consensus supercedes (Rogoff, 2003).

Tradition

tradition customs, stories, and beliefs handed down from generation to generation

Tradition is the handing down of customs, stories, and beliefs from generation to generation. In a culture, it is part of that group's heritage and, therefore, is cultivated in children as they grow up (Pleck, 2000). An example in the United States is learning the Pledge of Allegiance. In religion, tradition refers to the unwritten religious code handed down from leaders such as Buddha, Moses, Jesus and the Apostles, or Mohammed. In a family, tradition is implemented in the way it celebrates holidays and tells stories. The stories that families tell represent perspectives on events and relationships that are passed on. These stories give meaning to the family (Fiese et al., 1999).

Because tradition represents humans' ways of having solved certain problems in the past, through socialization the offspring of each generation receive a "design for living" from their ancestors—how to get shelter, how to feed themselves, how to dress, how to get along with one another. Traditional beliefs, attitudes, and values are also transmitted—the belief in God, the attitude that children should be protected, the value of hard work.

Tradition also sets the patterns by which people interact with one another. Social interaction refers to who does what in the society (roles) and how it is done (behavior). In some cultural groups, it is traditional for the women to do the cooking; in other groups, the men do it. In some cultural groups, the elderly are considered the wisest and are revered; in other groups, they are considered obsolete and useless. In some cultural groups, a price is fixed in advance for an exchange in the marketplace; in other groups, the exchange is accomplished by an agreed-upon price only after a certain amount of bargaining. In some cultural groups, people greet one another by surnames; in other groups, first names are used. Traditions become unquestioned ways of doing things that stay with us, even though we may forget the reasons behind them, as described in the box.

IN CONTEXT A bride served baked ham, and her husband asked why she cut the ends off. "Well, that's the way Mother always did it," she replied.

The next time his mother-in-law stopped by, he asked her why she cut the ends off the ham. "That's the way my mother did it," she replied.

And when Grandma visited, she too was asked why she sliced the ends off. She said, "That's the only way I could get it into the pan" (James & Jongeward, 1971, p. 97).

Rituals and Routines

ritual a ceremonial observation of a prescribed rule or custom

Rituals connect us with our past, define our present, and give us a future direction (Dresser, 1999; Pleck, 2000). A **ritual** is a ceremonial observance of a prescribed rule or custom. The symbols or symbolic actions embrace meaning that cannot always be easily expressed in words. Some familiar examples of rituals are the baptism or naming ceremony; the communion, signifying acceptance of a church's beliefs; the bar or bas mitzvah, signifying the age of responsibility; graduation, signifying an accomplishment; and the Navajo ritual called the Blessing Way, signifying "for good hope." Rituals serve not only a socialization function but a protective one as well, because they provide stability, something the child can "count on" in spite of change (Parke & Buriel, 2006).

The ritualization of behavior is a way of creating respect for traditions (Fiese, 2006). A ritual evokes appropriate feelings. The ritual of saying the Pledge of Allegiance evokes feelings of loyalty and reaffirms national identity. The ritual of saying grace evokes feelings of humility and thankfulness. The ritual of marriage signifies faithfulness and procreation.

Rituals that signify changes in individuals' status as they move through the cycle of life are called **rites of passage**. The most common rite of passage occurs at puberty to acknowledge passage from the state of childhood to adulthood and celebrate the transformation. Some rites involve a circumcision ceremony, as in some African or Australian tribes; some involve parties, such as a debutante ball; some involve the recitation of knowledge, as in the bar mitzvah. Graduation from high school is an American rite of passage. The ritual serves as a mechanism of socialization in that it announces to the rest of society that a certain individual has a new position and will fill a new role in the society, and it makes the individual aware of the new status and its accompanying roles and responsibilities.

rites of passage rituals that signify changes in individuals' status as they move through the cycle of life

Routines are repetitive acts or established procedures. In families, they may include bedtime, mealtime, and anything else done on a regular basis. They play a part in socialization because children come to know what to expect, giving them security and a chance to practice appropriate behaviors (Laible & Thompson, 2007).

routines repetitive acts or established procedures

Symbols

Symbols are acts or objects that have come to be generally accepted as standing for or representing something else (Vander Zanden, 1995), especially something abstract. The dove is a symbol of peace; the cross is a symbol of Christ's death; the circle is a symbol of the Great Spirit. The significance of symbols as socializing mechanisms is that they are powerful codes, or shorthand, for representing aspects of the world (Hewitt, 2003) that trigger certain behaviors individuals have learned to associate with them. For example, a crown conjures up the image of authority and all the attitudes associated with it. The resultant behavior would be respect and obedience. A country's flag conjures up feelings of patriotism. Saluting the flag would be the socialized behavior.

symbols acts or objects that have come to be generally accepted as standing for something else

According to anthropology professor Leslie White (1960, p. 73):

> All culture (civilization) depends upon the symbol. It was the exercise of the symbolic faculty that brought culture into existence and it is the use of symbols that makes the perpetuation of culture possible. Without the symbol there would be no culture, and man would be merely an animal, not a human being.

The symbol to which White is referring is language. Language makes it possible to replace behavior with ideas and to communicate these ideas to the next generation.

Apprenticeship Methods of Socialization

How do you learn a behavior from someone who has already mastered it?

Apprenticeship is a process in which a novice is guided by an expert to participate in and master tasks. According to Rogoff (1990, 2003), all the methods of socialization discussed so far are imparted in the child's macrosystem by means of various apprenticeships. In other words, the child, or novice, is guided to participate in various social activities and master tasks by someone who has more expertise. This person could be a parent, a sibling, a relative, a teacher, a peer, a coach, or some other member of the community.

apprenticeship a process in which a novice is guided by an expert to participate in and master tasks

IN PRACTICE

Socializing Skills for Life

"The Game of Life," a board game launched in 1960 by the Milton Bradley Company (now a division of Hasbro, Incorporated), simulates the road from high school to retirement. Recommended for children age 9 and up, it is a tool for teaching decision-making skills. It allows children to make choices about college, jobs, insurance, and investments while they negotiate life—wages, marriage, children, taxes, home ownership, and medical emergencies. Like real-life decisions, they don't always turn out as planned. For example, in the game you can choose to pay for insurance or go without it and save money; but if you land on the wrong square, you have to pay the penalty for being uninsured.

Recently, Hasbro Incorporated, which has introduced many adaptations of the game over the years, has partnered with Visa for a new version. A major outcome of the partnership is the replacement of cash with a branded Visa card. The new edition of the game ("Twists & Turns") will replace the lessons on money management with credit card usage. This updated "Game of Life" will provide players with a Visa-branded card at the start of the game and an electronic "Life Pod" that will keep track of the players' financial data and monitor their game status. The player with the most accumulated cash and "life cards"—experiences such as having a child, inventing a worthy product, and so on—wins.

Designers of the new edition say it was time "to reflect the way people choose to pay and be paid." "It's a chance to learn how people use electronic payments in their daily life." You still win the game by accumulating the most points, but you can't get points if you spend more than you have.

Critics of the new version say it's a form of advertising, called product placement. The product, the Visa credit card, is being marketed to a child-adolescent audience, who will likely adopt it when adulthood is reached without having compared credit card and other payment options.

Source: Kristoff, K. M. (2007, April 1). Venerable finance game abandons cash for credit. *Los Angeles Times,* p. C3.

To illustrate how apprenticeship as a socializing method works, we look at how children learn to feed themselves. First, the child is totally dependent on his or her mother for nourishment. As the child matures physically and cognitively, he or she observes others feeding themselves and wants to try the activity independently. The mother, or caregiver, structures the feeding activities according to the capability of the child—at first providing soft food the child can grasp with the fingers, such as fruit or crackers. Then the caregiver might give the child a utensil, such as a spoon, a cup, or a pair of chopsticks, at first guiding it into the child's mouth until the child can handle it alone, offering support when needed. Thus, the caregiver and the child participate or collaborate in the activity together. When the child exhibits appropriate mastery, the caregiver transfers the responsibility for independent feeding to the child.

In sum, apprenticeship as a method of socialization progresses from the expert's *structuring* activities for the novice according to ability, to *collaborating* in joint activities so that support can be provided when needed, to *transferring* responsibility for the management of the activity when the activity is appropriately mastered.

The ages at which these progressions in apprenticeship take place vary according to the macrosystem in which the child grows up—culture, socioeconomic status, and religious beliefs are some significant influences. For example, in some families, self-feeding (drinking from a cup and using a spoon or fork) is expected by age 2, whereas in some other families, the child is breast-fed until age 2 (and in some families, age 4), thereby extending the apprenticeship progression from dependence to independence (Rogoff, 2003).

Outcomes of Socialization

How would you describe your affective, cognitive, social, and behavioral characteristics?

According to Grusec (2002; Grusec & Davidov, 2010), socialization involves the following outcomes:

1. the development of self-regulation of emotion, thinking, and behavior;
2. reciprocity and cooperation—the development of role-taking skills, strategies for resolving conflicts, and ways of viewing relationships;
3. the acquisition of a culture's morals and values, including the willingness to accept the authority of others; and
4. conformity to and adoption of practices and routines associated with the group.

A very brief overview of major socialization outcomes follows. Each will be discussed in more detail in Chapter 11 (affective/cognitive outcomes—values, attitudes, motives and attributions, and self-esteem) and Chapter 12 (social/behavioral outcomes—self-regulation/behavior, morals, and gender roles).

Values

What matters most to you in life?

Values are qualities or beliefs that are viewed as desirable or important. Socializing agents in microsystems influence the internalization of values. For example, what message did your parents give you about money? Work? Spirituality? Significant societal events (chronosystem and macrosystem influences) also affect values. For example, the Depression in the 1930s made people aware of the need to be thrifty.

values qualities or beliefs that are viewed as desirable or important

Attitudes

What are your views on racial profiling?

Attitudes are tendencies to respond positively or negatively to certain persons, objects, or situations. Like values, attitudes are learned from socializing agents. Some methods by which they are acquired are via instructions ("Don't play with Sam; he doesn't go to our church"), modeling (the teacher shows concern when Juan says his father is sick), and direct experience (Leslie plays with Rose, who has cerebral palsy). The macrosystem influences attitudes, too. America's experiences with terrorism have resulted in homeland security measures, such as racial profiling.

attitudes tendencies to respond positively (favorably) or negatively (unfavorably) to certain persons, objects, or situations

Motives and Attributions

What efforts and activities do you engage in to be successful?

Motives are needs or emotions that cause a person to act, such as the need for achievement. **Attributions** are explanations for one's performance, such as "I failed the test because there were trick questions" (*external* attribution) or "I failed because I didn't study" (*internal* attribution).

Most developmental psychologists agree that there is an inborn motive to explore, understand, and control one's environment (Mayes & Zigler, 1992; White, 1959), known as **mastery motivation**. Some children are also motivated to achieve mastery of challenging tasks, known as **achievement motivation** (Boggiano & Pittman, 1993; McClelland et al., 1953).

Socialization agents, individual abilities and beliefs, and task-related experiences with challenge, effort, success, and failure contribute to the motive to achieve.

motives needs or emotions that cause a person to act

attributions explanations for one's performance

mastery motivation the inborn motive to explore, understand, and control one's environment

Self-Esteem

How do you feel about yourself?

Recall that *self-esteem* is the value one places on his or her identity. Why do some children come to view themselves as competent and worthy, whereas others view themselves as incompetent and unworthy? Interactions with parents, peers, and significant adults who communicate approval, validation, and support influence self-esteem. Until recently, self-esteem has been viewed as a unitary, global construct. Susan Harter (1999) has examined more specific domains, including physical competence, academic competence, behavioral competence, and social acceptance.

achievement motivation the motivation to achieve mastery of challenging tasks

How do you keep yourself "under control"?

Self-Regulation/Behavior

Self-regulation is the process of bringing emotions, thoughts, and/or behavior under one's control. **Behavior** consists of what one does or how one acts in response to a stimulus.

behavior what one does or how one acts in response to a stimulus

Behavior in infancy consists mostly of biological reflexes (sucking to get nourishment, defecating to rid the body of waste), but as the child matures physically and cognitively, he or she becomes more capable of directing external behavior and internal thought processes (eating at regular intervals rather than on demand, using the toilet instead of diapers). A number of theories (relating to emotions, learned behavior, social experiences, cognitive development, and cultural activities) have been offered to explain the influence of socialization on the development of self-regulation (Bronson, 2000).

Why do you do "the right thing"?

Morals

Morals are an individual's evaluation of what is right and wrong. Morals involve acceptance of rules and govern one's behavior toward others.

morals an individual's evaluation of what is right and wrong

Theories of moral development involve (1) an *affective*, or emotional, component (moral feelings such as guilt, shame, and empathy); (2) a *cognitive* component (moral reasoning, such as a conceptualization of right and wrong and related decision making); and (3) a *behavioral* component (moral action, how one responds to temptations to violate moral rules such as lying, cheating, or stealing). Socialization influences include relationship with parents, experiences in school, peer interaction, and role models and experiences in the culture and community.

Does being male or female influence an individual's self-concept?

Gender Roles

Gender roles are qualities that an individual understands to characterize males and females in his or her culture. The term *gender* usually refers to psychological attributes, whereas the term *sex* usually refers to biological ones.

gender roles the qualities that an individual understands to characterize males and females in his or her culture

Biologically, males and females differ in their chromosomes (male—XY, female—XX), their hormones, and their physiques. They also differ in the social roles they assume based on societal expectations. The female's biological capacity to bear children is associated in many societies with the expectation that she will assume a nurturing, cooperative role. The male's hormones (testosterone) and his muscular physique are associated in many societies with the expectation that he will assume an assertive, dominant role.

Theories of gender-role development, explaining how children are socialized to assume behaviors, values, and attitudes considered appropriate for their sex, relate to feelings, behavior, cognitive development, and information-processing.

Summary

- Socialization involves aims, goals, methods, and outcomes. It is a reciprocal, dynamic process, with children playing a role in their own socialization as a result of their biology, their culture, and their individual life experiences.
- Socialization aims to develop a self-concept, enable self-regulation/control, and to empower achievement.
- The significant agents of socialization are the family, the school, the peer group, the media, and the community.
- The family is the child's introduction to society and therefore bears major responsibility for socializing the child. It is the child's first reference group for values and relationships.
- The school acts as an agent of society in that it is organized to perpetuate that society's knowledge, skills, customs, and beliefs. Child care has become an important socialization agent because of societal changes in the amount of time children spend being cared for by individuals outside the family.
- The peer group gives children experience in egalitarian types of relationships. Children learn to look at themselves from the group's point of view.
- The media, unlike other agents of socialization, do not involve direct personal interaction, but they teach many of the ways of the society via object interaction. Children

process media information, constructing meaning and transforming it into behavior.

- The community provides a sense of belonging and friendship. The population distribution and services provided in a community affects the interactions a child will have.
- Socialization is the process by which individuals learn the ways of a given society so that they can function effectively within it. These ways are transmitted via different methods: affective (attachment); operant (reinforcement, extinction, punishment, feedback, learning by doing); observational (modeling); cognitive (instruction, setting standards, reasoning); sociocultural (group pressure, tradition, rituals and routines, symbols); and apprenticeship (structuring, collaborating, transferring).
- The outcomes of socialization are affective/cognitive (values, attitudes, motives and attributions, self-esteem) and social/behavioral (self-regulation of behavior, morals, gender roles).

Activity

PURPOSE To understand the impact of agents of socialization on development.

1. Name the three most important things you learned from your parent(s) while growing up.
2. Name three people other than your parent(s) who had a major influence on you as a child or adolescent.
3. Describe each one's influence, using specific examples.
4. What methods of socialization did your parent(s) and the significant others in your life use?
5. Whom are you influencing in ways similar to the ones you have described?
6. What are your aims and methods of socialization?

Related Readings

Bandura, A. (1986). *Social foundations of thought and action: A social cognitive theory.* Englewood Cliffs, NJ: Prentice-Hall.

Bjorklund, D. P., & Pelligrini, A. D. (2002). *The origins of human nature: Evolutionary developmental psychology.* Washington, DC: American Psychological Association.

Brazelton, T. B. (1984). *To listen to a child.* Reading, MA: Perseus Books.

Cialdini, R. B. (2007). *Influence: The psychology of persuasion* (rev. ed.). New York: Collins.

Corsaro, W. A. (2005). *The sociology of childhood* (2nd ed.). Thousand Oaks, CA: Pine Forge Press.

Dresser, N. (2005). *Multicultural manners: Essential rules of etiquette for the 21st century* (rev. ed.). New York: Wiley.

Erikson, E. (1963). *Childhood and society.* New York: Norton.

Goleman, D. (2006). *Social intelligence: The new science of human relationships.* New York: Bantam Dell.

Rogoff, B. (2003). *The cultural nature of human development.* New York: Oxford University Press.

Resources

Cultural Policy Center—fosters research on the practical working of culture in our lives

http://culturalpolicy.uchicago.edu

Your Child: Development and Behavior Resources—website guide to Internet information on kids' development and behavior

http://www.med.umich.edu

Facts for Families—topics relating to childhood and adolescent issues

http://www.aacap.org

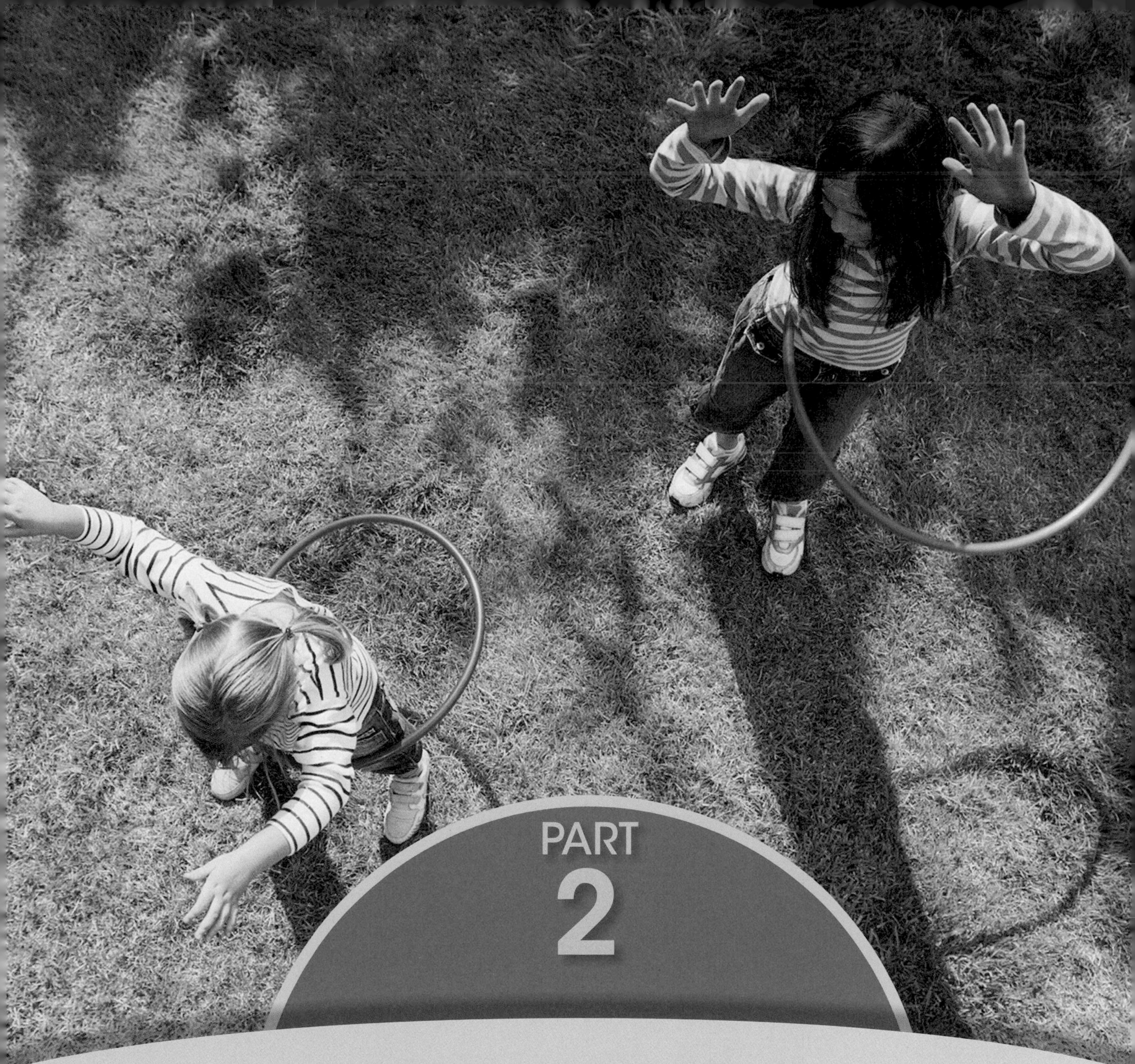

PART 2

Where and How Does Socialization Take Place?

DesignPics Inc./PhotoLibrary

3

Ecology of the Family

My soul knows that I am part of the human race, . . . as my spirit is part of my nation. In my very own self, I am part of my family.

—D. H. LAWRENCE

SOCIALIZATION SKETCHES

John Fitzgerald Kennedy

(1917–1963)

Time & Life Pictures/Getty Images

"If we cannot now end our differences, at least we can help make the world safe for diversity."

– JOHN F. KENNEDY

This quote reflects Kennedy's ideals for human relations. This chapter's Socialization Sketch describes the family influences, religious influences, and significant life experiences that influenced these ideals.

John Fitzgerald Kennedy (JFK) was the 35th president of the United States of America, serving from 1961 until his assassination in 1963. Not only was he the youngest to be elected to the highest office in the country, but he was the first Roman Catholic to become president of the United States. His 1961 inaugural address asked Americans to be involved citizens. "Ask not what your country can do for you; ask what you can do for your country." He also asked the nations of the world to join together to fight the "common enemies of man: tyranny, poverty, disease, and war itself."

Family

JFK was descended from Irish forbearers who immigrated to Boston. His grandfather, Patrick J. Kennedy, started as a saloon keeper and became a Boston political leader. His father, Joseph Patrick Kennedy, graduated from Harvard and became a bank president at age 25. He married Rose Fitzgerald, the daughter of Boston's mayor. As you can see, a family tradition was to retain relatives' names from previous generations.

JFK was born in 1917, the second of nine children. The family lived comfortably as the father's fortune increased. John attended private schools. The family was close and warm, although all four boys were competitive. The eldest brother, Joseph Jr., shone in school and sports. His career goal was politics. Joseph Jr. was killed while piloting a bomber in World War II.

Significant Experiences

Two trips to Europe during his college years gave JFK the opportunity to observe international power politics firsthand. At the time, his father was serving as ambassador to Great Britain. Returning to Harvard for his senior year, JFK wrote an honors thesis analyzing the British policies that led to the Munich Pact of 1938. He graduated cum laude from Harvard in 1940. He attended Stanford Graduate School of Business and spent time touring a number of countries in Latin America.

When war broke out in 1941, JFK volunteered for the army, but was rejected due to a football injury to his back. Determined to serve his country (as did his older brother), he did back-strengthening exercises and was accepted for service in the navy. JFK took command of a PT (torpedo) boat in the Solomon Islands. His boat was rammed and sunk by a Japanese destroyer. He rallied the survivors and managed to get them to an island, despite being injured himself. JFK was awarded the Purple Heart and the Navy and Marine Corps Medal.

After the war, JFK worked as a journalist covering the San Francisco Conference that established the United Nations. Having been exposed to international views and having grown up in a political family, he chose to run for the U.S. House of Representatives.

Significant historical events during JFK's administration centered around the protection of democracy and prevention of the spread of communism throughout the world. JFK's support of the civil rights movement exemplified the implementation of democratic principles at home.

Values

To illustrate JFK's commitment to world freedom and equality, he created the Peace Corps in 1961. The Peace Corps provided the opportunity for Americans to collaborate with community members in underdeveloped countries in the areas of education, agriculture, environmental preservation, community development, health care, and information technology. The sharing of people resources among diverse cultures was a first step toward world understanding.

In 1962, the Cuban Missile Crisis challenged JFK's commitment to world peace. An American spy plane had taken photos of Soviet missile sites under construction in Cuba. This caused Kennedy to be faced with a

Learning Objectives

After completing this chapter, you will be able to:

1. Describe the basic structure and functions of the family.
2. Explain the effects of transitions in family ties on children (divorce, single parenting, remarriage, dual-earner, kin custody, and cohabitation [heterosexual or homosexual partners]).
3. Discuss macrosystem influences (socioeconomic status, cultural orientation, and religious orientation) on families and the socialization of children.
4. Discuss chronosystem influences (sociopolitical, economic, and technological changes) on families and the socialization of children.
5. Define and discuss family empowerment.

dilemma: If the United States were to attack, the Soviets would retaliate, probably leading to a nuclear war; if the United States stood idle, due to the proximity of the weapons, it risked being attacked as well as appearing "weak" in the eyes of the world. Kennedy ordered a blockade of Cuba by the U.S. Navy. Negotiations took place to dismantle the missile sites and lift the blockade on the condition that ships bound for Cuba would not carry armaments. The United States also agreed to dismantle some of its missile bases in Turkey.

This peaceful resolution of a potential nuclear war had far-reaching historical consequences. Within a year (1963), the first "hotline" between Washington and Moscow was installed. Kennedy and Soviet Premier Khrushchev signed the Nuclear Test Ban Treaty, the first disarmament agreement of the nuclear age.

JFK's commitment to democracy at home was tested in 1963 when two African American college students prepared to enroll at the all-white University of Alabama. Alabama Governor George Wallace defied a court order and blocked the door. In response, President Kennedy called out the National Guard; the governor had to step aside. That evening, the president delivered his famous civil rights address, which later would be embodied in the Civil Rights Act of 1964, to the nation on television and radio. He called upon the American people to end the concept of "race" and its consequences of discrimination and inequality. "In short, every American ought to have the right to be treated as he would wish to be treated, as one would wish his children to be treated."

As we can see from this sketch, JFK's family influenced his socioeconomic status, his cultural and religious orientations, his values, his education, the early experiences to which he was exposed, his competitiveness, and his career.

- How did your family's socioeconomic status influence your socialization experiences and consequent developmental outcomes?
- How did your cultural or religious orientation influence your values?

What is the purpose of families and how do they work?

Family Systems

This chapter provides an understanding of what a family is, what a family does, how different families adapt to change, and how different families cope with external forces. Figure 3.1 shows a bioecological model of the contexts, or systems, involved in family interaction with other ecosystems over time. *Family systems theory* looks more within the family, viewing it as a whole, in terms of its structure and organizational patterns, and viewing its members in terms of how they interact with one another (Parke & Buriel, 2006). Family systems theory is used by many therapists to understand the different ways in which families carry out basic functions.

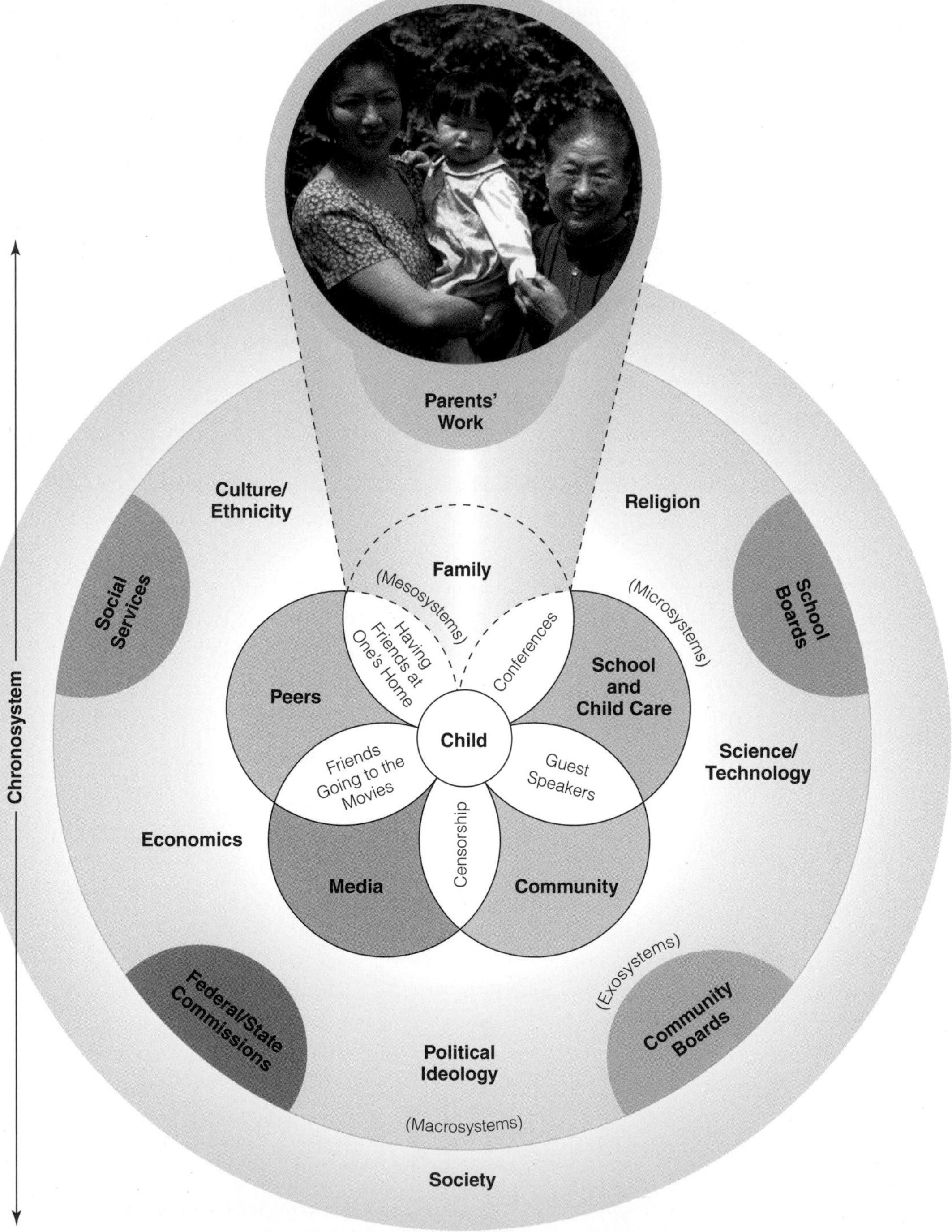

FIGURE 3.1 A Bioecological Model of Human Development

The family is a primary influence on the child's development.

Cengage Learning

In Chapters 1 and 2, the aims, methods, and outcomes of socialization were discussed, and the agents of socialization identified. Here, the family, the primary agent of socialization, is explored. A family is a microsystem. How a family is defined has important implications regarding issues of income tax filings, adoption and foster-care practices, employee benefits, property rights, inheritance, and so on. How states resolve the debate over the legality of same-sex marriage will also have significant effects on such issues.

The classic (structural-functional) definition of a family, according to sociologist George Murdock (1962, p. 19), is "a social group characterized by common residence, economic cooperation, and reproduction. It includes adults of both sexes, at least two of whom maintain a socially approved sexual relationship, and one or more children (biological or adopted) of the sexually cohabiting adults." How many families do you know that fit this classic definition?

Today, relationships that do *not* conform to Murdock's definition are more common than those that do, illustrating the impact of societal change on the family system's form and function. To accommodate changes in family patterns, the U.S. Bureau of the Census defines a **family** as "two or more persons related by birth, marriage, or adoption, who reside together." Thus, a family can be two or more adult siblings living together, a parent and child or children, two adults who are related by marriage but have no children, or adults who adopt a child.

family any two or more related people living in one household

Some states have legalized same-sex marriages. In 2004, Massachusetts became the first state to do so. Other states and cities have legally recognized certain unrelated people in caring relationships who live together in a household as a "family." These laws pertaining to "domestic partnerships," "reciprocal partnerships," or "civil unions" are intended to provide same-sex couples, foster parents, related pairs (mother/daughter, two brothers), and stepfamilies with rights and privileges related to health insurance policies, medical and educational decisions, employment leave policies, employment benefits, annuities, and pensions.

It is important to understand the changes in the concept of the definition of family structure, not only for legally related issues, but also because these changes affect the functions that families perform, the roles its members play, and the relationships its members have with one another, thereby affecting the socialization of children.

Family—Ideal or Real?

Is family a structure or function?
What were some of your family traditions?
What about your family was healthy/unhealthy?

Basic Family Structures

What is your concept of a family?

Families are organized in different ways around the world. A family consisting of a husband and wife and their children is called a **nuclear family**. For the children, such a family is the **family of orientation**, which means the family into which one is born. For the parents, the nuclear family is the **family of procreation**, the family that develops when one marries and has children (see Figure 3.2). In the nuclear family, the wife and husband depend on each other for companionship and the children depend on their parents for affection and socialization.

nuclear family a family consisting of a husband and wife and their children

family of orientation the family into which one is born

family of procreation the family that develops when one marries and has children

The significance of the nuclear family structure is that it is the main source of children and so provides the basis for the perpetuation of the society. Most societies assign responsibility for the care and socialization of children to the couple that produces or adopts them and sanction the sexual union of a male and a female by law or tradition—in our society, by legal marriage. The institution of marriage, then, serves not only to legalize a

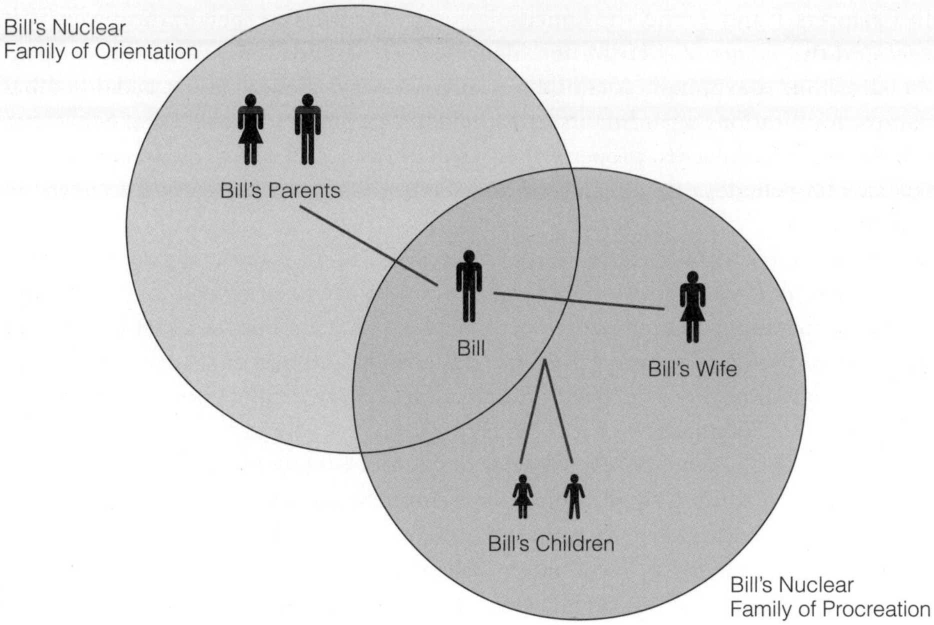

FIGURE 3.2 Nuclear Family

sexual union but also to fix the obligation toward children who result from that sexual union.

extended family relatives of the nuclear family who are economically and emotionally dependent on each other

The **extended family** pattern consists of relatives of the nuclear family who are economically and emotionally dependent on each other. They may or may not live nearby (see Figure 3.3).

In some cultural groups, such as Native Americans, Asian Americans, and Italian Americans, great emphasis is placed on the extended family (obligation to family supersedes obligation to the self). In these cultural groups, tradition assigns certain obligations and responsibilities to various members of the extended family—for example, who socializes the children, who decides how the family resources are allocated, and who cares for needy family members. Some cultures emphasize the mother's side of the family as having formal authority and dominance. These families are known as **matriarchal**. A contemporary example would be the royal family in Great Britain headed by Queen Elizabeth II. Other cultures emphasize the father's relatives as having formal authority and dominance. These families are known as **patriarchal**. This organizational pattern is much more common in the world than is the matriarchal. Examples of patriarchal families can be found

matriarchal family family in which the mother has formal authority and dominance

patriarchal family family in which the father has formal authority and dominance

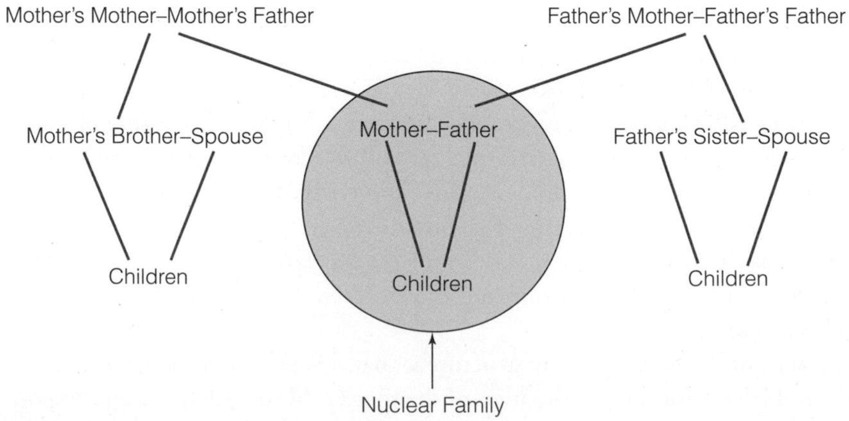

FIGURE 3.3 Extended Family

in literature (as in Biblical stories, Roman classics, or Shakespeare) and in the media (as in *The Godfather*, *The Sound of Music*, or the *Big Love* TV series).

In the United States, both sides of the extended family are generally regarded as equal, or **egalitarian**. Your mother's parents have as much legal authority and responsibility over you as do your father's parents. If something happened to your parents and they could no longer care for you, both sets of grandparents would have equal claim to your custody.

egalitarian family family in which both sides of the extended family are regarded as equal

Regardless of whether your extended family is matriarchal, patriarchal, or egalitarian, its main function is support; relatives are the people you turn to when you need help or when you have joys to share. Because, in today's society, many nuclear families do not have an extended family for support (for reasons that include moving, divorce, remarriage, and death), the people they turn to for help might be friends, neighbors, co-workers, or children's teachers (see Figure 3.4). These people assume some of the traditional support functions of the extended family and become one's *personal network* (Dean, 1984). People who have no such personal network have to rely on the *formal network* of society—professionals or government agencies—for support (Garbarino, 1992). Support services provided by the formal network are influenced by politics, economics, culture, and technology. For a political example, the federally funded preschool program Head Start was launched by the Democrats and later experienced a reduction in funding under the Republicans. For an economic example, the cultural norm of working for a living was a significant factor in changing government financial support for needy families—from welfare to workfare. For a technology example, cell phones and computers compete for family members' time together.

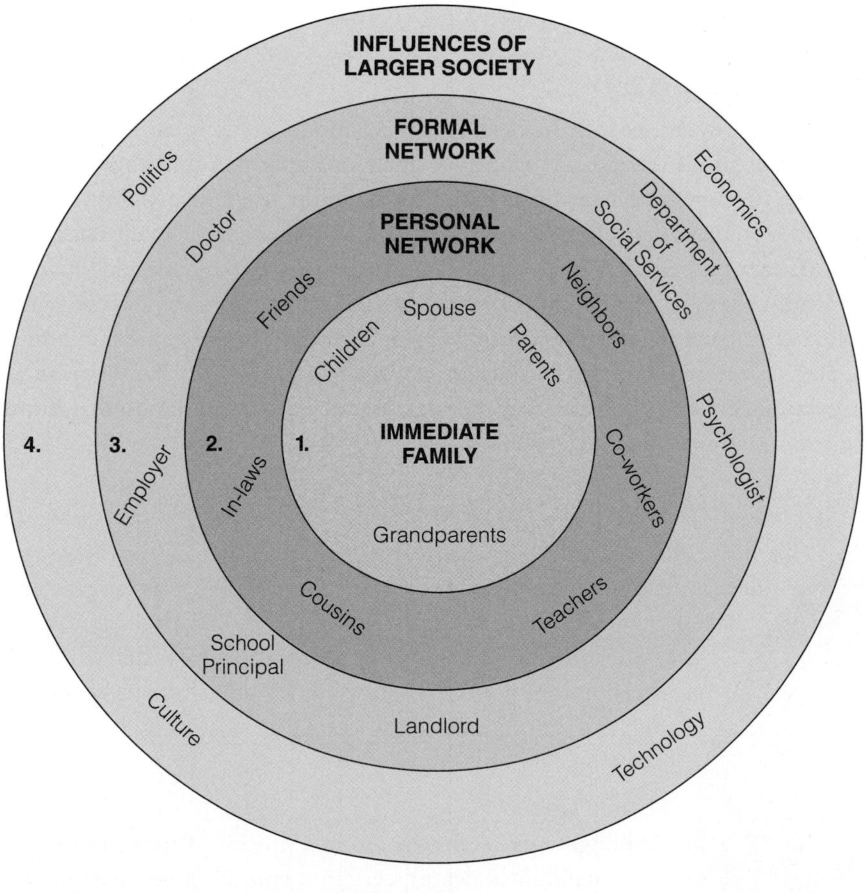

FIGURE 3.4 Sources of Family Support
Source: Adapted from Dean, 1984.

What do families do?

Basic Family Functions

The family performs certain basic functions, generation after generation, enabling it to survive and adapt. The following basic functions may vary by culture and may be impacted by economic, health, or social stresses.

- **Reproduction.** The family ensures that the society's population will be maintained; that is, a sufficient number of children will be born and cared for to replace the members who die.
- **Socialization/education.** The family ensures that the society's values, beliefs, attitudes, knowledge, skills, and techniques will be transmitted to the young.
- **Assignment of social roles.** The family provides an identity for its offspring (racial, ethnic, religious, socioeconomic, and gender roles). An identity involves behavior and obligations. For example, a Jewish person may not eat pork and may feel obliged to give to charity. A Chinese person may eat with chopsticks and defer to the authority of his or her elders. A person born into a high socioeconomic status may be pressured to choose a spouse from a similar family background. In some families, girls are socialized to do housework and be caregivers and boys to be breadwinners.
- **Economic support.** The family provides shelter, nourishment, and protection. In some families, all members except very young children contribute to the economic function by producing goods. In other families, one or both parents earn the money that pays for goods the entire family consumes.
- **Nurturance/emotional support.** The family provides the child's first experience in social interaction. This interaction is intimate, nurturing, and enduring, thus providing emotional security for the child. The family cares for its members when they are ill, hurt, or aging.

How has the family adapted to societal change?

Family Transitions

Throughout history, family structure has adapted to accommodate economic, social, political, and technological influences. Examples of such chronosystem influences include the Industrial Revolution, birth control, welfare reform, and no-fault divorce laws.

According to Coontz (2007), the origins of modern divorce patterns actually date back more than 200 years, to the historically unprecedented idea that marriage should be based on love. Ironically, she says, "the fragility of modern marriage stems from the same values that have elevated the marital relationship above all other personal and familial commitments; the concentration of emotion, passion, personal identity, and self-validation in the couple relationship and the attenuation of emotional attachments and obligations beyond the conjugal unit" (pp. 8–9).

Early American farm life required everyone's participation for family survival.

Lewis W. Hine [NCLC 00656]/Library of Congress Prints and Photographs Division

Structural Family Changes

Family composition is influenced by biological factors (fertility, age, health), cultural or religious beliefs, psychological factors (stress), and social factors (economics). Changes in family composition can include the addition of family members to the household, as by birth, adoption, remarriage, or relatives (kin) moving in; or the removal of family members, as by death, divorce, or children becoming adults and moving out.

Family Ties

Although families are always in a process of transition (marriage, childbirth, death), certain events affect the socialization of children more than others. Examples are divorce, single parenting, stepparenting, and cohabitation.

What influences family composition?

Changes in family ties are documented by the increase in divorce in the last 40 years and in the proportion of children living with only one parent. According to the Federal Interagency Forum on Child and Family Statistics (FIFCFS, 2010), nearly 70 percent of children age 0–17 lived with two parents, 26 percent lived with one parent, and 4 percent lived with neither of their parents. Parental divorce is not a single event but rather represents a series of stressful experiences for the entire family that begins with marital conflict before the actual separation and includes many adjustments afterward. Families must often cope with a reduction in family resources, assumption of new roles and responsibilities, establishment of new patterns of interaction, reorganization of routines, and probably the introduction of new relationships into the existing family (Hetherington & Clingempeel, 1992). Parents in conflict, especially those who have not separated, are less able to help their children regulate emotions and behavior, and less able to self-soothe their own stress (Kelly, 2000). When such parents do separate, attention toward children's needs is more likely to occur.

What events affect family ties?

As the divorce rate has risen, so has the frequency of remarriage (Department of Health and Human Services [DHHS], 2010). When a divorced person remarries, the children gain a stepparent. With the stepparent come additional kinship relationships. New roles and obligations, not derived from custom and tradition, have to be established.

In addition to family ties based on marriage, divorce, and remarriage, over the past decade there have been large increases in the number of individuals who live with a sexual partner of the opposite sex. As a result of the growing prevalence of cohabitation, the number of children born to unmarried parents has also increased (DHHS, 2010).

Divorce and the Law

What are the impacts of current divorce laws and custody arrangements on families and children?

In the 1970s, many states changed their divorce laws to reflect societal changes, such as the increased cost of living, employment of women, and father's increasing role in child care. Prior to then, the law permitted divorce only if one spouse committed such serious marital misconduct as adultery, cruelty, or desertion. Traditional divorce proceedings involved a determination of who was guilty and who was innocent. Child custody arrangements and financial settlements were intended to reward the innocent party and punish the guilty one. For example, a woman deemed to be the innocent party would not have to agree to a divorce unless her husband, deemed to be the guilty party, provided adequate support for her and the children. Further, judges would often divide property in accordance with family need. The mother and children retained the family home and enough support to avoid sudden poverty (Skolnick, 1987). Divorce cases were often costly financially and emotionally—to both parents and children.

Today, divorce law is "no-fault"; assigning blame is no longer a legal issue. Instead, divorces are granted on the basis of "irreconcilable differences" or "marital breakdown." The financial consequence, in most states, is that the family's assets are divided equally between the spouses, often necessitating that the family home being sold. Thus, in addition to the emotional impacts of the dissolution of a marriage, there are significant economic and social ones as well.

Divorce and the Family

How does the family adapt to divorce?

Effect on Family Functions

Divorce has certain consequences for family functioning and the socialization of children. Barring external social support, the effect of divorce on the custodial parent is that the responsibilities double. The single parent is responsible for financial support, child care, and home maintenance. Because the parent is usually under great stress, parenting is likely to diminish (Goodman, Emery, & Haugaard, 1998). The children may have to take increased responsibility for themselves and may have less time available to spend with the parent to receive love and security. In an attempt to prevent the consequences of divorce, some states are enacting mandatory waiting periods, mediation, and marital counseling before legalizing an application for divorce.

Dynamics

To assess the effect of divorce, one must examine how all the various members of the family deal with the transition, reestablish their role obligations to one another, and perform such functions as the following (Hetherington & Clingempeel, 1992):

- **Socialization/education.** Child rearing must continue; behavior must be monitored, values and morals imparted.
- **Assignment of social roles/authority.** Power for decision making within the family must be allocated and responsibilities for tasks assigned.
- **Economic support/domestic responsibilities.** The family must obtain enough money to provide for the support of its members. The physical well-being of the children must be provided for, and the residence must be maintained in a safe and healthy manner.
- **Nurturance/emotional support.** Caring and involvement toward one another are necessary to provide for the emotional well-being of family members.

A divorcing family's ability to carry on its former functions is affected not only by the coping skills of its members but also by societal forces, such as economic disparity for females, attitudes regarding the ideal two-parent family, and available informal or formal support services in the community (Coontz, 1997; Hetherington, 1989).

Regardless of their marital status, women do not earn income on the same scale as men. Sometimes a woman who heads a family must turn to her own family of orientation or to the government for economic assistance. Evidence has shown that children living in mother-only families were four times as likely to be poor compared to children living with two parents (Children's Defense Fund [CDF], 2010).

Socioeconomics

The change in the economic status of the family resulting from divorce means not only a change in family consumption habits, but often a change in housing. Moving in itself is a source of stress to the family; for one thing, former neighborhood supports are no longer available. Also, maintaining two households is costly when a parent lives in one place but must contribute to another.

Authority Distribution

Divorce affects the distribution of authority within the family. Before the divorce, the father may have had more authority because traditionally he had been regarded as the primary breadwinner, or authority may have been shared by both parents. After the divorce, however, the residential parent assumes day-to-day authority over the children, and the nonresidential parent becomes restricted to areas spelled out in the divorce agreement. Hetherington and Kelly (2002) found that both fathers' and mothers' authority over children, as indicated by their parenting practices, tended to deteriorate in the first two years following the divorce. There was less consistency, control, and affection.

Domestic Responsibility

Divorce affects the distribution of the domestic functions of the family. Before the divorce, both parents performed chores related to family functioning. If the mother was not employed outside the home, it was likely that she was primarily responsible for household duties and child care while the father was earning the money. In such cases, after the divorce, the mother was more likely to have residential custody of the children

(Hetherington & Kelly, 2002). Generally, she had to find work outside the home because of the reduction in the father's economic contribution to her and the children. In addition, she had to find someone to care for the children. The father, in turn, had to assume the domestic duties associated with his separate household or else hire someone to clean, cook, shop, and do laundry. If the mother was employed outside the home before the divorce, the father may have shared domestic responsibilities with her; so after the divorce, his chores became hers.

Emotional Support

The isolation of the nuclear family from relatives compounds the dilemma of the burdens thrust upon the divorced family—relatives cannot be called upon for help with child care, household duties, or emotional support. Because emotional support is one of the functions of the family, and divorce removes one adult from the context, the remaining adult no longer has someone with whom to share the burdens and joys of child rearing. Neither is there someone with whom to share the daily decision making and to provide needed psychological support.

Effects of Divorce on Children

How do children experience parental divorce?

The National Center for Health Statistics stopped publishing numbers of divorce and remarriage in 2000 because some states no longer count them. However, based on past data, almost one out of two marriages ends in divorce. Most divorces occur within the first ten years for both first marriages and first remarriages. Children experience a deep sense of loss, develop divided loyalties, and often feel helpless against forces beyond their control. In summarizing the last three decades of research on the effects of divorce, Hetherington and Kelly (2002) report that although children of divorced parents, as a group, have more adjustment problems than do children of never-divorced parents, the divorce *per se* is not necessarily the major cause of these problems; rather, the negative effects of conflict in troubled marriages can be observed in children years before the divorce takes place. Ahrons (2007) found similar results interviewing 173 grown children 20 years after the divorce.

Parental divorce involves a series of stressful interactions between children and their environment as the family restructures. However, not all children react to divorce in the same way (Lansforth, 2009). Children's reactions depend on the various personalities involved, their coping skills, and the parents' relations with their children, as well as with each other (Ahrons, 2007; Cowan, Powell, & Cowan, 1998). Reactions also depend on such factors as children's age and gender, how much family disharmony existed before the divorce, and how available other people are to the parents for emotional support, and to the children for role models (Kelly & Emery, 2003; Hetherington & Stanley-Hagan, 2002). Studies by Hetherington (1988, 1989, 1993) show that during and after parental divorce, children often exhibit marked changes in behavior, such as acting out, particularly in school. An analysis of academic achievement of high school students showed that those from divorced families had significantly lower achievement levels than those from married families (Hetherington & Kelly, 2002).

This girl waves goodbye to her Mom to spend time with her Dad.

Denise Hager/Catchlight Visual Services/Alamy

Child's Age and Divorce Effects

Preschool-age children's self-concept was found to be affected by divorce (Wallerstein & Kelly, 1996). In particular, the child's views of the dependability and predictability of relationships were disrupted. Some children blamed themselves for the breakup. For example, one 5-year-old child said, "If only I didn't whine like Daddy said, he wouldn't have left me." Even a year later, in a follow-up study, almost half the children in the sample still displayed heightened anxiety and aggression. These authors also found that school-age children responded to divorce with sadness, fear, feelings

TeachSource Video Activity

Go to the Education CourseMate website to watch the video entitled "Communicating with Families: Best Practices in an Early Childhood Setting." This video exemplifies co-parenting. The cooperation between the parents seems idealistic. Based on your own, or friends', experiences, how would you describe the reality of divorce for kids?

of deprivation, and some anger (Wallerstein, Corbin, & Lewis, 1988; Wallerstein & Kelly, 1996). They, like the preschool children, were still struggling after a year with the changes in their lives. School-age children had difficulty focusing their attention on school-related tasks.

In various studies (Amato, 2000; Hetherington & Clingempeel, 1992; Lansford, 2009), young children of divorce were found to be more dependent, aggressive, whiny, demanding, unaffectionate, and disobedient than children from married families. They feared abandonment, loss of love, and bodily harm. The behavior and fears expressed were due, in part, to the parents' preoccupation with their own needs, as well as to the ensuing role conflicts. When compared to parents of married families, divorced parents of preschoolers were less consistent in their discipline and less nurturant. Also, communication was not as effective, and they made fewer demands for mature behavior from their children.

Adolescents, unlike younger children, feel little sense of blame for the separation of their parents, but they feel resentment. They are often pawns in each parent's bid for loyalty: "She tells me terrible things about my dad; when I'm with him, he tells me terrible things about her." They are also still burdened by painful memories of the divorce ten years later (Wallerstein, Corbin, & Lewis, 1988) and even 20 years later, especially if one or both parents remarried (Ahrons, 2007).

Child's Gender and Divorce Effects

Gender influences the impact of divorce, with research showing that boys are harder hit. Two years after the divorce, many boys have trouble concentrating, do poorly on intelligence tests, and have difficulty with math. Also, they interact aggressively with their mothers, their teachers, and boys their own age. Monitoring of boys was lower in divorced non-remarried households, and the boys engaged in more antisocial behavior (Hetherington, 1993; Hetherington & Clingempeel, 1992). Girls tend to cry and whine to vent their sadness—and this gets them support. Although preadolescent girls seem to adjust to the divorce within two to three years, evidence has accumulated showing problems related to feminine gender-role development emerging at adolescence. Problems include difficult heterosexual relationships, precocious sexual activity, and confrontational exchanges with the mother (Ellis et al., 2003; Hetherington, 1993).

Children from a divorced family lack the live-in sex-role model of one parent, usually the father, who resides separately. As children grow, each parent interprets society to them. According to Lamb (2004), the father's role in the socialization of children is very important in that he not only models and teaches gender roles, he also models and teaches other values and morals. Opposite-sex role models for children, however, are available in the form of relatives, teachers, coaches, or community service personnel.

Child Custody Arrangements and Divorce Effects

Children involved in custody battles are the most torn by divorce (Kelly, 2000). To avoid this win/lose situation, some judges mandate joint custody, sharing responsibility for children; others rule based on the child's "best interests." The effects of various custody arrangements are discussed later.

Child's Emotional Support and Divorce Effects

Although divorce is upsetting to everyone involved, it is probably worse for a child to live in an embattled household. For parents, divorce is a very stressful time, and feelings of depression, loss of self-esteem, and helplessness interfere with parenting abilities. Parents must find support outside the family to bolster their confidence in themselves and their ability to parent. They must tell the child that even though they are divorcing each other, they are not divorcing the child. Relatives, teachers, friends, and community services are resources for support.

Child's Marriage Role Models and Divorce Effects

A serious long-range effect of divorce is the removal of marriage role models. Unrealistic expectations of future mates occur. Children may grow up idealizing the absent parent. Ideals are wishes for perfection; they are untempered by reality. For example, a child growing up in a two-parent home may experience such things as parents' disagreements and how they are (or are not) worked out, time demands on parents from sources outside the family, and physical affection from both parents. The child growing up in a single-parent home may fantasize situations and relationships regarding the missing parent; reality inevitably brings disappointment.

Single-Parent Custody

What is the effect on children of being raised by one parent?

In the United States, the percentage of children living with a single parent is about 26 percent. About four times as many children live with mothers as compared to fathers (FIFCFS, 2010).

Single parenthood can occur through death, desertion, divorce, births outside marriage (including via various reproductive technologies), and adoption without marriage. Single-parent custody refers to a judicial decision. To ensure children's legal status and rights, the federal government passed the Uniform Parentage Act of 2002. It provides a comprehensive framework establishing the parentage of children born to both married and unmarried couples, whether those children were conceived through sexual intercourse, assisted reproduction, or through a gestational agreement, such as surrogacy. Most states have variations of the federal law. Once parenting is established, the court may support orders for child custody, child support, visitation, health insurance, name change, and more.

Single-parent mothers experience economic as well as emotional and physical strain (Hetherington & Clingempeel, 1992; Peterson, 1996). Frequently, female-headed families are poor; at the least, a drop in the family's standard of living occurs if the woman was previously married (CDF, 2010).

Compared to children raised by single-parent mothers, little research has been done on children being raised by single-parent fathers. However, compared to single-parent mothers, single-parent fathers have more economic resources and have more authority over their children (Hilton & DeVall, 1998). However, compared to two-parent families, single-parent fathers, like single-parent mothers, have fewer economic resources (Patterson & Hastings, 2007).

Problems for fathers raising children are similar to those of mothers. In general, fathers find it difficult to obtain child-care help (day care, after-school care, housekeepers). Sometimes day-care centers' hours do not coincide with work hours, and the cost of a housekeeper or nanny is prohibitive. There is also role overload in having to work, care for children, and maintain the house. Social life suffers.

IN PRACTICE

Recommendations for Community Support of Single Parents

- Extend availability of day-care facilities to evening hours.
- Form babysitting cooperatives in neighborhoods or places of employment.
- Make transportation available for children to and from day care to parent's home or work.
- Provide classes on single parenthood and opportunities for support groups.
- Provide Big Sister programs (for girls from mother-absent homes) as well as Big Brother programs (for boys from father-absent homes).

While fathers' *economic* responsibility for their children has been the focus of public policy and consequent legislation; fathers' *emotional* responsibility has been ignored until recently (Amato, 1998, 2000). Fathers are now being included in prenatal, preschool, and elementary school programs. Many studies point to the benefit of the father's involvement in child rearing after parents separate (Amato, 1998); however, the father's influence is not always beneficial if the father has an antisocial personality or exhibits antisocial behavior (De Garmo, 2010).

Joint Custody

Joint custody is a contemporary solution to the quandary facing many judges: Which adult claimant should be given custody of a child? It also provides the rationale for father–mother involvement in child rearing, which enables the child to relate to both male and female role models (Bauserman, 2002).

Joint custody can refer to legal and/or physical custody arrangements. Joint *legal* custody divides decision-making authority for the child between the divorced parents. Typical areas requiring decisions include discipline, education, medical care, and religious upbringing. Sometimes *physical* custody is divided as well. For example, a child may spend weekdays with one parent and weekends and holidays with the other, or six months with one and six months with the other.

As the number of divorces has climbed, so has the number of states giving legal sanction to some form of joint custody. As a result, some nuclear families split by divorce are evolving into a new form, called the **binuclear family**, a pattern in which the children are part of two homes and two family groups. Binuclear families are not limited to joint custody cases, but parents without legal custody eventually tend to become less involved in the child's life.

binuclear family family pattern in which children are part of two homes and two family groups

An analysis of studies on children in joint physical or legal custody showed they were better adjusted than children in sole-custody settings and no different from married families (Bauserman, 2002). "Adjustment" included family relationships, self-esteem, emotional and behavioral adjustment, and divorce-specific adjustment.

The caveat in joint custody, however, is that usually the parents are divorcing because they can no longer communicate or cooperate with one another. So what may happen is that parents divide authority, and the joint-custody child, instead of having two decision-making parents, ends up having none because the parents can't agree. Lack of consensus or inconsistency is confusing to a child and may undermine discipline.

If the divorce was bitter, then the increased communication between the parents required by joint custody is likely to become more hostile, thereby exposing the children to even more conflict and psychological damage (Emery, 2004; Maccoby & Mnookin, 1992; Mason, 1998). Another problem occurs when parents use the child to communicate messages between them (Furstenburg & Cherlin, 1991)—"Tell your father to send the check or he won't get to see you next weekend"—and to inform each parent of the other's activities (Parke & Buriel, 2006).

Although joint custody gives children access to both parents, thereby avoiding the feeling of being abandoned by the noncustodial parent, some children, especially younger ones, are actually harmed by the inevitable continual separation and re-attachment. Preschool children have a very difficult time understanding why everyone can't live in the same house and "Why, if Mommy loves me and Daddy loves me, don't they love each other anymore?" School-age children express confusion and anxiety over their schedules, anxiety that spills over into school performance and relationships with friends (Francke, 1983). For example, a 6-year-old became obsessed with carrying his backpack everywhere because he was afraid of leaving his homework at one parent's house while he stayed at the other's. An 11-year-old girl felt that she could never be anyone's "best" friend because she didn't stay in one house long enough. To her, being a best friend meant being around all the time.

Kin Custody

"Kin" refers to blood relatives or those related by marriage or adoption. An increasing number of children are being raised by kin other than parents, the most common being grandparents raising grandchildren, especially since the Great Recession around 2007 (Livingston & Parker, 2010). Some of these families have informal arrangements (without legal custody or guardianship); others are part of the formal foster care system. Family relationships beyond the nuclear family are becoming increasingly important in American society (Bengston, 2001). Extended family members help care for children and provide emotional support.

This grandparent teaches her granddaughter how to use a toy.

Cengage Learning

Among children under age 18 not living with either parent, about 52 percent are cared for by a grandparent and about 25 percent are cared for by other relatives (FIFCFS, 2010). Some reasons for kin care are that the child's parents are deceased, the child was abandoned, or the court granted legal custody to the grandparent(s) because the parents were deemed unfit to nurture and support. Substance abuse, teen pregnancy, divorce, physical and mental illness, abuse, neglect, and incarceration are reasons cited. Many custodial grandparents do not fit the stereotype of senior citizens enjoying retirement activities (Smith & Drew, 2002). Their median age span is about 45 to 69 (Livingston & Parker, 2010), and some have to care for their own parents in addition to their grandchildren. The constant challenge leaves many grandparents physically, emotionally, and financially drained. The challenges faced by parenting grandparents are changes in relationships with their spouse and other family members, financial stress, possible feelings of uncertainty, isolation, anger, grief, fear, and worries about health or death (deToledo & Brown, 1995; Hayslip & Kaminski, 2005; Smith & Drew, 2002).

The challenge faced by children being raised by grandparents is to develop a sense of belonging and stability amid the transition from their own homes. Common feelings are grief, fear, anger, guilt, and embarrassment. Sometimes these feelings are exhibited in such acting-out behaviors as physical or verbal aggression, regression to immature behavior (crying, whining, bed-wetting), manipulation, withdrawal, and hyperactivity (deToledo & Brown, 1995).

Interethnic (Racial) and Interfaith (Religious) Families

When people with different heritages marry and have families, they face certain challenges not experienced by those couples who have similar backgrounds. This is also true of parents who adopt children of a different color or ethnicity than theirs. Because of obvious differences in physical traits, such as color or ethnic features, interethnic families, compared to interfaith families, are more likely to face the prejudices of others. In addition to the challenges of dealing with stereotyping, both interethnic and interfaith parents must deal with their cultural contrasts, as discussed in Chapter 1 (individualistic or collectivistic orientations), reflected by different values, communication styles, perceptions of appropriate gender roles, beliefs about parenting, and so on. They must decide how to carry on their cultural or religious traditions with their children. They must also enable their children to form a sense of identity (Crohn, 1995).

The number of interethnic and interfaith families has increased (Hitlin, Brown, & Elder, 2006). According to the American Academy of Adolescent and Child Psychiatry (AACAP, 2011), research has shown that multicultural children do not differ from other children in self-esteem, comfort with themselves, or number of psychiatric problems. Also, they generally have a tolerance for diversity even though some interracial families face discrimination in their communities. Some children report teasing, whispers, or stares from others when with their families.

This interethnic (racial) and interfaith (religious) family is coping with the challenges of socializing a child by parents with different backgrounds, ways of doing things, goals, and so on.

Rob Marmion/Shutterstock.com

Adolescents from interethnic families develop racial self-identities within overlapping contexts, creating a sense of self that reflects the social reality of their peer group, neighborhood, or school. For example, some adolescents who appear to be White may gravitate toward White friends, while also claiming a minority racial category on a college application to get special treatment (Hitlin, Brown, & Elder, 2006).

Stepfamilies

Because of the changing nature of families, as well as budgetary constraints, the U.S. Bureau of the Census no longer provides statistics on the number of children residing in stepfamilies. However, projections based on earlier data suggest that one out of three Americans is now a stepparent, a stepchild, a stepsibling, or a cohabiting member of a stepfamily (Stepfamily Association of America, 2000).

Because of the increase in the number of stepfamilies, the concept of family needs reexamining, according to the Stepfamily Association of America. Institutions such as schools, hospitals, and courts must adapt to the special needs of stepfamilies (Stewart, 2007). Most societal institutions have policies based on married families. Although they may be full-time parents to their spouses' kids, stepparents, in many cases, have no legal rights. For example, if a child needs emergency surgery, hospitals almost always require the consent of a biological parent or legal guardian.

In addition to legal issues, psychosocial issues present special problems for the stepfamily. Each family member has experienced the trauma of divorce, death, or separation from a parent or spouse. When a new family is formed, new problems are likely to arise. The impact of remarriage on a family is second only to the crisis of divorce (Hetherington & Kelly, 2002).

The interactions in stepfamilies are similar to those in any other family, which means they are sometimes tainted with anger, jealousy, value conflicts, guilt, and unrealistic expectations. One of the most common unrealistic expectations is the belief in instant love. Stepfamily relationships are, generally, instant; they do not evolve as they do in a family of orientation, where a child is born and grows.

Children in a stepfamily may feel abandoned by the noncustodial parent. Having to live with new rules and values, while still trying to deal with the old rules and values from both parents, places an enormous burden on the child. Also, the stepfamily often adds more children to the household. This involves adjustments in relating to new siblings. Thus, when families blend, all members are very much affected. In the early months of remarriage, there is likely to be less family cohesion, more poorly defined family roles and relationships, poorer family communication, less effective problem resolution, less consistency in setting rules, less effective disciplining, and less emotional responsiveness. Both stepmothers and stepfathers take a considerably less active role in parenting than do custodial parents (Bray, 1988, 1999). Even after two years, disengagement is the most common parenting style (Hetherington & Stanley-Hagan, 2002). Stepfamilies also may suffer from a lack of external support, fueled by a history of media myths—the wicked stepmother, the molesting stepfather (Rutter, 1994).

In general, families in which the custodial father remarries and a stepmother joins the family experience more resistance and poorer adjustment for children than do families in which the custodial mother remarries and a stepfather joins the family (Hetherington & Stanley-Hagan, 2002). The introduction of a stepparent may also strain the child's relationship with the noncustodial parent. Remarriage often presents children with loyalty dilemmas that they are too inexperienced to solve (Francke, 1983). If they like the stepparent, is that disloyal to their noncustodial parent? Or worse, will they lose the love of their biological parent? Does the noncustodial parent compete with the stepparent for the child's loyalty by buying the child things or by "putting the stepparent down"? Does the child view the stepparent as usurping the biological parent's role? ("She wants us to call her 'Mother.' I won't," said a 10-year-old girl. "He can't tell me what to do; he's not my real father," said a 7-year-old boy.)

Families in which both parents bring children from a previous marriage tend to be associated with the highest level of behavior problems (Bray, 1999). The addition of instant siblings to the family constellation is both bewildering and taxing to the children (Francke, 1983; Rutter, 1994). For example, overnight the birth-order hierarchy may shift. The child who has been the oldest may inherit an older brother; the child who has been the youngest may inherit a baby sister. Children often compete for attention, especially with the biological parent. Children who have differing histories of upbringing must now live under the same roof with new sets of rules. For example, children who were given choices at mealtime must now adapt to having to eat everything that is put on their plates or "no dessert." A child who has had to make his or her bed and clean his or her room now has to share a room with a child who has never had those responsibilities.

At least half of children living in stepfamilies are likely to face an additional strain—the birth of a half-sibling to their biological parent and the new spouse (Stewart, 2007). Not only is there yet another threat to securing parental love, but common sibling rivalry is intensified by half- versus full-blooded relationships (Francke, 1983; Rutter, 1994).

The complications in roles and relationships faced by the stepparents are evidenced by the increased risk of divorce among remarriages, especially those with children from a previous marriage. Whereas about 50 percent of first marriages end in divorce, for second marriages the estimated divorce rate is 60 percent (Stewart, 2007). Divorce is most likely to occur in remarried families during the first five years, the time in which the new stepfamily is trying to restructure and "refunctionalize" (Parke & Buriel, 2006). After five years, stepfamilies are as stable as married families of the same duration (Rutter, 1994).

In sum, the effect of remarriage on the child depends on several factors (Hetherington & Clingempeel, 1992; Hetherington & Stanley-Hagan, 2002):

- The presence of additional stressors (moving, finances, stepsiblings)
- The age, developmental status, and sex of the child
- The quality of the child's relationship with both biological parents (custodial and noncustodial)
- The quality of the child's relationship with the stepparent and siblings
- The temperament, personality, and emotional stability of the child and the parents
- The availability of parent substitutes or other social supports for the child
- The parenting styles of biological parents and stepparents
- The availability of social supports for the parents

Families of Unmarried Parents

Marriage is a legal contract with certain rights and obligations. It is society's institution for founding and maintaining a family. Families of unmarried parents include heterosexual adults who choose to live together without legal sanction and homosexual adults who live together unwed (with exceptions in some states) because society, in general, doesn't legalize their relationship. Such unconventional families are increasing (Stewart, 2007) and are discussed here because of their impact on children.

marriage a legal contract with certain rights and obligations

Unconventional families can give children love and stability, but it is more difficult because of the general absence of community supports. What makes things more challenging for unconventional families is the fact that traditional rights and obligations are not necessarily expected or implemented. For example, financial requirements for support of children under age 18 are not legalized for the cohabiting partner. The cohabitating partner is not automatically included in the child's school or social functions.

Most research on children growing up without a married mother and father reports a higher incidence of poverty, poor academic performance, emotional or behavioral problems, and substance abuse (CDF, 2010; Patterson & Hastings, 2007). However, numerous factors are involved in the circumstances under which children are born to unmarried parents that affect developmental outcomes. These factors include socioeconomic status, relationship of biological parents to each other and to the child, relationship of cohabiting adults (if not biologically related) to the child, child's characteristics (age, temperament, cognitive development), mother's and father's characteristics (age, temperament, education, parenting style, history of substance abuse, domestic violence, and/or child abuse), relationships with other children in the household or family, extended family relationships, and neighborhood characteristics (safety, supports, services) (Stewart, 2007). What makes these factors more salient in unmarried households with children is the lack of legal sanctions that accompany the marriage contract to ensure child protection.

Families of Same-Sex Parents

Families with same-sex parents are becoming more visible in society today (Patterson, 2002, 2006). Most common are two lesbian women living together raising children of one or both from their previous relationships with men. There are also lesbian relationships in which one or both of the women becomes artificially inseminated or adopts a child, as well as two gay men living together with custody of their biological or adopted children. There are bisexual and transgendered parents, too.

Many issues faced by families with homosexual parents are similar to those faced in divorced, stepparent, and various custodial arrangements (Patterson, 2002). According to the American Academy of Child and Adolescent Psychiatry (AACAP, 2006a), these issues apply to families with bisexual and transgendered parents, too. Overriding these, however, is how the family manages the stigmatizing attitude of society. Generally (some exceptions exist), society does not legally sanction homosexual marriages or families. Some cities and businesses, however, have implemented policies for domestic partnerships or civil unions; otherwise, housing, insurance benefits, emergency room visits, and school permission forms exclude the cohabiting partner.

Attitudes about homosexuality generally stem from one's personal feelings about one's own sexuality. These attitudes include fear, disgust, indifference, and acceptance. Because of perceived negative attitudes, many homosexuals, especially those raising children, hide their relationship by pretending to be heterosexual (Goldberg, 2009). Being open about their homosexuality renders them vulnerable to discrimination and ostracism.

Children of those who are open about their homosexual relationship may be teased by other children (Gollnick & Chinn, 2008)—"Why do you have two mommies?" or "Your dad is a ——." However, being secret, although arguably adaptive, is accompanied by the consequences of self-betrayal and disconnectedness from social support (Goldberg, 2009). New associations must be continually evaluated regarding the safety of disclosure. Many homosexual parents fear they will lose custody of their children if their sexual orientation is known (Patterson, 2009).

Research on children living with homosexual parents and their partners has focused on three fearful attitudes held by society in general: (1) that the children will become homosexual, (2) that they will be sexually molested, and (3) that psychological damage will result from the stigma of being raised by homosexuals. This research (Gartrell & Bos, 2010; Johnson & O'Conner, 2002; Patterson, 2006) has found no higher incidence of homosexuality among children raised by homosexuals than among those raised by heterosexuals, nor have there been any reported incidents of sexual abuse; also, children reared by homosexuals are not necessarily more psychologically troubled than children reared by heterosexuals.

However, as children approach adolescence and become concerned about their identities and sexual orientation, any family deviations from the norm among their peers can be magnified. The normal developmental changes that occur during adolescence, coupled with the problem of having to cope with a stigmatized parent, can multiply the potential problems facing the adolescent and his or her family. Variables affecting the adolescent's perception of the situation include his or her relationship with the biological parents, the partner, and friends; level of acceptance in the community; and self-confidence (Goldberg, 2009).

Families of Adopted Children

Families adopt children for many reasons, including an inability to conceive, the desire to care for a child without the sanction of marriage, the desire to care for a child with special needs (one who has been abused or neglected, has disabilities, or comes from another country), or the desire to make a foster care arrangement permanent. Regardless of the reason, the AACAP (2002b) recommends that the adoptive parent(s) tell the child about the adoption in a way the child can understand based on age and maturity. This enables the child to feel that his or her adoption was wanted by the family and is a positive experience.

Adoptive parents need to be prepared for children's interpretations of the adoption even years after the situation was explained (AACAP, 2002a). The child may create fantasies about the birth parents and may even deny the reality of the adoption (Pavao, 2005). The child may believe he or she did something bad and was sent away. Some children believe they were kidnapped by the adoptive parent(s). In adolescence, when identity formation is a normal challenge, the adopted child faces more complex issues, such as whether to tell friends, whether to contact the birth parent(s), what medical history is relevant, and loyalty. The identity issues are even greater in transracial adoptions. Some other issues may be fear of abandonment, painful reminders of identity at birthdays, a need to grieve for what is perceived to be lost, and dealing with the unknown (Eldridge, 1999).

Dual-Earner Families

Studies on dual-earner families have expanded in scope and coverage during the 2000–2010 decade (Bianchi & Milkie, 2010). A major trend was the increased diversity of families and workplaces. Families increasingly diverged from the two-parent family with breadwinner father and homemaker mother to single parent, stepparent, kin, unmarried, and same-sex parent families. Workplaces became more expandable in terms of space and flexible in terms of time. Work could take place anywhere a laptop could get Internet service, and 9 to 5 became 24/7. These changes influenced workers' home lives and the balance between work and family (Schieman, Milkie, & Glavin, 2009).

During the 2000–2010 decade, some studies showed that women's allocation of time to paid and unpaid work (cooking, laundry, cleaning, shopping, repairs, and child care) had generally become similar (Sayer, 2005). However, despite the increase in fathers' involvement in the home, men still gravitated toward stereotypical male chores, and child care remained much more the purview of mothers than fathers, just as paid work hours remained longer for fathers (Craig, 2006). Even though, in general, workplaces became more expandable and flexible, time conflicts between work and family remained (Jacobs & Gerson, 2004). Family demands, such as emergency repairs, care of sick children, shared family activities, and involvement in children's activities, often caused parents to have negative feelings, such as guilt, frustration, or anxiety (Bianchi & Milkie, 2010).

A mother dropping her daughter off at day care before going to work.

Cengage Learning

The lack of shared family time had consequences for children. For example, Crouter et al. (2004) found it to be related to risky adolescent behavior.

Maternal Employment and Child Well-Being

One of the largest topics in the literature on dual-earner families continued to be the relationship of parental employment, especially maternal employment, to child well-being (Bianchi & Milkie, 2010). Mother employment almost always improves the economic well-being of families with children, and often makes the difference between whether or not they can make ends meet. To the extent that mothers' working keeps children out of poverty and ensures that their basic material needs are met, it has important benefits (FIFCFS, 2010). Other benefits of dual-earner families include personal stimulation for the mother (if she enjoys her job), a closer relationship between father and children (because of his increased participation in family matters), and greater sense of responsibility for the children.

Reviews of the research on maternal employment (Bianchi & Milkie, 2010; Gottfried, Gottfried, & Buthurst, 2002; Hoffman, 2000) reveal that a variety of effects, depending on individual factors, result when a mother is employed outside the home. Individual factors influencing the impact of a mother's employment are the age, gender, and temperament of the child; the socioeconomic status cultural orientation of the family; whether the mother works full or part time; age of the child when she became employed; the quality of the parents' marriage; the mother's satisfaction with her job; the father's satisfaction with his job; and the father's involvement with the children and support of the mother.

Child-care arrangements constitute a mediating effect on the impact of maternal employment on the child. Brooks-Gunn, Han, and Walker (2010) examined the links between maternal employment in the child's first 12 months of life and cognitive, social, and emotional outcomes on the child at age 3, 4, 5, and 7. Data was used from the first two phases of the National Institute of Child Health and Development (NICHD) Study of Early Child Care (child care will be discussed in Chapter 5). Results showed some lower cognitive scores, as well as behavior problems at age 3, 4, 5, and 7 for children whose mothers who were employed during their first year compared to children whose mothers stayed home. However, among children whose mothers went to work after their first year of life, results were similar to children whose mothers worked part time or stayed home.

In general, employed mothers provide different role models than do mothers who remain at home. Also, employment affects the mother's emotional state—sometimes providing satisfactions, sometimes stress, and sometimes guilt—and this, in turn, influences the mother–child interaction. When the mother is satisfied with her career and does not feel guilty about working, her relations with her children are similar to those of nonemployed mothers who are content with their homemaking role.

New times call for reformed ideas of roles in the family and in children's socialization, as exemplified by this young boy who is cleaning the floor.

Marcel Mooij/Shutterstock.Com

One finding that has occurred frequently in various studies is that children of mothers employed outside the home, from kindergarten age through adulthood, have less stereotyped views of gender roles (Gottfried, Gottfried, & Buthurst, 2002; Parke & Buriel, 2006). These views are influenced by the mother's discussion of her work, as well as by the father's participation in household tasks and child care.

Some evidence suggests that mothers employed outside the home use different child-rearing practices than do mothers not so employed, particularly in the area of independence training. When mothers don't feel guilty about leaving their children in order to work, employed mothers tend to encourage their children to become self-sufficient and assume household tasks at an earlier age (Hoffman & Youngblade, 1999).

Children affect the mother's attitude about working and being a competent parent. A child's difficult temperament was found to be significantly associated with mother's work outcomes (quality of work and emotional rewards from combining work and family responsibilities) (Hyde et al., 2004).

IN PRACTICE

Coping Strategies for Dual-Earner Families

- Think of yourself as a household manager who delegates and supervises, rather than does.
- Determine your priorities, as well as what is really essential—clothes ironed or a game played with the children.
- Set aside routine "quality" time for your spouse and your children. For parents, uninterrupted time away from household and child-care duties will do. For children, any activity that raises the child's self-esteem is quality time—for example, talking about their day, reading to them, or playing a game with them.
- Establish traditions and rituals to which both parents and children can regularly look forward.
- Schedule time alone, time to pursue an interest, time to refresh their energies.
- Learn to say "no" sometimes. When invited somewhere or asked to help on a committee, you might respond, "Let me check and get back to you." This response gives you time to evaluate the invitation and see if it fits in with other commitments to family members.
- Advocate for family-responsive corporate policies such as leaves, flexible work hours, job sharing, child-care support, and seminars dealing with work/family issues.

Note: The American Psychological Association gives "Psychologically Healthy Workplace Awards" (www.apapractice.org/apo/psychologically_healthy.html).

Functional Family Changes

How are family functions affected by societal change?

Throughout history, families have been changing in the ways they execute their various functions, including reproduction, socialization/education, assignment of social roles, economic support, and nurturance/emotional support. Such changes in family functioning are adaptations to macrosystem influences, such as economics, political ideology, and technology.

Reproduction

Technological changes, such as birth control and reproductive assistance (donation of egg and sperm, in vitro fertilization, embryo transfer, surrogacy) have affected family size. Economics, too, has played a role. Many young people have chosen to postpone childbearing until they achieve financial stability. However, delaying conception until the late 30s affects fertility. Couples who have difficulty conceiving may then turn to technology for assistance or choose to adopt. In any case, family size has decreased in the past century compared to the past, when families had many children hoping some would survive to reproduce the next generation (FIFCFS, 2010).

Socialization/Education

The socialization/education domain of the family has decreased in the past century. Until the 19th century, children were educated at home. Education consisted of religious teachings and training to work on the farm, to work in the family business, or to perform household chores. The Industrial Revolution provided work outside the home and farm for women and children as well as men. Thus, the family could no longer be totally responsible for their children's education and training for the adult world. Gradually, schools took over this function.

The public, or "common," school emerged in the middle of the 19th century under the leadership of Horace Mann. The main rationale for compulsory, free public education was that families could no longer socialize their children for a productive role in the increasingly complicated U.S. economy. Schools were expected to teach good work habits and basic reading, writing, and arithmetic skills, as well as form good character. Today many states require that, in addition to these basics, schools teach such topics as sex education, substance abuse prevention, and anger management, things previously assumed to be the domain of the family.

Assignment of Social Roles

Social roles within the family are defined by which members perform what jobs, as well as the distribution of authority. Changes in family roles over time, as discussed here, illustrate chronosystem influences.

Wife/Mother

When the family was agrarian and self-sufficient, the wife was responsible for preparing food, making clothes, caring for the children, managing the house, caring for the animals, and cultivating the garden. Her husband had the authority in the family. When the economy began to change from agriculture to industry, and farms started to sell produce and animal products, men took over the responsibilities of making contacts for sales and transporting the goods, and the woman's role diminished.

Industrialization provided an opportunity for the expansion of women's roles, but few jobs were open to women initially. In the 19th and early 20th centuries in the United States, women were usually employed only as seamstresses, laundresses, maids, cooks, housekeepers, governesses, teachers, and nurses. Not until World War II did this pattern change. Today, more than half of all mothers with children under 18 are employed outside the home, occupying work roles similar to men.

Husband/Father

Traditionally, a man was responsible for economically supporting his wife and children; a wife was responsible for maintaining the household. This division of labor between husband and wife affected their parental roles (Mintz, 1998). In colonial families, children learned appropriate gender roles from both father and mother, because there was no sharp split between work and home. In 19th-century families, however, mothers assumed more child-rearing tasks because fathers worked in industry and were away from home much of the time.

Today, the role of father is being redefined by technological and ideological changes in our society. In many families, men are assuming more household and child-care responsibilities (Parke, 2002; Tamis-LeMonda & Cabrera, 1999). This is especially true in families in which the mother is employed. It is also true in cases where the parents are divorced and the father has custody, or partial custody, of the children. Today, many fathers are active participants in the socialization of their children.

Children

In preindustrial times, children contributed to the family work by helping adults on the farm, in the business, and in the home. Today, most adult family members work for pay outside the home and children rarely work at all. Work and family life are separate entities. Families have become consumption units rather than production units. Children used to be an economic asset, contributing to the family by doing chores or contributing wages earned outside the family. Now they have become an economic liability; they not only have to be sheltered, clothed, and fed until age 18 but have to be educated as well. In dual-earner families, the cost of child care must be added to the economic liability. Not only are children expensive to raise, but most cannot be counted on to provide economic support when their parents reach old age.

How has the balance of power changed?

Authority Patterns

Authority patterns in the family can be traced back in time. Similar to families in the Biblical era and ancient Rome, families in colonial America were patriarchal and extended.

The father was responsible for not only the economic survival of the family, but the socialization of the children as well. It was not until the 20th century that mothers gained status as family providers, influenced by political events. Their help was needed in the workforce while many men were engaged in the war effort (Coontz, 1997). It took implementation of the Civil Rights Act of 1964, which outlawed racial and gender discrimination, for women to gain more equal authority in the workplace and, consequently, at home. Now authority patterns in many families approach an egalitarian pattern, or some sort of collaborative one negotiated between the parents, with the father responsible for some tasks and the mother for others (Kaslow, 2001).

Economic Support

How has economic responsibility for family functioning changed?

A major function of the family remains the economic support of its members, but the scope of this responsibility has changed, as well as which family members contribute.

Until the 18th century, most American families were extended. They owned and occupied farms and plantations that were self-sufficient, producing most of what the family needed. Families built their own houses, grew their own food, and made their own furniture and clothing. Things the family needed but did not produce were usually obtained through barter. These early American families were economic units in which all members, young and old, played important productive roles. Thus, children were essential to the prosperity of the family. The boys helped cultivate the land and harvest crops; the girls helped cook, sew, weave, and care for domestic animals and younger children.

During the 19th century, farm families had begun raising crops to sell, using the proceeds to buy goods produced by others. Thus, families gradually became less and less self-sufficient. As industries grew, family members began to work for wages in factories and businesses. Money, then, became the link between work and family. The nuclear family became more common as houses were smaller and family providers had to be willing to move to where the work was (Coontz, 1997).

Today, most families require the economic contributions of both parents in order to afford food, clothing, shelter, services, and other goods needed for themselves and their children.

Nurturance/Emotional Support

How has family nurturance and emotional support changed?

The nurturing and emotional support function of families for the young (and sometimes the old) has remained fairly stable, but the range of the caregiving has diminished. For example, as medicine advanced, the family turned to doctors and nurses to provide health care. In the 19th century, health care as we know it today did not exist. There were no preventive inoculations (except for smallpox in the latter part of the century), no clinics, few hospitals, few medications, and doctors were few and far between. The sick were cared for by their families, as were the elderly. Today, we have insurance plans to cover costs of long-term care in residential facilities; we have disability plans; we have hospices to care for the dying. Because of the expense of caregiving outside the family, however, the importance of multigenerational bonds and links to extended kin needs to be reassessed (Bengston, 2001).

Macrosystem Influences on Families, Socialization, and Children

How do features of the macrosystem influence the socialization of children?

Specific effects of macrosystems (socioeconomic status, cultural orientation, and religious orientation) on socialization are examined to better understand how larger contexts can affect the way family systems operate.

On what basis are families ranked in society?

Socioeconomic Status

All societies have their own ways of ranking people, and they differ in the criteria used for placing people in certain classes or statuses. The term **socioeconomic status** (SES) generally refers to one's rank or position within a society, based on social and economic factors. Some societies, however, include inherited factors and stratify members by **ascribed status**; that is, family lineage, gender, birth order, or skin color determines a person's class. For example, in the British royal family marriages are expected to occur only with members of the nobility (there have been a few exceptions, however), and the firstborn son is automatically heir to the throne.

Other societies stratify members according to **achieved status**—that is, education, occupation, income, and/or place of residence determine an individual's class. The United States exemplifies a society in which status can be attained by achievement—Abraham Lincoln, the 16th president of the United States, was the son of a farmer. Academic achievement, trade skills, and athletic talent enable some youths from lower-class families to attain high status.

Traditional societies, those that rely on customs handed down from past generations as ways to behave, tend toward *ascribed status* for stratification; **modern societies**, those that look to the present for ways to behave and are thus responsive to change, tend toward *achieved status*. Stratification is based on the importance of individuals' contributions to a particular society's ability to function. For example, one person makes jewelry; another sells shoes; another is a doctor. Jewelry may be important to those who can afford it; shoes may be necessary for those who require foot protection; a doctor contributes to the well-being of everyone in the society. Thus, people in societies are not equally dependent on one another; some people are therefore more important to society than others and so are ranked higher in terms of social class or status. How a society stratifies or ranks people in social classes is shown by income earned and prestige acquired. In the United States, doctors are ranked high, whereas salespeople are ranked low.

It is more difficult for people to change their rank, or social class, in societies using *ascribed* criteria than in societies using *achieved* criteria. In societies using *ascribed* criteria, however, it is possible for achievements to change a person's ranking. For example, a person born into a lower-class family could become a soldier or a priest and thereby attain higher status. In contrast, in societies using *achieved* criteria, individuals' ascriptions (conditions of birth) affect their status. For example, those born into upper-class families will receive a head start on achievement because of their families' ability to educate them, live in certain neighborhoods, and buy certain material things.

When statuses are *ascribed*, roles are set in tradition. In other words, when one is born into a certain status, children are socialized primarily by modeling their elders and being instructed in the traditional ways. When statuses are *achieved*, however, as is the case in modern societies undergoing change, "the established system for assigning individuals to recognized statuses may break down. Wholly new statuses may come into existence" (Inkeles, 1969, p. 616). Thus, in societies that stratify by *achievement*, members may find themselves inadequately socialized to play the roles of the statuses they seek or have been assigned. For example, farmers who want to be competitive and profitable have to seek more technical knowledge than they learned from their parents. Society must then compensate for gaps in socialization by the family and rely on other institutions, such as the school or business, to prepare individuals for their new roles. Farmers may choose from courses such as plant pathology, genetics, animal husbandry, and economics for further expertise.

According to sociologist William Goode (1982), it is the family, not just the individual, that is ranked in society's class structure. This is an illustration of the macrosystem's

socioeconomic status rank or position within a society, based on social and economic factors

ascribed status social class, rank, or position determined by family lineage, gender, birth order, or skin color

achieved status social class, rank, or position determined by education, occupation, income, and/or place of residence

traditional society a society that relies on customs handed down from past generations as ways to behave

modern society a society that looks to the present for ways to behave and is thus responsive to change

This child learns the traditional skill of weaving as her mother supervises and provides help when necessary.

Paul Conklin/PhotoEdit

influence on a child's development, because the social class and status of the family help determine an individual's opportunities for education and occupation, as well as for social interaction. The members of the community in which the family lives, the children's friends, and the guests invited to the home generally come from the same social class. Even though U.S. citizens play down the existence of social classes, social scientists recognize that different groups in our society possess unequal amounts of money, prestige, influence, and "life chances" (Bornstein & Bradley, 2003). Despite its egalitarian principles, the United States has been widening the gap between rich and poor (U.S. Bureau of the Census, 2009a). See Figure 3.5 for a distribution of social classes in the United States.

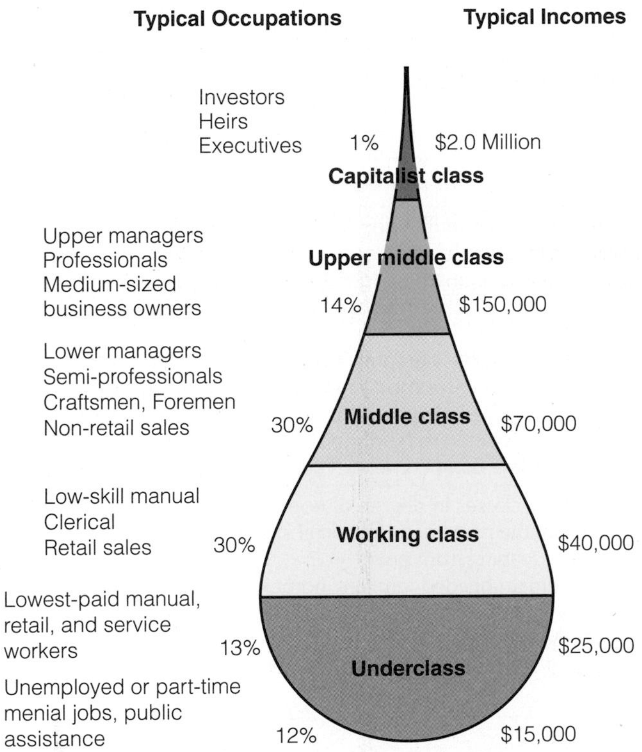

FIGURE 3.5 Social Class Structure in the United States
Children are socialized in the social class of their parents, establishing their "life chances."
Source: Gilbert, D. (2008). *The American class structure in an age of growing inequality* (7th ed.). Thousand Oaks, CA: Pine Forge/Sage, p. 13.

Social Class and Diversity

How does socioeconomic status influence socialization?

Sometimes, socioeconomic status is assumed to be related to ethnicity. However, studies have found that socioeconomic status actually exerts more influence on socialization than does race (Lareau, 2002; Patterson & Hastings, 2007). For example, Lareau (2002) found both White and Black middle-class parents made deliberate and sustained effort to stimulate children's cognitive and social development; whereas both White and Black lower-class parents viewed children's development as spontaneously unfolding as long as they were loved and cared for. Thus, different social classes (see Table 3.1 for descriptions) have different aims and methods of socialization, which, in turn, lead to different developmental outcomes for children, as discussed in the following paragraphs.

Upper Class

In upper-class families, the child is generally regarded as the carrier of the family's name, its heritage, and its status. The family is able to bear the maximum costs of child rearing (material goods, private schooling, setting up in business or career). Socializing children

Table 3.1 Social Class Descriptions

The following descriptions apply to the majority of people in a given socioeconomic class, but not to every person in the class (Gilbert, 2008; Macionis, 2009).

Upper Class	Inherited wealth, family tradition of social prominence extending back several generations Authority patterns—emphasis placed on extended family (often either patriarchal or matriarchal) Preparation for adult roles—appropriate child rearing for status, formal schooling for high-status occupations (medicine, law, or business), generally attend private schools and prestigious private colleges
Middle Class	Composed of business executives and professionals (upper-middle class), and salespeople, small-business owners, contractors, craftspeople farmers Earned status by achievement (education and/or hard work Authority patterns—emphasis placed on nuclear family (ties still maintained to extended family), egalitarian Preparation for adult roles—high value placed on achievement, respectability, and harmonious interpersonal relationships; education and ability to get along with others considered essential to adult success
Lower Class	Generally composed of semiskilled and unskilled workers Authority patterns—emphasis placed on extended family (close ties with relatives are maintained), patriarchal patterns more common (except where father is absent), distinction between male and female roles Preparation for adult roles—emphasis on respect for elders and importance of survival (class most affected by economic fluctuations), many experience being in debt, being laid off and/or being on welfare, children expected to help the family rather than further their own education (some don't complete high school)
Underclass	Differs from other classes in degree of hopelessness regarding upward mobility (stuck at the bottom of the social structure, perceive little chance of ever escaping from poverty) Composed of female-headed families, homeless alcoholics, drug users, mentally ill individuals who have been "deinstitutionalized," destitute elderly individuals, illegal aliens, rural families from economically depressed areas, those who cannot get an adequate education, job, or housing

in upper-class families to be responsible and to achieve is a challenge when such children already "have everything." Pressures to conform to family standards come not only from the nuclear family, but from the extended family (even the dead relatives) as well: "What would Grandfather Smith say?" Upper-class families often employ in-home caregivers. According to a study by Wrigley (1995) in Los Angeles and New York, many of the caregivers hired by upper-class families are poor women with little formal education who immigrated from developing countries in Latin America and the Caribbean. Often their values and beliefs about how children should be raised differ from those of the parents who employ them. Even though the parents provide instruction, the life experiences of the caregivers make implementation difficult.

Middle Class

In socializing children, middle-class parents are more likely to use reasoning and nonphysical forms of discipline (Bornstein & Bradley, 2003; Parke & Buriel, 2006). They tend to emphasize conformity to "what people will say" or "how it would look." Children are usually taught early to look toward the future. ("Eat your vegetables so you'll grow big and strong," "When you can use the potty, you'll be able to wear big-boy pants like Daddy instead of diapers.") Middle-class parents try to cultivate and foster children's talents through organized activities (Lareau, 2002).

Middle-class children are exposed to different language and cognitive experiences than are lower-class children. The structure and syntax of language used by the middle and upper classes is far more complex than that used by the lower class. For example, "I'd rather you made less noise, dear" might be what a mother from the middle class would say to her boisterous child, whereas "Shut up!" might be what a mother from the lower class would say (Bernstein, 1961; Hoff, Laursen, & Tardiff, 2002). Concept development is related to language development in that the use of complex language indicates a more abstract, as opposed to concrete, perception of reality. Thus, the child from a middle-class family learns the abstract meanings of words like *rather* and *less*; the child from a lower-class family gets a simple, concrete message, directly to the point.

Lower Class

Children from lower-class families are often identified in school as slow learners, aggressors, and truants. Studies comparing the relative intelligence of children from high- and low-socioeconomic-status families show that those from high-status homes score higher on IQ tests and achievement tests than do children from low-status homes (Ackerman, Brown, & Izard, 2004). The differences in intellectual, emotional, and social competence are more marked in later childhood and adolescence than in early childhood (Novotney, 2010; Sobolewski & Amato, 2005). Why is this so?

Social class membership begins exerting its influence before birth and continues until death (Conger & Dogan, 2007). Health care and diet of the mother affect the birth of the child. The incidence of birth defects is higher in the lower classes than in the middle and upper classes. Economic pressure and lack of opportunities affect the mental health of the lower-class family, as well as determine socialization practices (Parke & Buriel, 2006). Lower-socioeconomic-status parents have been found to be more dominant, controlling, and punitive than higher-socioeconomic-status parents, who have been found to be more verbal and democratic and to use various techniques. Economics, or lack of money, prevents lower-social-class parents from using an allowance as a reward. Children from lower-class families often cannot be sent to their rooms as a punishment, because there may be no room they can call their own to which they can be sent. Neither can such children have privileges removed for noncompliance, such as going to the movies, because they do not have those opportunities anyway. Thus, lower-class families frequently use directives and physical punishment for noncompliance, whereas middle- and upper-class families use reasoning and have more options available for reward and punishment (Conger & Dogan, 2007).

Underclass Children

The underclass, in essence, represents a contradiction to the concept that social mobility is available to anyone in America who is willing to work hard enough for it. How the underclass developed and what should be done about it remain debated issues among social scientists and public policymakers. The problems for underclass children include exposure to drugs and AIDS, child abuse, poor housing or homelessness, crime, insufficient health care, inferior education, insufficient child-care programs and other community services, and economic dependency on government (CDF, 2010). The federal government's response since 1996 has been to provide Temporary Assistance for Needy Families (TANF) while the parent(s) get job training and learn coping skills to become self-sufficient. Funds are available for intervention programs including parent education and quality child care (to be discussed in Chapters 5 and 10). These programs play a significant role in the developmental outcomes for underclass and lower-class children (Novotney, 2010).

Having too many responsibilities without adequate resources negatively impacts the present and future opportunities for parents and their children.

Tony Freeman/Photo Edit

Social Class Socialization Theories

operational definition contains terms that are identifiable and can be researched

Various theories have been advanced to explain social class contrasts in behavior, as well as in intelligence and competence. To be comparable, theories on socioeconomics must agree on an **operational definition** (one that contains terms that are identifiable and can be researched). Oakes and Rossi (2003) propose that socioeconomic status be defined in terms of:

1. *Material*, or financial, *capital* (economic resources)—exemplified by the financial resources the parent provides for the child's well-being, including enriching educational experiences
2. *Human capital* (knowledge and skills)—exemplified by the advanced education of the parent, which may influence his or her approach to socialization in regard to the priority placed on academic achievement along with the assistance he or she provides for school work.
3. *Social capital* (connections to, and the status and power of, individuals in one's social network)—exemplified by the parent's occupational status that may increase his or her capacity to be a mentor for success in the world of work, as well as serve as a link to important social resources in the community.

Social Selection Theoretical Model of Socioeconomics

One group of theories can be characterized as having a *social selection perspective.* This theoretical model hypothesizes that individual characteristics of parents, based on genes, personality dispositions, and physical traits, will predict their degree of achievement in terms of educational attainment, occupational status, and income (the major indicators of social class). In other words, it is the parents' genes, rather than socioeconomic status, that ultimately influence the life experiences of the children (Mayer, 1997).

Social Causation Theoretical Model of Socioeconomics

The other group of theories can be categorized as having a *social causation perspective.* It has been documented that social class affects the socialization strategies of parents and, consequently, impacts the development of children (Conger & Dogan, 2007).

There are two major *social causation* models to study the effects of socioeconomic status, as well as to develop ways of mediating them. One is the *family stress model* (FSM) (see Figure 3.6), which proposes that economic difficulties have an adverse effect on parents' emotions, behaviors, and relationships, which, in turn, negatively influence their socialization strategies (Conger & Conger, 2002). The FSM analyzes the stress-inducing properties of low socioeconomic statuses and their consequences. The second approach is the *extended investment model* (EIM) (see Figure 3.7), which focuses on the ways in which the resources possessed by families in higher socioeconomic statuses increase the tendency and ability of parents to promote the well-being and abilities of their children. The EIM assumes that parents from higher, compared to those from lower, socioeconomic statuses, have greater economic (such as income), social (such as occupational status), and human (such as education) capital. Examples of how such capital directly impacts children include having an adequate standard of living (housing, clothing, food, health care, and so on), providing learning materials in the home, having direct parent stimulation or supportive specialized trainers, and residing in a community environment that provides resources for the developing child such as parks, libraries, museums, and activities.

Thus, understanding the variables and linkages in the *social causation* model of the relationship between socioeconomic status, socialization, and child outcomes enables communities to develop intervention programs. For example, in her book *Common Purpose*, Lisbeth Schorr (1997) describes support programs that have strengthened families and neighborhoods in the United States. For example, a program called Youth

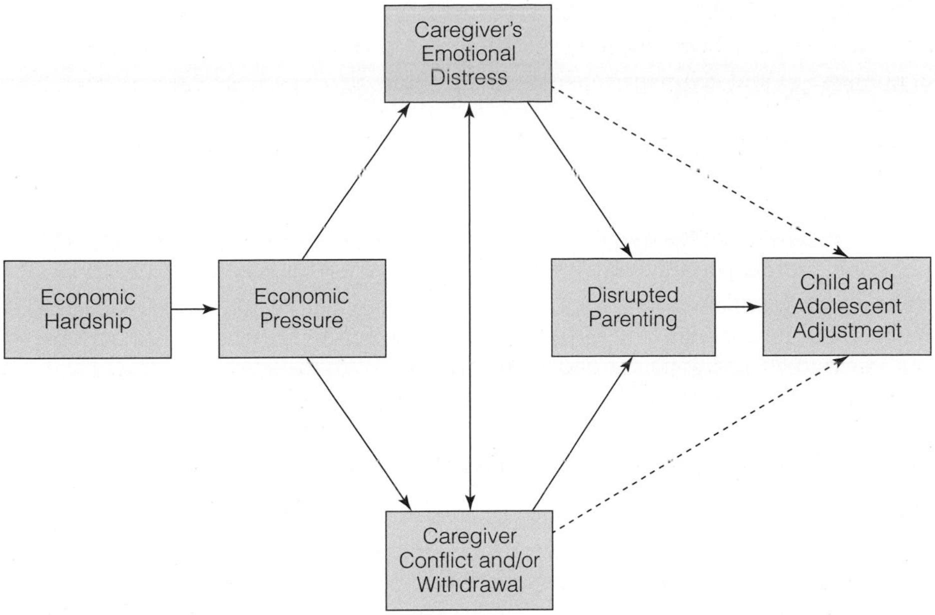

FIGURE 3.6 The Family Stress Model of Economic Hardship and Socialization
Source: Conger, R. D., & Dogan, S. J. (2007). "Social Class and Socialization in Families," In J. E. Grusec & P. D. Hastings (Eds.), *Handbook of socialization: Theory and research.* New York: Guilford, p. 438.

Build, begun in Harlem, New York, recruits adolescents from poor families to build and renovate low-cost housing. The youth are trained by journeymen in construction skills and the personal habits and qualities that contractors seek in entry-level workers. They also attend school and are trained in leadership skills that, together with job skills, will help them rebuild their own lives and provide them with the prospect of moving out of the lower class. What makes Youth Build successful is the caring support and commitment of its staff, as well as the sense of family and community among its members.

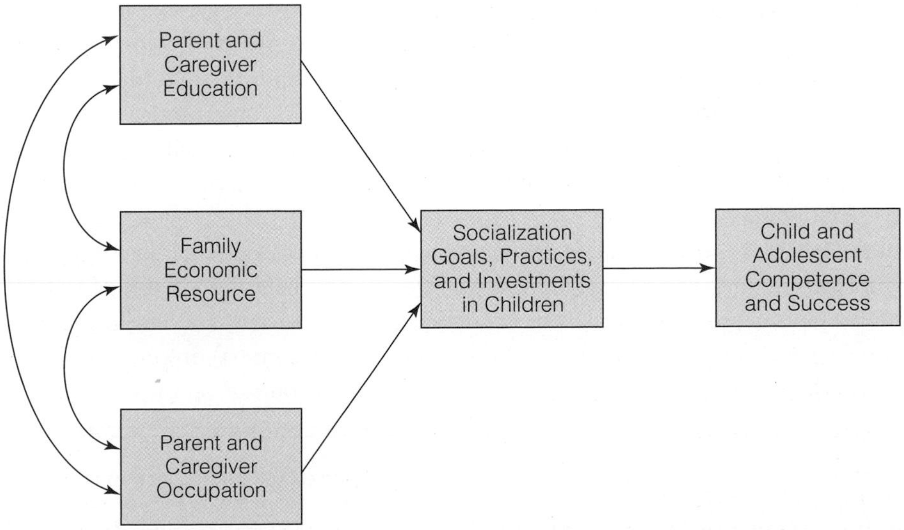

FIGURE 3.7 The Extended Investment Model of Resources and Socialization
Source: Conger, R. D., & Dogan, S. J. (2007). "Social Class and Socialization in Families." In J. E. Grusec & P. D. Hastings (Eds.), *Handbook of socialization: Theory and research.* New York: Guilford, p. 444.

IN PRACTICE

What Are the Implications of Socioeconomic Status Research for Professionals?

Delaying gratification. Professionals can provide children feedback on their behavior with cues or specific instructions and tangible, immediate rewards, such as small tokens (stickers, toys). For example, "You must do well in school so that you'll get a good job" or "You must take turns on the slide so the others will be your friends."

Socializing methods. Professionals can set standards (in advance) with reinforcement for compliance and consequences for noncompliance. For example, "We use our words to tell someone our angry feelings." "When I hear words, I will give you a sticker." "We do not hit anyone. If you hit someone, you get a warning; if you hit someone again, you will have to sit in the hall outside the room for five minutes."

Enhancing unique qualities of individuals. Professionals can enhance those aspects of class socialization that make the individual a unique, contributing member of society (helpfulness of kin, responsibilities given to children, ability to cope with adversity) while addressing those aspects of class socialization that hamper personality development (limited language, experiences, and cognitive stimulation).

What role does cultural heritage play in how families interact with children?

Cultural Orientation and Diversity

As discussed previously, culture is a macrosystem. One's cultural heritage involves the learned behavior, including the history, language, traditions, rituals, customs, beliefs, attitudes, morals, and values, shared by members of a social group (generally ethnic) to which that person belongs. The U.S. Census Bureau reaffirms the ascribed concept of race and ethnicity every 10 years (even though there is no scientific basis for such classification) (Bugental & Grusec, 2006). The census classifications are significant in that federal programs, such as school and community development grants, scholarships, affirmative action, and homeland security, are all based on the ascribed, or inherited, characteristics of ethnic groups.

Since this book deals with socialization goals, agents, methods, and outcomes, focusing on the learned cultural values of various groups and how they affect behavior is more relevant than comparing ethnically ascribed characteristics and their social or psychological consequences (which tends to be stereotypical). However, a general finding, reported by adults working with children and youths, is that children of color face more obstacles than white counterparts. These obstacles included access to high-quality health care, education, safe neighborhoods, and adequate support from communities where they live (W. K. Kellogg Foundation, 2010). Thus, in reality, race and ethnicity have socially constructed meanings based on stereotyping and prejudice, which affect developmental outcomes (Quintana et al., 2006).

Tonnies (1957), a German sociologist, compared the cultural values of diverse groups that shared a common heritage, explaining that differences in behavior are related to how each group adapts to political, social, and economic changes in society. He classified groups according to *gemeinschaft* characteristics (corresponds to low context) on one end of the spectrum, and *gesellschaft* characteristics (corresponds to high context) on the other.

gemeinschaft communal, cooperative, close, intimate, and informal interpersonal relationships

- **Gemeinschaft** groups
  - *Interpersonal relationships*—Communal, cooperative, close, intimate, and informal.
  - *Authority patterns*—Autocratic, established hierarchy with ascribed rights and obligations dispenses social sanctions and has political control, customs of the community are adhered to and respected, personal opinions and beliefs are private.

- **Gesellschaft** groups
  - *Interpersonal relationships*—associative, practical, objective, and formal.
  - *Authority patterns*—Democratic, public discussions and consensus established social sanctions and political control, fairness and equal rights are emphasized.

gesellschaft associative, practical, objective, and formal interpersonal relationships

Gemeinschaft and gesellschaft concepts applied to community relations will be discussed further in Chapter 10.

Because families are embedded in larger social groups, such as ethnic or religious communities, they can be similarly categorized, albeit generally, as *cooperative/interdependent* (*collectivism*) on one end of the spectrum (more likely found in gemeinschaft, or high-context, societies) and *competitive/independent* (*individualism*) on the other end (more likely found in gesellschaft, or low-context, societies). **Collectivism** emphasizes interdependent relations, social responsibilities, and the well-being of the group—"fitting in"; **individualism** emphasizes individual fulfillment and choice—"standing out" (Trumbull et al., 2001). Collectivism includes a "we" consciousness, group solidarity, sharing, duties and obligations, group decisions, and particularism or partiality toward group members; individualism includes an "I" consciousness, autonomy, individual initiative, right to privacy, pleasure seeking, and universalism or impartiality toward group members (Hofstede, 1991). About 70 percent of the world's cultures could be described as collectivistic (Trumbull et al., 2001).

collectivism emphasis on interdependent relations, social responsibilities, and the well-being of the group

individualism emphasis on individual fulfillment and choice

There are many minority cultures represented in the United States (aggregately referred to as "people of color"), and not all have the same status and power as the majority (White, Anglo-Saxon, Protestant, or Euro-American), even though equality is a value subscribed to in the United States. Being socialized in a family of a different cultural orientation from that of the school, which represents the majority orientation, can be problematic for the child (Trumbull et al., 2001). Table 3.2 outlines some areas of diverse socialization patterns, keeping in mind that there is variation within groups.

Cultural Orientation and Socialization Differences

Part of one's cultural orientation involves **norms**—the rules, patterns, or standards that express cultural values and reflect how individuals are supposed to behave. Some dimensions of differing cultural behavioral patterns were introduced in Chapters 1 and 2. This discussion examines cultural norms from the perspective of variations in human ways of adapting. In the 1960s, Florence Kluckhohn (1961; Kluckhohn & Strodbeck, 1961) developed a way of analyzing the seemingly limitless variety of cultural lifestyles. She

norms rules, patterns, or standards that express cultural values and reflect how individuals are supposed to behave

Table 3.2 Some Areas of Diverse Socialization Patterns in the United States

Socialization Areas	Majority Cultural Orientation ("Gesellschaft," Low Context, Individualism)	Minority Cultural Orientation ("Gemeinschaft," High Context, Collectivism)
Interpersonal	Competition and individual accomplishment; take risks; active learning style	Cooperation and group relationships; save face; passive learning style
Orientation Toward Time	Plan for the future, work and save now for a better future for yourself; efficiency, punctuality, time should not be "wasted"	Focus on the present, trust that the future will be provided for; units of time are undifferentiated; value the past, tradition, and ancestors
Valued Personality	Busy, materialistic, practical, assertive	Relaxed, spiritual, emotional, quiet
Relationship of Humanity to Nature	Control nature, use science and technology to "improve" nature	One with nature, respect and live with nature; belief in fate
Most Cherished Values	Independence, individual freedom, achievement	Dependence, loyalty to the group and tradition

Source: Kluckhohn, 1961; Maehr, 1974; Thiederman, 1991.

suggested that there are five basic questions that humans in all places and circumstances must answer. These questions greatly help our understanding of cultural diversity and socialization:

1. **How do humans relate to each other?** Do relationships have an individualistic orientation, where importance is placed on what one accomplishes and on personal rights and freedom? Or is importance placed on belonging to a group, such as family, peers, or community (a collectivistic orientation)? The Euro-American norm generally, as exemplified by the Bill of Rights, is personal freedom, whereas the Japanese norm generally, as exemplified by family loyalty, is commitment to the group.

2. **What is the significant time dimension?** Is it past, present, or future? Some cultures associate time with religious beliefs; for example, they live each day as it comes, believing that God will provide for the future. Other cultures, such as Euro-American, generally associate time with progress, and therefore generally plan for the future, even though it may require sacrifice in the present. Still others view the concept of time as subordinate to activities and interactions instead of dominating them. For example, some groups may approximate when an event will start or end (the party takes place when everyone gets there), whereas Euro-Americans generally tend to put events on a precise schedule (the party takes place from 8:00 to 12:00).

3. **What is the valued personality type?** Is it simply "being"? Is it "being in becoming"? Or is it "doing"? Some groups believe that a person "is being in becoming"—that one's deeds in this life determine the quality of one's next life. Euro-Americans generally stress "doing" to enhance the quality of one's present life.

4. **What is the relationship of humans to nature?** Are humans subjugated to nature? Are humans seen as existing in nature? Do humans have power over nature? Western cultures generally assume that nature can be controlled. An example is our use of pesticides, irrigation, and various other technologies that make farming more efficient. Some other cultures, however, are taught that land and all that grows on it are only lent, to be cared for and shared, not exploited.

5. **What are the innate predispositions of humans?** Are they evil? Neutral? Good? If one believes that humans are essentially bad, one assumes that the child's will must be broken and tends to use punitive and controlling measures to socialize the child—as was done by Calvinist and Puritan parents, for example. If one believes that humans are neutral (neither good nor bad), one assumes that the child can be molded and shaped by experiences provided by the adult. This philosophy was advocated by British philosopher, John Locke (1632–1704). If one believes that humans are essentially good, one assumes that the child will seek out appropriate experiences and develop accordingly. Jean Jacques Rousseau (1712–1778), a French philosopher, advocated such a belief.

What role does religion play in life?

Religious Orientation and Socialization Differences

Religion is a "unified system of beliefs and practices relative to sacred things, uniting into a single moral community all those who adhere to those beliefs and practices" (Durkheim, 1947, p. 47). Understanding some basic purposes of religion also helps us be more sensitive to diversity.

religion a unified system of beliefs and practices relative to sacred things

CourseMate

According to the U.S. Religious Landscape Survey (Pew, 2007), 78.4 percent of adults report belonging to various forms of Christianity, about 5 percent belong to other faiths, and 16.1 percent are not affiliated with any particular religion. See Table 3.3 for more details. For information about religious beliefs and practices, as well as social and political views, go to http://religions.pewforum.org/reports.

Religion is a macrosystem in that it influences patterns of gender roles, sexual behavior, marriage, divorce, birthrates, morals, attitudes, and child rearing. It also may affect one's dress, dietary habits, alcohol consumption, health care, and social interactions, including ethics (Gollnick & Chinn, 2008).

Table 3.3 Major Faith Traditions in the United States

Protestant	51.3%
Catholic	23.9%
Church of Latter Day Saints & other Mormon groups	1.7%
Jewish	1.7%
Buddhist	0.7%
Muslim	0.6%
Hindu	0.4%
Others	1.2%

Generally, religion provides people with "a way of facing the problems of ultimate and unavoidable frustration, of 'evil,' and the generalized problem of meaning in some nonempirical sense, of finding some ultimate why" (Williams, 1960, p. 327). Religion, its followers, and its influence on nonreligious dimensions of human life will likely continue as a significant force in American society (Greely, 2001).

Religion influences socialization in that it has been one of the major influences on human thought and behavior throughout history. It has profoundly affected individuals, families, communities, and cultures. It has motivated people to behave morally, philosophize about life's purpose, and speculate about an "afterlife." It has stimulated techniques, such as prayer, ritual, and meditation, by which believers can find psychological comfort. It has been an inspiring force in architecture, art, music, politics, business, health care, social work, and education (Fontana, 2003).

If the family subscribes to an organized religion, at birth children are often inducted into it via a public naming ceremony. The family's religious beliefs determine what is selected from the environment to transmit to the child. The family also interprets and evaluates what is transmitted. For example, Roman Catholics believe in strict obedience to authority and do not believe in divorce or birth control. Thus, children from Roman Catholic families are brought up to obey their parents and the church. They are also reared to believe in the sanctity of marriage and to believe that sex is for producing children.

Not only does religion influence families and their socialization of children, but it influences the community as well, in respect to values and behavior. The dominant religious group in the United States (Protestants) has undoubtedly influenced the political and economic foundations of our country (Weber, 1930). The **Protestant ethic** is a religiously derived value system that defines the ideal person as individualistic, thrifty, self-sacrificing, efficient in use of time, strong in personal responsibility, and committed to productivity. By following this value system, believers feel one can reach salvation. An example of the Protestant ethic's influence on politics is welfare reform—laws passed to require welfare recipients to work (be self-sufficient) after a certain amount of time receiving government assistance. Religious beliefs can affect communities when religious groups elect members to government offices and school boards to influence policies such as abortion laws, school prayer, and science curriculum.

Protestant ethic belief in individualism, thrift, self-sacrifice, efficiency, personal responsibility, and productivity

Every religion includes some beliefs that are shared by all its adherents. For example, Judaism teaches that a "good life" can be led only in a community; good Jews must always view their actions in terms of their effect on others. They believe in responsibility for others and regard charity as a virtue. Muslims give a percentage of their annual income to the poor. The ultimate goal of Buddhism is to be fully in the world and relate compassionately to others.

Through their beliefs and practices, most religions provide:

1. *A Divine Ideology*—enables individuals to comprehend events that happen to them; death, illness, financial crises, and injustices make sense if these are seen as

A bar mitzvah celebrates this 13-year-old boy's studies of Jewish history, culture, and prayer.

Miro Vintoniv/Index Stock/PhotoLibrary

part of a divine plan; helps fill the gap between scientific and technical knowledge and the unknown.

2. *Coping Mechanisms*—to help individuals accept and cope with crises without overwhelming psychological costs (for example, prayer helps people feel that they are "doing something" to meet the crisis); believing can help one avoid feeling that life's catastrophes are senseless.
3. *A Concept of Death*—provides structure to life (some religions preach hell for those who transgress in life on Earth and heaven for those who lead a good life); can give hope of a blissful immortality making the death of a loved one more tolerable and the thought of one's own death less terrifying.
4. *Establish an Identity*—gives meaning to life; many religious activities reflect pride and celebration; religious rituals symbolize faith, honor God, or remind members of the group of their religious responsibilities; rituals may include observing holidays, saying prayers, tithing, handling sacred objects, wearing certain clothing, and eating certain food or fasting (for example, Holy Communion commemorates the climactic meal of Jesus' life and his sacrifice for humankind; in partaking of the holy bread and wine, the communicant partakes of Christ).

Carl Jung (1938) wrote that religion provides individuals who have a strong commitment to traditional norms and values with moral strength and behavioral stability. In other words, religious people are more likely to comply with societal norms, especially if they believe that those norms are divinely sanctioned. They look upon social deviance as a form of religious deviance. This has been confirmed in research (Furrow, King, & White, 2004; Gorsuch, 1976) showing that moral behavior was consistently related to religious commitment.

How has societal change affected the socialization of children in families?

Chronosystem Influences on Families, Socialization, and Children

Families are not static; rather, they are dynamic and are continuously confronted by challenges, changes, and opportunities (Parke & Buriel, 2006). Some families can develop coping styles to adapt to changes and remain healthy and functional, but others may become victims of the consequences of change. They may experience stress, dissolution, or an unanticipated lifestyle. They are at risk for becoming unhealthy or dysfunctional. Chronosystem influences affecting the health of families include political changes, such as changes in the law (for example, welfare to workfare); economic changes, such as certain jobs becoming obsolete (for example, telephone operators); and technological changes, such as computers completing tasks faster, enabling more work to be done and hence increasing performance standards.

The general chronosystem effect on families is stress. According to the American Psychological Association (APA, 2007a), nearly half of the Americans surveyed believe stress has increased in the last year. Change in itself is not good or bad; how we react to it determines its worth. Selye (1956) defined stress as "the nonspecific response of the body to any demand" (p. 54). Others have defined **stress** as any demand that exceeds a person's ability to cope (Honig, 1986).

stress any demand that exceeds a person's ability to cope

- *Physical stressors* include disease, overexertion, allergies, and abuse;
- *Sociocultural stressors* include crowding, traffic, noise, bureaucracies, and crime;
- *Psychological stressors* include personal reactions to real or imagined threats and reactions to real or imagined pressure to achieve (Kuczen, 1987).

The APA (2007a) cited money and work issues as major stressors for 5 percent of Americans. Other major stressors were fulfilling work and family responsibilities, housing costs, and the impact of stress on personal relationships.

Stress is not new. In hunting-and-gathering societies, the fear of not finding food or shelter was a stressor. In agricultural societies, the unpredictability of the weather was a stressor. In industrial societies, working long hours was, and still is, a stressor. In information societies, information overload and excessive choice are stressors. One must make decisions in areas in which one has little or no expertise, and often facts and opinion are blurred. Children today face many of the same stressors of growing up that children a generation ago faced: separation anxiety, sibling rivalry, coping with school, peer pressure, being independent. However, children today also face stressors that were practically nonexistent a generation ago. Examples include the escalation of violence in families and communities, terrorism in the world (National Association of School Psychologists, 2001), and the bombardment of consumerism into homes, schools, extracurricular activities, and the media. Another stress is that family life has become fragmented. People are pressured by occupational and community demands for their time. Cellular phones, wireless computers, and e-mail have all contributed to merging the boundaries between family and other commitments, thus jeopardizing time for family.

Sociopolitical Changes

What are the consequences for families of social and political changes?

Sociopolitical changes influencing family functioning include foreign policy regarding immigration and war, and domestic policy regarding security, privacy, and social services.

Immigration Policies

Newcomers to this country usually occupy the lower-income jobs, require English language training, and may need housing assistance, health care, and other services until they adapt to American life. Children of immigrants have to accommodate to the culture of their parents as well as to that of their new country. Often they serve as "language and cultural brokers" for their non- or limited-English-speaking parents, assuming responsibility for translation and interpretation of transactions with U.S. society. How do parents maintain authority while depending on the child to transmit and receive information? How does the child maintain respect and not cause the parents to lose face (Orellana, Dorner, & Pulido, 2003)?

Apparently, parents' own limited cultural and language barriers to economic mobility influence the socialization of their children in that they stress educational success and specific occupational choice by using their own low status as a reference point. Evidence (Tseng, 2006) suggests that children of immigrants express higher educational, motivational, and economic mobility aspirations than do peers from U.S.-born families, even after accounting for the generally lower economic status of immigrant families.

Foreign Policies

War in a foreign country obviously affects the functioning of military families when one parent is called to duty. There have been documented increases in substance abuse, people seeking therapy, and individuals turning to spirituality for comfort (Kaslow, 2001). Children who have experienced loss of a loved one may react with emotional detachment or a seeming lack of feeling by exhibiting regressive or immature behavior, by acting out or exploding, or by continually asking the same questions because they cannot understand what happened (National Association of School Psychologists, 2001). Terrorism in the homeland affects the functioning of society as a whole and consequent safety and security policies. For example, terrorism has affected travel rules, communication procedures, and racial profiling. Flexibility in travel has diminished, affecting family visits and vacations. Mail is subject to inspection for fear of biological warfare (anthrax, for example). Families who have cultural backgrounds similar to that of terrorists are subjected to more searching and interrogation in public places. Some children have been ostracized and treated cruelly.

Domestic Policies

Social services, such as government financial assistance, have decreased. In 1996, the U.S. Congress abolished the Aid to Families of Dependent Children program. Welfare reform has brought changes in family structure and functions (Sealander, 2003). Recognizing that most poor families are headed by single parents, lawmakers in 1996 emphasized the responsibility of both parents to support their children. In addition to strengthening the child support enforcement system, the law included provisions designed to decrease childbearing outside of marriage and promote two-parent families (McLanahan & Carlson, 2002). What are the long-term consequences for parents, children, community support services, and society in general of these new welfare regulations, stronger paternity establishment, and stricter child support enforcement?

What economic changes affect families and children?

Economic Changes

Economic changes influencing family functioning may involve job uncertainty because of company buyouts, downsizing, and layoffs; the cost of living, requiring both parents to be employed; and the erosion of employee benefits, such as health insurance (Gallay & Flanagan, 2000).

Reduced levels of economic well-being have been found to increase parental stress, resulting in less affection toward children and less effective disciplinary interactions (Conger & Dogan, 2007). Children in such families were more likely to be reported by teachers as having behavior problems and negative social relations with peers (Mistry et al., 2002).

When both parents are employed, their family life may be at risk for fragmentation. The father works, the mother works, and the children go to child care or school, all requiring coordination. If working hours are staggered, the family may not eat together. Household tasks have to be done after work. If children have after-school activities, they have to be coordinated with the parents' already busy schedules. Then there are meetings—school, work, and community meetings. Hardly any time is left for family communication or shared leisure. Needless to say, this can cause stress. Children may feel rushed, tense, or out of control. And what happens when one parent is transferred to another city or state and the other parent's job doesn't allow for similar mobility? For single parents, the risk of fragmentation may be greater unless there is another supportive adult to assist with family functioning and buffer stress. Support and buffering have been shown to enable parents to perform multiple roles that, if they enjoy them, can contribute to their emotional well-being (Barnett & Hyde, 2001).

What technological changes affect families and children?

Technological Changes

Technological developments in science, medicine, industry, agriculture, transportation, communication, media, electronics, and so on have contributed to improvement in people's living standards—bettering health, widening opportunities for jobs and education, enhancing safety, cultivating efficiency, expanding people's access to information, and providing a wide choice of products.

Technological developments are associated with increased busyness, multitasking, distraction, confusion, and stress. For example, "Consumer technology is changing the way we live in time—collapsing, crunching, compressing it. Today technology is a self-perpetuating engine run by upgrades, add-ons, and refills" (Naisbitt, 2001, p. 31).

Digital technology is creating new styles of communication and interaction (Buckingham, 2006). Families are affected in that such technology provides endless opportunities for multidimensional use, for instantaneously accessing information, and for being perpetually connected (Montgomery, 2000), all the while creating a greater need for parents to supervise children's activities. Media technology has also created new ways to market to children. Websites designed for children contain brightly colored graphics, sound effects, music, and interactive games, beckoning children to buy the products that support them via pop-up and/or sound bite ads (Montgomery, 2001). Social networking, cell phones, and computer games all compete with family time, as well as impact children's learning (Clay, 2009).

Meeting the Challenge of Change: Family Empowerment

How can families be enabled to deal with change and associated stress?

As we have discussed, the family is a dynamic social system that has structure, functions, roles, and authority patterns. The way the system operates and adapts to change affects the relationships within it. Change can produce stress that affects all the individual members of the family. Examples are work transitions (downsizing, job change or loss), family transitions (birth, death, divorce, remarriage), health issues (illness, disability), economic issues (cost of living, credit), and community issues (traffic, crowding, safety).

How families cope with stress can be assessed by how they solve problems, how they communicate, how they adapt to change, their social supports, their spiritual beliefs, their self-esteem and personal adjustment, and absence of pathology, deviance, or drug use. Studies (Curran, 1985; Stinnett & Defrain, 1985) have shown that functional families that are resilient to stress are more likely to exhibit certain key characteristics—behaviors and values—than are families that are at risk for dysfunction when stressed. The overall general picture of functional families follows. The strength of each characteristic and the combination of characteristics, as well as how they are demonstrated, may vary from one family to another and may be influenced by cultural or religious orientation.

IN CONTEXT

- **Display of love and acceptance.** Members of strong families show their love and appreciation for one another.
- **Communicativeness.** Family members are spontaneous, honest, open, and receptive to one another. This means expressing negative as well as positive feelings.
- **Cohesiveness.** Family members enjoy spending time together. Sharing chores, resources, and recreational activities is considered important.
- **Communication of values and standards.** Parents in strong families have definite and clear values and make them known to their children.
- **Ability to cope effectively with problems.** Stress and crises are faced optimistically with the purpose of finding solutions.

empowerment enabling individuals to have control over resources affecting them

How can families that are stressed be helped? **Empowerment** is enabling individuals to have control over resources affecting them. Giving families access to knowledge and skills that enhance their ability to influence their personal lives and the community in which they live is the first step toward becoming resilient to stress (Vanderslice, 1984; Walsh, 2006). Empowerment is a process that evolves from analyzing one's own strengths and resources, becoming educated in skills one is lacking, and participating in the community. Empowerment is part of current federal social policy. For example, government funding to families is tied to becoming self-reliant instead of dependent. Rather than viewing families with problems as helpless, the government has various programs to help people help themselves, such as financial aid for a college education, vocational rehabilitation, child care, and health services. Public and private community agencies that help empower families will be discussed in Chapter 10.

The physical closeness between father and child is important to foster attachment and interdependence.

HIRB/Index Stock Imagery/PhotoLibrary

Summary

- The concept of family has changed to "any two or more related persons by birth, marriage, or adoption who reside together."
- The basic structures of a family are the nuclear and the extended family. A nuclear family consists of husband, wife, and children. An extended family consists of kin related to the nuclear family who are emotionally, and perhaps economically, dependent on each other. Extended families can be matriarchal, patriarchal, or egalitarian.
- The family's basic functions are reproduction, socialization/education, assignment of social roles, economic support, and nurturance/emotional support. The scope of the specific family functions has changed.
- Functional families maintain resilience and adaptability; dysfunctional families are at risk for breakup or for various problems.
- Family transitions affect family structure and functions. Divorce affects both parents and children according to certain variables. Different custody arrangements can cause problems.
- Children in a stepfamily have to form new relationships and accept new rules and new values, while still having to deal with the old relationships, rules, and values.
- Kin custody, usually grandparents, affects children's sense of belonging and stability.
- Families with parents who are unmarried by choice may affect children's economic and psychosocial stability.
- Families with same-sex parents can influence children if they become concerned about their sexual identities.
- Families of adopted children have varying socialization effects. Adopted children may have misunderstandings about their adoption, fears of abandonment, and identity issues.
- Dual-earner families have varying socialization effects according to age, gender, and temperament of the child, the socioeconomic status of the family, the quality of the parents' marriage, the mother's satisfaction with her job, the father's satisfaction with his job, and the father's involvement with the children, as well as the availability of quality child care and social supports.
- Macrosystem influences on families, socialization, and children are socioeconomic status and cultural and religious orientation. In traditional societies, social status is usually ascribed; in modern societies, social status is usually achieved. Socioeconomic status influences how children are socialized. Differences in social class child-rearing practices affect academic performance and behavior.
- Cultural orientation affects child socialization and consequent behavior patterns. Cultures differ in interpersonal relations, orientation toward time, valued personality type, relationship of humanity to nature, and most cherished values.
- Religious orientation influences families' socialization practices. Religion provides an ideology that enables individuals to comprehend events that happen to them and gives them an identity and a support system for traditional norms and values.
- Chronosystem influences on families, socialization, and children include sociopolitical and technological changes.

Activity

PURPOSE To understand the influence of certain family characteristics on socialization and development.

1. Of what socioeconomic status was your family of orientation? On what criteria did you base your answer?
2. List the values, beliefs, or attitudes supported by your cultural group.
3. List the values, beliefs, or attitudes supported by your religion.
4. What were some stresses your family of orientation experienced, and how did your family adapt?
5. What were three socialization goals communicated by your family of orientation? (Were they successful or unsuccessful?)
6. List three goals you have for yourself.
7. List three goals you have for your family of procreation.
8. Is there any connection between your family of orientation's socialization goals and your goals for your family of procreation?

Related Readings

Bria, G. (1998). *The art of family: Rituals, imagination, and everyday spirituality*. New York: Dell.

Cherlin, A. J. (2010). *The marriage-go-round: The state of marriage and the family today*. New York: Vintage.

Clapp, G. (2000). *Divorce and new beginnings: A complete guide to recovery, solo parenting, co-parenting, and stepfamilies* (2nd ed.). New York: Wiley.

Crohn, J. (1995). *Mixed matches: How to create successful interracial, interethnic, and interfaith relationships*. New York: Ballantine.

Galinsky, E. (1999). *Ask the children: What America's children really think about working parents*. New York: William Morrow.

Gilbert, D. L. (2008). *The American class structure in an age of growing inequality* (7th ed.). Thousand Oaks: Pine Forge/Sage.

Hetherington, E. M., & Kelly, J. (2002). *For better or worse: Divorce reconsidered*. New York: Norton.

Jacobs, J. A., & Gerson, K. (2004). *The time divide: Work, family, and gender inequality (The family and public policy)*. Cambridge, MA: Harvard University Press.

Johnson, S., & O'Conner, E. (2002). *The gay baby boom: The psychology of gay parenthood*. New York: NYU Press.

Pavao, J. M. (2005). *The family of adoption* (rev. ed.). Boston: Beacon Press.

Stewart, S. D. (2006). *Brave new stepfamilies: Diverse paths toward stepfamily living*. Thousand Oaks, CA: Sage.

Resources

Ohio State Human Development and Family Science Extension—all about aspects of family life
http://fcs.osu.edu/hdfs

National Stepfamily Resource Center—all about stepfamily issues
http://www.stepfamilies.info

NYU Child Study Center—all about children's issues
http://www.aboutkids.org

DesignPics Inc./Index Stock Imagery/PhotoLibrary

4

Ecology of Parenting

"Children behave as well as they are treated."

—UNKNOWN

SOCIALIZATION SKETCHES

Dr. Benjamin Spock

(1903–1998)

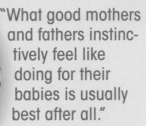

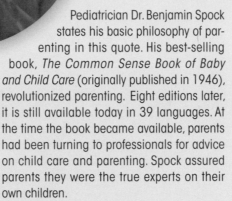

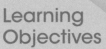

Hulton Archive/Getty Images

"What good mothers and fathers instinctively feel like doing for their babies is usually best after all."

— BENJAMIN SPOCK

Pediatrician Dr. Benjamin Spock states his basic philosophy of parenting in this quote. His best-selling book, *The Common Sense Book of Baby and Child Care* (originally published in 1946), revolutionized parenting. Eight editions later, it is still available today in 39 languages. At the time the book became available, parents had been turning to professionals for advice on child care and parenting. Spock assured parents they were the true experts on their own children.

Chronosystem

The trend in parenting in America prior to post–World War II was authoritarian, with strict rules for discipline and rigid scheduling for feeding, sleeping, toilet training, and so on. Spock urged parents to be flexible and view their children as having individual needs. The parenting view at the time was to avoid spoiling children by giving them attention when they cried. Spock urged parents to be affectionate with their children and enjoy them.

While Spock specialized in pediatrics, he realized he could help his young patients and their parents if he understood their psychological needs and family dynamics. So he embarked on a six-year study of psychoanalysis. As he applied what he learned to his patients and through discussions with parents, he developed the child-rearing philosophy that he shared in his book.

Family

Spock was born in New Haven, Connecticut. He was the eldest of six children, so he was involved in child care early on. He changed diapers, babysat, fed, and played with his siblings. His father was a prominent lawyer and his mother was a homemaker devoted to her children, running a strict household. Both parents had high expectations for their children to achieve.

School

Spock was an undergraduate at Yale University and a member of the Scroll and Key. He also was on the rowing team, winning a gold medal at the 1924 Summer Olympics. Spock attended medical school at Columbia University College of Physicians and Surgeons in New York, where he graduated first in his class. He did his residency training in pediatrics at the Weill Medical College of Cornell University in Manhattan and then in psychiatry at Cornell's Payne Whitney Psychiatric Clinic.

Community

During World War II, Spock served as a psychiatrist in the U.S. Navy Medical Corps. After this service, he held professorships at the University of Minnesota Medical School, the University of Pittsburgh, and at Case Western Reserve University, where he taught child development.

In 1957, Spock became one of the founders of the Committee for a Sane Nuclear Policy. He was politically outspoken and active in the movement to end the Vietnam War. His political views made him unpopular in some circles and hurt the sales of *Baby and Child Care*, but he persisted, convinced that his politics was related to a better world for children.

- What strong belief, one that was contrary to common practice, have you had for which you experienced criticism, and what did you do about it?
- Spock was criticized for his permissive parenting advice and blamed for "the 60s generation" of rebellious young adults raised on his book. Do you agree/disagree and why?

Learning Objectives

After completing this chapter, you will be able to:

1. Define parenting.
2. Discuss macrosystem influences on parenting (political ideology, culture, socioeconomic status, ethnicity/religion).
3. Explain chronosystem influences on parenting—how child-rearing attitudes have changed throughout history.
4. Describe the four basic parenting styles and how each affects a child's development.
5. Define and discuss developmentally appropriate parenting practices (guidance and discipline).
6. Define and discuss inappropriate parenting practices (physical, sexual, and emotional abuse) and causes of child maltreatment.

About Parenting

What is involved in parenting?

According to developmental psychologist, Jerome Kagan, **parenting** means implementing a series of decisions about the socialization of your children—what you do to enable them to become responsible, contributing members of society, as well as what you do when they cry, are aggressive, lie, or do not do well in school (Woodward, 1975). Figure 4.1 illustrates the socialization contexts affected by parenting. Parents sometimes find these decisions overwhelming. One of the reasons parenting can be confusing is that there is little consensus in the United States today as to what children should be like

parenting The implementation of a series of decisions about the socialization of children

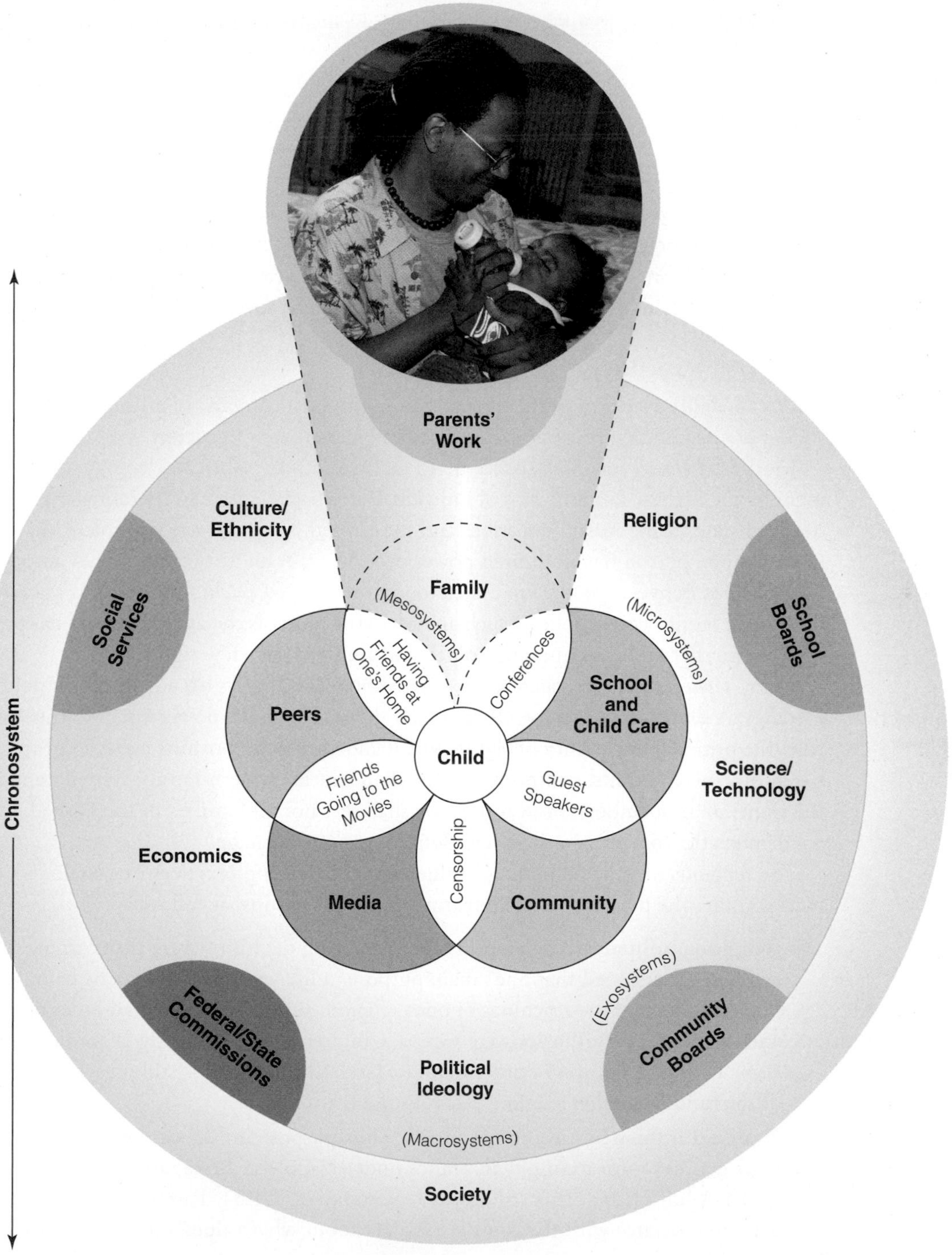

FIGURE 4.1 An Ecological Model of Human Development
Parenting is the means by which the family socializes the child.
Cengage Learning

when they grow up or what you do to get them there. Another reason parenting is confusing is that it is *bidirectional* and *dynamic*—an adult's behavior toward a child is often a reaction to that child's temperament and behavior, changing with time as the child develops (Lerner, 2006; Putnam, Sanson, & Rothbart, 2002). Thus, by influencing adults, children influence their own development. Causes for behavior are viewed from a circular rather than a linear perspective (Cowan, Powell, & Cowan, 1998). The concept of the *bidirectionality* of parenting is exemplified throughout this chapter.

Is Parenting a Fad or a Fact?

What parenting practices worked best for you?
What kinds of behavior did you engage in to manipulate your parents? Get attention? Get revenge?

How have societal values and practices influenced parenting?

Macrosystem Influences on Parenting

Whereas *parenthood* is universal, *parenting* is highly variable among different cultures and groups within societies. The purpose of examining the macrosystem influences on parenting is to provide an understanding of political, cultural, socioeconomic, and religious values or practices that, indirectly, have contributed to children's socialization and development.

What does politics have to do with child rearing?

Political Ideology

political ideology theories pertaining to government

autocracy a society in which one person has unlimited power over others

democracy a society in which those ruled have equal power with those who rule

Political ideology refers to theories pertaining to government. It influences parenting styles because children must be raised to function as citizens in society.

Most *traditional* societies subscribe to an aristocratic political ideology, or government by the highest-ranking class of individuals in a society; hereditary monarchs serve as heads of state (some Australian tribes and the United Kingdom are examples). A society in which one person has unlimited power over others is an **autocracy**. In an autocracy, relationships between people are understood in terms of a pecking order. The autocratic traditional family system follows such an order. The father is the authority who has power over the mother and the children; women and children have few rights.

Many *modern* societies, such as the United States, subscribe to a democratic political ideology. A **democracy** is a society in which those ruled have power equal to those who rule; the principle is equality of rights. In a democracy, relationships between people are based on consensus and compromise. The democratic modern family system considers the rights of all members. However, as we shall see, not all families in the United States are democratic; some retain their traditional autocratic heritage.

The religious or cultural heritage influences on parenting practices can be understood by examining the purposes of child rearing in various groups, as follows:

- **Religious influence.** Generations ago, parenting decisions were easier to make because it was assumed that one's main purpose in life was to serve God by being faithful and following the teachings of one's religion. Belief in a hierarchal order of status and obedience to authority were valued. Children were constantly exhorted to overcome their base natures in order to please God. This concept is still preached by some of the fundamentalist religious sects around the world.
- **National influence.** In some countries, one's purpose in life was held to be to serve one's country—for example, in France under Napoleon Bonaparte and in Germany under Adolf Hitler. This still holds true today in China. Parents and teachers are expected to agree with the country's leaders about what values and attitudes to instill in children.
- **Cultural influence.** In high-context macrocultures around the world, where interdependence is valued, it is assumed that children are born and raised to serve the purposes of the family. For example, in rural India children are trained to work at

jobs considered of value to their particular family; children defer to their elders and marriages are often arranged for the benefit of the family.

- **Progressive influence.** In low-context macrocultures, such as the United States, few children are brought up to believe that their principal destiny is to serve their family, their country, or God. Euro-American children are generally given the feeling that they are free to set their own goals in life. Achievement and competition are valued.

Socioeconomic Status

How does socioeconomic status affect child rearing?

A family's socioeconomic status, as discussed in Chapter 3, is its rank or position within a society based on social and economic factors, such as income, occupation, and education of the parents. In general, parents of *high socioeconomic status* have high incomes, engage in highly respected occupations, and are well educated; parents of *low socioeconomic status* have low incomes, hold unskilled or semiskilled jobs, and are poorly educated; parents of *middle socioeconomic status* have medium incomes, business or professional occupations, and a good education. It must be remembered that not all families can be classified according to the criteria listed here; some parents are very well educated and have very low incomes (graduate students, for example), and some parents have very high incomes and are not well educated (some businesspersons, for example). Also, there is as much variation within socioeconomic status groups as between them.

The following descriptive (not evaluative) generalizations are made on the basis of many research studies that compare the parenting styles of families of high and low socioeconomic status (Conger & Dogan, 2007; Hoff, Laursen, & Tardiff, 2002; Parke & Buriel, 2006), keeping in mind that variations exist within each class:

Parents of *low socioeconomic status:*	Parents of *high socioeconomic status:*
are likely to emphasize more obedience, respect, neatness, cleanliness, and staying out of trouble;	are likely to emphasize more happiness, creativity, ambition, independence, curiosity, and self-control.
are likely to be more controlling, authoritarian, and arbitrary in their discipline and are apt to use physical punishment;	are likely to be more democratic, using reason with their children and being receptive to their children's opinions.
are likely to use more short directives and varying tones of voice to communicate with children	are likely to talk more to their children, reason with them, and use complex language

A major reason why parenting styles differ according to socioeconomic status is that families tend to adapt their interactional patterns to the level of stress they are experiencing. All families experience stress, such as work problems, health problems, and relationship problems. However, parents with low incomes and other stressors related to poverty (housing, unsafe neighborhoods, job turnover) influence their well-being, the tone of their marriage, and the quality of their relationship with their children (Conger & Dogan, 2007; Cowan, Powell, & Cowan, 1998).

According to several studies (Conger & Dogan, 2007; McLoyd, Aikens, & Burton, 2006), economic hardship experienced by lower-class families is associated with anxiety, depression, and irritability. This emotional stress increases the tendency of parents to be punitive, inconsistent, authoritarian, and generally nonsupportive of their children. Such parenting techniques, such as commanding without explanation, require less time and effort than other methods, such as reasoning and negotiating. Expecting unquestioning obedience from children is more efficient than trying to meet the desires of all family members when one is experiencing stress.

New research (Novotney, 2009) shows that teens from upper and upper middle classes may be more self-centered, as well as depressed, than ever before. Privileged children are under a lot of parental pressure to achieve; their material advantage contributes to their self-absorption; and their exposure to media celebrities and commercialism promote false expectations regarding real life. The increase in depression among privileged teens may be due to fear of failure and not having developed skills to deal with disappointment.

What is the relationship between parental occupation and children's behavior?

Parental Occupation

Occupational role is a factor in socioeconomic status. When one performs a role, one takes on the behavioral expectations of that role through the process of socialization. For example, army officers will behave in an authoritarian manner, giving commands, whereas lawyers will use logic, reason, and explanation in performing their roles. Do the socialized role behaviors performed in one's occupation carry over into parenting styles?

Sociologist Melvin Kohn (1977, 1995, 2006) believes different social class occupations vary in the level of control individuals have over resources, including means of production, products, and people. Such control, then, affects their values and behavior. He analyzed the ways in which middle-class occupations in general differ from lower-class occupations. Kohn's early studies were done in the United States; his later studies extended to other countries, where he found the relationships between class, values, and behavior to be similar to those of the U.S. Specifically, middle-class occupations (such as teacher or office manager) typically require the individual to handle ideas and symbols, as well as be skilled in dealing with interpersonal relations. In contrast, lower-class occupations (such as construction worker or janitor) typically involve physical objects rather than symbols and do not involve as many interpersonal skills. Also, middle-class jobs often demand more self-direction in the prioritizing of job activities and in the selection of methods to get the job done than do lower-class jobs, which are more often routinized and subject to stricter supervision.

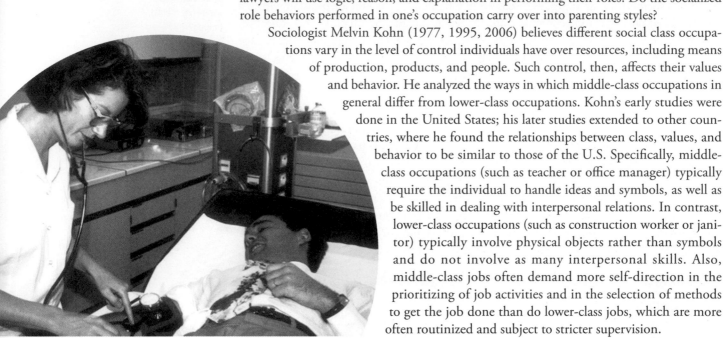

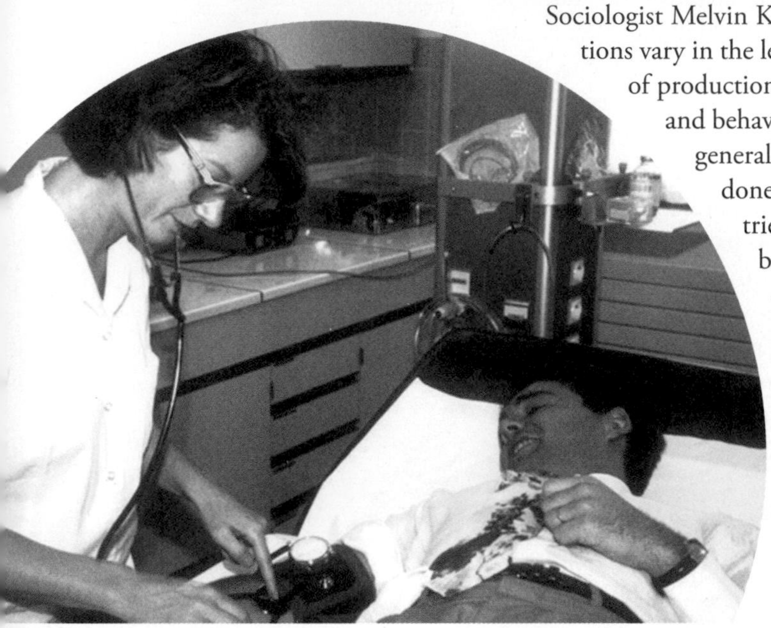

People who work in bureaucratic jobs, like those in a hospital, tend to incorporate the value of following the rules in their parenting styles.

Cengage Learning

Kohn also found parent–child relationship differences in middle- and lower-class families, which were most likely due to the different characteristics required in middle- and lower-class occupations. Generally, middle-class parents emphasize more self-direction for the child; lower-class parents emphasize more conformity. Specifically, Kohn found that middle-class parents were more concerned with their children's motives and the attitudes their behavior seemed to express, whereas lower-class parents were likely to judge their children's behavior in terms of its immediate consequences and its external characteristics. He also found that middle-class parents were more likely than lower-class parents to want their children to be considerate of others, intellectually curious, responsible, and self-controlled, whereas lower-class parents were more likely to want their children to have good manners, to do well in school, and to be obedient.

Similarly, Bronfenbrenner (1979) and others (Bronfenbrenner & Crouter, 1982; Crouter & McHale, 2005; Parcel & Menaghan, 1994) suggest that parents' workplaces affect their perceptions of life and the way they interact with family members. Consequently, parenting styles tend to be extensions of the modes of behavior that are functional in the workplace for parents.

How do culture and religion affect parenting and child development?

Culture and Religion

Traditional beliefs and practices that have been developed as adaptive survival strategies and passed from generation to generation are powerful and pervasive, even in modern times. However, as various cultural and religious groups become part of the mainstream, their values may change, as may those of the mainstream. This process can be observed in generational differences among grandparents, parents, and children (Parke & Buriel, 2006).

The culture and religion in which one grows up have indirect effects on parenting attitudes and consequent parenting styles (Greenfield, Suzuki, & Rothstein-Fisch, 2006; Parke & Buriel, 2006; Rogoff, 2003). To illustrate, Garcia-Coll (1990) reviewed the literature on cultural beliefs and care-giving practices and concluded that parenting goals and techniques depend to some extent on the nature of the tasks that adults are expected to perform or competencies that adults are supposed to possess in a given population. For example, in the United States (a complex, *modern* society), adults are expected to read, write, compute, and be economically self-sufficient. American children are thus expected to achieve in school, are given an allowance to learn the value of money, and are pressured to get a job at least by the time they finish their schooling. In the Fiji Islands (a simple, *traditional* society), adults are expected to farm, fish, and be able to make economic exchanges with relatives on the bigger islands (West, 1988). Fijian children are thus expected to relate to others in the community, to learn to help adults work, and to share resources.

Most religions delegate the teaching of their codes of conduct to parents. Parents have the divine duty to pass religious morals and values onto children—". . . And these words, which I command thee this day, shall be in thine heart: And thou shalt teach them diligently unto thy children" (Deuteronomy 6:5–7). Exemplifying codes of conduct are Judaism's and Christianity's Ten Commandments, Buddhism's Noble Eightfold Path, Islam's Five Pillars, Confucianism's Four Books, and Hinduism's Law-Books of Manu. Parenting and community behavior are influenced by these codes due to their longevity and basis in religious and civil law (Fontana, 2003).

Similarity in Parenting Across Different Cultures and Religions

A set of universal parenting goals was proposed by LeVine (1988, 2003):

1. Ensuring physical health and survival
2. Developing behavioral capacities for economic self-maintenance
3. Instilling behavioral capacities for maximizing cultural values, such as morality, prestige, and achievement

Cultures do, however, vary in the importance they place on these goals as well as how they implement them. Also, if one goal is threatened, it becomes the foremost concern and overrides the need to implement the others. To illustrate, if a society has a high rate of infant mortality, parents will concentrate more on the goal of physical health and survival; the pursuit of learning to participate economically and learning cultural values will be postponed until a later age, when the child's survival is relatively certain.

How various cultures prioritize these universal parenting goals may explain differences in maternal behavior toward infants (Richman et al., 1988). An example of a culture that prioritizes the parenting goal of physical health and survival is the Gusii of Kenya. Gusii mothers interpret holding the child as a form of protection from physical hazards such as cooking fires and domestic animals, and have no alternatives like cradle boards, playpens, or infant seats. This close physical contact enables Gusii mothers to quickly soothe their infants by cuddling them when they cry.

In contrast, an example of a culture that prioritizes the parenting goal of developing capacities for economic self-maintenance is the United States. American mothers verbalize with and gaze at their infants frequently. This reflects the belief that infants can communicate socially. By the time the American infant can walk, holding declines rapidly; infant seats, playpens, and high chairs are used to protect the locomotive infant from harm. This reduction in human physical contact reflects the value Americans put on separateness and independence.

Diversity in Parenting Across Different Cultures and Religions

Cultural values, as discussed in Chapters 1, 2, and 3, can be delineated on a continuum as being *collectivistic-oriented* or *individualistic-oriented.* To recap, *collectivistic* cultures emphasize interdependent relations, social responsibilities, and the well-being of the group; *individualistic* cultures emphasize individual fulfillment and choice.

These parents are going over their finances while their baby amuses herself with the toys they gave her.

Roy Morsch/Corbis

Collectivistic and *individualistic* orientations are exhibited by how diverse families differ in parenting styles and child-rearing practices (see Table 4.1 for a summary). For example, children socialized in a *collectivist* context are amused by people—by being held, teased, or shown how to do something; children socialized in an *individualistic* context are amused by things—by being given space, given toys, or *told* how to do something (Trumbull et al., 2001). Exemplifying a *collectivistic* orientation, at our department's Fall welcome picnic for faculty and students, I observed an Israeli parent trying to keep her 2½-year-old child occupied and away from the cooking area by continually talking to him. He was quite verbally adept for his age, and the attentive conversation seemed to distract him from examining the barbeque. Exemplifying an *individualistic* orientation, the American preschool-age children at the picnic were given toys to play with while their parents talked and cooked.

Some generalizations follow regarding *collectivistic* and *individualistic* cultural/religious orientations, as well as the specific family dynamics within them. These include differences in (1) authority roles, (2) communication, (3) display of emotion, (4) discipline/guidance of children, and (5) skills emphasized (Bugental & Grusec, 2006; Garcia-Coll, Meyer, & Britton, 1995; Parke & Buriel, 2006; Rogoff, 2003; Thiederman, 1991). Variations within the generalizations encompass the degree of adherence to traditional cultural/religious ways, the degree of assimilation into, and adoption of, mainstream ways, and the degree to which values are adopted from another culture or religion (perhaps due to intermarriage).

Cooperative/Interdependent (Collective) Orientation

General principles affecting socialization in collectively oriented groups can be delineated as follows:

1. **Authority Role**
   - Social roles are ascribed based on hierarchy (age and status respected).
   - Family structure is patriarchal, influenced by principles of order regarding roles and behavior.
   - Particularism is valued (individuals treated differently according to rank, gender, and/or situation); authority figures have more rights and privileges, as well as having more obligations and responsibilities to protect and care for others; mothers, grandparents, teachers each do certain things.

> Examples:
>
> - **Mary**, a ***Catholic American***, was socialized to believe in a hierarchical order of status and social roles (age and gender). This ensures people will maintain their appropriate behavior, as well as follow certain orderly principles (such as God's will regarding childbearing). She has also been socialized to respect, obey, and fear her parents and other authority figures.
> - **Habib**, a ***Muslim American*** who practices ***Islam***, was socialized to believe that one's relationship to God is that all things belong to Him and that wealth held by individuals is held in trust. He also believes that a portion of one's accumulated wealth is required to be given to those in need.

2. **Relationships**
   - Harmony is valued.
   - Family members place family needs above individual needs.
   - Children show obedience and loyalty to parents and are expected to care for elderly parents.
   - Believe that a cooperative social network extends from the mother and father union to the extended family of relatives and ultimately to the community; children are socialized by the extended, as well as the nuclear, family; old people traditionally pass on the cultural heritage to the younger ones; children are

taught to respect elders (age is a "badge of honor"—if you have grown old, you have done the right things)

> Examples:
>
> - **Angelo**, a ***Latino American***, was socialized to prioritize family needs and responsibilities. When his grandmother became ill, and his mother had to take her to the doctor, he had to stay home from school to care for his younger siblings.
> - **Winona**, a ***Native American***, has been taught that children are not permitted to communicate their opinions to older people. She also has been taught not to boast or cause another embarrassment. Children in her tribal group are socialized by all members of the community.

These children are engaged in a collective task.

Monkey Business Images/Shutterstock.com

3. **Communication**

- Communication tends to be more indirect, than direct—conversations might include inquiries about family members, health, or other seemingly unrelated matters to the purpose of the communication (such inquiries are necessary for assessing choice of language to be used and degree of familiarity with which certain topics can be discussed) (Stewart & Bennett, 1991).
- Nonverbal, more than verbal, communication (body language, gestures, touch, facial expression, eye contact) is used.

> Examples:
>
> - **Lee**, an ***Asian American***, and **Dakota**, ***a Native American***, were both socialized to rely on context (including nonverbal behavior and relational cues) in order to be able to completely understand what is being communicated in a conversation. They also learned to use silence and pauses in conversations to contemplate what was said and to think about how to respond.
> - **Akilah**, a ***Middle-Eastern American***, **Joe**, an ***Italian American***, and **Aloha**, a ***Hawaiian***, have learned to use interruption as a means of getting involved in a conversation (Thiederman, 1991).
> - **Kareem**, a ***low-income African American***, was encouraged to learn by adults who would ask "real" questions (those to which a child would not know the answer), such as "What's in that box?" (Heath, 1989). He experienced the acting out of conversations with body language and/or the use of a lot of teasing. Also, words sometimes were coined to enhance and further communication ("It's not what is said, but how it is said that is important") (Hale, 1994).

4. **Displays of Emotion**

- Some groups display emotions inwardly and others display them outwardly.
- Inward emotions are feelings rarely shown publicly; they can be expressed through a change in personal distance (stepping backward while engaged in a loud conversation), shunning (ignoring and avoiding a friend for boasting), or deviations in performing routines (knowing your wife is angry because she filled your teacup only halfway with lukewarm tea).
- Outward emotions are expressed through facial expressions, sound, body movement (however, facial expressions don't always reveal inner emotions).

The communication between these adults exemplifies a direct style. It also exemplifies an outward display of emotion in that the man is looking at and leaning his body toward the woman while he explains something; by the smile on her face, the woman is showing she understands and is pleased.

Cengage Learning

Examples:

- **Ami**, a ***Japanese American***, grew up learning that a smile can disguise embarrassment, mask bereavement, or conceal rage; whereas a straight face can hide happiness (Stewart & Bennett, 1991). Yet, up until she was about 5 years old, she, like other Japanese children, was expected to emote outwardly by whining and clambering on her mother after a separation, because this represents "amac," the child's enduring emotional dependence on the mother (Cole & Tan, 2007).
- **John**, a ***middle-class Euro-American***, was socialized not to whine and to exhibit self-control by modeling the ways in which adults show emotion (Cole & Tan, 2007).

5. **Discipline/Guidance**

- Age is equated with knowledge—children are not asked their desires, nor are they expected to communicate their opinions to older people; they are expected to be guided by adult wisdom.
- Children obey and imitate; they learn by doing—even when children play, an adult or older sibling is nearby to guide them as needed (Rogoff, 2003).
- A sense of obligation to parents is fostered by dependency and physical closeness between parents and child, which is continually reinforced as children grow older.
- The use of shame and guilt is enabled by the child's dependency on the mother; she controls the child's behavior by appealing to the child's sense of duty when the child deviates from her expectations.
- The child also learns related socialized behaviors to avoid shame and save face—reluctance to admit lack of understanding, to ask questions, to take initiative, to do something a new way, and to avoid confrontation or disagreement (a Japanese proverb says: "The nail that sticks out gets hammered down)."

Examples:

- **Han**, an ***Asian American***, experienced discipline/guidance through nurturance (responsive maternal care given to infants). In China, as well as in other Asian countries, infants seldom are allowed to cry for prolonged periods before they are picked up; they are fed on demand and weaned at a relatively late age; the young child is allowed to sleep with parents; and toilet training is gradual. Children so raised become dependent on their mothers to satisfy their needs.
- **Dalia**, a ***Middle-Eastern American***, experienced doting, indulgent care as a young child. This is common in Middle-Eastern cultures as a way of establishing strong emotional ties from children to their parents and families. Young children are not expected to follow rules, and misbehavior is tolerated. However, between age 5 and 7, parents gradually demand more discipline, and children are also expected to help younger siblings and elders (Kagicibasi, 1996).
- **Paloma**, a ***Native American***, experienced discipline/guidance that was subtly implemented as she grew up. Approval was indicated through a smile, a pleasant tone of voice, or a friendly pat. Children in her tribal group typically were corrected by adults lowering their voices. Neither physical punishment nor verbal praise were used; instead, frowning, ignoring, withdrawal of affection, shaming, and group pressure were the forms of social control used. Criticism of another is communicated indirectly through another family member, rather than directly.

- **Jose**, a ***Latino American***, was encouraged, as a child, to learn by observing, by doing, and by paying attention to the reactions of others. He, like other Hispanic children, is usually included in many adult activities. Self-regulation is socialized by adults who enable children to build new behaviors onto old; adults use feedback to help children improve. Praise in front of others is frowned upon because it may make the individual feel more important than others in the group (Trumbull et al., 2001).

6. **Skills Emphasis**

- Skills believed important for children to learn to get along in the group, as well as to become contributing adults, are brotherhood, sharing, spirituality, and personal integrity.
- Modesty and moderation are stressed (one doesn't talk for the sake of talking; one doesn't boast when one achieves; and one doesn't show emotions).
- Children are expected to do what they are capable of doing for their age (not to be perfect)—the goal is to improve on past performance (failure is not a concept)

Examples:

- **Honan**, a ***Native American***, grew up learning spirituality through rites and rituals. He was socialized to value cooperation highly and was discouraged from competing within the group (such as for attention). He learned that consensus on decisions facing the group is sought via discussions, rather than by voting and majority rule—the needs of the group supersede the needs of the individual. In his tribal group, personal items are readily shared because boundaries of property ownership are believed to be permeable.
- **Lupita**, a ***Latina American***, grew up in a family that emphasized cooperation and helpfulness. Hispanic children are generally taught to be sensitive to the feelings and needs of others. Also, there usually is more emphasis on interaction with people than with things.

Competitive/Independent (Individualistic) Orientation

General principles affecting socialization competitively-oriented groups can be delineated as follows:

1. **Authority Role**

- Achieved authority is valued—occurs through hard work (achievement is respected and admired).
- Universalism is valued (rules are the same for everyone).

Example:

- **Alice**, a ***Euro-American***, was socialized to believe in equal opportunity for all. When playing with her friends, a common saying was, "That's not fair!" (meaning: taking advantage), or "That's cheating!" (meaning: breaking the rules).

2. **Relationships**

- Relationships are compartmentalized (family, friends, school, work).
- Believe that behavior is governed by "Do unto others as you would have others do unto you," rather than by ascribed rights and obligations.
- A norm is informality; transience is common.
- Decisions are made democratically (equal rights and majority rule).

Example:

- **Richard**, a ***Euro-American***, was socialized that individual rights supersede rights of the group. His family put a fence around their property even though the neighbors objected to it. He also learned to value competition over collectivism. He chose to be on the swim team even though his best friend couldn't qualify.

3. **Communication**

- Communication can be direct and independent of context (such as in a memorandum), or indirect and dependent on context (such as in a face-to-face meeting).

Example:

- **Stacy**, a ***Euro-American***, was socialized by her lawyer parents to be pragmatic, specific, and come to the point quickly. She learned early to be comfortable with written and electronic messages; what is stated, *is* the message (the context in which it is said is not important). To encourage learning while growing up, her parents asked her "knowledge-training" questions ("What is this story about?").

4. **Displays of Emotion**

- Some groups of individuals, both *individualistic* and *collectivistic*, openly express feelings to others; some individuals close their feelings to others; and some individuals are open with those people with whom they are intimate and closed with all others.
- The display of emotions, open or closed, is likely an adaptive strategy developed and passed on regarding how best to get along with others (share your feelings with all, hide your feelings from all, or be selective).

5. **Discipline/Guidance**

- It is believed that there is a rational order in the world and individuals are agents of action ("Take the bull by the horns").
- It is assumed that problems and solutions are the nature of reality; children are socialized to solve problems they encounter.
- Discipline/guidance aims to be preventive (provide children with reasons for desirable behavior so they will internalize them and be self-directive).

Example:

- **Michael**, a ***Euro-American***, was socialized to believe in the importance of prevention (taking action in the present to avoid problems in the future—"A stitch in time saves nine"). He, like other Euro-American children, was socialized to avoid risks (Stewart & Bennett, 1991); yet he was also encouraged to engage in trial and error ("If at first you don't succeed, try, try again").

6. **Skills Emphasis**

- From a very young age, children are encouraged to make their own decisions.
- It is believed that the self is "located solely within the individual and the individual is definitely separate from others" (Lustig & Koester, 1999, p. 95);

children are expected to maintain clear boundaries between the self and others.

- Emphasis placed on individual achievement, self-expression, and personal choice.
- Competition between groups is believed to promote performance and "team spirit"; competition within the group is believed to promote creativity and productivity ("The early bird catches the worm").
- Personal responsibility for success or failure is ingrained in the culture—"The buck stops here" (Thiederman, 1991)—as exemplified by the legal system, which is charged with assigning responsibility for wrongdoings.

Examples:

- **Bill**, a ***Euro-American***, was socialized to place emphasis on competition; achievement is judged in terms of comparisons with self and others ("You swam faster today than you did yesterday"; "You got the highest grade in the class on the math test"). In his family, praise was given generously, not only for achievement, but to enhance his self-esteem (Trumbull et al., 2001). His parents emphasized personal responsibility for learning, behavior, and possessions.
- **Margaret**, a ***Jewish-American***, was socialized to believe in a basic tenet of Judaism: If one chooses to live a good life, being kind to others and sharing with those less fortunate, one will experience self-reward.
- **Mathew**, a ***Protestant American***, was socialized to believe in the "Protestant ethic"—that salvation is achieved through hard work, thrift, and self-discipline ("Where there's a will, there's a way"; "God helps those who help themselves").

Table 4.1 summarizes the differences between collective and individualistic parenting orientations.

Table 4.1 Summary: Collectivistic and Individualistic Parenting Orientations

	Collectivistic Orientation	Individualistic Orientation
Authority Role	Ascribed Hierarchal	Achieved Egalitarian
Relationships	Cooperative	Competitive
Communication	Indirect More emphasis on nonverbal (facial & body language) Dependent on context	Direct More emphasis on verbal Verbal (face-to-face) Independent of context
Displays of Emotion	Outward (facial & body) or inward (personal distance)	Open with all others or just with intimate others
Discipline/Guidance	Obedience Imitation Sense of obligation	Learn by doing Instruction and reasoning Sense of independence
Skills Emphasis	Sharing Helping Interaction with people Group loyalty	Decision making Individual achievement Self-expression Personal choice and responsibility

How has parenting changed over time?

Chronosystem Influences on Parenting

Parenting today raises new questions that previous generations seldom had to face. Should we have children? How many and how far apart? Terminate the unexpected or the imperfect child? Should we be strict or permissive? Should we stress competitiveness or cooperation? What activities should be encouraged? Because society is changing so rapidly and because of new advances in science and technology, parents cannot look to experience for answers as their parents could.

Several social scientists (Bronfenbrenner, 1989; Garbarino, Bradshaw, & Kostelny, 2005; Hewlett & West, 1998) are concerned that a number of developments—many beneficent in themselves—have conspired to isolate the family and to drastically reduce the number of relatives, neighbors, and other caring adults who share in the socialization of American children. Among the most significant forces are occupational mobility, the breakdown of neighborhoods, the separation of residential from business areas, consolidated school districts, separate patterns of social life for different age groups, and the delegation of child care to outside institutions. What today's parents lack is a support system.

Because of the nature of today's rapidly changing society, parents spend less time with their children. A majority of mothers hold jobs outside the home. Fathers often must travel in connection with their work and are away for days or even weeks at a time. Parents may have meetings to attend in the evenings and social engagements on the weekends. Various studies have found that lack of time together is perceived as the greatest threat to the family (Hochschild, 1997; Leach, 1994; Jacobs & Gerson, 2004). Given the changing nature of society and its pressures on the family's ability to function optimally, parenting today has become a "journey without a road map."

How have children been treated throughout history?

Historical Trends

A brief history of trends in the United States concerning the treatment of children and the role of parents follows.

Eighteenth Century

Before this time, it was not uncommon for children to be considered significant only if they contributed to their elders' welfare; no thought was given to their individual needs. If parents could not afford to care for them, they could be abandoned. Parenting was adult-centered.

humanism a system of beliefs concerned with the interests and ideals of humans rather than of the natural or spiritual world

tabula rasa the mind is a blank slate before impressions are recorded on it by experience

Beginning in the 18th century, however, there was some improvement in the way children were treated. Contributing to this reform was a reexamination of the writings of Locke, Rousseau, and Pestalozzi, all advocates of **humanism**—a system of beliefs concerned with the interests and ideals of humans rather than of the natural or spiritual world (Berger, 2007). British philosopher John Locke's (1632–1704) best-known concept was that a newborn's mind is a **tabula rasa**, a blank slate before impressions are recorded on it by experience, and that all thought develops from experience. Children are neither innately good nor innately bad. The influence of this concept on contemporary parenting has been to encourage parents and teachers to mold children's minds by providing them with optimal experiences.

During the 18th century in colonial America, children were needed to do endless chores. The father was the primary authority. Children were to be seen and not heard; immediate obedience was expected. Discipline was strict; those who disobeyed were believed to be wicked and sinful and were severely punished. Tradition and religion influenced child-rearing practices: "He that spareth his rod, hateth his son: but he that loveth him chasteneth him betimes" (Proverbs 13:24). "Train up a child in the way he should go: and when he is old, he will not depart from it" (Proverbs 22:6).

Parenting was also influenced by French philosopher Jean Jacques Rousseau (1712–1778), who believed that children are innately good and need freedom to grow because insensitive caregivers might otherwise corrupt them. Rousseau's writings influenced Johann Pestalozzi (1746–1827), who emphasized the importance of the mother as the child's first teacher. The mother is more likely than other adults to be sensitive to her child's needs. That the mother was most important in the upbringing of the child was corroborated by Robert Sunley's (1955) analysis of child-rearing literature from early-19th-century magazines, books, and journals.

Nineteenth Century

During the 19th century, parents were exposed to the ideas of psychologist G. Stanley Hall (1846–1924) who, like Rousseau, believed that young children are innately good and will grow naturally to be self-controlled adults, if not over-directed (Berger, 2007). This idea influenced many contemporary attitudes on child development and parenting. Parenting was becoming child-centered. Unlike the traditional emphasis on the needs of the parent, contemporary ideas of child rearing placed paramount importance on the individual needs and welfare of the child. However, parents still directed the child-rearing practices.

Although at the end of the 19th century, parenting literature was espousing love and affection for children in order to mold their characters, at the beginning of the 20th century, the discipline method advocated to mold character emphasized rewards and punishment. *Infant Care*, published in 1914 by the Children's Bureau, recommended strict child rearing. For example, thumb-sucking and masturbation were believed to damage the child permanently (Wolfenstein, 1953). At the beginning of the 20th century, the parenting literature advocated rigid scheduling of infants. Mothers were told to expect obedience, ignore temper tantrums, and restrict physical handling of their children (Stendler, 1950).

Early Twentieth Century

In the 1920s, applications of psychological theories began to appear in books and magazines. John B. Watson's theory of **behaviorism**, which held that only observable behavior (not what exists in the mind) provides valid data for psychology, and Sigmund Freud's theory of personality development, which dealt with non-observable (unconscious) forces in the mind were significantly influential for parents. Watson's theoretical view defined learning as a change in the way an individual responds to a particular situation: Behavior that is reinforced or rewarded will be repeated; behavior that is not reinforced will be extinguished or eliminated. Watson's theory applied to parenting in that conditioning of the child must take place early, with desirable behavior being reinforced and undesirable behavior being ignored. Freud's theory applied to parenting in that Freud believed it was necessary for children to express—rather than repress—emotions. He said that harmful early experiences can harm children's development (especially when these experiences are buried in the unconscious mind); that these can result in **fixations**, or arrested development, occurring at any time in life. Therefore, children's growing personalities must not be repressed, or else children will inevitably have problems as adults.

behaviorism the theory that observed behavior, rather than what exists in the mind, provides the only valid data for psychology

fixation a Freudian term referring to arrested development

Middle Twentieth Century

In the 1940s, mothers were told that children should be fed when hungry and be toilet trained when they developed physical control. This was very different from the rigid scheduling of feeding and toilet training previously advocated. Even handling of genitals was considered natural, whereas years before parents were warned to take every precaution to prevent it (Wolfenstein, 1953). Benjamin Spock, in the 1946 edition of *The Common Sense Book of Baby and Child Care*, advised parents to enjoy their children and their roles as parents. He advocated self-regulation by the child rather than strict scheduling by the parents. Spock wanted to encourage parents to have a greater understanding of children and to be more flexible in directing their upbringing. He based his recommendations on the writings of educators such as John Dewey (who believed children should learn by doing) and psychoanalysts such as Sigmund Freud (who believed children's psychological development occurred in natural stages and that healthy outcomes were influenced by parents).

Late Twentieth Century

Jerry Bigner (1979) analyzed the child-rearing literature in several women's magazines from 1950 to 1970. He found that in the early 1950s physical punishment—spanking—was condoned, but by the end of that decade it was discouraged on the grounds that physical punishment does no more than show a child that a parent can hit. Most articles encouraged self-regulation by the child. Parents were advised to hold, love, and enjoy their children and to emphasize the importance of children feeling loved. Parents were also urged to recognize individual differences, to realize that development is natural and maturation cannot be pushed. The extensive work of Arnold Gesell (Gesell & Ilg, 1943) influenced this view. He published norms, or average standards, of child development based on observations of children of all ages. He concluded that the patterns for healthy growth were biologically programmed within the child and that if the parents would relax, growth would occur naturally.

Toward the end of the 1950s, after the Soviet Union's successful launch of the first satellite into space, the concern for intellectual development in children became urgent. Jean Piaget's theories on cognitive development were of interest to professionals working with children. He emphasized that knowledge comes from acting in one's environment. Thus, the importance of giving children a stimulating environment and many experiences was reinforced.

Influenced by the mass media, which publicized scientific and humanitarian views on child rearing, many parents began to move away from the traditional *parent-centered* approach to child rearing, with its strict discipline, to a more *child-centered* approach, with more flexibility. However, in 1957, Spock revised the 1946 classic edition of his book on child care, which advocated a child-centered approach, to read, "Nowadays there seems to be more chance of a conscientious parent's getting into trouble with permissiveness than with strictness" (Spock, 1957). Spock realized the consequences of parents' focusing exclusively on what children need from them, rather than what the community will need from children when they grow up. Even though Spock continued to maintain his belief that children's needs should be attended to, subsequent editions of his book addressed the rights of parents—children need to feel loved, yet parents have the right to demand certain standards of behavior (Spock, 1957; Spock & Needleman, 1992). Other contemporary parenting views concur (Baumrind & Thompson, 2002; Parke & Buriel, 2006).

In sum, the trend in parenting attitudes in the United States over time has swung from parent-centeredness to child-centeredness to more of a balanced approach.

How do family members influence each other?

Family Dynamics

Family dynamics refers to what activities are going on, with whom, and how they "play out" over time. As discussed in Chapter 3, the structure and functioning of the family as a whole affect parenting. Here we discuss the particular characteristics of family members and how these members relate to one another, which also affect parenting (Bornstein, 2006).

A family enjoying mealtime together.

Monkey Business Images/Shutterstock.com

Parenting involves a continuous process of reciprocal interaction that affects both the parents and the children (Kuczynski, 2003). When one becomes a parent, one rediscovers some of one's own experiences in childhood and adolescence—for example, making snowmen, playing hopscotch, playing hide-and-seek, and running through the sprinklers on a hot day. When one becomes a parent, one's experience is expanded. Like a game involving strategies and counterstrategies, parenting requires continual adaptation to children's changing capacities. Parenting is time-consuming and difficult; it is also joyful and satisfying. Children are loving, open, and curious. What could be more gratifying than the first handmade card your child gives you that says "I luv u," or when your grownup child asks for your advice?

Children's Characteristics

What characteristics of children influence family dynamics and parenting practices?

Characteristics of children that influence family dynamics and parenting style in a bidirectional way include age and cognitive development, temperament, gender (Bornstein, 2006), and presence of a special need, such as a disability (Heward, 2008).

Age and Cognitive Development

As the child gets older and more mature physically and cognitively, parent–child interactions change. During infancy, parenting tasks are primarily feeding, changing, bathing, and comforting. As the child is awake more, play is added to the repertoire of activities. During the second year of life, physical and verbal restraint must be introduced for the child's safety. The child must be prevented from going into the street, from eating poisonous materials, from handling sharp objects, and so on.

During the preschool years, parenting techniques may expand to include reasoning, instruction, isolation (timeout), withdrawal of privileges (negative consequences), and reinforcement or rewards. As the children mature during school age, parents may encourage them to become more responsible for their behavior by allowing them to make certain decisions and to experience the positive as well as the negative consequences. For example, if a child requests a pet fish for his or her birthday, then the parents should allow the child to have the responsibility of feeding it. As children enter adolescence, parents may deal with potential conflicts by discussion, collaborative problem solving, and compromise. My son neglected to clean his room. It was "a waste of time" to make his bed and put his things away, since he would just be using them again. Because I like order and neatness, his behavior caused me to nag. After discussing his reasons for not complying with my standards and my reasons for him to do so, we agreed on a compromise: The day I cleaned house, he was to tidy his room; other days, he could keep the door closed, but not locked.

Researchers (McNally, Eisenberg, & Harris, 1991; Parke & Buriel, 2006) have found that although specific parenting practices change according to the age of the child, basic parenting styles remain quite stable over time. For example, a parent might isolate a preschooler who is hitting a younger sibling until some self-control is established. That

IN PRACTICE

Parenting and Prevention of Adolescent Problem Behavior

Studies have shown that adolescents whose parents are warm, affectionate, communicative toward them, and have certain standards for behavior are less likely to abuse drugs or engage in delinquent acts or join gangs than children who do not have good parental relationships (Baumrind, 1991; Greenberger & Chen, 1996; Grotevant, 1998; Steinberg & Morris, 2001).

Adolescence is a time when parent-child relations are tested. Many of the everyday demands of family life—doing one's assigned chores, being considerate of other members, communicating, adhering to standards (coming home on time, keeping appointments, writing thank-you notes, doing homework)—can become areas of conflict.

When parents react negatively to an adolescent's push for autonomy and become overly strict or overly permissive, the adolescent is more likely to rebel by exhibiting problem behavior (Collins & Laursen, 2004; Eisenberg et al., 2005).

The research also suggests that the effect of conflict between a child and one parent can be offset by a positive relationship with the other parent. Positive parent-child relationships can also negate the influence of a peer group that abuses drugs or alcohol and engages in delinquent behavior. Thus, parenting styles established in childhood have an impact on adolescent problem behavior.

parent might use reasoning and/or withdrawal of privileges for a school-ager who fights. Parenting practices may also change according to the situation. For example, a parent who usually gives a child instruction on how to behave in advance may resort to yelling when rushed. Thus, even though the methods may change, the goal of self-control and the emotional climate or style of attaining that goal remain stable.

Temperament

Temperament, introduced in Chapter 1, is the combination of innate characteristics that determine an individual's sensitivity to various experiences and responsiveness to patterns of social interaction. It is a central aspect of an individual's personality, and has been shown to be stable over time (Rothbart & Bates, 2006).

Temperament influences one's interactions with others—how infants respond to their caregivers and how caregivers respond to children—thereby illustrating the concept of bidirectionality. Thus, certain parenting styles may be elicited by a child's temperament (Putnam, Sanson, & Rothbart, 2002; Sameroff, 1994). For example, a very active child may have to be told more than once to sit still at the table or may have to be removed from the table to eat alone, whereas a less active child may only have to be told "Sit still at the dinner table so the food won't spill off the plate." Some methods of child rearing may have to be modified to suit a child's temperament. A child who has irregular patterns of hunger and sleep would be better suited to a more flexible "demand" feeding schedule, whereas a child who exhibits regularity is more suited to feeding at scheduled intervals.

In a classic longitudinal study of 136 children from infancy to adolescence, researchers Chess and Thomas (Chess & Thomas, 1987; Thomas, Chess, & Birch, 1970) isolated nine behavioral characteristics, which clustered into three general types of temperament. These temperamental types could be recognized by the second or third month of life. This model is still used by researchers today.

1. *Easy* children displayed a positive mood and regularity in body function; they were adaptable and approachable, and their reactions were moderate or low in intensity.
2. *Difficult* children were slow to adapt and tended to have intense reactions and negative moods; they withdrew in new situations and had irregular body functions.
3. *Slow-to-warm-up* children initially withdrew but slowly adapted to new situations; they had low activity levels and tended to respond with low intensity.

Although individual temperament seems to be established at birth, environmental factors, especially parenting styles, play an important role in whether or not a person's style of behavior can be modified. If the influences of heredity and environment blend well together, one can expect healthy development of the child; if they are incompatible, behavioral problems are almost sure to ensue (Thomas & Chess, 1977, 1980). Therefore, Thomas and Chess recommend that parents adjust parenting styles to their offspring's temperament, although they emphasize that "a constructive approach by the parents to the child's temperament does not mean an acceptance or encouragement of all this youngster's behavior in all situations" (1977, p. 188). Thomas and Chess refer to the accommodation of parenting styles to children's temperaments as **goodness-of-fit**. Infant temperament determines what kinds of interactions parents and infants are most likely to find mutually rewarding. However, just because infants are born with certain temperaments does not preclude them from adapting to certain behaviors demanded of them; the key is how the parents do it.

goodness-of-fit
accommodation of parenting styles to children's temperaments

1. *Easy* children tend to adapt well to various styles of child rearing.
2. *Difficult* children need consistent, patient, and objective parents who can handle their instability. For example, instead of expecting very active, distractible children to concentrate for long periods of time on their homework, parents can reward them for shorter periods of work with pleasurable breaks in between, as long as the task is finished.

3. *Slow-to-warm-up* children do best with a moderate amount of encouragement coupled with patience; parents and teachers should let these children adjust to change at their own pace.

Temperament first sets the tone for interaction. Children who are sociable (easy temperament) will communicate a different mood when they encounter people than will children who are more reserved (slow-to-warm-up temperament). Next, temperamental differences will determine the kinds of behaviors children may initiate. Active children (difficult temperament) will likely experience more things because they are constantly doing and on the go. They will probably have more social interactions because of their activities. Their temperament will elicit certain responses from others. For example, by being attentive to a child's frequent emotional expressions of joy, sadness, or even anger, a parent is likely to encourage those behaviors. On the other hand, if a parent ignores or sets consequences for such overt displays of emotion, that parent is likely to discourage those behaviors (Putnam, Sanson, & Rothbart, 2002).

Not only is a child's temperament influential on parenting styles; the parents' temperament, too, affects their parenting styles and how they respond to their child's behavior (Lerner, 1993). For example, an active parent may be impatient with an inactive infant; a sociable parent may feel rejected by a withdrawn child; a reserved parent may feel intimidated by an aggressive child.

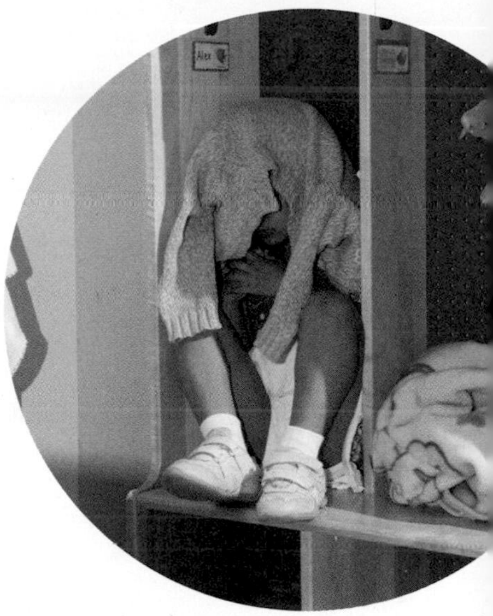

This child is exhibiting her difficult temperament by sulking in her cubby to protest having to go outside. Talking calmly to her will be more effective than demanding she comply, threatening punishment.

Cengage Learning

Gender

Parents provide different socializing environments for boys and girls (Leaper, 2002; Ruble, Martin, & Berenbaum, 2006), most likely because of their own socialization. Parents give children different names, different clothing, and different toys. Fathers, in particular, are more likely to act differently toward sons and daughters than are mothers (Fagot, 1995; Lamb, 2004; Parke, 2002). Also, fathers tend to be more demanding of their children than are mothers (Doherty, Kouneski, & Erikson, 1998; Lamb, 2004). Parents of school-age children were interviewed regarding parenting techniques used with their sons and daughters. Parents reported being more punishing and less rewarding with same-gendered children. Parents of girls emphasized cooperation and politeness; parents of boys emphasized independent and self-reliant behaviors (Power, 1987).

The types of play activities that are encouraged differ for boys and girls. There is also some evidence that parents encourage girls to be more dependent, affectionate, and emotional than boys. In addition, as boys get older, they are permitted more freedom than girls—for example, they are allowed to be away from home without supervision more than are girls (Basow, 2008). Besides parental effects on gender-role socialization, siblings and the child's own cognitive development have been found to be influential (McHale, Crouter, & Tucker, 1999). Gender-role socialization will be discussed more specifically in Chapter 12.

Presence of a Disability

The presence of a disability in a child influences family dynamics and parenting styles. The nature, onset, and severity of the disability as well as the availability of support systems are factors in how the parents cope.

Parental reactions to the diagnosis of a disability vary enormously; they may include grief, depression, and/or guilt (Meadow-Orlans, 1995). Another common reaction is anger—anger with God, fate, society, professionals, oneself, the other parent, or even the child. In addition, parents may also experience frustration as they seek an accurate diagnosis or referral of a child who has a problem that is not so readily identifiable.

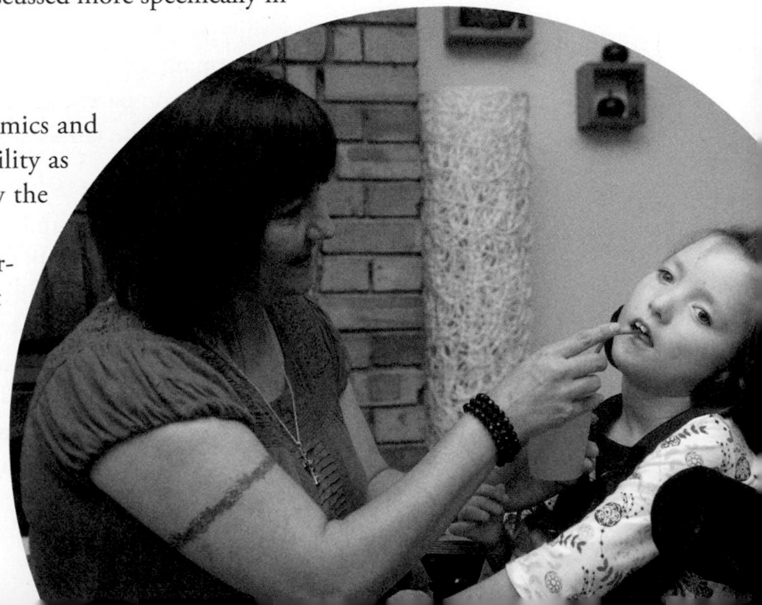

A mother caring for her child who is disabled.

Paul Doyle / Alamy

Society expects parents to love their children. When a parent experiences negative feelings at the birth of a child, that parent commonly feels guilt. Unable to accept their own feelings of rejection or hostility, parents may blame themselves for experiencing emotions unbefitting a good and loving parent, especially a parent of a child so in need of love and special care. Guilt may also be related to a parent's feeling that something he or she did, or failed to do, caused a child's disability.

Parenting is a difficult and complicated task. Parenting a child with a disability is even more so (Heward, 2008). Although most people will tolerate a 2-year-old's temper tantrum in a grocery store, they are apt to stare, or even make remarks, at a 10-year-old behaving in the same manner. Many parents have difficulty from time to time getting responsible babysitters, but parents of children with disabilities have even more. It is a challenge to change the diapers on a preadolescent, or care for a blind preschooler, or calm down a hyperactive child.

Not only is parenting a child with a disability more complicated and difficult, it is also more likely to cause major psychological stress in the parent, resulting in disturbed family interactions. According to Ann Turnbull and H. Rutherford Turnbull (2001), the parents of children born with disabilities may lose self-esteem. This can be transmitted to the child as overprotection, rejection, or abuse. The child may experience ambivalence, sometimes feeling love and sometimes anger. The frustrations of parenting a child with disabilities can tax anyone's patience. Parents worry about the care, the expense, and the future of their child. Some parents dedicate themselves totally to their child with disabilities. This pattern can lead to marital conflicts, neglect of other children, and family disruption.

What characteristics of families influence its dynamics and parenting practices?

Family Characteristics

Characteristics that influence family dynamics and consequent parenting style are size (number of siblings) and configuration (birth order, spacing, and gender of siblings), as well as parents' stage of life, marital quality, and abilities to cope with stress (Bornstein, 2006; Cowan, Powell, & Cowan, 1998).

Size

Both parents and children are affected by the number of children in the family. The more children there are, the more interactions within the family, but the less likely are individual parent–child interactions. Children in large families may have many resources to draw on for company, playmates, and emotional security. They may also have increased responsibility in the form of chores or caring for younger siblings. Parents in larger families, especially those with limited living space and economic resources, tend to be more authoritarian, tend to be more likely to use physical punishment, and tend to be less likely to explain their rules than are the parents of smaller families. The emphasis is on the family as a whole rather than the individuals within it (Bossard & Boll, 1956; Elder & Bowerman, 1963; Furman, 1995). However, it has also been found that the effects of family size on parenting style are mediated by parental education, occupation, social class, intactness of the family, and ethnic orientation (Blake, 1989; Bornstein, 2006).

Configuration

Not only does the number of children in a family affect child-rearing practices, but the spacing and gender of the siblings also influence parent–child interactions. With the birth of each sibling come different temperaments, different ages, and new relationships for parents to handle. Also, when adult children move back home, or when other relatives, such as grandparents, come to live with the nuclear family, authority patterns and relationships change.

According to Pew Research (2010), the multigenerational family household is making a comeback (it was a common American family configuration prior to World War II).

Influences on family configuration include the Great Recession, which began accelerating in 2007, and the big wave of immigration, dominated by Latino and Asian groups, which began around 1970. Today, many young people who can't afford places of their own choose to live with their parents. Aging adults who can't live independently (for health or financial reasons) move in with their younger relatives. To immigrants from some cultures, multigenerational households are the norm.

A number of studies (Furman, 1995; Sutton-Smith, 1982) have shown parenting practices with regard to firstborn and later-born siblings to differ even at the same age. Firstborns receive more attention, affection, and verbal stimulation than their later-born siblings. They also are disciplined more restrictively and are coerced more by their parents. More mature behavior is expected of them than of their siblings. Other findings have shown that mothers help their firstborns in solving problems more frequently than they do their later-borns. And mothers of firstborns apply more pressure for achievement than they do on their later-borns (Zajonc, 1976).

Judy Dunn (1988, 1992, 1993, 2007) has examined the socialization effects siblings have on each other, unlike the studies discussed earlier which explained the bidirectional influences of siblings on parenting behavior and differential parenting on siblings (McHale et al., 2000). Siblings provide opportunities for cooperation, competition, empathy, aggression, leading, following, and so on. Older siblings function as tutors or supervisors of younger brothers or sisters (Parke & Buriel, 2006). Dunn has shown that from 18 months on, children understand how to hurt, comfort, and exacerbate a sibling's pain. They understand what is allowed or disapproved in their families. They can even anticipate responses of adults to their own and others' misbehavior as well as comment on, and ask about, the causes of others' actions and feelings. Dunn concludes that the ability to understand others and the social world is closely linked to the activities and relationships with siblings and parents. It is important that parents monitor sibling interactions and intervene in conflicts. By explaining rights and fairness, as well as interpreting differences in abilities according to age, parents can enhance positive relationships between siblings.

What about only children? Only children experience more parent–child interaction, and their relationships with their parents are reported to be more positive and affectionate than those of children with siblings (Falbo & Polit, 1986). In a study of 2-year-olds with an unfamiliar peer in a laboratory room, Snow, Jacklin, and Maccoby (1981) observed that only children were more advanced socially than children with siblings, showing more positive behavior as well as assertive/aggressive behavior. Second-borns showed the least. Only children have also been shown to perform better academically in school than children who have siblings (Falbo & Polit, 1986).

Thus, being an only child does not seem to be harmful to development; rather, it may be beneficial. There are disadvantages, however, such as too much pressure from parents to succeed, loneliness, or not having anyone to help care for aging parents.

Parents' Life Stage

Parents go through six stages of changes in their expectations and practices for children from infancy to adolescence: (1) image making, (2) nurturing, (3) authority, (4) interpretive, (5) interdependent, and (6) departure (Galinsky, 1981).

Parents also go through changes in their relationships with their parents. Generational research shows that parents' relationships with their parents throughout childhood and adulthood impacts their parenting practices (Cowan, Powell, & Cowan, 1998). For example, mothers who reported having had an insecure childhood relationship with their parents have less effective parenting strategies with their preschool children than mothers who reported having had a secure relationship. Apparently, having a good "working" model to emulate influences parenting practices from infancy to adolescence.

Marital Quality

Marital quality contributes to children's development in that the parents form a coparenting alliance, cooperating with and supporting each other (Cowan, Powell, & Cowan, 1998). United parents are less subject to manipulation by their child. What child hasn't tried to get one parent to give in when the other parent has refused a request?

Research shows that children whose fathers are involved in their care do better socially and academically than children whose fathers play a marginal parenting role (Lamb, 2004; Parke, 2002). McHale (1995) found that parents who argued during a problem-solving task were also likely to be hostile and competitive when parenting their sons, and have different levels of involvement with daughters. Marital conflict may be so consuming for parents that they become less able to respond to their child's emotional needs and their parenting skills may diminish (Fincham & Hall, 2005).

Marital conflict culminating in divorce imposes a major disruption in relationships among all members of the family (Kelly & Emery, 2003). As was discussed in Chapter 3, divorce affects the parenting style of both the custodial and the noncustodial parent, with the custodial parent (usually the mother) becoming more authoritarian and restrictive, and the noncustodial parent (usually the father) becoming more permissive and indulgent, at least initially. Such a major stress also affects children's behavior, with children becoming more aggressive, rebellious, and manipulative.

Ability to Cope with Stress

Parents who are tired, worried, or ill and those who feel they have lost control of their lives are likely to be impatient, lacking in understanding, and unwilling to reason with their children. To see whether and how stress affects child rearing, Zussman (1980) created a stressful situation in which parents were observed interacting with their toddlers and preschool-age children. A laboratory playroom was equipped with play materials that were complex enough to require the children to request help. It was also equipped with such items as a breakable vase, a filled ashtray, and a stack of index cards. The parents were given mental tasks to perform while the children played in the room. Zussman found that when the parents were preoccupied with their task, they became less responsive to their preschool children (less likely to play with them, talk to them, help them) and more interfering, critical, and authoritarian with their toddlers.

What are the effects of real-life stress, such as divorce, illness, death, abuse, or financial problems, on parental interaction with children? In one study, Patterson (1982) obtained daily reports from a group of mothers concerning the occurrence of crises of varying magnitudes, including an unexpectedly large bill, a car breaking down, illness of a family member, and quarrels between spouses. The mothers were also asked to describe their moods, and family interactions were observed. The number of crises experienced was found to be a positive predictor of maternal irritability. Patterson found that the more often a mother becomes irritable, the less likely she is to deal with family problem solving, and that unsolved problems accumulate and lead to increased stress. Further, disrupted family interaction leads to an intolerant discipline style that in turn fosters antisocial behavior in the child (Patterson & Dishion, 1988).

Unemployment, with its consequent economic deprivation, is another cause of family tension. A considerable body of research has shown an association between paternal job loss and intrafamily violence, including partner abuse and child abuse (Luster & Okagaki, 1993; McLoyd et al., 2006). The possible explanations offered are the greater amount of time the father spends at home, which increases the possibility of conflict; an increase in the father's disciplinary role; a reaffirmation of the father's power in order to save face; and tension from diminished economic resources.

Finally, it has been shown that crises or stress do not always disrupt family functioning. The type of stressor, personalities, and relationships within the family, as well as the presence of social support networks outside the nuclear family, are influential factors (Cochran, 1993; Walsh, 2006; Yogman & Brazelton, 1986).

Authoritarian:	↑ Demandingness/Control	↓ Acceptance/Responsiveness
Authoritative:	↑ Demandingness/Control	↑ Acceptance/Responsiveness
Permissive:	↓ Demandingness/Control	↑ Acceptance/Responsiveness
Uninvolved:	↓ Demandingness/Control	↓ Acceptance/Responsiveness

FIGURE 4.2 **Dimensions of Parenting Styles**
Source: Based on Maccoby and Martin, 1983.

Parenting Styles

How do parents implement their roles as parents?

Parenting style encompasses the emotional climate in which child-rearing behaviors are expressed (Cowan, Powell, & Cowan, 1998). Parenting styles are usually classified by the dimensions of *acceptance/responsiveness* (warmth/sensitivity) and *demandingness/control* (permissiveness/restrictiveness) (Maccoby & Martin, 1983). Parents who are accepting/responsive give affection, provide encouragement, and are sensitive to their children's needs; parents who are unaccepting/unresponsive are rejecting, critical, and insensitive to their children's needs. Parents who are demanding/controlling set rules for children and monitor their compliance; parents who are undemanding/uncontrolling make few demands on children and allow them much autonomy. Parents who are neither responsive nor demanding are considered to be indifferent, or *uninvolved.* See Figure 4.2 for variations on the major dimensions of parenting styles.

Microsystem Influences: Between Parent and Child

What significant child outcomes are affected by the parent–child interaction?

A microsystem effect on children is the bidirectional parent–child relationship within the family. Research has shown parenting styles to have an impact on children's behavior, and vice versa, in such areas as attachment, self-regulation, prosocial behavior, competence, and achievement motivation. *Attachment*, introduced in Chapter 2, is an affectional tie that one person forms to another person, binding them together in space and enduring over time. *Self-regulation*, also introduced in Chapter 2, is the process of bringing one's emotions, thoughts, and/or behavior under control. **Prosocial behavior** involves behavior that benefits other people, such as altruism, sharing, and cooperation. **Competence** refers to a pattern of effective adaptation to one's environment; it involves behavior that is socially responsible, independent, friendly, cooperative, dominant, achievement-oriented, and purposeful. *Achievement motivation*, introduced in Chapter 2, refers to the tendency to approach challenging tasks with confidence of mastery.

prosocial behavior behavior that benefits other people, such as altruism, sharing, and cooperation

competence refers to a pattern of effective adaptation to one's environment; it involves behavior that is socially responsible, independent, friendly, cooperative, dominant, and achievement-oriented

uninvolved a style of insensitive, indifferent parenting with few demands or rules

Parenting styles, as we saw in Chapter 2, are usually described in terms of major dimensions or degrees: *authoritative* (democratic), *authoritarian* (parent-centered), and *permissive* (child-centered). More detailed definitions of the basic parenting styles can be found in the "In Practice" box. A fourth parenting style, **uninvolved**—insensitive, indifferent parenting with few demands or rules—is discussed later with inappropriate parenting practices.

Some classic contemporary books exemplifying the various parenting styles are:

- **Authoritarian.** *Discipline: The Brazelton Way* (Brazelton & Sparrow, 2003)
- **Authoritative.** *The New Dare to Discipline Book* (Dobson, 1996)
- **Permissive.** *The Successful Child: What Parents Can Do to Help Children Turn Out Well* (Sears, Sears, & Pantley, 2002).

TeachSource Video Activity

Go to the Education CourseMate website to access a learning module entitled "Early Childhood: Parenting." Which parenting style(s) do you believe you were exposed to as a child?

It must be realized that parents seldom fall into one category or one extreme; they are often a mixture. Parenting is so complex that it is often influenced by such factors as the

IN PRACTICE

Basic Parenting Styles

1. The ***permissive*** parent attempts to behave in a nonpunitive, acceptable, and affirmative manner toward the child's impulses, desires, and actions. He or she consults with him/her about policy decisions and gives explanations for family rules. He or she makes few demands for household responsibility and orderly behavior. He or she presents herself to the child as a resource for him/her to use as he/she wishes, not as an active agent responsible for shaping or altering his ongoing or future behavior. He or she allows the child to regulate his/her own activities as much as possible, avoids the exercise of control, and does not encourage him/her to obey externally defined standards. He or she attempts to use reason but not overt power to accomplish his/her ends (Baumrind, 1968, p. 256).
2. The ***authoritarian*** parent attempts to shape, control, and evaluate the behavior and attitudes of the child in accordance with a set standard of conduct, usually an absolute standard, theologically motivated and formulated by a higher authority. He or she values obedience as a virtue and favors punitive, forceful measures to curb self-will at points where the child's actions or beliefs conflict with what he or she thinks is right conduct. He or she believes in inculcating such instrumental values as respect for authority, respect for work, and respect for the preservation of order and traditional structure. He or she does not encourage verbal give and take, believing that the child should accept her word for what is right (Baumrind, 1968, p. 261).
3. The ***authoritative*** parent attempts to direct the child's activities but in a rational, issue-oriented manner. He or she encourages verbal give and take, and shares with the child the reasoning behind her policy. He or she values both expressive and instrumental attributes, both autonomous self-will and disciplined conformity. Therefore, he or she exerts firm control at points of parent–child divergence, but does not hem the child in with restrictions. He or she recognizes his/her own special rights as an adult, but also the child's individual interests and special ways. The authoritative parent affirms the child's present qualities, but also sets standards for future conduct. He or she uses reason as well as power to achieve his/her objectives. He or she does not base decisions on group consensus or the individual child's desires, but also does not regard himself/herself as infallible or divinely inspired (Baumrind, 1968, p. 261).

social context (for example, church versus Little League), the particular situation (Is the child in danger? Is the parent stressed?) (Grusec & Davidov, 2007); the child's age, gender, birth order, and siblings; the child's temperament, including how the child responds to parental demands (Kochanska, Askan, & Carlson, 2005); the parent's previous experience (Dunn et al., 2000), including how the parent was parented; the parent's temperament; and the parents' cultural or religious values (Parke & Buriel, 2006). In order to better understand the effects of parenting styles on children's behavior, researchers base their findings on the parenting styles observed most frequently in various situations.

The scolding a child gets from a parent for wrongdoing exemplifies the authoritarian parenting style.

BananaStock/Jupiter Images

Attachment

As mentioned in Chapter 2, attachment is an outcome of sensitive, responsive caregiving. It provides the basis for socialization because infants who are securely attached are willing to comply with parental standards.

Parenting behavior toward the baby influences attachment (Cummings & Cummings, 2002). When a parent responds appropriately, being sensitive and responsive to the baby's signals, the baby forms a *secure* attachment; when a parent responds inappropriately, inconsistently, or not at all, the baby tends to form an *insecure* attachment. According to Ainsworth and colleagues (Ainsworth et al., 1978), appropriately responsive caregiving involves paying attention to the baby's signals, interpreting them accurately, giving appropriate feedback, and responding promptly (enabling the baby to learn that his or her stimuli cause a response). For example, parents of securely attached babies synchronize their interactions according to the baby's activity (DeWolff & van IJzendoorn, 1997). When the baby is alert and active, they stimulate. When the baby is fussy, they soothe. When the baby is tired, they put him or her to sleep. Parents of insecurely attached babies may ignore the baby's signals; they may respond ineffectively or inappropriately. For example, a mother may give her baby a bottle or her breast when the baby is hungry, but be talking on the phone or reading rather than gazing at the infant to adjust to his or her needs.

The verbal give-and-take discussion between this father and son exemplifies the authoritative parenting style.

Frank Siteman/Index Stock Imagery/PhotoLibrary

To measure the quality of attachment in infants ages 1 to 2, researchers commonly use a classic experiment known as the *strange situation* (Ainsworth et al., 1978). In the strange situation, the parent brings the child to a laboratory playroom equipped with toys. The parent leaves the room briefly and the infant's behavior is monitored. A stranger enters the room and the infant's behavior is recorded. The stranger leaves and the parent returns. The following types of attachment have been observed in the strange situation

1. **Secure attachment (secure).** The infant actively explores the environment in the mother's presence, is upset when she leaves, and seeks contact when she returns. (The infant may accept the stranger's attention when the mother is present.)
2. **Resistant attachment (insecure).** The infant stays close to the mother, doesn't explore, becomes upset when the mother leaves, is wary of strangers, and resists physical contact with the mother when she returns.
3. **Avoidant attachment (insecure).** The infant shows little distress when the mother leaves, may ignore or avoid the stranger, and ignores the mother when she returns.
4. **Disorganized/disoriented attachment (insecure).** The infant is very upset by the strange situation and appears confused about whether to approach or avoid the stranger; when the mother returns, the infant may seek contact and then withdraw (Main & Solomon, 1990).

The significance of the quality of attachment is that it correlates with later intellectual and social development (Lamb et al., 1999). Securely attached infants tend to be more attentive, curious, and confident, exploring various physical environments, exhibiting more social competence with peers, and being more compliant with adults in the preschool years.

Self-Regulation and Prosocial Behavior

Baumrind's classic studies (1966, 1967, 1971, 1973) showed a strong correlation between parenting practices (studied via interviews) and observed self-regulation and prosocial behavior of American middle-class preschool children. Later studies (Brophy, 1989; Forman & Kochanska, 2001; Hart, DeWolf, & Burts, 1992) have supported Baumrind's findings that parenting style affects children's behavior. Table 4.2 outlines the relationship between parenting and children's behavior.

According to Baumrind, both the *authoritarian* and the *permissive* parents in her studies had unrealistic beliefs about young children. Whereas the strict or authoritarian parents thought the child's behavior must be constrained, the permissive parents tended to look at the child's behavior as natural and refreshing. Neither group seemed to take

Table 4.2 Relationship of Parenting Styles to Children's Behavior

Parenting Style	Characteristics	Children's Behavior
Authoritative (democratic) "Do it because. . ."	Controlling but flexible Demanding but rational Warm Receptive to child's communication Values discipline, self-reliance, and uniqueness	Self-reliant Self-controlled explorative Content Cooperative
Authoritarian (adult-centered) "Do it!"	Strict control (self-will curbed by punitive measures) Evaluation of child's behavior and attitudes with absolute standard Values obedience, respect for authority, and tradition	Discontent Withdrawn Fearful Distrustful
Permissive (child-centered) "Do you want to do it?"	Noncontrolling Nondemanding Acceptance of child's impulses Consults with child on policies	Poor self-reliance Impulsive Aggressive Hardly explorative Poor self-control
Uninvolved (insensitive and indifferent) "Do what you want."	Noncontrolling Nondemanding Indifferent to child's point of view and activities	Deficits in attachment, cognition, emotional and social skills, and behavior Poor self-control Low self-esteem

Source: Based on Baumrind (1967, 1971, 1991).

into account the child's stage of development—for example, the desire in early childhood to model parental behavior or the inability in early childhood to reason when given a parental command. Thus, Baumrind and others (Steinberg, 2001; Steinberg et al., 1994) endorsed the *authoritative* parenting style for adapting to the European American values of independence, individualism, achievement, and self-regulation. Authoritative parents take into account their children's needs as well as their own before deciding how to deal with a situation. They exert control over their children's behavior when necessary, yet they respect their children's need to make their own decisions. Reasoning is used to explain parenting policies, and communication from the children is encouraged. Children experience democracy at home.

Most early parenting research involved young children, but more recent studies have included adolescents in order to reveal the long-term effects of parenting styles (Baumrind, 1991; Holmbeck, Paikoff, & Brooks-Gunn, 1995; Steinberg, 2001). Dornbusch and his colleagues (Dornbusch et al., 1987) found that *authoritative* parenting is positively correlated, and *authoritarian* and *permissive* parenting negatively correlated, with adolescent school performance. Steinberg and his colleagues (Steinberg, Elmen, & Mounts, 1989; Steinberg et al., 1991) confirmed the relationship between authoritative parenting and academic performance. They explained it as being due to the effects of authoritativeness on the development of a healthy sense of autonomy and, more specifically, on the development of a healthy psychological orientation toward work. Thus, authoritative parenting influences not only how a child behaves in the early years but also how a child deals with responsibility, as exhibited in adolescence.

Authoritative parenting is *not* the norm among various cultural and socioeconomic groups in the United States and other countries. More common is the authoritarian style utilized by groups that closely adhere to their traditional cultural values (Greenfield, Suzuki, & Rothstein-Fisch, 2006). Cultural values, as we have discussed, are adaptive to the environment in which members of the group grow up.

Characteristic of some cultures, certain values, such as respect for elders and the need for social order, may influence child-rearing methods. For example, whereas authoritarian parenting is perceived by Americans and Europeans to be strict and regimented, stressing adult domination, it is perceived by Chinese people to be a means of training (*chaio shun*) and governing (*guan*) children in an involved and physically close way (Chao, 1994, 2001). The Chinese concept of authoritarianism comes from the Confucian emphasis on hierarchical relationships and social order. Standards exist, not to dominate the child, but to preserve the integrity of the family unit and assure harmonious relations with others (Greenfield, Suzuki, & Rothstein-Fisch, 2006).

Characteristic of lower socioeconomic statuses, certain conditions, such as lack of social supports or living in dangerous neighborhoods, may make strict discipline (authoritarian style) necessary to protect children from becoming involved in antisocial activities (Brody & Flor, 1998; Ogbu, 1994).

Thus, Baumrind's definition of authoritarian parenting (controlling without warmth) and child development outcomes (discontent, withdrawal, distrust, lack of instrumental competence) does *not* always apply cross-culturally or across social classes.

Socioemotional and Cognitive Competence

Competence, as defined earlier, refers to a pattern of effective adaptation to one's environment; it involves behavior that is socially responsible, independent, friendly, cooperative, dominant, achievement-oriented, and purposeful. Masten and Coatsworth (1998) reviewed studies on competence and resilience to stressful events in both favorable and unfavorable environments. They found the key ingredient in the development of adaptive skills leading to competence and resilience to be secure parent–child relationships and encouragement of cognition and self-regulation (includes attention, emotion, and behavior). Studies of factors that promote competence and resilience are significant for the development of early childhood intervention programs for children in unfavorable environments.

Burton White (1971) and his colleagues at Harvard (White & Watts, 1973) studied the relationship between parenting styles and the development of *competence* versus *incompetence* in preschoolers. First, they had preschool teachers rate children ages 3–6, representing different socioeconomic statuses, as "competent" or "incompetent" (see Table 4.3). Then, to find out when the differences in competence appeared, the researchers went into the homes of the competent and incompetent children who had younger siblings and observed the mother–child interaction from infancy to age 3.

No differences in competency were found between infants who were siblings of competent versus incompetent children. Yet by 10 months of age, differences in competency began to show up; by age 2, and often as early as 18 months, children could be classified as competent or incompetent. What is so significant about the period of development between 10 and 18 months? This period is the time when children begin to talk, walk, explore, and assert themselves. It is during this time that the parenting style is revealed—a good example of the bidirectionality of the parent–child relationship. How did the parenting styles differ?

Table 4.3 The Harvard Preschool Project: Differences in Learning

Competent Children	Incompetent Children
Get attention in socially acceptable ways	Remain unnoticed or are disruptive
Use adults as resources	Need a lot of direction to complete a task
Get along well with others	Have difficulty getting along with others
Plan and carry out complicated tasks	Lack ability to anticipate consequences
Use and understand complex sentences	Have a simplistic vocabulary

Parenting Style Differences of Mothers of Competent and Incompetent Children

Generally, the mothers of competent children were flexible, responding to their child as needed and adjusting the environment accordingly. In contrast, the mothers of incompetent children were either rigid, structuring the interaction with the child and the environment according to their standards; or they were lax, being unresponsive to the child and his or her environment. Specifically, mothers of *competent* children:

- Designed a safe physical environment at home so their children could explore and discover things on their own.
- Provided interesting things to manipulate; these could be pots and spoons as well as commercial toys.
- Spent no more than 10 percent of their time deliberately interacting with their children, yet they were always "on call" when needed.
- Made themselves available to share in their children's exciting discoveries, answer their children's questions, or help their children in an activity for a few minutes here and there while they went about their daily routines.
- Enjoyed their children and were patient, energetic, and tolerant of messes, accidents, and natural curiosity.
- Set limits on behavior and were firm and consistent in their discipline.
- Disciplined according to age—used distraction with infants under age 1; distraction and physical removal of either the child or the object from age 1 to 1½; and distraction, physical distance, and firm words after age 1½.

Mothers of *incompetent* children:

- Some spent little time with their children; they were overwhelmed by their daily struggles, and their homes were disorganized.
- Some spent a great deal of time with their children; they were overprotective and pushed their children to learn.
- Some provided for their children materially, such as giving them toys, but restricted their children's instinct to explore by ruling certain places and possessions out of bounds.
- Most used playpens and gates extensively.

In sum, White's research has shown that human competence develops between 10 and 18 months, and it is the parenting style that fosters competence. According to White (1995), the informal education provided by families for their children has more of an impact on a child's total educational development than does the formal educational system. Such an informal initial education essentially enables the child to "learn how to learn," or be motivated to achieve.

Research on school-age children confirms the connection between parenting style and competence/achievement in school (Grolnick & Ryan, 1989; Wigfield & Eccles, 2002). Other researchers (Gauvain & Perez, 2007) might classify White's findings as a social approach to cognitive development. The social processes involved are collaboration, guided participation, parent–child conversation, observational learning, and participation in socially organized activities.

To assess the relationship of the environment provided by families to the achievement motivation and consequent cognitive development of the child, Caldwell, Bradley, and colleagues (Bradley, 2002; Bradley, Caldwell, & Rock, 1990; Caldwell & Bradley, 1984) developed an assessment scale to determine the quality of the home environment for children under age 3. This scale, called HOME (Home Observation for the Measurement of the Environment), contains 45 items in the following six areas:

1. **Emotional and verbal responsiveness.** The parent responded to the child's vocalizations with verbal response.
2. **Avoidance of restriction and punishment.** The parent did not interfere with the child's actions or prohibit him or her more than three times during the observation.
3. **Organization of the physical and temporal environment.** The child's play environment was accessible to him or her and was safe.
4. **Provision of appropriate play materials.** The child had toys that were safe and age-appropriate, and that stimulated play.
5. **Parental interaction with the child.** The parent kept the child within visual range and looked at, touched, or talked to the child frequently.
6. **Opportunities for variety in daily stimulation.** The parent read stories or played games with child.

Studies examining the relation between young diverse preschoolers' HOME scores and their IQ scores, as well as later academic achievement in middle school (Wen-Jui, Leventhal, & Linver, 2004), showed a strong positive correlation (Bradley, Caldwell, & Rock, 1990). Also, as White's group discovered, the most critical time for influencing a child's achievement motivation and intellectual development is the first two years of life.

What about the relationship between home environment and adolescence? A HOME scale version was later developed to measure the quantity and quality of stimulation, support, and structure available to diverse children age 10 through 15 in their home environments. There was a significant relationship between family context and cognitive development (Bradley et al., 2000).

Mesosystem Influences: Between Parent and Others

How do links between parents and significant others affect child outcomes?

The impact of parental socialization techniques is enhanced by supportive links with other microsystems, such as the school and the community (Bronfenbrenner & Morris, 2006; Cochran & Niego, 2002). (See Table 4.4.) When family and school or community values are collaborative, positive child outcomes are likely; when family and school or community values are conflicted, the child is at risk for school failure, delinquency, and substance abuse (Sameroff, 2006; Wang, 2000). An example of where family and community (especially business community) values are likely to differ is in the amount of consumerism thrust at children through advertising, promotional games and rewards, and product displays.

Table 4.4 Bioecological Influences on Parenting Styles

Child Characteristics	Family Characteristics	Community Characteristics
Age and cognitive development	Size (number of siblings)	Supportive social environments
Temperament (easy, slow to warm up, difficult)	Configuration (birth order, spacing, gender of siblings)	Informal network: gemeinschaft relationships
Gender	Life stage Marital quality	Formal network: gesellschaft relationships
Presence of a special need	Abilities to cope with stress	

IN PRACTICE

Do You Need Help Parenting? Get a Coach

When most people become parents they do not realize the complexity and difficulty of parenting children.

Historically, and in some cultures today, new parents could rely on members of their extended families for advice and support. But today, as family generations disperse, the wise grandmother or aunt is unavailable. So, in a society accustomed to getting personal expertise (we hire trainers, nutritionists, therapists, and so on), it is a small leap to hiring a parenting coach.

Parenting coaches are generally professionals, including trained psychotherapists, child development specialists, educators, or social workers who have become entrepreneurs. The services, less expensive than traditional therapy, focus on solving specific problems, such as toilet training, sibling rivalry, bullies and victims, divorce, or school transitions. The coach may come to the home, or training sessions may take place in an office. The coach is also available for phone advice.

Source: Blankenstein, A., & Hall, C. (2007). "Need help, parents? Get a coach." *Los Angeles Times*, September 23, pp. B1, B14.

School

Families' links to schools via parent education, conferences with children's teachers, and participation in school activities can have positive effects on parenting (Epstein & Sanders, 2002; Epstein & Sheldon, 2006). Even parents of adolescents who take time to talk to their children about school, homework, and activities, and who show support and confidence in their abilities, have adolescents who are achievement-oriented (Wang & Wildman, 1995). Aspects of family involvement in schools are discussed in Chapters 6 and 7.

Community

The community is considered here to include social environments outside the family context of parenting. They can be supportive in helping parents cope with stress (Crnic & Acevedo, 1995). Relatives and friends are examples of *informal* supports; psychologists and employers are examples of *formal* supports. Each of these types of social support systems can provide instrumental (physical and financial) support, emotional support, and informational support (Bugental & Grusec, 2006). Formal support systems are discussed in Chapter 10.

Parenting practices are influenced by the neighborhood in which a family resides, such as rural or urban, safe or unsafe, stable or mobile (Bugental & Grusec, 2006). It has been found that when parents perceive their neighborhoods to be dangerous and low in social control, they place more restrictions on their children's activities (Cebello & McLoyd, 2002). To illustrate, residence in a neighborhood with high levels of crime, low levels of economic opportunity, poor transportation, and weak marital support can affect a single mother's commitment to seek employment and find child care (Duncan & Raudenbush, 2001). On the other hand, parents in lower-risk neighborhoods, with neighbors who have similar norms, expectations, and values about child rearing, are less likely to need so many restrictions (Parke & Buriel, 2006) because they feel connected and are more likely to intervene for the common good (Small & Supple, 2001).

What constitutes appropriate parenting behavior?

Appropriate Parenting Practices

Appropriate parenting practices involve knowledge of child development—what a child is capable of physically, emotionally, cognitively, and socially—as well as preventive and corrective methods for misbehavior.

Child protection agencies are required to use objective, standardized risk-assessment instruments, such as Child at Risk Field (CARF), to define parenting practices on a continuum from *appropriate* at one end to *inappropriate* at the other, in order to assess whether intervention is required (DePanfilis, 2006; Dubowitz & DePanfilis, 2000).

Appropriate parenting:

1. considers the child's age capacity;
2. maintains reasonable expectations for the child;
3. considers and works with the child's strengths/limitations/needs;
4. utilizes a range of acceptable disciplinary approaches;
5. gives basic care, nurturing, and support;
6. models self-control.

This mother is being responsive to her child.

Cengage Learning

The National Institute of Child Health and Human Development (2009) has put decades of parenting research into an easy-to-read booklet, *Adventures in Parenting*, that enables parents to make informed decisions based on the applicability of child development principles to their child (see http://www.nichd.nih.gov/publications). It is updated periodically online. The main principles are as follows:

- Respond to your child in an appropriate manner.
- Prevent risky behavior or problems before they arise.
- Monitor your child's contact with his or her surrounding world.
- Mentor your child to support and encourage desired behaviors.
- Model your own behavior to provide a consistent and positive example for children.

Developmental Appropriateness

Developmental appropriateness involves knowledge of children's normal growth patterns and individual differences. Appropriate parenting practices are influenced by parents' understanding of what is developmentally appropriate behavior in their child. Appropriate parenting practices can also reflect a knowledge of socialization methods (described in Chapter 2). For example, when is it appropriate to use *guidance*, a preventive socialization method, and *discipline*, a corrective socialization method?

developmental appropriateness involves knowledge of children's normal growth patterns and individual differences

Understanding why children misbehave can help parents choose an effective parenting method. Children sometimes misbehave because they are tired, hungry, uncomfortable, or sick. Sometimes children don't understand what is expected of them or why they did something wrong. Children may react to parental demands with anger, such as when they are told they can't have the candy displayed at the supermarket. They may misbehave when they are fearful, such as when left in a new and strange place. They may be jealous when a new sibling arrives and misbehave to get attention. They may feel hurt or disappointed when an adult lets them down, as by not fulfilling a promise or when parents divorce, and react with revenge.

Guidance and Discipline

Guidance involves direction, demonstration, supervision, and influence. One who guides "leads the way." **Discipline** involves punishment, correction, and training to develop self-control. One who disciplines enforces obedience or order. Both guidance and discipline are necessary socialization methods in child rearing. Sensitivity to the situation, the child's temperament, and the desired outcome are some of the factors involved in deciding which is appropriate at a particular time. (See Figure 4.3.)

guidance involves direction, demonstration, supervision, and influence

discipline involves punishment, correction, and training to develop self-control

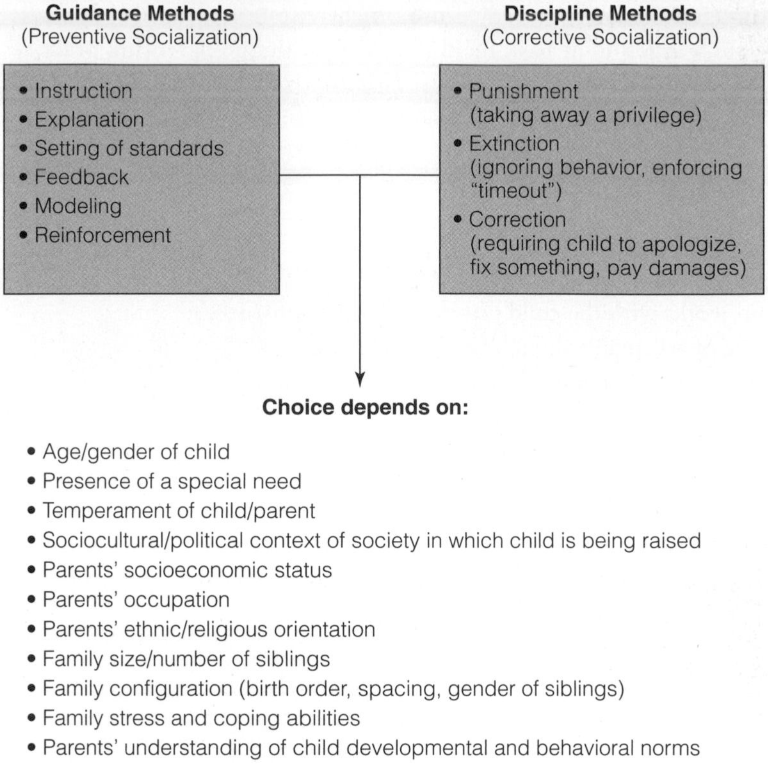

Guidance Methods
(Preventive Socialization)
• Instruction
• Explanation
• Setting of standards
• Feedback
• Modeling
• Reinforcement
Discipline Methods
(Corrective Socialization)
• Punishment
(taking away a privilege)
• Extinction
(ignoring behavior, enforcing "timeout")
• Correction
(requiring child to apologize, fix something, pay damages)
Choice depends on:
• Age/gender of child
• Presence of a special need
• Temperament of child/parent
• Sociocultural/political context of society in which child is being raised
• Parents' socioeconomic status
• Parents' occupation
• Parents' ethnic/religious orientation
• Family size/number of siblings
• Family configuration (birth order, spacing, gender of siblings)
• Family stress and coping abilities
• Parents' understanding of child developmental and behavioral norms

FIGURE 4.3 **Parental Practices: Guidance and Discipline**

What constitutes inappropriate parenting behavior?

Inappropriate Parenting Practices

Inappropriate parenting, as objectively defined by "child-at-risk" criteria (DePanfilis, 2006; Dubowitz & DePanfilis, 2000):

1. is based on the parent's needs;
2. demonstrates expectations that are impossible for the child to meet;
3. ignores the child's strengths/limitations/needs; shows an aversion to parenting;
4. employs extreme/harsh disciplinary approaches, including violence, threats, and verbal assaults;
5. generally does not provide basic care and/or support;
6. deliberately takes frustrations out on the child; is self-righteous.

Child Maltreatment: Abuse and Neglect

maltreatment intentional harm to or endangerment of a child

Maltreatment is any intentional harm to or endangerment of a child. It includes unkindness, harshness, rejection, neglect, deprivation, abuse, and/or violence (Cicchetti & Toth, 2005). It is a broader term than abuse and neglect and can be viewed as a continuum, with homicide at one extreme and parental force for disciplinary purposes at the other (Kalichman, 1999; Pagelow, 1982). Child maltreatment occurs in all economic, social, cultural, and religious groups (see http://childwelfare.gov).

Cultures differ in what constitutes maltreatment (Goodman, Emery, & Haugaard, 1998). However, it is generally agreed that maltreating parents fail to meet the physical or emotional needs of the developing child, and in many cases the trust the child places in the parent is betrayed (Starr, 1990). Child maltreatment constitutes inappropriate parenting in that it may result in child maladaptation (Bolger & Patterson, 2001; Maughan & Cicchetti, 2002).

Research (Cicchetti & Lynch, 1993; Cicchetti & Toth, 2005; Shonk & Cicchetti, 2001) suggests that maltreatment during childhood has far-reaching consequences in adulthood, such as inability to trust, low self-esteem, depression, relationship problems, sexual problems, learning difficulties, eating disorders, and alcohol or drug problems. A review of the research on child maltreatment (Maas, Herrenkohl, & Sousa, 2008) found a relationship between child maltreatment and youth violence perpetration, with physical abuse being the most consistent predictor of youth violence. The lack of normal nurturing during childhood may result in the adult need to replace the missing love and security with externals, such as drugs, alcohol, food, material objects, sex, gambling, and relationships (Farmer, 1989).

This boy was physically abused by his father for dropping a bottle of juice which broke on the floor.

ejwhite/Shutterstock.com

What can be done to help children who are maltreated? Although parents in our society have the fundamental right to raise their children as they see fit, the Fourteenth Amendment of the U.S. Constitution, which states that *everyone* has equal protection under the law, warrants legal intervention when the safety of the child is in jeopardy. Intervention may involve the filing of criminal charges, referral to community agencies for counseling and treatment, and/or removal of the child from the care and custody of the parent, guardian, or caregiver. Every state has child protective laws with varying procedures.

The federal Child Abuse Prevention and Treatment Act (CAPTA), as amended by the Keeping Children and Families Safe Act of 2003, defines, at minimum, child abuse and neglect as

- Any recent act, as failure to act, on the part of a parent or caretaker which results in death, serious physical or emotional harm, sexual abuse or exploitation; or
- An act, or failure to act, which presents an imminent risk of serious harm.

To better understand the forms child maltreatment may take, they are examined separately even though they may occur simultaneously. **Abuse** is defined as maltreatment that includes physical abuse, sexual abuse, and psychological or emotional abuse. **Neglect** is defined as maltreatment involving abandonment, lack of supervision, improper feeding, lack of adequate medical or dental care, inappropriate dress, uncleanliness, and lack of safety.

abuse maltreatment that includes physical abuse, sexual abuse, and psychological or emotional abuse

neglect maltreatment involving abandonment, lack of supervision, improper feeding, lack of adequate medical or dental care, inappropriate dress, uncleanliness, and lack of safety

Physical Abuse

Physical abuse is maltreatment involving deliberate harm to the child's body. Physically abused children include those who are intentionally bruised, wounded, or burned. Some physical abuse takes place under the guise of discipline. The places on children's bodies where they are wounded and the shape of the wound can give clues that indicate abuse rather than accident. Physical beating with a hand or an object, such as a belt or hairbrush, is the most common cause of physical abuse; other sources include kicking, shaking, choking, burning with cigarettes or scalding in hot water, freezing, and throwing the child around.

physical abuse maltreatment involving deliberate harm to the child's body

Physical abuse of children is more likely to occur in families where there is domestic violence—verbal conflict or physical aggression between partners (Dodge, Bates, & Pettit, 1990). Research shows a direct relation between physical abuse, aggressive behavior in children, and juvenile delinquency in adolescents (Maas, Herrenkohl, & Sousa, 2008; Rogosch et al., 1995). These effects may be due in part to modeling and in part to deficient abilities to process social information (Dodge, Bates, & Pettit, 1990). In other words, adolescents attribute hostile intentions to others, and they lack strategies to solve interpersonal problems.

Sexual Abuse

Sexual abuse occurs whenever any person forces, tricks, or threatens a child in order to have sexual contact with him or her. This contact can include such nontouching

sexual abuse maltreatment in which a person forces, tricks, or threatens a child in order to have sexual contact with him or her

IN PRACTICE

Things Parents Should Never Do

1. Never call children derogatory names.
2. Never threaten to leave your child.
3. Never say, "I wish you were never born!"
4. Never sabotage the parenting efforts of your spouse.
5. Never punish when you've lost control of yourself.
6. Never expect a child to think, feel, or behave like an adult.

behaviors as an adult's exposing himself or herself, or asking a child to look at pornographic material. It includes behaviors ranging from the sexual handling of a child (fondling) to genital contact, intercourse, and violent rape. In all instances of child sexual abuse, the child is being used as an object to satisfy the adult's sexual needs or desires. The offender often uses bribery, manipulation to secrecy with threats, and psychological power over the child because most sexual abuse occurs with an adult the child knows and trusts (Finkelhor, 1984). Both young girls and boys can be victims.

Children who are sexually abused often go through phases of (1) secrecy, (2) helplessness, (3) entrapment and accommodation, (4) delayed, conflicted, and unconvincing disclosure, and (5) retraction (Goodman et al., 1998). These phases can be explained by realizing that the child is vulnerable to a more powerful and knowledgeable adult. The adult demands secrecy and threatens the child if he or she tells—"I'll take your cat away." "Your mom will spank you." Thus, to enable the child to share, one must ensure a supportive and nonpunitive response.

Due to their nature, children are trusting and obedient. Due to their age and lack of experience, as well as their dependence on adults, they are vulnerable to incest and molestation. Most sexual assaults follow a gradually escalating pattern in which the perpetrator first attempts to gain the child's trust and affection before attempting sexual contact (Koblinsky & Behana, 1984).

Child victims may experience guilt, anxiety, confusion, shame, embarrassment, fear, sadness, and a sense of being bad or dirty. Every child reacts differently. Some child victims do not understand that the abuse is "sexual" in nature; therefore, they may find some elements of the abuse pleasant if the abuse is not forceful or scary.

The way certain adults view children provides a clue to why sexual abuse takes place. These adults feel that children in their care are their property to do with as they wish. A great myth of child abuse is that the child wants sex (O'Brien, 1984). Child sexual abusers also exhibit characteristics of low self-esteem, poor impulse control, and childish emotional needs (Koblinsky & Behana, 1984). They themselves were likely to have been abused as children.

incest sexual relations between persons closely related

Incest, or sexual relations between persons closely related, deserves special attention. The closer the victim and offender are emotionally, the greater trauma the victim experiences. Ongoing incest, or sexual abuse by someone close to the family, can disrupt necessary psychological developmental tasks of a child. Victims may develop poor social skills with peers their own age, often feel unable to trust people—yet desperately want to trust—and may become depressed, suicidal, self-destructive, and confused about their sexuality. A high percentage of drug abusers, juvenile runaways, and prostitutes have been sexually abused as children.

psychological or emotional abuse maltreatment involving a destructive pattern of continual attack by an adult on a child's development of self and social competence, including rejecting, isolating, terrorizing, ignoring, and corrupting

Psychological or Emotional Abuse

Psychological or emotional abuse is maltreatment involving a destructive pattern of continued attack by an adult on a child's development of self and social competence, taking the forms of rejecting, isolating, terrorizing, ignoring, and corrupting (Garbarino, Guttman, & Seely, 1986). Psychological or emotional abuse can occur when parents are inconsistent in their talk, rules, or actions; when they have unrealistic expectations of their children; when they belittle and blame their children; when they do not take an interest in any of their children's activities; or when they do not ever praise their children. For example, a mother leaving a dance class with her sobbing 5-year-old daughter said, "Why can't you learn the positions like the others? You always embarrass me. Sometimes I can't believe you're really my daughter."

Parents who psychologically abuse their children are prompted not by the child's misbehavior, but by their own psychological problems. They are usually people who received inadequate love and nurturing from their own parents (Helfer, Kempe, & Krugman, 1999). Parents may use a steady stream of verbal abuse that discounts the child's achievements and blows out of proportion every sign of misbehavior. Words like *always*, *never*, and *should* imply that a child invariably fails to live up to a parent's expectations. Psychologically abusive parents may display irrational expectations so that normal behavior is seen as a deficiency on the part of the child and a failure on the part of the parent. For example, forgetting to give the parent change from lunch money may be viewed as stealing rather than a mistake.

Psychological abuse is also associated with physical and sexual abuse as well as neglect. Exposure to domestic violence, a form of psychological abuse, also results in emotional, social, behavioral, and learning problems (Margolin, 1998; Maughan & Cicchetti, 2002).

Causes and Consequences of Child Maltreatment

Why does child maltreatment occur?

To understand the causes of child abuse and neglect, one has to examine not only the family interactions, but also the cultural attitudes sanctioning violence and aggression as well as the community support system (Rogosch et al., 1995). Figure 4.4 provides a model to illustrate the interaction among child, family, community, and cultural factors involved in maltreatment. For example, some influences on child maltreatment include the temperament of the child, marital distress, unemployment, and lack of community support, as well as cultural values such as tolerance for violence and a view of the child as property (Belsky, 1993; Emery, 1989).

Before predicting maltreatment, risk and resilient factors must be weighed (Cicchetti & Toth, 2005; Kalichman, 1999). *Risk* factors include those that are ongoing, such as parental history of being abused, and those that are transient, such as parent's loss of a job. *Resilient* factors include ongoing ones such as the child's easy temperament and transient ones such as an improvement in the family's financial status.

The Family and Maltreatment

As has been discussed, the process of parenting is very complex. It can be stressful and frustrating, as well as rewarding. Parenting involves the ability to continually give love, support, and guidance. Some individuals, because they themselves were never given love, support, or guidance, do not know how to give them to their own children.

Many abusers have a family history of being maltreated (Rogosch et al., 1995; Starr, 1990). A person who is maltreated feels unworthy, inadequate, and unacceptable. This results in low self-esteem. The next generation tends to model the parenting and attitudes to which it has been exposed. Therefore, unless it can be broken, maltreatment becomes a self-perpetuating cycle.

When children grow up under negative conditions, are scapegoated, are belittled, and are under constant criticism, they cannot develop their full potential or grow to be competent adults. They live out all the negative feelings they have developed as a result of the self-image they have received from their parents or caretakers and are thus prone to character and behavior disorders, self-doubt, and internal anger. They also have difficulty

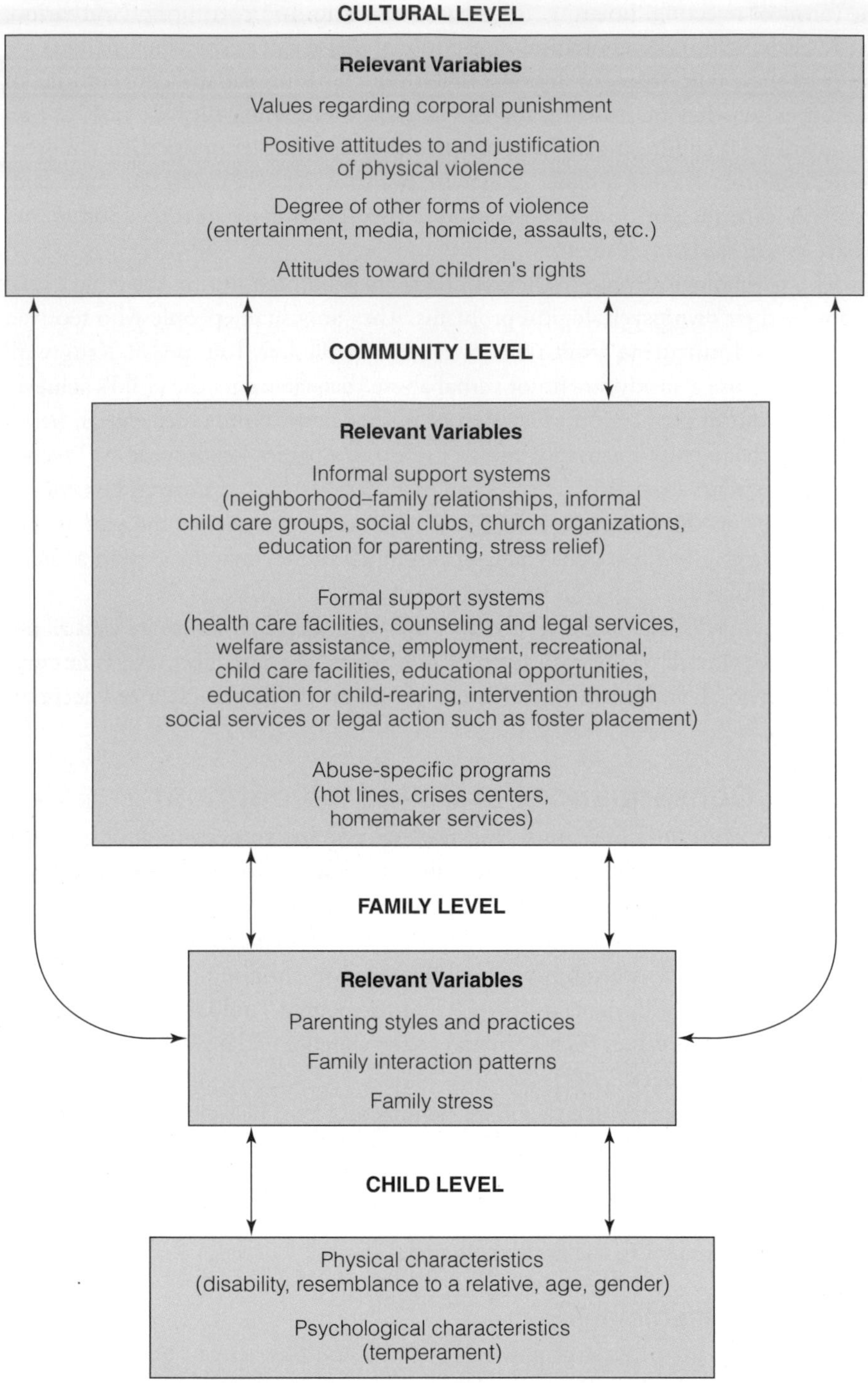

FIGURE 4.4 An Ecological Model of Risk and Resilient Factors in Child Maltreatment

Sources: Adapted from Parke and Lewis, 1981, p. 171; Cicchetti and Lynch, 1993; Cicchetti and Toth, 2005.

regulating their emotions and may avoid displaying their feelings; they have difficulty forming attachments and tend to avoid intimacy; they display more aggressive behaviors; and their cognitive development is often impaired (Lowenthal, 1999).

When life's stresses are added to feelings of inadequacy and lack of parenting skills, child abuse and neglect may be the result. Parents who face emotional problems, financial problems, and stress, who lack knowledge about child development, and who are immature may neglect or abuse their children. Abusive parents lack understanding of child development and consequently often have unrealistic expectations (Azar, 2002). They expect their children to eat when they are fed, not to be messy, to be obedient, to be quiet, and to give love. When children do not behave like adults, the parents lash out at them because their inability to conform to their parents' expectations serves as a reminder of their own inferiority (Farmer, 1989). When parents were themselves abused as children, their ability to control their feelings, in addition to their perspective of parenting, is affected.

IN CONTEXT Debby was reported for child abuse. She had tied her 3-year-old son to the bed because, earlier that morning, he had gone to his friend's house and had not telephoned his mother to report his whereabouts. The little boy sobbed, "But Mommy, I forgot my number." Often, abusive parents believe that their child's behavior is deliberate and purposeful (Helfer, Kempe, & Krugman, 1999). "She spit up on my new blouse because she was mad at me," said a mother of her 1-month-old daughter. "He ran in the street just to frighten me," said a mother of her 2-year-old son.

Parents who abuse their children often have psychological problems. Depression and alcoholism have been linked to abuse (Farmer, 1989; Small, 1987). Abusive parents are emotionally immature and need nurturing themselves. Thus, they look to the child to meet their needs (Farmer, 1989). This behavior, called *role reversal*, is the most commonly observed psychological characteristic in abusive parents (Farmer, 1989). Parents who are abusive, instead of seeing themselves as nurturers of the child, expect the child to meet their needs for love. When the child fails to meet this expectation, abuse results (Belsky, 1993). As one mother of a 3-week-old said, "When he cried all the time no matter what I did, that meant he didn't love me, so I hit him." These parents also lack appropriate knowledge of behavior management and developmental norms. Physical, or corporal, punishment is their only source of control.

The Child and Maltreatment

Certain physical and psychological characteristics have been associated more often with children who are abused than with those who are not (Belsky, 1993)—for example, behaviors such as crying, hyperactivity, and inability to give an acceptable response to the parent. Disabilities, such as mental retardation, were also found to be associated with abuse (Hershkowitz, Lamb, & Horowitz, 2007). Additionally, a child's appearance or behavior that reminds the parents of their own parents or of negative characteristics of themselves was found to contribute to a poor parent–child relationship. Such children may become scapegoats for buried negative feelings.

The Community and Maltreatment

Several researchers have examined effects of the community on maltreatment (Coulton, Crampton, Spillsbury, & Korbine, 2007). The ecology of child maltreatment involves neighborhood impoverishment, housing stress, unemployment, child-care burdens, and availability of alcohol (Freisthler, Merritt & La Scala, 2006). Researchers have also reported that isolation from the community and consequent lack of support is a significant characteristic of families who are abusive (Emery, 1989; Garbarino, 1977). Frequently, such families have no close relatives nearby or have few friends. Therefore, they have no one to turn to for guidance, comfort, or assistance when they need advice or have a problem. They have no one to relieve them of child-care responsibilities when they need to get away from the house occasionally.

The line between physical abuse and acceptable discipline sometimes depends on the interpreter (Kalichman, 1999). Society expects parents to socialize their children to behave acceptably, so to foster acceptable behavior, some parents use physical, or corporal, punishment. Although occasional spankings could not legally be classified as child abuse, parental use of corporal punishment as a means of dealing with behavioral problems may have future undesirable consequences, such as teaching the child to be aggressive to resolve conflicts. To help determine whether corporal punishment should be interpreted as abuse, James Garbarino has defined maltreatment as "acts of omission or commission by a parent or guardian that are judged by a mixture of community values and professional expertise to be inappropriate and damaging" (Garbarino & Gilliam, 1980, p. 7).

Summary

- Parenting means implementing a series of decisions about the socialization of a child.
- Parenting is conducted within various macrosystems, such as political ideology, culture, and economics.
- The socioeconomic status of a family influences parenting style. Generally, parents of lower socioeconomic status are more punitive, emphasizing obedience, whereas parents of higher socioeconomic status use more reasoning, emphasizing independence and creativity.
- Parental occupations (exosystems) influence parenting styles because skills required at work tend to be emphasized at home.
- Parenting styles and practices can be classified as cooperative/interdependent (collectivistic) on one end of the spectrum and competitive/independent (individualistic) on the other.
- Parenting is affected by chronosystem influences, such as historical trends and evolving family dynamics.
- Family dynamics involve the continuous and evolving bidirectional interactions affecting parents and children.
- Parenting styles include four basic types of parenting styles: authoritarian (adult-centered), permissive (child-centered), authoritative (democratic), and uninvolved.
- Appropriate parenting practices are influenced by parental understanding of developmental appropriateness, as well as guidance/discipline techniques. Guidance techniques are preventive, whereas disciplinary techniques are corrective.
- Inappropriate parenting is maltreatment—intentional harm to or endangerment of a child, including abuse and neglect. Parents who maltreat their children fail to meet the physical or emotional needs of the developing child.
- Children who are neglected are those who are abandoned, lack supervision, do not receive proper nutrition, need medical or dental care, are frequently absent or late for school, do not have appropriate or sufficient clothing, are unclean, or live in unsafe or filthy homes.
- Children who are physically abused are those who are intentionally bruised, wounded, or burned.
- Children who are sexually abused are those who are forced, tricked, or threatened to have sexual contact with an individual.
- Children who are psychologically or emotionally abused are those who are exposed to unreasonable demands that are beyond their capabilities; this type of abuse may include persistent teasing, belittling, or verbal attacks.
- Parents in families who abuse their children tend to have been abused themselves as children and/or have emotional problems. They lack knowledge of appropriate child development and have little or no support in their parenting role.

Activity

PURPOSE To examine your values relating to parenting.

1. Write the appropriate requirements for a parenting license. Include (a) physical requirements (health status, age, etc.); (b) psychological requirements (temperament, educational status, etc.); (c) social requirements (marital status, finances, etc.); and (d) experience with children.
2. What would you do?
    - Your 2-year-old has been coming into your bedroom for the past three nights at 3:00 A.M.
    - Three-year-old Charles spills his milk all over the table and begins to cry.
    - Your 4-year-old daughter tells you the 6-year-old boy next door likes to play "doctor."
    - Just as you walk out of the grocery store, you notice your 5-year-old son eating a candy bar that you did not purchase.
    - Your 6-year-old daughter does not want to go to school. You talk to the teacher to find out what the

problem is; the teacher says your daughter is shy and will not participate in class or interact with the other children.

- Your 7- and 9-year-old children have lately been arguing about everything. When they have nothing specific to argue about, like a toy, a game, or a television show, they tease each other.
- Your 9-year-old son is watching the news on television and asks, "What does 'rape' mean?"
- Bill, age 10, has recently begun to ignore your requests to put his things away. He also has been "forgetting" to do his regular chores.
- Your 11-year-old daughter asks to spend the night at a school friend's house, and you have never met the friend's parents.
- Your 12-year-old son makes an online purchase using your credit card.

Related Readings

Brazelton, T. B. (1992). *Touchpoints*. Reading, MA: Addison-Wesley.

Christophersen, E. R., & Mortweet, S. L. (2003). *Parenting that works: Building skills that last a lifetime*. Washington, DC: American Psychological Association.

Cleverly, J., & Phillips, D. C. (1986). *Visions of childhood: Influential models from Locke to Spock* (rev. ed.). New York: Teachers College Press.

Dreikurs, R., & Soltz, V. (1991). *Children the challenge: The classic work on improving parent–child relations*. New York: Penguin.

Faber, A., & Mazlish, E. (1999). *How to talk so kids will listen and listen so kids will talk* (rev. ed.). New York: Collins.

Faber, A., & Mazlish, E. (2004). *Siblings without rivalry* (expanded ed.). New York: Collins.

Garbarino, J., & Eckenrode, J. (1997). *Understanding abusive families: An ecological approach to theory and practice*. San Francisco: Jossey-Bass.

Ginott, H. G. (2003). *Between parent and child: The best selling classic that revolutionized parent–child communication* (rev. ed.). New York: Three Rivers Press.

Gordon, T. (2000). *Parent effectiveness training: The proven program for raising responsible children* (rev. ed.). New York: Three Rivers Press.

Satir, V. (1988). *The new peoplemaking*. Mountain View, CA: Science and Behavior Books.

Resources

American Academy of Child and Adolescent Psychiatry—Facts for Families (concise up-to-date information on issues affecting children, teenagers, and their families)

http://www.aacap.org

National Network for Child Care—Internet source of reviewed and research-based publications relating to caring for children

http://www.nncc.org/

Family Relations—information on parent education, parents forever (divorced, unmarried parents), families with teens

http://www.extension.umn.edu/family

Cengage Learning

5

Ecology of Nonparental Child Care

Give a little love to a child, and you get a great deal back.

—JOHN RUSKIN

Mark Wilson/Getty Images Entertainment/Getty Images

Learning Objectives

After completing this chapter, you will be able to:

1. Define and explain the different types of nonparental child care.
2. Discuss the characteristics of quality care as they relate to accreditation standards.
3. Discuss macrosystem, chronosystem, and mesosystem influences of nonparental child care on psychological, social, and cognitive development.
4. Describe the different socialization outcomes, curriculum models, ideologies, and practices as related to socialization.
5. Explain developmentally appropriate caregiving and the caregiver's legal role in protection from child maltreatment.

SOCIALIZATION SKETCHES

Yo-Yo Ma

(b. 1955)

"When you learn something from people, or from a culture, you accept it as a gift, and it is your lifelong commitment to preserve it and build on it."

—YO-YO MA

This quote expresses the American cellist Yo-Yo Ma's, philosophy of learning. It relates to the chapter you are about to read in that Yo-Yo Ma's early childhood care involved teachers in addition to his parents. It also ties into the chapter in that his socialization experiences enabled him to develop what Howard Gardner (2006) proposed as a new curriculum, "Five Minds for the Future." This curriculum aims to produce individuals with minds that are disciplined, synthesizing, creating, respectful, and ethical.

Yo-Yo Ma was recognized as a prodigy from the age of 5; he has become one of the world's most renowned instrumentalists. In his early childhood he learned important self-regulatory "tools" to succeed, first from his father and then from his teachers and mentors. He was an apprentice to such master musicians as Leonard Rose and Isaac Stern. These experiences exemplify the "Tools of the Mind" curriculum, discussed in this chapter.

Family

Yo-Yo Ma was born in Paris. His father, Hiao-Tsium Ma, a violinist and a professor at Nanjing University, had left China for Paris in 1936. His mother, Marina, a singer from Hong Kong and former student of Hiao-Tsium, emigrated to Paris, where she and Hiao-Tsium were married.

According to Yo-Yo Ma, his father was the pedagogue of the family—strict and very traditional. He was 49 when Yo-Yo was born, so he was set in his ways. He tutored Yo-Yo and his older sister in French, Chinese history, and music. Each day, Yo-Yo had to memorize two measures of Bach, so by the time he was 4 years old, he was playing a Bach suite (illustrating *the disciplined mind*). Yo-Yo and his sister were each sent to study music with well-known teachers.

When Yo-Yo was 7, the Ma family moved to the United States. His father got a position teaching music in New York City, where he founded the Children's Orchestra Society (directed today by Yo-Yo's sister). Yo-Yo continued to study the cello, attending different schools. He and his sister, who played the violin, performed at an event hosted and conducted by Leonard Bernstein. In attendance were President and Mrs. Kennedy. It was one of television's first "specials." Yo-Yo Ma was immediately noticed, not only for his extraordinary talent, memory, and virtuosity, but also for his "naturalness" on stage.

Peers

After graduating from high school, Yo-Yo attended a summer music camp. It was his first extended time on his own. He describes it as "wild"—suddenly he was free, without discipline. He became confused as to his purpose, his style of music, and his identity. On a National Public Radio (NPR) program (March 10, 2008), he said, "I grew up in three cultures: I was born in Paris, my parents were from China, and I was brought up mostly in America. When I was young, this was very confusing: Everyone said that their culture was best, but I knew they couldn't all be right."

Media

Yo-Yo's desire for artistic growth led him to experiment with various eclectic musical genres. His established artistry and respect have provided various opportunities to play with many renowned artists. Yo-Yo's career has been marked by his everlasting search for new ways to communicate with audiences. Yo-Yo continues to search for his individual voice, immersing himself in the music from many diverse cultures. "Every day I make an effort to go toward what I don't understand. This wandering leads to the accidental learning that continually shapes my life."

Community

Yo-Yo Ma is a ten-time Grammy award winner. A sampling of his virtuosity includes the soundtrack from *Crouching Tiger, Hidden Dragon*; *Appalachian Journey*, in conjunction with a Ken Burns documentary; *Hush* with Bobby McFerrin; and *Soul of the Tango*. This small sampling illustrates Yo-Yo's collaborations with various artists who served as "guides to their traditions." This interactive process has culminated in music extending beyond the boundaries of a particular genre (illustrating *the synthesizing mind*).

Yo-Yo Ma's experiences have led him to create "The Silk Road Project," a multidisciplinary collection of performing artists and scholars committed to exploring the cross-cultural musical influences of the Middle East and Asia on the classical tradition of the West. The legendary Silk Road represents the route traveled by caravans long ago. The project utilizes modern technology (such as digitization) to make obscure cultural traditions accessible to Western audiences (illustrating *the creating mind*). His ideal for the future is for cultures to become interdependent as "everyone has strengths" (illustrating *the respectful mind*). "We actually do have to live in one world . . . and all of this technology is making it more essential that we have a way of thinking about the whole because we know that the alternative is disaster. . . ." In 2006, Yo-Yo Ma was named to the honorary position of United Nations Peace Ambassador (illustrating *the ethical mind*).

- Have you had mentors in your childhood who were influential, and how so?

What is involved in nonparental child care?

Nonparental Child Care

nonparental child care, or day care the care given to children by persons other than parents during the parts of the day that parents are absent

extended day care the care provided for children before or after school hours or during vacations

Nonparental child care, or as it is sometimes called, **day care**, refers to the care given to children by persons other than parents during the parts of the day when parents are absent. Nonparental child care can begin as early as birth and extend into the school years until children are old enough to care for themselves. Most states have laws regarding the age at which children can legally be left unsupervised by an adult. Nonparental child care provided for children before or after school hours or during vacations is referred to as **extended day care**.

The care of children today, for a significant part of the day, is likely to be provided by caregivers other than parents. According to government statistics (FIFCFS, 2010), more than 70 percent of children ages 0 to 6, not yet in kindergarten, are in a child-care arrangement on a regular basis for all or part of the day with someone other than a parent. Also, more than 50 percent of children ages 6 to 14 receive some nonparental care before and after school. Because children are spending significant socialization time in nonparental care settings, and at very young ages, this chapter examines the influence of such child-care settings on development. Figure 5.1 shows a bioecological model of the systems involved in the process.

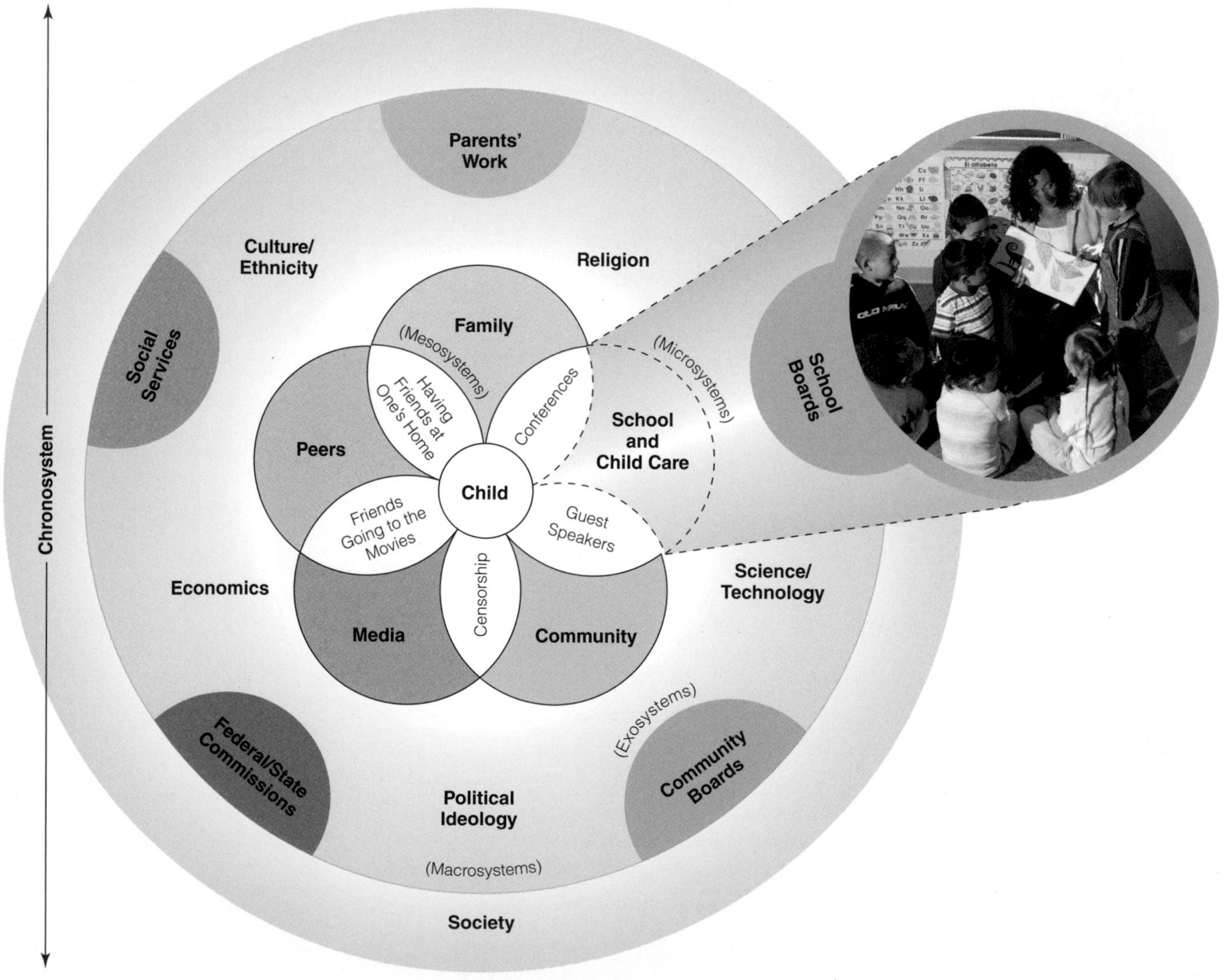

FIGURE 5.1 A Bioecological Model of Human Development
Child care is a significant influence on the child's development.
Astor 112/Cengage Learning

The availability, affordability, and adequacy of child care has become an increasingly serious concern as more and more parents jointly must contribute to the family income due to the rising cost of living.

To help employees balance their work and family responsibilities, the federal government passed the Family and Medical Leave Act (FMLA) of 1993. It allows qualified employees to take up to 12 weeks per year of unpaid leave for certain family and medical reasons, such as the birth and care of a newborn child or for the care of an adopted or foster child.

There are several different types of nonparental child care. A friend, relative, or sitter may come to the home and care for the child. The family may hire a nanny (someone who has received child-care training) to live with them. Families may cooperate and provide care by taking turns. Independent caregivers may provide care for children in their homes (family day care). Parents may take children to a center for care during the day. According to Clarke-Stewart and Allhusen (2002), children ages 3–5 are more likely than children younger than 3 to be cared for in a center-based program; children under the age of 3 are more likely to be cared for by parents, relatives, or independent caregivers in the child's home or the caregiver's.

Regardless of the type, *quality* child care involves certain basics: a caregiver who provides warm, loving care and guidance for the child and works with the family to ensure that the child develops in the best way possible; a setting (home or center) that keeps the child safe, secure, and healthy; and developmentally appropriate activities that help the child develop emotionally, socially, mentally, and physically (Clarke-Stewart, 1993; National Institute of Child Health and Human Development [NICHD], 2005). Many states require fingerprinting of caregivers so that background checks can be made through the police department.

The terms *nursery school, preschool, early childhood education*, and *child development program* are sometimes used to describe certain types of programs for young children. Because all care for children has an impact on their socialization or education, the terms *child care* or *day care* will be used to refer to nonparental caregiving.

Your Care as a Child

Who cared for you in your early years?
Will you be the primary caregiver for your children?
Are you and your present or future spouse employed, or do you plan to be?

Components of Optimal Quality Care

What is involved in quality care?

Given the patchwork of services that currently exists and the projected need for future child care, quality child care has become an issue of concern among working parents, professionals who deal with children, and legislators (Ghazvini & Mullis, 2002; Lamb, 2000; Lamb & Ahnert, 2006).

The term "quality" usually refers to a subjective evaluation of excellence; however, research has generated an objective definition by analyzing the physical, cognitive, social, and emotional components of the child-care setting. For example, the federal government initiated the National Day-Care Study (Ruopp et al., 1979) for the purpose of ultimately constructing national child-care standards of quality. The task was to identify key child-care components that best predicted good outcomes for children and to develop cost estimates for offering those components within programs. The study found the components of optimal quality child care—that is, the most significant predictors of positive classroom dynamics and child outcomes—to be:

- The size of the overall group
- The caregiver–child ratios
- Whether the caregiver had specialized training in child development or early childhood education

In classrooms that had smaller groups and whose teachers had specialized training, teachers could engage in more social interaction with the children. As a result, the children were more cooperative, more involved in tasks, more talkative, and more creative. They also made greater gains on cognitive tasks.

More recent studies have confirmed and expanded the National Day-Care Study findings (Ghazvini & Mullis, 2002; NICHD, 1996, 2005, 2010). Caregivers with specialized training in child development and developmentally appropriate practices have a more authoritative, rather than authoritarian, attitude toward child rearing, use more planned activities, are less stressed, and tend to communicate regularly with parents (Ghazvini & Mullis, 2002; NICHD, 2005). Today, measures such as the Infant/Toddler Environment Rating Scale and the Early Childhood Environment Rating Scale (Lamb & Ahnert, 2006) are available to assess quality.

In spite of such research on child-care quality and positive child outcomes, studies of child-care centers reveal that typical quality is still considerably below what is considered good practice by child development, psychology, and education specialists (Fragin, 2000; Cost, Quality, and Child Outcomes Study, 1995, 1999; NICHD, 2005).

What factors contribute to less than optimal quality child care?

- The education credentials of caregivers who work in child-care centers are often inadequate relative to the skills required (Fragin, 2000; NICHD, 1996).
- Staff turnover is high, ranging from 25 percent to 50 percent each year. This means that children are continually adapting to new caregivers, and administrators are constantly training new staff (Fragin, 2000; Whitebook, Howes, & Phillips, 1989).
- Staff compensation, including wages and benefits, is exceptionally low. Worker compensation is significantly related to quality of care provided (Whitebook, Howes, & Phillips, 1989).

A number of studies have examined the effects of varying levels of quality on children's behavior and development. Conclusions indicate a significant correlation between program quality (safe, stimulating environment) and socialization outcomes for children (Frede, 1995; Fragin, 2000; NICHD, 2005). Outcomes related to quality include cooperative play, sociability, ability to resolve conflicts, self-control, and language and cognitive development.

Given the research conclusions on quality child care, why do some parents choose otherwise? Mason and Duberstein (1992) found that the factors of availability and affordability of care overshadowed the factor of quality in some parents' choice of child care.

Advocacy, Accreditation, and Quality Child Care Standards

Advocacy, introduced in Chapter 2, is the process of supporting a person, group, or cause. An example of the process of advocacy is the work of the National Association for the Education of Young Children (NAEYC), an organization of professionals involved in early childhood education (see http://www.naeyc.org). Because national standards of quality do not exist, NAEYC took on the task of setting its own criteria, publishing a position statement on criteria for high-quality early childhood programs in 1984. Briefly, a high-quality program is:

> one which meets the needs of and promotes the physical, social, emotional, and cognitive development of the children and adults—parents, staff, and administrators—who are involved in the program. Each day of a child's life is viewed as leading toward the growth and development of a healthy, intelligent, and contributing member of society. (National Association for the Education of Young Children, 1984, p. 7)

Child-care programs that meet the criteria can voluntarily apply to the National Academy for Early Childhood Programs (a division of NAEYC) for accreditation, thereby receiving national recognition for high quality standards and performance. Accreditation specifics will be discussed later.

In 1986, NAEYC expanded its position on quality. With the proliferation of programs for young children and the introduction of large numbers of infants and toddlers into group care, NAEYC felt the need for a clear definition of *developmentally appropriate practice* (*DAP*), a term often used in the criteria for quality early childhood programs. *Developmental appropriateness*, as introduced in Chapter 4, involves knowledge of children's normal growth patterns and individual differences. In response to the trend toward increasing emphasis on formal instruction in academic skills (seen in many programs), NAEYC published specific guidelines for developmentally appropriate practices for programs servicing children from birth through age 8 (Bredekamp & Copple, 1997; Copple & Bredekamp, 2009). DAP views play as the primary indicator of children's development. Each child is viewed as a unique person with an individual pattern and timing of growth, as well as individual temperament, learning style, and family background. Both the program and interactions should be responsive to individual differences. Learning in a developmentally appropriate program emerges as a result of the interaction between the child's thoughts and experiences and the materials and people available. The curriculum should match the child's developing abilities while also challenging the child's interest and understanding (Bredekamp, 1986, Copple & Bredekamp, 2009).

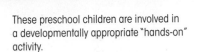

These preschool children are involved in a developmentally appropriate "hands-on" activity.

Cengage Learning

After much hard work, debate, and compromise involving numerous child advocate organizations, a federal child-care bill was eventually passed in 1990 (this became part of welfare reform in 1996). The bill included a Child Care and Development Block Grant to state governments, requiring them to designate a lead agency to direct their child-care programs, to set health and safety standards, and to allow eligible low-income families to choose any licensed child-care provider. In addition, the child-care bill included tax credits for working families with children if they have child-care expenses for one or more children under age 13 and pay for child care in order to work.

TeachSource Video Activity

Go to the Education CourseMate website to watch the video entitled "Preschool: Appropriate Learning Environments and Room Arrangements." How is "developmental appropriateness" exemplified and implemented?

How Does Accreditation Take Place?

While the law establishes minimum standards for quality child care, voluntary systems exist nationally to establish higher quality standards than the law provides for both child-care centers and family day-care homes (Helburn & Howes, 1996).

Child-Care Centers

In 1984, the National Association for the Education of Young Children (NAEYC) developed an accreditation system for child-care centers involving self-evaluations by staff and parents. Professional validators from NAEYC conduct visits to determine whether standards have been met; if they have, the program is accredited for three years. Standards are designed for programs serving children from infancy through age 8 in centers caring for more than ten children; school-age programs are eligible if a majority of the children are age 8 or younger.

The NAEYC accreditation standard criteria (see Figure 5.2), based on research and professional consensus, include staff qualifications and training, administration and staffing patterns (group size and adult–child ratios), physical environment, health and safety, and nutrition and food service. For example, for children ages 0 to 12 months, the standard is 6 to 8 children per group with an adult–child ratio of 1:3 to 1:4; for children ages 4 to 5 years, the standard is 16 to 20 children per group with an adult–child ratio of 1:8 to 1:10.

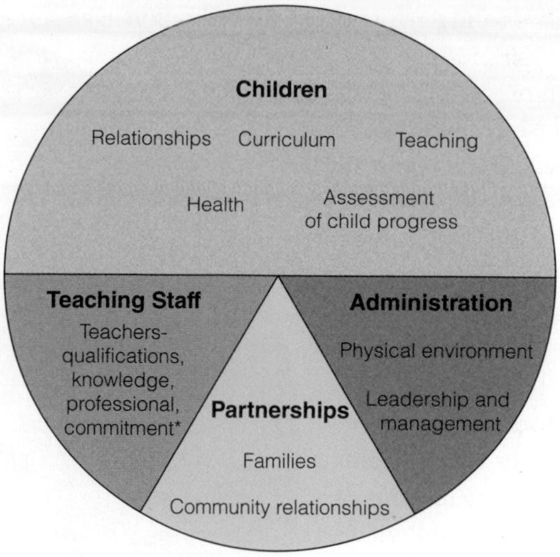

FIGURE 5.2 Conceptual Framework of Early Childhood Program Standards for NAEYC Accreditation

Source: NAEYC. 2007. NAEYC Early Childhood Program Standards and Accreditation Criteria: The Mark of Quality in Early Childhood. Washington, DC: NAEYC. Reprinted with permission from the National Association for the Education of Young Children (NAEYC). www.naeyc.org.
*Added by author for clarification.

Family Day-Care Homes

In 1988, the National Association for Family Day Care (now the National Association for Family Child Care, or NAFCC) began a program for voluntary accreditation of family child-care homes. The process includes self-evaluation as well as external validation of aspects of program operation, including health and safety, nutrition, indoor and outdoor play environments, interactions, and professional responsibility. Continuing education for the caregiver, such as cardiopulmonary resuscitation (CPR), is also required.

In-Home Care: Nannies

The oldest professional nanny organization in the United States is the International Nanny Association (INA). It includes nannies, nanny employers, nanny placement agencies, and nanny educators. Since 1987, INA has worked to professionalize the nanny industry by maintaining high standards of conduct, respecting and supporting families in their task of nurturing children, and promoting continuing professional growth. Background checks, referrals, conferences, and newsletters are some of their services.

What aspects of society have influenced child care?

Macrosystem Influences on Nonparental Child Care

Generally, child care and educational practices have been affected by three macrosystems: political ideology, economics, and science and technology. *Political ideology* is seen in values such as social responsibility (e.g., fostering adaptation of immigrants); competition (e.g., providing young children with learning opportunities to prepare for the future); and equal opportunity (e.g., assisting poor families and including ethnically diverse children and children with disabilities). The effect of *economics* can be seen in the need for both parents to work. *Science and technology* are reflected in the pressure to impart academic skills to all children as early as possible. To illustrate macrosystem influences, child care has been used during the 20th century for the following purposes:

1. **Social service.** The first day nurseries were established to care for the children of masses of immigrants to the United States during the mid-19th century. Day nurseries

were also established to care for the children of women who worked in factories and hospitals during wartime. The motivation to establish these day nurseries was social service to care for neglected children, and the care provided was essentially custodial (Clarke-Stewart, 1993).

2. **Enrichment.** The first cooperative nursery school was inaugurated at the University of Chicago in 1915. The purpose was to give the children of faculty opportunities to play in a supervised environment where they could develop impulse control, verbal skills, and knowledge about the world. Parent participation was required. Such nursery schools were popular with middle-class families from the 1930s to the 1960s. In the late 1960s, as a result of child development research and political pressure for the United States to compete globally—specifically to keep pace with Russian scientific advances—a new purpose was incorporated into nursery school programs: to stimulate intellectual growth (Clarke-Stewart, 1993).

3. **Parent employability.** Child-care services are used to enable women to seek job training and/or employment outside the home (Lamb, 2000). Economic necessity, including increases in the cost of living and in the number of single-parent families, has led to a growing reliance on nonparental care. Recent welfare reforms to increase employability have also contributed to this trend. The 1996 welfare law allows recipients of Temporary Assistance for Needy Families (TANF) to collect federally funded benefits for a maximum of 60 months. States can modify requirements with state funds. Recipients of TANF must be engaged in work-related activities (training, job search, job) within their state's time limit. The immediate effect of the imposed time limit for welfare was to increase the demand for available, accessible, affordable child care. Today, part of welfare reform is government funding of child care for qualifying families so that mothers of young children can be employed.

4. **Intervention.** In the 1960s, civil rights groups demanded equal opportunities in education, jobs, and housing. The Economic Opportunity Act, passed in 1964, funded preschool programs designed to compensate for the physical, social, and academic disadvantages of children who came from low-income families, were members of cultural minorities, had various disabilities, or were identified as abused. The purpose of such intervention was to provide children with skills they would be unlikely to get at home, enabling them to succeed in school and avoid poverty in adulthood. Intervention programs are usually comprehensive, including health and nutrition services, social services, and parental involvement. An example of a federally funded comprehensive preschool intervention program is Head Start. Its goal is to enable children from qualified families to enter school ready to learn. Public money spent to enhance the early childhood years would be more beneficial than public money spent to correct a deficiency in later childhood.

5. **Readiness.** Those who advocate that child care should be synonymous with early childhood education also believe the period in a child's life from birth to age 5 is a critical time for developing the physical, emotional, social, and cognitive skills they will need for the rest of their lives. That the formation of neural connections in the brain is most susceptible to stimulating experiences in the early years has been documented by scientific research (Shonkoff & Phillips, 2000). Such findings have influenced political policy. Some examples are: (1) Head Start, a preschool program, originating under the leadership of President Lyndon Johnson, to break the cycle of poverty through education; (2) the No Child Left Behind Act of 2002, passed under the leadership of President George W. Bush, to give public schools incentives to teach students what they need to know to be successful in life; and (3) the "Good Start, Grow Smart" Initiative, also passed during the Bush administration, to help states and local communities fund programs that will ensure young children are equipped with skills they will need to be ready to learn in school, such as prereading and language skills.

In sum, as a result of macrosystem influences, child care has become a service to families with children to provide custodial care, stimulating learning experiences, and socialization, to enable parents to work, and to implement early childhood education principles.

What is the correlation between society's traditional beliefs and consequent child-care policies?

Chronosystem Influences on Nonparental Child Care: Correlates and Consequences

The 1971 White House Conference on Children pointed to the need for quality child care as the most serious problem confronting families and children. Unfortunately, as the 21st century begins, the United States still has no official national policy or federal standards aimed at establishing a system of child care that is of good quality. Child-care standards continue to vary widely from state to state and family to family. Why is this so?

One reason is that traditional views of parenting in this country have delegated the primary responsibility for child care to the family. Some people in government and business support the "individualist" view that each family should be able to care for its own without outside assistance (Schorr, 1997).

Another reason is the fear of government involvement in what is considered a basic personal right: to bring up one's children according to one's values, one's religion, and one's culture. Federal involvement in private matters is seen by some as teetering on the brink of socialism. Is the underlying fear that if the government foots the bill for child care, then the government will call the shots?

In general, the federal government has not committed itself to implementing child-care standards (except in programs where federal funds are involved). This means the task is left to the states, local communities, private enterprise, professional organizations, and the consumer (visit the Education CourseMate website for this text to find a short guide on "How to Choose a Good Early Childhood Program").

What is the correlation between contemporary issues and consequent child-care policies?

The question regarding nonparental child care in the 1980s and 1990s was, "Is day care helpful or harmful to children?" Since today nonparental child care has become a fact of life, the question has changed to, "What ecological model of child care is most supportive of children and families?" (Ghazvini & Mullis, 2002; NICHD, 2005, 2010). The various controversial answers to both questions involve whether or not children should be enrolled in day care, the age at which children should be enrolled, whether such care should be full- or part-time, and the type of program that should be offered (for example, some believe the preschool experience should focus on learning how to get along with others, exploring the environment, and dealing with feelings; others believe the preschool experience should focus on academic skills, such as reading and math). The chronosystem reflects the following areas of concern that provided the bases for research at the time:

- **Separation from mother.** Much of the early concern regarding the effects of child care on the child's development was centered on the fear that separation from the mother, especially in infancy, would disrupt the natural mother–child bond of attachment and would result in psychological and social problems. Thus, most of the original research studies examined the effects of separation on the child. It should be noted that the infant separation studies were done in residential institutions, rather than in child-care centers as we know them today.
- **Child-care setting.** Concerns about quality child-care settings (physical environment, socio-emotional relationships, and intellectual stimulation) have spurred more recent studies to examine the overall effects of different child-care settings (home versus alternative) on children's social relationships with other children, their relationships with their mothers, and their intellectual development.

- **Ecological systems.** Today, concerns in the scientific community focus on the ecology of child care. Studies examine family factors, child-care factors (Clarke-Stewart & Allhusen, 2002; NICHD, 2005, 2010), and cultural factors (Lamb, 2000) that work together (mesosystems) to affect children's development. It is now well accepted that "childrearing has become a collaborative endeavor with children moving back and forth . . . between their homes and child care" (Phillips & Howes, 1987, p. 9). The mesosystem links may be supportive, competitive, or neutral. The next section discusses both classical and modern studies that emanated from chronosystems concerns.

Nonparental Child Care and Psychological Development

What are the effects of nonparental care on infants?

Most studies examining effects of nonparental care focus on the mother–child relationship. The following classic studies are examples.

1. **Spitz's Study.** One of the first studies to report the detrimental effects of separating infants from their mothers was done by Rene Spitz in 1946. He compared the development of infants raised by caregivers in a foundling home (a home for illegitimate and abandoned babies) to that of infants raised by their mothers in a prison. Each caregiver in the foundling home was responsible for at least eight infants. The mothers, who were all either mentally retarded or emotionally disturbed, were responsible for caring for their own infants in the prison. The infants raised in the foundling home had poor appetites and lacked interest in their surroundings; they exhibited severe depression, according to Spitz. As a result, they were retarded in their growth and mental development. The infants raised by their mothers in prison, on the other hand, developed normally. Even though the mothers in the prison were socially deviant, the one-on-one care and nurturance they gave their infants enabled the infants to exhibit normal development, whereas even though the caregivers in the institution were professionally trained, they had eight babies to nurture and probably could not establish emotional attachments with each one. Spitz supported "nature" care.
2. **Bowlby's Study.** In 1952, John Bowlby (1966, 1969, 1973) wrote that maternal love and care are the most important influences on an infant's future development. After reviewing studies on infants separated from their mothers, he concluded that any break in the early mother–child relationship could have severe emotional, social, and intellectual consequences. What Bowlby meant by "any break" was loss of the mother in infancy due to death or separation from the mother because of hospitalization, employment, or other circumstances such as neglect—being physically present but emotionally absent. He went on to say that being deprived of the early mother–child relationship would cause the infant to become depressed, physically and mentally retarded, or delinquent. Bowlby, too, supported "nature" care.
3. **Skeels's Study.** A 30-year longitudinal study completed in 1966 by Harold Skeels demonstrated that it is the quality of care (nurture) that affects children's development, not the relationship of the person who provides it (nature). Thus, the care can come from someone other than the child's mother. Skeels studied 25 infants who were institutionalized because they were deemed mentally retarded. Of these, 13 were later transferred to the institution for retarded women, where the infants were "adopted" by small groups of residents who lavished care and attention on them. The remaining 12 infants stayed where they were. After two years, the transfer group had gained an average of 28.5 points on an IQ test, but the control group had lost an average of 26.2 points.

Thirty years later, Skeels followed up on the original 25. He found that 11 of the 13 children who were transferred to the institution for retarded women had been adopted by families; 12 out of the 13 had achieved an education and become self-supporting adults with responsible jobs. Their own children had average IQs. Of the control group of 12 children who had remained institutionalized, 11 had survived; 4 were in institutions, 1 was a vagrant, 1 was a gardener's assistant at an institution, 3 were dishwashers, 1 was a part-time worker in a cafeteria, and 1 was a domestic worker.

In sum, Skeel's longitudinal study supported "nurture" care. It showed that

- children need care and nurturance to develop normally (in this respect, Skeels agrees with Spitz and Bowlby);
- care and nurturance can be provided by someone other than the mother (here Skeels disagrees with Spitz and Bowlby); and
- infants who are initially deprived can grow up normally if intervention by a caring, nurturing person is provided (Spitz and Bowlby did not even consider this possibility).

This child clings to his mother when left at child care because he is attached to her.

David Young-Wolff/PhotoEdit

Skeels's study has implications for society. If deprivational effects caused by neglect in infancy can be reversed by intervention, then we can enable many children to grow up to be independent, self-sufficient, responsible adults who are assets to society rather than liabilities. There are still many unresolved questions. Which children qualify for intervention? When do you intervene? What type of intervention is best? What kind of program do you provide, and for how long? Is day care worth paying for? Does the government or some other agency have the right to intervene? Is society willing to pay the cost of intervention? These questions will be discussed in more detail later.

4. **Contemporary Studies.** The significance of an infant's early attachment to a caregiver has been studied and related to nonparental child care.

During the first year of life children become attached to their primary caregiver—the person who holds them, comforts them, feeds them, and plays with them. This caregiver is usually the mother, but it can be the father, a grandparent, an older sibling, or another person not related to the child. Feelings of attachment distinguish this caregiver from others. When children are in strange situations or not feeling well, they want to be near the person they are attached to; no one else will do (indicating a *secure attachment*). On the other hand, when children are not attached to a significant person, they may cling when the person leaves or cry hysterically until the person returns, or they may ignore the person upon departure and avoid the person upon return, or they may cling to the person one moment and reject the person the next (indicating an *insecure attachment*).

Jay Belsky and colleagues (Belsky, 2009; Belsky & Rovine,1988) showed that babies less than 1 year old who receive nonparental care for more than 20 hours a week are at a greater risk of developing insecure attachments to their mothers; they are also at increased risk of emotional and behavioral problems in later childhood. Youngsters who have weak emotional ties to their mothers are more likely to be aggressive and disobedient as they grow older.

Others (Clarke-Stewart, 1992; 1993; Clarke-Stewart & Allhusen, 2005; Phillips & Howes, 1987) take issue with Belsky, saying the evidence is insufficient to support the claim that infants in full-time day care are at risk for emotional insecurity. That day-care infants exhibit different attachment behaviors than home-care infants may mean they have developed a coping style to adapt to the different people who care for them as well as the daily separations and reunions. In addition, the assessment of attachment procedures commonly used may not be an accurate way of comparing differences in attachment between infants reared in such diverse environments. Not all children who begin day care in infancy are insecurely attached, aggressive, or noncompliant, nor are they intellectually advanced. There are individual differences for day-care children just as there

IN PRACTICE

You have to work, so how do you deal with putting your child in someone else's care?

According to Lamb and Ahnert (2006), the onset of nonparental care is stressful for both mother and child. Even children who have a secure attachment to their mothers feel some anxiety. The onset of employment, as well as entry into day care, often affects parental behavior.

Parental sensitivity is a key determinant of a child's adjustment to nonparental child care. Choosing quality care, which tends to be best when evaluated and regulated by professionals (such as NAEYC accreditation) is the first step. The second is allowing time for sharing care with the caregiver until the child has adjusted to the transition. And third is staying involved with the caregiver, communicating about the child's behavior and development, and sharing concerns.

are for children reared at home (Clarke-Stewart, 1993, Clarke-Stewart & Allhusen, 2005; Honig, 1993).

In conclusion, recent data on psychological functioning of children who have attended day care in infancy are often confounded by the child's temperament and gender, family socioeconomic status, marital status, parent–child relationships, number of hours daily in care, and quality of care, including sensitivity and responsiveness of the caregiver (Langlois & Liben, 2003; NICHD, 1997, 2005, 2010). According to Lamb and Ahnert (2006), who reviewed the research, it now appears that nonparental care in itself does not reliably affect mother–child attachment. Adverse effects occur only when poor-quality day care coincides with such risky conditions as insensitive and unresponsive maternal behavior (NICHD, 1997). Thus, children in a quality child-care program, compared to children cared for at home, attach to their mothers similarly.

Nonparental Child Care and Social Development

What is the effect of putting infants, toddlers, and preschoolers with peers in child care?

Children in day care may be with peers from infancy. Infants stare at each other and touch each other. Toddlers may smile at each other, share toys, and fight over toys. Three-year-olds may play games, share, take turns, argue, and fight. Four-year-olds may also role-play. ("Let's play house. You be the mommy, and I'll be the baby.")

Results of a substantial number of studies on the social development of preschool children conclude that children attending some form of child-care program interact more with peers, positively and often negatively, and that they are less cooperative and responsive with adults than children in home care (Clarke-Stewart & Allhusen, 2002; NICHD, 2007).

Specifically, children who have had experience in a child-care program seem to be more socially competent than those who have not had such an experience. They are more self-confident, more outgoing, and less fearful. They are also more assertive and more self-sufficient. They know more about the social world—gender roles, taking the perspective of others, solving problems regarding getting along with another child, and emotional labels ("cheater," "crybaby," "bully"). While they are more socially competent, they have also been observed to be less polite, less respectful of others' rights, and less compliant with adult demands, as well as more aggressive and hostile to others (Clarke-Stewart, 1992; Clarke-Stewart & Allhusen, 2005; Lamb, 2000). Early individual differences in social competence have been found to remain stable through school age and early adolescence (Campbell, Lamb, & Hwang, 2000).

What is the effect of child care on intellectual outcomes?

Nonparental Child Care and Cognitive Development

Generally, the intellectual performance of children who attend a quality day-care program is higher than that of children from similar family backgrounds who do not attend a day-care program or who attend one of poor quality. For example, it has been shown that children, especially from low-income families, who attend a quality preschool program, even part-time, are more verbally expressive and more interactive with adults than children who do not (Burchinal et al., 2000; NICHD, 2007; Shonkoff & Phillips, 2000). It has also been demonstrated that children who attend quality child-care programs are better able to meet the requirements in the primary grades of elementary school and function at an increased intellectual capacity during their initial years of schooling; IQ scores show an increase of up to 10 points at the end of program implementation. Academic achievement in these children continues to be better through high school than for those who did not attend a quality preschool (CQO, 1999; Karoly, 1998; Schweinhart et al., 2005). Although longitudinal studies have shown that the increase in IQ scores is not permanent, there is a significant reduction in grade retention as well as in the need for placement in a special education program (CQO, 1999; Karoly, 1998; Schweinhart et al., 2005).

What child-care programs have been developed to modify the cognitive consequences of growing up disadvantaged?

Traditional preschool programs usually provide enrichment activities to children who already get basic intellectual stimulation at home. For children who do not have such an advantage, intervention programs were developed to provide compensation, or amends, for skills these children lack to succeed in U.S. public schools. Most research on the effects of day care on children's cognitive development has focused on intervention programs.

Many types of intervention programs were implemented in the 1960s and 1970s, using different curriculum models (discussed later). Although children enrolled in such programs fared better academically, socially, and emotionally than their nonparticipant counterparts (Karoly, 1998), the debate as to which type of intervention is best, for whom, for how long, and where (home or school) remains ongoing.

Even though intervention programs vary widely, most investigators concur that to enable the child to become competent cognitively, socially, and behaviorally, the child's family must be involved. Thus, the best type of intervention (among government-funded programs) is one that reinforces the strengths of the family as a child-rearing system and that enables the family to be the primary educator of its children, links the family to the formal educational system through involvement, and links the family to resources in the community so that the family can receive needed health and social services. These are known as family support programs. An example of such a program is the Child and Family Resource Program (CFRP), which began in 1973 as part of Head Start. It enrolled qualified families of children from birth through age 8, rather than just the children. It provided diagnostic medical, dental, nutritional, and mental health services as well as treatment. It also provided prenatal care and education for pregnant mothers. It assisted parents in promoting the development of infants and toddlers, as well as providing preschool comprehensive Head Start services for children ages 3 to 5. It eased the transition from preschool to elementary school and offered special development programs for children with disabilities. Finally, it provided services such as counseling, referrals to community agencies, family planning assistance, and help in dealing with emergencies or crises.

In sum, accurately predicting the cognitive, as well as social and behavioral, outcomes of intervention programs is difficult because of the numerous variables that must be taken into account, including quality of the mother–infant relationship, socioeconomic status of the family, educational level of the parents, stress on the family and coping skills, available family supports, temperament and gender of the child, spacing of the siblings, age at which the child enters the program and for how many hours per day, quality of the caregiver–infant relationship, caregiver–parent communication, and quality of the program (see Table 5.1).

This child's achievement motivation is enhanced by the teacher who is engaging him in a reading activity.

Cengage Learning

Table 5.1 Variables Influencing Child-Care Socialization Outcomes

Child-Care Variables	Family Variables	Child Variables
Type of care (in-home, family day care, center care)	Socioeconomic status	Age at entry into day care
Type of program (compensatory, enrichment)	Culture/religion	Gender
Compensation of caregivers	Family structure (two-parent, single, step, kin)	Health
Caregiver stress	Parental educational level	Temperament
Stability of caregivers	Mother employed part- or full-time	Security of attachment to mother
Adult–child ratio	Mother's attitude toward work	
Quality of day-care setting	Mother's attitude toward child care	
Sensitivity and responsiveness of caregiver to child	Mother's sensitivity and responsiveness to child	
Caregiver education/training	Roles and relationships between parents	
Caregiver ideology and attitudes toward child rearing	Father's involvement in child care	
Caregiver–parent communication	Parenting styles	
Part- or full-time day care	Stress/coping strategies Availability of social supports in community	

Mesosystem Influences on Nonparental Child Care

What collaborative links are available for child-care services?

The challenge of the future will be for society to provide more choices in quality child-care services because of the increased need. Links with school, community, government, and business must occur on a greater scale to increase the availability, accessibility, and affordability of child-care options (Smolensky & Gootman, 2003).

The types of child care most often used for infants and toddlers (younger than age 3) are relatives, family day-care homes (care in the home of a nonrelative), and day-care centers. Preschoolers (ages 3 to 4) are most frequently cared for in a child-care center or by relatives. The most common types of care (excluding self-care) for school-age children (ages 6 to 12) are family day-care homes and relatives (see Figure 5.3). A most striking trend, however, is the substantial growth in use of center-based care for children of all ages, especially by mothers who are employed full-time (Hofferth, 1996; Smolensky & Gootman, 2003).

School and Community Involvement in Nonparental Child Care

One way to increase child-care options is for the elementary school to extend the hours it is normally in session and to extend its services to include children younger than age 5. A majority of school-age children whose parents are employed care for themselves before and after school. Other children may be cared for by a neighbor. Still others may participate in a community program. Unsupervised children, contrary to popular belief, are not most likely to be found in impoverished, minority communities; rather, self-care is most common when mothers work full-time and parents are divorced or separated, regardless of income (Lamb, 2000).

At school, extended day care can be an effective link among child, family, and school. It can complement, support, and extend the school's educational purposes to the family in its education and nurturance of children. To illustrate, according to Schorr (1997), Edward Zigler, one of the founders of Head Start, envisioned the schools of the 21st century to include full day care and be the hub of social services for families. Bowling Park Elementary School in Norfolk, Virginia, is such a school. It includes infants and preschoolers and their

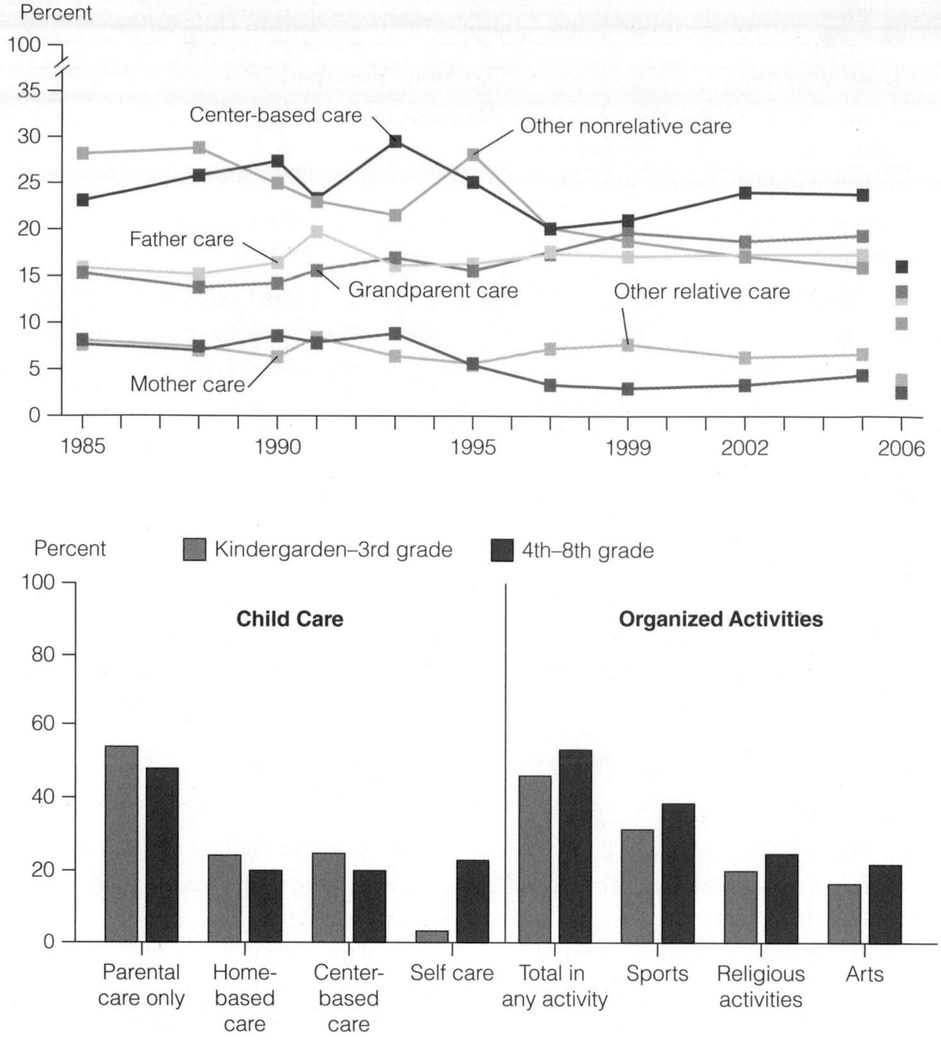

Figure 5.3 Who's Caring for the Children

Source: Children's Defense Fund, 2005 Federal Interagency Forum on Child and Family Statistics (2007). America's Children: Key Indicators of Well-Being, 2007. Washington, D.C.: US Government Printing Office.

parents, responding to family needs. A breakfast club provides an opportunity for parents to discuss parenting issues, children's books, and other matters, and adult education courses are offered. The concept is for children to feel connected to people who care.

A cooperative venture between school and community is an extended day-care program where the school district provides several schools as sites for the program and the YMCA provides the trained recreational leaders and transportation for children who attend schools not in the cooperative program. The male and female recreational leaders provide care that promotes the physical, social, emotional, and cognitive development of children. Games, crafts, and help with homework are some of the activities. An added bonus of this program for some children is the opportunity to develop a relationship with a male role model. Such opportunities are important for children living with single mothers.

Why is adult-supervised extended day care so important for children's well-being?

1. Research has found both boys and girls in fifth through ninth grade to be more susceptible to peer pressure when they were in an after-school situation in which there was no consistent adult control (Lamb, 2000; Smolensky & Gootman, 2003). They were also more likely to become involved in antisocial acts in their neighborhoods than children who attended an extended day program (Leventhal & Brooks-Gunn, 2000; Vandell & Su, 1999).

2. Data from the FIFCFS (2010) indicate that about 3 percent of children in kindergarten through third grade and about 22 percent of children in fourth through eighth grade are left alone to care for themselves outside of school hours while their parents work. There is no exact number of children under age 5 who are left alone all day, but a significant number are cared for by a sibling under age 14. Children who are unsupervised by adults after school are sometimes referred to as **latchkey children** because they carry keys to let themselves into their homes. Children involved in self-care are discussed in Chapter 10.

latchkey children children who carry their own key and let themselves into their homes

When the community provides child-care services, the quality of family life in a community is often improved (Garbarino, 1992). For example, Garbarino and Sherman (1980) found that support for child care in certain neighborhoods correlated significantly with a lower incidence of child abuse and neglect. This reduction in maltreatment resulted in a reduced need for more costly government social services to protect at-risk children, such as foster care. Provision of child-care services also affects the economics of the community by creating work for adults.

Government and Business Involvement in Nonparental Child Care

In some societies—for example, China, France, and Belgium—the government totally supports child care, through tax funds, to enable parents to work. In contrast, the current official policy in the United States is that the government will pay for child care (intervention programs) for disadvantaged families, defined by specific criteria, and will give tax credits to other families up to a maximum set by Congress. Some American businesses have become involved in supporting child-care services to attract and keep their employees (Smolensky & Gootman, 2003).

Nine government-funded early intervention programs, including the Perry Preschool Project in Ypsilanti, Michigan, were examined (Karoly, 1998). Beginning in 1962, researchers followed 123 poor African American children for 25 years, from age 3 or 4 to age 27. Compared to nonparticipating peers (children were randomly assigned to groups), children who had attended a "quality preschool" significantly outperformed those who had not. Specifically, the major findings of Karoly's review were the following:

- Gains in emotional or cognitive development for the child, typically in the short run, or improved parent–child relationships
- Improvements in educational process and outcomes for the child
- Increased economic self-sufficiency, initially for the parent and later for the child, through greater labor force participation, higher income, and lower welfare usage
- Reduced levels of criminal activity
- Improvements in health-related indicators, such as child abuse, maternal reproductive health, and maternal substance abuse

Thus, preschool, or early child care, does have lasting effects. It is beneficial for children because it starts them off on a more positive track. From the beginning, they experience greater success in school, which leads to pride in themselves, a greater commitment to school, and less disruptive behavior. Preschool is cost efficient, according to Schweinhart and colleagues (Schweinhart & Weikart, 1993; Schweinhart et al., 2005) and others (Karoly, 1998), because it reduces the need for special education and the likelihood of dropping out of school and ending up on welfare or becoming delinquent (see Figure 5.4). In terms of tax dollars, child care appears to be worth the expense (Karoly, 1998; Schweinhart et al., 2005). Government and business are beginning to agree with the research.

The federal government has committed to expanding existing programs, such as Head Start, to include more children. It has given block grants to states to develop programs according to need. For example, North Carolina has the Abecedarian Project, providing

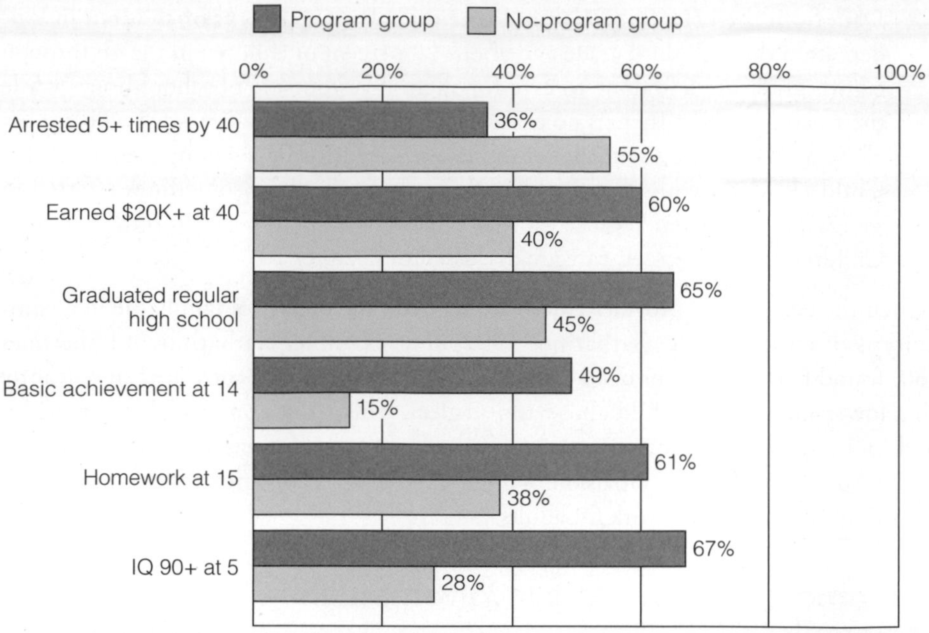

Figure 5.4 **High/Scope Perry Preschool Project: Lifetime Effects**

Source: From Lifetime Effects: The HighScope Perry Preschool Study Through Age 40, by Schweinhart, L.J., Montie, J., Xiang, Z., Barnett, W.S., Belfield, C.R., & Noes, M., © 2005, HighScope Educational Research Foundation. Used with permission.

individualized learning for children, links with the public schools, and services for families; Georgia has initiated public preschool for all 4-year-old children.

Some businesses provide child-care assistance for their employees, such as parental leaves, flexible scheduling, a list of community resources for parents to choose from (known as "resource and referral"), start-up funds or contributions to a community child-care center in return for preferential admission for employees' children, financial assistance to pay for child care, or on-site child care. Day-care facilities located at a parent's place of work can provide a beneficial link between family and community for children. For example, parents can visit children during breaks, and children can learn about the work their parents do by touring the workplace and meeting employees.

Some of the innovations businesses have implemented to support family life are outlined in Table 5.2. It has been found that employer-sponsored day care has several benefits (Galinsky, 1981, 1992):

- New employees are easier to recruit,
- employee absenteeism is lower,
- employees have a more positive attitude toward their work, and
- job turnover is lower.

Table 5.2 **Exosystem Link: Business Support for Families**

1. Child-care, elder-care, and ill/dependent assistance programs
2. National resource and referral service networks
3. Flextime programs to allow employees to adjust their workdays by as much as two hours in either direction
4. Extended leave-of-absence policies permitting up to a three-year break from full-time employment with part-time work in the second and third years
5. Work-at-home programs
6. Family-issues sensitivity training for managers and supervisors
7. School partnerships, including donations of equipment, time for employees to volunteer, or time for parent–teacher conferences
8. On-site employee-staffed child-care centers
9. Job-sharing programs
10. Parent education seminars

Nonparental Child Care and Socialization

Socialization Differences Between Types of Quality Nonparental Child Care

How do different types of child care and different child-care curriculum models affect socialization?

As has been discussed, there are different types of child care: care provided by an individual in the child's own home (*in-home care*), care provided in someone else's home (*family day care*), and care provided in a center either part- or full-time (*center-based care*). See Table 5.3 for a summary of the socialization effects of types of quality child care. Socialization is affected not only by the type of care, but also by the *curriculum* implemented (most often found in center-based care).

curriculum the goals and objections of an educational program, the teacher's role, the equipment and materials, the space arrangement, the kinds of activities, and the way they are scheduled

Socialization Outcomes of Four Theory-Based Nonparental Child-Care Curriculum Models

A **curriculum** includes the educational goals and objectives of the program, the teacher's role, the equipment and materials, the space arrangement, the kinds of activities, and the way they are scheduled.

Some examples of theory-based curriculum models are briefly described here. A curriculum translates theories about learning into action; consequently, different curricula have different socialization effects. Curricula can be generally categorized as **teacher-directed** (learning activities are planned by the teacher for all the children), or **learner-directed** (learning activities emerge from individual interest and teacher guidance). See Table 5.4 for a comparison. The four curriculum models we discuss are the *cognitively oriented curriculum*, *direct instruction*, *Montessori*, and *developmental interaction*.

teacher-directed curriculum a curriculum in which the learning activities are planned by the teacher for all the children

learner-directed curriculum a curriculum in which the learning activities emerge from individual interests and teacher guidance

The Cognitively Oriented Curriculum (Learner-Directed)

The **cognitively oriented curriculum**, developed by David Weikart and associates at the High/Scope Educational Research Foundation in Ypsilanti, Michigan, represents an

cognitively oriented curriculum a curriculum that attempts to blend the virtues of purposeful teaching with open-ended, child-initiated activities

Table 5.3 Socialization and Types of Quality Child Care[a] for Young Children[b]

	In-Home Care (Privately Funded or by Relative)	Family Day Care (Privately Funded)	Center-Based Care (Privately and Publicly Funded)
Physical Setting	Adult-oriented (valuable and breakable items moved)	Adult-oriented, but some specific child materials and play areas	Child-oriented (toys, educational materials, specific areas for play)
Caregiver Special Training	Unlikely	Some	More likely to have had college courses related to and experience with children (especially in public centers)
Adult-Child Interaction	Frequent and personal	Close	Mostly adult-directed and shared with other children
Activities	Mostly unplanned (generally around housekeeping chores)	Some planned	Planned curricula (group and individual)
Peer Interaction	Little	Varied	Much
Developmental Differences *(Based on a series of tests done in a laboratory playroom and observations at home)*	Scored lowest on assessments of cognitive ability, social understanding (taking another's perspective and empathy), cooperation, friendliness, and independence from mother	Scored highest on assessments of friendliness; lowest on independence from mother	Scored higher on assessments of cognitive ability, social understanding (taking another's perspective and empathy), cooperation, friendliness, and independence from mother
Socialization Outcomes *(Interpretation of results)*	One-to-one interaction and training by adult	Experience in complex interactions with children of different ages	Increase in social competence, maturity, intellectual development

[a] These are general differences *between* types of care; there are also differences *within* each type of care (Clarke-Stewart, 1987; Clarke-Stewart & Allhusen, 2005).
[b] Ages 2 to 4.

Table 5.4 Comparison of Teacher- and Learner-Directed Programs

Teacher-Directed Programs	Learner-Directed Programs
Characterized by drill, practice, direct praise for good work, and time spent in reading and math activities	Characterized by a variety of materials, more opportunities for choice and exploration, and more interpersonal contact
Children scored higher on reading and math achievement tests	Children scored higher on nonverbal reasoning and problem-solving tasks
Children showed more persistence and took responsibility for their failures	Children expressed responsibility for their successes
Children worked independently	Children worked cooperatively

Source: Miller and Dyer, 1975; Schweinhart and Weikart, 1993; Schweinhart, Weikart, and Larner, 1986; Stallings, 1974.

assimilation a Piagetian term for mental adaptation to one's environment by incorporating experiences

accommodation a Piagetian term for mental adaptation to one's environment by reconciling differences of experiences

equilibrium a Piagetian term for the state of balance between assimilation and accommodation, thereby allowing knowledge to be incorporated

TeachSource Video Activity

If you are not familiar with Piaget's theory of cognitive development, or need a brief review, go to the Education CourseMate website to watch the videos entitled "0–2 Years—Piaget's Sensorimotor Stage," "2–5 Years—Piaget's Preoperational Stage," "5–11 Years—Piaget's Concrete Operational Stage," and "12–18 Years—Piaget's Formal Operational Stage."

sensorimotor the first stage of Piaget's theory of cognitive development (ages 1½–2 years), in which the child uses senses and motor abilities to interact with the environment and understands only the here and now

preoperational the second stage in Piaget's theory of cognitive development (ages 2–7 years), in which the child uses symbols to represent objects, makes judgments based on appearances, and believes that everyone has the same viewpoint as he or she

application of Jean Piaget's theory of cognitive development to an educational program. It is classified as "learner-directed" because it attempts to blend the virtues of purposeful teaching with open-ended, child-initiated activities.

Piaget believed that humans adapt mentally to their environments through their interactions or experiences with people, objects, and events. He viewed the child as an active learner who explores, experiments, and plans, thereby constructing knowledge. Learning, or mental adaptation to one's environment, occurs by **assimilation** (incorporating experiences) and by **accommodation** (reconciling differences of experiences). An example of *assimilation* is seeing a bluebird for the first time. The experience is incorporated into one's mental concept of a bird. An example of *accommodation* is seeing a butterfly, calling it a bird, and being told it is not a bird but a butterfly. The experience results in adjusting the original mental concept of butterfly and accommodating the concept that all things that fly are not always birds. When one can assimilate *and* accommodate new information, according to Piaget, one is in **equilibrium**, a state of balance, thereby allowing the information to be incorporated. We continually assimilate and accommodate throughout our lives. However, we do not always reach equilibrium. When we cannot accommodate some new information at the time we encounter it, we reject it.

To minimize rejection in a child's learning experiences, Piaget recommends that all new experiences be planned in such a way that a child can make a connection or relationship to previous experiences. The implications of this recommendation for education are significant. If teachers can assess children's cognitive structures through parent conferences, observation, interviews, and tests, they can select appropriate learning activities and tasks that will promote cognitive growth. Otherwise, if a child lacks the cognitive structure for a given task, the child will fail; the new information will be rejected because the child cannot accommodate it at that particular time. For example, 4-year-olds generally have a poor understanding of equality. Thus, trying to convince a preschooler that the piece of cake on his plate is the same size as his sister's, even though a smaller plate makes her piece look larger, will be useless.

In addition to experiences or interactions with people, objects, and events, motivation is also a factor in intellectual development. According to Piaget, all children mature in a certain order.

1. **Sensorimotor stage** (*thinking is action*). Infants and toddlers understand their environment only through their senses and motor abilities that enable them to explore. It involves only understanding the here and now.
2. **Preoperational stage** (*thinking is based on appearances*). As preschoolers develop language, they understand that words symbolize objects, but they think everyone understands things as they do. They can also consider only one characteristic of a thing at a time. Children in this stage make judgments based only on how things appear.

3. **Concrete operational stage** (*thinking is based on reality*). By the time children reach school age, their understanding of the world expands to incorporate concepts about time, equality, weight, distance, and so on, but their understanding is limited to concrete, or actual, things they can see or manipulate. While children in this stage can apply logical, systematic principles to specific experiences, they still cannot distinguish assumptions or hypotheses from facts or reality.
4. **Formal operational stage** (*thinking is based on abstractions*). It is not until adolescence that children come to understand abstract concepts such as government and are able to use logical thinking. In this stage, children can think logically about abstract ideas and hypotheses as well as concrete facts.

concrete operations the third stage in Piaget's theory of cognitive development (ages 7–11 years), in which the child can apply logical, systematic principles to specific experiences, but cannot distinguish between assumptions or hypotheses and facts or reality

formal operations the fourth stage in Piaget's theory of cognitive development (ages 11 years and up), in which the child can think logically about abstract ideas and hypotheses as well as concrete facts

In the cognitively oriented curriculum, children are encouraged to become actively involved in constructing their own learning. The teacher observes the children individually, questions and evaluates them, in order to identify their developmental level. Knowing their developmental level enables the teacher to involve children in appropriate activities that they will be capable of accommodating. The teacher organizes the environment so that children can choose from an array of developmentally appropriate materials and activities. The teacher encourages goal setting and problem solving by asking the children to plan what they are going to do and how it is to be done. Meanwhile, the teacher is enabling the children to have key experiences that stimulate thinking processes, language development, and social development. Thus the child learns to make decisions, to set goals, and to solve problems by finding alternatives to plans that did not work out as anticipated (Hohmann & Weikart, 1995). A preschool child's goal might be to build a road with blocks. A third-grader's goal might be to make a book of the planets, with descriptions and drawings.

In a cognitively oriented program, the children's emerging abilities are "broadened and strengthened" rather than "taught." In other words, once an ability is recognized by the teacher, it is nourished by the activities the teacher then provides. Children are not pushed to achieve at another developmental level. They also are not taught facts *per se*; they learn to think for themselves. Emphasis is placed on self-direction, rather than external reinforcement from others (as emphasized in behavioral programs). For example, a child may choose to make an airplane at the workbench. The teacher asks the child what materials are needed to carry out the project. When the airplane is complete, the teacher asks the child to tell how the airplane was made. A discussion about how airplanes fly might follow.

The Direct Instruction Curriculum (Teacher-Directed)

The **direct instruction curriculum** is based on behaviorist principles of dividing learning tasks into small progressive segments and reinforcing mastery of them. The behaviorist theory of B. F. Skinner (1968) provides the foundation for the direct instruction curriculum. *Behaviorism*, introduced in Chapter 4, is the doctrine that observed behavior, rather than what exists in the mind, provides the only valid data for psychology. The direct instruction curriculum would be classified as "teacher-directed." Also known as academic preschool, the curriculum was initially developed at the University of Illinois by Carl Bereiter and Siegfried Engelmann. It was later elaborated by Engelmann and Wesley Becker at the University of Oregon. The program was based on the idea that waiting for children to become academically ready was not a very sound educational practice, especially for children from lower socioeconomic groups. Those who subscribe to behaviorism believe that it is possible to ensure learning and that the school can create readiness through behavioral principles of reinforcement and individualized instruction, whatever the IQ or background of the child. Therefore, in the behavioral approach to education, learning is mastery of specific content. The content and sequence are determined by the teacher or the school—whoever is responsible for planning the curriculum. Learners

direct instruction curriculum a curriculum based on behaviorist principles

A teacher-centered activity in that the children were given similar materials and they are following the teacher's directions.

Cengage Learning

receive immediate feedback for their responses. Incorrect responses require repetition of the task; correct responses are reinforced, and the learner progresses to the next task.

The Bereiter–Engelmann (1966) preschool program, which was specifically designed for children from low-income families, implements the behavioral approach to learning. Bereiter and Engelmann believe that children from low socioeconomic levels are behind in language development. This lag causes them to have difficulty understanding what is required of them in school. To catch up with their age-mates, they need intense instruction in structured, detailed, sequential skill building. Concepts are organized explicitly and concisely in presentation books for teacher use. All the teacher needs to do is teach the lessons exactly as they are presented in the book. The Bereiter–Engelmann program also prescribes classroom management techniques, such as rewarding students for correct responses, instructional pacing techniques (how much time to spend on a topic or with a child), and group management—for example, using hand signals to cue students to respond. The program is designed to foster IQ gain and improve achievement test performance in the early school years (Horowitz & Paden, 1973).

A revised form of the Bereiter–Engelmann program for use in elementary schools stresses hard work, focused attention, and achievement in reading, language, and arithmetic. The direct instruction curriculum uses few of the play materials normally seen in many early childhood programs. The reason for this is to minimize environmental distractions that could tempt the children to leave the task at hand and explore. Children are expected to be quiet, respond to the teacher, and not interrupt or leave their seats without permission.

The Montessori Curriculum (Learner-Directed)

Dr. Maria Montessori was a physician in Italy at the turn of the century. She developed methods of working with children who were mentally retarded and later adapted them for use with children of normal intelligence in her *Casa del Bambini*. Her principles of education were described in a journal in the United States in 1909 and eventually became very popular in many parts of the world. Trainers were sent to her school to learn her methods and apply them in early childhood programs.

Montessori (1967) believed that children should be respected and treated as individuals and that adults should not impose their ideas and wishes on them. Children must educate themselves. The Montessori curriculum is classified as "learner-directed."

Children naturally absorb knowledge just by living. However, there are sensitive periods when children absorb knowledge most easily. The role of the adult should be to recognize these sensitive periods and prepare the children's environment for the optimum use of these periods of learning (Montessori, 1967). In order for teachers to take advantage of these sensitive periods, they must be keen observers of children's behavior. They also have to know when to encourage the child, when to divert the child, and when to leave the child alone.

Montessori curriculum a curriculum based on individual self-directed learning with the teacher as facilitator; materials provide exercises in daily living, sensory development, and academic development

A **Montessori curriculum** involves children of different ages. The teacher, called a directress or director, prepares the classroom environment for the children so that the children can do things independently, thereby facilitating individual self-directed learning. Sometimes the younger children learn from the older ones. The teacher introduces materials to the children by demonstrating the correct way to use them. The children are then free to choose any materials with which they wish to work. Children work on the floor or on child-sized furniture. The Montessori program provides material designed for exercises in daily living, sensory development, and academic development (Miller & Dyer, 1975). Exercises in daily living include gardening, setting the table, buttoning buttons, and folding clothes. Sensory development includes work with shapes, graduated cylinders, blocks, and puzzles. Academic materials include large letters, beads and rods for counting, and equipment for learning about size, weight, and volume. All the materials are designed in such a way that children can determine whether they have succeeded in using them properly. Reward for success or reprimand for failure is nonexistent in a Montessori school (unlike behavioral programs). Rather, each child is encouraged to persist as long as possible on a chosen task because each child is respected as a competent learner.

The Montessori curriculum fosters reality training. For example, toys such as replicas of furniture or dress-ups are not included. Children use real things instead of play things and do real tasks, such as setting the table with real silverware and ironing with a real iron.

Since only one of each type of equipment is provided in a Montessori classroom, a child must wait until the child using a particular piece of equipment is finished. The intent of this is to help children learn to respect the work of others and to cope with the realities of life.

The Developmental Interaction Curriculum (Learner-Directed)

The Bank Street curriculum, developed by Elizabeth Gilkeson and associates at the Bank Street College of Education in New York City in 1919, focuses on the development of self-confidence, responsiveness, inventiveness, and productivity (Gilkeson & Bowman, 1976). It is classified as "learner-directed." The program is also referred to as the **developmental interaction curriculum** because it is individualized in relation to each child's stage of development, while providing many opportunities for children to interact and become involved with peers and adults. The curriculum was influenced by the writings of John Dewey (1944), who believed that children are naturally curious and learn by exploring their environment, and Sigmund Freud (1938), who believed the interactions in the first five years of a child's life are significant in forming the child's personality.

developmental interaction curriculum a curriculum that is individualized in relation to each child's stage of development while providing many opportunities for children to interact with peers and adults

The curriculum is designed to help children understand more fully what is already known to them. Learning is organized around children's own experience bases. Gradually, children's orbit of knowledge and understanding is enlarged by enabling children to explore in greater depth things already familiar to them. Teachers must continually assess children's progress in order to challenge children to experience new levels of complexity (a feature similar to the Montessori curriculum).

The classroom is arranged to include a variety of interest centers where children can pursue special projects, ample storage space giving children easy access to materials, a quiet area for reading, a library, musical instruments, and art materials. There are also places for the care of animals and plants.

All areas of the curriculum are integrated through the development of themes or units—for example, community helpers, animals, seeds, and so on. Concepts are built around the theme. For example, seeds grow into plants such as wheat; plants such as wheat are used to make ingredients for food such as flour; ingredients are combined and cooked to make food such as bread. Activities are built around the concepts. For example, children might plant seeds and bake bread. The activities lead to other learning engagements. For example, cooking leads to math—measuring, counting, adding, weighing. Children might look at books about seeds, take a trip to a bakery, and so on. Motivation to learn comes from the pleasure inherent in the activities themselves; extrinsic rewards, such as praise or tokens commonly used in behavioral programs, are generally not used in the Bank Street curriculum to influence children's learning, choice of activities, or behavior. The teacher gains the children's cooperation by showing care, concern, and support.

How can a preschool curriculum be developed to prepare young children to adapt to a changing world?

New Nonparental Child Care Curricula

Howard Gardner (2006), educational psychologist, says that accelerated change, due to globalization, science, technology, and mounting quantities of information, calls for new ways of learning and thinking in school and work. Gardner describes a curriculum defining five cognitive abilities necessary for socialization geared toward future achievement outcomes:

The Five Minds for the Future Curriculum

1. *The disciplined mind*—socialization toward mastering at least one way of thinking that is characteristic of a scholarly discipline, craft, or profession. The disciplined mind can focus on improving and mastering a skill.
2. *The synthesizing mind*—socialization toward integrating ideas from different disciplines into a coherent whole and the ability to communicate that integration.
3. *The creating mind*—socialization toward having the capacity to uncover and clarify new problems and questions, and pose possible and novel solutions.
4. *The respectful mind*—socialization toward awareness and appreciativeness of differences between human individuals and between human groups.
5. *The ethical mind*—socialization toward the ability to evaluate one's own work and the needs of society, conceptualizing how all citizens can work for the common good.

How can a preschool curriculum contribute to socializing children to develop these five "minds"? The Tools of the Mind curriculum gives children an early start.

The Tools of the Mind Curriculum

The "Tools of the Mind" curriculum is based on Vygotsky's (1978) sociocultural theory of learning (introduced in Chapter 2). Tools of the Mind is designed to help children become intentional and reflective learners. Children (novices) learn the tools of their culture by engaging in activities with more expert others (masters).

To be ready for the formal learning of tools required in a complex culture that takes place in school (reading, writing, calculating), socialization must include certain self-regulatory skills ("school readiness" is discussed further in Chapter 6). Cognitively, self-regulatory tools include paying attention, ignoring distractions, planning one's activities, staying on task, and reflecting upon one's thinking. Behaviorally, self-regulatory tools involve controlling behavior and emotional impulses, delaying gratification until appropriate, being motivated to achieve, and cooperating with others. These self-regulatory skills are implemented by activities in the Tools of the Mind curriculum and relate to the five future minds described by Gardner. The following are examples of "tool" activities that foster the five minds:

- *The disciplined mind* is fostered by "graphics practice"; children draw on white boards, starting and stopping to musical cues. They verbally repeat what to write to help them focus on the task.
- *The synthesizing mind* is fostered by "venger drawing." Working in small groups, teachers help children plan and discuss various ways to incorporate a geometric shape into a drawing. Each child creates a unique representation of what was discussed.
- *The creating mind* is fostered by "play planning"; children describe what they are going to do during playtime and represent their plan on paper, drawing and/or writing at their own level.
- *The respectful mind* is fostered by "buddy reading"; children "read" to each other, using external mediator cards to remind them of their roles as they take turns reading and listening, thereby engaging in a cooperative partner activity.
- *The ethical mind* is fostered by "collection-making"; children work in a cooperative partnered math activity, taking turns counting and checking the items in their group's collection using a one-by-one correspondence.

Current research (Diamond et al., 2007) shows that such self-regulatory skills have a stronger association with school readiness than IQ or entry-level reading or math skills. Thus, the Tools of the Mind curriculum fosters adaptive skills that can be applied in various situations (school, work, life) and are the basis for more complex learning.

How Nonparental Child-Care Ideologies Relate to Socialization Practices

How do concepts of child rearing affect socialization practices in child care?

ideology concepts about human life and behavior

An **ideology** involves concepts about human life and behavior. It has been well documented, as discussed in past chapters, that cultural or religious ideology influences socialization practices. People from different cultural and economic backgrounds hold different views of what constitutes appropriate child care (Epps & Jackson, 2000; Honig, 2002); yet much of the existing literature on child-care practices has been focused on a monocultural model of optimum care (Bromer, 1999; Greenfield et al., 2003; Miller, 1989).

In a study examining the nature of early socialization in quality day-care centers serving infants and toddlers from families of different social classes, Miller (1989) found differences in language and social interaction according to the socioeconomic status of the center's clientele. She also discovered that parents tend to seek out and employ caregivers outside the family whose child-care ideologies generally match theirs. Miller focused on the verbal interactions and role expectations between adults and children because language, according to Bernstein (1961), mediates and is mediated by one's perception of reality as well as one's social role. Thus, the language of caregivers who spend much of the day talking and responding to children has an impact on the development of values, roles, and culture-specific behaviors. Table 5.5 illustrates the differences between the day-care centers' ideologies and consequent relationships with children, as well as the different curricula at each.

The significance of Miller's description of socialization in child-care facilities for children under age 3 is its attempt to analyze different cultural ideologies that may be typical of various socioeconomic statuses and may unwittingly contribute to structures of social inequity in the larger society. Also, when nonparental child care complements family ideology and behavior, it is more likely to be beneficial for the child; when it differs, it is more likely to be harmful (Lamb, 2000). This was also found to apply to differences between caregiver and parental attitudes regarding child-rearing practices—for example, authoritative versus authoritarian styles (Ghazvini & Mullis, 2002).

Table 5.5 Social Class, Ideology, and Child Care

Center A	Center B	Center C	Center E
Served lower-class, semi-skilled, and unskilled workers	Served lower middle-class	Served upper middle-class, highly educated professionals	Served upper-class, affluent, elite executives
Crying typical of babies, not considered to represent a need; usually caregiver ignores	Crying almost always represents a need, usually tired or hungry; babies told to stop	Crying always represents a need; caregiver responsible for finding solution; if nothing works parent is called	Crying typical of babies, not considered to represent a need; usually caregiver ignores
"Make" child clean up spilled milk			"Invite" child to clean up spilled milk
Children treated as underlings with few rights; obedience to caregivers was expected, and resistance to authority demands was punished	Children expected to depend on caregivers, compete with peers for attention, and development would take normal course; children's resistance to authority demands was tolerated	High level of give-and-take between children and caregivers; caregiver adjusted expectations and demands to gain child's cooperation	Caregivers controlled children's time, space, and objects; children who resisted authority demands were ignored first, then firmly redirected
Curriculum based on conformity, group cohesion, adaptation to few resources, and rote learning	Curriculum based on maintaining safety, adherence to set routines, and avoidance of conflict	Curriculum based on achievement of responsible independence	Curriculum based on compliance, conformity, and high-quality performance

What does knowledge of child development have to do with caregiving and teaching?

Developmentally Appropriate Caregiving

maturation developmental changes associated with the biological process of aging

Maturation refers to developmental changes associated with the biological process of aging. There are individual differences within the "average" ages at which children reach certain developmental milestones, such as walking, talking, and controlling bladder and bowels. Maturation is a significant factor in being "ready" to learn.

Caregivers or teachers who implement developmentally appropriate practices "must know about child development and the implications of this knowledge for how to teach, the content of the curriculum—what to teach and when—how to assess what children have learned, and how to adapt curriculum and instruction to children's individual strengths, needs, and interests. Further, they must know the particular children they teach and their families and be knowledgeable as well about the social and cultural context" (Bredekamp & Copple, 1997, p. 16; Copple & Bredenkamp, 2009). Some aspects of developmentally appropriate caregiving involve observation, sensitivity to children's needs, and responsiveness. Teachers create a stimulating environment, plan engaging activities, enable children to initiate learning, and facilitate self-regulatory behavior in children. In order to enhance children's development, ongoing assessment of their learning must take place and be reflected in the planned activities. Collaboration with families is essential.

How can caregivers work with parents for optimal child outcomes?

Collaborative Caregiving

To provide a beneficial caregiving environment for children, it is critical for professionals who care for infants and children to collaborate with families regarding ideologies and socialization goals (Bromer, 1999; Greenfield, Suzuki, & Rothstein-Fisch, 2006). At opposite ends of a continuum are cultural frameworks (ideologies) for socialization, *individualism* versus *collectivism* (see Figure 5.5). The primary goal in an individualistic society is independence. Children are encouraged to be autonomous and self-fulfilled; social responsibilities are motivated by personal choice. The primary goal in a collectivistic society is interdependence. Children are encouraged to be subordinate and responsible in relating to others; achievements are motivated in terms of service to the group, usually the family (Greenfield, Suzuki, & Rothstein-Fisch, 2006). In a diverse society, such as the United States, both parents and caregivers represent different degrees of individualism and collectivism. Differences between parents and caregivers can, for example, be observed in attitudes about sleeping arrangements (should the baby sleep alone or with its parents?), carrying (should the baby be carried in a baby carrier close to the mother's body or in an infant seat physically separate from but in view of the mother?), feeding (should the baby be fed whenever it cries, or should a certain schedule be adhered to?) (Bhavnagri, 1997).

For another example, diversity in socialization goals between parents and caregivers can also be observed in communication styles with infants. Some mothers tend to label objects verbally so the child will learn the names of things in the environment ("That's a car. It's red. Look! It has four wheels."). Other mothers tend to focus more on the sharing of an object than on labeling it ("Here's the car. I give it to you; you give it to me. Thank you!") (Greenfield, Suzuki, & Rothstein-Fisch, 2006).

Perhaps parents and nonparental caregivers should set aside "transition time" when the child enters a child-care setting. During this time, parent and caregiver observe each other interact with the child and discuss socialization goals, methods, and outcomes. Observation and discussion should take place at regular intervals. Evidence for this recommendation comes from a study of child-care facilities in three Canadian cities with major immigrant influx (Bernhard et al., 1998). The investigators found

In this classroom parents and teachers are collaborating in an activity with the children.

Cengage Learning

that parents and teachers were unaware of their basic differences in socialization goals, particularly regarding respect for authority, social skills, and learning. Also, there were substantial differences over what constitutes appropriate parenting at home. Thus, there needs to be more linkage between home and child care in order to provide developmentally appropriate practices for diverse groups of children (Bredekamp & Copple, 1997; Copple & Bredekamp, 2009).

Independence Oriented		**Interdependence Oriented**
Individual achievement is valued. • Competition is encouraged. • Toys promoting individual enjoyment or mastery are provided. • Self-help skills are reinforced.	**Values**	Group cohesiveness is valued. • Mutual help is encouraged. • Toys promoting turn taking or collaboration are provided. • Helping others is reinforced.
Object-focused activities are emphasized. • Children are stimulated and learn from playing with toys and things. • Babies are put on mats or in playpens to play with things.	**Activities**	People-focused activities are emphasized. • Children are stimulated and learn from observing and interacting with people. • Babies are held by adults most of the time.
Communication of feelings is openly expressive. • Children are encouraged to talk about feelings of happiness, sadness, fear, or anger. • Children are permitted to question rules and authority figures.	**Communication**	Communication of feelings is restricted. • Children are expected to subordinate their feelings to promote the harmony of the group. • Children are not permitted to question rules or authority figures.

FIGURE 5.5 Dimensions of Cultural Frameworks for Socialization in Caregiving Settings
Source: Adapted from Bromer, 1999; Rosenthal, 2003.

IN CONTEXT Collaborative caregiving also refers to the support child caregivers can provide to parents because of their knowledge of child development and developmentally appropriate practices. Support includes the following:

- Listening to parents
- Empathizing
- Translating emotional responses into concrete ones that can be acted on
- Modeling methods of guidance and discipline
- Providing opportunities for support groups and parent education
- Enabling the family to link with services in the community

Caregivers and Child Protection

What is the caregiver's legal responsibility in suspected cases of child maltreatment?

Political ideology in the United States (a macrosystem) regarding children is that they should be protected from harm and maltreatment. If the family doesn't do this, then the government must. Child protection laws have been enacted, such as the Child Abuse Prevention and Treatment Act (CAPTA) of 1974, which was amended and reauthorized

Physical abuse, exemplified by the bruise on this child's eye, must be reported to child protective services.

George Glod/Superstock

as the Keeping Children and Families Safe Act of 2003. This act defines maltreatment and lists professionals who must report suspected cases to their local child protective agency. Child caregivers and educators are among the mandated reporters. Sometimes caregivers notice that a child's appearance, behavior, or way of interacting differs from that of the other children. Caregivers with child development training and experience are able to recognize deviations from what is considered normal development. States vary in their specific definitions of maltreatment and their procedures as to when and how to report it. (Please go to the Education CourseMate website for this book to see a detailed listing of the "Indications of Possible Maltreatment.") Intervention programs for maltreatment are discussed in Chapter 10.

Children who are maltreated do not usually "tell." They may be distrustful of all adults. They are even unlikely to express hatred toward abusing parents. They have little understanding of the parents' behavior. Often children believe the abuse occurred because they did something wrong. Thus, they may be confused and even frightened by another adult's concern. They may also worry about their parents' retaliation if they tell (O'Brien, 1984). With this understanding, child caregivers and educators can be involved in identifying, supporting, providing a stable environment, and modeling ways to express feelings appropriately and to resolve conflicts.

Summary

- Nonparental child care, or day care, refers to care given to children by persons other than parents during the day or part of the day. It can be at the child's home, at another home, or in a center.
- Components of optimal quality care include (1) a caregiver who provides warm, loving care and guidance for the child and works with the family to ensure that the child develops in the best way possible; (2) a setting that keeps the child safe, secure, and healthy; and (3) activities that help the child develop emotionally, socially, mentally, and physically.
- Quality care is also judged by whether the program is developmentally appropriate. Objective measures of quality include size of the overall group, caregiver–child ratios, and caregiver training in child development.
- Nonparental child care and early childhood educational practices have been affected by macrosystems—political ideology, culture/ethnicity, economics, and science/technology.
- Chronosystem influences in nonparental child care are evidenced by historical changes in the United States. Child care began in this country as a social service (custodial focus) for immigrants. By the 1960s, child-care programs began to flourish (educational focus) because of the increase in mothers of young children entering the labor force.
- Studies have examined the emotional, social, and intellectual correlates and consequences of child care for the child. Children who attend quality day-care programs do not differ in their attachment to their mothers from children cared for at home. Children in day-care programs differ somewhat from children who are not in day care in their relationships with peers; those in day-care programs tend to be more self-sufficient, outgoing, and aggressive with others. The intellectual performance of children who attend day care is higher than that of children from similar family backgrounds who did not attend a quality child-care program.
- A federally funded program for children who are disadvantaged, Head Start provides intervention to enable such children to enter school ready to learn. There are many kinds of intervention programs, but for the child to become a competent member of society, the child's family must be involved.
- A mesosystem influence on nonparental child care includes links with the school and community. Schools can extend hours to care for children and include those under the age of 5. Child care in the community is beneficial economically. It is less costly to fund child-care programs with tax dollars than it is to fund other services such as special education, welfare, or programs for juvenile delinquents. Child care also provides work for adults in the community.
- Another mesosystem influence on nonparental child care involves links with government and business. Government provides funding of child care and tax credits to families using child care. Business may provide services for their employees, such as leaves, flextime, financial assistance for

child care, resources and referrals, in-kind contribution to child-care facilities in the community, and/or on-site care.

- Different types of nonparental child care (in-home care, family day care, center-based care) have different effects on socialization because of the varying opportunities for interacting with adults, other children, and materials.
- Different curriculum models have different effects on socialization because of the specific skills a program emphasizes.
- Four theory-based curriculum models found in center-based nonparental child-care programs include the cognitively oriented, direct instruction, Montessori, and developmental interaction curricula. Teacher-directed curricula, such as direct instruction, generally produce children who score higher on achievement tests. Learner-directed curricula, such as Montessori and developmental interaction (as well as the cognitively oriented curriculum), generally tend to foster autonomy, problem-solving skills, and cooperation.
- New preschool curricula aiming to prepare children for a changing world are "The Five Minds" and the "Tools of the Mind."
- The ideologies of caregivers influence their socialization practices. These ideologies affect caregivers' language and social interaction with children.
- Caregivers or teachers who implement developmentally appropriate practices must know about child development and how to teach curriculum accordingly.
- To provide a beneficial caregiving environment for children, it is critical for professionals who care for infants and children to collaborate with families regarding socialization goals, including their position along the spectrum of individualism versus collectivism.
- Political ideology in the United States regarding children is that they must be protected. Caregivers and educators are mandated by law to report child maltreatment, including physical abuse, neglect, sexual abuse and exploitation, and emotional abuse or deprivation.

Activity

PURPOSE To assess the socialization that occurs in the child-care facilities in your community.

1. Look in the phone book or online and choose two child-care facilities in your community to visit. Note whether they are half- or full-day facilities and whether they serve infants/toddlers, preschoolers, and/or school-agers.
2. Describe each facility—physical setting, teacher–child ratio, ages of children, hours, fees, equipment (outdoor and indoor), toys, and creative materials.
3. Observe the interaction between the adults and the children. Describe.
4. Observe the interaction between the children. Describe.
5. What kind of curriculum is implemented? Describe.
6. Is there parent involvement and/or education in the program? Describe.
7. Are there support services (health, nutrition, counseling, referrals) for families of the enrolled children? Describe.

Related Readings

Bedrova, E., & Leong, D. (2007). *Tools of the mind: The Vygotskian approach to early childhood* (2nd ed.). Upper Saddle River, NJ: Prentice-Hall.

Bender, J., Flatter, C. H., & Sorrentino, J. (2005). *Half a childhood: Quality programs for out-of-school hours.* Nashville, TN: School Age Notes.

Elkind, D. (1987). *Miseducation: Preschoolers at risk.* New York: Knopf.

Helfer, M. E., Kempe, R. S., & Krugman, R. D. (Eds.). (1999). *The battered child* (5th ed.). Chicago: University of Chicago Press.

Isenberg, J. P., & Jalongo, M. R. (2003). *Major trends and issues in early childhood education* (2nd ed.). New York: Teachers College Press.

Leach, P. (2010). *Child care today: Getting it right for everyone.* New York: Knopf.

Resources

CYFERnet—practical research-based information on children, youth, and families

http://www.cyfernet.org

National Association for the Education of Young Children—promoting excellence in early childhood education

http://www.naeyc.org

National Institute of Child Health and Human Development—national research study on the relationship between child care and child development

http://www.nichd.nih.gov

Dynamic Graphics/Jupiter Images

6

Ecology of the School

"The direction in which education starts a man will determine his future life."

—PLATO

SOCIALIZATION SKETCHES

Carlos Santana

(b. 1947)

Wire Image/Getty Images

"Peace has never come from dropping bombs. Real peace comes from enlightenment and educating people to behave more in a divine manner."

— CARLOS SANTANA

Santana's quote refers to the importance of diverse people learning to get along together. The following Socialization Sketch relates to this chapter in that Santana gives credit to the schools he attended, and their teachers, for giving him the motivation to achieve. He is "giving back" to education by helping the National Education Association (NEA) recruit people of color to become teachers.

Grammy Award–winner Carlos Santana became famous as a Mexican Latin rock guitarist in the late 1960s and early 1970s with his band, "Santana." They created a blend of salsa, rock, blues, and jazz fusion. Over the next few decades, Santana continued to work on his melodic, blues-based guitar lines set against Latin percussion. In the 1990s he experienced a resurgence of popularity. It's unusual for a rock musician's popularity to span four decades.

Santana has recently done television spots for the National Education Association. He says, "Do you love music? Do you love art, books, science? We all love something. Whatever you love, think about teaching it."

Family

Carlos Augusto Alves Santana was born in Autlan de Navarro, Jalisco, Mexico. He lived with his parents, two brothers, and four sisters. His father was a mariachi violinist. Carlos began playing the violin when he was 5 years old, occasionally performing with his father's mariachi orchestra when his family moved to Tijuana. When he was 9, he became interested in the guitar, playing rhythm and blues, rock and roll, and blues music. Soon he was performing in bands in the Tijuana area. By age 10, he was being sexually abused, keeping it a secret and escaping into his music. It wasn't until he was married that he told his secret—his wife got him into therapy. Now he shares his story to help others shed their shame.

When Carlos was 13, the Santana family moved to San Francisco, California. He graduated from Mission High School in 1965, working as a dishwasher to help the family. He enjoyed the San Francisco music scene, often sneaking into performances of his favorite artists. In 1966, he formed his own band.

School

Santana shares what teachers have meant in his life. He talks of Mr. Knudsen, who was particularly special because he knew something Carlos didn't know about himself. When Santana came to the United States, Mr. Knudsen took the time to review his grades from Mexico. "They were pathetic." Yet Mr. Knudsen told Carlos he believed he could be successful, that he had a great imagination and an "eye for art." He also said he'd heard Carlos was a pretty good musician. On a school field trip to an art museum in San Francisco, Mr. Knudsen said that in the real world of art or music there was no room for 50-50; if you want to follow your dream, you have to give 100 percent. Santana cried—no one had ever believed in him or cared about him as an individual person with such passion.

Therefore, Carlos Santana is trying to get the message out about teaching. "A truly great teacher has to have a great heart—a capacity for passion and compassion." Teachers must have "the ability to impact young people's minds to the point where they would never allow themselves to be placed in a situation where they feel they are a lesser person, or a loser, and that's where teachers of color can make a difference." It's important for kids to have role models: someone who understands, someone to motivate, someone to emulate.

Santana and his wife established the Milagro Foundation in 1998 to support educational programs in music and art. It also provides musical instruments to kids from low-income and at-risk families.

Learning Objectives

After completing this chapter, you will be able to:

1. Define the school's function as a socializing agent.
2. Discuss the macrosystem influences on the school affecting its function—educational policy, school choice, diversity, and equity.
3. Discuss the chronosystem influences on schools—societal change, technology, health, and safety.
4. Discuss the mesosystem influences on schools—linkages between school and child, school and family, school and media, school and community.

Media

Carlos Santana was honored as Person of the Year (2004) by the Latin Academy of Recording Arts and Sciences. He has come a long way since he played songs on his guitar for tourists on the streets of Tijuana. Carlos Santana has been labeled a "crossover" musician, uniting all different kinds of music. His *Supernatural* CD is a graceful synchrony of musical styles. Santana believes that is how it should be in the classroom with students and teachers of all different backgrounds—if you can learn to harmonize, you can help change the world for the better.

- What characteristics of Santana make him an effective role model for young people?
- Do you agree with Santana that children learn best when they pursue their interests and the teacher guides them?

Source: Academy of Achievement (http://www.achievement.org)

What is the purpose of the school from the perspectives of society and the individual?

The School's Function as a Socializing Agent

The school is society's formal institution where learning takes place. This chapter examines the school as a microsystem in which children develop. To better understand the socialization function of the school, macrosystem influences (political ideology, economics, culture, religion, and technology) and their changes over time (chronosystem influences) are discussed. Also relevant to understanding the school's function as a socialization agent are the linkages, or mesosystems, between school and family, school and peer group, school and media, and school and community. Figure 6.1 shows a bioecological model of the systems involved in the process.

The school's function as a socializing agent is that it provides the intellectual and social experiences from which children develop the skills, knowledge, interests, and attitudes that characterize them as individuals and that shape their abilities to perform adult roles. Schools exert influence on children by

- their educational programs leading to achievement;
- their formal organization, introducing students to authority; and
- the social relationships that evolve in the classroom.

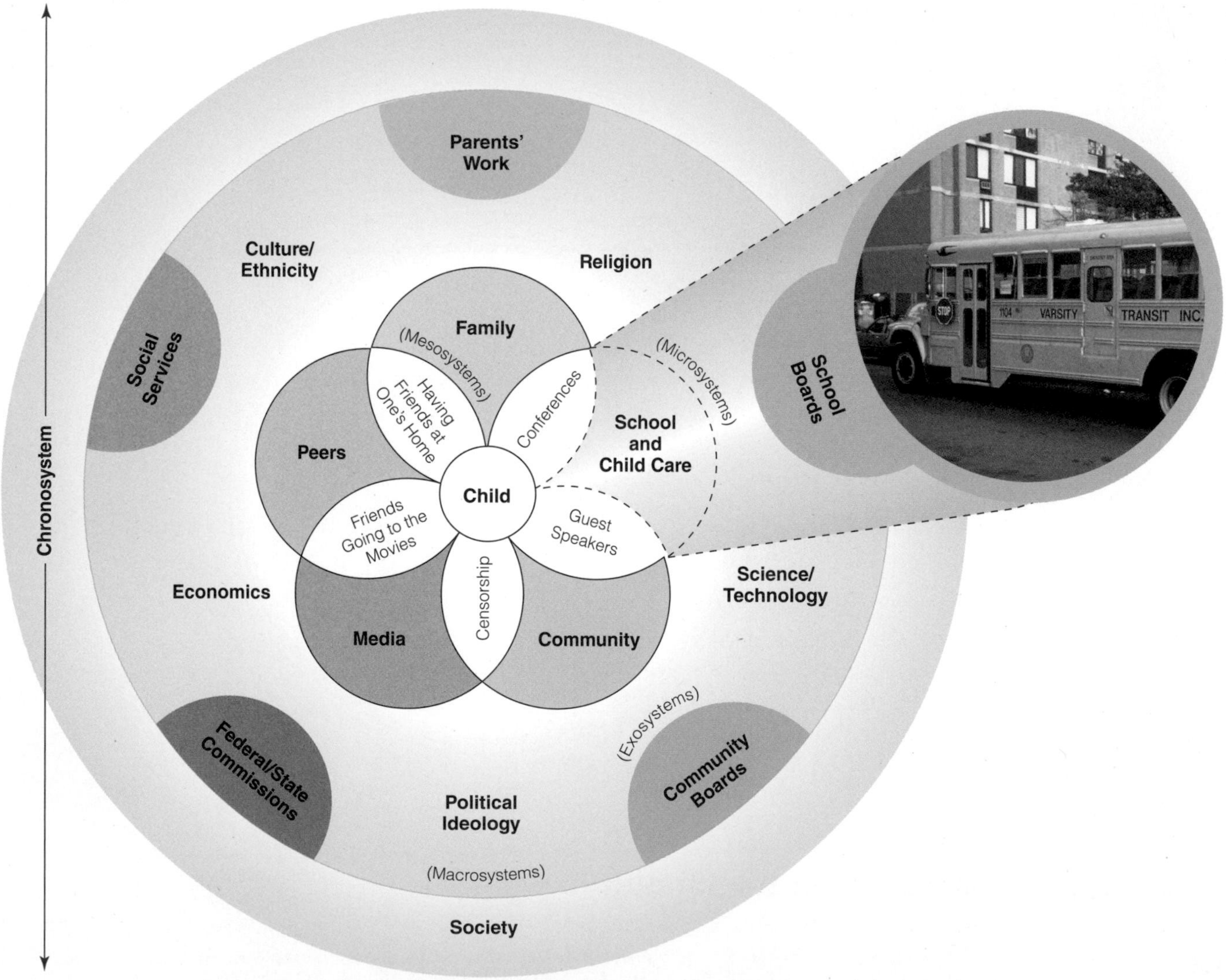

FIGURE 6.1 A Bioecological Model of Human Development
The school is a significant influence on the child's development.
Cengage Learning

Table 6.1 Goals for Schooling in the United States

A. Academic Goals
   1. Mastery of basic skills (reading, writing, arithmetic) and fundamental processes (communicating ideas, using information resources)
   2. Intellectual development (accumulate general knowledge; think rationally, independently, and critically; solve problems; be curious)

B. Vocational Goals
   3. Career/vocational education (select a suitable occupation based on interest and abilities, develop appropriate work attitudes and habits, become economically independent and productive)

C. Social, Civic, and Cultural Goals
   4. Interpersonal understanding (various values, relationships, cultures)
   5. Citizenship participation (understand history and representational government, make informed choices, contribute to the welfare of others and the environment)
   6. Enculturation (awareness of values, behavioral norms, traditions, achievements of one's culture and other cultures)
   7. Moral and ethical character (evaluate choices, conduct, develop integrity)

D. Personal Goals
   8. Emotional and physical well-being (develop self-awareness, coping skills, time-management skills, healthy habits, physical fitness)
   9. Creativity and aesthetic expression (develop originality in problem solving, be tolerant of new ideas, appreciate various forms of creativity)
   10. Self-realization (evaluate abilities and limitations, set goals, accept responsibility for decisions made)

Sources: Goodlad, 1984; Johnson et al., 2004.

Some of these influences are intentional, such as instruction in a specific subject, and some are unintentional—for example, competitive grading and its effect on motivation.

The primary purpose of education, from *society's* perspective, is the transmission of the cultural heritage: the accumulated knowledge, values, beliefs, and customs of the society. To transmit culture and maintain it, society needs trained people who can assume specialized roles as well as develop new knowledge and technology. The purpose of education from the *individual's* perspective is to acquire the necessary skills and knowledge to become self-sufficient and to participate effectively in society.

The school's function in the United States can be described as

- *universal* in that it is open to all,
- *formal* in that it is methodical, and
- *prescriptive* in that it provides directions based on custom.

Society's expectations are expressed in goals—academic, vocational, social, civic, cultural, and personal—described more specifically in Table 6.1. These goals emerged from a detailed study of schooling led by John Goodlad (1984) in a sample of communities across the United States representing urban, suburban, and rural areas as well as different socioeconomic statuses. Elementary, junior high, and high schools were included in the observations. Questionnaires were given to teachers, parents, students, and administrators regarding their goals for education.

Macrosystem Influences on Schools

What societal factors play a significant role in how the school functions?

The school reflects macrosystem influences of society—specifically, its traditional values and future goals. The citizens of the society implement these values and goals. In a democratic society, the role of the school is continually debated by its citizens until a consensus is reached regarding funding, standards, curricula, teacher education, class size, attendance requirements, assessment, and so on. This consensus translates into educational policy.

What factors are involved in developing educational policy?

Educational Policy

Influential macrosystem factors in developing educational policy are political ideology, economics, culture, religion, and science/technology.

Political Ideology

The basic political ideology for which the United States of America stands is democracy—as Abraham Lincoln put it, "government *of* the people, *by* the people, *for* the people." A democratic society presumes freedom from government oppression. Citizens in a democratic society, although diverse, are presumed to have equal rights and equal opportunities. For a democracy to function, its educational policy must involve educating citizens

- to discuss and compromise on issues pertaining to them as individuals and as a group;
- to select competent leaders to rule by the will of the majority; and
- to evaluate the equity of the rules as well as the leaders' implementation of them.

Exercising one's right to vote, thereby participating in decision making, is how this occurs. It wasn't until after the Civil War, however, that schooling became public, thereby offering all children, regardless of socioeconomic status, an equal opportunity to be educated and exercise their voice in government. The concept of equality has been expanded since the days of the writing of the Constitution to include race, creed, color, gender, age, national origin, and disability, implemented in various laws discussed in following pertinent sections.

Economics

How much society is willing to pay for the education of its citizens is influenced by values of equality of opportunity, concepts of knowledge and skills required for the future, and affordability of programs and curricula funded by taxes or other public or private resources. Educational policies are generally under the jurisdiction of the states, rather than the federal government; as a result, expenditures per pupil vary widely throughout the country, among and even within states. For example, New Jersey, ranked first among the states in per pupil spending for public education, spent about $11,793; Utah, ranked last, spent about $4,900 per pupil (National Center for Education Statistics, 2007). A major cause of school funding inequalities is that most states rely heavily on local property taxes for financing education. Thus, property taxes in wealthier districts usually generate adequate monies, while property taxes in poorer districts do not. To address the achievement gap between disadvantaged students and their peers, Congress passed the No Child Left Behind Act (NCLB) in 2001, mandating that all students meet certain proficiency standards in basic subjects, pass achievement tests, and that schools meet certain health and safety requirements. Federal funding is tied to the school's ability to meet these standards. More details of the NCLB are discussed later.

TeachSource Video Activity

Go to the Education CourseMate website to watch the ABC News video entitled "No Child Left Behind (NCLB): Good Intentions, Real Problems." Do you think school funding should be tied to children's test scores? Why or why not?

Culture

Traditional values of the macroculture are imparted via the school curriculum and classroom management (Ballantine & Spade, 2004). A challenge facing educators is how to balance equity with diversity, enabling children to assimilate the macroculture while maintaining their distinctive microcultural heritage or identity. This challenge is exemplified by diverse holidays celebrated in the classroom and by what information is included in textbooks—for example, the perspectives of Native Americans and those of the colonists who came to America from Europe regarding Thanksgiving are presented.

Scientific knowledge is one of the national education goals.

Cengage Learning

Religion

The first amendment to the Constitution guarantees freedom of religion and requires separation of church and state. This means educational policy mandates that public schools cannot promote a *particular* religion, nor can they inhibit religious beliefs. The word "God" is in many government documents, such as the Declaration of Independence and money. In 1956, Congress adopted "In God we trust" as the official motto of the United

States. This policy has been debated throughout the country's history, as exemplified by such issues as school prayer, appropriate science curriculum, extracurricular activities in public school facilities, and school vouchers (discussed in the next section).

Science/Technology

Advances in science and technology have affected not only school curricula but the methods of teaching (Oppenheimer, 2003). Technological aids for teaching include television, video recorders and players, computers, and other digital devices. Most of these are interactive, enabling children to enhance learning and develop skills. Scientific research on how children process information has broadened teaching methods to include active participation and discovery in addition to passive recitation and rote learning. Teaching methods will be discussed in Chapter 7.

In addition, more advanced courses are being taught in schools. Part of President George W. Bush's educational policy was to enable American children to meet the challenges of a changing world. In 2006, Congress passed the American Competitiveness Initiative, committing funds to schools for more advanced courses, especially in math, science, and languages critical to national security and global competitiveness.

School Choice

What options do parents have regarding the education of their children?

Macrosystem influences can be seen in society's policies regarding school choice. Generally, students are assigned to a public school in the local district where they live. Educational policies—hiring teachers and staff, curricula, amount of attendance time required, textbooks, assessment procedures, class size and composition, extracurricular activities, school expenditures, and rules and regulations—are made bureaucratically by each school district in compliance with state requirements. Since individual schools differ in how these policies are implemented, families are allowed to choose among schools because

1. school choice is consistent with a democratic form of government that promotes freedom;
2. choice will foster competition among schools to better educate students; and
3. individual students will be more empowered to succeed in some schools than in others (Olsen & Fuller, 2007).

Magnet Schools

In the 1970s, as schools accommodated the federal requirement to desegregate, the concept of magnet schools emerged as one solution to the unpopularity of forced busing of children from their neighborhoods to distant schools in order to create racial balance. A **magnet school** is a public school that offers special educational programs, such as science, music, or performing arts, and draws students from different neighborhoods by choice.

magnet school a public school that offers special educational programs, such as science, music, or performing arts, and draws students from different neighborhoods by choice

School Vouchers

Many people believe that private schools have more successful educational outcomes than do public schools, because of less bureaucracy, more family involvement, smaller classes, and students' backgrounds. Families who send their children to private school must pay tuition as well as school taxes for public schools. Since the 1970s, there has been much political pressure in various states to give public financial support to private schools. One mechanism is the **school voucher**—a certificate issued by the federal government in the amount the local school district would normally spend on that child's education at his or her assigned public school, which parents can apply toward tuition at a private school or used for reimbursement for home schooling expenses. Supporters claim that in a free market system, private schools should have as much right as public schools to be supported by the government. They argue that the best schools will attract the most students, thereby thriving and multiplying, and the worst schools will be eliminated or will improve to attract "customers" (Tozer, Violas, & Senese, 2008).

school voucher a certificate issued by the federal government in the amount the local school district would normally spend on a given child's education at his or her assigned public school, which parents can apply toward tuition at a private school or used for reimbursement for home schooling expenses

The NCLB provides guidelines for school choice and vouchers. It includes private and faith-based schools, which can now apply for federal funds. It offers parents new options to prevent their children from being stuck in schools assessed as needing academic improvement or in schools assessed as being dangerous. If a school has a poor track record for two years, parents can transfer their children (transportation included) to public schools with track records of academic success and safety (parents have the right to inspect instructional material and assessments). The NCLB sets out requirements for funding school improvement, teacher qualifications, and testing.

Charter Schools

charter school a school, authorized and funded by a public school district, formed by a group of parents, teachers, or other community members with a shared educational philosophy

In response to the controversial nature of vouchers, many states have passed legislation to allow families to have more alternatives for their children—hence the creation of charter schools. A **charter school** is a school that is formed by a group of parents, teachers, or other community members with a shared educational philosophy and that is authorized and funded by a public school district. The charter that is granted states educational goals, methods, and outcomes. Like any other public school, the charter school must meet state educational standards. Charter schools can choose among various scientifically based curricula to implement. The school has explicit responsibility for improved achievement, as measured by standardized tests.

Home-Based Schools

Some families, believing that any mechanism involving public school improvement will not benefit their child, choose to provide home-based education. Although specific requirements vary from state to state, generally, home schools must have credentialed teachers and follow a prescribed curriculum. Some home-based education is combined with charter schools. Many families who choose home schooling do so because they believe it is the parents' right to control their children's education and to teach morals and values (usually religious) as they see fit.

Diversity and Equity

How can the school meet the diverse needs of individuals while also providing everyone with equal opportunities?

All the macrosystem influences on school previously discussed relate to how diverse groups in society, such as those characterized by gender, culture, religion, or disability, are enabled to have equitable opportunities to achieve. Here we examine the effects of those macrosystem influences on school; in the next chapter, we examine how such diverse groups are treated as part of the student population in the classroom.

Gender

Until 1972, when Title IX of the Education Amendments Act was passed, gender inequities were common in schools. These inequities included different curriculum opportunities for males and females (boys took "shop" and girls took "home economics"), different academic and career advising, different amounts of money allocated to athletic and extracurricular activities, and different portrayals in textbooks. The opening section of Title IX states:

> No person in the United States shall, on the basis of sex, be excluded from participation in, be denied the benefits of, or be subjected to discrimination under any education program or activity receiving federal financial assistance.

Every public school and most colleges and universities in the United States are covered by Title IX, which prohibits discrimination in school admissions, in counseling and guidance, in competitive athletics, in student rules and regulations, and in access to programs and courses, including vocational education and physical education. Title IX also applies to sex discrimination in employment practices, including interviewing and recruitment, hiring and promotion, compensation, job assignments, and fringe benefits.

Culture

The macrosystem ideology that the school is responsible for socializing diverse cultural groups is wedded to American immigration policy; those who live and work here must learn good citizenship. They must accept democratic values as well as adhere to the laws and principles of the Constitution.

Macrosystem philosophies regarding how diverse cultural groups should be socialized, especially by the school, are *cultural assimilation* (microcultures assume attributes of the macroculture), *melting pot* (all cultures blend into one), and *cultural pluralism* (micro- and macroculture coexist).

- **Cultural assimilation** is the process whereby a minority (subordinate) cultural group takes on the characteristics of the majority (dominant) cultural group. The school has traditionally served the socialization needs of the majority culture. For a long time it was felt that in order for diverse cultural groups to be assimilated into society, they had to adapt to the majority culture's ways. Examples of assimilation are the use of English as the official language on public documents, English immersion programs in schools, and celebrating American holidays.
- **Melting pot**, a concept gaining popularity in response to major increases in immigration, was that society should socialize diverse groups to blend into a common culture. The term became popular in 1908 after the premiere of a play by that name, written by Israel Zangwill. Advocates of the melting-pot theory believed that the new emerging U.S. culture must be built not on the destruction of the cultural values and mores of the various immigrant groups, but on their fusion with existing U.S. civilization, which itself was never purely Anglo-Saxon but a product of the interaction of Anglo-Saxon elements with French, Spanish, Dutch, Native American, and African American components. An example of the melting-pot philosophy is *Esperanto*, a language invented in 1887 for international use. It is based on word roots common to the main European languages. Currently, there is an Esperanto League of Cyberspace.
- **Cultural pluralism** involves a mutual appreciation and understanding of various cultures and the coexistence in society of different languages, religions, and lifestyles. Kallen (1956), who coined the term, theorized that the majority (dominant) culture benefits from coexistence and constant interaction with other cultural groups—in other words, "unity in diversity." The various minority (subordinate) cultural groups, or microcultures, should accept and cherish the common elements of U.S. cultural, political, and social mores as represented by the public schools, but they should, by their own efforts, support supplemental education for their young (such as language training or religious school) to preserve their family's cultural awareness and values.

cultural assimilation the process whereby a minority (subordinate) cultural group takes on the characteristics of the majority (dominant) cultural group

melting pot the idea that society should socialize diverse groups to blend into a common culture

cultural pluralism mutual appreciation and understanding of various cultures and coexistence in society of different languages, religious beliefs, and lifestyles

An example of the socialization philosophy of cultural pluralism is the concept of multicultural education—learning experiences that encourage interest in many cultures within the society rather than in just the mainstream culture.

Language

An increasing number of children with limited English proficiency (LEP) are attending U.S. schools and are at risk for failure. Research shows that disproportionately high numbers of some diverse students enter school unprepared for academic work (Haskins & Rouse, 2005) and do not finish school, and disproportionately high numbers of those who do remain in school are achieving far below their potential (Bennett, 2010).

The teacher is sensitive to cultural pluralism in the classroom. Here, she is encouraging diverse children to work together to learn about places other than the United States.

The federal government has tried to equalize opportunities for diverse groups through legislation. In 1974, Congress passed the Equal Educational Opportunity Act, requiring schools to take "appropriate action" to overcome the language barriers of students who cannot communicate in English.

The NCLB consolidated existing federal programs and grants for the education of LEP and recent immigrant students under the Elementary and Secondary Education Act of 1965 (ESEA). The new Language Acquisition State Formula Grant Program (ESEA, Title III) allocates 80 percent funding according to the population of LEP students and 20 percent according to the population of recently arriving immigrants. The law gives the states flexibility in designing and administering programs while emphasizing achievement of English proficiency rather than encouraging bilingual curricula. Recipients of Title III money are subjected to strict accountability standards (funding is tied to continually improved student achievement).

According to the National Center for Education Statistics (NCES) (2007), since the 1960s all statistically delineated racial/ethnic groups whose educational achievements were followed showed an increase in the percentage of adults who had completed high school and continued their education in college. Also, the percentage of White, Black, Hispanic, Asian/Pacific Islander, and American Indian/Alaska Native adults with bachelor's degrees increased. Despite these gains, however, progress has varied and differences persist on the following examples of educational performance indicators.

1. The percentage of families with children in poverty was higher for Black, American Indian/Alaska Native, Hispanic, and Native Hawaiian or Other Pacific Islander families than for White and Asian families.
2. The percentage of students who spoke a language other than English at home was higher among Hispanic and Asian elementary and secondary students than among elementary and secondary students of all other racial/ethnic groups followed in the study.
3. On the National Assessment of Educational Progress (NAEP) reading assessment, higher percentages of Asian/Pacific Islander and White fourth graders and eighth graders scored at or above "proficient" than did American Indian/Alaska Native, Black, and Hispanic students at the same grade levels. On the fourth- and eighth-grade mathematics assessment, a higher proportion of Asian/Pacific Islanders scored at or above "proficient" than did fourth and eighth graders of all other races/ethnicity groups followed in the study.
4. A larger percentage of Black than White, Hispanic, and Asian/Pacific Islander students received financial aid, while a smaller percentage of Asian/Pacific Islanders received financial aid than any of the other race/ethnicity groups followed in the study.

Communication Style

Research indicates that children's individual communication styles vary; they have been shown to be related to socialization in the family's culture (Banks, 2007). Likewise, teachers often communicate in the style of their own culture. Sometimes the contrast in styles interferes with the child's ability to learn. For example, the time a teacher waits for a child to respond to a question and the time the teacher waits before talking again were compared between a Euro-American and a Navajo teacher of the same group of third-grade Navajo students (White & Tharp, 1988). The Navajo teacher waited considerably longer than the Euro-American teacher after the children responded before talking again. What was perceived by the Euro-American teacher as a completed response was often intended by the child as a pause, which the Euro-American teacher had interrupted. In contrast to Navajo students, who preferred long wait times between responses, Native Hawaiian students preferred "negative" wait times; that is, the listener speaks without waiting for the speaker to finish (White & Tharp, 1988). This is often interpreted by teachers from other cultures as rude interruption, but in Hawaiian society it demonstrates involvement and relationship (Tharp, 1989).

Nonverbal behavior is another variation in communication style that is related to cultural socialization—for example, eye contact. Children from Euro-American families are generally taught to look directly at an adult when being spoken to, while children from Asian American, Latino American, Caribbean, and southern African American families are generally taught to lower their eyes. Avoidance of eye contact may be interpreted as disrespect (Dresser, 2005). Teachers must develop an awareness of how cultural background affects actions. The next chapter will explore the ecology of teaching a diverse student population.

Religion

As was discussed in Chapter 3, religion is a significant socializing mechanism in the transmission of values and behavior. Traditions, rituals, and religious institutions reinforce the values taught in families.

Religious pluralism flourishes in the United States. There are about 2,000 different religious groups, and with the influx of immigrants from Asia, Africa, and the Middle East, non-Western religions such as Islam, Hinduism, and Buddhism are joining the ranks of Protestantism, Catholicism, and Judaism (Gollnick & Chinn, 2008).

Although political ideology in the United States advocates separation of church and state (including public school), the two often intersect. For example, the phrase "One nation, under God" is now in the Pledge of Allegiance, and the phrase "In God we trust" appears on U.S. currency. The degree to which religious ideologies intersect with public school curricula and policies is significant in the socialization of all children who attend public school. Issues that have been controversial are school prayer, the curriculum (teaching evolution, sex education), censorship of certain books, and the celebration of certain holidays. Teachers need to be sensitive to the values of the families in the community in the context of a diverse society, while at the same time implementing the educational goals of the school district.

Sometimes the line between secular and nonsecular education is a fine one and must be determined by the courts. Legally, schools may teach the Bible as part of the history of literature (as a story), but they may not teach it as religion (as a holy document). Reading of scriptures and reciting prayers is a violation. Public schools may teach the scientific theory of evolution, but not biblical creationism. Dismissing children an hour early from public school for religious instruction is permitted.

How are secular and nonsecular distinguished? Secular deals with worldly experiences, nonsecular with spiritual ones. How can the Bible represent both, yet only be allowed to be taught as literature? Literature consists of writings in prose or verse, whereas the Bible also consists of sacred religious scriptures. Therefore, biblical stories can be taught minus their spiritual messages.

President George W. Bush established the Center for Faith-Based and Community Initiatives to provide opportunities for faith-based and community organizations to apply to the U.S. Department of Education for grants, such as programs for early reading, family literacy, and after-school activities, in order to help ensure that no child is left behind.

Disability

As a result of changes in the law—that education is a right, not a privilege—the school has become a designated agent for identifying children with special needs, such as disabilities, and including them in educational activities that are available to all children.

A **disability** refers to the reduction of function or the absence of a particular body part or organ. An **impairment** refers to physical damage or deterioration. A **handicap** is defined as something that hampers a person—a disadvantage or hindrance.

Children with disabilities are those who have been evaluated as having mental retardation, a hearing impairment, deafness, a speech impairment, a visual impairment, a serious

disability reduction in the functioning of a particular body part or organ, or its absence

impairment physical damage or deterioration

handicap something that hampers a person; a disadvantage, a hindrance

emotional disturbance, autism, an orthopedic impairment, another health impairment, deaf–blindness, multiple disabilities, a traumatic brain injury, or specific learning disabilities and who, because of those impairments, needs a special education and related services.

The terms *disability* and/or *impairment* are used today instead of *handicap* in order to dispel negative stereotypes. People in wheelchairs are disabled. They are handicapped only when they try to enter a building with steps. A person may be handicapped in one situation but not in another. For example, Ray Charles was handicapped in *reading* music because he was blind. He certainly was not handicapped, however, in *playing* music. Thus, for children with disabilities, the main aim of socialization should be to minimize the effects of their disabilities and to maximize the effects of their abilities.

Some common assumptions about individuals with disabilities can affect interaction with them. Assuming that individuals with disabilities are helpless can lead to solicitude or overprotectiveness. The assumption that individuals with disabilities are incapable can lead to ostracism or neglect.

handicapism assumptions and practices that promote the deferential and unequal treatment of people because they are different physically, mentally, or behaviorally

Assumptions and practices that promote the deferential and unequal treatment of people because they are different physically, mentally, or behaviorally is called **handicapism**. The word *handicap* is thought to be derived from the practice of beggars who held "cap in hand" to solicit charity, thereby indicating a dependent position (Biklen & Bogdan, 1977). The media have contributed to certain attitudes associated with disabilities. For example, children's stories tell of evil trolls, hunchbacks, or witches (who are old and deformed in some way), thus promoting an attitude of fear. Though handicapism has a long history, the media today are trying to include people with disabilities in TV shows and advertisements. Teachers need to be sensitive to handicapism and view children as individuals with abilities and disabilities, as applicable.

Ideological Background for Socialization of Individuals with Disabilities

Historically, we can delineate four stages of attitudes toward people with disabilities that have affected their socialization (Hallahan, Kauffman, & Pullen, 2009).

1. During the pre-Christian era, people with disabilities tended to be banished, neglected, and/or mistreated.
2. During the spread of Christianity, they were protected and pitied.
3. In the 18th and 19th centuries, institutions were established to provide separate education.
4. In the latter part of the 20th century, there was a movement toward accepting people with disabilities and integrating them into the mainstream of society to the fullest extent possible ("full inclusion"). Currently, laws enable individuals with disabilities to receive a free and equal education and to compete for jobs without discrimination.

A child with disabilities can be integrated into the classroom with the support of special equipment and assistance from the teacher.

Wadsworth/Thomson Learning/Cengage Learning

In 1975, Congress passed the Education for All Handicapped Children Act, which required that children with disabilities be educated in a regular public classroom whenever possible. It applied to children ages 3 to 21. In 1986, an amendment was passed to serve children from birth to age 3 in order to minimize the risks of developmental delays because of lack of appropriate services early on. In 1990, the name of the Education for All Handicapped Children Act was changed to the Individuals with Disabilities Education Act. In 1991, the Americans with Disabilities Act was passed to ensure nondiscriminatory treatment of people with disabilities in areas of their lives such as employment, use of public facilities, transportation, and telecommunications.

The Individuals with Disabilities Education Act (IDEA)—An Equitable Response to Diversity

The Individuals with Disabilities Education Act (IDEA), passed in 1990, provides federal money to states and local agencies to educate children with disabilities ages 3 to 21.

The equitable response of IDEA to diversity is the concept of inclusion. **Inclusion** is the educational philosophy of being part of the whole—that children are entitled to participate fully in their school and community. In 2004, IDEA was modified to conform to applicable requirements of the No Child Left Behind Act, such as parental choice and academic accountability for student progress, and to add requirements for transition services to promote post-school employment or education. While individuals from 3 to 21 are classified by specific disability to receive benefits of the law, IDEA allows states to use the category "developmental delay" for preschool children with special needs because of the possible effects of early categorization. Each state has specific criteria and evaluation procedures for determining children's eligibility for early intervention and special services, including what constitutes developmental delay (McLean, Wolery, & Bailey, 2003).

inclusion the educational philosophy that all children are entitled to participate fully in their school and community

Many children are diagnosed early by physicians as having specific conditions, such as cerebral palsy or spina bifida. However, many other children are at risk for developmental delays or disabilities as a result of environmental variables such as abuse, exposure to toxins or disease, or poverty (McLean, Wolery, & Bailey, 2003). Such children are often not identified prior to their contact with social workers or teachers. Thus, early childhood professionals are significant identifiers of children with special needs. This identification can occur through informal observations of children, screening with developmental scales, and vision and hearing screening (Meisels & Shonkoff, 2000).

IDEA requires *nondiscriminatory evaluations*, appropriate to a child's cultural and linguistic background, of whether a child has a disability and, if so, the nature of the disability. A reevaluation must occur every three years. Parental approval is required. There are over six and a half million documented children with disabilities eligible to be served by IDEA (National Center for Educational Statistics, 2008).

The main purpose of the act is to guarantee that all children with disabilities have available to them a free and appropriate public education. The principal method of guaranteeing the fulfillment of that purpose is the **individualized education program (IEP)**. The IEP is basically a form of communication between the school and the family. It is developed by the group of people responsible for the child's education—the parents, the teacher, and other involved school personnel. Any child receiving special education services must have an IEP, which is generally written at the beginning of each year and reviewed at the end, but can be extended for up to three years in certain cases in which long-term planning is deemed more appropriate. The exact format varies, depending on the particular school district; however, all IEPs must include the following:

individualized education program (IEP) a form of communication between school and family, developed by the group of people (teacher, parent, and other involved personnel) responsible for the education of a child with special needs

1. A statement of the child's present levels of educational performance.
2. A statement of annual goals, including short-term objectives.
3. A statement of the specific special education and related services to be provided to the child, and of the extent of the child's participation in regular education environments, including initiation dates and anticipated duration of services.
4. Required transition services from school to work or continued education (usually by age 14 to 16).
5. Objective criteria, evaluation procedures, and schedules for determining whether instructional objectives are being met.

In sum, the IDEA requires that students with disabilities be placed in the *least restrictive environment* (LRE). This means that they should be included in school programs with students who are not disabled to the maximum extent appropriate. Supplementary services such as attendants, tutors, interpreters, transportation, speech pathology and audiology, psychological services, physical and occupational therapy, recreation, and medical and counseling services enable inclusion. Supplementary aids such as wheelchairs, crutches, standing tables, hearing aids, embossed globes, braille dictionaries, and books with enlarged print also enable inclusion. Inclusion can be for the entire day or appropriate portions of the day.

What societal changes have affected schools?

Chronosystem Influences on Schools

Chronosystem influences on the school include its adaptation to societal change in general and to specific developments such as new technology (computers and software), health (substance use/abuse, obesity), and safety (violence and emergency preparedness). What aspects of past knowledge must be taught for survival in the present, and what coping skills must be taught for survival in the future?

From its inception, the public school system was intended to be a vehicle for social change. Schools, however, do not execute their functions in a vacuum. As we have discussed, they are affected by macrosystems such as political ideology, economics, culture, religion, and technology, and are linked to other microsystems such as the family and community. They must teach children from diverse backgrounds with diverse skills. Therefore, in order to equalize opportunities, schools must implement a variety of programs, such as computer literacy, conflict resolution, and health education, in addition to basic reading, writing, and arithmetic. "The school has become a potential intervention site for almost every social problem affecting children" (Linney & Seidman, 1989, p. 336).

What changes have occurred in schools?

Adaptations to Societal Change

Elementary schools traditionally taught academic skills and good citizenship. Gradually, development of critical thinking skills, individuality and self-concept, and interpersonal relationship skills crept into the curriculum. The reasons for the gradual changes were many. The classic writings of John Dewey (*Democracy and Education*, 1944), Jean Piaget (*To Understand Is to Invent*, 1976), B. F. Skinner (*The Technology of Teaching*, 1968), and Carl Rogers (*Freedom to Learn*, 1969), to name a few, influenced educational practices. More recently, the work of Lev Vygotsky (*Mind and Society*, 1978) has been adapted for the classroom. We discussed the "Tools of the Mind" curriculum (based on Vygotsky's theory) in Chapter 5.

The political climate from the late 1950s to the early 1970s was supportive of educational change, as evidenced by the passage of legislation providing federal money for new programs. For example, the Economic Opportunity Act of 1964 provided federal money for preschool programs for disadvantaged children, and the Elementary and Secondary Education Acts of 1965 (Title I), incorporated into the No Child Left Behind Act of 2001 (NCLB), provided federal aid to education. As discussed previously, federal funds for students with LEP, recent immigrants, and the education of individuals with disabilities became available in the late 1970s. Thus, government support allowed schools to benefit more children by individualizing programs to meet individual needs. However, during the 1980s, federal aid to education was reduced; public education was felt to be the responsibility of the states.

A 1983 report, titled *A Nation at Risk: The Imperative for Educational Reform*, by the National Commission on Excellence in Education (NCEE), helped create a public demand for change in the public schools. The report charged that U.S. citizens "have lost sight of the basics of schooling" and that "the educational foundations of our society are presently being eroded by a rising tide of mediocrity that threatens our very future as a nation and a people" (NCEE, 1983).

As the 21st century approached, debates regarding the function of school had not changed very much. To address the charges made by the NCEE report, government, business, and educational leaders developed six national education goals, announced in 1990 and reconfirmed in 1999 in the Educational Excellence for All Children Act (National Education Goals Panel, 1999). They stated that by the year 2000:

1. All children in America will start school ready to learn.
2. The high school graduation rate will increase to at least 90 percent.
3. American students will leave grades 4, 8, and 12 having demonstrated competency in challenging subject matter including English, mathematics, science, history,

and geography; and every school in America will ensure that all students learn to use their minds well, so they may be prepared for responsible citizenship, further learning, and productive employment in our modern economy.

4. American students will be first in the world in science and mathematics achievement.
5. Every adult American will be literate and will possess the knowledge and skills necessary to compete in a global economy and to exercise the rights and responsibilities of citizenship.
6. Every school in America will be free of drugs and violence and will offer a disciplined environment conducive to learning.

The passage of the NCLB in 2001 was intended to motivate schools and students to fulfill the goals and standards set for them. Reaching the goals requires significant improvements in a wide range of services for children, including health care, child care, parent education, and family support (Comer, 2004). It also requires many changes in schools, teacher education, and testing.

The NCLB Act:

- increases accountability for states, school districts, and schools;
- provides greater choice for parents and students. particularly those attending low-performance or unsafe schools;
- gives more flexibility to states and local educational agencies (LEAs) in the use of federal education dollars; and
- mandates a stronger emphasis on reading, language arts, mathematics, and science.

Every state receiving NCLB funding must develop both content standards (what students are expected to know) and academic achievement standards (how students will acquire the skills to master the content) in these subject areas. The standards must be aligned with assessments in the same subject areas for grades 3–8 and high school. Assessment results must be classified by poverty, race, ethnicity, disability, and limited English proficiency to ensure that no group is left behind. To ensure that every child can read by the end of third grade, the Reading First Initiative was passed (schools can apply for Federal grants to include scientifically based reading instruction and diagnostic assessments in grades K–3). School districts and schools that fail to make adequate yearly progress (AYP) toward statewide proficiency goals will, over time, be subject to improvement, corrective action, and restructuring measures aimed at getting them back on course to meet state standards. Schools that meet or exceed AYP objectives or close achievement gaps are eligible for State Academic Achievement Awards. States must report school safety statistics to the public on a school-by-school basis, and LEAs must use federal Safe and Drug-Free Schools and Communities to improve.

Technology

Schooling for the future includes being prepared for the world of work and technological change. Learning to use computers is now essential to successful functioning in society. This is a good example of the impact of a macrosystem (technology) and a chronosystem (change) on a microsystem.

The computer is an interactive tool that can enhance learning in a variety of subjects. It can present and store information, motivate and reward learners, diagnose and prescribe, provide drill and practice, and individualize instruction (Oppenheimer, 2003). It can support a wide range of learning styles because it enables children to construct their own knowledge (Plowman, Stephen, & McPake, 2010; Prensky, 2010). The computer's effectiveness as a tool for learning depends on how it is used by teachers and students, as well as the software selected.

Computers are not really new to education. In the past, computers were used mainly for programmed instruction, which involves reading information and answering questions.

TeachSource Video Activity

Go to the Education CourseMate website to watch the ABC News video entitled "Technology Is Making Teaching and Learning More Fun." In your early schooling, was technology integrated in the classroom? If so, how? If not, recall a situation(s) where it could have been.

Technological advances affect what and how children learn.

Cengage Learning

Depending on one's responses, one branches into different program areas or goes back for more information and practice. The learning that occurs is determined by reacting to the program rather than discovery by the learner, although sometimes children discover different ways to get the same result by experimenting with different commands. Today, educational software includes interactive games (such as Leapster), websites to visit (such as PBS Kids), and discussion groups via safe chat rooms (such as kids.com).

The digital revolution has hit education with more and more classrooms plugged into the whole wired world. But are schools making the most of new technologies? Are they tapping into the learning potential of today's digital generation? Collins and Halverson (2009) argue that the knowledge revolution has transformed our jobs, our homes, and our lives, and therefore must also transform our schools. To keep pace with a globalized technological culture, American education must go well beyond the walls of the classroom to include online social networks, distance learning with anytime, anywhere access, digital home schooling models, video-game learning environments, and more.

Computers can be used for collaboration and research (Collins & Halverson 2009). Students can network with each other in the classroom on projects. With Internet access they can access information from libraries, universities, government databases, and any online service subscribed to by their school. With computer-interactive multimedia capabilities, such as graphics, sound, and compact discs, students can access museums and planetariums, learn about other countries, or go back in history. New software is being developed for learning via computer simulation. For example, the standard biology laboratory experiment of dissecting a dead frog can now be simulated. Some driver education programs start students on computers.

In sum, computers contribute to schooling for the future in that they can individualize instruction to accommodate different learning styles; they can be used for routine tasks, thereby freeing teachers to provide more creative ones; they can help develop self-directed learners, logical or hypothetical thinkers, and problem solvers; and they can provide access to infinite information. Parents and teachers must enable children to develop critical thinking skills to evaluate appropriate software, as well as the plethora of information on the Internet. In doing research on the Internet, students must learn to distinguish facts from opinions and reliable resources from unreliable ones.

Health and Safety

The NCLB contains provisions for the Safe and Drug-Free Schools and Community Act (SDFSCA). States can apply for federal funds to implement programs grounded in scientific research that prevent illegal use of substances and violence. Parents and communities are required to be involved and new programs must be coordinated with other public programs to foster a safe, drug-free learning environment that fosters school achievement.

Substance Use/Abuse

Substance use and abuse remain major problems among high schoolers, with over half of American teenagers having tried an illicit drug by the time they finish high school. Inhalant use has increased in eighth graders (National Institute on Drug Abuse [NIDA], 2008). Substances include tobacco, alcohol, and various drugs as well as performance-enhancing supplements. The use of mind- and physical-altering chemicals has dangerous effects on development and deleterious effects on school performance. Students under the influence of such substances are not in a state of readiness to learn, and there may be long-term impairment of cognitive ability and memory. Substance abuse is frequently associated with lack of motivation and self-discipline as well as reduced school attendance. Special services are often required to help the student learn. Substance abuse is also correlated with antisocial and violent behavior (NIDA, 2008).

The use of substances in school by some students impairs the educational environment for others. Along with the family and community, schools must be involved in dealing with the substance use and abuse problem. The National Institutes of Health (2003), following guidelines from the NCLB, has identified ways for schools to participate in promoting the health of children and preventing substance abuse:

- The school must provide factual information about the harmful effects of drugs.
- Collaboration with parents and community members must occur to support and strengthen students' resistance to substances.
- The school should provide such services as confidential identification, assessment, and referral to appropriate treatment programs for users and abusers.
- Substance use should be monitored within the school, establishing clear guidelines and penalties for usage.

Can schools require students to submit to random drug tests in order to participate in extracurricular activities (such as sports, drama, band, or Academic Decathlon)? Random drug tests typically involve selecting students at random, calling them out of class, and directing them to a bathroom where they must provide a urine sample in a container. A teacher usually waits outside the bathroom stall and seals the container for transport to the testing lab. The Supreme Court (*Earl v. Board of Education of Tecumseh, Oklahoma, Public School District*, 2002) held that drug testing did not violate students' rights under the Fourth Amendment to be free from warrantless searches. The rationale in the decision was that students in public school are under the temporary custody of the state and, therefore, have limited privacy rights, especially when a search is deemed necessary for their own protection.

Obesity

Since 1980, the percentage of children who are overweight has more than doubled, while rates among adolescents have more than tripled (Hedley et al., 2004) (see Figure 6.2).

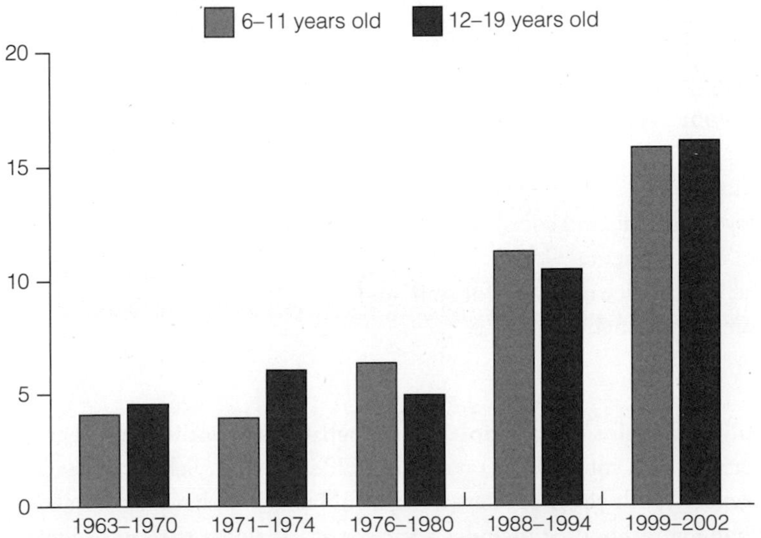

FIGURE 6.2 Percentage of Overweight U.S. Children and Adolescents

Source: Wechsler, H., McKenna, M. L., Lee, S. M., and Dietz, W. H. (2004). The role of schools in preventing child obesity. *The State Education Standard.* National Association of State Boards of Education, p. 5.

According to Hedley and colleagues (2004), obesity in children and adolescents is a major concern because:

- Several weight-related conditions that were observed primarily among adults have been increasingly diagnosed in young people. For example, ten years ago type 2 diabetes was almost unknown among young people, but in some communities it now accounts for nearly 50 percent of new cases of diabetes among children and adolescents.
- Many overweight young people have at least one additional risk factor for heart disease, such as high cholesterol or high blood pressure.
- Childhood overweight also is associated with social and psychological problems, such as discrimination and poor self-esteem.
- Children and adolescents who are overweight are more likely to become overweight or obese adults.

According to the National Association of State Boards of Education (NASBE, 2000), "Health and success in school are interrelated. Schools cannot achieve their primary mission of education if students and staff are not healthy and fit physically, mentally, and socially." Thanks to the efforts of educators and policymakers, many schools are making important contributions to our nation's struggle against the obesity epidemic. Schools play an especially important role in tackling obesity because:

- Over 95 percent of young people are enrolled in schools (NCES, 2007).
- Promotion of physical activity and healthy eating have long been a fundamental component of the American educational experience, so schools are not being asked to assume new responsibilities.
- Research has shown that well-designed, well-implemented school programs can effectively promote physical activity, healthy eating, and reductions in television viewing time.
- Emerging research documents the connections between physical activity, good nutrition, physical education and nutrition programs, and academic performance (Wechsler et al., 2004).

Schools can help students adopt and maintain healthy eating and physical activity behaviors. The Centers for Disease Control and Prevention (CDC, 2011) publishes guidelines, available online (http://www.cdc.gov/healthy youth), that identify school policies and practices most likely to be effective in promoting lifelong physical activity and healthy eating through a Coordinated School Health Program (CSHP) approach. A CSHP integrates efforts of the eight components of the school community that can strongly influence student health:

1. health education;
2. physical education;
3. health services;
4. nutrition services;
5. counseling, psychological, and social services;
6. healthy school environment;
7. promoting the importance of health for staff; and
8. family and community involvement.

TeachSource Video Activity

Go to the Education CourseMate website to watch a video from the BBC Motion Gallery entitled "Childhood Obesity and School Nutrition." Based on what you have learned in this section, what can you do to improve your (or your child's) nutritional habits?

Violence

violence behaviors that intentionally threaten, attempt, or inflict harm on others

The National Academy of Sciences defines **violence** as "behaviors by individuals that intentionally threaten, attempt, or inflict harm on others" (Elders, 1994). School violence is a subset of youth violence. Youth violence refers to harmful behaviors that may start early and continue into young adulthood. It includes a variety of behaviors such as bullying, slapping, punching, and weapon use. Victims can suffer serious injury, significant social and emotional damage, or even death. The young person can be a victim, an offender, or a witness to the violence—or a combination of these.

Understanding the factors that make some individuals more likely to commit violent acts helps in designing programs to address the problem. Such risk factors include (CDC, 2010):

1. **Individual Risk Factors**
   - History of violent victimization
   - Attention deficits, hyperactivity, or learning disorders
   - History of early aggressive behavior
   - Association with delinquent peers
   - Involvement in gangs
   - Involvement with drugs, alcohol, or tobacco
   - Low IQ
   - Poor academic performance
   - Low commitment to school or school failure
   - Poor behavioral control
   - Deficits in social, cognitive, or information-processing abilities
   - High emotional distress
   - Antisocial beliefs and attitudes
   - Social rejection by peers
   - Exposure to violence and conflict in the family
   - Lack of involvement in conventional activities

2. **Relationship Risk Factors**
   - Harsh, lax, or inconsistent disciplinary practices
   - Low parental involvement
   - Low emotional attachment to parents or caregivers
   - Low parental education and income
   - Parental substance abuse or criminality
   - Poor family functioning (e.g., communication)
   - Poor monitoring and supervision of children

3. **Community/Societal Risk Factors**
   - Diminished economic opportunities
   - High concentrations of poor residents
   - High level of transiency
   - High level of family disruption
   - Low levels of community participation
   - Socially disorganized neighborhoods
   - Low emotional attachment to parents or caregivers
   - Low parental education and income
   - Parental substance abuse or criminality
   - Poor family functioning (e.g., communication)
   - Poor monitoring and supervision of children

Parents, teachers, students, and communities are very concerned about the rise in school violence. The shootings of 12 students and a teacher in 1999 at Columbine High School in Colorado was the first school incident alerting society to the negative outcomes of being rejected by peers, of being victims of bullying, and, most important, of being disengaged from family, school, and community. This led to the development of school programs addressing bullying and victimization (to be discussed in Chapter 8) as well as respect and conflict resolution. Other school shootings have since occurred all over the country. For example, in 2007, a student, who had been diagnosed with an anxiety disorder, shot 32 people at Virginia Polytechnical University and then committed suicide. This led to reexamination by the school of privacy issues regarding psychological evaluations as well as the passage of more permissive gun laws by the state. The federal government has developed guidelines for emergency preparedness (see next section) and grants for violence prevention programs.

To have an optimal environment for learning, schools must be safe. Violence transcends all socioeconomic levels of schools and communities. Its roots are found in a family's dysfunctional way of solving problems, as well as in a community's racism, sexism, classism, and high unemployment. Children who grow up in families that practice spousal or child abuse or neglect are more likely to exhibit aggressive behavior in school. They may also model the violent behavior they see in their neighborhood (Dodge, Coie, & Lynam, 2006). Children who are exposed to violence in the contexts of home, school, and community are most likely to perceive violence as the normal means of conflict resolution, and that violence is acceptable and is an effective way to solve problems (Sylvie & Windle, 2010).

The incidence of hate-motivated violence is rising (National Education Association, 2009). The National Education Association (NEA) defines hate crimes as "offenses motivated by hatred against a victim based on his or her beliefs or mental or physical characteristics, including race, ethnicity, and sexual orientation." Not only has there been an increase in hate incidents in school, but websites targeted to promote intolerance have proliferated. The NEA believes that preventing hate-motivated violence requires a comprehensive, coordinated educational effort in schools and communities, along with federal legislation.

What is being done to ensure school safety? Some schools have hired security guards, installed metal detectors, installed camera surveillance, required students to carry photo identification, and/or given teachers cellular phones, but these are reactive measures to a problem the roots of which lie in a "socially toxic environment." To be proactive and cut those roots, all of a child's ecological systems have to participate, as discussed in the following sections.

Macrosystem

The *macrosystem*, or government, can implement laws, such as NCLB, which mandates safe schools. It can increase law enforcement in communities. It can provide funding for preventive programs in schools and families, such as implemented by the Office of Safe and Drug-Free Schools (OSDFS). Violence prevention in schools may involve having more counselors available to students and training teachers to intervene with children who are social isolates, bullies, or victims. Violence prevention in families may involve parent education and/or counseling.

Exosystem

The *exosystem*, such as business, can provide jobs, financial assistance to rebuild impoverished communities, and role models for youth. Businesses can support schools by giving time and money, offering opportunities for field trips, providing guest speakers, and funding after-school activities.

Mesosystem

The *mesosystem*, as exemplified by the link between schools and families, can empower families to share the responsibility for creating a safe school environment. This can mean accompanying young children to and from school, providing older children with cell phones, being involved in school activities, supporting school policies regarding safety and conflict resolution, and monitoring children's behavior (including those who are withdrawn, as well as aggressive). The mesosystem, as exemplified by the link between communities and families, can provide services to support families (examples will be discussed in Chapter 10), thereby proactively contributing to the prevention of violence.

Microsystem

The *microsystem*, referring here to the school itself, can implement a curricular priority at all grade levels of anger management (learning cues to when angry feelings get out of

IN PRACTICE

Preventing Violence in Young Children: What Strategies Can Help Children Resolve Conflicts before They Escalate into Violent Behavior?

1. *Emotional regulation:* Enable children to verbalize angry feelings and presumed cause (young children may need some suggested words). Redirect anger to appropriate physical activity (pounding Play-Doh, running).
2. *Empathy:* Role-play to get the other person's perspective.
3. *Problem solving:* Discuss solutions to conflict that are agreeable to all parties involved.
4. *Mediation:* Involve adult or trained peer to listen to all perspectives and give assistance in working out a compromise.

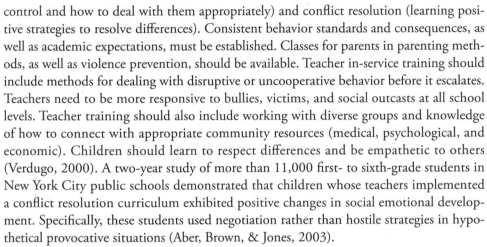

School violence has become a national concern. These students must subject to being searched before they can enter the school.

Michael Newman/PhotoEdit

control and how to deal with them appropriately) and conflict resolution (learning positive strategies to resolve differences). Consistent behavior standards and consequences, as well as academic expectations, must be established. Classes for parents in parenting methods, as well as violence prevention, should be available. Teacher in-service training should include methods for dealing with disruptive or uncooperative behavior before it escalates. Teachers need to be more responsive to bullies, victims, and social outcasts at all school levels. Teacher training should also include working with diverse groups and knowledge of how to connect with appropriate community resources (medical, psychological, and economic). Children should learn to respect differences and be empathetic to others (Verdugo, 2000). A two-year study of more than 11,000 first- to sixth-grade students in New York City public schools demonstrated that children whose teachers implemented a conflict resolution curriculum exhibited positive changes in social emotional development. Specifically, these students used negotiation rather than hostile strategies in hypothetical provocative situations (Aber, Brown, & Jones, 2003).

To conclude, in a changing society, the challenge continually facing educators is how to transmit the society's diverse cultural heritage and also prepare individuals for the future. See Table 6.2 for a summary of macrosystem/chronosystem influences on the school.

Emergency Preparedness

According to Margaret Spellings, Secretary of Education (U.S. Department of Education [USDE], 2007), "Knowing how to respond quickly and efficiently in a crisis is critical to ensuring the safety of our schools and students. The midst of a crisis is not the time to start figuring out who ought to do what. At that moment, everyone involved—from top to bottom—should know the drill and know each other."

Children and youth rely on and find great comfort in the adults who protect them. Teachers and staff must know how to help their students through a crisis and return them home safely. Knowing what to do when faced with a crisis can be the difference between calm and chaos, between courage and fear, between life and death. Schools need to be ready to handle crises, large and small, to keep our children and staff out of harm's way and ready to learn and teach. The OSDFS has developed a guide, *Practical Information on Crisis Planning: A Guide for Schools and Communities* (USDE, 2007).

The dictionary's definition of a crisis is, "An unstable or crucial time or state of affairs in which a decisive change is impending, especially one with the distinct possibility of a highly undesirable outcome." Additionally, the dictionary notes that "crisis" comes from the Greek word meaning "decision." In essence, a crisis is a situation where schools could be faced with inadequate information, not enough time, and insufficient resources, but in which leaders must make one or many crucial decisions.

Table 6.2 Summary: Macrosystem/Chronosystem Influences on the School

Political Ideology	No Child Left Behind Act—funding based on performance standards Permits school choice (magnet schools, vouchers, charter schools) • Value of equal opportunity—leads to intervention programs for social problems, compensatory programs, financial aid, and scholarships • Achievement and competitiveness issues—results in curriculum changes, teacher competency standards, transition programs from school to work
Economics	Cost-effectiveness—affects programs, curricula, class size, and school improvements Accountability (testing)—enhances preparation of students for future employability
Diversity and Equity	Diverse student population (gender, culture, religion, disability)—results in more individualized approaches to learning • Inclusion—leads to adaptation to society
Science/ Technology	Technological advances—leads to increased knowledge and new approaches to learning based on scientific research • Computers—results in increased access to information and more opportunities for skill development (reading, writing, math) and collaborative learning
Health and Safety	Government grants for health programs (substance abuse, obesity) and safety (violence, emergency preparation)

Emergency plans need to address a range of events and hazards caused both by both nature and by people, such as:

- Natural disasters (earthquake, tornado, hurricane, flood)
- Severe weather
- Fires
- Chemical or hazardous material spills
- Bus crashes
- School shootings
- Bomb threats
- Medical emergencies
- Student or staff deaths (suicide, homicide, unintentional, or natural)
- Acts of terror or war
- Outbreaks of disease or infections

A review of the crisis literature reveals that experts identify four phases of crisis management (USDE, 2007):

1. *Mitigation/prevention* addresses what schools and districts can do to reduce or eliminate risk to life and property.
2. *Preparedness* focuses on the process of planning for the worst-case scenario.
3. *Response* is devoted to the steps to take during a crisis.
4. *Recovery* deals with how to restore the learning and teaching environment after a crisis.

What linkages are influential in the school's ability to socialize?

Mesosystem Influences on Schools

Mesosystem influences on the school include its linkages with other ecosystems. Because children in the United States spend approximately 180 days per year for approximately 13 years in school, including kindergarten (and more, if they attend preschool), the schools they attend and the teachers they encounter play significant roles in their socialization. The school, in designating programs and curricula, selects which experiences a child will have, hence determining which aspects of culture are to be transmitted.

School–Child Linkages

Certain psychological characteristics of a child, such as learning style, may determine which type of learning environment is optimal for that child's development. **Learning style** is defined as that consistent pattern of behavior and performance by which an individual approaches educational experiences. According to Bennett (2010), it is the composite of characteristic cognitive, affective, and physiological behaviors that serve as relatively stable indicators of how a learner perceives, interacts with, and responds to the learning environment. It is influenced by the cultural experiences of home, school, and society.

learning style a consistent pattern of behavior and performance by which an individual approaches educational experiences

Learning style, then, is an aspect of socialization. How schools and teachers respond to the child's learning style affects the child's educational experience. Learning styles can be observed in children by various criteria. For example, does the child learn best by watching? By listening? By moving his or her body? Does the child achieve more alone or in a group? Is the child better at breaking down a whole task into components (analysis) or relating the components to each other to form a new whole (synthesis)? Is the child motivated by pleasing the teacher? By concrete rewards? By internalized interest? Does the child need much or little structure to carry out a task? Learning styles will be discussed in more detail in Chapter 7.

School–Family Linkages

Socialization of the child begins in the family; the school extends the process by formal education. The outcome of this joint effort depends to a considerable extent on the relationship between family and school. Many research studies, from preschool to elementary school to high school (Epstein & Sheldon, 2006), have provided evidence showing that when schools work together with families to support learning, children tend to succeed in school and afterward. These studies point to family involvement in learning as a more accurate predictor of school achievement than socioeconomic status. Specifically, when families (1) create a home environment that encourages learning, (2) express high (but not unrealistic) expectations for their children's achievement and future careers, and (3) become involved in their children's education at school and in the community, then children from low-socioeconomic-status and culturally diverse families are enabled to fare comparably to middle-class children.

As discussed, the school has traditionally been less effective in educating children from low-socioeconomic-status families. The reasons generally cited for the school's lessened effectiveness are (1) the fewer resources available for education in poor communities, (2) the expectations of the teachers (most teachers are middle class), and (3) the lack of certain preschool experiences expected of children their age by public schools. For example, sitting still at the table when working or eating is generally expected of school-age children. But some children do not have a table at home large enough to accommodate all the family members at one time, so there are no formal sit-down meals; instead, family members eat "on the run." Consequently, until these children learn to conform to sitting still as well as other school-expected behaviors, they will have trouble in school.

This parent supervises his child's homework, emphasizing the importance of effort and hard work.

jgroup/Big Stock Photo

It has been demonstrated that the effectiveness of school as a socializing agent depends on the degree of consistency, or supportive linkages, between children's home environment and their educational environment (Berger, 2007; Haskins & Rouse, 2005). Most federally funded programs require that schools and families work together.

If, however, the family does *not* believe the school is a very significant socializing agent, parents will not take much interest in the work the child brings home. They may ignore the teacher's requests for help to change the child's behavior, and may even relate negative experiences they had at school to the child. Besides a lack of consensus on goals, another problem that may discourage the family from being involved in school is a mismatch in how children are socialized to learn at home and at school. The home environment is a significant influence on a child's readiness to learn in school. See the In Practice Box, "What Is Involved in Children's Readiness to Learn?"

Thus, the school needs to interact with the family so that socialization goals for the child are complementary rather than contradictory. For example, in studies of students in the early grades (Darling & Westberg, 2004), those children (of all reading levels) who were asked to read to their parents gained in reading skills (a school goal), whereas the control group of children did not. The key to forming complementary goals for the child is communication. The school and the family need to talk to each other about their attitudes regarding education and parenting. What are the parents' expectations for the child's achievement and behavior at school? What are the school's expectations for the child's activities at home?

How Families Become Involved in School

There are three major types of family involvement: (1) decision making—determining school programs and policies; (2) participation—working in the classroom as paid or volunteer instructional assistants; and (3) partnership—providing home guidance to their children to support learning and extend school goals. Yale University psychiatrist Dr. James Comer (2004) found that involving parents of culturally diverse children in these three areas overcame parent distrust of the school.

Families also become involved in school and education when they vote. They elect people to serve on the local school board to make decisions about educational goals, school facilities, budget allocations, personnel, student standards of achievement and conduct, and evaluation methods. This interaction is indirect, but nonetheless influential (see Figure 6.3). Direct interaction occurs when families go to the school their children attend and talk to the administrators and teachers. Successful schools are those that work at developing partnerships with families and communities (Berger, 2007; Epstein & Sheldon, 2006).

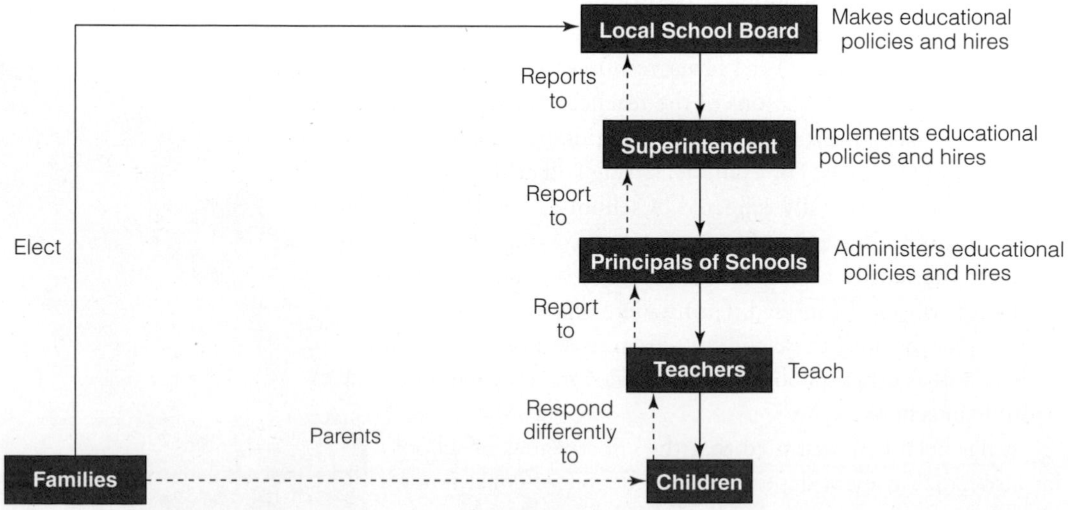

FIGURE 6.3 **Child-Family-School Linkages**

IN PRACTICE

What Is Involved in Children's Readiness to Learn?

The nation's primary educational goal is that all children will come to school "ready to learn." The concept of "school readiness" is multifaceted, encompassing the physical health, social-emotional, cognitive, and linguistic status of children. There is abundant evidence that poor children lag behind their more advantaged counterparts on most if not all aspects of readiness. The effects of poverty manifest themselves early in a child's life. Children in low-income families have more health problems, are more likely to have behavioral or developmental problems, are less likely to see a pediatrician on a regular basis, and are less likely to live in a safe home environment that nurtures their development (U.S. Department of Health and Human Services [USDHHS], 2008). At the end of preschool, they score up to one standard deviation below the norms on measures of language and early math; thus, they require intervention to enable them to meet NCLB proficiency standards (Moore et al., 2009).

Illustrating the significance of child, family, and school linkages, the challenge of reaching this goal for macrosystems, microsystems, and mesosystems is to employ the following strategies (Boyer, 1991, pp. 136–143):

1. *A healthy start.* Good health and good schooling are inextricably interlocked. Every child, to be ready to learn, must have a healthy birth, be well nourished, and be well protected in the early years of life.
2. *Empowered parents.* The home is the first classroom. Parents are the first and most essential teachers. All children, as a readiness requirement, should live in a secure environment where empowered parents encourage language development.
   a. Parents must speak frequently to children and listen to them.
   b. Parents must read to children.
   c. Parents must build a bridge between home and school.
3. *Quality preschool.* Many young children are cared for outside the home. These children need high-quality programs that not only provide good care but also address all dimensions of school readiness.
4. *A responsible workplace.* If each child in America is to come to school ready to learn, we must have workplace policies that are family friendly, offering child-care services and giving parents time to be with their young children.
   a. Employers should provide available leave time.
   b. Employers should allow flexible scheduling.
   c. Employers should enable job sharing.
   d. Employers should provide a link to community child-care services.
5. *Television as a teacher.* Next to parents, television is the child's most influential teacher. School readiness requires television programming that is both educational and enriching.
   a. Commercial companies selling children's products should help underwrite quality programs.
   b. Communities should establish a ready-to-learn public access channel.
6. *Neighborhoods for learning.* All children need spaces and places for growth and exploration. They need safe and friendly neighborhoods that contribute richly to a child's readiness to learn.
   a. Neighborhoods should have well-designed indoor and outdoor parks.
   b. Neighborhoods should provide readiness programs in libraries, museums, and zoos.
   c. Neighborhoods should establish ready-to-learn centers in malls where college students can volunteer their services.
7. *Connections across the generations.* Connections across the generations will give children a sense of security and continuity, contributing to their school readiness in the fullest sense.
   a. Communities should build bridges between child care and senior citizen centers.
   b. Communities should build bridges between child care and community schools and teachers.

School–Peer Group Linkages

Children's attitudes about learning can be influenced by the peer group to which they belong. The peer group can thus help or hinder the school's role in socialization. The In Context box gives two examples.

IN CONTEXT Brian is not too sure of his status with his peers in class. The high school he attends has a strong tradition of academic excellence and has many intramural scholastic competitions. Brian's peers expect best efforts, which are rewarded by social recognition. Those who lag are put down. Brian works very hard academically to meet the standards of his peer group.

Todd, on the other hand, has a group of friends who believe it is not "cool" to carry books, give evidence of having done homework, or work hard academically. Todd, in choosing a group of friends whose value it is to "keep cool," probably is not working up to his full potential academically.

That peers influence the educational process was demonstrated by Coleman (1961) in his classic study on adolescents in schools. He found that in most high schools, boys value athletic ability and girls value popularity. That this is still true today is evidenced by the labeling of peer groups in junior high school and high school (Kinney, 1993): "brains," "nerds," "jocks," "populars," "normals," "unpopulars." Thus, students who depend on their peers for approval are less likely to endorse school and family values of academic success.

Research has established that under certain circumstances, such as attaining a superordinate goal (a group grade), the use of peers in a cooperative learning setting (students share responsibility for solving academic tasks and preparing reports) increases student achievement more than a teacher-directed setting. In addition, working together in a cooperative learning setting improves student self-esteem, social relations (particularly in the area of ethnic relations), and acceptance of students with disabilities who have been included (Johnson & Johnson, 1999; Slavin, 2006).

School–Media Linkages

Schools are linked to media through their use in the classroom as well as by media-related experiences outside the classroom that may influence student learning.

Many schools and teachers use the Public Broadcasting System (PBS) to complement their lessons. PBS offers a service called "Teacher Source" that provides educational support for prekindergarten through 12th grade. Schedules of local broadcasting of PBS shows are available online, as are related lesson plans and activities. PBS videos on arts and literature, health and fitness, math, science and technology, social studies, history, and early childhood can be purchased.

An example of media material that can be used with preschoolers is *Barney & Friends*. *Barney & Friends* was developed to address the interests and needs of young children ages 2 to 5. The programs are designed to enhance the cognitive, emotional, social, and physical development of the young child. Music, stories, examples, repetition, and positive reinforcement are some of the techniques used to teach social interaction, cooperation, sharing, language development, and coping with new experiences (such as going to the dentist, moving, and going to school).

An example of the use of media by students in a middle and junior high school in Escondido, California, is the production of their own news program (with the help of a teacher) on the school's television network, Channel B. In addition to reporting "goings-on," the program has background music; sometimes there are guests; and once a week there is a lesson in American Sign Language.

An example of media material that can be used with high schoolers is the opera adaptation of Shakespeare's *Romeo and Juliet*. Some activity ideas are to have students research the Shakespearean era, write an opera that addresses a problem, and compare Shakespeare's *Romeo and Juliet* with modern film adaptations.

Many schools and teachers subscribe to Channel One, a for-profit TV news program, including commercials, beamed directly into U.S. schools. Schools participating in Channel One receive satellite dishes, wiring, VCRs, DVDs, and television monitors for each classroom. The programs must be shown in class. They consist of news sprinkled with ads aimed at children (Gatorade, Phisoderm, bubble gum).

Computers in the classroom are necessary interactive tools to prepare children for the future. Some schools have enough computers for several students in a class to share; others have laptops for all; some schools are experimenting with other digital devices, such as iPads. An example of how computers are being used in the classroom is that the teacher has the students write essays on a topic for other students to read and make comments. Writing for others improves skills. Also, students use social networking when studying a piece of literature and write blogs for others in the class to discuss.

School-Community Linkages

Communities allocate resources for schools. They may use tax money to fund school construction or services. They may pass laws requiring builders to include a school in a new housing development. They set school boundaries (districts), thereby influencing the socioeconomic and/or cultural composition of schools.

Communities and School Size

Generally, large schools are found in large communities, and small schools are found in small communities. Communities with ample budgets can afford to have more schools per capita, hence smaller schools and classes. Studies relating the size of a school to socialization (Lee, 2004; Leithwood & Jantzi, 2009) have found that students in small schools (fewer than 400 students) engage in a greater variety of activities than students in large schools (more than 760 students). Students in small schools also hold more leadership positions than those in large schools. Although there may be more choices of activities in large schools, students have to compete for acceptance to teams and extracurricular activities, such as the newspaper. Consequently, many students don't "try out." Thus, the size of the school influences the kind of socializing experiences students have, because participation in extracurricular activities contributes to leadership skills, responsibility, cognitive and social competence, and personality development.

Several studies (Smerdon & Borman, 2009) found that students attending small schools had higher achievement, better discipline, better attendance, and higher graduation rates than did students attending large schools. Students and families reported more satisfaction with smaller schools. As a result of these studies, some communities have begun to offer schools within schools as a way of reorganizing the administration of existing large schools.

A study on what makes adolescents feel connected to schools (McNeely, Nonnemaker, & Blum, 2002) found students' connections with their schools to be associated with:

- **School size.** The smaller the school (down to 600 pupils), the more connected students felt.
- **Discipline policies.** Harsh discipline, such as zero tolerance, made students feel less connected, though safer.
- **Student friendships.** Adolescents are more connected to school when they have more friends there because they are less socially isolated.

Schools sometimes link up with business to promote a goal for children. This is an assembly featuring the Power Rangers (a media-related business of toy and clothing tie-ins to the famous TV characters) promoting health and fitness via their Empower program.

AP Photo/Beth Hall for Saban Brands

Communities and Class Size

Communities vary in their school districts' policies regarding class size. The size of the classes within a school influences socialization. Classes are considered "large" if they have more than 25 students, "small" if they have fewer than 20 students, and "regular" if they are in between. Prior to the implementation of the Federal Class-Size Program and similar initiatives in

Many schools require children to do community service. This girl raised money for the San Francisco Food Bank by collecting and recycling empty cans.

Kei Hoshino Quiqley

several states, more than 85 percent of our students were in classes with over 18 children, and about 33 percent were in classes of 25 or more students (U.S. Department of Education, 2000).

In large classes, as the size of the group increases, participation in discussion by each child decreases; interaction with the teacher also decreases (Benitez, Davidson, & Flaxman, 2009). In small classes, more learning activities take place and the greater interaction among students enables them to understand one another, resulting in an increase in cooperative behavior. Teachers have more time to monitor students' "on-task" behavior and can provide quicker and more thorough feedback to students. Also, potential disciplinary problems can be identified and resolved more quickly (U.S. Department of Education, 2000).

Community Businesses and Schools

The businesses in a community can support schools by donating resources and time ("Adopt-a-School"). A business can donate equipment, offer expert guest speakers, provide field trips, and/or offer apprenticeship training to students. Such supportive linkages enable children to understand the connection between school learning and the world of work, as well as discover new role models to emulate.

Community Services and Schools

Many schools require students to participate in the community by providing service, for example, by picking up trash at a local park, volunteering in a hospital, tutoring, and so on. For actual curricula, see http//learning.blogs.nytimes.com/2010/08/16 (Ojalvo, 2010). Service-learning, which involves incorporating community service experiences into students' school work, has long been viewed as a positive educational reform option. Beginning in the 1970s, educators began paying more attention to this teaching option, and the 1990s saw an array of initiatives to help promote the practice (Institute of Education Sciences, 1999). Even preschools are getting involved in community service. Albert (2010), a preschool director, requires her students to decide which nonprofit organization they want to support before they graduate and come up with a plan as to how to be supportive. For example, a 5-year-old girl was very upset seeing a man eat food out of a trash can. She decided to raise money for the San Francisco Food Bank by collecting empty cans and turning them in for recycling money. She raised $1,000!

Summary

- The school is an agent of socialization. It is a setting for intellectual and social experiences from which children develop the skills, knowledge, interest, and attitudes that characterize them as individuals and that shape their abilities to perform adult roles.
- Schools influence children through their educational policies, leading to achievement; through their formal organization, introducing students to authority; and through the social relationships that evolve in the classroom.
- The primary purpose of education from society's perspective is the transmission of the cultural heritage—the accumulated knowledge, values, beliefs, and customs of the society.
- The function of education from the individual's perspective is to acquire the skills and knowledge needed to become self-sufficient and to participate effectively in society.
- The school's function as a socialization agent is affected by the larger macrosystem context—political ideology, economics, culture, religion, and technology. Macrosystem influences are also demonstrated by society's policies concerning diversity and equity with regard to gender, culture, religion, and disability.
- The school's response to gender equity involves implementation of Title IX of the Education Amendments Act, which prohibits sex discrimination.
- The school's response to cultural diversity is via the No Child Left Behind Act.
- The school's response to religious pluralism involves sensitivity to which religious values intersect with educational goals.
- The school's response to children with disabilities is to provide special education and related services as required.

The Individuals with Disabilities Education Act guarantees that all children with disabilities will have available to them a free and appropriate education.

- Chronosystem influences on the school include its adaptation to societal change in general and its adaptation to specific developments such as technology, health (substance use/abuse and obesity), and safety (violence and emergency preparedness).
- Schooling for the future involves being prepared for the world of work and technological change.
- To maintain an effective environment for learning, schools must provide healthy and safe conditions. Substance use/abuse is a significant problem in schools, as is obesity, since both affect children's health and ability to learn. Schools have adopted programs to address violence and emergency preparedness
- Mesosystem influences on the school include its links with other ecosystems: school–child, school–family, school–peer group, school–media, and school–community. Linkages supportive of education will have beneficial socialization outcomes for the child.
- Family involvement in the school is the most important influence on children's educational success because the family is the primary socializer of children, and the family influences children's readiness to learn in school.
- Family involvement can occur in decision making, participation, and/or partnership.
- Peers influence student motivation to succeed.
- Media in school (TV, videos, computers) expand and individualize children's learning opportunities.
- Schools and communities are linked in terms of government tax monies allocated to the school (affecting size and resources) and in terms of local businesses that give support (financial, equipment, speakers, field trips).

Activity

PURPOSE To understand the school's role in influencing the socialization of children.

1. Attend a school board meeting where a controversial issue (school rules, dress code, curriculum, extracurricular activities, use of federal funds) is discussed. Agendas can be obtained in advance by contacting the school district office.
2. Describe the issue in at least a paragraph, giving background information if possible.
3. Explain the views of (a) the board, (b) the school administration, (c) the teachers, and (d) the parents and/or students.
4. What was the outcome of the discussion?
5. What was your opinion of the experience?

Related Readings

Berger, E. H. (2007). *Parents as partners in education: Families and schools working together* (7th ed.). Upper Saddle River, NJ: Prentice-Hall.

Collins, A., & Halverson, R. (2009). *Rethinking education in the age of technology: The digital revolution on schooling in America.* New York: Teachers College Press.

Comer, J. P. (2004). *Leave no child behind: Preparing today's youth for tomorrow's world.* New Haven, CT: Yale University Press.

Epstein, J. L. (2001). *School, family, and community partnerships: Preparing educators and improving schools.* Boulder, CO: Westview Press.

Gollnick, D. M., & Chinn, P. C. (2007). *Multicultural education in a pluralistic society* (8th ed.). Upper Saddle River, NJ: Prentice Hall.

Higginbotham, E., & Andersen, M. L. (2009). *Race and ethnicity in society: The changing landscape.* Belmont, CA: Wadsworth.

Kauffman, J. M., & Hallahan, D. P. (2004). *Special education: What it is and why we need it.* Boston: Allyn and Bacon.

Lareau, A. (2000). *Home advantage.* Lanham, MD: Rowman & Littlefield.

Mazur, A. J., & Doran, P. R. (2010). *Teaching diverse learners: Principles for best practice.* Thousand Oaks, CA: Corwin Press.

Ravitch, D. (2010). *The death and life of the great American school system: How testing and choice are all undermining education.* New York: Basic Books.

Schumacher, D., & Queen, J. A. (2006). *Overcoming obesity in childhood and adolescence: A guide for school leaders.* Thousand Oaks, CA: Sage/Corwin Press.

Resources

American Academy of Child & Adolescent Psychiatry—provides resources and information for families on many topics (Facts for Families)
http://www.aacap.org

National Network of Partnership Schools—working together for student success
http://www.csos.jhu.edu/P2000/

U.S. Department of Education—promoting educational excellence for all Americans
http://www.ed.gov

Cengage Learning

7

Ecology of Teaching

"A teacher who can arouse a feeling for one single good action, for one single good poem, accomplishes more than he who fills our memory with rows on rows of natural objects, classified with name and form."

—GOETHE

SOCIALIZATION SKETCHES

Amy Sussman/Stringer/Getty Images Entertainment/Getty Images

Learning Objectives

After completing this chapter, you will be able to:

1. Describe the teacher's role as a socializing agent.
2. Explain how the teacher's leadership style, management style, and expectations of students affect learning.
3. Describe how student differences, based on gender, cultural background, socioeconomic status, learning style, disability, at-risk, and resilience, affect teacher interaction and learning.
4. Explain macrosystem influences on teaching—philosophies, classroom contexts, accountability, standardization, and developmental appropriateness.
5. Describe mesosystem influences on teaching—family involvement in learning.

Amy Tan

(b. 1952)

"I think books were my salvation, they saved me from being miserable."

— AMY TAN

In this quote, Amy Tan, best-selling novelist, refers to her love of books because they served as an escape from reality—a difficult childhood and adolescence. She exemplifies concepts of cultural contrasts between the macroculture and microcultures discussed in this chapter. Her most famous book, *The Joy Luck Club*, adapted into a play and a movie, tells the stories of four immigrant mothers and their daughters which gradually unfold during their weekly mah-jongg games. The book focuses on the chasms between two cultures and two generations. It traces the transformation of the mothers from young girls into old women and of the Chinese daughters into Americanized adults.

Family

Amy Tan was born in Oakland, California. Her parents were immigrants from China. Her father, John Tan, was an electrical engineer and a Baptist minister who came to America to escape the turmoil of the Chinese Civil War. Her mother, Daisy, had divorced an abusive husband in China at the expense of losing custody of her three daughters. She was forced to leave them behind when she escaped on the last boat to leave Shanghai before the Communist takeover in 1949. Her marriage to John produced three children, Amy and two brothers.

Amy's parents had high expectations for their children to succeed in America. Schools were chosen accordingly and Amy was to become a doctor. It is not unusual for traditional Chinese parents to make life-path decisions for their children. It was also not unusual for such parents to use fear to control their children "for their own good." However, Amy was a little girl who didn't like being told what to do, so she didn't listen. In an interview in 1992 for the Academy of Achievement: A Museum of Living History (http://www.achievement.org), she said of her parents, "They just didn't understand. They didn't know how much the smallest amount of recognition would have meant to me and how the small amount of criticism could undo me."

Amy's father and brother both died of brain tumors within a year of each other. Amy's mother moved the children to Switzerland to finish high school. By then, Amy and her mother were in constant conflict.

Community

Growing up in an American macroculture, Amy was exposed to role models other than her parents. She saw other kids get Bs, and even Cs, on their report cards whose parents said, "That's OK, you tried. Here's some money for candy." Amy got scolded for the one B among all As on her report card.

While Amy was forbidden to read certain books, like *Catcher in the Rye*, she managed to read them anyway. These forbidden things had a great influence on her philosophy of life. She said, "I'm a very strong advocate for freedom of speech, freedom of expression, and the danger of banning books. The danger is in creating the idea that somebody else is going to define the purpose of literature and who has access to it."

Amy did a lot of things out of anger in her childhood through young adulthood. She hung out with bad peers and she dropped out of the college her mother had chosen for her, switching majors from pre-med to linguistics and literature at another college. She credits her change in behavior and perspective to her friendship with a kind, good, and loving man, now her husband, who reminded her of her father. His stability and support enabled her to realize that her mother parented out of love and Chinese tradition and so deserved her respect and forgiveness.

Amy Tan gives advice to kids whose parents are immigrants or first generations in this country. She says she understands how difficult it is growing up in two cultures and being confused as to who you are (Am I Chinese, Korean, Indian, or whatever, or am I an American?) and being different from most of the kids in your neighborhood. However, if you have the opportunity to go back to the country of your parents or ancestors, as I did, you will find out how many American assumptions you have and it will give you a sense of perspective. The idea is that your identity is not foisted upon you; it is what you create. "I realize now that the most important thing that is an American Dream—in looking at people living in other countries, in looking at the life my sisters had not growing up in this country—is the American freedom to create your own identity."

- What cultural and/or generational conflicts did you experience growing up?
- What is your definition of the American dream?

Who was your best teacher and who was your worst?

The Teacher's Role as a Socializing Agent

IN CONTEXT My *best* teacher was Mr. Grazer* in seventh grade. He was very handsome; you could easily look at him all day and absorb whatever he was saying. I loved him because he was genuinely interested in us, his students. He would ask us what we planned to do with our lives; you just wanted to succeed to have his approval. I continued to return to my old junior high school, even when I was in college, just to tell him of my accomplishments.

My *worst* teacher was Mr. Moore* in high school. He taught chemistry, the first class in which I failed an exam. It seemed like he enjoyed yelling at us, as a class and individually, more than he liked teaching. He especially chose the girls in the class to belittle for achievement efforts or behavior. Once he made me do time in detention because I turned around to lend the person seated behind me a pencil. I was too intimidated regarding my scientific abilities to choose physics to meet my science requirement the next year.

* The names have been changed to preserve their anonymity.

For more than 30 years, I have asked my students to think back over their education in elementary, middle, and high school and remember the characteristics of their best teacher and those of their worst. Though the exact wording differs, without fail "best" teachers are interesting, competent, caring, encouraging, and flexible, yet have demanding standards; "worst" teachers are boring, incompetent, distant, demeaning, and rigid with inflexible standards, or inconsistent with lax standards. After exploring reasons for students' choices, the message becomes quite clear: "Best" teachers make students want to learn and reinforce their efforts, while "worst" teachers turn students off.

My informal surveys about good teachers correspond to formal research on effective role models. According to Albert Bandura (1986, 1989), models whom children imitate are perceived as being warm and as having prestige, control over resources, and the potential to reinforce or punish behavior. Later research confirmed this. Primary-grade students reported good teachers to be caring, responsive, and stimulating (Daniels, Kalkman, & McCombs, 2001).

This chapter examines the teacher's role as a socializing agent along with his/her bidirectional relationship with the student and its impact on learning. (See Figure 7.1.) The student comes to school with a unique combination of family and cultural background, learning style, abilities, motives, and interests. The teacher also comes to school with a unique combination of family and cultural background along with certain abilities and characteristics, such as teaching style, ways of management, and expectations. Student–teacher interactions take place in a classroom environment that may enhance or detract from learning.

The most powerful socializing influence of the school lies in those who translate program goals into action—the teachers (Brophy & Wentzel, 2010). Teachers provide the environment for children's learning. They understand children's needs, interests, and abilities and can feel empathy for children's fears of failure. Teachers can encourage children to explore, to satisfy their natural curiosity, and to love learning—to love it so much that it becomes part of their lives forever. Teachers also play a major role in helping children learn to deal with positions of authority, to cooperate with others, to cope with problems, and to achieve competence.

The teacher is responsible for selecting materials relevant to the learner, for managing the group dynamics in the classroom, and for interacting individually with each child (Prensky, 2010; Sadker & Zittleman, 2009). More specifically, effective teachers:

- Organize the classroom environment to provide time and opportunity to learn.
- Involve students in planning motivating learning activities.
- Communicate high expectations for student success.

- Adapt learning activities to the needs and abilities of students.
- Ensure success for students by providing guidance and support as they progress through the curriculum.

The teacher–student relationship forms a different social experience for each child and, therefore, leads to different developmental outcomes. One explanation relates to **perception**, a biological construct that involves interpretation of stimuli by the brain. Factors such as maturation, attentiveness, past experiences, and emotions influence how a student perceives things, events, and interactions. A teacher's perception, and consequent presentation of information, are also influential in student learning. Does the teacher accommodate for different perceptions of the learning material? Another explanation relates to the child's home environment: Is it supportive of learning? Are there socialization contrasts between home and school? Is there communication between home and school?

perception a biological construct that involves interpretation of stimuli from the brain

We will first examine characteristics of the teacher, and then characteristics of the student, that influence learning.

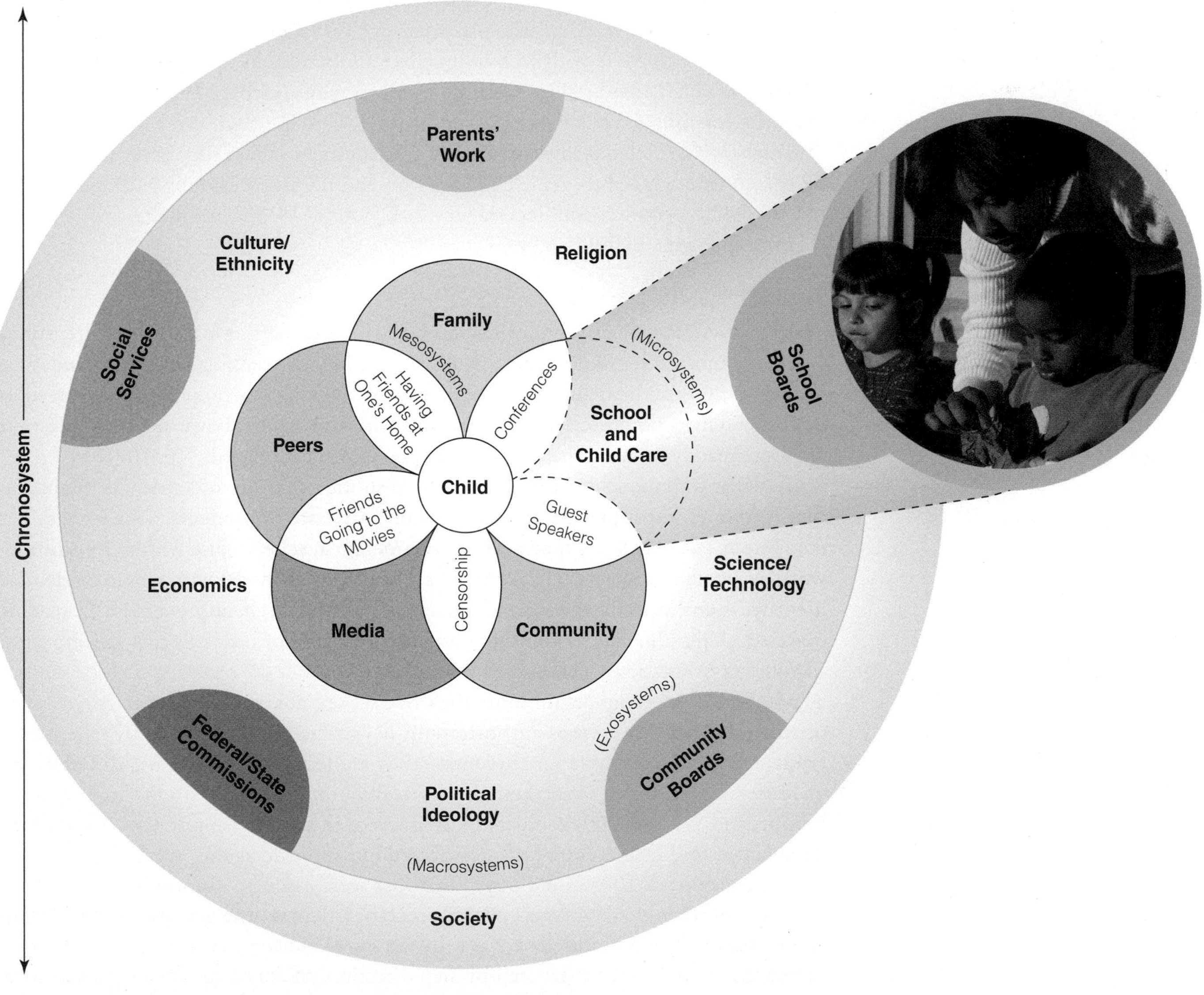

FIGURE 7.1 A Bioecological Model of Human Development
The teacher and student interact in the microsystem of school to affect learning outcomes.

GFOW 4203/Cengage Learning

What characteristics of teachers foster student learning?

Teacher Characteristics and Student Learning

For me, it was Mr. Grazer's knowledge of who did well at what, who was friends with whom, and how to use those facts to make everyone want to improve academically and socially. Teachers who try to work closely with each child and who understand group dynamics are more likely to provide a successful and rewarding learning environment. Studies have found that successful or effective teachers are those who are warm, enthusiastic, and generous with praise, and have high status. Also, successful teachers communicate well and are responsive to students. Conversely, unsuccessful or ineffective teachers are aloof, critical, and negative. They tend to communicate in ways that are difficult for students to understand and are unresponsive to students' needs. Teachers who are warm and friendly in their relationships with children are likely to encourage favorable rather than aggressive behavior and constructive, conscientious attitudes toward schoolwork (Good & Brophy, 2007; Daniels, Kalkman, & McCombs, 2001; Wayne & Youngs, 2003).

When teachers communicate with children, learning is influenced; when teachers ask questions, verbalization is elicited from the child. For example, teachers' verbal styles have been found to have an impact on the development of language skills in preschool children (Smith, 2001). Teachers who use expansive verbal descriptions and who encourage the children to converse with each other effect an increase in their students' verbal skills. It was also found that teachers who use reinforcement (verbal praise, smile, touch) can foster the learning of certain tasks.

Teacher–child relationships are significant factors in school success. A sample of kindergarten through eighth-grade children who had negative relations with teachers early on, marked by conflict and dependency, had poor academic and behavioral outcomes (Hamre & Pianta, 2001).

How does the teacher's behavior enable student learning?

Teachers as Leaders

Teachers are role models for learning and behavior. Teachers' impact on socialization and success in motivating student learning is explained by the classic research of Bandura and Walters (1963) on modeling, mentioned earlier: "Models who are rewarding, prestigeful or competent, who possess high status, and who have control over rewarding resources are more readily imitated than are models who lack these qualities" (p. 107).

Students who model their teachers pick up subtle behaviors and attitudes about learning. It follows, then, that the most important influence on students' achievement is the competent teacher. More specifically, a competent teacher is one who is committed to work, is an effective classroom manager, is a positive role model with whom students can identify, is enthusiastic and warm, continues efforts for self-improvement in teaching, possesses skill in human relationships, and can adapt his or her skills to a specific context (Brophy & Wentzel, 2010; Good & Brophy, 2007).

Mr. Grazer was a model (in more than one sense), able to engage a diverse classroom of students. Mr. Moore was authoritarian; it was his way or no way. Teachers direct, guide, and set an example for students—they are leaders. Teachers use different styles of leadership to accomplish their goals. To illustrate, a classic study done by Lewin, Lippitt, and White (1939) compared the effects of three leadership styles—authoritarian, democratic, and **laissez-faire** (a policy of letting people do as they please; permissive)—on three groups of 10-year-old boys. The boys were assigned randomly to one of three after-school recreational groups engaged in craft activities. The groups were led by three adults who behaved in different ways. In the *authoritarian* situation, the leader determined the group's policy, gave step-by-step directions, dictated each boy's particular task, assigned children to work with one another, was subjective in his praise of the children's work, and stayed aloof from group participation. In the *democratic* situation, the leader allowed the boys to participate in setting group policy, gave the boys a general idea of the

laissez-faire a policy of letting people do as they please; permissive

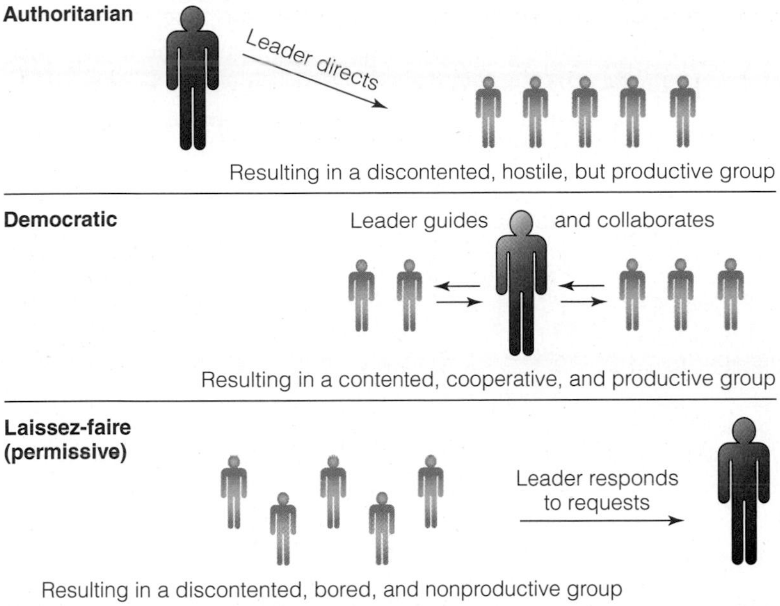

FIGURE 7.2 **Teachers and Leadership Styles**

steps involved in the project, suggested alternative procedures, allowed them to work with whomever they wished, evaluated them in a fair and objective manner, and tried to be a member of the group. In the *laissez-faire* situation, the leader gave the group complete freedom to do as they wished, supplied material or information only when asked, and refrained almost completely from commenting on the boys' work.

The style of leadership was shown to have a definite effect on the interactions within each group. The boys in the authoritarian situation showed significantly more aggression toward one another and were far more discontented than the boys in the democratic condition. They also produced more work than the other two groups. The boys in the democratic group showed less hostility, more enjoyment, and continued to work even when the leader left the room, which was not true of the other two groups. Finally, the laissez-faire group accomplished relatively little; the boys were frequently bored and spent much time "fooling around." (See Figure 7.2.)

How do teachers' leadership styles influence the learning environment in the classroom?

Good and Brophy (2007) report several studies finding that a teacher who is clearly the leader and authority and who directs the class toward specific goals (*direct instruction*) promotes achievement. In this learning environment, little emphasis is placed on discussion, student ideas, discovery learning, or other types of *indirect instruction*. The NCLB Act, with its standardization and assessment criteria, has caused many teachers to reformulate their teaching styles.

Prensky (2010) found that students prefer indirect instruction. Effective teachers are those who are partners with students in learning; they can motivate students to be curious by asking appropriate questions. For example, rather than lecture and have students take notes, teachers ask questions and suggest topics to explore; students find answers doing research.

Rogoff (2003) views the teacher's leadership role as that of a mentor who guides participation. For example, when a teacher shows a child how to be more successful at doing math problems (addition, subtraction) by putting the numbers in boxes on graph paper, the teacher is not only guiding the child's participation but is also providing support

This teacher is a powerful influence on learning through her ability to stimulate the children's interest and engage their involvement.

BananaStock/Jupiter Images

zone of proximal development (ZPD) Vygotsky's term for the space between what a learner can do independently and what he or she can do while participating with more capable others

for success from one level to the next. This is known as "scaffolding," like you might see on a building being constructed. Thus, teachers facilitate children's capacities to reach their full potential. Lev Vygotsky (1978) called the space between what a learner can do independently and what he or she can do while participating with more capable others the **zone of proximal development (ZPD)**. The effective teacher is one who is sensitive to the student's zone of development and provides appropriate independent, as well as collaborative, activities to enhance learning.

TeachSource Video Activity

Go to the Education CourseMate website to watch the video entitled "5–11 years: Lev Vygotsky, the Zone of Proximal Development, and Scaffolding." Can you relate some activities you experienced in which you learned this way?

IN CONTEXT My mother wanted to learn how to use the word-processing program on my computer. I demonstrated a few commands and let her practice, telling her to call me if she got stuck. When she felt she had mastered the basics, I showed her how to do more complicated things. With my assistance, my mother was able to learn more quickly than she would have on her own.

What does a teacher's managing ability have to do with a student's learning ability?

Teachers as Managers

Mr. Grazer's teaching style motivated me—he actually was the person who encouraged me to write. In contrast, Mr. Moore squashed my desire to continue learning science. Kounin (1970) studied classroom management techniques and consequent student learning. His classic research showed that the key to successful management lay in preventive, rather than consequential, measures. The differences between successful and unsuccessful classroom managers lay in the planning and preparation of instruction, so that inattention and boredom were prevented.

Kounin found that student inattentiveness and misbehavior were often linked to problems of discontinuity in a lesson, which in turn were linked to inadequate preparation by the teacher. For example, a teacher who is giving instructions on how to do a book report and stops to find some appropriate books in the closet is likely to have lost the students' attention by the time the books are located. On the other hand, if a teacher has the exemplary books displayed on a table while the book report instructions are being given, it is likely that inattentiveness will be prevented.

Did you ever have teachers who had "eyes in the back of their heads"? Such teachers seem to know what their students are doing without looking and therefore are quick to react to potential problems. Kounin refers to this type of teacher behavior as "with-it-ness." Teachers who are "with it" respond immediately to incidents rather than waiting, quash minor problems before they turn into major ones, do not overreact to incidents, and focus accurately on the individuals involved in the incident rather than blaming someone wrongly. When students realize that the teacher knows what is going on, they are less likely to become involved in unproductive behavior.

Well-managed classrooms appear to run by themselves, with the teacher spending most of the time teaching rather than dealing with behavior problems. During a review of videotapes of their classes, teachers who were effective managers often referred to the preventive and anticipatory measures they had taken to avoid classroom problems—for example, encouraging student self-regulation (Emmer & Stough, 2001).

Another characteristic of successful classroom managers is the ability to "overlap"—that is, to deal with more than one activity at the same time (Good & Brophy, 2007). For example, while working with a group of students in one corner of the room, a teacher provides an appropriate motivating statement to a child who is wandering about, not involved in an activity ("Nadia, I'd like to read the paragraph you wrote so we can think of another one"). Also, transitions from one activity to the next are smooth, not disruptive: "When you complete the chapter, you may work on the computer"; rather than "All books away; it is time for your test now."

Teachers' Expectations

Do teachers' expectations affect the achievement and behavior of students?

Mr. Moore believed science was for boys, homemaking for girls. This was a powerful "downer" for me, because I had thought of becoming a doctor. Since achievement was not expected from the girls in Mr. Moore's class, it did not occur. To document the significance of expectations, Rosenthal and Jacobson, in their book *Pygmalion in the Classroom* (1968), described a classic experiment in which they had all the teachers in an elementary school give a test to their students that was designed to identify intellectual "bloomers" (those who would show an academic spurt during the year). Actually, the test was a nonverbal IQ test and, unknown to the teachers, did not predict future intellectual spurts. After the test, however, the researchers provided the teachers with a list of bloomers. The bloomer list was not based on the test; instead, it was a random list of names from the teachers' rolls. Eight months later, all the children were retested with the same IQ test. The designated "bloomers" did, in fact, demonstrate significant intellectual growth; those in the first and second grades showed the most growth. This study raised the question, Are teachers trapped by their self-fulfilling prophecies for their students?

Rosenthal and Jacobson's study generated a lot of controversy because of methodological weaknesses and the inability of others to replicate the original results. However, studies observing actual teacher behavior in the classroom have shown the effects of expectancy (Sadker & Zittleman, 2009). For example, in a longitudinal study of more than 1,500 middle school students whose teachers predicted their performance in math, there was a greater impact on future math achievement for low achievers, whose performance was overestimated, than for high achievers, whose performance was underestimated (Madon, Jussim, & Eccles, 1997). These findings demonstrate the power of "living up to expectation."

Brophy and colleagues (Good & Brophy, 2007; Brophy & Wentzel, 2010) explain the real-world effect of teacher expectations as follows: Teachers usually receive data about students at the beginning of the school year (test scores, past grades, family and health information, comments by previous teachers), which influence their expectations of students for achievement and behavior. Because of these expectations, the teacher tends to treat students differently. Students then react to the teacher differently. The students' behavior and achievement reinforce the teacher's expectations. Gradually, the students' self-concepts, motivation, and levels of aspiration reflect these expectations. If continued throughout the year, the students' performances will match or fulfill what the teacher expected or prophesied at the beginning of the year.

In addition to students' past records of achievement and behavior, teachers' expectations can be influenced by certain student characteristics, such as socioeconomic class, cultural background, gender, personality, physical attractiveness, speech characteristics, and handwriting (Good & Brophy, 2007; Sadker & Zittleman, 2009).

IN CONTEXT Ms. Karns has a child named Roy in her third-grade class who has moved several times and has below-normal achievement scores recorded in his cumulative folder. As Ms. Karns reviews the folders belonging to the other children in her class, she finds three children (Sarah, Andrew, and Cary) who have consistently scored well above normal on achievement tests and whose folders also contain notes from previous teachers about what a joy each one was to teach. Upon observing Ms. Karns midyear, we find that she waits less time for Roy to answer her questions than she does for Sarah, Andrew, or Cary. We also find that she is more critical of Roy than she is of the others and demands less of him in terms of work.

Of course, not all teachers translate their expectations into the type of behavior described in the box. Some teachers do not form expectations that continue throughout the year; rather, they change their expectations on the basis of the students' performance.

Teacher expectations about students do not have a direct impact on student behavior; it is only when these expectations are communicated to the students, and selective reinforcement results in shaping their behavior, that teacher expectations have an impact. By becoming aware of possible biases in their behavior caused by their expectations, teachers can make a conscious effort to interact objectively with each child.

Which students turn teachers on to teaching? Which ones turn them off?

Student Characteristics and Teacher Interaction

Students who are engaged, interested in what I have to say, and willing to participate in class turn me on; I feel myself becoming more animated and willing to delve into topics of interest. Students who doze, who come in late or leave early, who won't participate no matter what, turn me off; I find myself struggling to make the material more interesting and becoming exhausted in the process.

Teacher–student interaction is bidirectional, with teachers eliciting responses in students and students, through their behavioral, cognitive, and affective qualities, eliciting responses in teachers (Bloom, 1982). According to Lillian Katz (1995), teacher–student interaction is specific and limited in that it relates to school matters. The intensity of affect between teacher and student is supposed to be low and somewhat detached, because teachers cannot get too emotionally involved with their students; otherwise they would lose objectivity (in their ability to evaluate, for example). Teachers must maintain rationality and intentionality in their curriculum goals. They must exhibit impartiality toward individual students, as their scope of responsibility is to the whole group. Teaching a group of students from diverse backgrounds is a big challenge, especially when the group is large. The bidirectional relationship of teacher and student, which in turn affects socialization, is a complex dynamic reflecting factors such as gender, cultural background, socioeconomic status, learning styles, and disability.

Do teachers treat boys and girls differently?

Gender

Research shows that teacher–student interaction differs according to the gender of the student (the gender of the teacher does not seem to matter), though even when confronted with documentation (such as video recording), most teachers are unaware of inequities (Sadker & Zittleman, 2009). Studies consistently show that boys have more interactions with teachers than do girls (Streitmatter, 1994; Ruble, Martin, & Berenbaum, 2006). Teachers are more responsive to the disruptive behavior of boys than of girls and are more likely to reprimand boys (Frawley, 2005). When children request attention, teachers generally respond to boys with instructions and to girls with nurture. In addition, girls receive more attention when they are close to the teacher, whereas boys are given attention from a distance.

Studies also show that the feedback received by boys and girls on the intellectual quality of their work differs: Boys receive considerable criticism for failing to obey the rules, whereas girls receive criticism related to their performance; and boys attribute their failure to do well to lack of effort, whereas girls attribute their failure to do well to lack of ability (Dweck, 2002). Do some girls, then, give up trying to be successful when they reach high school because of the responses their elementary teachers have given them?

Why do girls perform better academically than boys in elementary school, but falter in high school? For example, girls do not do as well as boys in science and math by the time they reach adolescence (American Association of University Women [AAUW], 1991; Maccoby & Jacklin, 1974). There is evidence that girls generally take fewer advanced math classes than do boys in high school and college (AAUW, 1991; Sadker & Sadker, 1994; Sadker & Zittleman, 2009).

Richard Whitmire (2010), author of *Why Boys Fail*, worries about boys being shortchanged in K–12. He reports that only 40 percent of young men are enrolled in college as compared to 60 percent of young women. He points to the emphasis of today's schools on order, sitting still, and passive learning—methods much better suited to girls than boys. Boys have higher dropout and lower graduation rates, as well as lower grades and test scores than do girls.

Other experts, such as Susan McGee Bailey (Whitmire & Bailey, 2010), principal author on the 1991 *AAUW Report*, rejects these concerns, contending that ingrained sexism and gender roles continue to hamper K–12 schooling for both boys and girls. She says that race, gender, and income issues interact in complicated ways. Income and race gaps are larger than gender gaps, as documented in reading and math scores on the National Assessment of Educational Progress data.

How can teachers be more equitable? Teachers must be trained to foster assertive and affiliative skills in both girls and boys. School curricula and textbooks should be monitored for gender stereotypes and should provide positive role models for both girls and boys. Gender-role socialization will be discussed in more detail in Chapter 12.

Culture

Do teachers engage in cultural stereotyping?

Cultural background is a factor in teacher–student interaction in that both teacher and student come to the relationship with certain socialization experiences influencing their values, morals, attitudes, motives, behaviors, and roles. We discussed socialization in families of diverse cultural backgrounds in Chapters 3 and 4. Here we focus on the impact of such diverse socialization on teacher–student interaction. Diverse socialization yields diverse perspectives on what to learn, how to learn it, and how to show it has been learned. The role of teacher and school is to implement the values and traditions of society and so take on the responsibility of acculturation.

The United States is composed of many diverse cultural groups. According to the National Center for Education Statistics (2007), the majority of individuals in the United States classify themselves as non-Hispanic white, but numerous minority groups include those of Latino origin, African American origin, Native American/Alaskan origin, Asian–Pacific Island origin, and others. Americans speak many languages. The number of people 5 and older who speak a language other than English at home has more than doubled in the last three decades, at a pace four times greater than the nation's population growth, according to a U.S. Census Bureau report (2007). The largest language groups are Spanish (Texas, California, and New Mexico), French (Louisiana and Maine), German (North Dakota and South Dakota), Slavic languages (Illinois, New York, New Jersey, and Connecticut), Chinese (California, New York, Hawaii, and Massachusetts) and Korean (Hawaii, California, and New Jersey). The language data that the Census Bureau collects is vital to local agencies in determining potential language needs of school-aged children, for providing voting materials in non-English languages as mandated by the Voting Rights Act, and for researchers to analyze language trends in the U.S. Projections of population growth to the year 2020, based on life expectancies, fertility rates, and immigration, suggest that the gap between majority and minority cultural groups is narrowing. This trend, plus the movement toward a global economy, points to the importance of understanding cultural diversity. Examples of possible misunderstandings follow.

IN CONTEXT As the preschool teacher was helping the children settle down on their mats for naptime, she noticed red marks on Jenny Truong's neck and forehead. She asked Jenny how she got them and Jenny replied that her father put them there. The teacher, suspecting child abuse, reported it to the police. People from various Asian countries believe that internal winds cause illness. However, by bringing the wind to the surface, the illness can leave and that person will be healed. The way this is done is by "scratching the wind away," or "coining." A coin dipped in oil or menthol is vigorously rubbed against the head, neck, chest, back, or wherever the symptoms are exhibited. The skin is rubbed until it turns red (Dresser, 2005).

One day a fifth-grade teacher noticed that Juanita, normally a tidy youngster, had a brown smear of dirt on one arm. That day and the next, the teacher said nothing. However, when Juanita came to class with the mark on her arm the third day, the teacher told her to go wash her dirty arm. When Juanita said it was not dirty, the teacher told her not to argue and to do as she was told. Juanita complied. Several days later, Juanita was taken out of school by her parents to attend the funeral of her sister. Two weeks had passed and Juanita had still not returned to school, so the principal went to her home to find out why. Juanita's mother told the principal that when someone is ill, each family member places a spot of oil and soil somewhere on the body. "We are one with nature. When someone is ill, that person is out of balance with nature. We use the oil and soil of our Mother, the earth, to show her we wish our sick one to be back in balance with nature. When Juanita's teacher made her wash her arm, our oneness with nature was broken. That is why her sister died. The teacher caused her death; Juanita can never return to her class" (Garcia, 1998).

What can teachers do to be equitable regarding diverse groups?

Respect for cultural as well as religious differences requires teachers to be sensitive to a variety of customs. Asking appropriate questions and listening carefully can help avoid misunderstandings. The National Association for the Education of Young Children (NAEYC) has taken the following position:

> For optimal developmental and learning of all children, educators must accept the legitimacy of children's home language, respect (hold in high regard) and value (esteem, appreciate) the home culture and promote and encourage the active involvement and support of all families, including extended and nontraditional family units. (NAEYC, 1996a, p. 5)

Teacher sensitivity can be used to enable children to be tolerant and respectful of differences. When a kindergarten boy from India was called "garbage head" by his classmates because his hair smelled of coconut oil, the teacher planned a series of activities in which she and the children compared coconut oil to a variety of shampoos, conditioners, mousses, and gels. After much discussion about all the different things people put on their hair, the children came to realize that everyone's hair has a particular smell and coconut was simply one of a vast array (Ramsey, 2004).

Understanding diversity in *microcultures*, or minority groups, involves examining the *macroculture*, or majority group. Historically, political and social institutions in the United States developed from a Western European tradition. The English language came from England, and the American legal system is derived from English common law. The American political system of democratic elections comes from England and France (Gollnick & Chinn, 2008). American formal institutions (representing the macroculture), such as government, schools, business, and health and welfare agencies, reflect White European Protestant influences often referred to as the *Protestant ethic*.

What are some generalized values of the macroculture?

Although the macroculture includes people who are not White, of European descent, or Protestant, certain basic values are shared to some degree by all members of the macroculture. Generally, the American macroculture (briefly discussed in Chapter 1 as a low-context macrosystem), is characterized by the following (Arensberg & Niehoff, 1975; Stewart & Bennett, 1991; Williams, 1960):

- **Emphasis on active mastery** rather than passive acceptance—individuals are responsible for what happens to them.
- **Valuation of the work ethic**—industriousness, ambition, competitiveness, individualism, independence.
- **Achieved status**—based on occupation, education, and financial worth, rather than inheritance.
- **Stress on assertiveness** rather than humility.

- **Valuation of fairness**—equal opportunities in social, political, and economic institutions rather than hierarchal privileges.
- **More interest in the external world of things and events** than the internal world of meaning and feeling—achievement and success are measured by the quality of material goods purchased.
- **Emphasis on change, flow, movement**—new and modern are better than old and traditional; emphasis is on future rather than past or present.
- **Belief in rationalism** rather than traditionalism—not accepting things just because they have been done before; there has to be a logical reason for doing something.
- **Emphasis on peer relationships** rather than superordinate–subordinate; advocates equality, or horizontal relationships, rather than hierarchy, or vertical relationships.
- **Focus on individual personality** (individualism, independence) rather than group identity and responsibility (collectivism, interdependence)—idealizes an adaptive and outgoing personality rather than a conventional, introverted one.
- **Objective, impersonal relationships to others** tend to the norm rather than subjective, personal ones; communication is direct or confrontational.
- **Principles of right and wrong** characterize personal life and community affairs, rather than shame, dishonor, or ridicule.

How are these values exemplified in young children's behavior? Most children in the United States learn that nature is something you conquer and exploit. In the sandbox they often "build roads" or "dig to the other side of the world" (Ramsey, 2004). Children are also encouraged to be actively engaged rather than "bored," as evidenced by the quantity of toys parents bring on long car rides.

What are some generalized values of the microculture?

The degree to which individual U.S. citizens subscribe to the general values of the macroculture depends, in part, on the values of the microculture, or minority group, to which they belong (the microculture was briefly discussed in Chapter 1 as a high-context macrosystem). The degree may also depend on how much an individual must interact with formal societal institutions for support (Gollnick & Chinn, 2008). For example, one who receives a government loan to further his or her education must comply with regulations by proving attendance at a college or university and following the prescribed schedule for repayment. To better understand possible areas of differences between macroculture (mainly individualistic) and microculture (mainly collectivistic) values in school, some generalities about microcultures follow.

- **Orientation toward the extended family**—the child is considered an important member of the family group; the family provides a psychological support system throughout the individual's life. Cousins are considered as close as brothers. Emphasis is placed on cooperation, helping those in need, and respect for elders. Family matters may take precedence over school attendance.
- **Fostering of sharing and group ownership**—to a child who has not been socialized to understand individual ownership ("These are *your* crayons"), *your* may mean belonging to the group. Thus, if Lee cannot find his pencil, he borrows Steve's without asking because whatever belongs to the group, the child regards as his or hers, too.
- **Humility**—children are socialized not to "show up" (demonstrate individual superiority over) their peers. Children from collectivistic cultures may not exhibit competitive behaviors in classroom settings, such as responding to "Who has the best work?" However, when performance is socially defined as benefiting the peer society ("Which group has read the most books?"), children from collectivistic cultures compete well.
- **Learning occurs by observation and being patient**—at home, children from collectivistic cultures may not be rewarded for curiosity and for asking questions; parents may even use legends and fables to discourage curiosity.

- **Respect and compliance shown by no eye contact** rather than by looking directly at an adult, as is expected in the macroculture.
- **Ascribed status**—more characteristic of collectivistic cultures where status is based more on who you are (family name) than what you have achieved.
- **Present-time orientation**—more common than future-time orientation. Time is viewed as a continuum, with no beginning and no end. Ceremonies, for example, begin when the participants are ready, rather than punctually at the scheduled time.

How do individualistic and collectivistic orientations affect socialization?

Until recently, most of the research on child development has been carried out in the context of the dominant macroculture, which has an individualistic orientation. Consequently, the development of children from European American, middle-class families has come to be considered the norm for all children regardless of the cultural or economic context they inhabit (Bennett, 2010). Thus, to get a broad perspective on child development and to foster understanding of culturally diverse children, the socialization backgrounds of collectivistic cultures will be compared to those of individualistic cultures. The following discussion comprises generalizations from research.

> The continuum of individualism/collectivism represents the degree to which a culture emphasizes individual fulfillment and choice versus interdependent relations, social responsibility, and the well-being of the group. Individualism makes the former a priority, collectivism, the latter. (Trumbull et al., 2001, p. 4)

Generally, the school is oriented toward the European American value and tradition of individualism, whereas most minority ethnic groups are oriented toward that of collectivism. To enable teachers to meet the challenges of education in a pluralistic society, Trumbull and colleagues (2001) describe how the individualistic–collectivistic continuum approach to different cultures can be applied in the classroom. They give the following example of an individualistic and a collectivistic response to the same situation (p. 6):

> At the end of the school day, when it is time to clean up, Salvador isn't feeling well. He asks his friend, Emanuel, to help him do his assigned job for the day, cleaning the blackboard. Emanuel isn't sure he'll have time to do his job and help Salvador.
> *Individualistic response*: The teacher gets a third person to do Salvador's job, as Emanuel has his own responsibility.
> *Collectivistic response*: The teacher tells Emanuel to help Salvador with his job.

These children are learning to cook by guided participation. Each child is observing, modeling, and doing.

Cengage Learning

Understanding Socialization Contrasts Between Home and Classroom to Enable Equitable Teaching

Diverse cultures have diverse perspectives on such things as objects/people, possessions, achievement, and social roles. Children are socialized according to the perspectives of their family's cultural heritage.

- **Objects/people.** Children socialized in individualistic cultures generally learn about physical objects as a means toward independence. Parents give children toys and teach them how to use various materials so they can amuse and help themselves. Parents use direct oral language to communicate instructions. Children socialized in collectivistic cultures generally are amused and helped by other people. Holding, touching, and modeling how to carry out a task tend to be the dominant forms of communication. In school, where verbal instructions are often given, children who are not accustomed to that manner of learning may have difficulty. Demonstrating and working alongside the student may be more helpful.

■ **Possessions.** In collectivistic cultures, the emphasis on social relationships and getting along extends to possessions. Personal items, such as clothing, books, and toys, are often considered family property and are readily shared. In individualistic cultures, emphasis generally is on having and taking care of your own things—"that's mine!" is often heard. In school, where much emphasis is placed on producing one's own work and keeping one's things tidy in one's desk, children who are used to communal tasks and property may have difficulty adjusting. Teachers might incorporate cooperative activities in the classroom to allow such children an opportunity to contribute.

■ **Achievement.** Individualistic cultures tend to stress individual achievement and competition: "Who read the most books?" Related is the sense of self-expression and personal choice: "Who knows the answer?" "Which club do you want to join?" Collectivistic cultures tend to stress group affiliation and cooperation: "How is your friend feeling today?" "Let's let him hold your teddy bear." Related is the belief in the need for group harmony and saving face: "We need to help Maria with her math so she won't be embarrassed in class." Teachers might be cognizant of their use of praise for a child in front of the group. Although this is thought to reinforce desired achievement and competition and to foster self-esteem, it may have the opposite effect on children who interpret it as upsetting group harmony and causing embarrassment.

■ **Social roles.** Children socialized in collectivistic cultures are generally taught to respect a hierarchy of authority roles, with grandparents, parents, teachers, and other adults possessing knowledge and being worthy of respect. Thus, they may not be very responsive if a teacher asks their opinion (their status in the age hierarchy implies they do not know enough to have one) or inquires whether they have questions (indicating that the material the teacher taught was not understood may be considered disrespectful). Children socialized in individualistic cultures are generally taught egalitarian principles in social roles; everyone has certain rights that must be respected, such as the right to voice an opinion. Collectivistic cultures usually have more rigid gender roles than do individualistic cultures. When I taught preschool, some little girls would always arrive clothed in pretty dresses, in spite of the suggestion to all parents that their children wear clothes suitable for climbing on the outdoor equipment and easily washable. Teachers might structure some learning activities using group structures and group leaders. Children in the group help each other and ask pertinent questions via the group leader, who serves as mediator between the group and the teacher. As the children become more competent with various school subjects, they can experience being a group leader.

Socioeconomic Status

Do all children have an equal opportunity to succeed in school?

It has been well documented that family socioeconomic status affects school readiness and later academic achievement (Duncan & Magnuson, 2005; Sirin, 2005). "Since the term 'socioeconomic status' (SES) refers to one's social position as well as to the privileges and prestige that derive from access to economic and social resources, . . . it may be difficult to measure directly a family's access to resources or its position in a social hierarchy" (Duncan & Magnuson, 2005, p. 2). Therefore, researchers typically use one SES indicator, such as occupation, or combine several indicators, such as occupation, income, and parental education, into scales that reflect families' relative positions in a social hierarchy. We discussed the influence of the family's socioeconomic status on socialization in Chapters 3 and 4. Here we relate it to the impact of learning in school.

To understand the relationship between families' disparate socioeconomic circumstances and children's achievement, Duncan and Magnuson (2005) examined four components of SES: income, education, family structure, and neighborhood.

- **Income.** Children from birth to age 5 whose families' incomes were below the poverty line were found to score lower on a standardized test than children from families with average incomes. This is most likely due to the more stimulating learning environment of books, newspapers, educational games, and activities available in families able to afford such things.

- **Education.** Children whose parents finished high school and had some college education routinely score higher on cognitive and academic tests than do children of parents with less education. Despite the heterogeneity of children in all social classes, teachers often stereotype children's potential based on their socioeconomic status and base expectations for achievement accordingly (Ramsey, 2004).
- **Family structure.** Single-parent families are likely to have fewer resources than dual-parent families. Young children living with single mothers are more likely to be poor (FIFCFS, 2010). Financial and time constraints may limit a single parent's ability to supervise and discipline children and to provide a supportive and stimulating environment. On average, children raised by single parents have lower social and academic well-being than do children of intact marriages (Childrens Defense Fund, 2010). Part of the explanation is economic insecurity in young or single-parent families. Another part is parental conflict and strain in divorcing families. Finally, the many transitions experienced by children in young and single-parent families may result in feelings of instability.
- **Neighborhood.** Children growing up in high-poverty urban communities plagued by violence, gangs, drug activity, old housing, and vacant buildings may experience stress, a lack of positive role models, a lack of institutional resources (school, protective services), and negative peer influences (Duncan & Magnuson, 2005).

In sum, the lack of preparedness for school of children from low-SES families affects the teacher–student relationship. Low-SES families tend not to have physical or emotional resources for educational support. Many home experiences taken for granted in middle-class families, such as books, computers, and trips, are unavailable in poor families. Because low SES can be a self-perpetuating cycle, poor parents themselves may not have received an adequate education growing up and, therefore, may lack knowledge of readiness and supportive educational activities to provide for their child, such as language stimulation, reading, and games.

The differential treatment of groups of people because of their class background, and the reinforcement of those differences through values and practices of societal institutions such as schools, is known as **classism**. As has been discussed, socioeconomic class is based on income, educational attainment, occupation, and power. Where a family falls on the continuum from poor to rich affects the manner in which its members live, how they think and act, and the way others react to them (Gollnick & Chinn, 2008).

classism the differential treatment of people because of their class background and the reinforcing of those differences through values and practices of societal institutions

Dealing with life's inevitable inconveniences is dependent on class. For example, if your car breaks down, do you bring it to a service station for repairs, rent a car, and go about your business? Or do you ask a relative or friend to help you fix it while you depend on others and public transportation to take you where you need to go? When you get sick, do you go to a doctor knowing that whatever the treatment, it will be covered by your insurance? Or do you go to bed and try to heal yourself? Likewise, in the classroom children who have access to books, computers, and trips can navigate more successfully through school projects than those who have few resources at home.

What are the consequences of classism?

The consequences of classism in school are subtle, but significant. One consequence is that students of lower socioeconomic status are more likely to be assigned to low ability groups in their early years, setting them on a track that is difficult to alter (Gollnick & Chinn, 2008).

How do you learn best?

Learning Styles

Children have different ways they learn best, and teachers have different ways they teach best. When I was in school, I liked listening to interesting lectures. I liked organization and analysis. When I had difficulty, I appreciated help from a neighboring student. I disliked being put into groups and given a task. I hated laboratory assignments. My daughter, on the other hand, loved working in groups and hated analytical tasks. She also liked writing creative stories. She was not too fond of lab work, either. I liked teachers who were structured and followed a plan; my daughter liked teachers who were innovative in their approaches to curriculum. Student learning style and teacher teaching style can be viewed as bidirectional, with one influencing the other.

Some children learn more effectively by observation, modeling, and apprenticeship rather than through verbal instruction, the teaching method most commonly used in American schools. To illustrate, Joan tells how she learned to prepare salmon as a child. After watching her mother, she was allowed to gradually take on portions of the task and to ask questions only if they were important. Once she told her mother that she didn't understand how to do "the backbone part." So her mother took an entire fish and repeated the deboning because, according to her, it is not possible to understand "the backbone part" except in the context of the whole fish.

Researchers (Hilliard, 1992; Tharp, 1989; Park, C.C. 2001) suggest that children develop learning or cognitive styles based on the socialization they receive in their families and peer groups—although there are still many unanswered questions about cognitive styles. Children who live in families that are structured—members have defined roles, specific times are set aside for eating and sleeping, the family uses formal styles of group organization (relating to a leader, pursuing goals, receiving feedback)—have been observed to have an *analytical cognitive style*. Children who live in families that are less structured—roles are shared, individuals eat when hungry and sleep when tired—are more likely to exhibit a *relational cognitive style*.

What is the relationship between cognitive style and socialization in families?

Orientation Toward Persons/Objects

Children from collectively oriented families tend to be more oriented toward feelings and personal interaction, and are more proficient at nonverbal communication, than are children from individually oriented families (Bennett, 2010; Hale-Benson, 1986; Hale, 2004). This is because children from collectively oriented families generally get a lot of experience interacting with people (Hale-Benson, 1986; Hale, 2004). Communication in these interactions may differ from that experienced by children from individually oriented families. In a collectively oriented conversation, talking may traverse from topic to topic rather than following a linear sequence from the beginning of the story to the end as occurs in an individually oriented conversation (Ramsey, 2004). Children from individually oriented families generally learn to focus on objects; they usually have numerous opportunities to manipulate things and discover properties and relationships. These experiences with objects help prepare them for school, which is also object-oriented, using books, computers, learning centers, and so on.

Field Dependence/Independence

Some children exhibit a holistic, concrete, social approach to learning (Bennett, 2010). This style of learning, referred to as *field-dependent*, usually implies that the person works well in groups and perceives things in terms of the whole context. A *field-independent* learning style, on the other hand, describes an analytic and logical approach to tasks and usually implies that the person relates well to impersonal, abstract information, independent of the context. Children who tend to be more field-dependent likely were socialized to be open, warm, committed to mutual dependence, cooperative, sensitive to the feelings of others, and respectful of adults and social convention (Greenfield, Suzuki, & Rothstein-Fisch, 2006; Park, C.C., 2001; Soldier, 1985).

Demonstration is a socialization method related to the field-dependent learning style, with its intended outcome

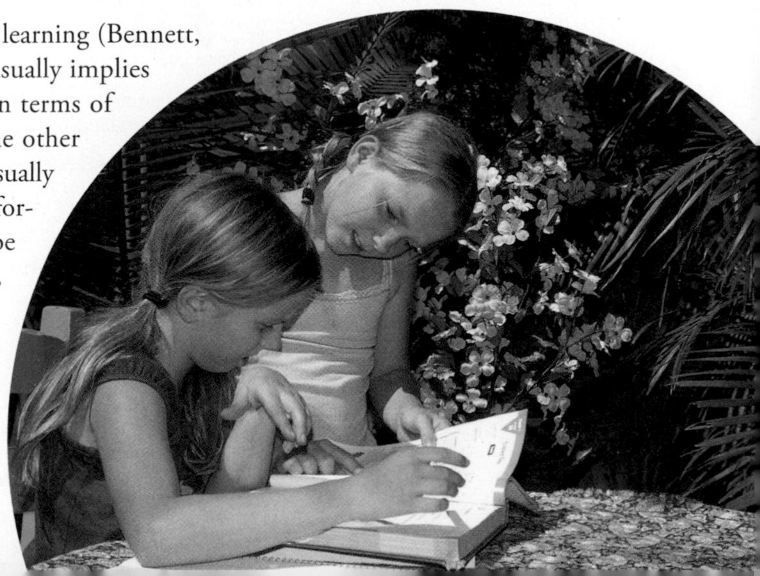

An example of a novice being coached by a more expert peer.

nicoblue/Big Stock Photo

being visualization (Bennett, 2010). Adults demonstrate how to perform a task correctly, expecting the child to eventually master it internally (by visualization); guidance is gentle and supportive. Disapproval is indirectly communicated via silence or shame (Shibusawa, 2001). Children also learn through careful observation, noticing, for example, the behavior and expressions of adults, the changing weather conditions, the terrain, and so on. After observing an adult do a task, the child takes over small portions of the task under the guidance of the adult; the child becomes an apprentice. When the child feels ready to do the whole task, he or she practices it in private. Thus, failures are not seen and don't cause embarrassment, but success is demonstrated for the adult with pride (Rogoff, 2003). In contrast, direct verbal communication of instructions and standards, feedback, external rewards, and punishment are socialization methods related to the field-independent learning style.

Values for Learning

Families that value effort and hard work as well as the importance of group identity (in that one's performance reflects upon the family or teacher) socialize children to be top performers on achievement tests (Magno, Profugo, & Mendoza, 2008; Stevenson & Lee, 1990).

Families that value hierarchical roles socialize children to view the teacher as the complete source of knowledge. These children may be less inclined to participate in class discussions or share ideas, and may be reluctant to work with other students on group projects. They have been taught that the student's job is to listen, take notes, memorize, follow directions, and recite. In their families, children's ideas are not requested, nor are they valued. They are taught not to ask questions, argue, or challenge the teacher (Dresser, 2005).

How can teaching be adapted to diverse cognitive styles?

Because all children learn differently, Howard Gardner (1999) recommends that teachers adapt the curriculum to the following multiple intelligences he believes encompass human capability (see Figure 7.3):

TeachSource Video Activity

Go to the Education CourseMate website to watch the video entitled "School Age Children: Multiple Intelligences." Which one(s) of these intelligences best describes you? Give an example.

1. **Logical-mathematical:** skills related to solving logical problems and performing mathematical calculations (generally qualities of scientists, mathematicians)
2. **Linguistic:** skills related to the meaning, sound, and rhythm of words as well as the use of language (generally qualities of authors, journalists, poets)
3. **Bodily-kinesthetic:** ability to coordinate parts of the body and manipulate objects skillfully (generally qualities of athletes, dancers, surgeons)

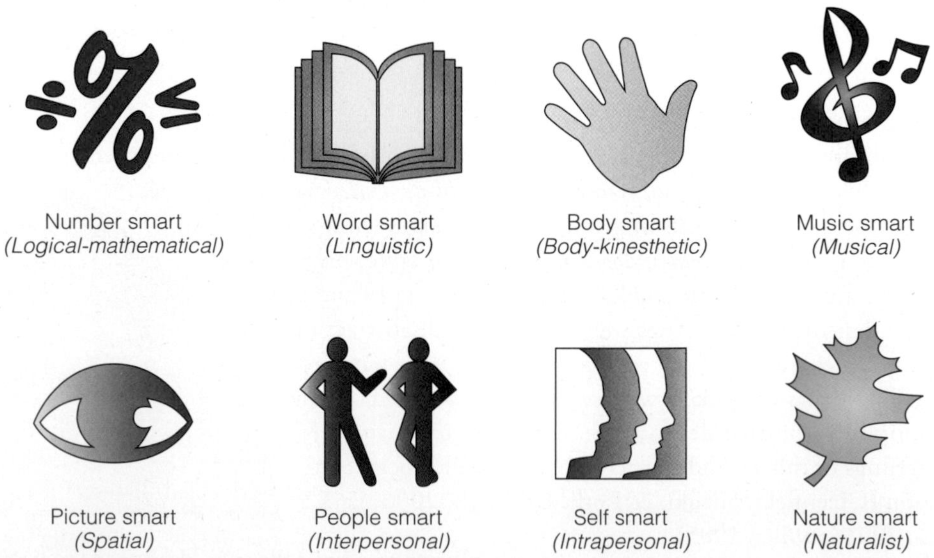

FIGURE 7.3 **Gardner's Multiple Intelligences**

4. **Musical:** ability to produce pitch and rhythm and appreciate musical expression (generally qualities of musicians, composers, singers)
5. **Spatial:** ability to form a mental model of concrete objects and manipulate parts in relation to each other (generally qualities of architects, engineers, artists)
6. **Interpersonal:** ability to analyze and respond to behavior, feelings, and motives of other people (generally qualities of psychologists, teachers, salespeople)
7. **Intrapersonal:** ability to understand one's feelings and motives, using such knowledge to adapt one's behavior accordingly (generally qualities of actors, lawyers)
8. **Naturalist:** ability to discriminate among living things and be sensitive to the natural environment (generally qualities of botanists, zoologists, ecologists)

Disability

What experiences (personal or other) have you had with disability?

Did you know that before 1975, children with disabilities could not attend public school in most states? Today, thanks to legislation discussed in Chapter 6, all children have the right to a free and equitable education. Here we examine the teacher–student interaction as it is affected by the presence of a disability. Not only have laws been passed to give individuals with disabilities equal access rights, but educators have modified the teaching environment to include the following (Hallahan, Kauffman, & Jullen, 2009):

1. *Individualized instruction*, in which the child's abilities rather than prescribed academic content provide the basis for teaching techniques.
2. *Adaptation of the curriculum to various learning styles*, whereby visual, auditory, and tactile learners are motivated to succeed.
3. *Collaboration with various professionals*, so that services such as medical, physical therapy, speech therapy, and counseling are provided.
4. *Peer tutoring*, in which children with greater abilities help those who are in need.

Some examples of how the educational environment and teaching strategies can be modified to include young children with disabilities are available in Appendix D on the Education CourseMate website.

The Individuals with Disabilities Education Act (IDEA), discussed in Chapter 6, requires that children with disabilities be placed in the "least restrictive environment." This means inclusion with nondisabled peers whenever appropriate. In order to determine and maintain optimal placement, IDEA requires that an individualized education program (IEP) be written annually (IDEA 2004 allows for IEP long-term planning for up to three years in certain cases) and reviewed by (1) the child, (2) the parent, (3) the teacher, (4) the professional who has evaluated the child most recently, and (5) the principal or school district special resource person. The IEP must specify educational goals, methods for achieving those goals, special educational/resource services to be provided to meet the child's needs, and appropriate assessment measures. The NCLB provides modifications for children with disabilities.

TeachSource Video Activity

Go to the Education CourseMate website to watch the video entitled "Bobby: Serving a Student with Special Needs in an Inclusive Elementary Classroom." How does the teacher implement an IEP for Bobby?

Identification and Assessment of Children with Disabilities

How do families of children with disabilities find out what public services are available to them?

Congress passed PL 99-457 in 1986, a law which addressed the needs of infants, toddlers, and preschoolers with disabilities. It also recognized that families play a large role in the socialization of children with disabilities. Consequently, PL 99-457 provides that, whenever appropriate, the preschooler's IEP will include instruction for parents; it then becomes an individualized family service plan (IFSP). A variety of programs are available to meet the needs of preschool children with disabilities. These can be home-based or center-based and can be full- or part-time.

The purpose of preschool intervention services, as defined by Congress, follows:

1. To enhance the development of infants and toddlers with disabilities and to minimize the potential for delay.
2. To reduce educational costs by minimizing the need for special education and related services after infants and toddlers with disabilities reach school age.

3. To minimize the likelihood of institutionalization of individuals with disabilities.
4. To enhance the capacity of families to meet the special needs of infants and toddlers.

For children with certain kinds of disabling conditions, identification can occur at birth—for example, Down syndrome and various physical deformities. Behaviors not usually exhibited by normal infants can be identified shortly after birth—for example, extreme lethargy, continual crying, convulsions, and paralysis. However, many disabling conditions, such as learning disabilities, are not readily apparent and may not be suspected until later.

Teachers and others who work on a daily basis in preschool programs are in a unique position to assess young children. By observing and recording specific child behaviors that occur excessively, or that occur instead of appropriate behaviors, the teacher can identify children who may have potential disabilities.

Teachers and parents can observe behavior using a variety of techniques: anecdotal records, checklists and rating scales, time samples, and measurements of behavior.

- *Anecdotal records* report a child's adaptive behavior in various situations.
- *Checklists and rating scales* are used to compare a child's development against norms or averages.
- *Time samples* record everything a child does for a certain period of time each day (for example, from 9:00 to 10:00 for five consecutive days).
- *Measurements of behavior* record the frequency of a behavior, the duration of the behavior, the antecedents of the behavior, and the consequences of the behavior.

The teacher observation form (an assessment of general development for preschool children) provides a model that may be used to indicate the necessity for referral to other professionals—a pediatrician for health problems; an otologist for auditory problems; an ophthalmologist for visual problems; a neurologist for neurological problems; an orthopedist for bone, joint, or muscle problems; a psychologist or psychiatrist for emotional problems; and so on. To view an example of a teacher observation form, see Appendix D on the Education CourseMate website.

Assessment, of course, is meaningless unless adequate follow-up and services are provided for children who need them. Services may involve corrective or supportive medical services (such as prosthetics or physical therapy) and/or special educational programs (such as professional in-home training or child attends a center). Services may also involve social work or counseling (such as parent training in special care or linking the family to services to which the child is legally entitled). Assessment must be an ongoing process; hence, the IEP or IFSP, previously discussed, is used. When children are continually assessed, their performance can indicate the need to modify the special program.

Any program designed to meet the special needs of children with disabilities must involve the family (Heward, 2008). Recognizing that parents are family members with myriad responsibilities and individual needs and preferences has a profound influence on parent–professional relationships in special education settings. The same concept of individuation embraced by the field of special education as pertinent to children and youth also applies to parents and other family members.

How can individuals with disabilities be integrated into the community and become contributing members?

Inclusion

The community, through legislation, has facilitated integration of individuals with disabilities into society. Not only do people with disabilities have a right to receive an appropriate education; they also have the right to equal employment opportunities and the right to enjoy the services provided by the community.

The Americans with Disabilities Act (ADA), passed in 1990, serves as a "bill of rights" for individuals with disabilities in order to guarantee equal opportunity. It bars discrimination in employment, transportation, public accommodations, and telecommunications. This law guarantees access to all aspects of life—not just those that are federally funded—for people with disabilities. The law specifies that "reasonable accommodations" be made according to the disability a person has. For example, telephone companies must provide services so that individuals with hearing or voice impairments can use ordinary telephones; all new construction and renovations of facilities must be accessible to those with disabilities; employers must restructure jobs and modify equipment as reasonably required.

A child with disabilities can be included in school activities through special transportation services.

Cengage Learning

Risk and Resilience

Risk refers to endangerment or vulnerability to negative developmental outcomes. Children at risk are more likely to drop out of school, abuse substances, engage in violent behavior, become pregnant, be unemployed, and commit suicide. Risk factors affecting infants and children can be classified as *genetic* (such as mental retardation), *prenatal* (such as drug exposure), *perinatal* (such as health care), and *environmental* (such as poverty) (Rickel & Becker, 1997). Children considered to be at risk tend to come from families that lack social support networks, experience unemployment, exhibit depression, engage in substance abuse, have poor marital relations, and/or practice domestic abuse (Walsh, 2006).

Resilience refers to the ability to withstand and rebound from crisis or persistent challenges. Resilient children are more likely to have close friends, be in families with supportive marriages, attain a high level of education, and master vocational skills, despite growing up in a difficult or traumatic environment (Garbarino, 1995a; Rickel & Becker, 1997; Walsh, 2006). For example, psychologist Emmy Werner (1993) began studying infants at risk in Hawaii more than 40 years ago. The children came from families who were chronically poor, alcoholic, and abusive. Expecting negative developmental outcomes for the children, she was surprised to find that approximately one-third of those she followed grew into emotionally healthy, competent adults.

Why are some children at risk for psychological, social, or academic problems, whereas other children with similar characteristics are resilient?

risk endangerment; vulnerability to negative developmental outcomes

resilience the ability to withstand and rebound from crisis or persistent challenges

What enabled these children to become resilient to a traumatic childhood? The resilient children had a sense of autonomy and personal responsibility; they related to others positively; perhaps most significantly, they had established a bond with an adult caregiver or mentor. Apparently, the "substitute" parent and positive relationships and experiences act as buffers against negative developmental outcomes.

> These buffers make a more profound impact on the life course of children who grow up under adverse conditions than do specific risk factors or stressful life events. They appear to transcend ethnic, social class, geographical, and historical boundaries. Most of all, they offer us a more optimistic outlook than the perspective that can be gleaned from the literature on the negative consequences of perinatal trauma, caregiving deficits, and chronic poverty. They provide us with a corrective lens—an awareness of self-righting tendencies that move children toward normal adult development under all but the most persistent adverse circumstances. (Werner & Smith, 1992)

The implications of such research are profound. The findings mean that parents, schools, community services, and others can help children develop into healthy, contributing adults by working together to build a socially nourishing environment (Comer, 2004; Garbarino, 1995a).

Schools have the potential to provide optimal socialization experiences and foster resiliency in children. In his book *Leave No Child Behind*, Comer (2004) describes the success of one model. The Comer model, implemented in hundreds of schools all over the United States, is based on the principle that good relationships promote healthy development, which is inextricably linked to learning. Schools using the Comer model are an extension of the family, and the family is a reflection of the learning environment fostered by the school. Others agree that the school must work with families as well as children, and this has been documented by much research (Epstein & Sanders, 2002). Specifically, when families get involved in school, their children:

- Get better grades and test scores.
- Graduate from high school at higher rates.

Example of families working together with the school.

Cengage Learning

- Are more likely to go on to higher education.
- Behave more positively.
- Are more achievement-oriented.

What aspects of poverty put children at risk?

Poor Children at Risk

Poverty puts children at risk for negative developmental outcomes. According to the FIFCFS (2010), 18 percent of children 0 to 17 years old were classified by federal income standards as "poor." Poor families face many challenges besides their standard of living. Some of these include having both parents working outside the home, reliance on child care, inadequate health care, malnutrition, lack of adequate housing, and unsafe communities. In his book *Savage Inequalities*, Jonathan Kozol (1991) describes many poor neighborhoods and schools as being near chemical plants or sewage dumps, in ill repair, and plagued by crime and drugs.

The community's failure to support the school—because of economics and values—affects the teacher–student relationship. As we discussed in Chapter 6, schools in poor communities often lack money for school improvements, resources, and smaller classes. Teachers also have to motivate students to achieve in the face of **learned helplessness**—the perception, acquired through negative experiences, that effort has no effect on outcomes (to be discussed in more detail in Chapter 11). The difficulty comes from the belief, common in poor families, that there is little connection between educational achievement and making a living (Macleod, 2008). Thus, delinquency and dropping out present additional challenges to teachers.

learned helplessness the perception, acquired through negative experiences, that effort has no effect on outcomes

How does substance abuse in the family affect the child in school?

Families, Substance Abuse, and Children

The teacher–student relationship is affected by the child's exposure to the use/abuse of substances by family members. Substance abuse has been consistently linked with poor parenting and poor family functioning; addicted parents' primary relationship is with drugs, not with their children (National Center on Addiction and Substance Abuse [CASA], 1998).

Prenatal Substance Exposure

One group of children from at-risk families are those prenatally exposed to drugs or alcohol. (Postnatal exposure poses risks, too, as discussed in the next section on alcohol.) Commonly abused drugs include crack cocaine, heroin, marijuana, tranquilizers, and stimulants. Substance-exposed infants exhibit low birth weight, sleeping and eating disorders, and increased irritability. They experience not only physical and health problems but psychological and behavioral ones as well (National Institute on Drug Abuse [NIDA], 2010; Tyler, 1992).

A recent study by Bergin and McCullough (2010) investigated characteristics of the babies of 41 low-income mothers who had used alcohol, cocaine, and other substances while pregnant. These 41 babies were compared to a group of other babies who were matched with them on factors like birth weight that increase the risk of developmental problems, but who were not exposed to drugs prenatally. All of the babies were tested at 12 months on the quality of their attachment to their mothers, and the mothers were tested on their sensitivity and involvement (this latter assessment was based on two hours of videotaped interaction between each mother and her baby). The researchers found that mothers who displayed sensitivity to their babies' signals and who involved themselves in social interaction with the babies were the ones whose babies showed healthy development of attachment. The researchers concluded that sensitive, loving care can offset some of the problems prenatally exposed babies usually experience. Parents need to continue such involved care by being supportive of their children's learning at home and at school.

In conclusion, the research on the later effects of being exposed prenatally to drugs is unclear because of intervening variables such as socioeconomic status, parental care, and support from others.

Family Alcohol Abuse

Another group of children at risk for negative developmental outcomes are those whose parents abuse alcohol. According to the American Academy of Child and Adolescent Psychiatry (AACAP, 2002d), one in five adult Americans lived with an alcoholic while growing up. **Alcoholism** is a chronic, progressive, and potentially fatal disease. It is characterized by excessive tolerance for alcohol and by physical dependency and/or pathologic organ changes as direct or indirect consequences of the alcohol ingested.

alcoholism a chronic, progressive, and potentially fatal disease characterized by excessive tolerance for alcohol and by physical dependence and/or pathologic organ changes

Alcohol consumption during pregnancy can produce abnormalities in the developing fetus. Alcohol interferes with the delivery of nutrients to the fetus, impairs the supply of fetal oxygen, and interferes with protein synthesis (AACAP, 2006d).

A specific cluster of abnormalities appearing in babies exposed prenatally to alcohol abuse (heavy drinking) was described and named *fetal alcohol syndrome* (FAS) by Kenneth Jones and his colleagues (Jones et al., 1973). Among the distinguishing features of this syndrome are prenatal and postnatal growth retardation and facial abnormalities, including small head circumference; widely spaced eyes; short eyelid openings; a small, upturned nose; and a thin upper lip. Most FAS children have mental retardation. FAS is the leading known preventable cause of mental retardation. Now warnings of possible birth defects are required on alcoholic beverages and in establishments that serve alcohol.

Behavior problems appear in infancy and persist into childhood; the most common are irritability, hyperactivity, poor concentration, and poor social skills. Sometimes affected children display other physical problems such as defects of the eyes, ears, heart, urinary tract, or immune system (Aaronson & MacNee, 1989).

The consequences of living in an alcoholic family are particularly difficult for young children and adolescents because alcoholism affects the process of socialization of values, morals, attitudes, behavior, gender roles, self-control, and self-concept. The effects of alcoholism depend on the child's age, gender, relationship to the drinking and nondrinking parents, and relationship to other family members or other social networks.

Children whose parents abuse alcohol are prone to a range of psychological difficulties, including learning disabilities, anxiety, attempted and completed suicides, eating disorders, and compulsive achieving. The problems of most such children remain invisible because their coping behavior tends to be approval-seeking and socially acceptable. They do their work, do not rock the boat, and do not reveal their secret. Many are high achievers and eager to please. Yet their adaptation to the chaos and the inconsistency of an alcohol-abusing family often results in developing an inability to trust, an extreme need to control, an excessive sense of responsibility, and denial of feelings, all of which result in low self-esteem, depression, isolation, guilt, and difficulty maintaining satisfying relationships. These and other problems often persist throughout adulthood (Brown & Newman, 2010; Tubman, 1993; Woititz, 1990).

The child is often embarrassed by his or her parents. The ashamed child does not invite friends home and is afraid to ask anyone for help. The child also feels anger toward the alcoholic parent for drinking and may be angry with the nonalcoholic parent for lack of support and protection. The child may even feel guilty, perceiving himself or herself as the cause of the parent's drinking (AACAP, 2002d).

Although the child tries to keep the parent's alcoholism a secret, teachers, friends, relatives, or other caring adults may sense that something is wrong. The following behaviors may signal a problem (AACAP, 2002d):

- Failure in school; truancy
- Lack of friends; withdrawal from classmates
- Delinquent behavior, such as stealing or violence
- Frequent physical complaints, such as headaches or stomachaches
- Abuse of drugs or alcohol
- Aggression toward other children

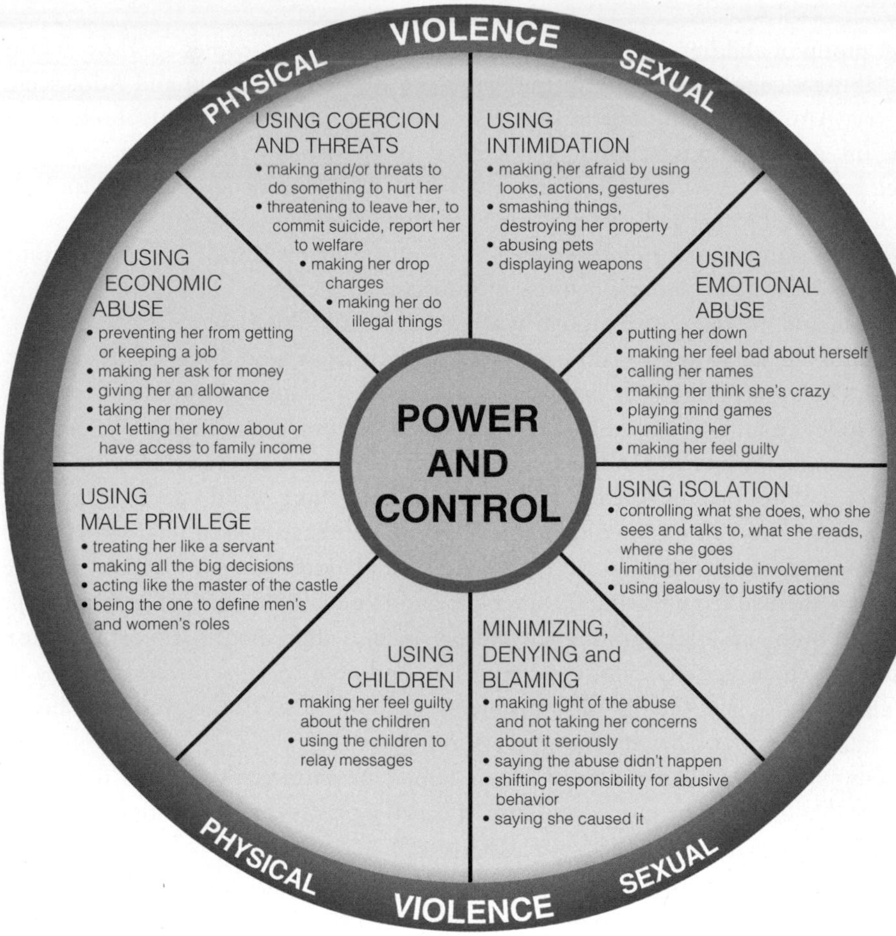

FIGURE 7.4 **Domestic Abuse Intervention Model—Power and Control**

- Risk-taking behaviors
- Depression or suicidal thoughts or behavior

Whether or not their parents are receiving treatment for alcoholism, these children can benefit from programs such as Al-Anon and Alateen. Therapists can help these children understand that they are not responsible for their parents' drinking problems. Therapists can also help the family, particularly when the alcoholic has stopped drinking, develop healthier ways of relating to one another (AACAP, 2002d).

How does violence in families affect the child in school?

Familes, Violence, and Children

Violence in families includes child maltreatment and domestic abuse. Various types and observable signs of maltreatment were explained in Chapter 4; here the masked effects that interfere with development are discussed. (See Figure 7.4.)

Domestic violence can be defined as "the systematic abuse by one person in an intimate relationship in order to control and dominate the partner" (Kearny, 1999, p. 290). Abusive behavior can be physical, emotional, mental, and/or sexual. Domestic violence is found in all socioeconomic classes and cultures (CDC, 2009). Most is experienced by women, although some men experience it too (Kearny, 1999). The government plays a significant role in preventing negative outcomes from domestic violence. It has passed laws making violence against women a crime and provided funding for shelters, counseling, and hotlines (National Coalition Against Domestic Violence, 1999).

Children who are exposed to domestic violence often experience the following feelings (Kearny, 1999, p. 291).

IN PRACTICE

What Supportive Strategies Can Teachers Use for Children Exposed to Domestic Violence?

Breaking the silence surrounding domestic violence and providing appropriate intervention can help. Specific preventive strategies include the following:

- **Identification.** Be alert to changes in emotional, social, and/or learning behaviors. Ask the child, "What is wrong?" (Does the child not want to go home? Is the child unusually attached to his or her teacher? Is the child withdrawn? Is the child aggressive or a bully?)
- **Support.** Be available to listen to the child and acknowledge his or her feelings without being judgmental. Help the child develop ways to release his or her feelings appropriately.
- **Modeling.** Exhibit nonviolent, cooperative ways of solving problems.

Children living in a violent environment often exhibit similar behavior with their peers, modeling their family interactions. Also, exposure to violence may desensitize children and adolescents so aggression becomes part of the "norm" (Center for Children and Families in the Justice System, 2002). Chapter 6 listed some strategies to resolve conflicts before they escalate into violent behavior: emotional regulation, empathy, problem solving, and mediation.

- **Anger.** They are angry at the abuser for perpetrating the violence, at the victim for tolerating it, or at themselves for not being able to stop it.
- **Fear/terror.** They are afraid that the mother or father will be seriously injured or killed, that they or their siblings will be hurt, that others will find out and then the parents will be "in trouble," or that they will be removed from the family.
- **Powerlessness.** Because they are unable to prevent the fights from happening, or to stop the violence when it occurs, they feel out of control.
- **Loneliness.** They feel unable or afraid to reach out to others, feeling "different" or isolated.
- **Confusion.** They are confused about why it happens, choosing sides, what they should do, what is "right" and "wrong." They are also confused about how the abuser can sometimes be caring and at other times violent.
- **Shame.** They are ashamed about what is happening in their home.
- **Guilt.** They feel guilty that they may have caused the violence, or that they should have been able to stop it but couldn't.
- **Distrust.** They don't trust adults because experience tells them that adults are unpredictable, that they break promises, and/or that they don't mean well.

Macrosystem Influences on Teaching

How is teaching in the classroom influenced by factors in the larger society?

Macrosystem influences on teaching include philosophical and theoretical foundations of teaching and learning that have undergone change over the years; classroom and curriculum contexts affected by school administration; and policies and procedures regarding accountability for achievement (standardization and individuation).

Philosophies of Teaching and Learning

Why do some teachers direct children, whereas others let children find their own direction, in the learning environment?

Philosophies of teaching range from emphasis on the learner, with the goal of expanding an individual's knowledge (*learner-directed*), to emphasis on the teacher, with the goal of methodically presenting new knowledge to the student (*teacher-directed*). One root of the learner-directed teaching philosophy comes from the Greek philosopher Socrates (469–399 B.C.E.), who believed "Knowledge is virtue." He developed the *Socratic method*,

Children working on various projects in a learner-directed classroom.

Bob Daemmrich/PhotoEdit

eliciting knowledge from individuals by questioning their statements until a satisfactory logical conclusion was reached. Another root of learner-directed learning can be traced back to Rousseau's *Emile* (1762). Rousseau concentrated on the development of the child rather than the subjects to be taught. His thesis stated that *how* learning occurs is more important than *what* is taught.

One root of the teacher-directed philosophy comes from the psychologist B. F. Skinner (1904–1990), who believed that any student can be conditioned to learn any subject, provided the tasks involved are divided into small, sequenced steps and the learner is reinforced appropriately for desired responses or behaviors (positive consequences for desirable behavior and negative consequences for undesirable behavior). This became known as the *behaviorist method.* Another root of teacher-directed learning can be traced back to Plato's (427–347 B.C.E.) *Republic.* Plato's thesis stated that the mind is what it learns, so the content of the curriculum is vital for an educated society. Teacher-directed educational environments usually subscribe to the philosophy that the functions of the school are to impart basic factual knowledge (reading, writing, arithmetic) and to preserve the American cultural heritage (Sadker & Zittleman, 2009; Tozer et al., 2008). Those who support this philosophy believe that education should include homework, tests, memorization, and strict discipline. They view the school as a place where hard work and obedience are expected. The teacher structures the curriculum. Subjects chosen are based on the teacher's, school's, or community's goals.

There are many types of educational programs, based on various philosophies of teaching and learning (Joyce, Weil, & Calhoun, 2009). For the sake of simplicity, the programs discussed here are categorized according to their emphasis on who takes responsibility for the learning that takes place—the teacher or the learner (see Table 7.1).

Teacher-directed learning environments generally focus on helping students engage in specific thinking processes—remembering information, relating new information to prior knowledge in order to build schemas that organize ideas, and developing understanding. The general methods used are lecturing, tutoring, and guidance. Learner-directed learning environments generally focus on activities, skills, and collaborative discussions used in those contexts to construct knowledge. The general methods used are inquiry, scaffolding, research, and collaboration (Blumenfeld, Marx, & Harris, 2006).

What does research say about the effects of teacher-directed and learner-directed programs on socialization?

Classroom Contexts and Socialization Outcomes

In reality, most programs emphasize both teacher and student responsibility for learning, but to different degrees. Because different programs provide different learning environments, experiences, and interactions, the school's program influences a child's development and socialization in a particular way.

Studies (Chall, 2000; Good & Brophy, 1986, 2007) have indicated that students in traditional, teacher-directed classrooms tended to perform better academically than students in modern, learner-directed programs. Why? Most likely it was because standardized tests are based more on teacher-directed goals than on learner-directed ones.

In a study (Daniels, Kalkman, McCombs, 2001) of students in learner-directed classrooms, the kindergartners, first graders, and second graders reported being more interested in schoolwork and learning than did students in teacher-directed classrooms. The children in the teacher-directed classrooms showed significant signs of becoming alienated from school.

We can conclude, then, that different patterns of competence emerge as a result of the different experiences that children have in various programs. Social competence is enhanced in instructional settings where students interact with each other and the teacher to accomplish educational goals; academic competence is fostered in instructional

Table 7.1 Teacher- and Learner-Directed Classroom Contexts

Teacher-Directed (Traditional)	Learner-Directed (Modern)
Structure	
Day is organized by teacher and divided into time segments according to subject	Program is prepared by teacher based on student abilities and interest; time spent on activities depends on interest; activities not divided into specific subjects
Management	
There are many rules for appropriate behavior (being moral, having manners, following directions, paying attention, being quiet, sitting still, being neat)	Teacher encourages children to discuss standards of conduct and take responsibility for their behavior
Curriculum	
Predetermined by teacher and/or textbook	Subjects determined by student ability and interest
Emphasis on reading, writing, arithmetic, science, social science	Activities and problem-solving experiences based on student interest
Knowledge considered an end in itself; what is studied is preparation for life	Knowledge considered a means to an end, the process of living; subject matter grows out of experience
Motivation	
Extrinsic (grades)—success mainly a function of how well the required tasks are mastered according to teacher's standards	Intrinsic (child's interests)—success is mainly a function of self-evaluation (based on accomplishment of a self-chosen goal)
Advancement determined by subjects and tests passed, time spent in system	Advancement according to activities chosen and skills developed
Competitive activities	Cooperative activities
Method	
Teacher teaches generally the same thing at the same time to all students or a group of students	Learning is individualized and students are responsible for their own learning
Teaching style is dominative	Teaching style is integrative
Teaching of content	Teaching of process
Direct encouragement of children's participation	Indirect encouragement of children's participation

settings where students are motivated and rewarded for accomplishing the teacher's educational goals. The success of learning environments in achieving their goals depends on the knowledge and experiences of the teacher, the learner, and the relationship between them. General goals of all curricula should encompass creating adaptive learners, effective information users, collaborative workers, and citizens who understand how knowledge is generated in different disciplines (Blumenfeld, Marx, & Harris, 2006). Research on curriculum models and learning environments is ongoing.

How can teachers structure and manage classroom activities to encourage certain socialization outcomes?

To encourage certain socialization outcomes, instructional settings can be organized into "goal structures" (Johnson & Johnson, 1999). The three types of goal structures are **cooperative**, in which students work together to accomplish shared goals; **competitive**, in which students work against each other to achieve goals that only a few students can attain; and **individualized**, in which one student's achievement of a goal is unrelated to other students' achievement of that goal. Each type of goal structure, according to Johnson and Johnson, promotes a different pattern of interaction among students. A cooperative goal structure promotes positive interpersonal relationships, such as sharing, helping, trust, and acceptance. A competitive goal structure promotes comparisons and mistrust and for some, achievement motivation. An individualized goal structure promotes student–teacher interaction and responsibility for oneself. Table 7.2 describes the conditions under which each goal structure is most effective in promoting the desired learning.

cooperative goal structure students working together to accomplish shared goals

competitive goal structure students working against each other to achieve goals that only a few students can attain

individualized goal structure one student's achievement of the goal is unrelated to other students' achievement of that goal

An interesting application of the cooperative type of goal structure, as it relates to socialization, was described by Aronson and Patenoe (1996). The goal of the activity was to get students in a newly integrated classroom to interact positively with one another.

Table 7.2 Classroom Management: Goal Structures and Socialization

Goal Structures	Type of Instructional Activity	Importance of Goal for Socialization	Student Expectations	Expected Source of Support
Cooperative	Problem-solving; divergent thinking or creative tasks; assignments can be more ambiguous with students doing the clarifying, decision making, and inquiring	Goal is perceived as important for each student, and students expect group to achieve the goal	Each student expects positive interaction with other students; sharing ideas and materials; support for risk taking; making contributions to the group effort; dividing the task among group members; capitalizing on diversity among group members	Other students
Individualized	Specific skill or knowledge acquisition; assignment is clear and behavior specified to avoid confusion and need for extra help	Goal is perceived as important for each student, and each student expects eventually to achieve this goal	Each student expects to be left alone by other students; to take a major part of the responsibility for completing the task; to take a major part in evaluating his/her progress toward task completion and the quality of his/her effort	Teacher
Competitive	Skill practice; knowledge recall and review; assignment is clear with rules for completing specified skills or knowledge	Goal is not perceived to be of large importance to the students, and they can accept either winning or losing	Each student expects to have an equal chance of winning; to enjoy the activity (win or lose); to monitor the progress of his/her competitor to compare ability with peers	Teacher

Source: Adapted from Johnson, D. W., and Johnson, R. T. (1999). *Learning together and alone: Cooperative, competitive, and individualized learning* (5th ed.). Reprinted by permission of Allyn and Bacon, Needham Heights, MA.

The students were divided into small groups and given tasks in which they had to cooperate with each other in order to succeed. Each student was given a piece of information that the rest of the group needed in order to finish the task. All the members had to share their pieces of information with the others. Aronson called this "the jigsaw-puzzle method." The results were higher achievement, a decrease in social insults, higher self-esteem, and improved attitudes toward school. Several successful adaptations of cooperative goal structures have been developed to include children with disabilities and those who are ethnically diverse and to prepare students for an increasingly collaborative workforce (Slavin, 2006).

Thus, the way teachers manage the classroom environment, including arranging the room, planning the activities, observing behavior, and organizing groups, affects the socialization taking place in that classroom.

How are teachers accountable for meeting the standards of the NCLB?

Teachers and the No Child Left Behind Act

As applied to education, **accountability** refers to making schools and teachers responsible for student learning or achievement outcomes. It means that educational expenditures must be justified. Educational accountability is a result of rising costs, poor student performance in the business world, the need to compete in global markets, and the desire to maintain leadership in the world in science and technology.

accountability making schools and teachers responsible for student learning or achievement outcomes

The No Child Left Behind Act of 2001, which is a model for *standards-based education*, requires annual testing in all states. Although states and local school districts vary in specifics, generally, student achievement is tested in reading, writing, math, and science throughout elementary and middle school and on graduation from high school.

One key goal of the federal reauthorization of the Elementary and Secondary Education Act (ESEA), also known as the No Child Left Behind (NCLB) Act of 2001, is that all students are taught by highly qualified teachers (HQT) by the end of the 2005/06 school year. To this end, each local educational agency (LEA) must develop a plan to ensure that all elementary, middle, and high school teachers who are assigned to teach core academic subjects meet the NCLB requirements:

- Have at least a bachelor's degree from an accredited institution of higher education;
- Hold full state certification; and
- Demonstrate subject-matter competence for each NCLB core academic subject they teach.

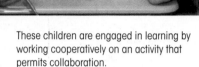

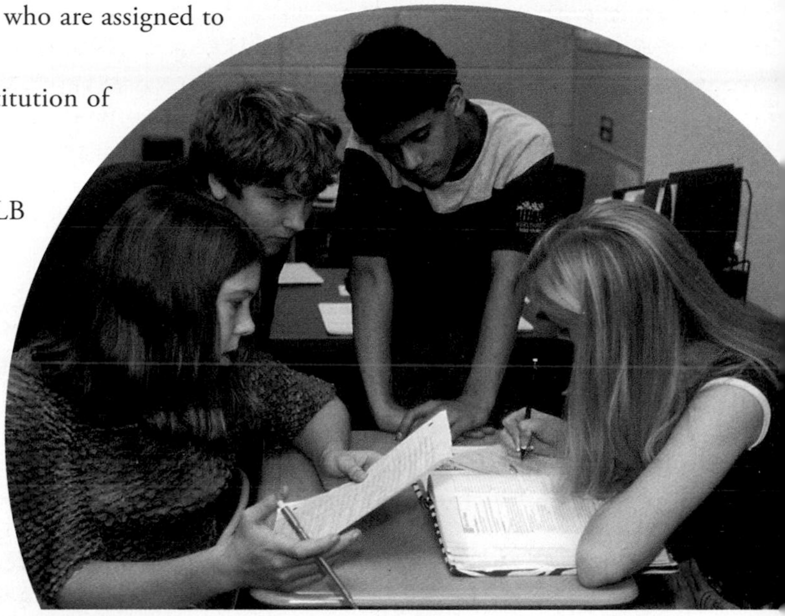

These children are engaged in learning by working cooperatively on an activity that permits collaboration.

Cengage Learning

NCLB recognizes two types of teachers: elementary school teachers and middle/high school teachers. The options available for demonstrating subject-matter competency differ for each classification and type of teacher. They also differ by state (check your state's Department of Education's credentialing standards). In California, out-of-state NCLB HQT compliance may be transferable if the issuing state's requirements are at least as rigorous as those of California.

Self-contained elementary school teachers must demonstrate competence in the areas generally taught as part of the elementary school curriculum. California has standardized tests for teacher competency, such as the Multiple Subjects Credential.

In California, the NCLB Core Academic Subjects for middle/high schools are defined as:

- Mathematics (including math intervention and California Exit Exam–math classes);
- Biological sciences, chemistry, geosciences, physics;
- Social science (history, government, economics, geography);
- Foreign languages (specific);
- Drama/theater, visual arts (including dance), music; and
- English/language arts/reading (including reading intervention and California High School Exit Exam–English classes).

Middle and high school teachers in California must pass a competency exam in the subject(s) they teach, such as the Single Subject Credential. While teachers and schools are held accountable for students' performance, and continual improved performance, in NCLB subject areas, flexible modifications exist for diverse students with English language limitations and for students with disabilities.

School Readiness and Developmentally Appropriate Assessment

How should "readiness-to-learn" be evaluated?

Many educators feel a major effect of the NCLB is that academic achievement, including school readiness, has come to be redefined as children's ability to earn a passing score on required *standardized tests*. By relying on test results to signify whether children are ready for school, achievement gaps and low test scores can very possibly be explained as being caused by poverty, family circumstances, or other outside factors.

According to the NCLB and the national goal that every child who enters school is ready to learn, states and LEAs have developed various standards of readiness. For example, the San Francisco Unified School District hired a research company to statistically assess the skills children need to be well prepared for kindergarten so that children could be tested accordingly. The Basic Building Blocks of School Readiness fall into four categories: (1) Self-Care and Motor Skills, (2) Social Expression, (3) Self-Regulation, and (4) Kindergarten Academics (see Figure 7.5).

For another example, the state of *South Carolina* turned to experts in early childhood education to address the school readiness issue for its K–2 schools (Freeman & Brown,

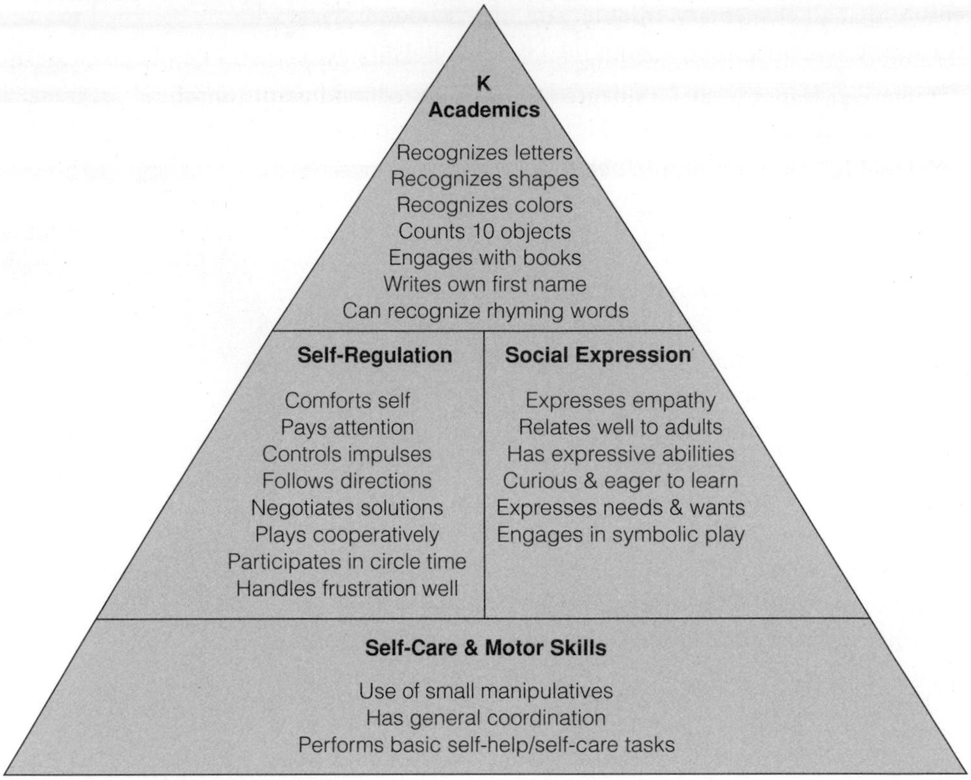

FIGURE 7.5 **Basic Building Blocks of School Readiness**
Source: Applied Survey Research. (2007). Children's readiness for kindergarten in San Francisco: Comprehensive report (www.library.ca.gov), p. 15.

2008). Rather than asking "Is this child ready for school?" the state created a program assessment system that reframed the question of school readiness by asking "Is this school ready for all children?" This developmentally appropriate approach avoided on-demand tests, focusing instead on a school's ability to meet research-based criteria shown to enhance children's growth, development, and learning—that is, their chances for school success. As a result, the state's *kindergarten* and first-grade performance-based *authentic assessment* instrument, which is based on the Work Sampling System (Meisels et al., 2001), has been left intact and uncompromised. **Authentic assessment**, a practice in which evaluations are based on real performance showing mastery of a task (such as building a model of a house) rather than standardized test performance (figuring out the square footage of a house in a math problem). **Standardized tests**, a practice in which an individual is compared to a norm on scientifically selected items, have been developed to assess kindergarten readiness.

authentic assessment evaluation based on real performance, rather than test performance, showing mastery of a task

standardized tests tests in which an individual is compared to a norm on scientifically selected items

The National Association for the Education of Young Children (NAEYC, 1988, 1995) asserts that standardized school readiness tests are developmentally inappropriate for young children because each child comes from a unique set of family experiences. What one family makes available for its children, another does not. Some children travel extensively; others seldom go outside their immediate community. Some children speak a language other than English. Some have had preschool experiences; others remained at home. Also, maturational differences influence children's ability to perform well on standardized tests—for example, the ability to listen and follow instructions, control a pencil, and sit still for a certain period of time.

NAEYC and other professional organizations, such as the Association for Childhood Education International (ACEI), support the use of authentic assessments as a school readiness measure. Preschool teachers can evaluate a child's readiness to learn by compiling a portfolio of a child's writing or art with accompanying descriptive notes rather than relying solely on standardized paper-and-pencil tests.

Mesosystem Influences on Teaching

Mesosystem influences on teaching include community support and family involvement. Community support can be financial, as in donations and grants to school programs; it can be service-oriented, as in making professional resources available to teachers; it can be extensions of the learning environment, as in providing guest speakers to classrooms and enabling class field trips. Family involvement and collaboration with teachers are important throughout school, but are especially important before the child enters formal school so that appropriate attitudes toward future learning are developed. Families help ready children for school and support school goals. (See Figure 7.6.)

What links to other microsystems foster student learning in the classroom?

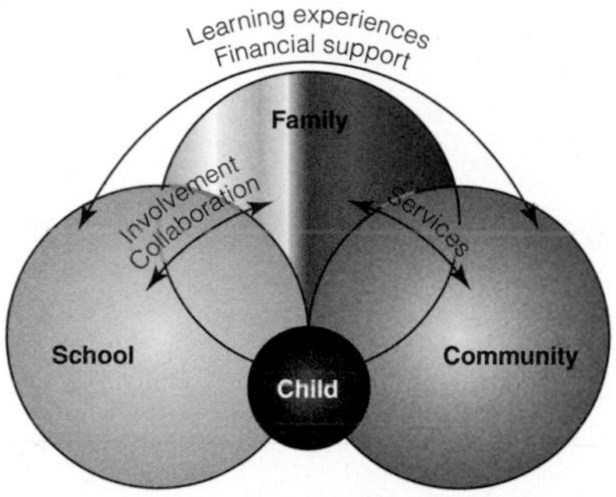

FIGURE 7.6 Mesosystem Influences on Teaching: Fostering Student Learning

Source: Center for Children and Families in the Justice System. (2002). http://www.lfcc .on.ca.

IN PRACTICE

Family Involvement in Learning

What strategies can teachers implement to involve families in learning?

1. Recognize and show that parents are significant contributors to their child's development. Call on parents for advice, help, support, and critical evaluations.
2. Present a realistic picture of what the child's program is designed to accomplish.
3. Maintain ongoing communication with parents. Provide written information regarding due process procedures, parent organizations, and other relevant matters as well as oral and written information about the child's progress.
4. Show parents you care about their child. Call, write notes, spend time listening to parents' concerns.
5. Keep parents informed as to how they can help their child at home. Enable parents to enjoy their children.
6. Use parents' ideas, materials, and activities to work with the child.
7. Know community services and resources so you can refer parents when necessary.
8. Be yourself. Don't appear to know all the answers when you don't; don't be afraid to ask for advice or refer parents to others.
9. Recognize that diverse family structures and parenting styles will influence parent participation.
10. Help parents grow in confidence and in self-esteem (Heward, 2008).

What strategies can families implement to prepare children to learn?

1. Express your love.
   - Spend time with your child.
   - Talk and listen.
   - Help child to be independent (let child do things of which he/she is capable).
2. Use everyday opportunities to teach about the world.
   - Talk about scenery, weather, news.
   - Figure things out together—how much time has passed, how to divide the pie, how to repair the toilet.
   - Enable the child to follow directions.
   - Plan together (activities, goals).
3. Encourage questions.
   - How does this work?
   - Why did this happen?
4. Give approval for trying new things.
   - Reward accomplishments.
   - Make it understood that mistakes happen—what can we learn?
   - Stimulate creativity.

5. Instill a love of books.
   - Model reading.
   - Read to your child.
   - Answer questions.
   - Visit the library.
   - Tell stories, and have child tell them too.
6. Get involved in school.
   - Talk about school positively.
   - Visit school.
   - Encourage attendance.
   - Support homework.
7. Limit TV viewing.
   - Select appropriate programs.
   - Encourage reading and imaginary and physical activities.
   - Discuss programs with child.
8. Encourage writing.
   - Have child write and/or draw thank-you notes, messages, stories.
9. Develop math concepts.
   - Cook together.
   - Play games.
   - Give allowance money to save and spend.
10. Develop science concepts.
   - Encourage collections.
   - Observe plants and animals.
   - Visit museums.
11. Develop social studies concepts.
   - Discuss current events.
   - Observe national holidays.
   - Demonstrate good citizenship by being well informed, discussing decision making, voting.
12. Get involved in the community (Hatcher & Beck, 1997).
   - Visit workplaces (post office, fire department, factory, office).
   - Visit historical sites.
   - Participate in community service.
13. Be a model of lifelong learning (Rich, 1992).
   - Confidence ("I can do it.")
   - Motivation ("I want to do it.")
   - Effort ("I'm willing to try hard.")
   - Responsibility ("I follow through on commitments.")
   - Initiative ("I am a self-starter.")
   - Perseverance ("I finish what I start.")
   - Caring ("I show concern for others.")
   - Teamwork ("I work cooperatively with others.")
   - Common sense ("I use good judgment.")
   - Problem solving ("I use my knowledge and experience effectively.")

Summary

- Teachers are significant socializing agents in that they translate school curricula goals into action. Effective teachers are warm, enthusiastic, and generous with praise, and have high status.
- The teacher plays a major leadership role in helping children learn to deal with positions of authority, to cooperate with others, to cope with problems, and to achieve competence. Types of leaders include authoritarian, democratic, and laissez-faire (permissive).
- Classroom management goal structures (cooperative, individualized, competitive) have different socialization effects.
- Teachers' expectations of children often influence their interactions with them and, consequently, the children's performance. Teachers need to be aware of their responses to gender, to children from diverse cultural groups (individualistic and collectivistic orientations), to children from various social classes and religions, to children with disabilities, and to those at risk for negative developmental outcomes because of poverty, substance abuse, or violence in the family.
- The U.S. macroculture—usually defined as White Anglo-Saxon Protestant—generally shares certain values. The degree to which individual Americans subscribe to the general values depends, in part, on the microculture or minority group of which the individual is a member. Diverse cultural groups can be classified according to where they best fit along a continuum of individualistic versus collectivistic orientations.
- Learning, or cognitive, styles are aspects of socialization that have implications for education. Two types are an analytical, field-independent cognitive style and a relational, field-dependent cognitive style.
- Children with disabilities are enabled to have positive developmental outcomes via legislation. The Individuals with Disabilities Act (IDEA) requires that an individualized education program (IEP) be written annually, specifying educational goals, methods, and resources/services required to meet the child's needs.
- Children at risk for negative developmental outcomes, such as children from families experiencing poverty, substance abuse, and/or domestic violence, need special support from teachers and other adults to enable resiliency and achievement motivation.
- Macrosystem influences on teaching include curriculum philosophies, as well as policies on accountability and standardization. Philosophies of teaching and learning range from teacher-directed programs to learner-directed ones and various combinations.
- Teacher-directed (traditional) educational environments usually subscribe to the philosophy that the functions of the school are to impart basic factual knowledge and preserve the American cultural heritage.
- Learner-directed (modern) educational environments subscribe to the philosophy that the function of the school is to develop the whole child, physically, socially, and emotionally as well as cognitively. Curriculum emerges from the child's interests and abilities and is constructed accordingly.
- Socialization outcomes differ according to the setting. Children in traditional (teacher-directed) settings perform better on academic tasks and are "on-task" more often than children in modern (learner-directed) settings. Children in modern settings tend to have a more positive attitude toward school, are involved in more cooperative work, and show more autonomy than do children in traditional settings.
- The NCLB requires schools and teachers to be accountable for student learning. In order to receive public funding, schools administer standardized assessment exams and students must meet proficiency standards in basic subjects for their grade. Teachers must meet criteria for quality.
- "School readiness" encompasses health, nutrition, and social/emotional factors. Families can enable children to be ready by nurturing, communicating, encouraging learning, and getting involved in school. Schools can enable "readiness" by individualizing the curriculum, providing activities that are developmentally appropriate, and using authentic assessments rather than relying on standardized tests.
- Mesosystem links between teachers, families, and communities play a significant role in implementing the nation's number-one education goal—that all children will come to school "ready to learn."

Activity

PURPOSE To understand the teacher's influence on socialization.

1. Choose two elementary school classrooms (same grade) to observe. One should be primarily teacher-directed, or traditional; the other should be primarily learner-directed, or modern. (You may have to go to two different schools.)
2. Describe the physical arrangement of each classroom environment.
3. Describe the activity going on during the time of your observation in each classroom. How are simultaneous activities (computer work and reading group, for example) handled? What about transitions from one activity to another?
4. Describe the social interaction (for example, warm/hostile, flexible/inflexible, caring/uncaring) between the teacher and children in each classroom. Note teachers' responses to gender and ethnic diversity (and disability, if included).
5. Can you draw any conclusions regarding the socialization of the children in each classroom?

Related Readings

Bennett, C. E. (2010). *Comprehensive multicultural education: Theory and practice* (7th ed.). Boston: Allyn and Bacon.

Brown, W. K., & Newman, T. A. (2010). *Children from alcoholic families (family matters)* (5th ed.). Tallahassee, FL: William Gladden Press.

Geffner, R. A., & Jouriles, E. N. (1998). *Children exposed to marital violence: Theory, research, and applied issues.* Washington, DC: American Psychological Association.

Genishi, C., & Dyson, A.H. (2009). *Children, language, and literacy: Diverse learners in diverse times.* New York: Teachers College Press.

Hallahan, D., Kauffman, J., & Pullen, P. C. (2008). *Exceptional learners: Introduction to special education* (11th ed.). Boston: Allyn and Bacon.

Holt, J. (1970). *How children learn.* New York: Dell.

Joyce, B. R., Weil, M., & Calhoun, E. (2009). *Models of teaching* (8th ed.). Boston: Allyn and Bacon.

Macleod, J. (2008). *Ain't no makin' it* (3rd ed.). Boulder, CO: Westview Press.

Moss, W. L. (2004). *Children don't come with an instruction manual: A teacher's guide to problems that affect learners.* New York: Teachers College Press.

Resources

American Educational Research Association—promotes educational research and its practical application

http://www.aera.net

Center for Research on Education, Diversity & Excellence—assists nation's population of diverse students, including those at risk for academic failure, to achieve academic success

http://www.cal.org/crede

Council for Exceptional Children—the voice and vision of special education

http://www.cec.sped.org

Cengage Learning

8

Ecology of the Peer Group

"Without friends no one would choose to live, though he had all other goods."

—ARISTOTLE

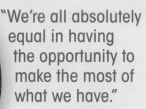

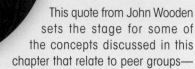

AP Photo/hf

Learning Objectives

After completing this chapter, you will be able to:

1. Define peer group and explain its functions as a socializing agent.
2. Discuss developmental tasks relating to the peer group.
3. Delineate the stages of play and exemplify peer activities during early childhood, middle childhood, and adolescence.
4. Describe the stages of friendship.
5. Discuss acceptance, neglect, and rejection by the peer group, explaining peer sociotherapy to help rejected children gain acceptance.
6. Describe peer group dynamics and the effects of peer group social hierarchies, including bullies and victims.
7. Explain the dynamics of leadership in adult-structured groups.

SOCIALIZATION SKETCHES

John Wooden

(1910–2010)

"We're all absolutely equal in having the opportunity to make the most of what we have."

— JOHN WOODEN

This quote from John Wooden sets the stage for some of the concepts discussed in this chapter that relate to peer groups—cooperation, friendship, support, goal orientation, competition, and sportsmanship. Basketball's coaching legend, John Wooden was able to instill in his diverse players his philosophy of selfless teamwork. It was this philosophy accompanied by hard work that enabled him, in his last twelve years as coach for UCLA, to win ten National Collegiate Athletic Association (NCAA) championships. In the 27 years he led the Bruins, they never had a losing season. Their record of 88 consecutive winning games will probably never be surpassed. Coach Wooden always credited his team's success to this spirit of selfless teamwork—"Always think of passing the ball before shooting it," he told them.

Wooden viewed his role of coach as that of a teacher (he was licensed to be a high school English teacher).

Family

John Wooden was born on his parents' farm near Centerville, Indiana. Life was difficult for the family. The farm had neither running water nor electricity; money was often in short supply. John, his three brothers, and his parents worked on the farm, which supplied most of their food. In later years, Coach Wooden credited his success to the habits of discipline and hard work he learned on the farm.

In 1924, the Woodens, like many farm families, went bankrupt and lost their farm. The family moved to Martinsville, a small town in Indiana that took great pride in the performance of its high school basketball team. Wooden, who had shown a gift for the game from grade school days, soon became a star player on his high school team. The team went to the state championship three years in a row, and won it twice. While still in high school, John met Nellie Riley. By his own account, it was love at first sight, and the two teenagers decided to marry as soon as John finished college.

John credits his parents, especially his father, for his values. His father read to the family every evening. He read poetry and the Bible. All the sons worked their way through college and all majored or minored in English. John tells of his father trying to get across the message, "Never try to be better than someone else. Learn from others and never cease trying to be the best you can be at whatever you're doing."

When John graduated from eighth grade, his father gave him a little card, saying, "Son, try to live up to this." One side contained a seven-point creed "Be true to yourself, help others, make friendship a fine art, drink deeply from good books, make each day your masterpiece, build a shelter against a rainy day by the life you live, and give thanks for your blessings and pray for guidance every day." John kept it until it wore out and he had to get a replacement, which he carried with him all the time.

School

John started playing basketball in grade school. The court was the schoolyard, which had to be shoveled each time it snowed. When John moved to Martinsville, the high school had a huge gymnasium that had more than enough seats to be filled by the townspeople.

In high school, John had a particularly influential math teacher who helped him think about the meaning of success. He was very strict and he made students concentrate. Once, he had them define success in class. John tells of a little verse he brought to class, "At God's footstool, to confess, a poor soul knelt and bowed his head. 'I failed,' he cried. The master said, 'Thou didst thy best. That is success.'"

Community

In all his years as coach, John Wooden prohibited his players from any use of profanity, and consistently avoided it himself. Yet he developed a fearsome reputation at UCLA among opposing teams for the fanciful harangues he directed at officials and opposing players from the bench.

Coach Wooden said of the game of basketball, "It is such a team game. It's a beautiful game when it's played as a team. To me, it's not beautiful when it's individual, one working one on one and making a fancy dunk."

Wooden says he tried to explain to his players that every person has a role and every role is important. Even the players who don't play that much have a role, and their turn to play will come, too, when they are ready.

Wooden recalled one of his proudest moments. He overheard one of his players, an African American, reply to a reporter's question about racial tensions on the team: "You don't know our coach. He doesn't see color. He just sees ballplayers."

Years after retiring, Wooden still remained close to many of his former players. He died peacefully in Los Angeles at the age of 99. His record of accomplishment remains unmatched.

- What are the characteristics of a successful coach?
- What socializing methods are used by the coach and the team members?
- What is involved in being a team player?

Source: http:www.achievement.org.

Why is the peer group considered to be a socializing agent?

peers individuals who are of approximately the same gender, age, and social status and who share interests

The Peer Group as a Socializing Agent

The peer group is a microsystem in that it comprises relationships, roles, and activities. **Peers** are equals, individuals who are usually of the same gender, age, and social status and who share interests. Although *outwardly* the peer group appears to comprise equals, *inwardly* the dynamics of the peer group reveal that some members are more equal than others (Adler & Adler, 1998; Steinberg, 2010). Interactions, dynamics, and social hierarchies in the peer group will be discussed later.

Experiences with peers enable children to acquire a wide range of skills, attitudes, and roles that influence their adaptation throughout life (Rubin, Bukowski, & Parker, 2006). Peer groups are significant socializers, contributing beyond the influence of family and school because (Bukowski, Brendgen, & Vitaro, 2007):

- They satisfy certain belonging needs.
- They are often preferred to other socializing agents.
- They influence not only social development, but cognitive and psychological development as well.

Today, as more mothers are being employed outside the home, more and more children are being cared for in group settings. Consequently, children are experiencing social interaction with peers today earlier and for longer periods of time than they were a generation ago. Also, school-age children and adolescents who are not supervised by adults after school are more likely to turn to their peers for support. In this chapter, we examine various peer group influences; Figure 8.1 shows a bioecological model of the systems involved in the process.

How do peers contribute to normal development?

The Significance of Peers to Human Development

Peer groups are significant to human development because they satisfy certain basic needs: the need to belong to a group and interact socially, and the need to develop a sense of self (a personal identity). Belonging to a peer group enables one to have social interactions with others and have experiences independent of parents or other adults. By interacting socially with others, we derive an opinion of ourselves. We referred to this concept in Chapter 2 as the "looking-glass self" (Cooley, 1909/1964) and the "generalized other" (Mead, 1934). We think of ourselves as having pretty hair, cute freckles, or a large nose because others tell us so. We think of ourselves as clever, as fast runners, or as good at drawing by comparing our skills to those of others.

IN CONTEXT *What were some of the things you did growing up to be accepted by peers? An example of what I did follows:*

When I was 13 years old, I sneaked out of the house to go to a party in my neighborhood when I was supposed to be babysitting for my brother. I was so scared my parents would come home while I was gone, or my brother would wake up and not find me, that I had a horrible time. I ended up telling my friends my parents would be home early, so my friends would not be mad at me for leaving.

Belonging Needs and Social Interaction

Although the need to belong to groups and to interact with others is characteristic of humans, individual differences in intensity and amount exist. Some differences are due to *nature*, or temperament, and some are due to *nurture*, or socialization experiences. Child–peer relationships are bidirectional. For example, individual temperamental characteristics, such as shyness or sociability, may influence a child's ability to make friends. These temperamental traits affect parent responses in that parents of shy children may have to provide more encouragement to have peer experiences than do parents of sociable children (Rubin, Bukowski, & Parker, 2006). Also, parents who provide opportunities for

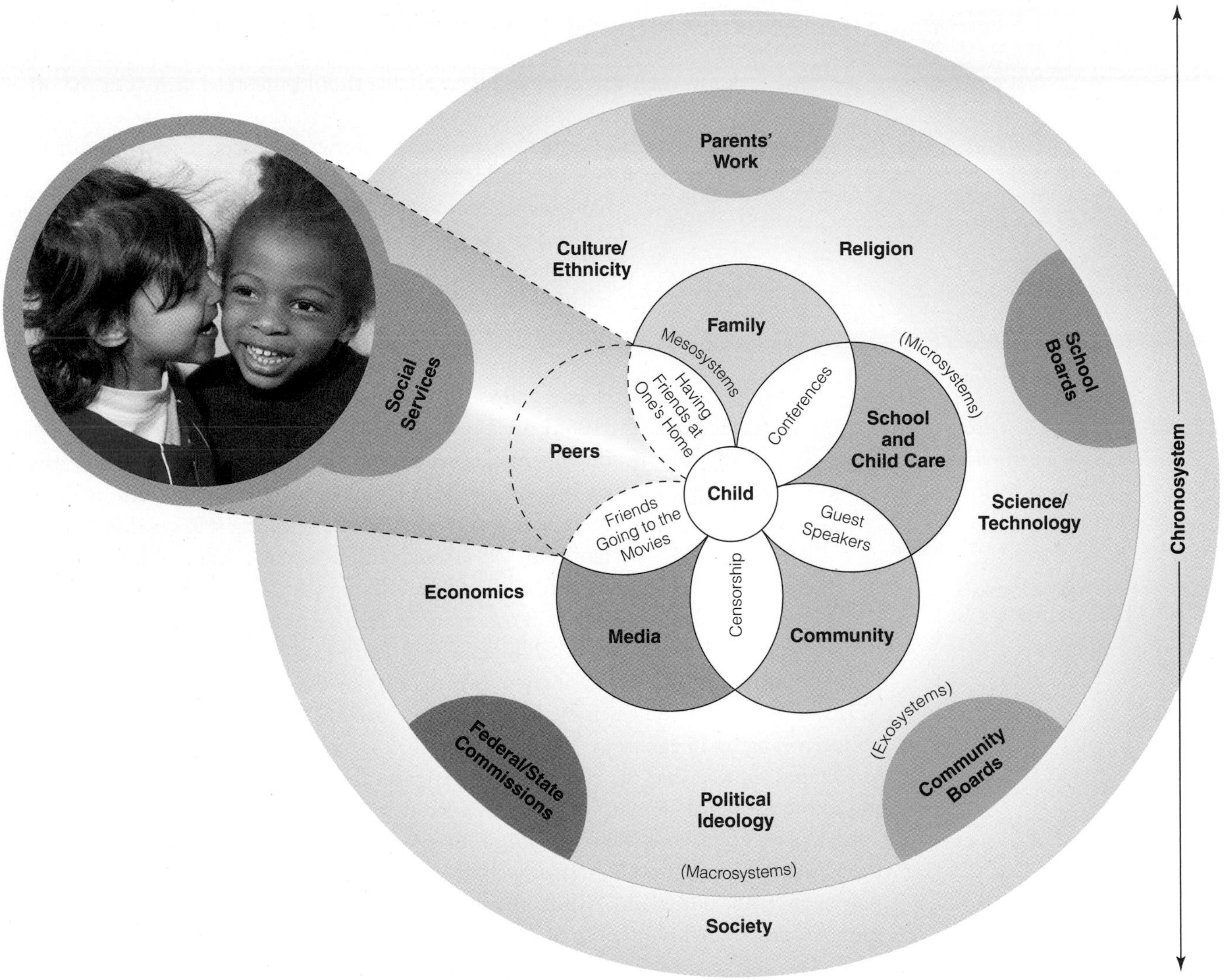

FIGURE 8.1 A Bioecological Model of Human Development
Peers are a significant influence on the child's development.

Cengage Learning

their children to have contact with peers may coach their children to interact positively and may intervene when negative behavior occurs (Pettit & Mize, 1993). Parent–child relationships from infancy to middle childhood will be examined to better understand how they influence peer relationships.

Infancy/Toddlerhood (Birth to Age 1½ or 2 Years)

The sense of belonging develops first within the family. A baby gets the feeling he or she "belongs" to his or her mother when the mother holds, soothes, and meets the baby's needs. Babies whose mothers or caregivers are sensitive and responsive to their needs—for example, feeding them when they are hungry and comforting them when they are frightened—are *securely attached* (Ainsworth, 1979; Rubin, Bukowski, & Parker, 2006; Hay, Caplan, & Nash, 2009). The importance of attachment in socialization was discussed in Chapter 2. Attachment theory suggests that the child who enjoys a secure attachment relationship with his or her caregiver is likely to possess a model to imitate for responsiveness to others (Rubin, Bukowski, & Parker, 2006; Ladd, 2005; Schneider, Atkinson, & Tardif, 2001). In addition, it is believed that a secure attachment provides a secure base for exploratory behavior (Ainsworth, 1973, 1979, 1982). Infants and toddlers

These babies are already interested in each other as distinct human beings.

Myrleen Ferguson Cate/PhotoEdit

who are secure in their relationship with their caregivers feel confident in leaving them to explore their environment (including objects and people) because they know their caregiver will be available should the need arise. On the other hand, babies who are *insecurely attached*, those who have experienced parental rejection or inconsistency of care, tend to avoid peer relationships (Ladd, 2005; Troy & Sroufe, 1987).

Babies who form secure attachments during their first year are described at age 3½ as socially involved with their peers. Children who are securely attached tend to approach others with positive expectations more readily than do children who are insecurely attached (Ainsworth, 1979; Jacobson & Wille, 1986; Rubin, Bukowski, & Parker, 2006). They are often leaders proactively engaged in activities (Park & Waters, 1989). In contrast, a child who has experienced insecure attachments, in which his or her needs were met insensitively or inconsistently, may have negative expectations toward peers, acting as if peers will be rejecting (Howes, Matheson, & Hamilton, 1994). Such children may exhibit withdrawal or aggressive behavior (Rubin, Bukowski, & Parker, 2006).

After toddlerhood, a gradual shift occurs in the relative importance of adults and peers in children's lives (Harris, 2009). Children who attend preschool increasingly look to their peers for attention and decreasingly seek proximity to their caregivers (Hartup, 1983). This was demonstrated in a classic field study by Corsaro (1981) done in a preschool with children ranging in age from 2 years 11 months to 4 years 10 months. Field notes and videotapes showed that the children rarely engaged in solitary play and that when they found themselves alone, they consistently tried to gain entry into ongoing peer activities: "Can I play? I'll be your friend." Also, children who were involved in peer activities often protected the interaction by resisting children who attempted to gain access: "You can't play; you're not our friend." Thus, the more important peers become to the child, the more expansive are his or her social experiences.

Early Childhood (Ages 2 to 5 or 6 Years)

Preschool children's social interactions are affected not only by how secure they feel in their attachment to their mothers but also by the willingness of adults to provide opportunities for social interaction (Ladd & LeSieur, 1995). For instance, where the family resides determines the number of same-age children living nearby. The willingness of parents to invite other children to their home or to take their child to another's home, and whether or not a child attends a preschool program, affect the amount of social interaction that can take place.

Parenting styles in Euro-American groups (discussed in Chapter 4) have been found to influence children's competence in interacting with peers. *Authoritative* (democratic) parenting has been associated with children's social-behavioral competence and confidence (Baumrind, 1973; Ladd, 2005). *Authoritarian* (adult-directed), *permissive* (child-directed), and *indifferent/uninvolved* parenting styles, in contrast, have been linked to low competence in social interaction (Ladd & LeSieur, 1995; Ladd & Pettit, 2002). It is likely that children model parental interactions with their friends.

Middle Childhood (Ages 6 to 12 or 13 Years)

By school age, opportunities for social interaction increase. Children spend most of the day with other children—in class, on the school bus, and in the neighborhood. Children no longer need adults to structure their social interactions. In the middle years, children become more and more dependent on the recognition and approval of their peers, rather than of adults. Their sense of belonging extends and expands (Rubin, Bukowski, & Parker, 2006).

Interestingly, however, it was found that children whose parents took an active role in arranging and organizing their peer relations (inviting specific children to the home, encouraging the child to participate in a school or community group, and discussing the child's friends and interactions) tended to develop closer, more harmonious ties with peers (Ladd & LeSieur, 1995).

Adolescence (Ages 12 or 13 to ~18 Years)

Adolescents generally delineate their belonging needs and consequent social interactions according to the closeness of the relationship. The closest relationships and most intimate social interactions, such as sharing feelings, occur with one or two "best" friends; next are relationships with about six to ten peers who are friends who do things together (the "clique"); finally, there are relationships with the larger, more loosely organized peer group (or the "crowd") with which the adolescent identifies (Steinberg, 2010).

Sense of Self

Throughout development, peer relationships contribute to the self-concept, including one's perception of his or her personal identity (Who am I?) and self-esteem (How do I feel about myself?).

Infancy/Toddlerhood

Infants as young as 6 months look at, vocalize to, smile at, and touch other infants, thereby distinguishing themselves from others (Hay, Caplan, & Nash, 2009). As babies develop, relations with peers change, becoming more reciprocal. For example, at about a year, their smiles, vocalizations, and playful activities are often imitated or reacted to (Howes & Matheson, 1992). During the second year, toddlers use words to communicate and can coordinate their behavior with that of a playmate (Rubin, Bukowski, & Parker, 2006).

Early Childhood

When children begin to play in groups, generally after age 2 or 3, they have a chance to play a variety of roles that were not available to them in the family context. Now they have to grapple with and work through issues of power, compliance, cooperation, and conflict (Kemple, 1991; Ladd, 2005). Such issues contribute to the development of a sense of self and personal identity, giving children the opportunity to be assertive regarding ownership and to negotiate regarding desires: "That's my puzzle; you can't play with it." "If you let me ride the bike, I'll let you hold my doll."

Middle Childhood

For the middle-years child (ages 6 to 12 or 13), the peer group is attractive because it provides opportunities for greater independence than does the family, thereby enhancing the sense of self. Did you ever build a fort or a tree house when you were a child? The underlying idea, of course, was for the group to have a place of its own, where it could be independent of adult supervision and where unwanted children could be excluded.

In the peer group, children can say what they feel without being told "You should not say things like that." Or they can make suggestions without being told "You're too young to do that." Or they can do things without being told "It will never work" (as an adult might say).

Middle-years children, especially toward preadolescence (age 11 to 13), long to find others like themselves, to know that others share their doubts, their fears, their wishes, and their perceptions. The peer group is an important source of self-confirmation in that children learn, by comparing their thoughts and feelings with those of others, that they are not

Example of early childhood peers sharing, playing, and cooperating.

Cengage Learning

really different or "weird." Thus, belonging to a group clarifies personal identity and enhances self-esteem. The concern about acceptance in the peer group is often exhibited by gossip. Researchers (Cillesen & Mayeaux, 2004; Teasley & Parker, 1995) have found that much gossip among middle-years children is negative, involving defamation of third parties. "Did you hear that Jane actually bribed Sam to go to the party with her?" Children like to discuss who their friends are and who their enemies are. "Don't you just hate Brian? He's such a dork!"

The peer group, in addition to clarifying and supporting one's identity, also provides role models for one to incorporate into one's self image. Peers show what is worth doing and how to do it. It was probably your friends who taught you how to dance and to like popular music, as well as influencing what style of clothes you wore.

Adolescence

Adolescence (about age 13 to 18) is a time in our society when peer group activities escalate. One reason is that adolescents are not fully included in the adult world of responsibility and recognition for contributions. Therefore, they turn to peers. Adolescents often experience differences in the values of the family and those of the peer group. For example, academic achievement is an important value in some families, whereas among some groups of adolescents, athletic performance seems to be more important (Steinberg, 2010). Normally, which values are adolescents more likely to adopt—their family's or their friends'? According to Hans Sebald (1989, 1992), adolescents turn to their parents with regard to scholastic or occupational goals—in general, *future-oriented decisions*. They turn to their friends with regard to clothing, social activities, dating, and recreation—in general, *present-oriented decisions*. On *moral issues*, parental values dominate; on *appearance*, such as grooming, peer values dominate (Martino, Ellickson, & McCaffrey, 2009; Niles, 1981).

In sum, the process of achieving a sense of self involves the major task of balancing group identification with personal autonomy while simultaneously forging an individual role within the group. To participate in group activities, one must develop the required skills to engage in its games, as well as master the rules and agreements that govern its activities. In reaching a balance between group identification and personal autonomy, children must weigh loyalty to group norms against individual norms and parental norms. They need to develop their roles in the group structure (leading or following, for example) and cope with feelings of being accepted, popular, unpopular, or rejected (Bukowski, Brendgen, & Vitaro, 2007; Grusec & Lytton, 1988; Rubin, Bukowski, & Parker, 2006).

Parent versus Peer Influence

Parenting styles (discussed in Chapter 4) have been found to be associated with the relative importance of adult versus peer influence on children (Mounts, 2002). Parents affect child–peer relationships by influencing with whom their children interact. In addition, the parent–child relationship affects the socializing outcomes of peer groups as follows.

- *Authoritative* parents—those who are warm, accepting, neither too controlling nor too lax, and consistent in their child-rearing management—generally have children who are attached and who internalize their values. These children have little need to rebel or to desperately seek acceptance from peers (Fuligni & Eccles, 1993; Rubin, Bukowski, & Parker, 2006), because they are included in family decision making and feel socially competent (Ladd & Pettit, 2002). They usually associate with friends who share their values, so they are not faced with negative peer influences (Fletcher et al., 1995). These findings may be due to the individualistic-oriented values of independence and equality that tend to be common in families who exhibit the authoritative parenting style (Greenfield, Suzuki, & Rothstein-Fisch, 2006).

- *Authoritarian* parents—those who are very strict, cold, and do not adjust to their adolescent's need for greater autonomy—typically have children who alienate themselves from parental values and are attracted to the peer group to gain understanding and acceptance (Fuligni & Eccles, 1993; Rubin & Burgess, 2002). These adolescents are at risk for negative peer influences. However, such adverse effects of authoritarian parenting do not necessarily hold true in some culturally diverse families with a collective orientation (Chao, 1994) because the collective-oriented values of interdependence and respect of the hierarchal order tend to foster cooperation, not rebellion (Chen, Chung, & Hsiao, 2008).
- *Permissive* parents—those who indulge their children by not providing standards, rules, or behavioral consequences and/or who ignore their children's activities—typically risk having children who are unpopular and who, as adolescents, may be drawn to peer groups that are antisocial, having a negative influence on their values and behavior (Bukowski, Brendgen, & Vitaro, 2007; Rubin & Burgess, 2002). This is because the peer group provides the structure and support such children don't get from parents.

Regardless of parenting style, the peer group may provide one with a desired connection to the community and positive social support.

Psychological Development: Emotions

How do peer relations predict adult life course development?

Individuals who do not have normal peer relations are affected in their later psychological development. Studies have indicated that poor peer relations in childhood are linked to later development of neurotic and psychotic behavior and to a greater tendency to drop out of school (Bukowski, Brendgen, & Vitaro, 2007; Hartup, 1983; Ladd, 2005; Rubin, Bukowski, & Parker, 2006). Psychologists actually find that sociometric measures (measures of patterns of attraction and rejection among members of a group, discussed later in the chapter) taken in the elementary grades predict adjustment in later life better than other educational or personality tests: The child's peer group seems to serve as a barometer, showing current and predicting future adjustment problems (Asher & Paquette, 2003; Hymel, Bowker, & Woody, 1993).

Why is this so? One's ability to deal with the social world depends on communicative skills, a repertoire for coordinating one's actions with those of others, reciprocity, cooperation, and competition. These competencies develop through interactions and experiences in the peer group. In addition, peer groups have certain norms for behavior, sometimes positive (cooperation, for example) and sometimes negative (exclusion of some children or rebelliousness, for example). Children learn to compete for status in the peer group by *compliance* with group norms (*followership*) and *creation* of group norms (*leadership*) at appropriate times. Sometimes I have to go along with the group; sometimes I come up with the idea of what to do. Even though one might have occasions to lead and to follow, generally statuses, or social hierarchies, remain fairly stable in the group, with those who don't fit in being cast out or leaving on their own (American Academy of Pediatrics, 2002).

Social Development: Social Competence and Conformity

Does being socially competent mean conforming?

Social competence involves behavior informed by an understanding of others' feelings and intentions, the ability to respond appropriately, and knowledge of the consequences of one's actions. Being part of a social group involves conforming to group norms.

According to Harris (2009), children not only learn the importance of conforming to be accepted by the peer group; they also learn through experience such aspects of social competence as the dynamics of power, manipulation, and popularity, as well as how to negotiate these attributes. Social competence and the degree of social conformity that individuals exhibit depends on their age, the situation, and their personal values.

social competence behavior informed by an understanding of others' feelings and intentions, the ability to respond appropriately, and knowledge of the consequences of one's actions

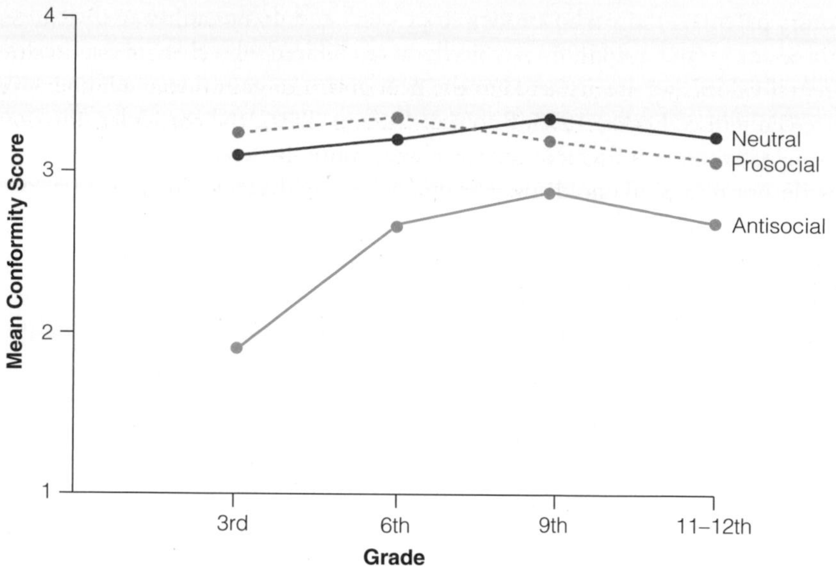

FIGURE 8.2 Conformity Peaks
Prosocial conformity peaks at sixth grade, whereas antisocial conformity peaks at ninth grade.
Source: T. J. Berndt (1979). Developmental changes in conformity to peers and parents. *Developmental Psychology*, 15, 608–616. Copyright © 1979 by the American Psychological Association. Reprinted by permission.

■ **Age.** Studies have shown that children are most susceptible to the influence of peers in middle childhood and become less conforming in adolescence (Berndt, 1979; Brown, Clasen, & Eicher, 1986; Foster-Clark & Blyth, 1991) (see Figure 8.2). Even when it is known to be wrong, middle-years children still go along with the majority opinion of the group (Berenda, 1950). In a classic study, 90 children ages 7 to 13 were asked to compare the lengths of lines on 12 pairs of cards. They had already taken this same test in school. This time, however, the children participating in the experiment were tested in a room with the eight brightest children in their class. Answers were given aloud. These eight children had been instructed beforehand to give 7 wrong answers out of 12. The results pointed to the power of group influence. Whereas almost all the subjects had given correct answers to the seven critical questions in the original test taken in school, only 43 percent of the 7- to 10-year-olds, and only 54 percent of the 10- to 13-year-olds, gave correct answers on the second test in the group setting. The rest changed their former answers to match the group's, which were intentionally incorrect.

■ **Situation.** Social conformity is even more apparent in ambiguous situations where children are unsure about what they should do or are supposed to do (Cohen, Bornstein, & Sherman, 1973; Hartup, 1983; Steinberg, 2010). For example, Thomas Berndt (1979; Berndt & Ladd, 1989) gave a questionnaire to students ranging from third to twelfth grade, asking how they would respond to various hypothetical situations (*prosocial, neutral, antisocial*). A question exemplifying a *prosocial* situation asked the students whether they would help a classmate with a report if asked by their peers, instead of doing what they wanted to do, which was helping another classmate operate the film projector. A question exemplifying a *neutral* situation asked the students whether they would go to a movie if asked by their peers, even if they were not particularly interested in that movie. A question exemplifying an *antisocial* situation asked the students whether they would steal some candy if a peer wanted help in doing it.

■ **Personal Values.** One of Berndt's (1979) findings was that conformity to antisocial behavior and neutral situations peaked in the ninth grade and then dropped off to previous levels. Another finding was that conformity to prosocial behavior peaked in the sixth grade and then dropped. In general, the sixth- to ninth-graders exhibited the most conforming behavior. The results are plotted in Figure 8.2. Berndt also found that whether or not people conformed to the group depended on their feelings about the particular situation—how "good" or "bad" they felt about it. Students were more likely to conform to situations they did not feel very "bad" about. Thus, personal values do affect one's likelihood of conforming to the peer group.

Cognitive Development: Social Cognition

Why are preadolescent children (age 11 to 13) more susceptible to peer group influences than children of other ages?

Much documentation has been accumulating regarding the connection between social development and cognitive development (Ladd, 2005; Rubin, Bukowski, & Parker, 2006). This connection is referred to as **social cognition**—conceptions and reasoning about people, the self, relations between people, social groups' roles and rules, and the relation of such conceptions to social behavior (Shantz, 1983). Collaboration with peers through language and play enables the child to construct thoughts (Berk & Winsler, 1995). The social interactions with peers also contribute to the child's cognitive understanding of his or her culture (Rogoff, 2003). Even though children interact with one another increasingly from infancy on, the ability to cope with complex social messages increases with age and stage of cognitive development.

social cognition conceptions and reasoning about people, the self, relations between people, social groups' roles and rules, and the relation of such conceptions to social behavior

■ **Social Cognition in the Preoperational Stage.** Young children ages 2–7 are in the stage of cognitive development that Jean Piaget (1952) termed *preoperational*. The preoperational stage is characterized by intuitive, rather than logical, thought. Preoperational children are poor at understanding relationships between objects, events, and people. For example, children under age 7 do not have the cognitive ability even to be aware of peer pressure to conform or the consequences for deviance. They have difficulty taking another's point of view and cannot, therefore, project what the peer group thinks of them.

■ **Social Cognition in the Concrete Operational Stage.** Young children ages 7–11 are in the stage of cognitive development that Piaget (1952) termed *concrete operational*. The concrete operational stage is characterized by the ability to apply logical, systematic principles to help interpret specific or tangible experiences, but also by the inability to distinguish between intangible assumptions, or hypotheses, and facts, or reality.

According to David Elkind (1981a), concrete-operational children make theories about reality (situations and people) assumed to be true without examining or evaluating contradictory data (**assumptive realities**), no matter how illogical they are. For example, U.S. children of this age who have seen a globe at school might try to dig a hole in the ground to get to China, because China is on the other side of the globe (I used to do this at the beach). No amount of adult logic in terms of distances can dissuade them. Concrete-operational children also assume they are clever. David Elkind calls this **cognitive conceit**, the exhibition of too much faith in one's reasoning ability and cleverness. The concept of cognitive conceit is illustrated in some favorite stories of children of this age—for example, *Peter Pan* (a child who outwits Captain Hook, an adult) or *Alice in Wonderland* (a young girl who makes the queen look like a fool).

assumptive reality a theory about reality assumed to be true without examining or evaluating contradictory data

cognitive conceit Elkind's term for children in Piaget's stage of concrete operations who put too much faith in their reasoning ability and cleverness

Because children under age 11 often think they know it all, they sometimes feel they do not have to pay attention to the opinions of others, be they adults or other children. "I don't have to" (a common remark at this age), then, is not really defiance but a statement of concrete-operational children's beliefs about their abilities (Piaget, 1952).

■ **Social Cognition in the Formal Operational Stage.** From about age 11 and on, children are in the stage of cognitive development that Piaget (1952) termed *formal operational*. The formal operational stage is characterized by the ability to think logically about abstract ideas and hypotheses, as well as concrete facts; one can now construct all the possibilities of a proposition—the ones related to fact and the ones contrary to fact. The child now understands the *form* behind a concept and can add ideas to or subtract them from it. Preadolescent children, then, can conceptualize their own thoughts and discover the arbitrariness of their assumptions. They also discover rules for testing assumptions against facts (**reality testing**). This leads to diminished confidence in their ability, especially their cleverness. Preadolescent children are aware of the reactions of others and the need to conform to their expectations. This new awareness exhibits itself in the **imaginary audience**—the belief that others are as concerned with one's behavior and appearance as one is oneself. Thus, preadolescent children believe they are the focus of attention, and they strive extra hard to be like their peers so that they will not stand out.

reality testing testing assumptions against facts

imaginary audience the beliefs that others are as concerned with one's behavior and appearance as one is oneself

As children approach adolescence (ages 13 to 15), the imaginary audience comes to be regarded as an assumption to be tested against reality. As a consequence of this testing, adolescents gradually come to recognize the difference between their own preoccupations and the interests and concerns of others. Therefore, conformity decreases because adolescents realize that they are expected to conform to some situations but can be independent in others. Adolescents have also developed better social skills and a greater reliance on their own judgment.

One reason preadolescent children are more conforming than other age groups is that their level of cognitive development is capable of logical thought; that is, they can project how others react and evaluate their assumptions. However, they have not yet had the experience of testing their assumptions on reality.

IN CONTEXT

An example of cognition and conformity occurred when my daughter began junior high school. She refused to take the backpack I had bought her for her books. She said, "All the kids will laugh at me; only kids in elementary school use backpacks." I asked her what the junior high kids used to carry their books. Exhibiting preadolescent assumptions, she did not know exactly (she had not been there yet), but she thought they used satchels. For the first week of school, she carried her books loosely in her arms. When the second week of school came, she grudgingly put her books in the backpack, saying she was tired of dropping books and that her arms ached. One day after school had been in session for about a month, I picked up my daughter at school. I noticed that a lot of kids had backpacks. I said nothing, but I thought to myself, "She assumed all the other kids would have satchels and she didn't want to be different. She had to make sure that enough other kids had backpacks before she would take hers to school." Can you remember being reluctant to do something before you saw others do it? What were your concerns?

Another reason preadolescent children are more conforming than other age groups is that they are entering Erikson's (1963) fifth psychosocial stage of development—*identity versus identity (role) confusion* (Who am I, and what is my role in life?). Erikson's stages were discussed in Chapter 2. In the process of finding an identity, preadolescent children repeat the crises of the earlier stages—*basic trust versus basic mistrust* (Do I generally trust people, or distrust them?); *autonomy versus shame and doubt* (Am I confident I can be independent, or am I doubtful about my ability to be independent?); *initiative versus guilt* (Do I feel good about starting new things or meeting new people, or do I feel guilty?); and *industry versus inferiority* (Do I feel competent about my abilities, or inferior?).

"The growing and developing youths, faced with this psychological revolution within them, and with tangible adult tasks ahead of them, are now primarily concerned with what they appear to be in the eyes of others as compared with what they feel they are"

(Erikson, 1963, p. 261). They are trying out roles and using the reactions of others to judge how well the roles fit their self-concept. Thus, in the process of wondering "Who am I?" children beginning this psychosocial stage of development tend to "temporarily overidentify to the point of apparent complete loss of identity, with heroes of cliques and crowds" (p. 262).

Erikson explains the clannishness and cruelty of excluding those who are different from the group as a defense against a sense of identity confusion. Preadolescent children who are on the brink of entering the identity-versus-role-confusion stage look to the peer group for their identity. The group's symbols and rituals (ways of dressing, ways of behaving, attitudes, opinions), as well as its approval and support, help define what is good and what is bad, thereby contributing to the development of ego identity. Identifying with a group and excluding those who are not like the members of the group helps children identify *who they are* by affirming *who they are not*. As preadolescence gives way to adolescence, young people begin to derive an identity from the accumulation of their experiences, their abilities, and their goals. They begin to look within themselves rather than to others for who they are. The peer group, then, serves to mediate between the individual and society, playing a powerful role in shaping the individual's identity (Adler & Adler, 1998).

These girls feel more comfortable in their classroom reading together rather than each doing it alone.

Cengage Learning

Peer Group Socializing Mechanisms

Typical socializing methods include reinforcement (approval and acceptance), modeling (imitation), punishment (rejection and exclusion), and apprenticeship (when a novice learns from an expert).

What socializing mechanisms does the peer group employ to influence behavior?

Reinforcement

One important way in which children influence each other is through reinforcement, or giving attention. Approving another's behavior (smiling, laughing, patting, hugging, verbalizing praise) increases the likelihood of that behavior's recurring (Kindermann, 1998). The behavior could be sharing, or it could be aggression against another (Martin & Pear, 2010). Reinforcement also involves acceptance into the group. Criteria for acceptance will be discussed later.

Sometimes reinforcement is unintentional, but it is still effective. To illustrate, studies of preschool children (Dodge, Coie, & Lynam, 2006) have shown that they react to physical aggression (bullying) by becoming passive, assuming a defensive posture, crying, telling the teacher, retrieving their property, or retaliating with aggression. When a child responded to the aggression with reinforcers, such as passiveness, defensiveness, or crying, the aggression tended to be repeated on the same victim. When the child responded with proactive behavior, such as telling the teacher, retrieving property, or counter aggression, the aggressor or bully tended to behave differently toward the former victim. Thus, passivity unintentionally reinforces aggression toward the victim; action serves to redirect the aggression away from the victim.

Using reinforcement as a behavior modification technique requires waiting for the behavior to appear and then reinforcing it (Martin & Pear, 2010). To determine whether certain social stimuli functioned as reinforcers, Furman and Masters (1980) observed and recorded rates of laughter and praise (*positive* reinforcers); crying, physical attack, and disapproval (*negative* reinforcers); and other expressions (*neutral* reinforcers) in preschool children. They found that behaviors classified as positive reinforcements were twice as likely to be followed by similar affective behaviors, whereas punitive acts (negative reinforcers) were more than five times as likely to be succeeded by negative behaviors. Parents and teachers need to be alert to patterns of peer reinforcement so that peers can be used effectively to help change negative or disruptive behavior.

This boy is intent on modeling his friend's agility at playing the game.

Cengage Learning

Modeling

Children also influence each other through modeling, or imitation (Kindermann, 1998). Modeling is related to conformity. Observing a child behave in a certain manner can affect another's consequent behavior in three different ways (Bandura, 1989).

- The observing child may learn how to do something new that he or she could not do previously (such as drawing a picture of a dog) or would probably not have thought of (such as riding a bike with "no hands").
- The child may learn the consequences of behavior by observing someone else. For example, pinching another results in being punished by the teacher, or getting to the swings first results in getting the longest turn.
- A model may suggest how a child can behave in a new situation. For example, when the children lined up at the edge of the pool for their first dive, Maureen was first. She said, "I can do it. I've watched my brother hundreds of times." As the instructor was showing her how to hold her arms and keep her head down, the others watched nervously. In a second, she hit the water, and in another few seconds she popped up smiling. The others relaxed.

In a classic study by Bandura, Ross, and Ross (1963), children who were shown a film in which a model struck a doll, sat on it, and screamed at it later copied the model's aggressive behavior when given a similar doll to play with. Other researchers (Hartup, 1983; Hartup & Coates, 1967) studied a group of 4- and 5-year-old children who were asked to watch one of their classmates work out problems. The classmate, the model, received some trinkets for doing the task. This model put aside some of the trinkets for a mythical child. The children who watched were then asked to do the problems, and the model left the room. They were also given trinkets and were also given the opportunity to save some trinkets for "the other child." Another group of 4- and 5-year-olds, who did not watch a model do the problems and exhibit altruistic behavior, were asked to do the same problems, were given trinkets, and were given the opportunity to save some for "the other child." The children who observed altruistic behavior gave more trinkets than those who did not.

The extent to which modeling influences behavior depends on the following factors (Bandura, 2001):

- **Situation.** Active behavior is more likely to be imitated than passive behavior.
- **Model.** A model who is perceived to be similar to the observer and has desirable or admirable traits is more likely to be imitated than one who does not seem similar or who has traits not particularly desirable to the observer.
- **Observer.** The observer's cognitive and physical ability to reproduce the observed behavior also influences modeling. The observer must understand and remember the behavior and must be able to perform the verbal and/or motor functions involved.

Studying children in preschool classes has shown that a great deal of imitation, some positive and some negative, of both verbal and motor acts occurs in day-by-day interactions (Grusec & Abramovitch, 1982). Imitation seems to decrease from preschool to age 10, perhaps because deferred, rather than immediate, imitation and other subtle forms of observational learning become more favored as children get older. Dominant children in a group are imitated more often by others, but they imitate others as well (Grusec & Lytton, 1988).

As a socializing method, modeling has broader effects than reinforcement. A large number of children can be influenced by one carefully selected model, whereas direct reinforcement requires one-to-one interaction between the teacher and the learner. Modeling can provide a means of inducing behavior that otherwise might not occur. It may give the child an idea for doing something never done before, or it may remind the child of something done before and induce the child to repeat it (Bandura, 2001).

Punishment

Still another way in which children influence each other is through punishment—teasing, physical aggression, or rejection by the group. Such behavior begins in preschool (Crick, Casas, & Ku, 1999). Criteria for rejection will be discussed later. An extreme of such punishment is being a victim of bullying. *Victims* are usually withdrawn, passive, shy, insecure, and have difficulty asserting themselves in a group. *Bullies* are usually dominant, aggressive, impulsive, angry, and have a low frustration tolerance. Bullying and victimization require adult intervention strategies, to be discussed later (Coloroso, 2003; Olweus, 1993).

Sometimes children are rejected or punished by peers because of physical characteristics (being overweight, for example) or behavioral characteristics (bragging, dominating, or criticizing, for example) (Adler & Adler, 1998; Coie, Dodge, & Kupersmidt, 1990; Parkhurst & Asher, 1992). The consequence of being punished by exclusion and teasing by the peer group is described in the box "Peers, Power, Pecking Order, and Punishment." The social dynamics of inclusion, exclusion, and social hierarchies are discussed later.

Apprenticeship

Yet another way peers influence each other is through apprenticeship, in which someone with more expertise (the expert) helps someone with less (the novice). Examples of apprenticeship referred to in this chapter are peers having introduced you to hip-hop music, having taught you to dance, or having "educated" you about sex. The concept of apprenticeship as a method of socialization was discussed in Chapter 2. Traditionally, the word *apprenticeship* has been used in the world of work—a beginner becomes an apprentice under a master until he or she learns a trade well enough to succeed alone.

Lev Vygotsky (1978) postulated that a more knowledgeable person, such as a teacher or an expert peer, initially guides the learner's, or novice's, activity. Gradually, the two begin to share problem-solving functions, with the novice taking the initiative and the expert peer correcting and guiding when the novice falters. Finally, the expert peer cedes control and acts as a supportive audience.

IN CONTEXT An illustration of Vygotsky's hypothesis might be your learning how to ride a two-wheel bike from a friend who has mastered the skill. Your friend shows you how to get on the bike, how to balance, how to pedal, and how to stop. You get on the bike while your friend supports it. Your friend holds on while you pedal. After many falls, you can finally balance and pedal at the same time, so your friend lets go (but runs after you yelling instructions on how to stop).

Vygotsky believed that engaging in such apprenticeship activities advances the novice's level of development. Vygotsky suggested that the boundaries for a novice's learning abilities lie between (1) his or her *actual* development, or what he or she can do independently, and (2) his or her *potential* development, or what he or she can do while participating with more capable others. He called this space the *zone of proximal development* (ZPD), discussed in Chapter 7. Examples of how schools implement ZPD are peer collaboration on projects, peer tutoring, and peer counseling.

IN CONTEXT A personal example of ZPD is my husband, who has a talent for drawing. I persuaded him to take an art class to develop his ability further. The students in the class submitted their drawings every week for peer review and suggestions for improvement, while the instructor served as a moderator. At the end of the course, my husband's drawings were significantly more elaborate and sophisticated than when he began the class. Peer review is a technique also used in other classes, such as writing and speech.

cliques friends who view themselves as mutually connected and do things together

crowds loosely organized reference groups of cliques

IN PRACTICE

Peers, Power, Pecking Order, and Punishment

Peer groups in schools are manifested in the formation of cliques—friends who view themselves as mutually connected and doing things together—and crowds—loosely organized reference groups of cliques. Cliques and crowds are significant contributors to children's and adolescents' quests for identity.

In elementary school, cliques are hierarchical friendship groups based on popularity and prestige. By the time children reach high school, the clique social hierarchy is stratified. Typically, one finds "jocks," "preppies," or "populars"; "brains," or "nerds"; and "loners," or "unpopulars" (Eder, 1995; Kindermann & Gest, 2009). High school social life was popularized in the media by the TV show *Beverly Hills 90210*. By interacting within and between friendship groups, children learn what kind of social competence they possess. The high-status clique is the "populars"; below them are the "wannabes" (the group that hangs around hoping for inclusion); next are smaller, independent groups; and at the bottom of the social hierarchy are the "social isolates" (those who only occasionally find playmates) (Adler & Adler, 1998).

Cliques are dominated by leaders. They are exclusive in nature, so that not all individuals who desire membership are accepted. The critical way that cliques maintain exclusivity is through careful membership screening. Acceptance or rejection of potential new members is linked to the power of the leaders. Leaders derive their power through popularity and use it to make decisions and influence social stratification (pecking order) within the group (Adler & Adler, 1998).

In their observations of preadolescents in school, Adler and Adler (1998, p. 76) found that the popular clique "set the tone for, and in many ways influenced, the behavior of the entire grade." Maintaining membership takes a concerted effort at conforming to desires of the leaders. The exclusivity of membership is a reward for those who are "in" and a punishment for those who are "out." The "wannabes" try to be "cool" by imitating the "populars"—wearing the same clothing and hairstyles, buying the same music, and using the same vocabulary (Eder, 1995). Their conforming behavior is reinforced because, occasionally, they are invited to participate in clique activities even though they are not fully accepted into the group.

Those who are "out," the "social isolates" (the "loners," "drifters," "dweebs," "nerds"), are excluded because they are different in some way—appearance, behavior, and/or language. Those who are "in" or the "wannabes" treat them poorly by teasing and laughing at them. It is as though everyone in the pecking order offsets his or her own insecurities by humiliating the individuals who are lower in status (Thorne, 1993). The exclusion of the "social isolates" from nearly all of the cliques' social activities, coupled with the extreme degradation they suffer, takes a heavy toll on their feelings of self-worth.

The significance of these findings from peer group studies was manifested in 1999 at Columbine High School in Littleton, Colorado, where two social isolates, Eric Harris and Dylan Klebold, shot and killed 12 students and a teacher, as well as themselves. Interviews with students and community members pointed to the injustice and harassment done to Harris and Klebold by the "jocks," combined with their disengagement from caring adults (Wilson & Mishra, 1999). That such rage was acted out, when cliques and cruelty have been around for years in children's groups, poses a disturbing question. In 1961, James Coleman studied 11 high schools of varied socioeconomic statuses and found similar peer group stratification, similar values (athletes having the highest prestige; brains and unpopulars, the lowest), and similar behavior. The adolescents in his study seemed to accept things as "normal" for high school life; so why did the Columbine tragedy occur?

Peers are influenced by other ecosystems, such as media and community. According to Greenfield and Juvonen (1999), Harris and Klebold acquired knowledge from the broader society (macrosystem) beyond home and school. They had:

1. *role models* (media showing heroes engaged in violence to accomplish goals);
2. *tools* (guns and assault weapons available for purchase along with Internet instructions on how to construct a bomb);
3. *social validation* from Internet groups; and
4. *opportunities* to practice their objectives (via violent video games).

Peer behavior, especially bullying and victimization, has not only been influenced by ecosystems, but has influenced ecosystems as well. For example, according to the National Conference of State Legislators (2008; http://www.NCSL.org), since 1999 many states have passed laws to address harassment, intimidation, and bullying. Many schools and businesses also have rules.

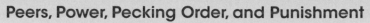

Macrosystem Influences on the Peer Group: Developmental Tasks

What does society expect the peer group to accomplish?

Developmental tasks, discussed in Chapter 2, are midway between an individual need and a societal demand. Macrosystem influences on the peer group involve reinforcing the values and traditions of society. The peer group, in turn, provides the setting and the means for children to achieve some of the expected developmental tasks of early and middle childhood (Havighurst, 1972; Zarbatany, Hartmann, & Rankin, 1990), especially social competence. This means that children must learn to get along with others, develop morals and values, learn appropriate social and cultural roles, and achieve personal independence while formulating an identity (Rubin, Bukowski, & Parker, 2006).

Getting Along with Others

How do children learn the give-and-take of relationships?

Playing with children of the same age is a vehicle for socializing the capacity to "get along" by learning to give and take. Getting along involves recognition of the rights of others. The peer group provides children with opportunities for understanding the limitations that group life places on the individual: "At my house I can play with my Legos all I want, but at preschool I have to share." "When I'm with my friends, I can't always have my way. We talk about what we're going to do on Sunday, trying to please everyone. If Barbara, Joan, and Carol want to go shopping and I don't, the group tells me if I come with them, they'll stop by my favorite ice cream place on the way home. Even though I don't get my way, I get the feeling I'm wanted and that the group is trying to please me. I agree to go shopping."

The ability to get along is developmentally progressive in that it involves both seeing things from another's perspective and verbal communication (Grusec & Lytton, 1988). It depends, then, on increasing cognitive abilities as well as social experiences. Some studies (Lamb & Ahnert, 2006; NICHD, 2007) have shown that young children who are in child-care centers are more socially competent than those who are cared for at home, but are also more aggressive. It is likely that these children learn early how to "stick up" for themselves and compete for toys.

Getting along with others is related to the ability to empathize. As children develop, they become increasingly able to empathize with others—first on an emotional level, then on a behavioral level. For example, it has been found that by the end of the first year, babies often cry when they observe another baby crying; by the middle of the second year, they pat or hug the crying baby; by the end of the second year, they offer specific kinds of help, like a toy or a Band-Aid (Saarni, Mumme, & Campos, 1998). Then they also begin to empathize cognitively. For example, the studies of Zahn-Waxler and colleagues (Zahn-Waxler & Radke-Yarrow, 1990; Zahn-Waxler et al., 1992; Zahn-Waxler, Robinson, & Emde, 1992) showed that during the second year, children's responses to the distress of others become increasingly differentiated and their ability to comfort increasingly effective. They were more likely to empathize with family and friends than they were with strangers. They were also more likely to verbalize their empathy and respond sensitively: "Please don't cry; I'll let you play with my doll."

Developing Morals and Values

How does the peer group contribute to children's concepts of right and wrong, worthy and unworthy?

The development of *morals* (distinguishing right from wrong) and *values* (determining what is worthwhile) occurs in a social setting. By interacting with others, the child comes to know what is and what is not acceptable behavior. Children learn morals and values from parents and other adults through instruction, reasoning, modeling, reinforcement, and punishment; they learn morals and values from peers through real experiences (learning by doing).

Most studies of the development of morals and values involve school-age children and adolescents who are capable of articulating judgments about hypothetical dilemmas, as will be discussed in Chapter 11. However, research by Judy Dunn (1988, 2004) on the

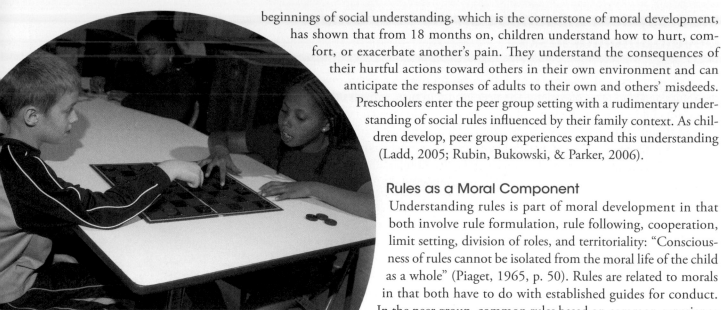

In game playing, children's moral development is influenced by practicing such activities as rule-following, cooperation, and limit-setting.

Cengage Learning

beginnings of social understanding, which is the cornerstone of moral development, has shown that from 18 months on, children understand how to hurt, comfort, or exacerbate another's pain. They understand the consequences of their hurtful actions toward others in their own environment and can anticipate the responses of adults to their own and others' misdeeds. Preschoolers enter the peer group setting with a rudimentary understanding of social rules influenced by their family context. As children develop, peer group experiences expand this understanding (Ladd, 2005; Rubin, Bukowski, & Parker, 2006).

Rules as a Moral Component

Understanding rules is part of moral development in that both involve rule formulation, rule following, cooperation, limit setting, division of roles, and territoriality: "Consciousness of rules cannot be isolated from the moral life of the child as a whole" (Piaget, 1965, p. 50). Rules are related to morals in that both have to do with established guides for conduct. In the peer group, common rules based on common experience begin to develop. These rules may be devised to meet a specific situation; they may be copied from adults' rules or those of older children. Between the ages of 3 and 7, children sometimes observe the rules of the group and sometimes not. Even when playing together, children of this age play "each one on his own" (Piaget, 1965, p. 27)—everyone has his or her own views of the way the game is played—without any real regard for the codification of the rules.

Around the age of 7 or 8, children "begin to concern themselves with the question of mutual control and of unification of the rules" (Piaget, 1965, p. 27), even though their understanding of the rules may be rather vague. At 11 or 12, children fix the rules in their groups; everyone in the group understands and observes them. For example, in the game of Four Square, whoever misses the ball is out. Everyone knows that rule. However, some groups will make rules regarding how the ball is returned, like "no babies." A "baby" is a ball bounced so lightly that it barely comes off the ground and, therefore, is almost impossible to get. Thus, if a child wants to belong to the group, the rules must be respected and obeyed. If "babies" are not allowed, one cannot use them if one wants to continue to play with the group. Learning the conditions attached to belonging to the group, then, is the way children are socialized as to the requirements for participation. It is also a way in which children develop morality.

Types of Morality

morality of constraint behavior based on respect for persons in authority

morality of cooperation behavior based on mutual understanding between equals

Piaget (1965) contrasts two types of morality. One type, *heteronomous morality* or **morality of constraint**, consists of behavior based on respect for persons in authority. It is imposed by a prestigeful and powerful source, usually the parent or another adult. This type of morality fosters the ideal that to obey the will of the authority is good; to obey one's own will is bad. Such morality is fostered in the family and in school. The other type, *autonomous morality* or **morality of cooperation**, consists of behavior based on mutual understanding between equals. It involves the acceptance of rules because they are necessary for the continuance of group life. If one wants to participate in the group, one freely accepts the rules; the rules are imposed on oneself by oneself. This type of morality emerges from the mutual respect of the children in the group. Thus, peer group participation—participation among equals—helps foster morality of cooperation, whereas morality of constraint is more likely to be fostered in authoritarian, adult-dominated situations, such as the family or school.

In our society, we must obey certain rules because they were imposed by an authority, whether or not we agree (draft registration, for example). We also impose certain rules on ourselves for the benefit of group life (compromise with a neighbor regarding the property line, for example). To participate effectively in society, then, children need both types of morality training. To exemplify, studies (Ladd, 2005; Ladd & LeSieur, 1995; Ladd & Pettit, 2002) have shown that children who come from homes with moderate to high levels of discipline and control (authoritative parenting) and who have had a great deal of peer group experience tend to be autonomous, socially competent, and have strong moral character. In contrast, children who come from homes characterized by low levels of discipline and control (permissive parenting) or high levels of punitiveness (authoritarian parenting), and who have had a great deal of peer group experience, tend to be "peer conformists" or "chameleons."

It would seem, then, that the peer group helps children in the *process* of developing morals (learning by doing), whereas the *level* of moral development is greatly influenced by parenting styles (learning by reasoning). According to a study by Walker, Hennig, and Krettenaur (2000), parent and peer context for moral reasoning differ by the quality of verbal interactions (parents provided more cognitive stimulation than did friends). Research (Kerns, Contreras, & Neal-Barnett, 2000; Martino, Ellickson, & McCaffrey, 2009) documents the importance of contingent linkages between parents and peers in moral behavior.

Learning Appropriate Sociocultural Roles

How do peer experiences contribute to children's understanding of how to behave in group situations?

Although the family imparts sociocultural roles, such as *independence* and *interdependence*, the peer group gives the child opportunities to try out roles learned at home (Greenfield, Suzuki, & Rothstein-Fisch, 2006). The child gains an understanding of the individual's responsibility in a group situation. For example, does one exercise *autonomy* and respect peers' right to free choice ("I want to play Scrabble; what game do you want to play?"); or does one exercise *empathy*, anticipating the desires of peers ("I know you like to play chess, so let's play that")? Does one communicate in a *direct, assertive* manner ("I want to try your new bike") or in an *indirect, passive* manner ("That's a nice new bike you got")? Does one *compete* with peers for *individual* recognition or *cooperate* with peers for *group* recognition? Does one *confront* conflict or *avoid* it?

An example of how appropriate sociocultural roles are learned can be seen when children who have never had to share things at home or who have never had to take turns learn to do so in the peer group or else be excluded. From the peer group, children receive feedback about their behavior and skills. Your peers will not hesitate to tell you when you are acting dumb. Children not only learn the sociocultural roles of cooperation and appropriate behavior from each other, they also learn how to compete. They evaluate their skills in terms of whether they can do better than, as well as, or worse than others in the group. They also learn methods of conflict resolution.

IN CONTEXT An example of cultural conflict is when an immigrant girl from a collectively oriented culture on a Los Angeles high school volleyball team drank from the water bottle of an American girl. On some teams observed in various collectivistic cultures, water bottles are routinely passed around so all team members can drink. In the United States, an individualistically oriented culture, one's water bottle is one's personal property, besides which, Americans believe that sharing personal items is sharing germs. The American girl was very angry and adult intervention was required to quell the conflict (Greenfield, Suzuki, & Rothstein-Fisch, 2006).

In preschool settings in different countries, the peer group serves as a vehicle by which children learn certain cultural values. For example, in China, children learn to conform to the group through the teacher's structuring the activities accordingly, criticizing those who don't conform and praising those who do. In Japan, children learn to get along in the peer group through the teacher's encouragement and noninterference. In the United States, children learn to respect other children's rights through the teacher's interceding in conflicts, explaining why they are hurtful or unsafe, and providing a consequence (Tobin, Wu, & Davidson, 1989).

Sex and Gender Roles

Sex is a broad term encompassing (1) an individual's biological characteristics, (2) the psychological construct of appropriate male/female behavior (gender role), (3) sex education, and (4) sexual activity.

Gender Role

Gender role is sociocultural in that children learn from their peers what is culturally acceptable and admirable for boys and girls (Best, 1983; Ruble, Martin, & Berenbaum, 2006; Thorne, 1993). For example, Jerry, age 4, wanted to join a group of girls who were playing with their dolls. Jerry had a doll at home that he bathed and dressed while his mother or father bathed his baby sister. When Jerry approached the girls, they said, "Boys don't play with dolls!" Peer pressure for *appropriate* gender-type play has been observed to begin as early as age 2 (Maccoby, 1990, 2000; Serbin, Powlishta, & Gulko, 1993).

Peer groups generally segregate boys and girls beginning in preschool (Maccoby, 1990, 2000; Ruble, Martin, & Berenbaum, 2006). In the preschool years, girls become interested in small group games in small spaces, games that allow them to practice and refine social rules and roles (for example, playing in the house corner). Boys engage in larger group games that are more physically active and wide-ranging. These games tend to have a more extensive set of explicit rules that involve reaching a defined goal. The games tend to be competitive (for example, the "good guys against the bad guys," in the form of Batman or Darth Vader, with the goal being "to save the world"). Thus, segregated peer group play leads to different outcomes for boys and girls in achievement motivation, personal relationships, and self-concept (Dweck, 1981). Gender roles will be discussed in more detail in Chapter 12.

Sex Education

The peer group is often the imparter of information about sexuality. Children and adolescents share their knowledge with each other—knowledge they may have gained from their families, from the media, from school, or from friends. With their limited cognitive ability, they often have an incomplete understanding of normal sexual development, which, combined with their friends' incomplete understanding, distorts the total picture of sexuality.

In the United States, adolescents receive information on sex and sexuality from parents, school, peers, and media (Katchadourian, 1990; Somers & Surmann, 2004).

- Parents transmit their attitudes about sex, love, and marriage.
- Schools provide information on topics including: abstinence, sexually transmitted diseases, menstruation, semen production, and pregnancy.
- Topics discussed with peers include: love, contraception, ejaculation, homosexuality, intercourse, masturbation, petting, and prostitution.
- The media present the excitement of sex without the consequences.

Thus, knowledge about the *mechanics of reproduction* apparently comes from parents and school, but knowledge about sexual *behavior* apparently comes from peers and the media.

Regarding the danger of sexually transmitted diseases and the consequences of teen pregnancy, adults need to be "tuned in" to the role that peers and other socializing agents play in sex education. They need to talk to children before puberty about love, marriage, sex, and reproduction and continue to communicate throughout adolescence, being "askable," available, and willing to answer questions.

Observations of elementary school children in the United States demonstrate that girls and boys are very aware of the opposite sex and what is expected of heterosexual behavior (Best, 1983; Ruble, Martin, & Berenbaum, 2006; Thorne, 1993). Children continually talk about who "loves" whom and who is "cute." As preparation for later heterosexual relations, children play chase-and-kiss games. Usually, the girls try to catch the boys and kiss them, pronouncing they have "cooties." The others who watch will engage in laughing and teasing.

In the United States, the onset of sexual activity is influenced by peers, gender, and the media (Brooks-Gunn & Furstenberg, 1989). One's peers establish the norm for initiating sex. Assumptions (rather than actual knowledge) about what one's peers are doing has been found to be associated with sexual behavior (actual behavior is difficult to research because of disclosure reluctance). In adolescents, studies have found parenting styles and arguments with teens over dating to be associated with sexual initiation (Longmore et al., 2009). Historically, boys have been much more likely to engage in sexual intercourse earlier than girls. This may have been due to peer pressure "to become a man" as well as not having to bear the consequences of becoming pregnant. However, the gender gap in the onset of sexual activity has narrowed (Moore & Rosenthal, 2006). This may be due to media influence portraying females as sexual seductresses as well as easier access to contraception. The American Psychological Association (APA, 2007b) concluded in its report on the sexualization of girls that virtually every form of media (TV, music, movies, magazines, sports media, video games, the Internet, and advertising) portrays girls as sex objects, meaning they are valued only for their physical appearance (attractiveness and sex appeal) or for their sexual behavior rather than for being unique individuals with thoughts and feelings. Parental influence on sexual behavior is believed to outweigh peers and the media if there is a feeling of connectedness and support as well as open communication (Ikramullah et al., 2009; Small & Luster, 1994; APA, 2007b). However, as a family's socioeconomic status decreases, teen sexual activity has been found to increase. Also, teens from single-parent families report a higher incidence of sexual activity, whereas those teens who attend church, do well in school, and are on academic rather than vocational tracks report lower activity.

How does the peer group contribute to individuality?

social support resources (tangible, intellectual, social, emotional) provided by others in times of need

Achieving Personal Independence and Identity

As discussed earlier, peer groups enable children to become increasingly independent of adults. "Individuals juggle different and often conflicting images of self between the childish self shown to their families and the maturing self shown to their peers" (Adler & Adler, 1998, p. 198). In addition, as children get older, peers become increasingly important as social support (Jackson & Warren, 2000; Rubin, Bukowski, & Parker, 2006). **Social support** refers to the resources (tangible, intellectual, social, emotional) provided by others in times of need. Tangible support includes sharing toys, clothes, and money. Intellectual support includes giving information or advice. Social support involves companionship. Emotional support involves listening and empathy. Boys' and girls' use of social supports differs (Jackson & Warren, 2000). Boys tend to have more extensive social supports and girls, more intimate ones. Boys look to their social supports for affirmation; girls look to theirs for help to solve a problem.

Children develop their identities through meaningful interactions and accomplishments in the peer group. Children begin to view the peer group as a reference group beginning about age 7 or 8 and increasing through adolescence (Rubin, Bukowski, & Parker, 2006).

- Peers provide validation for the self: "Do you like my hair?" "C'mon, let's play ball." "I have a secret to tell you."

Telling secrets is a way of gaining support from a peer while beginning to separate from dependency on adults.

Cengage Learning

- Peers provide encouragement to try new things: "I'll join Girl Scouts if you will too." "Do you want to go camping with me 'n' my dad?"
- Peers provide opportunities for comparison: "I beat Sam in the race." "Sally made the team, but I didn't."
- Peers enable self-disclosure. Children are more likely to disclose their innermost feelings to trusted friends than to adults (Parker & Gottman, 1989): "I'm in love with Brad; I let him French kiss me." "I copied my report from the Internet."
- Peers provide identity: "I want to be a *popular* when I go to high school next year."

According to Ungar (2000), in a study of high-risk adolescents, the participating youths indicated that adopting the behavior and appearance of peers was a conscious strategy to enhance personal and social power. Identification with the peer group enabled the young person to avoid feelings of alienation, especially if there were family problems, in that peers served as a source of support. Participants described peer groups as a means to assert both individual and collective identities. In other words, peer influence was bidirectional: The members shaped the group, and the group, in turn, shaped the members.

How does children's play change throughout development?

Chronosystem Influences on the Peer Group: Play/Activities

Chronosystem influences on the peer group refer here to changes in structure, activities, and relationships as peers grow and develop psychologically, socially, and cognitively. Because child-initiated play is the main activity that occurs in peer groups, it is discussed first; adult-initiated play is discussed later.

How does play contribute to developmental outcomes?

The Significance and Development of Play

play behavior enjoyed for its own sake

"**Play** is behavior that is enjoyed for its own sake" (Evans & McCandless, 1978, p. 110). It is significant to development for many reasons. Play, according to Jean Piaget (1962), is the way the child learns about his or her environment because its interactive nature allows for construction of knowledge. Vygotsky (1978) and others (Berk & Winsler, 1995; Scarlett et al., 2004) describe play to be an imaginary situation governed by social rules.

Play contributes to development in that it enables the child to separate thought from actions and objects. It also enables the child to move from impulsive activity to planned goals and self-regulation (instead of taking a desired toy, the child asks permission to play with it). Anna Freud (1968) viewed play as an acceptable way to express emotions and impulses. Groos (1901) described play as a way for children to practice skills necessary for adult life, such as working with others, cooperating, negotiating rules, and so on. According to Elkind (2001), it best sets the stage for academic learning. For example, imaginative play enhances children's language development; exploring properties of objects stimulates their curiosity about science; games are a precursor to developing math skills. By observing a child's play, therapists and educators can learn what the child feels and understands.

Years ago, in a classic study based on observations of nursery school children at "free play," Mildred Parten (1932) examined developmental changes in their social play according to type of social interaction: solitary, onlooker, parallel, associative, and cooperative.

- **Solitary.** The child plays alone and independently. The child seems to concentrate on the activity rather than on other children who may be nearby. Solitary play is typical of infant/toddlers.
- **Onlooker.** The child watches other children playing. Conversations with the others may be initiated. Though there is no actual engagement in the play being observed, the child is definitely involved as a spectator. Two-year-olds engage in a considerable amount of onlooker play.

- **Parallel.** The child plays alone, but with toys like those that other children are using, or plays in a manner that mimics the behavior of playing children. Parallel play is common among 2- and 3-year-olds, but diminishes as the child gets older.
- **Associative.** Social interaction and communication are involved in associative play, but with little or no organization. Children engage in play activities similar to those of other children; however, they appear to be more interested in being associated with each other than in the tasks at hand. Associative play is common among 3- and particularly among 4-year-olds.
- **Cooperative.** Social interaction in a group characterizes cooperative play. The activity is organized, and the group has a purpose—for example, a group building a fort together, a group playing "store," or a game of baseball. Cooperative play is the prototype for the games of middle childhood. Cooperative play begins to be exhibited by 4- to 5-year-olds.

An example of parallel play.

Cengage Learning

Contemporary research shows that these play forms emerge in the order suggested by Parten, but earlier forms may coexist with later forms, rather than being replaced by them (Howes & Matheson, 1992). However, the complexity of the form does change with age (Rubin & Coplan, 1992). Children will combine *type of activity* with *type of social interaction* (what Parten classified as "stage of play"). For example, when children engage in the activity of pretending, they may do it solitarily or cooperatively (Hughes, 2010).

Brian Sutton-Smith (1971) categorized play by type of activity: imitative, exploratory, testing, and model building.

- **Imitative play.** During the first year of life, the baby imitates the parent. During the second year of life, the child can put together parts of acts already imitated or observed in new combinations. In the third year, children imitate whole roles, such as mother or father. Most of this early imitative play consists of imitation of the important and powerful people in children's lives. Between 4 and 6, imitative social play tends to be governed by one player acting as a central person and the others acting in satellite roles, by players taking turns and alternating the roles, or by all the players doing much the same thing at the same time.
- **Exploratory play.** In the first year, the child explores—touches, tastes, and manipulates. In the second year, the child also empties, fills, inserts, puts in and out, pulls, stacks, and rolls. In the third year, the child arranges, heaps, combines, transfers, sorts, and spreads. Novel manipulations are a delight to the child and can be manipulations of objects or of words.
- **Testing play.** In many types of play, what children are actually doing is testing themselves. During the second year, children test their motor skills. They pull wagons, lift objects, climb, run, and jump. As children get older, they test themselves in games. They compete with others to measure their skills, both physical and intellectual. They also test their emotions, such as fear and anger.
- **Model-building play.** About age 4, model-building play becomes explicit, when blocks are organized into buildings, trucks into highway traffic, dishes into tea parties. Children begin to put elements of their experiences together in unique ways.

As can be seen, children's play becomes more complex and interactive with age. The increasingly social nature of play requires a combination of physical/motor skills, interpersonal skills, and cognitive skills. Through play, children discover their capacities. They explore and test their physical and mental abilities against their own standards and in comparison to others. Children often issue a challenge just to see if they can make their bodies and minds do what they want them to: "I bet I can climb to the top of that tree"; "I can figure out that puzzle in five minutes!"

Young children often engage in *rough-and-tumble play*. This type of play involves fighting, wrestling, and/or chasing. It is viewed more as "mock" aggression than "real" aggression (Hughes, 2010). Children in many cultures exhibit it, as do young animals. Thus, it may have evolutionary survival roots to develop protective skills in the young.

A very common type of *pretend play* among young children is "superhero/heroine play" (Kostelnik, Whiren, & Stein, 1986). Superheroes and heroines emerged in radio, comics, movies, and television. Some examples are Buck Rogers (1920s), Superman and Batman (1930s), Wonder Woman (1940s), Captain Video (1950s), the Hulk (1960s), Luke Skywalker and Princess Leia (1970s), HeMan (1980s), Ninja Turtles and Power Rangers (1990s), and Spiderman and Powerpuff Girls (2000s). Some super heroes/heroines are classic, as evidenced by the popular 2010 Halloween costumes: Batman, Cat Woman, Spiderman, Wonder Woman, Superman, and Supergirl. What super characters have in common is that they possess powers children wish they themselves had: They are good, strong, can fly, swim under water, change the shape of their bodies, and overcome all obstacles they may encounter. In other words, they are in control—no one tells them what to do, they know what is right, and they have respect and approval from others. Unfortunately, in this kind of play, some children exploit being in control by intimidating others and, therefore, cause hostile and hurt feelings.

Superhero/heroine play allows children to experience power and prestige unavailable to them in their daily lives. It also provides them with concrete models whose behavior is easy to emulate, unlike real-life models, whose behavior is often too ambiguous or complex for children to figure out. Finally, it gives children a chance to experience concretely abstract values such as honor, justice, courage, honesty, and mercy. Some preschools ban superhero/heroine play because it usually involves aggression, but others use it to enable children to be creative rather than imitative, such as "How would Spiderman fix that broken chair?" (Levin, 1998).

Do babies play?

Infant/Toddler Peer Activities

Peer groups emerge early in the child's life, the time varying according to the family situation, including attachment and play patterns, the availability of age-mates, and the temperament and social competence of the child (Ladd, 2005; Parke, 1990).

Observations of babies in institutions have shown that even at 2 months babies are oriented toward the movements of a baby in an adjoining crib (Bridges, 1933). Between 6 and 8 months, babies look at each other and sometimes touch each other; between 9 and 13 months, they sometimes fight, mainly over toys (Hay, Caplan, & Nash, 2009). During the second year, toddlers interact positively with peers, once conflicts over toys have been resolved (Hughes, 2010). They imitate each other (Asendorpf & Baudoniere, 1993) and show responsiveness (Howes, 1988, 2009).

Do preschoolers have friends?

Early Childhood Peer Activities

From age 2 to age 5, peer interaction increases in frequency and becomes more complex (Rubin, Bukowski, & Parker, 2006). Sometime about age 3 or 4, children begin to enjoy playing in groups—at first usually on an informal and transitory basis (Howes, 1988, 2009; Coplan & Arbeau, 2009). Young children, however, are limited in their friends. Playmates come from the immediate neighborhood—or from school, if parents are willing to chauffeur or have friends over.

Successful social relationships depend on the ability of one person to take the point of view of another, the ability to empathize, and the ability to communicate. Generally, children under 3 not only cannot take another's point of view or empathize, they also lack the skills for effective two-way communication. Even though some children under age 3 do

IN PRACTICE

Play in Peril

According to results of several studies commissioned by the Alliance for Childhood (Miller & Almon, 2009), children in all-day kindergartens were found to spend four to six times as much time being instructed, tested, or prepared for tests (about two to three hours per day) as in free play or "choice time" (30 minutes or less). See Figure 8.3. Classic play materials like blocks, sand and water tables, and props for dramatic play have largely disappeared.

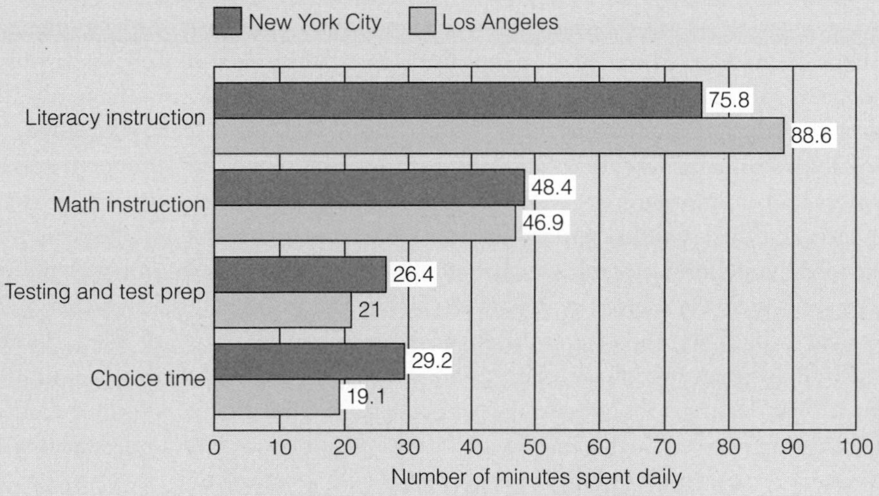

FIGURE 8.3 Daily Kindergarten Schedule in Two Cities

Source: E. Miller and J. Almon. (2009). *Crisis in the kindergarten: Why children need play in school.* Alliance for Childhood (http://www.allianceforchildhood.org).

The following are some of the Alliance's recommendations:

1. Restore child-initiated play and experiential learning with the active support of teachers to their rightful place at the heart of kindergarten education.
   - Provide time and space for play to kindergartners every school day, both indoors and during recess.
   - Make room in kindergarten for all types of play that contribute to children's development, including make-believe, sensory, language, construction, large- and small-motor, and mastery play.
2. Reassess kindergarten standards to ensure that they promote developmentally appropriate practices, and eliminate those that do not.
   - Replace one-size-fits-all kindergarten standards with flexible guidelines based on well-grounded knowledge of children's cognitive, social, emotional, physical, and creative development.
   - Change developmentally inappropriate practices that cause normal child behavior and learning patterns to be wrongly labeled as misbehavior, attention disorders, or learning disabilities.
3. Use alternatives to standardized assessments in kindergarten, such as teacher observations and authentic assessment of children's work.
4. Give teachers of young children quality preparation that emphasizes the full development of the child and the importance of play, nurtures children's innate love of learning, and supports teachers' own capacities for creativity, autonomy, and integrity.
   - Give teachers professional development, mentoring, and other support in learning how to encourage and support play, especially with children who have had limited opportunity to engage in creative play or who have poor self-regulation skills.
   - Help teachers communicate with parents about the importance of play and ways to support it at home and in the community.

exhibit some prosocial behaviors, such as empathy, they also exhibit some antisocial behaviors, such as selfishness and aggressiveness. According to Dunn (1988, 2004), children begin to exhibit social understanding in the family setting by 18 months; then they must have experiences with peers to implement their understanding of social situations effectively.

Developmental advances in cognition and language enable preschoolers to engage in increasingly complex social interactions. They participate in more cooperative ventures, but they also exhibit more aggression. They direct more speech to their peers as well (Rubin, Bukowski, & Parker, 2006).

What do school-agers do informally with their peers?

Middle Childhood/Preadolescent Peer Activities

The middle years (ages 6–12) represent a change in the proportion of social interaction involving peers; approximately 10 percent of the social interaction for 2-year-olds involves peers, whereas for 6- to 12-year olds it is more than 30 percent. The remainder is spent with siblings, parents, and other adults (Rubin, Bukowski, & Parker, 2006). The settings of peer interaction also change during the middle years, from supervised (home and preschool) to more unsupervised (neighborhood). The increased social interaction with peers and the expanded settings for peer group activities in the middle years are accompanied by the formation of informal groups. *Informal* groups are initiated and overseen by youngsters themselves, as opposed to *formal* groups (to be discussed later), which are organized by adults and occur in adult-supervised settings (Brown & Dietz, 2009).

As children reach school age, they spend some of their time hanging around informally, talking, teasing, "roughhousing," and bike riding, but they often move spontaneously into group games. Such games involve the development of skill, understanding, and acceptance of rules, and the ability to cooperate as well as compete.

Games and Development

As children's physical and mental capacities and interests mature, the quality of their games changes; they tend to reflect the culture, and they are apt to be more gender-specific (Hughes, 2010; Scarlett et al., 2004). For girls, there are jump rope, hopscotch, jacks, dolls, and playing house or school. Boys play baseball, football, cars, trains, cops and robbers, or spacemen. According to Sutton-Smith (1972), games involving verbal and rhythmic content, such as guessing games, have traditionally been played predominantly by girls, whereas physically active games and organized sports have traditionally been played mostly by boys. Chasing and teasing games have been played by both genders. Title IX of the Education Code, passed in 1972, which prohibited sex discrimination in school activities, has enabled girls to have more opportunities to play organized sports.

- **Cognitive influence.** Game patterns change with cognitive development, as children become more capable of handling complex rules and strategies. According to classic studies by Sutton-Smith (1972), children ages 6 to 9 enjoy simple games with dramatic content (cops and robbers). Older children like games requiring strategy, such as checkers or chess, as well as organized team sports.
- **Psychological influence.** Games also change with children's psychological development. For example, their self-concepts change. Sutton-Smith (1972) points out that in younger children's games, such as Simon Says or Giant Steps, the person who is "It," operating from a home base, is safe and has power to control the moves of the others. The structure of these games provides a nonthreatening opportunity for children to venture into a leadership role. From about age 10 on, the games enjoyed involve a central figure who is vulnerable to attack by others who seek the leadership role (King of the Castle). Older children also enjoy competitive games, in which one wins and one is defeated, because these types of games offer the experience of competence.
- **Sociocultural influence.** Children's games reflect the culture in which they live. For example, according to Parker (1984), competitive games, such as soccer, basketball, or football, offer practice in territorial invasion. Card games offer practice in bluffing

and calculating odds. All games involve memory, manipulation, and strategizing. Thus, games offer opportunities for children to practice skills they will need in adult life (Hughes, 2010).

Today, children generally spend less time in spontaneously organized play (stick-ball, hide-and-seek, marbles, jacks) than they did a generation ago because children can buy many prepared board games with printed instructions and rules, as well as computer, digital, and video games. The sandlot neighborhood versions of baseball and football have given way, for many children, to organized sports supervised by adults, such as Little League and AYSO, that come with rule books and procedures. One reason is safety; parents fear letting their children play unsupervised because of traffic, crime, and kidnapping issues. Another reason is to provide structured time after school, especially when both parents are employed. Adult–peer group linkages are discussed later in more detail. Although children gain many physical, cognitive, and social skills from adult-organized play, they are not getting many opportunities to experience making and revising their own rules and enforcing them with their peers.

In recent years, girls' access and participation in sports has increased.

John Neubauer/PhotoEdit

Media technology enables many preadolescents to spend time connecting with peers via cell phones and computers—talking, texting, and sharing information on social networking sites.

Adolescent Peer Activities

How do adolescents "hang out"?

Adolescents like to "hang out"—talk, watch TV, listen to music, play video games, be seen, see who else is "hanging" with whom, wait for something to happen (/Steinberg, 2010). In early adolescence, most activities occur with same-sex peers, whereas in later adolescence, activities that attract and include the opposite sex are favored, such as parties, sporting events, and concerts. Adolescents, when not engaged in organized school, sports, or community activities, spend a lot of time on their appearance—clothing, makeup, jewelry, body art—and connecting with friends via cell phones and computers. According to Roberts and Foehr (2004), the average 11- to 14-year-old spends more time with media than in any other waking activity. Media influences will be discussed in greater detail in Chapter 9.

Peer Group Interaction

Why is peer group interaction easy for some children and difficult for others?

The relationships children form when interacting with peers, as well as why some children are successful in making friends, vary based on a variety of factors, such as ability to make friends and acceptance, neglect, or rejection by the group.

Development of Friendship

How do children make friends?

Like other activities children engage in as they develop, their social relationships and friendships also become more complex. With age, friendships become more distinctive, longer-lasting, and closer. They encompass acquaintances, "just friends," "good friends," and "best/close friends" (Berndt & McCandless, 2009).

Howes (1988, 2009) studied the social interaction and friendship formations of young children in a child-care setting. Although young children's social competence is limited by their cognitive development, apparently early experience with peers enhances interaction skills. She found that 13- to 24-month-old toddlers differentiated friends among available playmates at their child-care center. These friendships were marked by emotional responsiveness (happiness in seeing each other or comforting in times of stress). Children 25 to 36 months were able to distinguish between the emotional and play components of friendship by approaching different peers when in need of comfort and when wanting to run or wrestle.

Selman and Selman (1979) interviewed more than 250 individuals between the ages of 3 and 45 to get a developmental perspective on friendship patterns. They delineated the following five stages: (1) momentary playmateship (early childhood, to 4 years); (2) one-way assistance (early to middle childhood, 4–9 years); (3) two-way, fair-weather cooperation (middle childhood, 6–12 years); (4) intimate, mutually shared relationships (middle childhood to adolescence, 9–15 years); and (5) autonomous interdependent friendships (adolescence to adulthood, 12 years on).

These preschool girls are enjoying each other while they share a meal.

Photo courtesy of Michael Berns

Early Childhood

Most children under age 4 and some older ones are in the first stage—*momentary playmateship*. They are unable to consider the viewpoint of another person and can think only about what they want from the friendship. Friends are defined by how close they live ("He's my friend; he lives next door") or by their material possessions ("She's my friend; she has a dollhouse and a swing set").

Early to Middle Childhood

The second stage is *one-way assistance*. From about age 4 until about age 9, children are more capable of telling the difference between their own perspectives and those of others. However, friendship is based on whether or not someone does what the child wants that person to do ("He's not my friend anymore; he didn't want to play cars"). Youniss and Volpe (1978), in a study of the friendships of children between 6 and 14, found that the 6- and 7-year-olds thought of friendship in terms of playing together and sharing material goods ("She plays dress-up with me"; "She always shares her candy with me").

Middle Childhood

In the third stage—*two-way, fair-weather cooperation*—children 6 to 12 acknowledge that friendship involves give-and-take. However, they see friendship as mutually serving individual interests rather than mutually cooperating toward a common interest ("We are friends; we do things for each other"). Youniss and Volpe (1978) found that 9- and 10-year-olds regard friends as those who share with one another ("Someone who plays with you when you don't have anyone else to play with"). At this age, children emphasize similarities between friends, as well as equalities and reciprocities ("We all like to collect baseball cards. We trade them and give doubles to our friends who are missing those. No one brags"). Children of this age are beginning to recognize that friendship is based on getting along—sharing interests, ideas, and feelings.

> **TeachSource Video Activity**
>
> Go to the Education CourseMate website to watch the video entitled "5–11 Years: Peer Acceptance in Middle Childhood." What feelings did you have and what behavior did you engage in during this age about being accepted and having friends?

Middle Childhood to Adolescence

The fourth stage is one of *intimate, mutually shared relationships*. Children between 9 and 15 can view a friendship as an entity in itself. It is an ongoing, committed relationship that incorporates more than just doing things for each other; it tends to be treasured for its own sake and may involve possessiveness and jealousy ("She is my best friend. How can she go to the movies with Susan?"). Youniss and Volpe (1978) report that the 12- and 13-year-olds in their study carried the earlier principles of equality and reciprocity further ("If someone picks on me, my friend helps me. My friend does not leave me to go off with some other kids").

Adolescence to Adulthood

Finally, there is the fifth stage of *autonomous interdependent friendships*. About age 12, children are capable of respecting their friends' needs for both dependency and autonomy ("We like to do most things together and we talk about our problems, but sometimes Jason just likes to be by himself. I don't mind").

Are there gender differences in friendships? Generally, girls refer to a best friend as someone you can have an intimate conversation with and who is "faithful" more than do boys; boys refer more to the companionship nature of best friends and the sharing of activities (Lever, 1978; Maccoby, 1990; Rose & Smith, 2009).

Acceptance/Neglect/Rejection by Peers

Who is accepted by the group and why?

The significance of being accepted, neglected, or rejected by peers came to the attention of the media in 1999 when two rejected adolescents shot 12 students and a teacher at the school they attended in Colorado, as we discussed earlier. Apparently the athletes who repeatedly teased them were the targets for retaliation. Which children are readily accepted by the group? According to several studies (Asher & McDonald, 2009; Rubin, Bukowski, & Parker, 2006), a child's acceptance by peers and successful interactions with them depend on a willingness to cooperate and interact positively with other children. Children who are popular with their peers tend to be healthy and vigorous, capable of initiative, and well poised. They are also adaptable and conforming, as well as dependable, affectionate, and considerate.

Certain physical and intellectual factors can also affect a child's popularity. Studies have shown that, on average, children who are physically attractive are more popular than those who are not (Adams & Crane, 1980; Adler & Adler, 1998; Ritts, Patterson, & Tubbs, 1992). A study of 6- to 10-year-old boys (Hartup, 1983) revealed that those with muscular physiques were more popular than those who were skinny or plump; this is consistent with findings that athletic ability is related to popularity (Adler & Alder, 1998; Coleman, 1961). Children who are more intelligent have been found to be more popular than those who are less intelligent (Berndt, 1983; Rubin, Bukowski, & Parker, 2006). Other studies have shown that the ability to use language and communicate ideas effectively helps in peer acceptance (Gottman, Gonso, & Rasmussen, 1975; Kemple, 1991). In general, popular children approach others in a friendly manner, respond appropriately to communications, interpret emotional states correctly, and are generous with praise and approval. See Table 8.1 for a summary of characteristics of children who are accepted, versus those who are neglected or rejected, by their peers.

Table 8.1 Summary of Characteristics of Children Accepted/Neglected/Rejected by Peers

Accepted	Neglected/Rejected
Cooperative	Shy
Positive in interactions	Withdrawn
Capable of initiating interaction	Dishonest
Adaptable and conforming	Unsporting attitude when losing
Understands emotional expressions	Incapable of initiating interaction
Shows concern for others	Socially unskilled
Able to communicate effectively	Unable to interpret others' emotional states
Happy	Unable to communicate easily
Dependable	Whiny
Affectionate	Disruptive
Considerate	Miserly with praise
Well-poised	Bossy
Generous with praise	Aggressive
Intelligent	"Different" physically, behaviorally, academically
Friendly	Negative social reputation
Self-confident (not conceited)	
Physically attractive	
Athletic ability	
Prosocial behavior	
Positive social reputation	

Family interaction patterns play a role in children's successful integration into the group (Hartup, 1996; Ross & Howe, 2009). In the family, children learn to express and interpret various emotions such as pleasure, displeasure, attachment, and distancing. Children also learn to respond to such emotional expressions and to regulate their behavior according to family requirements. Thus social competence, which leads to peer acceptance, begins in the family.

Which children are neglected or rejected by the group?

The rise and fall of children's likes and dislikes causes almost every school-age child to feel neglected or rejected at some point by other children. The child not asked to play, not chosen to be on the team, not invited to the party, or excluded from the club feels that a crucial part of his or her world has been shattered. Lack of acceptance by the peer group early on is linked to later maladjustment (Ladd, 2005).

The reason a child is neglected or rejected may be shyness, lack of social skills, antisocial behavior, or prejudice on the part of the group. Children who do not know how to initiate a friendship, who are withdrawn, who misinterpret others' emotional states, who have difficulty communicating, who are bossy, who are disruptive in class, and/or who rarely praise their peers are not readily accepted by the group. Also, children who are poor losers, who cheat or whine, and who are aggressive are not welcome in most children's groups. Antisocial behavior is the most consistent correlate of peer rejection (Asher & McDonald, 2009; Coie & Cillesen, 1993; Coie, Dodge, & Kupersmidt, 1990). Research on excluded childhood groups shows that certain categories, such as ethnic or racial, and those with stigmas, such as obese or disabled, are more likely to be rejected by peer groups (Killen, Rutland, & Jampol, 2009). For example, *Blubber*, by Judy Blume (1974), a classic story, is about an overweight girl who is the brunt of her fifth-grade classmates' teasing and scapegoating: "She won't need a coat this winter; she's got her blubber to keep her warm."

Sometimes children are rejected for reasons they cannot change or even understand. They may be teased and ostracized from the group because they are different physically (weight, height, skin color); behaviorally (accent, speech impediment, style of dress, religious preference); academically (learning disabled, gifted); or even in their names (Killen, Rutland, & Jampol, 2009; Langlois, 1986; Sandstrom & Coie, 1999).

IN CONTEXT

The *Los Angeles Times* published this story in 1982.

A 9-year-old boy named Alfonse wrote a letter to Senator Alfonse D'Amato (R-NY), asking him how he got his name. The boy couldn't ask his father why he was named Alfonse, because his father had died. He wrote that he hated his name because the kids at school joked about it. D'Amato wrote back that the name Alfonse means "prepared for battle," and when you're young, "you'd better be." D'Amato also wrote that when he asked his father why he was named Alfonse, his father replied, "Son, your Uncle Alfonse was a very wealthy man, and that's how we got the down payment on the house." The senator recommended that young Alfonse tell his friends to call him Al.

Family problems can have damaging effects on children's peer relations (Baker, Barthelemy, & Kurdek, 1993; Ladd, 2005; Ross & Howe, 2009). For example, children whose parents are getting a divorce may act out feelings of anger and fear at school, eliciting rejection from peers in the process. Children who have a parent who is an alcoholic may be reluctant to bring friends home and may avoid making close friends out of embarrassment. Likewise, children who are abused, children of homosexual parents, or children whose parents have a disability or health impairment may isolate themselves to avoid judgment by others.

sociometry techniques used to measure patterns of acceptance, neglect, and rejection among members of a group

How can children who are neglected or rejected by peers be helped?

Peer Sociotherapy

Techniques known collectively as **sociometry** have been developed to measure patterns of acceptance, neglect, and rejection among members of a group. Sociometry was originally used in school classrooms but is now widely used in other settings, such as recreational, work, and prison environments. Contemporary researchers typically use sociometry to identify the extent to which children prefer to be with certain peers (Cillesen, 2009; Parkhurst & Asher, 1992).

A sociometric rating is easy to conduct; it involves asking children questions anonymously about each other and tabulating the results. For example: Who is your best friend? With whom would you prefer and not prefer to work on a project? With whom would you share a secret? Preschoolers can be shown photographs of classmates and asked with whom they like and dislike playing. Children with the most "liked" votes are popular; those with the most "disliked" responses are neglected or rejected.

Sociometric results can help adults facilitate the inclusion of neglected or rejected children into the group. By careful observations, adults can assess where the neglected or rejected child needs intervention (Kemple, 1991)—*social* (Does the child cooperate? share? boast?); *emotional* (Does the child interpret others' emotions correctly? empathize?); *language* (Does the child make relevant responses to peers' communications? communicate desires clearly?); or *physical* (Does the child resort to aggression to resolve conflicts?). Adults can then choose appropriate intervention strategies or sociotherapy.

Selman and Selman's (1979) developmental stages of friendship have been used in peer **sociotherapy**, an intervention to help children who have trouble making and keeping friends learn to relate to others. By assessing their levels of social relationships with others, a therapist or teacher can sometimes help children to move on to the next developmental level.

sociotherapy an intervention to help children who have trouble making and keeping friends learn to relate to others

Children who have difficulty making friends can be helped by giving them a chance to play with younger children. Some researchers (Bullock, 1992; Howes, 1988, 2009) have found that socially withdrawn preschoolers become more sociable after they have had a chance to play, one-on-one, with children one to two years younger than themselves during play sessions. The researchers conclude that being with younger children gives socially withdrawn children a chance to be assertive in initiating and directing activity. Once they experience success with younger children, they are better able to interact with children their own age.

Children who have difficulty reading other children's social cues may benefit by watching others who interact successfully. This can be done in real situations with an adult coach, watched on video, or performed by puppets (Bullock, 1992).

Also, having a friend in a new situation, such as school, or in a stressful situation, such as divorce, helps the child cope and better adjust to what is going on (Ladd, 1990, 2005). This is another reason why it is important to enable children to make friends.

In order to help children who are not readily accepted by their peers get along better, Oden and Asher (1977) identified four categories of social skills, based on the research on popularity: *participation* (playing with others, paying attention); *communication* (talking and listening); *cooperation* (taking turns, sharing); and *validation/support* (offering encouragement or help).

A group of unpopular school-age children were coached on these specific skills. The coaching sessions involved demonstration (instruction and role modeling), discussion (explanation and feedback), and shaping by reinforcing desired behavior (behavior modification). A year later, the group of unpopular children who were coached showed more sociability and acceptance by peers than the control group of unpopular children who were not coached. Coaching strategies have been used successfully with preschool as well as school-age children (Mize & Ladd, 1990).

Another study (Sandstrom & Coie, 1999) found that elementary school children who were initially rejected could improve their status with peers by participating in extracurricular activities and by having their parents monitor their social interactions (arranging for play with cooperative peers, intervening in conflicts). See the In Practice box for suggestions on how to improve children's social skills.

IN PRACTICE

Improving Children's Social Skills

The following are some guidelines that teachers and parents can use in monitoring children's interactions to improve their social skills (Asher, 1982; Bullock, 1992).

Model

- Observe how others interact positively.
- Imitate behaviors and communications that were successful in promoting friendship.

Participate

- Get involved with others.
- Get started on an activity, a project, or a game.
- Pay attention to the activity.
- Try to do your best.
- Help someone who is younger.

Cooperate

- Take turns.
- Share the game, materials, or props.
- Make suggestions if there's a problem.
- If there is disagreement about the rules, work out a mutually agreeable alternative.

Communicate

- Talk with others.
- Say things about the activity or about yourself.
- Ask a question about the activity.
- Ask a question about the other person.
- Listen when the other person talks.
- Look at the other person to see how he or she is doing.

Validate and Support

- Give some attention to the other person.
- Say something nice when the other person does well.
- Smile.
- Have fun.
- Offer help or suggestions when needed.

What social mechanisms establish order and control within the peer group?

Peer Group Dynamics and Social Hierarchies

The peer group is a microsystem with dynamic roles and relationships affecting its participants. Unlike the microsystems of family, school, and community, the peer group is generally unencumbered by adult guidance. The peer group uses informal social mechanisms to develop norms, statuses, alliances, consequences, and feelings about self (Thompson, Cohen, & Grace, 2002). These social mechanisms are illustrated in the box "Peers, Prestige, Power, and Persuasion."

How does one become part of the "in" group and gain status within it?

Inclusion and Exclusion

Adler and Adler (1998), who studied groups of boys and girls ages 8 to 12 (tweens) in a predominantly white, middle-class community for eight years, found dynamics in peer cliques to include techniques of *inclusion* (recruitment of new members, treatment of "wannabes," friendship realignment, ingratiation) and *exclusion* (out-group subjugation, in-group subjugation, compliance, stigmatization, expulsion).

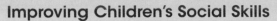

Wiseman (2009), author of *Queen Bees and Wannabes*, reports that tween girls' experiences in cliques impact their teen years, future relationships, and overall success. Clique dynamics, which include the different roles girls play in and outside of cliques—Queen Bees, Targets, and Bystanders—define how they and others are treated. Self-confidence can easily be undermined. Inclusionary and exclusionary techniques engaged in by the clique, girls' power plays—from fake apologies to fights over IM and text messages—as well as how they handle their conflicts over boys are very influential in shaping their behavior as adults. Tweens are influenced not only by the "goings-on" in the real world, but by the virtual one as well. Social networking and texting enable the rapid spread of gossip, making clique inclusion, status, and exclusion very transitory.

This child is being teased by the group leader.

Jacky Chapman/PhotoLibrary

Clique Inclusionary Techniques

Recruitment of a new member into a clique is usually by invitation; if a member meets and likes someone, that individual is afforded "probationary" status until the other members agree to include him or her (Adler & Adler, 1998; Wiseman, 2002). "Wannabes" sometimes gain entry by doing nice things for members of the clique or by doing something to gain their respect, such as helping the school team win. The hierarchical structure within the clique, with shifts in status and power, causes friendship loyalties to be compromised.

Higher-status members often co-opt lower-status members to maintain their popularity. Lower-status members might abandon their lower-status friends in order to gain favor with a higher-status member, thereby moving up the social hierarchy. Ingratiation, or currying favors with clique members, can be directed both upward, toward peers of higher status (for example, adulation), and downward, toward peers of lower status (for example, domination).

Clique Exclusionary Techniques

Out-group subjugation, such as teasing, picking on, and being mean to those outside the clique, serve to solidify the cohesiveness of the group and assure the strength of the group's position with other groups (Adler & Adler, 1998; Wiseman, 2002). In-group subjugation occurs when high-level insiders harass or ridicule low-level insiders for dominance. Lower-status members then need to comply with leaders' or high-status members' wishes in order to gain favor. Stigmatization, such as branding a member as a tattletale, a cheat, or a crybaby, is used to disempower a clique member who falls into disfavor. Expulsion, or being cast out of the group permanently, occurs when a member engages in a serious infraction of the group's rules or stands up for his or her rights against the dominant leaders.

TeachSource Video Activity

Go to the Education CourseMate website to watch the video entitled "12–18 Years: Cliques, Crowds, and Conformity in Adolescence." What were your experiences like in middle and high school regarding cliques?

Bullies/Victims

An extreme example of the dynamics and social hierarchies in peer groups is bullying. **Bullying** is aggressive behavior intended to cause harm or distress. It occurs repeatedly over time in an unbalanced relationship of power or strength. It can occur in many forms, including physical violence, teasing and name-calling, intimidation, and social exclusion (APA, 2005; Salmivalli & Peets, 2009).

Who gets "picked on," by whom, and why?

bullying aggressive behavior intended to cause harm or distress; it occurs repeatedly over time in an unbalanced relationship of power or strength

Dan Olweus (1993) has extensively studied bullies and their victims at school. He defines *bullying*, or victimization, as being "exposed, repeatedly and over time, to negative actions on the part of one or more other students." Negative actions, or harassment, include threats, taunts, teasing, name-calling, and making faces or dirty gestures, as well as hitting, kicking, pinching, and physically restraining another.

Bullying that occurs online is known as "cyberbullying." Preteens and teens who subscribe to websites such as MySpace, Facebook, or YouTube, and who socialize online through chat rooms, can send hurtful e-mails, instant messages, photos, and video clips to, or about, victims. For some targeted young people, Internet harassment can be devastating, especially since there is virtually no limit to the number of recipients such rumors can reach (Patchin & Hinduja, 2006). Some examples of malicious rumors that appeared anonymously on the

IN PRACTICE

Peers, Prestige, Power, and Persuasion

William Golding's classic novel *Lord of the Flies* (1954) is about a group of English schoolboys, ranging in age from 6 to 12, who are marooned on a desert island when their plane crashes. The adults are killed, and the youngsters, despairing of rescue, set out to build their own society. At first, the older boys try to draw on their memory of English society, but they do not remember enough, and there are no elders they can turn to for guidance. They establish their own system of socialization, first by investing authority in a leader chosen on the basis of appearance and perceived power (he possesses a conch shell) and then by setting up rituals to provide order amid the chaos. In the beginning, the boys try to cooperate, making shelters, gathering food, and keeping signal fires going. Ralph takes on the leadership role, trying to impose order by delegating responsibilities for survival chores. Piggy, Ralph's spectacled, chubby friend, dispenses logic and rationale for the necessary decisions. His thick spectacles come in handy for lighting fires. However, disagreements and conflict soon give way to savagery. The other boys would rather play, swim, or hunt the island's wild pig population than plan for survival. Soon they begin to ignore Ralph's rules, and Jack challenges them outright. Jack, the leader of his subgroup of savages, starts luring Ralph and Piggy's followers to join him. Ralph and Piggy now become the hunted, instead of the hunters, as emotion overtakes reason. Piggy, the continual reminder of adult standards of behavior, is brutally killed before the rescuers arrive. The children have forgotten how they were socialized to resolve differences appropriately, such as by negotiation, and resort to competition for status and power, using aggressive means to get them.

A parallel example of peer group dynamics is the "reality" TV series *Survivor*. A group of adult contestants are castaways on a deserted island. Each week, the survivors compete in grueling physical competitions in games as well as for resources to survive. The prize for which they are competing is to be the last one left on the island and, hence, the winner of a million dollars. What begins as fun turns into manipulation and maliciousness. Every week, the group meets with its leaders in a Tribal Council to vote one contestant off the island. Everyone must explain the rationale behind his or her vote. The ejected member must give a farewell speech, describing his or her experiences and feelings. Unlike the children in *Lord of the Flies, Survivor* adults do remember how to negotiate differences, but like the children, they engage in competition for status and power, using manipulative means to get them.

IN PRACTICE

What Can Be Done about Bullies and Their Victims?

- Awareness, supervision, and involvement by adults of children's behavior, including their e-communications (for strategies, see http://www.bnetsavvy.org)
- Interventions with bullies by parents, teachers, and peers that do not reinforce harassment
- Home and class rules with consequences, training in alternative behaviors, role playing, cooperative learning
- Interventions with victims to get them to tell adults of their harassment and enable them to get support and training to be assertive and to respond in nonreinforcing ways to threats (ignoring, humor)

Sources: Grannetti and Sagarese, 2008; Long, 2008; Olweus, 1993.

Internet included an e-mail saying a certain girl had gonorrhea and was spreading it, or a photo of a boy changing in the locker room, taken with a cell phone camera.

According to Giannetti and Sagarese (2008), because cyberbullying is a relatively new phenomenon, school and law enforcement officials are still sorting out legal issues. Most of what is done online is protected as "free speech." Internet service providers (ISPs) contend they are merely conduits for individuals to post information, so they generally won't get involved in using their technology to trace the perpetrator unless it is a legal matter. Since most cyberbullying originates on home computers or personal consoles, school administrators resist getting involved. Hiding behind the anonymity of the computer emboldens bullies; kids feel free to say things they would not likely say face-to-face, and they believe they won't get caught.

Bullies tend to have the following characteristics (Olweus, 1993):

- Domination needs—need to feel powerful, superior
- Impulsive, low frustration tolerance, easily angered
- Usually physically stronger than peers
- Difficulty adhering to rules
- Generally oppositional, defiant, aggressive
- Show little empathy
- A relatively positive self-concept
- Engage in antisocial behavior

Victims tend to have the following characteristics (Olweus, 1993):

- Usually physically weaker than peers
- Poor physical coordination
- Exhibit fear of being hurt or hurting themselves
- Cautious, sensitive, quiet, passive, submissive, shy
- Anxious, insecure, unhappy
- A relatively negative self-concept
- Difficulty asserting themselves
- Often relate better to adults than peers

Antisocial Behavior: Gangs

Why do some individuals join gangs and engage in antisocial behavior?

A **gang** is a group of people who form an allegiance for a common purpose and engage in unlawful or criminal activity (Jackson & McBride, 2000). Gangs are of concern not only because of their antisocial activities, but also because of their increase (Goldstein, 1991; National Gang Center [NGC], 2009). Gangs usually consist of males, although there are female gangs; they are not co-ed. Gang members identify themselves through names, clothes, tattoos, slang, sign language, and graffiti. The problem of gangs is spreading throughout our society like a plague. They are present in neighborhoods and schools, affecting businesses, recreation, and education (Landre, Miller, & Porter, 1997; NGC, 2009). Gang violence has tragic consequences; gangs deal drugs, steal, hurt, and kill. Innocent bystanders are often victims (U.S. Department of Justice, 2000).

gang a group of people who form an alliance for a common purpose and engage in unlawful or criminal activity

Researchers organize the risk factors for gang membership and delinquency according to five developmental domains: individual, family, school, peer group, and community. This framework has its origins in Bronfenbrenner's bioecological model of human development (Bronfenbrenner & Morris, 2006). Indeed, research shows that risk and protective factors in these five domains function as predictors of juvenile delinquency, violence, and gang membership at different stages in social development, as affected by the timing of the respective domains of influence (NGC, 2009). Studies also show that antecedents of gang involvement begin to come into play long before youths reach a typical age for joining a gang. For the highest risk youth, a stepping-stone pattern appears to begin as early as ages 3–4 with the emergence of conduct problems, followed by elementary school failure at ages 6–12, delinquency onset by age 12, gang joining around ages 13–15, and serious, violent, and chronic delinquency onward from mid-adolescence (Howell & Egley, 2005). For more information on risk factors, prevention, and programs, go to http://www.nationalgangcenter.gov.

While sometimes peer group dynamics can result in negative or antisocial behaviors, and "hanging around with the wrong crowd" is often blamed for delinquency and substance abuse, in reality the single most consistent characteristic of delinquents is lack of support and socialization by their families (Jackson & McBride, 2000; Rutter, Giller, & Hagell, 1998). Antagonistic relationships between parents are often found in families with antisocial children (Patterson, 2002). When children do not have their needs met in their families, they often turn to their peers. There is also a relationship between peer rejection and delinquency (Bagwell et al., 2000).

Poor neighborhoods with poor-quality schools, limited recreational and employment opportunities, and adult criminal subcultures tend to be predictive of juvenile gang activity (Farrington & Loeber, 2000).

Social change, microsystems (family, school, community) under stress, and consequent lack of support for children tend to be associated with an increase in delinquency rates (Sheldon, Tracy, & Brown, 2000). Many young people lack positive adult role models. The gap between the consumerism perpetuated by the media and reality may entice young people to turn to delinquency. Personality factors may contribute to the reasons some adolescents become delinquents. It is known that those who become delinquent are more likely to be defiant, ambivalent to authority, resentful, hostile, impulsive, and lacking in self-control (Goldstein, 1991; Howell & Egley, 2005). Those who get poor grades in school, have been reported for classroom misconduct, and have trouble getting along with other children and teachers show a greater tendency to become delinquents (Ladd & LeSieur, 1995; Landre, Miller, & Porter, 1997; NGC, 2009). Thus, the peer group may be the setting in which preexisting antisocial behavior due to family factors, social change, personality characteristics, or being out of synch with the school is reinforced (Goldstein, 1991; Rubin, Bukowski, & Parker, 2006).

What is the appeal of gangs?

Gangs give members companionship, guidance, excitement, and identity (Goldstein, 1991). When a member needs something, the others come to the rescue and provide protection (Landre, Miller, & Porter, 1997). Gang members have experienced failure and alienation in their lives. They tend to live in depressed or deprived environments, which their families may be helpless to change. Because they feel they can't accomplish anything individually, gang members band together to exercise influence over their lives (Jackson & McBride, 1985).

The homes of gang-oriented children are characterized by either high permissiveness or high punitiveness (Patterson, 2002). The parents of such peer-oriented children also show less concern and affection; by such passive neglect, rather than active maltreatment, they push their children to look to peers for support (Ladd & LeSieur, 1995; NGC, 2009). Youngsters living with both biological parents are less susceptible to pressure from peers to engage in deviant behavior than youngsters living in single-parent homes or with stepfamilies. Thus, the stability of the home is an important protector against pressure toward deviant behavior (Steinberg, 1987).

For a summary of ecological forces in the formation of gangs, see Table 8.2.

Table 8.2 Ecological Forces in the Formation of Gangs

Cultural group. Gangs are usually made up of one cultural group, thereby being a source of identity and support.

Socioeconomics. Gang members usually come from poor families in densely populated areas where there is competition for resources; recently there are increasing numbers of gangs in middle-class neighborhoods.

Family structure. Gang members usually come from families with minimal adult supervision, or a family that has a gang lineage.

Belief system. Gang members believe they are victims and blame society for their problems and they are justified in protecting themselves outside of society's rules.

Source: Jackson and McBride, 2000.

Prosocial Behavior: Peer Collaboration, Tutoring, and Counseling

What positive outcomes can result from peer dynamics?

Peer group dynamics, often with the help of adults, can have positive outcomes for participants. Collaboration, tutoring, and counseling are methods encouraged by adults to enable peers to be supportive of one another. Peers who *collaborate* learn to solve problems through consensus. Peers who *tutor* learn how to analyze and synthesize information for others. Peers who *counsel* learn how to care, help, and give support to others.

Peer collaborations with different outcomes are discussed by Piaget and Vygotsky. According to Piaget (1965), when children interact, they discover that others have opinions and perspectives different from theirs. As a result, they reorganize their cognitive structures (accommodate) to fit discrepant information. Thus, Piaget believed that cognitive development was more likely to result from *conflict* with same-age peers than from interaction with older children and adults (Berk & Winsler, 1995). Vygotsky (1978), on the other hand, believed that cognitive development resulted from *collaboration* with peers. Peer conflict could only contribute to heightened understanding if the disagreement was compromised or resolved. Vygotsky emphasized the importance of mixed-age groups that provide each child opportunities to interact with more knowledgeable companions and give each child a chance to serve as a resource for others. Expert peers can serve as mentors, models, or tutors, whereas novice peers can be apprentices. Adults must guide collaborative activities, teaching social and problem-solving skills, intervening when necessary (Berk & Winsler, 1995).

Peer tutoring is exemplified by inclusion programs, in which a child with a disability is assisted, academically and/or socially, by a classmate (Vaughn, Bos, & Schumm, 1997). Peer tutoring provides a zone of proximal development (ZPD), discussed earlier, in which what one is capable of learning independently is potentially increased by participating with more capable others.

An example of peer counseling is "positive peer culture," or PPC (Vorrath & Brendtro, 1985). PPC involves a group of peers with an adult leader. It is designed to "turn around" negative youth subculture and mobilize the power of the peer group to foster positive behavior. A person is asked not whether he or she wants to *receive* help, but whether he or she is willing to *give* help. As the person becomes of value to others, his or her feelings of self-worth are enhanced (Vorrath & Brendtro, 1985). PPC is predicated on the belief that delinquent youth, who are often rebellious and strong-willed, have much to contribute when redirected. Those who have encountered difficulties in their lives are often in the best position to help others. PPC provides students with what they do not get from other socializing agents: care and a sense of responsibility—for themselves and others.

IN CONTEXT A group home for troubled girls had severe drug-abuse problems. The result of the many attempts to suppress this activity was a cold war between staff and youth. Suspicion, searches, and restriction became commonplace. That was a year ago. Now staff members no longer police students for drugs, and the climate of intrigue is gone. As a new girl enters, her peers confiscate any drugs she may have and tell her, "We don't have to use dope around here." Drug problems are dealt with openly in a helpful, matter-of-fact way. Group members state with strong conviction that when a person has good feelings about herself, she no longer needs to get high on drugs.

Mesosystem Influences on the Peer Group

How do links with groups in the community affect peer group outcomes?

Adults play a significant role in "setting the stage" for peer group experiences. Earlier, the adult role was discussed in terms of secure attachment and arranging for friends to get together in the home. The neighborhood in which a child lives influences whether the peer group has positive or negative effects (Kowaleski-Jones, 2000; Steinberg, 2010).

Neighborhoods that include parents who are involved in schools, who participate in organized activities for children (sports, arts, Scouts), and who monitor their children tend to have children who provide positive peer influences for one another. On the other hand, neighborhoods that include parents who are disengaged from school and community activities tend to have children who provide negative peer influences for one another. Thus, parents can influence whether a child's peer group experiences are positive or negative by knowing who their child's friends are and by being involved in their child's activities.

How do adult- and child-structured peer groups differ?

Adult-Structured Peer Groups

Peer groups linked to and structured by adults include team sports, clubs, Scouts, and church groups. They differ, because of their organization, from the informal peer groups (neighborhood or school groups of friends) that have been discussed so far, which are formed and maintained by the children themselves. Whereas child-structured groups are casual and informal, adult-structured groups are purposeful and formal.

Adult-structured and child-structured groups differ in their socializing influences on children (Adler & Adler, 1998). When adults organize groups, there are rules, guidelines, or suggestions about appropriate or expected behavior in an activity. Adults supply the structure through verbal instructions, praise, criticism, feedback about the activity or the child's performance, and modeling ways to perform the activity. The structuring of a setting influences the behavior that goes on within it. For example, formal groups organized by adults encourage children to play according to established rules, to be compliant, and to seek guidance as well as recognition from adults; groups organized by the children themselves encourage children to be active and assertive with peers, to take initiative, and to behave independently (Huston et al., 1986; Mahoney et al., 2005). Studies of preschool children have found that girls prefer more adult-structured groups (Carpenter, Huston, & Hart, 1986; Powlishta, Serbin, & Moller, 1993). A similar pattern of gender differences has been shown to exist for school-age children (Carpenter, 1983; Maccoby, 1990, 2000).

Groups structured by adults are also characterized by the different values that are imparted to children. Clubs may be formed at church, at school, or in the community. A church club may serve the purpose of fellowship—getting to know children of similar religious backgrounds. A school club may provide extracurricular activities for interested children—for example, computer club, chorus, or drama club. A community club may be for recreation (the Y) or for character building (Scouts). For example, the ideology of the Boy and Girl Scouts of America is to foster patriotism, reverence, leadership, and emotional development. Children are encouraged to develop self-reliance by accomplishing certain tasks to earn merit badges—for example, water safety or cooking.

How do adults affect peer group interaction?

Adult-Mediated Group Interaction

How adults mediate, or structure, the social interaction within a peer group—specifically, whether it is *competitive* or *cooperative*—influences children's behavior. To illustrate, psychologist Mustaf Sherif (1956) and his colleagues (Sherif et al., 1961) conducted a classic series of naturalistic experiments in which middle-class, white, Protestant boys, 11 years old, were recruited and sent to a camp during the summer. Within a few weeks, adult mediation brought about two sharply contrasting patterns of behavior in this sample of normal boys. The sample was divided into two separate groups (the Rattlers and the Eagles), who did not know each other. The counselors/observers were able to transform each group into a hostile, destructive, antisocial gang through various strategies, such as competitive sports in which winning was all-important and letting each group know the other group was "the enemy." Then, within a few days, the counselors/observers were able to change these groups into cooperative, constructive workers and friends who were concerned about the other members of the community. Various problems at the camp were set up to foster a cooperative spirit. For example, a water line was deliberately broken so that the two groups of boys would have to work together to fix it. Another time, the camp truck broke down on the way to town for food. The boys had to help get the engine started.

Several findings emerged from Sherif's (1956) and his colleagues' (Sherif et al., 1961) naturalistic experiments regarding peer group behavior.

- Groups tend to *stratify*, with some individuals assuming more dominant roles and others more submissive ones.
- Groups develop *norms*—standards that serve to guide and regulate individuals' actions as members of a group.
- Frustration and competition contribute to hostility between groups.
- Competition *between* groups fosters cohesiveness *within* groups.
- Intergroup hostility can often be reduced by setting up a *superordinate*, or common, goal that requires the mutual efforts of both groups. When overriding goals that are real and important for all concerned need to be achieved, then hostility between groups diminishes.

The significance of these studies of peer group dynamics is that they suggest strategies for enabling children to work together. The findings on cooperation and competition were implemented by a team of researchers at Johns Hopkins University (Johnson & Johnson, 1999; Slavin, 2006). A Team Games Tournament (TGT) was developed to see if cooperation in a competitive setting would increase academic achievement. In TGT, four or five children of varying academic ability, gender, and race are put on each team. Teams are equated on average ability level. Individuals *compete* with individuals who are members of other teams. Each person's game score is added to those of the others on the team to form a team score. Team members *cooperate* by studying as a group and helping each other prepare for the tournament. TGT has had positive effects on mathematics achievement in junior high school, language arts achievement in elementary school, and, in general, on attitudes toward subject matter and classroom procedures. Increases have occurred in class solidarity, fostering friendships among girls and boys as well as among children of differing cultural backgrounds. A sample sociometric test—a measure of acceptance or rejection by the group, discussed earlier—revealed that children who succeeded as team members were liked more than when they succeeded as individuals.

Adult Leadership Styles

What effect does adult leadership style have on group dynamics?

Groups led by adults can differ markedly according to the kind of leadership provided, as was exemplified by teachers' leadership styles in Chapter 7. Leadership style influences socialization, as illustrated by a classic series of studies (Lewin, Lippitt, & White, 1939; Lippitt & White, 1943) that distinguished three kinds of adult leadership and measured their effects on groups of 10-year-old boys. The boys were organized into clubs and worked on such activities as soap carving, mask making, and mural painting. The three kinds of leadership were categorized as follows:

- **Authoritarian.** Policies, activities, techniques, and delegation of tasks were dictated by the leader. Praise and criticism of the group members' work was subjective. ("You are good at that.") The leader did not participate actively in the group's activities.
- **Democratic (authoritative).** Policies and activities were determined by group discussion. The leader presented techniques and delegation of tasks in terms of alternatives from which the group members could choose. Praise and criticism were objective. ("Your soap carving has a lot of detailed work; it must have taken you a lot of time to do that.") The leader participated in the activities.
- **Laissez-faire (permissive).** Policies, activities, techniques, and delegation of tasks were left up to the group members. The leader supplied materials for the projects and was available for information, if requested. Comments about the group members' work were very infrequent. The leader did not participate in the group's activities.

Children working together on a task under the supervision of a democratic leader.

Cengage Learning

Because each adult in the studies rotated through the three leadership styles, differences in the group's behavior were determined to be a function of the style of leadership, rather than the leader's personality. Children in the groups with *authoritarian* leaders became either submissive or aggressive. The boys were discontented with the activities and worked less constructively when the leader left the room. They tended to be competitive with one another. Children in the groups with *democratic* leaders had high morale. The boys were involved in their group goals and were cooperative. They sustained their level of activity even when the leader left the room. Children in the groups with *laissez-faire* leaders were disorganized and frustrated. The boys made efforts to mobilize themselves as a group, but were unable to sustain their efforts.

In all three situations, the behavior of the adult set the tone for group effort (see Table 8.3). Within each situation, children got different messages about how to make decisions and work with others toward a goal.

What role do sports play in socialization?

Team Sports

Sports are organized interactions of children in competitive and/or cooperative team or individual enjoyable physical activities (Humphrey, 2003). In the United States, sports are not only a major form of recreation, but are also considered a means of achieving physical health. Sports are also regarded as a way for children to learn leadership skills, loyalty, and other desirable traits, and as valuable training in competitiveness and give-and-take relationships. Organized sports are also a vehicle for promoting the development of talent.

The American attitude toward sports is revealed by the statistics: More than 41 million U.S. children age 6 and older play competitive sports (Hilgers, 2006). This includes Little League baseball, Pop Warner football, soccer, hockey, swimming, track, and gymnastics (Poinsett, 1997). Most local youth sports organizations belong to national associations, which set guidelines for the games and the coaches.

Do all children benefit from the experience of playing sports?

According to Murphy (1999), many do not. Some children do learn a lot about themselves and their capabilities, about their potential for improvement (however modest), about the value of teamwork, about the fun of sports, and about the lifelong importance of physical fitness (Baltzell, Ginsberg, & Durant, 2006; Poinsett, 1997). Other children, however, are humiliated by their experience in organized sports. Perhaps they are being pushed to succeed by their parents; not being able to live up to their parents' expectations, they become discouraged and end up hating the sport or themselves. I remember watching many Little League games while my son was involved. It was not uncommon to hear a father yell to his son from the stands, "You dummy, how could you miss that ball? Wake up!"

Table 8.3 Socialization Effects of Leadership Styles

Adult Leadership Style	Children's Outcomes
Authoritarian	Aggressive Submissive Discontented Competitive
Democratic	High morale Cooperative Self-supporting, cohesive
Laissez-faire	Disorganized Frustrated Nonsupporting, fragmented

Thus, not every child needs organized sports to develop physical, cognitive, and psychosocial skills; not every sport is age-appropriate; and not every coach is best suited for every child. See "Children and Sports: Choices for All Ages" (Mayo Clinic, 2006; http://www.cnn.com/HEALTH/library).

IN CONTEXT When I was 11 years old, I was on a softball team. I desperately wanted to be the pitcher, but I wasn't chosen. My throwing was accurate, but it wasn't fast enough. The coach put me in center field because I was also a good fielder. I was so crushed that I almost quit. What I didn't understand then was that the team already had a good pitcher, but the shortstop made a lot of errors and the right and left fielders were daydreamers. The coach's logic was to put me in center field because I could catch and throw; and because I could also run fast, I could get the balls missed by the others. It took me quite a few games to understand that teamwork makes everyone play better because teamwork coordinates all the individual abilities. No matter how good one person on the team is, if the others are not playing well, the team can't win. I wanted to be the pitcher because I wanted to be the star. I learned that stars don't succeed without the support of the cast.

What role does the coach play in socialization?

The value a coach places on competing and winning, rather than on learning and playing, impacts children's attitudes about themselves and others, as well as about the sport. Winning can mean several things. It can mean self-improvement and a sense of accomplishment when a player's performance improves, or it can mean beating the other team. When winning is narrowed down to beating the other team, undue pressures are put on children (Baltzell, Ginsberg, & Durant, 2006; Humphrey, 2003). If children are ridiculed, belittled, or threatened when they fumble, or if the coach gives attention only to the better players, then some children are not benefiting from participating on that team. On the other hand, if the coach gives extra support to those lacking in confidence, they will benefit in more ways than just improving their athletic skills. Thus, sports training can be of benefit in developing an attitude of positive thinking and setting goals that go beyond what one currently thinks one can do. A significant factor is that coaches consider the developmental needs of children and foster an environment based on respect for effort, rather than just for winning (Murphy, 1999).

IN CONTEXT At a gymnastics competition I saw a girl fall off the bar. She was not hurt, but her confidence was shaken. Her coach told her the mistake and made her do the routine again correctly even though it would not count for points. The girl took a deep breath, focused, and completed her flip on the bar. Everyone applauded. The girl learned not to give up if perfection is not achieved on the first attempt and that effort can be as appreciated by the audience as much as the performance.

Summary

- The peer group is a microsystem in that it comprises relationships, roles, and activities. Peers are a group of equals, usually of the same age, gender, and socioeconomic status, who share the same interests.
- Peer groups are significant to human development because having a group of friends meets the needs of belonging and social interaction as well as promoting a sense of self and personal identity.
- The peer group influences the sense of self by providing opportunities for comparisons with others. It also influences personal identity by providing opportunities for independence from adults and allows children to "learn by doing."
- As children enter the middle years of childhood (ages 6 to 12 or 13), the peer group becomes increasingly important. Experiments show that children become more susceptible to the influence of peers in middle childhood

(especially around preadolescence, ages 11 to 13) and become less conforming in adolescence.

- The relative importance of adult and peer influence on children depends on parenting style, particular values, and cultural background. Children of authoritative parents are less likely to be influenced by peers than are children of authoritarian or permissive parents.
- In achieving a personal identity, a major task for the child is to balance peer group identification with personal autonomy while forging an individual role within the group.
- The socializing mechanisms that peers employ to influence one another's behavior are reinforcement (approval and acceptance), modeling, punishment (rejection and exclusion), and apprenticeship (novice learns from expert).
- Macrosystem influences on the peer group enable children to accomplish certain developmental tasks: getting along with others, developing morals and values, learning appropriate sociocultural roles (including gender roles, sex education, and sexual activity), and achieving personal independence and identity.
- Play has cognitive, social, psychological, and adaptive functions for adult life. Parten identified categories of play based on social interactions: solitary, onlooker, parallel, associative, and cooperative. Sutton-Smith identified four types of play based on activities: imitative, exploratory, testing, and model building.
- As children develop, their play and their social relationships become more complicated. Selman and Selman delineated five stages of friendship: momentary playmateship; one-way assistance; two-way, fair-weather cooperation; intimate, mutually shared relationships; and autonomous, interdependent friendships.
- Children who are readily accepted by the peer group tend to be healthy, vigorous, initiating, well-poised, adaptable, conforming, dependable, affectionate, considerate, happy, enthusiastic, concerned for others, and self-confident.
- Children who are neglected or rejected by the peer group tend to have difficulty initiating a friendship, have difficulty communicating, rarely praise their peers, and are shy, poor losers, cheaters, whiners, or aggressive. Sometimes children are rejected because they are different physically, behaviorally, in style of dress, academically, or in their names.
- Sociometry is a set of techniques to measure acceptance, neglect, and rejection among members of a group. Peer group dynamics and social hierarchies involve norms, statuses, alliances, consequences, and outcomes that are related to self-esteem.
- Peer groups can have negative effects on children. Bullies who victimize children can cause psychological as well as physical harm. The anonymity and potential breadth of cyberbullying can have devastating effects.
- Antisocial gang behavior usually occurs in the peer groups whose members lack family support and live in poor, unsupportive neighborhoods. Gangs are allegiances that engage in unlawful activities.
- Prosocial behavior in peer groups includes peer collaboration, tutoring, and counseling.
- Mesosystem influences on peer groups emerge from links with adults. Groups structured by adults differ from those structured by children in that adults provide values, rules, and suggestions.
- Groups led by adults can differ markedly according to the kind of leadership provided by the adult. Leaders are classified as authoritarian, democratic (authoritative), and laissez-faire (permissive).
- How adults mediate, or structure, the social interaction within a peer group (competitive or cooperative) influences children's behavior.

Activity

PURPOSE To understand peer influences at different ages on attitudes, values, and behavior.

1. Choose at least six children (two preschoolers, age 4–5; two elementary school children, age 7–9; and two middle school children, age 11–13). Separately ask each one the following questions, marking parents (P) or peers (pr) in the appropriate column in the chart.
2. Write a summary of about a page on which choices were most influenced by parents and which were most influenced by peers. Explain. Did you notice an age difference regarding peer influence? Explain. Did you notice a personality difference, such as being shy or outgoing, in those children who chose peers over parents or vice versa? Explain.

	Preschool	Elementary School	Middle School
1. Whom do you tell about what happened at school (your mom or dad or your friends)?			
2. Whom do you ask about which TV shows you should watch?			
3. Who has helped you decide what you want to be when you grow up?			
4. Who most often helps you decide who your friends should be?			
5. Whom do you talk to most about games or sports you would like to play?			
6. If someone hurts your feelings, whom do you talk to about it?			
7. Who suggests books to you to read (or toys to play with)?			
8. Whom do you ask about what you should wear?			
9. If something exciting happened to you, whom would you tell first?			
10. Who tells you about snack foods to try?			

Related Readings

Adler, P. A., & Adler, P. (1998). *Peer power: Preadolescent culture and identity*. New Brunswick, NJ: Rutgers University Press.

Dunn, J. (2004). *Children's friendships: The beginnings of intimacy.* Malden, MA: Blackwell.

Elkind, D. (2007). *The power of play*. Philadelphia: Da Capo Lifelong Books.

Franzese, R. J., Covey, H. C., & Menard, S. (2006). *Youth gangs* (3rd ed.) New York: Charles Thomas.

Harris, J. R. (2009). *The nurture assumption:Revised and updated.* New York: Free Press.

Humphrey, J. H. (2003). *Child development through sports.* New York: Routledge.

Kohut, M. R. (2007). *Bullies and Bullying: A complete guide for teachers and parents.* Ocala, FL: Atlantic Publishing Group.

Scarlett, W. G., Naudeau, S. C., Salonius-Pasternak, D., & Ponte, I. C. (2004). *Children's play.* Thousand Oaks, CA: Sage.

Thompson, M., Cohen, L., & Grace, C. O. (2002). *Best friends, worst enemies: Understanding the social lives of children.* New York: Ballantine Books.

Wiseman, R. (2009). *Queen bees and wannabees: Helping your daughter survive cliques, gossip, boyfriends, and the new realities of the girl world.* New York: Three River Press.

Resources

American Psychological Association—scientific and professional organization representing psychology in the United States

http://www.apa.org

Kids Sports Network—good sports . . . have good sports experiences

http://www.ksnusa.org

Office of Juvenile Justice and Delinquency Prevention—serving children, families, and communities

http://www.ojjdp.gov/

9

Cengage Learning

Ecology of the Mass Media

"The medium is the message."

—MARSHALL MCLUHAN

Learning Objectives

After completing this chapter, you will be able to:

1. Explain how mass media affect children's socialization.
2. Describe chronosystem influences on media (how new technology affects media devices, content, and usage).
3. Discuss how various macrosystem influences (politics, economics, technology) affect media use.
4. Discuss the main concerns regarding the impact of screen media (TV and movies) on children.
5. Describe mediating influences on television viewing and socialization outcomes.
6. Explain how mesosystems (community, school, family, and peer group links) affect television programming and viewing.

SOCIALIZATION SKETCHES

Francis Ford Coppola

(b. 1939)

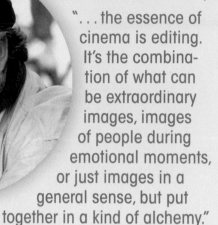

AF archive/Alamy

"... the essence of cinema is editing. It's the combination of what can be extraordinary images, images of people during emotional moments, or just images in a general sense, but put together in a kind of alchemy."

– FRANCIS FORD COPPOLA

This quote from Francis Ford Coppola, American film director, producer, and screenwriter, sets the stage for this chapter because it refers to the important role of the director in shaping the message of the particular media. A film director is a person who directs the actors and crew in the making of a film. The director controls a film's artistic and dramatic aspects, while guiding the technical crew and actors. Coppola is widely acclaimed as one of Hollywood's most influential screen directors.

This socialization sketch represents many concepts regarding media discussed in this chapter. The process of making a film involves taking an initial story idea through scriptwriting, shooting, editing, directing, and distribution to an audience. It takes place all over the world in a huge range of economic, social, and political contexts, and uses a variety of technologies and techniques.

Coppola is an individual who had to cope with a disability growing up, forcing him to discover his interests and abilities, which enabled him to later fine-tune them and enter the media field.

Francis Ford Coppola's precision in directing is illustrated in his most famous film, *The Godfather* (an epic chronicling the saga of the Corleone family), which became a massive success with both critics and public. Along with its even more acclaimed sequel (*The Godfather II*), it is one of the highest-grossing films of all time, and appears on every list of the best films ever made.

Coppola has continued to create magic in cinema, winning multiple Academy Awards for *The Godfather II*, and directing such legendary films as *The Conversation* and *Apocalypse Now*. Today, he is more productive than ever and, both by his personal example and by his generous sponsorship of young filmmakers, he has left a significant mark on the history of motion pictures.

Family

Francis Ford Coppola was born in Detroit, Michigan, to a family of Italian ancestry (his paternal grandparents were immigrants). He received his middle name in honor of Henry Ford, as he was born at the Henry Ford Hospital. His father, Carmine Coppola, was the first flautist for the Detroit Symphony Orchestra. Francis was the second of three children. The family moved to New York when Carmine got a job as first flautist for the NBC Symphony Orchestra. Francis spent the remainder of his childhood in New York.

At about age 9, Coppola contracted polio, an infectious disease, leaving him bedridden and isolated at home for about a year and a half. He was paralyzed for some of that time, so he watched TV, listened to the radio, and played with his tape recorder. This allowed him to indulge his imagination with a homemade puppet theater. He was given a copy of the Tennessee Williams' play *A Streetcar Named Desire*, which he eagerly read. This experience was instrumental in developing his interest in theater. Eager to be involved in film-craft, he turned out 8-mm features edited from home movies.

School

As a child, Coppola was a mediocre student but was very much interested in technology and engineering; his friends nicknamed him "Science." He liked inventing and building things in his basement at home. He took music lessons and became proficient on the tuba.

In high school, Coppola worked on the lighting of drama productions. He loved stories and literature, so he thought he would be a playwright. After graduating from Great Neck North High School on Long Island, he entered Hofstra University in 1955 to obtain a major in theater arts. There he won a playwriting scholarship, which furthered his interest in directing theater. This was not approved by his father, who wanted him to study engineering.

While pursuing his bachelor's degree, Coppola was elected president of the university's drama group. Under his leadership, it merged with the school's musical comedy club and they staged a new production each week. Coppola also founded the cinema workshop at Hofstra, and contributed prolifically to the campus literary magazine. He won awards for theatrical production and direction, and received a prestigious award for his outstanding contributions to the school's theater arts division.

Significant Experiences

When Coppola happened to see Soviet filmmaker Sergei Eisenstein's silent movie *Ten Days That Shook the World* (a dramatization of the October 1917 Bolshevik Revolution), he was profoundly impressed, particularly by the quality of editing in the movie. It was then Coppola decided he would go into cinema rather than theater. After graduating from college, Coppola chose to enter UCLA's graduate Film School Program.

Coppola says that the movie art form is exciting because "it combines so many other art forms." The essence of editing is putting a number of images together a certain way, "becoming something quite above and beyond what any of them are individually. I was struck, I remember, on 'Ten Days That Shook The World,' how although it was a silent film, there were sequences where you actually almost could hear the machine guns firing, because of the way it was edited. So it's a form of alchemy, of magic, that is very appealing. I think cinema, movies, and magic have always been closely associated." It's the creation of illusions and magic through technology that Coppola has succeeded in doing.

- What was your favorite movie and why?
- Have you read a book and later seen the movie? What was your reaction to the interpretation of the story and editing?
- Have you had a significant experience that clarified a goal you wanted to pursue?

Source: http://www.achievement.org.

7. Discuss the role of print media as socializers of children.
8. Discuss the role of sound media (popular music) in the socialization process.
9. Discuss the impact of interactive and multimedia (computers and games) on socialization outcomes.

What is meant by "mass media" and "the medium is the message"?

mass media the form of communication in which large audiences quickly receive a given message via an impersonal medium between the sender and the receiver

Understanding Mass Media

Media, the plural of *medium*, refers to a type of communication. A medium is an intervening means through which a force acts or an effect is produced. Figure 9.1 illustrates the media's contribution to socialization of the child. **Mass media** refers to the form of communication in which large audiences quickly receive a given message via an impersonal medium between the sender and the receiver. The meaning of the message varies with the type of media. Examples include newspapers, magazines, books, radio, television, movies, videos, popular music, computers, and various multimedia.

Long before people recorded events as history, the medium used to share group traditions and values was oral stories, which were passed from one generation to the next. The

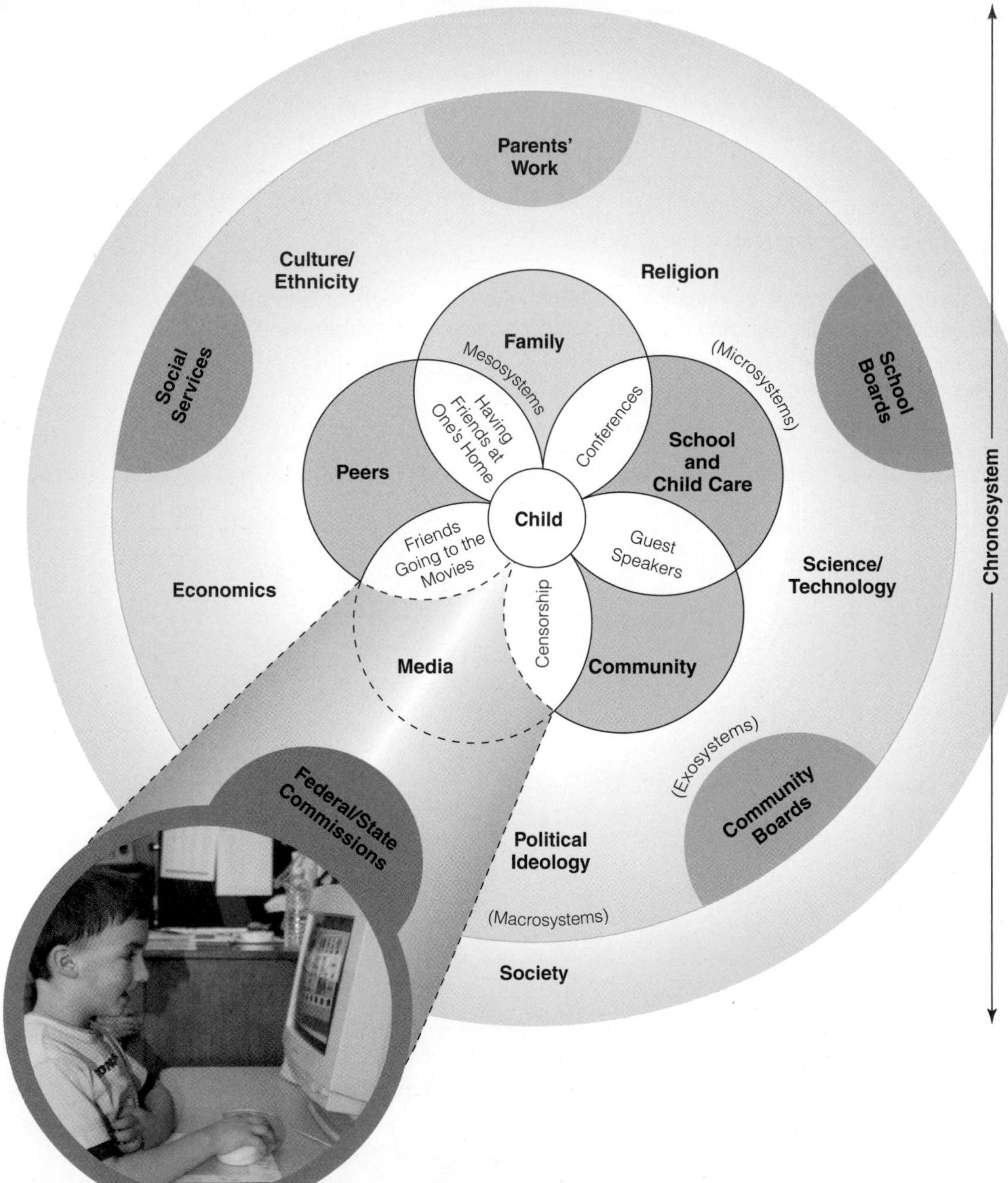

FIGURE 9.1 A Bioecological Model of Human Development

The media contribute to the socialization of the child.

GFOW 2724/Cengage Learning

oral tradition was personal (face-to-face). A significant feature of this type of communication was that it could be adapted to the interest and understanding of the listener. When the printing press was invented and stories could be written, now it was the reader who had to adapt his or her understanding to the storyteller's message. When the electronic media revolution occurred and television became a medium for storytelling, business became linked to the viewing experience. Now stories are told not by elders, not by teachers, but by economic enterprises with something to sell (Comstock & Scharrer, 2007; Gerbner et al., 2002).

How do media affect socialization?

Media affect socialization because they influence values, beliefs, attitudes, and behavior. As communications theorist Marshall McLuhan's (1964) famous aphorism stated, "The medium is the message," meaning that media are external extensions of the human being and "the 'message' of any medium is the change of scale or pace or pattern that it introduces into human affairs" (p. 8). In other words, the mass media are shapers, spreaders, and transformers of **culture**. The mass media are *shapers* of culture in that their form and content affect us in some way (for example, they influence the products we buy). The mass media are *spreaders* of culture in that they extend our capacity as human beings to process information and, in so doing, transform us in some way (for example, they enhance our ability to multitask). The mass media are *transformers* of culture in that new media create new environments, as well as new ways of looking at existing environments.

culture (recap) the learned behavior, including knowledge, beliefs, art, morals, law, customs, skills, and traditions that is characteristic of the social environment in which an individual grows up

To illustrate, digital technology has already revolutionized the communications industry—computers, phones, print, photo media, and more, use digital code (a series of zeros and ones) to transmit information. As of 2009, all TVs had to be digital, or have a converter, in order to receive programming. The FCC required the change from analog to all-digital broadcasting to free up airwave frequencies for public safety communications (police, fire, emergency rescue, and security). Also, since digital technology is a more efficient way of transmitting data, it allows for expansion including improved images and sound quality, as well as making more options available for consumers (such as high-definition TV, more programs, and multimedia services).

What are the shared effects of various media on children in general? What are the diverse effects on children as individuals who experience media at different ages, with varying backgrounds and perceptions? What immediate and long-term effects have been cultivated by media exposure? The outcomes for children of mass media experiences are sometimes difficult to sort out because of the many variables involved—variables that change over time (such as child's age or a family's economic situation) and that may be bidirectional (such as a child's cognitive ability enabling him/her to understand a TV show while at the same time the show is enhancing his/her cognition). According to reviews of the research (Comstock & Scharrer, 2007; Hofferth, 2010):

- Child variables include age, cognitive ability, gender, social experience, and psychological needs.
- Family variables include economics, affecting what media are purchased (videos, books, CDs, computers, game consoles, cell phones, MP3 players); time, including what alternative leisure activities are pursued (games, sports, museums, trips); and mediation, or how much adult supervision accompanies media exposure.
- Bidirectional variables include what the child brings to the media experience to change it (for example, computer knowledge can enable one to download various software) and how the media experience changes the child (for example, surfing the Internet can provide vicarious experiences such as travel). "It is not what the media does to people but what people do with the media" (Lull, 1980, p. 198).

Media and their messages can change experience, enhance experience, or interfere with experience. Books or television can, for example, *change* the neutral experience of going to sleep into a frightening one for a child, by showing monsters coming out from under a bed. Movies can employ computer graphics and simulations to alter reality. Television can *enhance* the experience of a parade by providing close-up shots, supplying comments, and increasing the pace of the action. Computers equipped with multimedia graphics and sound can enable the user to make infinite combinations and projections with the available information, thereby enhancing the computer user's experience. Television and movies can also *interfere* with the experience of imagining what a storybook character looks like by choosing an actor with certain characteristics to play the role.

Extending our human capacity to process information changes the way we perceive reality. We can, via television and the Internet, see and hear things happening all over the world. Satellite communications have transformed the world into a "global village" by compressing time and distance. According to McLuhan (1989), we now live in a global village that has become a global theater. Because of the electronic media revolution, we perceive ourselves differently from the way people did 60 years ago. Whereas learning about the world through reading is solitary, single-sensory, and gradual, learning about the world through television, videos, and computers is massive, multisensory, and immediate. For example, how many of you get a video clip of the news on your computer home page?

How has new technology affected media devices, content, and usage?

Chronosystem Influences on Mass Media

The media scene has changed drastically in the last few years as new devices, with the capability to combine different types of media in miniaturized forms for customized use, have emerged. One can be connected to someone or something via sound, text, and/or picture 24/7. The media environment affecting children today is characterized by availability, variety of choices, proliferation of portable devices, facility of use, and affordability (Kaiser Family Foundation [KFF], 2010; Roberts & Foehr, 2008). This means kids have access to multiple TV and radio channels, DVDs, CDs, game consoles, MP3 players, and cell phone apps. The technology enables individuals to choose what they will watch or listen to, and when and where they will do so. An impact of such flexibility is that while communication with others is facilitated, media usage for entertainment or learning becomes more personal than social. For example, games can be played on a computer rather than face-to-face with a friend; TV shows can be viewed alone rather than with family; information can be gleaned from the Internet rather than a teacher.

Media technology has been undergoing change over the past 100 years, from books to radio to movies to television to computer to multimedia. Now the widespread use of communications satellites and digital technology has enabled almost instantaneous delivery of media content and has changed mass communication from a national to a global enterprise (Perse, 2001). Cable TV, satellite dishes, and wireless technology have multiplied the available programming. The VCR, DVR (digital recorder such as TiVo), and computer have added to the choices. The decreasing cost of such technologies has afforded families the opportunity to own multiple TV sets and other devices. Technology that combines media gives viewers the ability to choose and control available programming. Parents who own such devices can preselect what children watch based on what they consider appropriate.

Even though media technology has changed, concerns regarding its influence on children remain the same. "In general, proponents of media innovation argue that the new technology benefits children by opening up new worlds to them, while opponents argue that new media might be used to substitute for real life in learning ethical principles, undermining children's morality" (Wartella & Jennings, 2000, p. 32). Research on children and media has spanned such areas as which demographic groups of children are gaining access to new technologies, what their preferences are for different genres, how much time is being spent and what other activities are being displaced, and how the content of various media exposure may be affecting children (Hofferth, 2010; Roberts & Foehr, 2008).

Over time, every new communication medium that has become available for popular use has elicited concern regarding its effects, especially on children and adolescents (Hofferth, 2010; Pecora, 2007). For example, the introduction of broadcast radio in the 1920s, touting its educational and entertainment benefits, elicited parental concerns about the decrease in family communication and the effect of violence in programming (Wartella & Jennings, 2000). Television emerged as a mass medium in 1948 and critics said:

> It brought the world to everyone's living room, but most particularly it gave children an earlier look at far places and adult behavior. It became the greatest and loudest salesman of goods, and sent children clamoring to their parents for box-tops. It created heroes and villains, fads, fashions, and stereotypes, and nowhere so successfully, apparently, as with the pliable minds of children. (Schramm, Lyle, & Parker, 1961, pp. 11–12)

Dominating the media scene today are interactive media, such as computers, game consoles, and cell phones. While these offer the potential for expanded learning and socialization of children, they also increase the risk of exposure to content and experiences that may be inappropriate for children (Comstock & Scharrer, 2007; Wartella & Jennings, 2000). The influence on children's development of active participation in such media, compared to passive participation in radio and television, is of special concern. Research on interactive media is discussed later.

Chronosystem influences on media involve not only technological changes but content changes as well. As we will discuss, violence, sex, and advertising have increased over time. The media appeal to different ages and diverse populations has also changed. For example, more television shows and movies are geared toward children and adolescents. Shows are available in different languages. Shows are available with closed captions for people with hearing impairments. Nontraditional relationships are more visible. Reality-based, or unscripted, entertainment is becoming more and more popular, especially when viewers can participate by calling or e-mailing their opinions to the broadcaster. Viewers can also blog to each other via computer websites. Advertising is changing from separate, timed commercials to placement of sponsors' products within shows (for example, a Coke can or bottle is placed on a table, as in *American Idol*). Advertisements have also infiltrated the movie theater as well as the Internet.

IN CONTEXT What Is the Digital Generation? The digital generation is composed of "digital natives" and "digital immigrants," terms coined by educator, Marc Prensky (2010). Digital natives are those born into a digitized world. Digital immigrants are those who had to learn about digital devices to survive. Digital natives communicate in text rather than in person, get information by surfing rather than by asking an expert, share by posting rather than calling, and click, click, click. Digital natives use e-mail, e-commerce, e-books, e-cards, e-entertainment, e-network, e-communication, e-banking, e-library, e-news, e-pals, e-forums, e-photos, e-courses, e-diplomas . . . and can figure out how to program a remote control much more easily than their digital-immigrant parents.

Macrosystem Influences on Mass Media

What influence do politics, economics, and technology have on the broadcasting media?

In order to understand the impact of the media on children, we must examine the broadcast system under which radio and television operate and the macrosystem influences on it (politics, economics, technology). Politics includes the laws under which the media operate. Economics include corporate sponsors for the shows. Technology includes the type of medium as well as its content.

The mass communication system in the United States is generally characterized by private ownership and dedicated to corporate profits (this does not, of course, apply to public TV). The broadcast media are subject to regulation by the Federal Communications Commission (FCC) and the Federal Trade Commission (FTC). The FCC has jurisdiction over policies related to the media industry, including restrictions on content and the structure of ownership. The FTC is charged with consumer protection, such as ensuring that advertising and marketing practices are not harmful or misleading. Because Congress deems the airways "public," the government, through an agency, can legally issue licenses and control transmitters in the interest of the people. In addition to federal regulations, there are also state and local laws pertaining to broadcasting. Cable channels, because they do not use the public airwaves, are not under the same obligation to serve the public interest as broadcast television.

The FCC can award a license to broadcast when such an action is "in the public interest, convenience, or necessity," though licensing standards are unclear. There are no comparable FCC rules for cable or satellite (pay) television or videocassettes. In 1984, the FCC lifted some of its restrictions when the Reagan administration moved to deregulate and to reduce government intervention. The FCC held that marketplace competition could best serve children's interests. Two trends resulted from this shift in policy: Educational content declined and advertising increased. These developments led Congress to enact legislation known as the Children's Television Act of 1990. This law imposed a limit of 10.5 minutes of commercials for each hour for children's programming on weekdays and 12 minutes an hour on weekends. In 1996, the FCC expanded this act by ruling that all commercial stations must broadcast at least three hours of children's educational or informational programs per week.

The media industry responds to public disapproval of programming or content via self-regulation. For example, in 1997, most of the television industry implemented a rating system intended to give parents advance information about the content of programs (see the In Practice box, "Parental Guidelines"). Specifically, the guidelines address the level of violence, foul language, and sexually suggestive content. Television manufacturers now must install V-chips—computer chips that can be programmed to block undesirable programs—in all new sets. They are also available as add-ons for existing TVs. These V-chips enable families to set their own viewing standards.

TV and radio make their profits from advertising. The broadcaster sells the advertiser time. Advertisers choose the vehicle—the program—that will expose the demographic audience best suited for their commercials. Within this system, control over content really rests with the audience. If the audience is not interested in the content of a program, the program is dropped. Thus, the tastes and interests of viewers and listeners serve as indirect but powerful controls.

The main emphasis of mass communication in the United States is on entertainment (Comstock & Scharrer, 2007; KFF, 2010). Generally, the major media aim their content at the broadest spectrum of viewers in order to gain the attention of the largest number of consumers for the products advertised on their programs. A major result is that the broadcast media must continually produce a "mass culture" geared to popular or majority tastes. However, with the availability of new technologies such as cable, satellite, video, and computers, audiences have become more fractionated, so advertisers have to target their products to special interests. Audience fractionation increases as family income increases (Roberts & Foehr, 2004, 2008), because more TV sets and other technologies are available to those with higher socioeconomic status.

Yet, as long as the broadcast media in the United States are designed to attract audiences to sell products, they will convey messages that are likely to influence attitudes and behavior (Comstock & Scharrer, 2007). Parents, then, must be cognizant of what is, and is not, appropriate for their children to watch, listen, and interact with. The website of the American Academy of Child and Adolescent Psychiatry (www.aacap.org) has a section, "Kids and Pop Culture," that provides reviews and articles by experts on TV, movies, books, music, video games, and Internet sites to help parents and other caregivers make healthy media decisions.

Children and Screen Media: Television and Movies (Videos, DVDs)

Why the special concern for children regarding TV and movies?

Television includes network and cable shows received on a TV set. Movies include productions made for the theater and for home viewing on a TV set in video or DVD format. According to national studies by the Kaiser Family Foundation (2010), the American family remains strongly connected to television, even though other media are available and are used in addition to TV (multimedia use is discussed later). Families use TV for entertainment, education, news, and consumer information.

TeachSource Video Activity

Go to the Education CourseMate website to watch the video entitled "Children and Television Viewing." Why and how does television engage children's attention?

Television and movies have evoked many concerns, especially about their content, their socializing effects on children, and potential public response. Television has certain properties that distinguish it from other media, including its attention demands, the brevity of its sequences, the rapid succession of presented material, and its visual orientation (Singer & Singer, 2001).

Children are a special audience in regard to the medium of television (Hofferth, 2010; Pecora, 2007). Because of cognitive immaturity, they are generally assumed to be more vulnerable than adults to the amount of time spent watching TV and to believing that the images they see are real, that violence is the way to solve problems, that one should buy what is advertised, and that the values, stereotypes, and behavior portrayed on TV constitute the way one should be. "Television is a particularly appealing medium to young children in part because many of its images and modes of representation are readily understood; it does not require the child to learn a complicated system of decoding as does reading, for example" (Huston, Zillman, & Bryant, 1994, p. 5). As a result, television has important socializing potential. As children develop, both the amount and content of their viewing changes. Increased cognitive abilities enable them to decode the audio and visual messages of TV, making the medium more entertaining and informative (Huston et al., 2007).

Television, Movies, and Change

How have TV and movies affected our lives?

Advances in television broadcasting have created changes in the sleep habits, meal arrangements, use of leisure time, and conversation patterns of millions of U.S. families (Andreasen, 2001; Hofferth, 2010). Mass communications have also created changes in our culture. New products advertised via television, magazines, newspapers, and the Internet can be adopted in a very short time. The rapid spread of other cultural forms, such as fashion fads, hairstyles, and types of music or sports, can be stimulated by the media. All of these changes have given rise to some concern, which can be better understood if we look back in time:

> It has never been much of a secret . . . that movies influence manners, attitudes, and behavior. In the fifties, they told us how to dress for a rumble or a board meeting, how far to go on the first date, what to think about Martians or, closer to home, Jews, blacks, and homosexuals. They taught girls whether they should have husbands or careers, boys whether to pursue work or pleasure. They told us what was right and what was wrong, what was good and what was bad; they defined our problems and suggested solutions. (Biskind, 1983, p. 2)

Since the introduction of TV, what kind of programming was available for children?

Pecora (2007) traced the history of children's TV from its inception. She states that children's shows were usually broadcast on Saturday morning or late afternoon. In the 1950s there were cartoons, such as *The Wonderful World of Disney*; children's entertainment, such as *The Howdy Doody Show*; action-adventure, such as *The Lone Ranger*; popular

IN PRACTICE

Parental Guidelines (TV and Movies)

Television

There are two categories of ratings, one for children's programs and one for programs not specifically designed for children. In addition to age-appropriateness, content ratings have been added as descriptors.

The following categories apply to programs designed solely for children:

All Children. *This program is designed to be appropriate for all children.* Whether animated or live action, the themes and elements in this program are specifically designed for a very young audience, including children ages 2–6. This program is not expected to frighten young children.

Directed to Older Children. *This program is designed for children age 7 and above.* It may be more appropriate for children who have acquired the developmental skills needed to distinguish between make-believe and reality. Themes and elements in this program may include mild fantasy or comedic violence, or may frighten children under the age of 7. Therefore, parents may wish to consider the suitability of this program for their very young children. Programs containing fantasy violence that may be more intense or more combative than other programs in this category are designed as TV-Y7-FV.

The following categories apply to programs designed for the entire audience:

General Audience. *Most parents would find this program suitable for all ages.* Although this rating does not signify a program designed specifically for children, most parents may let younger children watch this program unattended. It contains little or no violence, no strong language, and little or no sexual dialogue or situations.

Parental Guidance Suggested. *This program contains material that parents may find unsuitable for younger children.* Many parents may want to watch it with their younger children. The theme itself may call for parental guidance and/or the program contains one or more of the following: moderate violence (V), some sexual situations (S), infrequent coarse language (L), or some suggestive dialogue (D).

Parents Strongly Cautioned. *This program contains some material that many parents would find unsuitable for children under age 14.* Parents are strongly urged to exercise greater care in monitoring this program and are cautioned against letting children under the age of 14 watch unattended. This program contains one or more of the following: intense violence (V), intense sexual situations (S), strong coarse language (L), or intensely suggestive dialogue (D).

Mature Audience Only. *This program is specifically designed to be viewed by adults and therefore may be unsuitable for children under 17.* This program contains one or more of the following: graphic violence (V), explicit sexual activity (S), or crude, indecent language (L).

When a program is broadcast, the appropriate icon should appear in the upper left corner of the picture frame for the first 15 seconds. If the program is longer than one hour, the icon should be repeated at the beginning of the second hour. Guidelines are also displayed in TV listings in a number of newspapers and magazines.

Movies

G	General Audiences	All ages admitted.
PG	Parental Guidance Suggested	Some material may not be suitable for children.
PG-13	Parents Strongly Cautioned	Some material may be inappropriate for children under 13.
R	Restricted	Under 17 requires accompanying parent or adult guardian.
NC-17	No One 17 and Under Admitted	

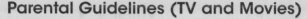

music/dancing, such as *American Bandstand*; and some educational shows, such as *Captain Kangaroo*.

In the 1960s, public TV broadcasts became available and shows such as *Sesame Street* and *Mr. Rogers' Neighborhood* were viewed. Children's shows on other networks began to appear; they were supported by advertising dollars instead of being funded by the network. The quality of many of these children's shows came under criticism, especially for violent content (superheroes such as Spiderman became prevalent) and for commercialism (ads aimed at children).

In the 1970s, a citizens' advocacy group, Action for Children's Television (ACT), petitioned the FCC, requesting age-specific programming and advertising limits in children's TV. Little of substance has changed on network TV since the 1960s, while choices for children have increased on public TV. Diversity first appeared in the form of *The Harlem Globetrotters* on CBS in 1970. Gender diversity was also part of this decade, as in such shows as *Josie and the Pussycats*.

The 1980s saw cable and home video enter the media scene. For the first 30 years, the network stations dominated the children's television industry. Now there was serious competition with cable stations, such as Nickelodeon and the Disney Channel. To lure audiences back and attract more viewers, the networks introduced toy tie-ins with the Smurfs on Saturday morning TV. The FCC responded to objections to such commercialism by deleting ACT's recommendations for advertising limits, saying the marketplace should determine children's programming. And so it did. "By the end of the decade the children's TV and toy markets were dominated by story lines built around multiple characters designed to sell—programs became a showcase for licensed products" (Pecora, 2007, p. 20).

During the 1990s, childhood consumerization expanded. Now junior brands of many adult products and merchandise (such as personal care items, designer clothing, or foods) were available for children, or marketed to them. In addition, a new market was identified—"tweens." Tweens were not only targets for products, but for programming, as well. For example, Nickelodeon introduced *Nick at Night*, a series of original half-hour, live-action programs for the tween audience. Significant political activity took place in this decade on behalf of children: The Children's Television Act of 1990 (described later) was passed.

"As we enter the new millennium, digital technology has brought dramatic changes to the landscape of children's television as the Internet and video games vie for attention" (Pecora, 2007, p. 33).

Theories Regarding How Screen Media Influence Children

How do TV and movie viewing impact children's developmental outcomes?

- **Social Cognitive Theory.** According to Bandura (2001), media contribute to children's learning by enabling them to observe role models behave on screen. Children identify with role models perceived to have prestige. Active behavior is more likely to be imitated than passive behavior. If the role model's behavior is rewarded (for example, accomplishing a goal, getting money or material objects, or receiving recognition), it is also likely to be imitated. Thus, children can learn positive or negative things from TV and movies. Their consequent behavior depends on other variables (discussed later), especially adult mediation.
- **Cultivation Theory.** Gerbner and colleagues (Gerbner et al., 2002) believe media content affects viewers' beliefs about the world and, consequently, alters their behavior. For example, exposure to violent media leads to a belief that aggression can resolve problems with no adverse effects. According to cultivation theory, then, the more time one is exposed to violence, the more likely that individual will engage in violent acts.

- **Motivation Theory.** Rubin (2002) believes that the impact of media depends on how media are used (entertainment, learning, background noise), and the individual abilities and characteristics of the user. For example, young children are more susceptible to media influence due to their cognitive immaturity—they don't have the skills to evaluate what they view, and so are gullible. Whether media is used alone, with peers, or with adults makes a difference in socialization outcomes.
- **Displacement Theory.** According to some researchers (Anderson, Huston, Schmitt, Linebarger, & Wright, 2001), media used for entertainment may displace important developmental activities such as play, hobbies, games, sleep, studying, reading, physical activities, and social engagements, especially conversations with family and friends, For example, the active process of reading a book—imagining characters, developing vocabulary, and appreciating plot development—might be displaced by the passive process of watching TV or a movie.

As Urie Bronfenbrenner (1970b) said in an address to the National Association for the Education of Young Children:

> Like the sorcerer of old, the television set casts its magic spell, freezing speech and action, turning the living into silent statues so long as the enchantment lasts. The primary danger of the television screen lies not so much in the behavior it produces—although there is danger there—as in the behavior it prevents: the talks, the games, the family festivities and arguments through which much of the child's learning takes place and through which his character is formed. Turning on the television set can turn off the process that transforms children into people.

How do TV and movies shape us?

Screen Media and Socialization Outcomes

Watching TV and movies impacts socioemotional development and relationships, physical development and health, psychological development and behavior, cognitive development and achievement, as well as moral development and values.

Socioemotional Development and Relationships

Socioemotional development involves establishing and maintaining relationships with others. The statistics on TV viewing habits indicate that, on average, children spend three to five hours a day in front of the television set and often do it with little parental monitoring (Comstock & Scharrer, 2007; KFF, 2010). Young children from economically and educationally disadvantaged backgrounds spend even more time watching TV than do children from more affluent, better-educated families (Comstock & Scharrer, 2007; Roberts & Foehr, 2004). Even with the availability of other media (computers, mobile devices, CD players), TV viewing time increased (Roberts & Foehr, 2008). Thus, time spent watching TV affects interpersonal relationships, especially family interactions and shared time. Interpersonal relationships involve communication, compromise, and resolution of problems. Shared time with family helps strengthen relationships—playing games, engaging in hobbies, going places together. If children have few experiences listening to others, responding to them, negotiating, and compromising, their socioemotional development will be negatively affected.

Physical Development and Health

Physical development and health are influenced by physical activity and nutrition. Time spent watching TV is time that potentially could be used for physical activity. There is evidence linking heavy media consumption and obesity (Escober-Chavez & Anderson, 2008). A study found that children who watched four or more hours of TV per day were significantly more likely to be obese than children who watched an hour or less (Crespo et al., 2001). Another study of preschoolers (ages 1–4) found that a child's risk of being overweight increased by 6 percent for every hour of television watched per day. If that child had a TV in his or her bedroom, the odds of being overweight jumped an additional 31 percent for every hour watched. Preschool children who had TVs in their bedrooms watched 4.8 hours more of TV or videos per week than those who did not (Dennison, Erb, & Jenkins, 2002).

Psychological Development and Behavior

Psychology refers to the mind, including perception, emotions, attitudes, motives, and consequent behavior. Perception of a particular thing may vary among individuals due to their biology and experiences. Also, the form, style, and content of a show may influence how one perceives it.

What effects does the way screen media presents information have on children's perceptions of reality?

Television as a medium presents information in particular forms (for example, animation, live, scripted) and styles (for example, action, drama, news). The forms generally used in children's programming are perceptually salient (high action, special visual and auditory effects) as opposed to less striking ones (dialogue, moderate action). According to a study by Huston and colleagues (2007), both younger and older children attended to perceptually salient features. Children also attended to content that was moderately comprehensible (too easy was boring and too difficult was frustrating). While comprehensibility changes with cognitive development, formal features that elicit attention can serve as guides for children to distinguish important from unimportant content.

"Producers use film and video conventions as implicit cues to appeal to particular audiences to convey particular connotations. For example, the advertisements for girls' and boys' toys differ in form. Commercials for boys' toys are made with rapid action, quick cuts, and scene changes, and local sound effects; commercials for girls' toys are made with dreamy or tinkling music, scene changes marked by dissolves, and quiet sounds" (Huston et al., 2007, p. 52).

This child is engaged in imaginative play.

My Childhood Memories/Alamy

Children recognize these sex-typed cues. Formal features are not only cues for sex-typing, but for fiction and reality, too. Perceptions of reality fall into two categories: factuality (Did it happen in the real and unrehearsed world, or was it constructed and scripted for TV?) and social realism (How similar is the TV portrayal to an actual event?). According to Huston et al. (2007), judgments about factuality occur in a developmental sequence (7-year-olds understand better than 5-year-olds that fictional characters do not retain their TV roles in their off-TV lives). Generally, children over the age of 8 also understand that fictional shows are made up, scripted, and rehearsed. Preschool children understand that animated content is not real, but believe other content to be so. Individual differences occur based on levels of cognitive development. Children make factual judgments primarily based on genre (news is factual; drama is not), which in turn depends on formal production features (such as talking heads or graphics). Regarding the perception of social realism, Huston and colleagues state that children use content cues, often comparing the actions they see on TV to their knowledge about the real world. However, formal features (such as a laugh track) can influence perceptions.

Because children have not experienced much of the real world, they accept what TV portrays as the truth and neglect to test it against reality. According to "cultivation theory," TV fosters the growth of preferences, attitudes, behaviors, and fears engendered by what is portrayed, especially among heavy viewers (Comstock & Scharrer, 2007; Gerbner et al., 2002).

What are the effects of viewing the prevalent violence in screen media?

"Television and movies, by their very nature, have the ability to introduce children to frightening images, events, and ideas, many of which they would not encounter in their entire lives without the mass media" (Cantor, 1998, p. 3). An example is *violence*, defined as the "overt expression of physical force against others or self, or compelling action against one's will and pain of being hurt or killed or actually hurting or killing" (Gerbner et al., 1978). Violence on TV is measured in terms of *prevalence, rate*, and *role*. Prevalence is the extent to which violence occurs in the program; rate is the frequency of violent episodes;

and role is the number of characterizations of violence or victimization. Violence on television is a concern because, over the years, there has been an increase in violence on children's Saturday morning programs as well as on prime-time television (8:00 to 11:00 P.M.) (KFF, 2003)

The National Television Violence Study (NTVS) (Center for Communication and Social Policy, 1998; KFF, 2003) has demonstrated that there is a great deal of violence on American television, and today there are more venues and channels available on which to find it. In addition, much of this violence is portrayed in formulaic ways that glamorize, sanitize, and trivialize aggression. An example of programming with violent content that is popular with children is *Super Hero Squad Show*. The NTVS concludes that not all violence portrayed on TV has similar effects on children. Characterization in which the perpetrator is attractive is more likely to influence the viewer's identification and modeling. When violence is justified, goes unpunished, or shows no harm or pain to the victim, it is also more likely to influence viewer behavior. The concern is not only with the prevalence of violence, but that it is portrayed as necessary and relatively harmless (Comstock & Scharrer, 2007).

Although it may be difficult to prove that excessive viewing of televised violence can or does provoke violent crime in any specific individual, it is clear that children who watch a great deal of televised violence are more prone to behave aggressively than are children who do not watch TV violence (Comstock & Scharrer, 2007; Perse, 2001). The NTVS (Center for Communication and Social Policy, 1998; Murray, 2007) demonstrated that the context in which most violence is presented on TV poses the following risks for viewers: (1) learning to behave violently, (2) becoming desensitized to violence, and (3) becoming fearful of being attacked. Characteristics of the child, such as age, real experiences, temperament, and cognitive developmental level, as well as parental mediation (AACAP, 2002b) influence the impact of viewing violence. Explanations from psychological research for these findings come from theories of learning, attribution, and arousal.

Are children likely to learn and remember new forms of aggressive behavior by watching them on TV? If children learn and remember, will they practice the behavior? Research shows that children do learn and remember novel forms of aggression seen on TV or in films (Comstock & Scharrer, 2007). They are more likely to remember the behavior learned by observation if they have tried it at least once. Whether or not children will practice the behavior depends on the similarity of the observed setting to their real setting; that is, if they imitate an observed aggression and it "works" (is reinforced) in solving a problem or attaining a goal, it is likely to be repeated. For example, a young child who sees Superman punching a criminal to retrieve a bag of money and prevent innocent bystanders from getting shot might be likely to try the observed aggressive behavior to take a toy away from another child, not having comprehended the concept of the Superman scene—that aggression is justifiable for protection. If the child's aggressive behavior results in getting the toy, the child is likely to repeat the behavior. Thus, children may learn aggressive behavior from TV, but whether or not they perform it depends on factors within the child, such as anger, as well as the situation (Huston & Wright, 1998; Perse, 2001).

Does watching violence on television influence people's attitudes about aggressive behavior? In psychological theory, attitudes include attributions, rules, and explanations that people gradually learn from observations of behavior. Therefore, for individuals who watch a great deal of television, attitudes will be built on the basis of what they see, and the attitudes will, in turn, have an effect on their behavior.

According to research, children learn, remember, and practice aggressive behavior they have seen on TV and film.

Sky Bonillo/PhotoEdit

Apparently, young children are more willing to accept the aggressive behavior of other children after viewing violent scenes (Paik & Comstock, 1994). However, studies have shown that children's attitudes are changed if adults discuss the program (Huston & Wright, 1998). In an experimental study (Huesmann et al., 1983), one group of children who regularly watched violent programs were shown excerpts from violent shows. They then took part in discussion sessions about the unreality of television violence, as well as alternative strategies to solve conflicts, and wrote essays. Another group, who also watched many violent programs, was shown nonviolent excerpts followed by a neutral discussion of content. The children who took part in the sessions on unreality and alternative strategies exhibited significantly less aggressive strategies in their essays than those in the control group.

The more television children watch, the more accepting they are of aggressive behavior and the more likely they are to attribute it as justifiable (Comstock & Scharrer, 2007). It has been shown that persons who often watch television tend to be more suspicious and distrustful of others, and they also believe there is more violence in the world than do those who do not watch much television (Comstock & Scharrer, 2007; Perse, 2001). This may be explained by the notion that television cultivates beliefs and perceptions about reality (Gerbner et al., 2002).

Does viewing violence on TV decrease one's sensitivity to violence in real life?

Research shows that repetition of violence in the media results in classical desensitization (Comstock & Scharrer, 2007). **Desensitization**—the gradual reduction in response to a stimulus after repeated exposure—is used in behavior therapy to overcome fears. For example, the more one is exposed to riding in an airplane, the less one should fear flying. A news story several years ago depicted this very kind of desensitization. A masked burglar gagged and tied a woman to a chair while he robbed her home of valuables. He told her 5-year-old son to watch television and not to call the police until the show was over. Four hours later, the son phoned. Apparently, the boy's emotional sensitivity to the real event had been so reduced that he did not react immediately. Also, the boy may have been so accustomed to seeing similar events on TV that he did not realize the seriousness of the real event.

desensitization the gradual reduction in response to a stimulus after repeated exposure

Another response to viewing televised violence is an increase in aggressive behavior resulting from the increase in general arousal (excitement) that occurs. According to Murray (2007), neurological studies of children's brains while they viewed violent and nonviolent shows revealed activity in certain areas of the brain when violence was viewed. The activated areas of the brain were those normally involved in arousal and attention, detection of threat, episodic memory encoding and retrieval, and motor programming.

What are the long-term effects of continuous arousal? A longitudinal study examined the relation between TV-violence viewing at ages 6 to 10 and adult aggressive behavior about 15 years later for a sample growing up in the 1970s and 1980s. Follow-up archival data and interview data revealed that childhood exposure to media violence predicts young adult aggressive behavior for both males and females. Identification with aggressive TV characters and perceived realism of TV violence also predicted later aggression. These relationships persisted even when the effects of socioeconomic status, intellectual ability, and a variety of parenting factors were controlled (Huesmann et al., 2003).

Cognitive Development and Achievement

What sorts of things do broadcast TV and movies teach children?

Children's cognitive development varies by age and experience. The attention of young children (under age 5) can be captured by bright colors, moving objects, various sounds, and things shown on screen that are similar to what they have experienced (Comstock & Scharrer, 2007). However, young children often have trouble distinguishing reality from fantasy and need adult mediation to do so. Children under age 8 are more easily persuaded by television messages than are older children, believing what is said to be true, because they take things literally, rather than figuratively (Stabiner, 1993). Although most children by age 3 can distinguish program content from commercials, children under age 8 seldom understand that the purpose of the ad is to sell something. Whereas children under age 8 do not understand the persuasive intent of advertising and are, therefore, particularly vulnerable to its appeals, children over age 8, who are more aware of the purposes of advertising, are still apt to be persuaded by appeals that are subtly deceptive or misleading (Comstock & Scharrer, 2007; Kunkel, 2001). For example, they don't understand product disclosures or disclaimers, comparative claims, the real meaning of endorsements by famous characters, or the use of premiums, promotions, and sweepstakes (Council of Better Business Bureaus, 2010).

Every hour of broadcast television is carefully planned to contain enough minutes for "commercial messages." By selling commercial messages to advertisers, TV stations are able to defray the costs of their programs and make a profit. Commercials are cost effective for the advertisers due to the wide audience. Federal regulation of TV commercials is handled by the FTC, while the Council of Better Business Bureaus (CBBB) has a self-regulatory Children's Advertising Review Unit. More recently, however, ads not only appear on TV, but also in movies, video games, on the Internet, and on cell phones. Should these venues be regulated as well?

Child-directed commercials include toys, cereal, snacks, beverages, and fast-food restaurants (Calvert, 2008). Many are concerned that non-nutritional ads have contributed to the problem of obesity. Why advertise to children? Children and youth today have money—from allowances, gifts, and doing chores. They also can be quite persuasive with parents. ("Please, please, pretty please buy me that Pokémon; I've been good.") How parents handle their children's exposure to advertising and their requests for products can mediate the role commercialism plays in a child's developmental outcomes (Calvert, 2008). Children have decades of buying power ahead of them and, unlike adults, have no preconceived product preferences. They are open to suggestion and are impulsive (Kunkel, 2001; Stabiner, 1993). Advertisers report that children start asking for brand names as early as 2 years old. One successful way to gain a child consumer is to give the child a sense of power or importance. For example, Kool-Aid was marketed as a product "just for kids." Also, it contained coupons that children could save and trade in for toys (Stabiner, 1993).

Despite increased awareness of the purpose of advertising, even older children find commercials convincing, especially if endorsed by a celebrity (Comstock & Scharrer, 2007). For example, in a study of 8- to 14-year-old boys, celebrity endorsement of a racing toy made the product more attractive; including live racetrack footage led to exaggerated estimates of the toy's features as well as decreased awareness that the ad was staged (Ross et al., 1984).

New technologies available for TV to reap more advertising dollars include attention-getting production features (action, sound effects, music), repetition, branded environments (popular characters used to sell products ranging from food to vacations), and free prizes, which are effective in attracting children's attention, making them remember the product and influencing their purchasing choices (Calvert, 2008). Marketers have also begun to use stealth advertising, wherein the intent of the ad is concealed (for example, a planted fake news story intended to draw attention to a product). In this approach, the line between content and commercial is blurred. Whereas the Children's Television Act of 1990 prohibited such marketing on children's programs, some stealth advertising does occur, as in "toy tie-in" marketing, wherein featured characters on children's TV shows correspond to toys sold in the marketplace (Levin, 1998). In essence, these are program-length commercials and constitute unfair soliciting of children (Huston & Wright, 1998; Strasburger, Wilson, & Jordan, 2008).

Marketing products to children has become common.

Laura Dwight/Corbis

Adolescents are affected by TV commercials (as well as print and Internet), too. When smoking or drinking are glamorized in the media, the likelihood that teenagers will experiment with cigarettes or alcohol increases (Strasburger, Wilson, & Jordan, 2008).

Likewise, social marketing on TV designed to promote healthful behaviors has been effective in preventing tobacco use, promoting condom use, and improving nutrition, to name a few (Evans, 2008).

What about all those ads for medications? According to Neil Postman, New York University Professor of Communication Arts and Sciences:

> A commercial teaches a child three interesting things. The first is that all problems are resolvable. The second is that all problems are resolvable fast. And the third is that all problems are resolvable fast through the agency of some technology. It may be a drug. It may be a detergent. It may be an airplane or some piece of machinery, like an automobile or computer. (Postman, 1994, pp. 43–45)

Advertising sells more than products; it sells a message. These ads exemplify equating sexual desirability with purchasing the product.

Michael Newman/PhotoEdit

The essential message of a commercial, then, is that people have problems—lack of confidence, lack of friends, lack of money, lack of health, and so on, and these problems are solvable through the product advertised.

According to James McNeal, author of *Children as Consumers* (1987), advertisers are attuned to children's developmental stages and their needs for peer approval, status, and independence. The basic advertising message being communicated, then, is "things make the person." The most common appeal employed in advertising to children is associating the product with fun and happiness without providing any factual product-related information (Kunkel, 2001).

What do children learn from broadcast TV about diversity?

stereotype an oversimplified representation of members of a particular group

A **stereotype** is an oversimplified representation of members of a particular group. Stereotypes generally conform to a pattern of dress or behavior that is easily recognized and understood. Humans categorize people to simplify their mental processing. Generally, stereotypes are less real, more perfect or imperfect, and more predictable than their real-life counterparts. Some stereotyping on television may be unavoidable because of the format; 30- or 60-minute programs do not allow for full character development. Many diverse groups—women, older people, African Americans, Italian Americans, Hispanic Americans, Asian Americans, Native Americans, and Middle Eastern Americans—claim that television and movies either ignore them or distort them. According to a study by Children Now (2003), while 40 percent of American youth under age 19 are children of color, few of the faces they see on TV represent their heritage. Thus, TV not only fails to accurately reflect the world in which young people live, but it also sends a message that society values some groups more than others, finding them worthy of attention. Although there has been some progress in increasing Latinos' presence in prime time, Latinos continue to be cast as characters with low-status occupations. Arab/Middle Eastern characters are most likely to be portrayed as criminals. Males outnumber females two to one in prime-time TV and women are significantly younger than their male counterparts (Children Now, 2003).

What are the effects of screen media viewing on children's reading and communication skills?

There is concern that time spent in front of the TV has been responsible for the general decline in reading levels and scores on standardized achievement tests (Hofferth, 2010). TV viewing takes time away from other pursuits, such as reading, hobbies, attending concerts, and visiting museums—pursuits that enhance cognitive development.

The research on TV and reading, however, has been inconclusive (Comstock & Scharrer, 2007). According to research reviews (Comstock & Scharrer, 2007; KFF, 2003), there is no doubt that children read fewer books when television is available to them. This is probably because it is human nature to opt for the activity requiring less effort (entertainment) rather than the activity requiring more effort (reading). However, literacy begins at home, and the way parents use media exerts a major influence on children's use of leisure time (Adams & Hamm, 2006).

What is the effect of TV/video viewing on academic achievement?

The effect of TV/video viewing on academic achievement depends on age, program content, and whether there is an adult present to co-view and comment on programming. A longitudinal study (Zimmerman & Christakes, 2005) found viewing before age 3 was negatively related to later academic achievement, whereas viewing at and beyond age 3 was positively related to subsequent achievement.

Another longitudinal study (Anderson et al., 2001) following more than 500 children from preschool to adolescence found that the content of television shows has a significant impact on academic achievement. Specifically, viewing educational programs as preschoolers was correlated with higher grades in school, reading more books, placing more value on achievement, greater creativity, and less aggression. Early exposure to educational programming was also associated with higher grades in high school English, math, and science. These associations were more consistent for boys than for girls, with the exception of girls who watched violent programs as preschoolers. These findings held true even after taking into account family background.

And finally, co-viewing with an adult who extends learning by drawing attention and asking and answering questions can have a positive academic influence (Kirkorian, Wartella, & Anderson, 2008).

Do infant/toddlers learn from watching "educational" videos/DVDs?

A recent study by DeLoache and colleagues (DeLoache et al., 2010) found that infants who watched an unidentified baby video did not actually learn the vocabulary words that the video purported to teach. The researchers recruited 96 families with children between 12 and 18 months of age to participate in a month-long study. Some children watched a best-selling infant-learning DVD several times a week, half of them watching alone and half with a parent. Another group had no exposure to the DVD, but their parents were asked to try to teach them the vocabulary words from the DVD in everyday interactions.

Before and after the month of vocabulary work, all of the children were tested on their knowledge of a list of words that appeared in the DVD. The results showed that those infants who regularly watched the DVD over four weeks learned very little from their exposure to it, regardless of whether they had watched alone or with a parent. They knew no more of the words from the DVD than did children who had never seen it.

This study extends DeLoache's earlier research showing that very young children often don't understand symbols that are obvious to adults (DeLoache, 1991). Thus, infants who watch "educational" videos/DVDs may not relate the images (symbols) on the screen to what is present in the real world. Research concludes that the best way to help babies develop language is by talking to them, in the ordinary way that parents talk to their children.

What is the effect of TV and movie viewing on the perpetuation of morals and values?

Moral Development and Values

As discussed in Chapter 2, *morals* refer to an individual's evaluation of what is right and wrong; *values* refer to qualities or beliefs that are viewed as desirable or important. They influence attitudes, motives, and behavior.

Children not only watch "kid vid" (TV shows especially for children) but spend much of their viewing time watching "adult" programs (action/dramas, situation comedies, news). The problem is that an adult knows about certain aspects of life—its tragedies, its contradictions, its unfairness, its mysteries, its joys—that a child does not have the intellectual capability or life experience to comprehend. What television does is communicate the same information to everyone simultaneously, regardless of age, level of education, or experience. And, in the quest for new material to hold its audience, television has been increasingly exposing its audiences to life experiences previously considered forbidden: explicit sexuality, adultery, family violence, incest, corruption, extreme violence, pornography, and horror. Consequently, "with TV's relentless revelation of all adult secrets, it is not inconceivable that in the near future we shall return to the 13th- and 14th-century situation in which no words were unfit for a youthful ear" (Postman, 1994). If so, what values are being perpetuated?

Excitement, adventure, power, and violence are more likely to be the themes on TV and screen, rather than prosocial values. According to Comstock and Scharrer (2007), as viewers get older they get much less information on cooperation, peace, and obeying the laws than do preschool children.

Shows exhibiting socially desirable behaviors that benefit others do influence children's values. Studies have shown that children who watch altruistic behavior (generosity, helping, and cooperation) on television become more altruistic themselves (Comstock & Scharrer, 2007; Perse, 2001). For example, in a classic study, children who watched a prosocial episode of *Lassie*, in which Lassie's master risked his life by hanging over the edge of a mineshaft to rescue Lassie's puppy, exhibited more prosocial behavior than did children who watched a neutral episode of *Lassie* (Sprafkin, Liebert, & Poulos, 1975). However, merely watching prosocial behavior on the screen has few lasting effects unless an adult watches the show with the child, discusses the positive behavior, and encourages the child to model it. Unfortunately, research shows that not many adults do so (Comstock & Scharrer, 2007; Dorr & Rabin, 1995).

What do screen media tell us about sexuality?

The frequency of sexual references on TV has increased steadily over the last two decades. The number of sexual scenes has nearly doubled since 1998, according to a study by the Kaiser Family Foundation (2005). Television and movies have increasingly included talk about sex, nudity, profanity, and sexually explicit activities. Sex appeal and sexual activity are glamorized. Unfortunately, much less attention is paid by the media to the potential consequences of casual sexual behavior (Comstock & Scharrer, 2007;

IN PRACTICE

Sexualized Childhood

In their book, *So Sexy, So Soon: The New Sexualized Childhood,* Levin and Kilbourne (2009) accuse the media of sexualizing children. They say that American children are exposed to a barrage of sexual images in television, movies, music, and the Internet. Young children are being socialized to believe that buying certain clothes, consuming brand-name soft drinks, and owning the right possessions will make them sexy and cool; and the most important thing is to be attractive to the opposite sex. The result is that kids are having sex younger and with more partners than ever before. Eating disorders and body image issues are common as early as grade school. Levin and Kilbourne stress that there is nothing wrong with a young person's natural sexual awakening, but it is wrong for media to commercialize sex and sexuality. They offer advice to parents on how to limit children's exposure to the marketing of sex and how to engage them in age-appropriate conversations about sex and the media. The following are some examples of the book's advice:

- Limit exposure to sexualized media by learning about "what's out there" and using rating systems to help determine age-appropriateness.
- Teach media literacy by discussing with children what they see or hear—"You wouldn't show your private parts to everyone, would you?" "Is there another way for that guy to get what he wants besides fighting?"
- Learn what shows, movies, and toys are popular so you can talk to kids about them.
- Challenge kids' imaginations to go beyond the narrow scripts of certain toys—"What else does Barbie do besides get dressed up?" "Can these action toys find lost kittens or puppies?"
- Let children know you are available to answer their questions about what they've seen or heard in the media.
- Talk to other parents about how they deal with sexualized media. Talk to your child's school, as well.

KFF, 2005). TV is also bolder about sexual activity than it was several years ago (Comstock & Scharrer, 2007; KFF, 2005). The shows of the 1970s that caused a furor only talked about sex, whereas the shows in the late 1980s began to present sex acts visually. Men and women are now seen in bed together. Moreover, these presumably copulating couples are typically not married to each other. Finally, sex acts previously considered taboo, such as sexual abuse, incest, rape, and prostitution, are now openly discussed and depicted on TV (Lorch, 2007; Strasburger, Wilson, & Jordan, 2008).

A significant portion of adolescents' information about sexuality comes from TV programming (Lorch, 2007). Watching shows depicting premarital, extramarital, or nonmarital sex affects the moral values of young teens in that they report such sexual behavior to be acceptable (Malamuth & Impett, 2001). However, family discussions of values can intervene (Bryant & Rockwell, 1994).

Why is it so difficult to determine the causes and effects of media experiences?

Mediating Influences on Screen Media and Socialization Outcomes

In a comprehensive review of all evidence on the effects of television on children, Comstock and colleagues concluded that television is indeed a major socializer of children (Comstock & Scharrer, 2007). However, it is difficult to pinpoint the exact effects of television on behavior because of other mediating or intervening influences, such as the viewer's cognitive developmental level, psychological needs, attitudes, motives, habits, interests, values, morals, beliefs, and experiences (Huston & Wright, 1998; Perse, 2001) (see Figure 9.2).

> Children are not just recipients of media messages; they choose the content to which they are exposed, and they interpret the content within their own frames of reference. They receive media messages in contexts of family, peers, and social institutions, all of which may modify or determine how children integrate messages into their existing store of information and beliefs. (Huston & Wright, 1998, p. 1027)

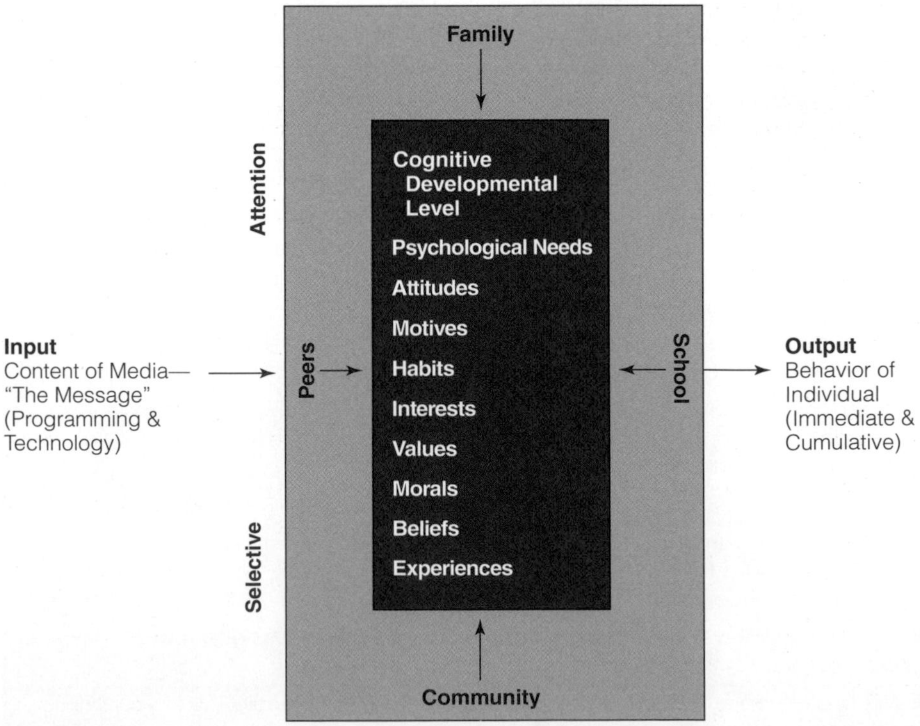

FIGURE 9.2 Mediating Influences Affecting the Outcomes of Media Messages on the Viewer

Selective Attention

Selective attention involves choosing stimuli from one's environment to notice, observe, and consider. Our senses (sight, hearing, touch, taste, and smell) are equipped to respond to stimuli in the environment. However, it is impossible to pay attention to everything going on about us; thus we select, or consciously attend to, only some of the available stimuli. Selective attention is crucial to learning because children's perceptions and concepts of the world depend on which aspects of it get their attention.

What role does selective attention play in the influence of TV viewing?

selective attention choosing stimuli from one's environment to notice, observe, and consider

Infants/toddlers show elevated attention to loud noises, bright colors, and movement. Preschool children show elevated attention to animation, strange voices, lively music, auditory changes, and rhyming, repetition, and alliteration.

Older children pay attention to more complexities as they gain in cognitive development. They are now able to understand story plots and characters. They are attracted to action, adventure, and family situation comedies. School-agers need to attend to visual techniques more than adolescents to understand the story line (Comstock & Scharrer, 2007). In general, media cues that attract attention are "outstandingness," novelty, contrast, and how closely the cue is related to the viewer's frame of reference. This partially explains the finding that variations in media experiences are related to age, race and ethnicity, gender, socioeconomic status, and various indicators of social and psychological adjustment, such as happiness or anger (Roberts & Foehr, 2004). Although television programmers may be able to attract the audience's attention by manipulating the level of "outstandingness," novelty, or contrast, it is ultimately up to the viewer to decide whether that message belongs in his or her frame of reference.

Adult Involvement

Why is significant adult mediation important?

Parents, especially, can mediate the amount and level of attention given to TV by their children by being the primary socializers in their children's frames of reference. Children are more likely to attend to messages on TV that conform to their family's interests, attitudes, beliefs, and values. Parents, teachers, and older siblings are probably most important in determining television programming effects on children (Comstock & Scharrer, 2007; Roberts & Foehr, 2004). Early evidence of this importance was found in a first-year evaluation of *Sesame Street*. It was shown that those children who watched the show with their mothers and talked to them about the show learned more than did other children (Ball & Bogatz, 1970). This finding was supported by later research on the vocabulary development of preschoolers (Rice et al., 1990).

Several studies (Huston & Wright, 1998; KFF, 2010; Perse, 2001) support the value of significant others' involvement in children's television viewing. For example, one study (Wilson & Weiss, 1993) showed that co-viewing a show with older siblings increased preschoolers' enjoyment of and decreased their arousal to a scary program. Another study (Haefner & Wartella, 1987) showed that co-viewing changed 6- and 7-year olds' evaluations of certain characters in two programs.

Co-viewing with an adult can change the viewing experience for a child. Adult viewers can analyze and evaluate content. They can tune out irrelevancies, absorb complicated plots, and understand underlying messages. For the most part, children cannot. As mentioned previously, young children cannot distinguish fantasy and reality; their understanding is based on appearances. They do not know what is fact and what is opinion. They have neither the experience nor the knowledge to enable them to comprehend the basis of many events that occur in the world. Yet they are exposed to the whole world through the television screen before they have even developed an understanding of their own immediate world. We do not expect children to read a book before they can recognize letters. Adults, then, must develop strategies to mediate children's television viewing according to their values and their children's cognitive developmental level.

In viewing TV with their children, parents can mediate the messages that are broadcast.

Image Source/Jupiter Images

Parents can mediate television viewing by (AACAP, 2001):

1. controlling the number of hours of television exposure,
2. checking ratings and evaluating what kinds of programs may be viewed,
3. viewing television with their children and discussing the programs, and
4. arranging family activities other than television viewing.

What role do links with other microsystems play in media socialization?

Mesosystem Influences on Screen Media

Mesosystem influences on television and movies consist of linkages with the community, the school, the peer group, and the family. These linkages affect the pervasiveness of media exposure, types of media and messages experienced, adult mediation, and the impact of socialization outcomes.

How has the community responded to concerns about broadcast (free) TV?

Community–Media Linkages

The community's response to free, broadcast commercial programs has been to develop alternatives—such as the following:

1. **Public Broadcasting Service.** PBS is a nonprofit broadcasting service to an alliance of local community and educational stations who are members. It is financially supported by the Corporation for Public Broadcasting and by annual membership fees of licensees as well as by selling time to advertisers. Supplemental funds come from grants from the National Endowment for the Humanities, from universities, and from big corporations, with the aim of providing more specialized, diversified, and high-quality programs to reach specific age, social, and cultural groups. PBS offerings as well as interactive activities are available on their website (www.pbs.org).

2. **Cable and Satellite Television.** Families that pay for cable television or have purchased satellite dishes can view certain channels that show movies, sports, and educational programs. One such channel, available only through cable or satellite TV, is Nickelodeon—a television channel for children. Every day there are shows for children ages 2 to 15. For example, there are songs for young children, adventures for middle-years children, and talk shows for teenagers. Cable and satellite TV also provides music television stations that feature live performances of popular music.

3. **Recording Devices.** The business community has provided expanded uses of television. In many homes, television sets are currently used as display terminals for videotapes or DVDs and video games. Families that have home recorders or DVRs can play a more active role in selecting and managing their leisure time. VHS tapes or DVDs of selected movies, instruction, or games can be rented or purchased to show at home. Recorders also enable you to record TV shows you don't want to miss.

The proliferation of videos and discs makes movies produced for the big screen accessible and affordable. Unless adults mediate the selection, young people can be exposed to such things as violence, sexuality, and different values (AACAP, 2006c), as was discussed in regard to TV.

4. **Public Interest Groups.** Public interest groups, such as Action for Children's Television (ACT), whose advocacy efforts ended with the passage of the Children's Television Act of 1990, and the Center for Media Literacy, have been formed to pressure broadcasters for change, to lobby the government for regulations, and to educate the public to monitor its own viewing habits and those of its children. They have been influential in reducing violence on children's TV, reducing the number of commercials on children's shows, and preventing program hosts or celebrities from advertising on their shows, as well as developing the rating system for television and movies. Media literacy strategies for children, parents, and teachers are available on the CML website (http://www.medialit.org).

School-Media Linkages

How does the school influence media use?

Many teachers use educational TV as part of their curriculum, and millions of school-age children receive a portion of their regular instruction through television. PBS was founded in 1969, at which time it took over many of the functions of its predecessor, National Educational Television (NET). It airs a variety of programs specifically developed for the classroom, referred to as Educational Television (ETV)—some are national, others are local. Digitization has enabled PBS to provide interactive activities, such as educational games.

Educational institutions that were granted airwave licenses can broadcast their own programs. Some institutions are leasing their airwave licenses to wireless companies to provide them with multimedia services (TV and Internet). Schools that subscribe to cable TV can get educational programs from "Cable in the Classroom," which offers numerous multimedia services (http://www.ciconline.org). Supporters of television in the classroom suggest that it provides memorability, concreteness, and emotional involvement, and also stimulates reading, encourages class discussion, and promotes student interactions (Greenfield, 1984). However, educational TV has been criticized because many programs are financed by corporations that advertise their products on the show. It is felt that the classroom should not be a marketplace (Calvert, 2008).

In sum, the Corporation for Public Broadcasting (2004) concludes that educational TV in the classroom

- Reinforces reading and lecture material
- Aids in the development of a common base of knowledge among students
- Enhances student comprehension and discussion
- Provides greater accommodation of diverse learning styles
- Increases student motivation and enthusiasm
- Promotes teacher effectiveness

Peer-Media Linkages

How does the peer group use media to foster its influence?

Although research demonstrates that parents can mediate the effects of TV, according to a study by Nathanson (2001), parental influence may wane when children reach adolescence and face pressure from peers. Nathanson studied peer mediation of antisocial television and found that it occurs frequently and it promotes more positive orientations toward violent programs, leading to greater aggression.

The peer group can exert influence via the digital devices that allow individuals to keep connected. Cell phones with instant text messaging, cameras, MP3 players, and Internet connections enable users to interact 24/7. The ability to connect with friends is a significant factor in being part of a peer group (KFF, 2010; Roberts & Foehr, 2004). "If you don't talk online with people, you might miss something that happened, and then when you see the kids at school, you won't know what they're talking about."

Social networking websites, such as MySpace, Facebook, and YouTube, as well as instant messaging (IM), e-mail, and chat rooms enable kids to connect with groups of people. In addition to being a source of social engagement, such technology can be a way for youth to experiment with different "personas." An adolescent may be a "brain" in high school math, but becomes "DarthVader69" online. Social networking sites can also be sources of gossip since they serve as peer connections. A rumor about someone can be spread in seconds, too short a time to check the rumor's validity.

Special interest websites, such as for sports or a certain music genre, are also sources of peer connection. File sharing among peers who have similar interests can further such connections.

Family-Media Linkages

How can families optimize the media experience for children?

Parents must exercise their primary responsibility in regulating and monitoring their children's viewing habits. In a democratic society, it is ultimately the viewer who bears responsibility for the effects of television; families must accept that responsibility by not viewing what is offensive and/or by supporting public interest groups.

Unfortunately, several studies (Comstock & Scharrer, 2007; Roberts & Foehr, 2004; Warren, 2005) indicate that parental involvement in children's viewing is infrequent. Some children are allowed to watch what and when they want. Other children are restricted to how early and how late they may watch. Still others have restrictions on their total viewing time per day. And some children are restricted to viewing certain approved shows. Although many shows are viewed with other family members, especially siblings, two intensive, longitudinal studies of young children and their families concluded that parents do not use the time to mediate the shows (St. Peters et al., 1991; Desmond, Singer, & Singer, 1990).

Parental involvement is difficult for many families, because both the parents may work, or be too busy. In still other families, parents aren't involved because the child has his or her own personal media devices.

Why is it harder to study the socialization effects of print than of screen media?

Children and Print Media: Books and Magazines

Compared to screen media, such as television, print media are more difficult to investigate scientifically because they are often long, have complex structures, and provoke more individual imagery than does television. Thus, it is difficult to separate the socializing effects of the *content* of the book or magazine from the socializing effects of the *interpretation* of the reader.

Unlike the screen media, where the visual image is provided, the print media describe in words the images of the writer. These words must then be translated into visual images by the reader. Obviously, reading is much more personal than is television viewing because the visual images readers conjure up from printed words depend on their vocabulary, reading ability, and real-life experiences.

Also, it is difficult to compare the socialization effects of books and TV because, until children gain a fair amount of reading skill, adults usually read books to them. This means adults are present to explain, answer questions, and adjust the tempo of the book to the child's level of understanding and interest. In addition, adults choose most of the books young children read. Parents and relatives buy them. Teachers assign certain books, and librarians choose which books will fill the library shelves. Thus, adults play a large role in determining the influence books will have on children, whereas this has not been the case with television viewing.

What do we know about the socialization potential of the print media?

How Books and Magazines Socialize Children

According to Roberts and Foehr (2004), children's and adolescents' exposure to print media is influenced by the socioeconomic status of the family and the educational level of the parents—more income means more resources for printed material; greater education means a higher value placed on books and reading.

The role that print media are known to play in socialization is that of passing on culture to the next generation, as illustrated by the prologues to each chapter in this book. The print media teach history, values, morals, ideals, and attitudes. Print-based culture is still the primary basis for information about education, religion, and government (Gerbner et al., 2002). The core of an educated person is **literacy**, being able to communicate through reading and writing. According to Postman (1986, p. 2), "the written word endures, the spoken word disappears." That print media make a powerful contribution to literacy may seem obvious, but why?

literacy the ability to communicate through reading and writing

Different media elicit different thinking skills (Healy, 1990; Strasburger, Wilson, & Jordan, 2008). Meringoff (1980) and colleagues (Char & Meringoff, 1981) compared young children's abilities to comprehend and reproduce narratives presented in different media (stories in print versus stories on television and radio). They found that even when the same soundtracks were used, television focused children's attention on the actions of characters, whereas radio or book format directed attention to the quality of the language. Children were more likely to consider television as an experience apart from themselves when answering questions about the program, whereas they were more likely to include their own personal experiences when answering questions about stories in books. As was said earlier, print and screen media require different ways of processing information.

Books are written language. Language, as was discussed in Chapter 2, enables socialization to take place. Language makes ideas and communication of these ideas possible; language also makes it possible to replace action with thoughts. Language is a vehicle by which individuals can express emotions (Rovenger, 2000). Language enables humans to internalize attitudes of others. Language is the means of passing on the cultural heritage from one generation to the next.

What impact does language have on socialization?

Magazines are written language, too, but they are infused with pictures and advertisements, sometimes in greater proportion than their articles. Thus, a socializing effect of magazines is consumerism. Magazines usually cater to special interests, such as fashion, sports, celebrities, music, computers, science, or pets, thereby contributing to the knowledge base of their readers. Teenagers often turn to magazines for advice on such things as relationships, appearance, and "cool" things to have (Kaiser Family Foundation, 2004).

Jim Trelease (2006), in *The Read-Aloud Handbook*, cites evidence stressing the importance of reading for building knowledge. Reading aloud improves children's *listening comprehension*, a skill that must occur before *reading comprehension*. It is the activity of reading aloud to children that enables them to become successful readers. Reading aloud is so important because it enhances attachment, and socialization begins with personal attachment. Reading aloud also provides a model for children to imitate. As Gail E. Haley said in the 1971 Caldecott Medal acceptance speech (the **Caldecott Medal** is an award given yearly by the Association for Library Services to Children for the most distinguished American picture book for children):

Caldecott Medal award given yearly for the most distinguished picture book for children

> Children who are not spoken to by live and responsive adults will not learn to speak properly. Children who are not answered will stop asking questions. They will become incurious. And children who are not told stories and who are not read to will have few reasons for wanting to learn to read.

Ellen Spitz, in *Inside Picture Books* (1999), analyzes books that adults have read to children for generations like *Goodnight Moon* (Brown, 1947) and *Where the Wild Things Are* (Sendak, 1963). She discusses how well-known picture books transmit psychological wisdom, convey moral lessons, and shape tastes. Hidden in these familiar stories are the anxieties of childhood, such as fear of separation and loss, or threat of aggression. Reading to children builds a special bond between the reader and listener.

Unfortunately, according to Zuckerman and Khandekar (2010), who developed the "Reach Out and Read" program, most American parents are not reading to children.

- Fewer than half (48%) of young children in the U.S. are read to daily, meaning that more than 13 million children under 5 go to bed every night without a bedtime story.
- The percentage of children read to daily drops even lower (to 36%) among low-income families, whose children face the highest risk of literacy problems.
- Even among high-income families, however, more than two out of every five children are not read to daily.

The Reach Out and Read program (http://www.reachoutandread.org) utilizes pediatricians and trained health professionals to discuss with parents, at their children's regular well visits, the importance of reading aloud to children. Pediatricians also recommend, and in some cases provide, appropriate books. Reach Out and Read is nationwide and is currently implementing Quality Improvement Initiatives to increase the proportion of eligible patients receiving books and parents receiving early literacy guidance at well-child visits.

How do print media influence children's development?

Language, Reading, and Cognitive Development

Books enhance language, reading skills, and comprehension, as well as overall cognitive development. The relationship of children's language to the amount of reading they do and the amount that is read aloud to them has been examined in numerous studies. Many studies have found that children who are read to often and who read a lot on their own are more advanced in their language development than children who are rarely read to and do not read very much on their own (Dickinson & Smith, 1994; McLane & McNamee, 1990; Senechal & LeFevre, 2002; Zuckerman & Khandekar, 2010).

By reading aloud to children, adults can enhance children's language development as well as the desire to read on their own.

Cengage Learning

Part of the explanation for the effect of reading on language development, compared to talking and/or other media, is that literary language is more structured and more complex. The language in children's books is more complex and richer in syntactic patterns than the language used in children's television programs (Healy, 1990; Postman, 1992).

Books also enhance reading development (Desmond, 2001). Research indicates that children who are read to learn to read earlier and more easily than children who are not read to. According to a study of mother–child book reading in low-income families (H. Raikes et al., 2006), book reading to children during the preschool years is reliably linked to language and cognitive development. For English-speaking children, the effects of having books read to them began to show up between 14 and 24 months regarding comprehension and vocabulary. For Spanish-speaking children, positive associations between book reading and language and cognitive development were apparent by 36 months. The difference between the two groups may have been due to differences in book availability and reading patterns by the mothers. Other studies have demonstrated that children who had been read to and had their questions answered learned to read early (Barclay, Benelli, & Curtis, 1995; Senechal & LeFevre, 2002; Zuckerman & Khandekar, 2010).

What is the impact of early reading on later cognitive outcomes? Although most children learn to read at school, preschool children who are read to develop emergent literary skills, such as understanding that words tell stories and words are made up of different letters (Whitehurst & Lonigan, 1998). Letter recognition has been found to correlate with future reading achievement scores (Lonigan, Burgess, & Anthony, 2000).

Books nourish cognitive development. Not only do they provide information and concepts, they also provide vicarious experiences and stimulate the child's imagination. For example, *The Very Hungry Caterpillar* (for preschoolers) by Eric Carle (1986) helps teach a child the days of the week, how to count to five, and how a caterpillar becomes a butterfly, all in bright pictures.

Books can be used to help children gain an understanding of themselves and others across time and space (Norton & Norton, 2010). For example, *The Three Pigs* (for preschoolers) by David Wiesner (2001) was the 2002 winner of the Caldecott Medal. The book is an adaptation of the classic folktale. The pigs are huffed and puffed off the page into a new world. Transformations occur as the pigs boldly enter new stories, make new friends, and ultimately control their own fate.

What are the effects of books and literature on children's psychosocial development?

Psychosocial Development

Books and literature can help children understand the realities of life. They provide children with models of behavior, helping children understand the consequences of certain behaviors; they provide values with stories to illustrate them; they can enable children to cope with problems in their lives; and they offer an opportunity for children to understand their feelings as well as the feelings of others.

1. **Role models**—models of behavior, models of gender roles, and models of occupational roles (Rovenger, 2000). For example, *Mothers Can Do Anything* (for preschoolers) by Joe Lasker (1972) demonstrates the variety of jobs mothers can hold, including scientist, linesman, artist, and lion tamer.

2. **Values** (Bennett, 1993). For example, Linda Sue Park's (2001) *A Single Shard* (for school-agers) was the 2002 winner of the **Newbery Medal**, an award presented yearly by the American Library Association (ALA) for the most distinguished contribution to American literature for children. The book is about dedication to one's dreams. The story takes place in 12th-century Korea where Tree-ear, an orphan, becomes fascinated by the artistry and craft of some potters who live nearby. Despite great odds, Tree-ear's courage, honor, and perseverance enable him to become an apprentice to the master potter, Min. He achieves great happiness by fulfilling his dream of becoming an artist.
3. **Cope with problems** (Bettelheim, 1976; Cashdan, 1999; Rovenger, 2000). For example, some fairy tales and folk stories deal with aggressive and negative traits of human beings and indicate ways of coping with them. Folk and fairy tales are appealing to children because they explain things in terms to which children can relate. Folk and fairy tales lie at the root of every culture and, despite geographical differences, have many similarities in theme (Campbell, 1968; Norton & Norton, 2010). Common themes found in folk tales include tribal history, local history, myth, legend, tricksters, and entertainment.
4. **Understand feelings** (Rovenger, 2000). For example, in the 2010 Newbury Medal winner, *When You Reach Me* (for tweens) by Rebecca Stead (2009), the underlying theme is being able to see situations through other people's eyes. Miranda, the main character, also learns that giving or withholding small acts of kindness or meanness can have big consequences. Miranda gains and loses friends and grapples with normal sixth-grade angst, but her worries take on a new twist when she discovers mysterious notes from someone who tries to convince her that things can be seen that have not happened yet.

Newbery Medal award given yearly for the most distinguished contribution to American literature for children

Concerns about Children and Books and Magazines

What concerns are associated with print media?

Books can elicit some of the concerns that were described earlier in this chapter regarding television, such as fantasy being confused with reality, violence, the perpetuation of certain values (such as sexual explicitness and offensive language), stereotyping, and even commercialism (toy tie-ins, clothing, or movies).

Concerns about books sometimes translate into "challenged and banned books." A "challenge" is an attempt, via a formal, written complaint, to remove or restrict materials based on the objections of a person or group; a "ban" is the removal of those materials. Challenges attempt to remove material from school curriculum or the library, thereby restricting the access of others. According to the American Library Association (www.ala.org, 2008), the top three reasons for challenging books are that they contain material considered to (1) be "sexually explicit," (2) have "offensive language," and (3) be "unsuited to age group."

Fantasy and Reality

The degree to which books should reflect reality leads to controversy regarding how the characters solve problems and how they are portrayed (Norton & Norton, 2010). Some books have young characters who overcome obstacles, apparently caused by adults, through real problem solving or through fantasy. For example, Maurice Sendak's *Where the Wild Things Are* (1963) illustrates Max's imagination when, because of his misbehavior, his mother sends him to his room without supper. This book was banned in some schools because its illustrations were regarded as "frightening" to young children and because of its message. Others highly recommend the book because readers can identify with Max and his strong feelings expressed through fantasy.

The Goosebumps books, a series of monster mysteries by R. L. Stine, were introduced to school-agers through school book clubs. There are five basic plots written in a clipped style thick with thumps and gasps. They are advertised on TV and have games and toys for children to act out the plots, thereby blurring the boundaries of fantasy and reality (Gellene, 1996). Critics say they don't promote literacy but do promote commercialism. Another example of the business strategy of "toy tie-ins" is Mattel Corporation's American Girl—dolls that come with books, movies, clothing, and furnishings.

A popular series for older school-agers is *Harry Potter* by J. K. Rowling. Apparently, these best sellers are stimulating children's imaginations through their blend of fantasy, magic, mystery, and reality. Attendance at the movies and video purchases, as well as book sales, attest to *Harry Potter*'s popularity. Harry is an 11-year-old English boy who became an orphan when his "good wizard" parents died saving him from an evil wizard. The action surrounds Harry's dual life among the "muggles" (ordinary human beings, including his cruel foster parents) and his teachers at the Hogwarts School of Witchcraft and Wizardry, and his progress toward initiation as a sorcerer/magician. The classic theme of the power of magic still attracts readers. Some people, however, object to the witchcraft theme, saying it is antireligious. It has appeared on the ALA's most challenged book list since 1999.

Violence

Children were exposed to violence in stories and fairy tales long before there was television, and it has been shown that children imitate aggression from storybooks, just as they do from television (Neuman, 1995). Bettelheim (1976) and Cashdan (1999) believe that fairy tales help children cope with their strong emotions on an unconscious level: "It seems particularly appropriate to a child that exactly what the evil-doer wishes to inflict on the hero should be the bad person's fate—as the witch in 'Hansel and Gretel' who wants to cook children in the oven is pushed into it and burned to death" (Bettelheim, 1976, p. 144).

In *The Witch Must Die*, Cashdan (1999) explores how fairy tales help children project their own inner struggles with good and evil onto battles enacted by characters in the stories. According to Cashdan, the violence we, as adults, see in literature for young children, especially in fairy tales, is really a catharsis, a mechanism for release of strong feelings. A well-written book also enables the reader to empathize with the human suffering of people's inhumane acts because the author has time to develop the characters (Huck et al., 2004).

Stereotyping

Stereotypes continue to appear in children's books, textbooks, and magazines as they do on TV. Males, European Americans, and middle-class families tend to be overrepresented. Men and boys are more likely to be active and presented in adventuresome or exciting roles; females are more likely to be passive or dependent and presented in inconspicuous or immobile roles. Fairy tales, especially those made into Disney movies, are good examples (*Cinderella, Snow White and the Seven Dwarfs, Beauty and the Beast*).

Children's literature, specifically award-winning books in the 1980s–1990s, present more equitable portrayals of gender and cultural diversity (Dellman-Jenkins, Florjancic, & Swadener, 1993; MacLeod, 1994) than were present in the 1960s–1970s. What about the 21st century? Hamilton and colleagues (2000) studied top-selling children's books from 2001 as well as a seven-year sample of Caldecott award–winning books, for a total of 200 books. They found nearly twice as many male as female titles and main characters. Male characters appeared 53 percent more times in illustrations. Female main characters nurtured more than male main characters did, and were seen in more indoor than outdoor scenes. Occupations were gender stereotyped. Overall, few differences in sexism were found between Caldecott Award–winning books and other books.

Some changes have occurred in elementary school textbook gender-role stereotyping. Since 1972, when Scott, Foresman and Company was the first publisher to issue

IN PRACTICE

Examining Textbooks for Biases

A problem with depending solely on a textbook for classroom instruction is that sometimes the validity of its content is not questioned. Sadker and Zittleman (2009) recommend critically examining textbooks for the following biases:

1. *Invisibility:* the underrepresentation of certain groups
2. *Stereotyping:* the attribution of rigid roles to certain groups
3. *Selectivity and imbalance:* the interpretation of issues and situations from only one perspective
4. *Unreality:* the exclusion of sensitive and controversial topics
5. *Fragmentation and isolation:* separating issues, information, and contributions of certain groups from main instructional materials rather than integrating them
6. *Linguistic bias:* the omission of feminine and ethnic group references, pronouns, and names
7. *Cosmetic bias:* the superficial appearance of a well-balanced curriculum, giving the illusion of equity

guidelines for improving the image of women in textbooks, all major publishers have issued recommendations for reducing inequities in instructional materials. Although basal reader books have tried to become more equitable in their inclusion of previously underrepresented groups, reality is still misrepresented (Sadker & Zittleman, 2009). For example, in an attempt to correct previous imbalances, males from cultural minority groups are overrepresented in working roles, as compared to the actual makeup of the labor force. Individuals with disabilities, on the other hand, are underrepresented in basal reader series. People over age 55 not only are underrepresented, but are often shown walking in parks, rocking in chairs, and being cranky. Finally, relatively few of the families portrayed in basal readers have single parents, even though about half the children reading these books are likely to spend at least part of their childhood with only one parent.

Concern about the effects of school textbooks on gender-role stereotyping, attitudes about cultural minorities and people with disabilities, and acquisition of values has caused some state boards of education to adopt guidelines for purchase.

What about magazines and stereotyping?

Magazines for teenagers have been around for decades; for example, *Seventeen*, a magazine for teenage girls, was first published in 1944 and still dominates sales. It has articles on fashion, cosmetics, celebrities, and relationships (Massoni, 2010). Teenage boys prefer to read magazines about sports, cars, or computers (Comstock & Scharrer, 2007). Many magazines have websites that solicit reader feedback, providing forums and chat rooms where teens can blog to other teens. Some magazines use the web to recruit "cool hunters" to stay informed about emerging trends in the youth culture (Kaiser Family Foundation, 2004).

Massoni (2010), a sociologist, has written the first cultural history of the origins of *Seventeen* and its role in shaping the modern teen girl ideal. Using content analysis, interviews, letters, oral histories, and promotional materials, she shows how *Seventeen* helped create the modern concept of "teenager." The early *Seventeen* provided a generation of thinking young women with information on citizenship and clothing, politics and popularity, adult occupations and adolescent preoccupations. In the latter part of the 20th century, however, economic and social forces converged to reshape the magazine toward teen consumerism.

One study (Evans et al., 1991) sampled ten issues each of three widely circulated female-oriented magazines (*Seventeen*, *Sassy*, and *YM*) to identify messages directed at teenage girls and how they related to female identity. The conclusion was that the road to happiness for girls is to attract males by physical beautification (presumably by purchasing the products advertised in the magazine). Many articles implied that female self-esteem should be related to body image, physical attractiveness, and satisfaction with one's weight. According to psychiatrists Derenne and Beresin (2006), who reviewed changes in ideal female body type throughout history, the ideal of beauty has been difficult to achieve and has been shaped by social context. "Current mass media is ubiquitous and powerful, leading to increased body dissatisfaction among both men and women" (p. 257). They conclude that exposure to mass media (television, movies, magazines, Internet) is correlated with obesity and negative body image, which may lead to disordered eating.

What makes popular music different from other media?

Children and Audio Media: Popular Music

Throughout time and across cultures, people have always created and listened to music. It is a form of communication, emotional expression, art, celebration, tradition, and enjoyment. Music expresses aspects of the culture as it changes through history; for example, popular music through the years has ranged from patriotic "Yankee Doodle" to jazz to rock (Sklaroff, 2002). "Pop" music usually refers to rock, but other types of music, such as hip-hop, R&B, and alternative, which may go in and out of vogue, also have a socializing effect. Popular music is an example of how the tastes and preferences of young people have fueled the billion-dollar music industry (Comstock & Scharrer, 2007). What sets today's popular music apart from television and books is that it is an expression of the subculture of youth and also that it effectively alienates many adults (AACAP, 2004).

The media of records, radio, television, videos, MP3 players, and CDs provide the ways and means for popular music today. For example:

> With its origins in the music of slaves and other downtrodden groups, rock music has always spoken to values and points of view outside the mainstream, values frequently divergent from or in opposition to adult culture. . . . Rock music offers an antidote to and an escape from the unrelenting socialization pressures that emanate daily from family and school. Popular music does not tell its listeners to delay gratification and prepare for adulthood. Rather, it tells young people that the concerns they have today are of importance, that they merit expression in music, and that one ought to value one's youth and not worry so much about the future. (Larson, Kubey, & Colletti, 1989, pp. 584, 596–597)

For most young people, music use is driven primarily by the motivation to control mood and enhance emotional states (Strasburger, Wilson, & Jordan, 2008). Music's ability to communicate emotion and influence mood has been widely noted. Even preschoolers and infants as young as 8 months can reliably discriminate "happy" and "sad" music (Roberts, Christenson, & Gentile, 2003).

According to reviews of the research on popular music (Christenson & Roberts, 1998; Roberts & Foehr, 2004), children's interest in rock music accelerates at about the third and fourth grades, and by early adolescence, teens listen to music (radio, CDs, MP3 players, music videos) from two to five hours each day. Girls listen more than boys. African Americans and Latino Americans watch music videos more than European Americans.

Music preferences become more specific as children get older. Boys generally prefer the louder forms of rock; girls generally prefer softer, more romantic forms. Cultural background and socioeconomic status also play a role in music choice. African Americans report a preference for soul, rap, and rhythm and blues; Latino Americans lean toward salsa; European Americans say they like all types of rock (Roberts & Foehr, 2004).

Popular music provides many adolescents with a means of identifying with a particular group or performer (Larson, 1995), especially when real positive role models are lacking in the young person's life. Going to concerts, collecting rock stars' music, wearing certain clothing, adopting certain hairstyles, and getting tattooed or body pierced can all be part of an adolescent's search for identity—it's a style to "try on," a group of which to be a part. Performers are powerful image-makers; their effect on children depends on the role of other significant socializing agents, such as family and friends.

Teens at a rock concert.
Shae cardenas/Shutterstock.com

> Music style, defined as the selection of a certain type of music and a personal style to go with it, is one of the most powerful identifying markers in the school crowd structure. Within any high school it is usually easy to classify many subgroups of adolescents according to their music preferences (e.g., "metalheads," "goths," "alternatives," "hip-hop," "punkers," "rastas," etc.). These labels may change as music changes, but the underlying processes of adolescent subcultures are likely to remain the same. (Roberts, Christenson, & Gentile, 2003, p. 158)

What effect do music lyrics have on listeners?

The medium of vocal music is a socializing influence in that it engages one's attention and emotions with the sound while espousing certain values with the lyrics (AACAP, 2004). However, motivation, experience, knowledge, and self-concept are factors in the interpretation of the lyrics (Strasburger, Wilson, & Jordan, 2008). For example, some studies (Prinsky & Rosenbaum, 1987; Thompson, 1993) have discovered that preadolescents and adolescents often don't understand or attend to the underlying themes in the lyrics. Other studies (Larson, 1995) report music listening as a fantasy experience to explore possible selves (images of power and conquest, rescue by an idealized lover). This effect is magnified by music videos (discussed later) with their visual as well as audio components (for example, MTV) (Strouse, Buerkel-Rothfuss, & Long, 1995) and is reduced by the presence of family members who disapprove (Thompson & Larson, 1995). Christenson and Roberts (1998) found that teenagers who report watching music videos or music television shows do so to find out what is "cool," rather than learning any social values. However, they also found that the more important music is to an adolescent, the more importance he or she places on lyrics relative to other elements of music gratification. In addition, attention to lyrics was highest among fans of controversial music—music that is alienated from the mainstream (whether it be 1960s protest folk or rock or the heavy metal and rap of today).

Some (Arnett, 1991; Roberts & Christenson, 2001) suggest that adolescents' fascination with the despairing lyrics of some types of music is a *symptom* of alienation, not its *cause*. For some teens, drug use and careless behavior provide an escape from a chaotic family environment. Acting on the lyric suggestions reflects an absence of parental supervision. For most fans, heavy metal music serves not as a source of anger and frustration, but as a release. A study (Anderson, Carnagey, & Eubanks, 2003) was done on 65 female and 74 male college students to find out the effects of songs with violent lyrics on aggressive thoughts and feelings. It was demonstrated by word completion and interpretation tests that the college students who heard a violent song felt more hostile than those who heard a similar (same artist and genre) but nonviolent song. The concern is that repeated exposure to violent lyrics may contribute to the development of an aggressive personality.

The question that remains is whether the songs *reflect* the values of a particular generation or *influence* that generation's values. Concern centers on the issue of contagion.

contagion the phenomenon in which an individual exposed to a suggestion will act on it

Contagion is the phenomenon in which an individual exposed to a suggestion will act on it. For example, there is a concern regarding the language and the social criticism set to rhyme (rap) in the music genre hip-hop. Also of concern to adults is the potential for alienation of the youth who listen, because the lyrics generally are self-assertive expressions of disgust with the establishment. However, rap and hip-hop remain popular and have been commercialized. The artists themselves, their style of dress, or the genre's lyrics and beat are used to sell products (Fedorak, 2009). Adults fear the contagious effect such role models may have on their children regarding language, violence, sexuality, substance abuse, and anti-establishment messages.

The mass media have cultivated hip-hop culture, commodifying the music, dancing, graffiti art, language, and style of dress (Watkins, 2005). Today, many advertisements aimed at the youth generation are set to hip-hop music or rap rhyme. Russell Simmons and Sean "P. Diddy" Combs are examples of rappers who have capitalized on hip-hop's business appeal, having recognized that hip-hop is about aspiration and creating a better life. Many hip-hop artists have become prominent in screen media as well as audio. Many have used hip-hop as a means of political activism to call attention to urban blight, poverty, gang violence, racism, drugs, authoritarianism, and global issues. The catchy beat beckons attention. As quoted on the back cover of *Can't Stop Won't Stop: A History of the Hip-Hop Generation* (Chang, 2005), hiphop "draws from the fire, verve, rage, injustices, pains, victories, and creativity of a whole generation of marginalized, forgotten, pissed-on, and pissed-off youth."

Some rock stars try to contribute positively to the community by agreeing to be role models for anti-drug campaigns, or by donating their time for rock concerts to raise money for Third World countries. For example, in 2005, free worldwide concerts ("Live 8") were held to redirect activism from the streets to politics with the goal of making poverty history. Their message was broadcast in more than 140 countries on the radio and the Internet.

What about music videos?

MTV, or Music Television, first introduced in 1983, is a highly controversial provider of entertainment because of its ability to captivate young audiences. MTV is a 24-hour rock music, cable television channel that promotes new songs by accompanying them with visual dramatization. Some of these videos have been criticized for their violence, sexism, substance abuse, and sexual content (AACAP, 2004; Strasburger, Wilson, & Jordan, 2008; Villani, 2001), as well as stereotyping of groups with diverse cultural backgrounds (Rich et al., 1998). A concern about the marriage of music to television is that many adolescents in the United States view MTV, or other music video channels, at least once a week (Roberts & Foehr, 2004). Mental images once formed by rhythm, beat, and perceived lyrics are now created by special effects on video. Another concern is the commercialism. Music videos show images that sell a product (Villani, 2001); therefore, what messages are really being promoted must be questioned. For example, many preadolescents and adolescents are influenced by the clothing, jewelry, hairstyles, and body art adorning music artists.

What is the impact of new media technology that enhances interaction and multiusage?

Children and Digital Media: Interactive and Multimedia

In the 20th century, "each new media technology brought with it great promise for social and educational benefits, and great concern for children's exposure to inappropriate and harmful content" (Wartella & Jennings, 2000, p. 31).

Interactive and multimedia are technologies that enable the user to participate actively, such as computers, video games, digital devices, and cell phones. According to Roberts and Foehr (2008), the total amount of media used by young people (ages 8–18) each day has increased to more than eight hours, excluding schoolwork, with most of the increase coming from video games and computers. Much of the media exposure is multidimensional and flexible, meaning that more than one medium is used at a time (for example, going online while watching TV), or using one medium for various purposes (for example, accessing the Internet via cell phone). Even children ages 0–6 spend as much time with TV, computers, and video games as playing outside (KFF, 2003a).

While it is difficult to generalize about the impact on children of new media technology, most psychologists and educators agree that it is empowering in that children's sense of self-efficacy is enhanced by being able to easily access information, entertainment, and communication. According to Brooks-Gunn and Donahue (2008), the implication for parents is the need to educate themselves about new media technology, to teach children media literacy skills, and to set limits. The implication for educators is the need to use new media technology to help children learn by incorporating digital media into the curriculum for enrichment, skill practice, and independent research (Prensky, 2010).

Children, Computers, and the Internet

The Internet, formerly known as the Arpanet by the U.S. Department of Defense, was first constructed to form a network that would always be operable under any form of attack because there was no central distribution point. This network soon came to be used by universities to share information with each other and was later adopted by the private sector and individuals. The Internet created public space and removed barriers to communication, such as time and space. This public network is neither owned nor controlled by any individual or institution; free speech prevails. As an international network, the Internet encompasses many different cultures. Websites, social networking sites, e-mail, instant messaging, and chat rooms create what McLuhan called a "global village."

The Internet is a pool of information. Whatever may be of interest to you, no matter how major or minor, is potentially there. Information is typically stored on the web pages posted by individuals and content producers. Because websites are not categorized, search engines have emerged as a means to sort and index the sites. Websites sometimes provide means for feedback from visitors, and forums can be created wherein collaboration can take place. It can be a challenge to distinguish objectivity from subjectivity (Alexander & Tate, 1999; Livingstone, 2009). Information on the Internet is multidimensional rather than linear. Topics can expand in various directions through hyperlinks among websites. One has to take care not to get sidetracked.

Some of the problems with Internet technology, besides appropriateness of content on certain websites (discussed later), are:

1. piracy issues over illegal transferring of copyrighted material,
2. privacy issues regarding the ability to track online usage patterns and gain access to personal data,
3. the capacity to hack into unauthorized information,
4. viruses and worms that can destroy data on computers, and
5. unsolicited junk mail, or "spam."

Since more than two-thirds of U.S. children have access to computers at home, and virtually all have access at school (Roberts & Foehr, 2008), what interactive websites have been designed specifically for them? Some websites are educational; some are for entertainment; and some are a combination ("edutainment"). An example of an educational site is PBS Kids' "Africa," wherein a spider explores Africa's amazing places, its civilization, and its culture. An example of an entertainment site is Disney's "Pirates of the Caribbean Online," a virtual world for children to adopt avatars and play games. An example of an "edutainment" site is Disney's Club Penguin. The *Club Penguin Times* is a virtual gazette, distributed monthly to the estimated 6.7 million users of Club Penguin. It supplies educational information related to various games, and children ages 6 to 14 supply much of the content by submitting poems, jokes, reviews of events, and questions to "Aunt Arctic." "Today not only are American young people surrounded by media in their homes and schools, but the portability made possible by the increased miniaturization of digital media means they can remain connected anywhere they wish" (Roberts & Foehr, 2008, p. 12).

IN CONTEXT "Facebook" for Kids

My granddaughters, age 10 and 11, have begged to get Facebook, as some of their friends network. Social networking sites, such as Facebook, do not allow kids under age 13 to join. However, "Togetherville," a social network for 6- to 10-year-olds, was recently created. It's free to join, and kids' accounts must be created by their parents using their own Facebook logins. Parents can approve or reject their children's friends and see what types of activities their kids are engaging in. Kids have separate logins from their parents. There are games, prescreened YouTube videos, and educational applications, but no ads. Parents can send their kids virtual gifts, review their activities on the site, or look at virtual art the kids have created (http://www.npr.org, May 18, 2010).

How do children cope with access to all kinds of information on the Internet without having developed critical thinking skills, or distinguish between commercial interests and educational ones?

Reading comprehension via the Internet requires different skills from reading comprehension via traditional book reading, according to Leu and colleagues (Leu et al., 2005). Reading online is a process that requires knowledge about how search engines work and how information is organized within websites—knowledge that many students lack. Internet reading also requires a higher level of inferential reasoning and comprehension-monitoring strategies that help readers stay on task. Programs are being developed to train teachers to teach online digital literacy, including strategies to search for, navigate, critically evaluate, and synthesize online information. One of the most challenging aspects of online reading is understanding how to strategically evaluate a long list of search results to determine which link, if any, to pursue (Coiro & Dobler, 2007).

Leu and colleagues (2005) asked 50 of the best seventh-grade readers from school districts in rural South Carolina and urban Connecticut to assess the reliability of a slickly designed website about the mythical "endangered Pacific Northwest Tree Octopus." Though the site is a known hoax, all but one child claimed it was scientifically valid. Even after the participants were informed the site was a joke, about half of the children were adamant that it was truthful. Thus, it is important that children learn online digital literacy skills, as they can easily get conned by misinformation.

There is concern regarding the disparities of opportunities for children of different socioeconomic statuses to learn to use computers effectively as tools in their lives and to experience enriched learning in the classroom (Hofferth, 2010; Jackson et al., 2006; Roberts & Foehr, 2008). Thus, some children may lag behind in the very skills needed to succeed in our increasingly computer-dependent society. Are we creating a gap between the information-rich and the information-poor?

Jackson and colleagues (2006) did a longitudinal field study designed to assess the effects of Internet use in low-income families. Most of the 140 urban child participants were about 13 years old, of African American heritage, from poor, single-parent families. At the beginning of the study, the children were underperforming in school, scoring at the 30th percentile on standardized reading tests. Every family was provided with a home computer and Internet access. Participants completed periodic surveys regarding Internet use and participated in home visits. Jackson found that children who used the Internet more frequently had higher scores on standardized reading tests after six months and higher grade point averages 1½ years after the study began than children who used it less frequently. Why was this so? Jackson's analysis is that the Internet is more of a fun learning environment compared to traditional ways of developing academic performance.

What about the socializing effects of computers outside the educational domain?

Some fear that children who have home computers will become social isolates and choose solitary activities over interactive ones. So far, this has not been widely proven. One study (Sleek, 1998) over a two-year time span of people who regularly log on to the Internet, found that as use of the Internet increased, the number of social activities engaged in and social support experiences decreased. On the other hand, children often *use* a computer to attract playmates, as by sharing software and games via e-mail or social networking sites. They also use it to communicate with friends. On the negative side, the computer can be a source of gossip and cyberbullying. Also, kids who don't have access to an e-mail account or social networking site are often excluded from peer group activities, like an invitation to a birthday party sent via a multiple list e-mail. In the classroom, the computer serves as a means for children to engage in collaborative activities (Plowman, Stephen, & McPake, 2010; Prensky, 2010).

According to some studies (Gross, 2004; Valkenburg & Peter, 2007), adolescent boys and girls use online digital technology similarly (computers or cell phones) to socially interact. They spend about an hour a day e-mailing or text messaging their friends, usually about school, friends, plans, and gossip. Apparently, as the teens reported, such communication makes them feel closer. However, according to research by Turkle (2011) on the effects of social networking, people are increasingly functioning without face-to-face contact, resulting in a feeling of alienation. She says that teens' identities are no longer being shaped by self-exploration, but by how their online persona is perceived by their network of friends. In addition, online digital communication can be the source of dangerous connections with strangers. Teens at risk for such include those with a history of depression or abuse (Wolak, Mitchell, & Finkelhor, 2003).

Some risks or problems of children "surfing" the Internet include (AACAP, 2001):

What about online access to inappropriate or offensive information?

1. Accessing areas that are inappropriate or overwhelming
2. Being exposed to online information that promotes hate, violence, and pornography
3. Being misled and bombarded with intense advertising
4. Being invited to register for prizes or to join a club where they are providing personal or household information to an unknown source

Finding pornography on the Internet is as easy as "googling" the word "sex." Boys are more likely to seek out pornography than girls and use increases with age (Wolak, Mitchell, & Finkelhor, 2007). However, some exposure to sexually explicit sites is unsought, as in junk e-mails (spam) or pop-up ads. What can parents do? Parents can now, with certain software, block out parts of the Internet (pornography, for example) to which they don't want their children exposed. The problem with such software filters is that they block access to websites via certain banned words; thus, it may block "breast" links not only to pornography but also to cancer. Some states have laws banning sending spam to children.

Parents can register their e-mail address to block inappropriate messages online. Most importantly, parents should monitor their child's Internet activity, learning the technology, limiting online time, and discussing various risks (AACAP, 2001; Rosen, 2007).

Video games actively engage children in media technology.

Holos/Getty Images

Regarding privacy, the Federal Trade Commission passed the Children's Online Privacy Protection Act (COPPA), which is continually being revised. The primary goal of COPPA is to give parents control over what information is collected from their children online and how such information may be used. The rules protect children from data gathering by online marketers by requiring parental permission prior to obtaining information.

Regarding inappropriate and offensive content on Internet sites, the Federal Communications Commission has issued rules implementing the Children's Internet Protection Act (CIPA), a federal law enacted by Congress in 2001 to address concerns about access to offensive content over the Internet on school and library computers funded with public money (http://www.fcc.gov/cgb).

What are the influences on a child's development of playing computerized games?

Children and Computerized Video/DVD Games

Computerized games represent a fusion of digital media technology. Electronic interactive games such as Nintendo or Wii, played on the TV screen, computer monitor, or digital device, are a qualitatively different form of play than traditional play—interaction takes place between the players and an intangible for a wide range of experiences rather than an interaction with other players or tangible materials (balls, dolls, game boards) (Scarlett et al., 2005). "Video games are the first medium to combine visual dynamism with an active participatory role for the child" (Greenfield, 1984, p. 101). Table 9.1 categorizes types of electronic games (Scarlett et al., 2005, p.117).

Children find electronic games appealing because of their (a) graphics and realism; (b) gradual, or levels of, challenge; and (c) ways of encouraging interaction (Scarlett et al., 2005). Electronic games have been developed for infants and toddlers, preschoolers, school-agers, adolescents, and adults. Electronic play for infants and toddlers (occurring jointly with parents) may serve as a distraction from the developmental task of developing a sense of self, which involves recognizing that they are separate beings (Anderson & Evans, 2001). However, for older children Schmidt and Vandewater (2008) have found that electronic media, particularly video games, can enhance visual spatial skills, such as visual tracking, mental rotation, and target localization. Gaming may also improve problem-solving skills. Some games can be educational in that they reinforce certain skills, such as math, spelling, or reading, or require players to use certain strategies (Hofferth, 2010).

The main concern with these interactive electronic games is the prevalence of aggression, sex, and gender-role stereotyping, as well as the rule-bound logic designed by the programmers (Anderson, Gentile, & Buckley, 2006; Dietz, 1998; National Institute on Media and the Family, 2001; Provenzo, 1991). Playing video games is more than interacting with the game physically (using a joystick, mouse, or finger to manipulate characters and objects); it also involves interacting with the game psychologically and emotionally in that you become the characters on screen.

A meta-analytic, multicultural review of the literature on violent video games and aggression, empathy, and prosocial behavior (Anderson et al., 2010), which analyzed 130 research reports on more than 130,000 subjects worldwide, concluded that exposure to violent video games makes kids more aggressive and less caring—regardless of their age, sex or culture. Many states have banned the sale of violent video games to children, finding they are made for adults, but such rulings have been overturned in most cases due to

Table 9.1 Computer and Video Game Ratings

EC (**Early Childhood**): contains content that may be suitable for ages 3 and older. Contains no material that parents would find inappropriate.

E (**Everyone**): contains content that may be suitable for ages 6 and older. Titles in this category may contain minimal cartoon, fantasy, or mild violence or infrequent use of mild language, or both.

E10+ (**Everyone 10 and Older**): contains content that may be suitable for ages 10 and older. Titles in this category may contain more cartoon, fantasy, or mild violence; mild language; and minimal suggestive themes.

T (**Teen**): contains content that may be suitable for ages 13 and older. Titles in this category may contain violence, suggestive themes, crude humor, minimal blood, simulated gambling, or infrequent use of strong language.

M (**Mature**): contains content that may be suitable for persons ages 17 and older. Titles in this category may contain intense violence, blood and gore, sexual content, or strong language.

AO (**Adults Only**): contains content that should only be played by persons ages 18 and older. Titles in this category may include prolonged scenes of intense violence, graphic sexual content, and nudity.

Source: www.esrb.org.

challenges by video game industry groups, which claim such games are protected forms of expression under the First Amendment.

Video games portray gender roles stereotypically and contribute to the role media play in socializing sexism. A content analysis of images of video game characters from top-selling American gaming magazines showed male characters (83 percent) are more likely than female characters (62 percent) to be portrayed as aggressive. Female characters are more likely than male characters to be portrayed as sexualized (60 percent versus 1 percent), scantily clad (39 percent versus 8 percent), and as showing a mix of sex and aggression (39 percent versus 1 percent). A survey of teens confirmed that stereotypes of male characters as aggressive and female characters as sexually objectified physical specimens are held even by non-gamers (Dill & Thill, 2007). Why do TV producers and video game manufacturers produce more video games for boys than girls? Males play video games more than females (Anderson, Funk, & Griffiths, 2004; Scarlett et al., 2005). This may be because males tend to be attracted to their action-oriented, often violent, content. The male demand for such aggressive games may arise from a need to have strong role models, rather than from male hormones.

Also of concern regarding electronic games, computers, and the Internet are the increasing opportunities for extension of real experiences to virtual ones (Anderson, Funk, & Griffiths, 2004). Multimedia technology enables children to interact with simulated characters, assume multiple identities, and chat with strangers who may also have simulated identities (Subrahmanyam et al., 2001). How do children shift from reality to simulation and back to reality, and what is the outcome?

Still another concern is the possible link between electronic media use and attention deficits. According to Schmidt and Vandewater (2008), a small positive relationship was found between heavy electronic media use and mild attention problems in school.

In a review of the research on video game playing, the National Institute on Media and the Family (2001) summarized the positive and negative influences on children as follows:

Positive Influences

- Games provide an introduction to information technology.
- Games can give practice in following directions.
- Some games provide practice in problem solving and logic.
- Games can provide practice in use of fine motor and spatial skills.
- Games can provide an opportunity for adult and child to play together.

Negative Influences

- Practicing violent acts may contribute more to aggressive behavior than passive viewing of violence.
- Games are often based on plots of aggression, competition, and stereotyping.
- More often, games do not present opportunities for independent thought or creativity.
- Games can confuse reality and fantasy.
- Academic achievement may be negatively related to overall time spent playing video or computer games.

In sum, adults should become cognizant of available technology, software, and games. They should use video game ratings to determine developmental appropriateness for their child. The Entertainment Software Rating Board is a nonprofit, self-regulatory body that independently assigns ratings, enforces advertising guidelines, and helps ensure responsible online practices for interactive software. They should also limit the time spent playing games, with homework and chores being done first. In addition, they should discuss the game content with the child, explaining discrepancies between reality and fantasy (AACAP, 2006d).

Summary

- Mass media include screen, print, audio, and multimedia. Media are intervening means through which forces act or effects are produced. They are shapers, spreaders, and transformers of culture.
- Chronosystem influences on the media are mainly related to new technology.
- Macrosystem influences on mass media include politics (laws), economics (corporate sponsors), and technology (medium and message).
- The socializing effect of television viewing is complicated due to mediating influences—selective attention, psychological needs, attitudes, motives, habits, interests, values, morals, beliefs, and experiences, as well as co-viewing with an adult.
- Theories of how screen media influence children's socialization outcomes include social cognitive, cultivation, motivation, and displacement.
- Watching TV and movies impacts children's socioemotional development and relationships, physical development and health, psychological development and behavior, cognitive development and achievement, as well as moral development and values.
- Mesosystem influences on the media include linkages with the community, school, and family. The community's linkage to the media (broadcast television) has been to develop alternatives. The school's linkage to the media is to teach critical viewing skills as well as to use educational television programs in the classroom. The family's linkage to the media is to help children develop critical viewing skills, to set limits, and to co-view with children whenever possible.
- Print media (books and magazines) describe in words the images of the writer. The socializing effects of print media on young children are usually mediated by adults. Print media influence language, reading, and cognitive development, as well as literacy.
- Audio media/popular music engage children's attention and emotions with the sound while espousing certain values with the lyrics. Popular music provides many adolescents with a means of identifying with a particular group or performer, influencing dress, behavior, friends, and self-concept.
- Interactive and multimedia include computers, video games, digital devices, and cell phones. Concerns regarding children's usage focus on the effects on social interaction, the reduced time spent on other activities, the impact of aggressive, sexual, and stereotypical games, the confusion of reality with fantasy, and the access to information without the necessary critical skills.

Activity

PURPOSE To increase your awareness of television's impact.

1. Monitor a child's (or your own) television viewing behavior for a week, using the chart that follows as a model.
2. Note the total viewing hours for the week.
3. Keep track of the time spent in other leisure activities for a week.
4. Analyze your findings to determine what types of shows are viewed and the potential impact of their content and commercial messages on viewers.

Date, Day, Time	Name and Type* of Show	Description of Action (Conflicts/Cooperation)	Description of Role Portrayal (Cultural, Gender, or Occupation)	Number and Kind† of Time Advertisements

* Comedy, sports, news, drama, cartoon, musical, mystery, and so on.
† Food, toy, beverage, medicine, public service, and so on.

Related Readings

Adams, D. M., & Hamm, M. (2006). *Media and literacy: Learning in the information age: Issues, ideas, and teaching strategies.* Springfield, IL: Charles C. Thomas.

Anderson, C. A., Gentile, D. A., & Buckley, K. E. (2006).*Violent video games effects on children and adolescents: Theory, research and public policy.* New York: Oxford University Press.

Cantor, J. (1998). *"Mommy, I'm scared": How TV and movies frighten children and what we can do to protect them.* San Diego: Harcourt Brace.

Cashdan, S. (1999). *The witch must die: How fairy tales shape our lives.* New York: Basic Books.

Chang, J. (2005). *Can't stop won't stop: A history of the hip-hop generation.* New York: St. Martin's Press.

Fedorak, S. (2009). *Pop culture: The culture of everyday life.* Toronto: University of Toronto Press.

Livingstone, S. (2009). *Children and the Internet: Great expectations, challenging realities.* Cambridge, UK: Polity.

Norton, D. E., & Norton, S. E. (2010). *Through the eyes of a child: An introduction to children's literature* (7th ed.). Upper Saddle River, NJ: Prentice-Hall.

Perse, E. M. (2001). *Media effects and society.* Mahwah, NJ: Lawrence Erlbaum.

Plowman, L. Stephen, C., & McPake, L. (2010). *Growing up with technology: Young children learning in a digital world.* New York: Routledge.

Rosen, L. D. (2007). *Me, my space, and I: Parenting and the net generation.* New York: Palgrave Macmillan.

Spitz, E. H. (1999). *Inside picture books.* New Haven, CT: Yale University Press.

Trelease, J. (2006). *The read-aloud handbook* (6th ed.). New York: Penguin Group.

Turkle, S. (2011). *Alone together: Why we expect more from technology and less from each other.* New York: Basic Books.

Resources

Center for Media Literacy (CML)—produces and distributes several media literacy resources

http://www.medialit.org

Kidsnet—provides program ratings, study guides, and media guides for children and their parents

http://library.temple.edu/collections/urbana/kidsnet/?bhcp=1

Awesome Library—includes 24,000 carefully reviewed "kid-safe" resources, including the top 5 percent in education; the site also includes an index of other kid-safe search engines

http://www.awesomelibrary.org/

Burke/Trilio Productions/FoodPix/Getty Images

10

Ecology of the Community

"No man is wise enough by himself."

—TITUS MACCIUS PLAUTUS

SOCIALIZATION SKETCHES

Ralph Nader

(b. 1934)

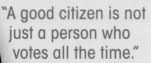

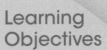

Charley Gallay/Getty Images

"A good citizen is not just a person who votes all the time."

— RALPH NADER

Ralph Nader's quote is his philosophy of community responsibility and involvement, concepts that will be exemplified in this chapter. Nader is America's most renowned and effective crusader for the rights of consumers and the general public, a role that has repeatedly brought him into conflict with both business and government.

In his famous book *Unsafe at Any Speed* (1965), Nader asked why thousands of Americans were being killed or injured in car accidents when the technology already existed to make our cars safer. The automobile industry resisted Nader's suggestions furiously, but public outcry forced government and industry to apply new safety standards, and to include devices like shoulder harnesses and air bags, which have saved thousands from death or injury.

Ralph Nader's concept of full-time citizenship led him to form groups such as Public Citizen, which have exposed corporate and governmental negligence and corruption as well as winning important new protections for Americans as citizens and consumers.

Ralph Nader continues his efforts to make government and business accountable to the people, and to make all Americans aware of their rights and of their own power to defend them.

Family

Ralph Nader was born in Winsted, Connecticut, to Nathra and Rose Nader, Lebanese immigrants who operated a restaurant and bakery. Nader's dream of becoming a "people's lawyer" was instilled in him in adolescence by his parents, who, in noisy free-for-alls, conducted family seminars on the duties of citizenship in a democracy.

"From my parents, and from reading American history, I got the idea that one person can change things. 'So many of the major steps forward in our society's progress started with just a handful of people.' For example, the abolitionist movement against slavery, the women's right to vote movement (started with six women in an upstate New York farm house), the Civil Rights movement, environmental rights, and the whole labor movement.

"My family used to converse at dinner time around the table, talking about all kinds of issues—from local, neighborhood issues to world issues. Adults and children went back and forth in a lively and very critical manner.

"During our early years my mother would relate historical sagas to us for five or ten minutes every lunch hour, when we would come home from school, and it would be continued the next day. 'I think that built into us a sense that freedom involves responsibility.' The whole family got involved in the local community. At first, it was little issues. We went to the town meeting and we talked about how the town could get a sewage system, instead of dumping the sewage in a local river.

"We had a library very near our home and we spent a lot of time in the library. Our family didn't have television to distract us; nor did we did have video games. We did have a lot of personal interaction. Our parents never lectured us. They gave us proverbs, history, and they set an example for us. They were active in the local community. We were encouraged to question things and to think for ourselves.

"One time when I was nine or ten years old, I came home from school, went into the back yard, it was a nice Spring day, and my dad said to me, 'Well Ralph, what did you learn in school today? Did you learn how to believe, or did you learn how to think?' I didn't understand the difference until a teacher stated an incorrect fact and I corrected her, ending up in the dunce chair."

School

In school, certain teachers and books influenced Nader. A history teacher who wrote the quote, "Gone: One minute, sixty seconds. Don't bother looking for it, you will never find it again," stands out. Beginning at about age 10, Nader became fascinated by the early muckrackers' books on Standard Oil and the Chicago meat plants.

Following his graduation from high school in 1951, Nader entered the Woodrow Wilson School of Public Affairs at Princeton University.

Learning Objectives

After completing this chapter, you will be able to:

1. Define a community and explain its five functions.
2. Describe how a community influences socialization, including physical, social, and personal factors in the community.
3. Explain how the community serves as a support system, including the preventative, supportive, and rehabilitative services it provides.
4. Describe how mesosystems (community links to family and school) influence and care for people with economic, health, social, and disability-related problems.
5. Explain the value of volunteerism for the community.
6. Define child advocacy and explain how the community protects children who are maltreated.

He graduated magna cum laude in 1955 with a major in government and economics. Nader enrolled in Harvard Law School. He became an editor of the *Harvard Law Review*, and after graduating with honors, set up a small legal practice and traveled widely. He became distressed by the indifference of American corporations to the global consequences of their actions, and he began to speak against the abuse of corporate power.

Community

Ralph Nader grew up in a small town where there were a lot of streams and a lot of woods. People did a lot of fishing. "Everything was within ten or 15 minutes' walk. You could go to the lakes, the rivers, the streams, the library, the schools, the stores, the city hall, the county courthouse, the firehouse, the hospital, not to mention your friends' homes, all the doctors', dentists' offices, the banks, all within ten, 15 minutes' walk."

Growing up in that kind of atmosphere contributed to the sense of wanting to preserve something. The town was to "human scale"; it had about 10,000 people. At one time, it had over 50 factories that produced clocks, pins, Waring blenders, and such. It was somewhat self-sustaining in that "One day you could hear the moo of the cows, and the next day you would be drinking their milk." There was the town meeting form of government. You could go to the town meeting, and with other citizens could, in effect, enact laws just by voting at the meeting or in a referendum.

Nader's community experiences growing up influenced him to become an advocate for consumers. He created an organization of energetic young lawyers and researchers (often called "Nader's Raiders") who produced systematic exposés of industrial hazards, pollution, unsafe products, and governmental neglect of consumer safety laws.

Nader is widely recognized as the founder of the consumers' rights movement. He played a key role in the creation of the Environmental Protection Agency, the Occupational Safety and Health Administration, the Freedom of Information Act, and the Consumer Product Safety Commission. He has continued to work for consumer safety and for the reform of the political system through his group Public Citizen.

- Have you ever felt an injustice that made you angry enough to try to right the wrong?
- Do you believe that one person, or a group of people, can change something related to powerful institutions, such as government or business?

What constitutes a "community," and what does it do?

Community: Structure and Functions

A *community*, introduced in Chapter 2 as one of the significant *microsystems* (see Figure 10.1), is a group of people living in the same geographic area (neighborhood, town, or city) under common laws; it is also a group of people sharing fellowship, a friendly association, and common interests. The word *community* derives from the Latin *communis*, which means "shared." The concept of sharing can refer to space, norms, values, customs, beliefs, rules, or obligations. The spatial aspect of community may be small and nearby, as when one refers to one's neighborhood; or it may be large and far-reaching, as when one refers to one's country or to society in general.

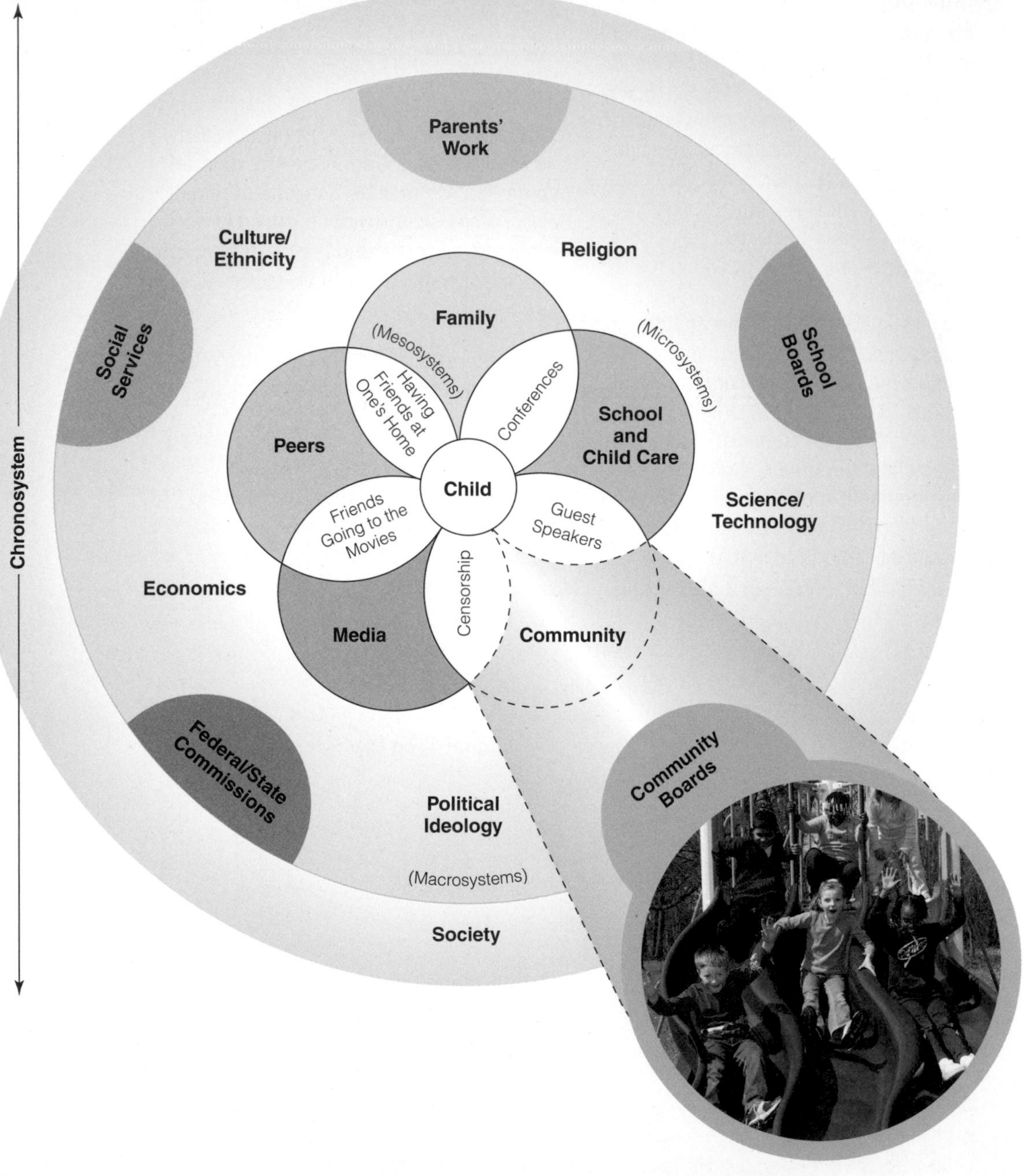

FIGURE 10.1 A Bioecological Model of Human Development
The community in which the child grows up is a significant influence on his or her development.

ECA_ASH/Cengage Learning

A community serves both the individual and the group. If children are to grow up to be contributing members of adult society, they need positive role models, mentors, and leaders. They need to experience democracy in action—involvement, discussion, collaboration, and compromise.

Community ecology comprises the psychological and practical relationships between people and their social, as well as physical, environment. Thus, the crucial component of a community is the relationship of people to one another and the sense of belonging and of obligation to the group.

community ecology the psychological and practical relationships between humans and their social, as well as physical, environment

The sense of community was exhibited when Hurricane Katrina hit New Orleans and other areas of the Gulf Coast. People from all over the country came to assist those who were stranded without shelter or food. The American Red Cross coordinated a fundraising drive with the help of technology. Internet websites donated space for Red Cross ads, as did TV and radio stations and bank ATMs. Donations poured in. People all over the country opened their homes to victims as well as their pets. Airlines provided for travel. Disasters such as this make people realize the importance of community—that people need people to survive.

The need for community is both psychological and practical, or economic. *Psychologically*, humans need companionship and the emotional security that comes from belonging to a social group whose members share the same ideas and patterns of behavior. *Practically*, humans need to cooperate with others in order to share in the necessities of life—food, shelter, and security. Therefore, a community is structured to have five functions (Warren, 1988):

1. **Production, distribution, consumption.** The community provides its members with the means to make a living. This may be agriculture, industry, or services.
2. **Socialization.** The community has means by which it instills its norms and values in its members. This may be tradition, modeling, and/or formal education.
3. **Social control.** The community has the means to enforce adherence to community values. This may be group pressure to conform and/or formal laws.
4. **Social participation.** The community fulfills the need for companionship. This may occur in a neighborhood, church, business, or other group.
5. **Mutual support.** The community enables its members to cooperate to accomplish tasks too large or too urgent to be handled by a single person. Supporting a community hospital with tax dollars and donations is an example of people cooperating to accomplish the task of health care.

Communities, small or large, perform these functions in many different ways. The ways in which a particular community performs these functions influence the socialization of children growing up there.

The Community's Influence on Socialization

How did the neighborhood(s) in which you grew help shape you?

The neighborhood or neighborhoods (nearby geographic areas) in which we grew up conjure up rich imagery of what constitutes a sense of community. We may picture a small town with a mini-mall, the gas station, and the movie theater; the outlying streets with a church or two, the school, and homes separated by bushes or fences. We may picture apartment houses grouped closely together on the street, with the bus stop on the corner and the park and school several blocks away. We may picture acres of farmland and the town, miles away, with a large mall that we visited only once a week. We may picture a large housing tract with lawns, cars, bicycles, and no sidewalks.

My Neighborhoods and Neighbors

When I was growing up in a suburb of New York City, the kids played in the street. Houses faced each other in rows, and the street was the commons. We played stickball, hopscotch, jump rope, and hide-and-seek. We biked and roller-skated in the street. The only traffic was from the residents, who knew to watch out for the children. We knew who our neighbors were because at dinnertime, one or another's mother would open the front door and call. If someone got hurt, we would knock on that person's door to get adult help.

When I was married and living in the Cornell University housing development, the apartments faced each other in attached rows along a long sidewalk. The children would play there and on play equipment at the end of the walkway. Several times a year, someone would organize a potluck supper for the block, so everyone could meet each other and welcome newcomers.

When I started a family, we lived in a suburb where the homes were on large lots. It was in Michigan, where it was cold in the winter and hot in the summer. People did not "hang out" outside. My son took the school bus to school and played with the neighbor kids in someone's backyard. I stayed home to care for my new baby daughter. For the first time in my life, I felt isolated in my neighborhood.

When my second child was two years old and my husband got a job in California, we moved. We chose a neighborhood where the houses faced each other and the street ended in a cul-de-sac. The kids played in the street, easily supervised by any adult looking out a window. Potlucks were regular holiday events, set up in the street or at the neighborhood pool. Neighbors worked together on school and community issues. They helped when someone was ill or had serious problems.

Looking back at the neighborhoods in which I lived, I realize that what mattered most was the relationship with neighbors, not the house or the socioeconomic status of the community.

Part of the imagery of the neighborhood in which we grew up involves the people who lived there. How did they earn a living? We may picture farmers, shopkeepers, laborers working in factories or mines, or people rushing to and from work dressed in business suits.

How did the people in our community instill in us their norms and values? We may visualize the schools we attended or the clubs we belonged to. We may remember some community traditions like the Fourth of July picnic when everyone brought food to share, or the annual school music festival when every class had certain songs to sing, or we may remember the razzing from the boys on the street when we wore our new shoes.

How did our community enforce its rules? We may picture everyone watching over everyone else and knowing that if we did something wrong, Mrs. Nader would be sure to tell Mother. We may picture the police officer on the corner or the sheriff's car patrolling the streets. We may picture the neighborhood bully beating up someone for being a "rat fink."

How did the people in our neighborhood community socialize with one another? We may visualize our mothers gathered in someone's kitchen or on the street in front of someone's house, a group of men entering a bar after work, a group of adults dancing in the church social hall. Or we may remember our homes filled with company on various occasions.

How did the people in our neighborhood community help one another? We may recall the flurry of activity after the Masons' house burned down. Everyone contributed clothing, food, or household items. We may think of the Garcias' house after their 2-year-old was killed by a car—people crowded inside, talking quietly and crying. We may picture the hospital room where our father spent several weeks—filled with plants, flowers, and cards from friends. We may picture the waiting room of a medical clinic and the cries of sick children, or people waiting in line to fill out forms at a government office.

The community is a socializing agent because it is where children learn the role expectations for adults as well as for themselves. It is in the community that children get to observe, model, and become apprentices to adults; it is in the community that children get to "try themselves out." Socialization requires active involvement:

> For the things we have to learn before we can do them, we learn by doing them. We become just by doing just acts, temperate by doing temperate acts, brave by doing brave acts . . . states of character are formed by doing the corresponding acts. (Aristotle, *Metaphysics*, Book 1, Ch. 1)

Factors that make a community "family-friendly," according to a survey of leaders from 90 cities and towns across the United States by the National League of Cities (Meyers & Kyle, 1998) and from 33 cities in Canada by the Institute of Marriage and Family Canada (Walberg & Mrozek, 2010), are

- Education (quality academic programs and safe schools)
- Recreation (facilities and opportunities)
- Community safety
- Citizen involvement
- Physical environment (clean, safe, attractive, well cared for)
- Employment opportunities (good jobs, economic growth)
- Cost of living
- Neighborhood quality (housing affordability, good government, cultural opportunities, specific supports for children and families).

Physical Factors

What physical characteristics of the community affect how people behave?

Research has shown that certain characteristics of the physical environment of the community influence the behavior of those who live there, especially children (Bell et al., 2005). These characteristics are population density and composition, noise, arrangement and types of houses, and play settings.

Population Density and Composition

Population density refers to the number of people occupying a certain area of space. High population density can have positive effects on social relationships in that people have many opportunities to mingle, provided there are spaces (places to sit or play) to do so (Etzioni, 1993).

High population density can also have negative effects, such as excessive social contact, reduced behavioral freedom, scarcity of resources, personal space violations, and inability to maintain desired privacy (Bell et al., 2005). Studies (Bell et al., 2005; Evans & Stecker, 2004) have demonstrated a relationship between residential density and susceptibility to learned helplessness. *Learned helplessness*, introduced in Chapter 7 and discussed further in Chapter 11, is a sense of apathy that develops when people perceive that they have no control over events, that their actions no longer influence outcomes. Additionally, communities characterized by high density tend to be associated with more violence and higher crime rates than low-density communities (Limber & Nation, 1998).

Population composition refers to the stability or mobility of people in a neighborhood as well as to their homogeneity or heterogeneity. The rate of population turnover in a neighborhood is a measure of the stability or mobility of its residents. This rate indirectly affects the socialization of children in that it influences the interactions with newcomers, as well as the degree of community involvement (Bell et al., 2005; Garbarino, 1992). The degree of transience in a neighborhood affects both those who remain and those who move.

Interaction with a variety of people is possible in this densely populated community; however, some people may experience a feeling of being crowded.

Adisa/Big Stock Photo

Compared to cities, small towns provide more opportunities for close interactions and the people tend to be more similar.

Deklofenak/Shutterstock.com

When people do not plan to remain in a neighborhood more than a few years, they tend not to get involved in community activities and it's difficult for their children to establish close friendships. Those who do remain in the neighborhood make fewer efforts to establish close personal ties with newcomers whom they expect to depart.

Homogeneous neighborhoods include people of similar backgrounds; *heterogeneous* neighborhoods include people of differing backgrounds. Neighborhoods differ in the extent to which they include people of differing ages, income levels, religions, and cultural and educational backgrounds (Garbarino, 1992). Children who grow up in *homogeneous* neighborhoods—for example, many suburban neighborhoods—have few opportunities to interact with children or adults who differ in their backgrounds and values. Children whose neighborhoods are accessible to a larger town only by car have little opportunity even to observe the work world of adults. Children who grow up in *heterogeneous* neighborhoods—for example, some urban neighborhoods—are more likely to have opportunities to interact with children of differing backgrounds at school or on the playground. Because stores and businesses are more accessible, children have more opportunities to interact with adults in their work roles.

Noise

Noise is sound that is undesired or interferes with that to which one is listening. High levels can lead to hearing loss, increases in arousal levels, and stress. It can interfere with attention (Evans, 2006).

A study conducted by the California Department of Health Services linked freeway noise to poorer school test scores (Savage, 1983). The study compared third- and sixth-graders in two comparable sets of nine schools, one set located near freeways and the other farther away. The children in the noisy schools generally did less well academically in reading and mathematics than their counterparts in quieter schools. One sixth-grader said, "We can't hear the teacher, and she gets mad because we don't hear what she says." Another child said, "You can't concentrate when the trucks are passing." Noise interferes with verbal communication and may affect productivity (Bell et al., 2005).

Another study (Clark et al., 2006), reports on the first cross-national epidemiologic study known to examine exposure–effect relations between aircraft and road traffic noise exposure and reading comprehension. Participants were 2,010 children aged 9–10 years from 89 schools in three countries, the Netherlands, Spain, and the United Kingdom. Analysis of the pooled data concluded that aircraft noise exposure at school was linearly associated with impaired reading comprehension; the association was maintained after adjustment for socioeconomic variables. Aircraft noise exposure at home was highly correlated with aircraft noise exposure at school and demonstrated a similar linear association with impaired reading comprehension. Road traffic noise exposure at school was not associated with reading comprehension in either the absence or the presence of aircraft noise. Research (Evans, 2006) showed the effect of noise on performance depends on the type of noise, the complexity of the task, and individual factors such as personality and adaptation level.

Community Design

Community design refers to the way houses and streets are arranged. Design affects the social interactions among people living in a neighborhood as well as their physical activity (AAP, 2009; Bell et al., 2005).

When houses face the street or a courtyard, people have a common place of contact. Children living in such a setting usually play on the court or sidewalk or in the street, provided there is not much traffic. This direct access to the outside maximizes the potential for parental supervision. In other words, children can be watched from inside simply by looking out. On the other hand, houses that have no common area, such as apartments, minimize the potential for parental supervision. When children in such houses leave to play, their actions cannot be supervised unless the children are accompanied by a parent or other adult.

The physical design of the community affects children's opportunities for physical activity. Parks and green spaces afford opportunities for physical recreation. Arrangement of streets, sidewalks, and bicycle lanes provides opportunities for walking, running, skating, or bicycling, Environments that promote more active lifestyles among children and adolescents, as well as health and nutrition education, will be important to enable them to achieve physical fitness and avoid obesity (AAP, 2009).

A modern playground can stimulate imaginative play.

Svetlana Mihailova/Shutterstock.com

Play Settings

Play settings influence socialization by the types of activities that occur in them and by whether or not adults are present to supervise. Some communities provide playgrounds for children, and the type of equipment available appears to affect their use (Rivkin, 1995; Scarlett et al., 2005).

A classic study (Hayward, Rothenberg, & Beasley, 1974) comparing different playground settings (traditional, modern, adventure) found that the availability of play materials clearly influenced the play activity.

- The *traditional* playground setting had swings, a slide, a teeter-totter, and a sandbox.
- The *modern* playground had various sculptures on which children could climb, crawl, and slide.
- The *adventure* playground had old lumber, tires, crates, bricks, and rocks.

Children were interviewed and observed in each of the settings. Preschool children, often accompanied by adults, used the traditional and modern playground more often; school-age children and teenagers used the adventure playground more often. The children in the traditional and modern playgrounds were involved in using the equipment, whereas children in the adventure playground were involved in expressing ideas and fantasies.

Economic Factors

How do economic characteristics of the community affect people's lives?

Economic factors in a community play a central role in shaping the daily lives of families who live and work there. Local economic systems vary depending on the jobs, goods, and services provided by the business sector of the community. When a local plant closes, the employees are forced to find work elsewhere, often at lower wages. Often they have to bridge the income gap by working more hours. Thus, wage earners have fewer hours to spend with their families.

Community economics affect the costs of housing, transportation, education, and health care, all of which have risen steadily since the 1970s and today consume substantially more of a typical family's income than they did then. In recent decades, the average working family's tax burden has also risen.

Children's economic well-being is directly related to that of their families. When families have an adequate income, they are better able to meet their children's material, intellectual, and emotional needs and help them become healthy, productive adults. Yet today, children, especially those in single-parent families, are the poorest Americans (FIFCFS, 2010). Failure to address the economic needs of families, especially the threat of poverty, leads to social consequences affecting individuals, families, and the whole community. Examples of such ills are

- more crime and delinquency,
- more substance abuse,
- more school failure,
- more child abuse and neglect,
- more teenage childbearing,
- more unhealthy children, and
- lower productivity by tomorrow's labor force.

These problems impose enormous costs on the community, including expenditures for treatment of illnesses and chronic health conditions, special education, foster care, prisons, and welfare (Evans & English, 2002). Social problems related to poverty and their costs are discussed in more detail later.

Community economics, specifically unemployment, is related to how children in families are socialized. There is evidence that economic hardship threatens the psychological well-being of parents and undermines their capacity for supportive child rearing. When parents have difficulty coping financially and share their problems with their children, children experience increased psychological distress (McLoyd, Aikens, & Burton, 2006).

A Pulitzer Prize–winning journalist, Julia Cass (2010), chronicled the toll poverty is inflicting on America's children for the Children's Defense Fund. She spent time with poor children in Quitman County, Mississippi, children displaced by Hurricane Katrina in Baton Rouge, Louisiana, and children of newly poor families in Long Island, New York. Cass found that despite government programs put in place over the past generation, poor children remain poor, with their future in jeopardy. In addition, the current economic crisis continues to drag more and more families into poverty. At the end of 2010, more than one in five families were living in poverty, a number of them in extreme poverty. This is the highest child poverty rate the nation has experienced since 1959.

According to Cass (2010), Long Island "is not the kind of place one would expect to find in a report on poor children and families. It is the birthplace of the suburban American dream, a national symbol of the single-family suburb." Unlike Baton Rouge, and Quitman County, Long Island's two counties, Nassau and Suffolk, have an educated work force, well-run governments, and a long history of stability and affluence. Long Island's child poverty rate is low compared with the two Southern states: 5 percent in Nassau and 7 percent in Suffolk. Demographically, too, Long Island is different: Its population is 80 percent White, 13 percent Hispanic, 9 percent Black, and 6 percent Asian (U.S. Bureau of the Census, 2009b). Cass describes newly poor families in Long Island as having fallen from middle class to working poor and from working poor into poverty because of the recession, the housing crisis, the gap between wages and cost of living, and the insufficient safety net. She says that families are living in motels, food pantries are emptying, and outreach agencies are running out of funds to help with a month's rent or an overdue utility bill.

Cass (2010, pp. 41–42) reports that the new faces of poverty—the families that now seek help—are diverse:

- An Italian American father, with a teenage son, whose paycheck doesn't cover expenses since his wife became incapacitated with muscular sclerosis and cannot work.
- A White, college-educated schoolteacher with three children whose divorce and child with special needs have pushed her into the working poor.
- A Hispanic couple (Brazilian and Ecuadorian), with a 3-year-old daughter, who achieved the American dream—well-paying work and a suburban house—and lost both.
- A couple (White and Asian) whose work dried up and whose house was damaged by fire. They and their son and daughter live in a motel room.
- A Hispanic single, working mother of three (second-generation Guatemalan) who was evicted from her low-income rental housing unit because the owner hadn't paid the mortgage and the bank foreclosed on the property.

What perceived social and personal characteristics of the community affect people's relationships?

Social and Personal Factors

In addition to the physical and economic characteristics of a community, certain other factors, less tangible and more individualistic, influence socialization. These factors include the neighborhood setting and the patterns of community interaction.

The Neighborhood Setting

The neighborhood, referring to people and places nearby, is the geographic setting in which children generally spend their unstructured time (Garbarino, 1992). The neighborhood is where children explore, interact with other children, observe adults engaged in work or other activities, and have various experiences themselves.

Neighborhood settings differ not only in the physical environments (streets, parks, facilities) available for children, but also in the social environments (who is available to interact with whom). Since children are minimally mobile, they play close to home and interact with those who live close by. A classic study by Medrich and his colleagues (Medrich et al., 1981) examined how children in different neighborhoods spent their time after school. Five neighborhoods (their names were changed for publication) exemplify how different settings affect children's daily experiences and hence their socialization. Were any of these similar to neighborhoods you grew up in?

IN CONTEXT

Five Neighborhoods

Mountainside

Mountainside has no sidewalks, and its streets are hilly. The houses are set back from the road, and you get a feeling of isolation. The shops, library, school, park, and recreation center are clustered in "the village" at the base of the hill, several miles from most of the houses. Children spend most of their free time close to home because it's not easy to get around in this neighborhood—the hills are too steep for bicycles. They play baseball and soccer in diamonds they have painted on the streets. They build tree houses and rope swings and share them with other neighborhood children. The children interact with few adults other than their parents, and that doesn't seem to bother them. They have to rely on their parents to drive them to lessons or recreational facilities.

Rosewood

Rosewood is a neighborhood with sidewalks and connecting streets on which the children ride their bicycles and play softball. There are few boundaries between the houses. The neighborhood is centered on the school. Anyone can get there within a seven-minute walk, and many children use the playground as a meeting place. Rosewood is heterogeneous in character and dense with children. The majority of children are European American, but a large proportion are African American. Friends are chosen on the basis of similarities in age and race.

Bancroft

Bancroft is a neighborhood with no sidewalks or street lamps. The roads are narrow and patched with asphalt. Most houses cannot be seen from the street. Yards are separated by fences. In Bancroft, both parents are apt to work, and children are frequently left on their own when not at school; children are expected to stay close to home after school so parents know where they are. Children's time is often spent in the company of brothers and sisters. Children rarely leave their block except to go to school, run an errand, or keep an appointment. This may be because the school and park both front on streets heavy with traffic.

Glenn

Glenn begins where the trucking companies and shipping warehouses along a freeway exit end. The houses look like fortresses. There are a lot of apartments. Neighbors sit on banisters, and children hang around the streets. Although buses and large trucks run through continually, there are no stop signs. Shops and churches are located mostly in one area; all have locked gates because vandalism rates are high. There is a park with a recreation center that many people frequent. Glenn is a neighborhood with strong ties based on cultural heritage. Friendships seem to be formed along cultural lines, and tightly knit adolescent gangs are common.

Eastside
Eastside is a neighborhood with stark streets and debris collecting at the curbs. Yards are fenced, and most lack trees. Despite its physical appearance, the neighborhood is vibrant with street life. Many Eastside families migrated from the South and talk with one another about relatives back there or recent visits. The children congregate on the street. Many go to the community center, where they are eligible for free lunch. Friendships are formed easily according to whoever is nearby. Not only are peers considered to be friends to children, but so are neighbors and shopkeepers. Children have a lot of comfortable relations with different adults. The schoolyard can be reached in five minutes, and children often gather there to play. Age doesn't seem to matter regarding playmates, but skills count. It is not uncommon to find a broad age range of children getting together to play ball.

These examples illustrate how the neighborhood setting affects children's mobility, exposure to adults, friendship patterns, and types of play (Berg & Medrich, 1980; Medrich et al., 1981).

Patterns of Community Interaction

Community interaction is an important factor in development because, according to Bronfenbrenner (1979, 1989), the developmental potential of a setting—in this case, the community—is enhanced as a function of the number of its supportive links with other settings the child might be in, such as the family or school. Factors impacting patterns of community interaction are the size of the community, social diversity, shared norms, and valued type of social relationships.

Size of Community

Patterns of interaction vary considerably with the size of a community. In a small town, one person may interact directly with almost every other person in a given week or month. In contrast, a resident of a large city might conceivably roam the streets without ever seeing a familiar face.

Interaction in a small town involves close contact with relatives, friends, and acquaintances. Because of this, people in a small community tend to be involved in each other's lives—their marriages, their children, their illnesses, and their employment are subjects of discussion, concern, and gossip. Interaction in a large city, on the other hand, involves less personal contact but more impersonal interactions. For example, interactions with co-workers, bankers, clerks, and bus drivers may occur daily, but only in the context of the specific roles they perform. For personal interactions, residents of large cities must rely on immediate family members and voluntary associations (church, PTA, lodge, club).

Social Diversity

The degree to which an environment contains a diversity of roles and experiences for children to learn from and for parents to draw upon affects families and children. A diverse setting contains a variety of businesspeople as well as a variety of ages and cultural groups. Such a setting provides many opportunities for interaction and for children to learn what community relations are all about. Such a setting also affords families a choice of social networks on which they can rely for support (Sampson, 2001). A setting in which people are socially similar (economics, occupation, culture, and/or religion) affords children a narrow view of the larger society.

Shared Norms

Communities have norms that facilitate congenial social interactions. The norms of a small town are more homogeneous than those of a large city, and are also more widely understood and accepted (Garbarino, 1992). In a small town, shared convictions about what is right or wrong, proper or improper, tend to be passed on from generation to generation and become institutionalized, meaning the unwritten local customs become the common law. Such consensus implies similar socialization goals among parents, teachers, and community leaders.

Examples of institutionalized convictions mediated by the community include "Honor thy father and mother" (community members ask children if their parents know where they are before inviting them into their homes), or disapproval of wearing shorts in certain places. Social control is achieved through fear of gossip and of being rejected.

Large cities, which bring together people from a wide variety of cultural, religious, regional, educational, and occupational groups, are not as likely as small towns to have shared convictions regarding norms for social interaction. Therefore, large cities must rely more on formal rules and regulations than on informal methods for influencing behavior. For example, in a small town it is highly unlikely that you would play your stereo loudly at 11:00 P.M. Your behavior is regulated by courtesy to your neighbor. In a large city, however, where neighbors often do not know each other, behavior might have to be regulated by rules restricting noise to certain hours. Social control is achieved via formal sanctions.

Valued Types of Social Relationship

Ferdinand Tonnies (1957/1987), in his book *Gemeinschaft und Gesellschaft*, considered to be a classic, defines two basic types of social relationships (first discussed in Chapter 3). *Gemeinschaft* relationships are mutually dependent and caring. People relate to each other because they are kin, because they live in a particular locality, or because they are like-minded and wish to pursue a common goal. **Gemeinschaft** interpersonal relationships are communal, cooperative, close, intimate, and informal. There is mutual trust and concern, as well as willing cooperation. *Gesellschaft* relationships, on the other hand, are independent and contractual. People relate to each other because it is a practical way of achieving an objective, like paying for services rendered. **Gesellschaft** interpersonal relationships are associative, practical, objective, and formal. They are characterized by individualism and mutual distrust. Typically, interactions are for a particular purpose. Children who primarily experience gemeinschaft relationships have socialization experiences that are very different from those of children who primarily experience gesellschaft relationships (see Table 10.1).

gemeinschaft communal, cooperative, close, intimate, and informal interpersonal relationships

gesellschaft associative, practical, objective, and formal interpersonal relationships

What kind of social relationships did you primarily have in the community or culture in which you grew up, and how did they influence you?

Table 10.1 Basic Social Relationships

Gemeinschaft	Gesellschaft
Mutually dependent	Independent
Caring	Contractual
Informal	Formal
Intimate	Associative
Trusting	Mistrusting
Kin	Employers/managers
Friends	Employees
Neighbors	Business associates
Special-interest groups	Achievement objectives
Collectively oriented	Individually oriented

How can the community contribute to children's learning experiences?

The Community as a Learning Environment

The community is a setting that provides much potential for learning (Decker & Decker, 2001). Libraries, museums, zoos, farms, businesses, people's experiences, and collectibles (family heirlooms, antiques, photographs, and so on) are all rich sources for involving children (Hatcher & Beck, 1997).

IN CONTEXT Petco Park in San Diego, California, opened its doors for free admission to families and children for a huge science exposition in March 2010. Expo day is one of the signature events of the San Diego Science Festival, a month-long celebration of science and learning that takes place at schools, libraries, universities, and public locations (http://www.sdsciencefestival.com). The event is run by UC San Diego in partnership with public agencies and private companies in the region. The goal is to make science accessible to everyone through hands-on activities. There is also live entertainment, such as fire and ice experiments, interactive activities such as the "Moon Walk Challenge," animals such as reptiles for handling, and exhibitions such as live butterflies.

To illustrate the community's potential for learning, an experiment was initiated in Philadelphia to try a "school without walls" (Brenner & Von Moschzisker, 1971). Students in grades 9–12 were chosen by lottery from eight school districts; neither economic nor academic background was a factor. There was no school building; each of the eight areas had a headquarters with office space for staff and lockers for students. All teaching took place within the community. Art was studied at the art museum; biology was studied at the zoo; vocational education took place at various business locations. A higher than average percentage of students who attended went on to college. The School Without Walls is currently a magnet school (students apply for entrance) in the Washington, D.C., area and is known for its high student achievement.

Many school districts have *alternative schools*, as well as *home schooling*, that follow this model. The philosophy of alternative education is that the child, like the adult, learns the art and technique of citizenship, not through lectures on civics, but from involvement in real issues (Hatcher & Beck, 1997). Some high schools and colleges have combined work–study programs, in which students can apply theoretical knowledge learned in school to practical experience at work. Existing schools can find many ways of using the community as an educational resource—inviting guest speakers to class, going on field trips, and working on a community project (such as planting trees, participating in a parade, or raising money for individuals in need).

Today, many high schools, middle schools, and some elementary schools around the country require students to perform community service in order to graduate. The National and Community Service Trust Act of 1993 gives grants to schools to develop and implement student involvement projects. Projects can include environmental conservation, hospitals, child-care facilities, law enforcement, and social service agencies, to name a few.

Part of the National School Goals 2000, reform strategies discussed in Chapter 6, is the commitment of communities to learning. The business community can facilitate child socialization by fostering school and related educational work or recreational projects in several ways. Members of the business community can

- provide specific schools with materials, financial aid, human resources, and professional support (some communities refer to such a project as "Adopt-a-School");
- serve on school advisory councils or on school boards; and
- offer schools the use of business settings for job placement or offer field sites for work experience programs.

Some examples of partnership activities supported by the Daniels Fund (http://www.danielsfund.org, 2005) are (1) the Annapolis, Maryland, Symphony Orchestra Adopt-a-School program that puts professional musicians in string music classes monthly to develop students' skills and encourage participation in the strings program. The program culminates in an annual Side by Side Concert, where the students perform with the professional musicians; and (2) the Sierra Sacramento Valley Medical Society places physician and medical student volunteers in local schools to augment preventative health education.

In sum, the community becomes a place and a resource for learning when citizens (parents, educators, businesspeople, religious groups, service providers, legislators) are committed to mutually beneficial goals that focus on the positive growth and development of children (Decker & Decker, 2001; Pagano, 1997).

The Community as a Support System

How can the community service families?

The community can provide *informal support* to families, as when neighbors watch each other's children or share resources (gemeinschaft), or it can provide *formal support* through its publicly or privately funded community services (gesellschaft). Community services are necessary for several reasons.

- **Increasing population.** As more people compete for available resources, more people need supportive services to survive—job assistance, housing assistance, financial support, food subsidies, and medical care. As people live longer, the number of years that they are likely to depend on Social Security payments for support in their retirement years, as well as on Medicare for their health insurance, increases. As advances in science occur, more people's lives are prolonged. These people may have diseases or disabilities that prevent them from working; they, too, will need financial assistance as well as other services to survive.
- **Changing nature of the family.** Births to teenagers, divorces, single-parent families, and employed mothers mean an increasing need for such services as financial assistance, social services, and child care. The mobility of families has caused separation from relatives. When relatives are unavailable, families turn to the community for support.
- **Increasing urbanization of communities.** The centralization of industries in certain areas, with the consequent migration—from rural to urban areas—of people seeking employment, has increased the number of people living in a smaller amount of space. People living in cities must turn to the community for various kinds of services. Because of the high density of people living in a small area, for example, the community is expected to provide open-space areas for recreation. Rural areas, because they are less populated, have fewer public services than urban areas.

Chronosystem and Macrosystem Influences on Community Services

How have changes in the macrosystem over time (the chronosystem) affected community services?

An aspect of the macrosystem, political ideology, is influential in determining what services government leaders believe to be worthy of support; for example, the Head Start preschool program was launched under President Lyndon Johnson. Political ideology also refers to legislation; for example, the No Child Left Behind Act was passed under President George W. Bush.

Another aspect of the macrosystem, economics, relates to various sources of funding for a community service. Agencies providing services may be *public*, *private*, or a *combination*.

- **Public agencies.** Financed by taxation, they are administered within the legal framework of the local, state, or federal government. For example, an outcome of the

1910 White House Conference on the Care of Dependent Children was the establishment of the U.S. Children's Bureau, the oldest federal agency for children, for the purpose of protecting children from harm. Since then the role of government in the protection of children has expanded in scope, as well as in the economic resources allocated to programs from tax monies. The Children's Bureau is now administered by the U.S. Administration for Children and Families in the Department of Health and Human Services. The Children's Bureau works with state and local agencies to develop a number of programs that focus on preventing the maltreatment of children, protecting them from abuse, and providing permanent placement if their home is not safe.

- **Private agencies.** Financed by donations, membership dues, corporate contributions, consultation fees, investment income, foundation grants, publication sales, or conference fees, they are established by individuals or philanthropic, religious, fraternal, or humanitarian groups; their management is the responsibility of a board of directors. The nation's oldest and largest membership-based child welfare organization is the Child Welfare League of America (CWLA, 2002), founded in 1920. CWLA's member agencies directly provide at-risk children and families with services in the areas of child abuse prevention and treatment, kinship care, juvenile justice, family foster care, adoption, positive youth development, residential group care, child day care, family-centered practice, and adolescent parenting and pregnancy prevention. CWLA's trained staff address such issues as behavioral health care, substance abuse, housing and homelessness, and HIV/AIDS.
- **Combination agencies.** Using both public and private sources of money, these may get government grants to implement research or innovations and private donations to provide services over and above what is funded by the grant. For example, the Office of Community Services, run by the Administration for Youth and Families, was set up by the federal government to work in partnership with states, communities, and other agencies to provide a wide range of human and community development services and activities that ameliorate the causes and characteristics of poverty and otherwise assist persons in need. Various agencies, public or private, can submit applications for competitive funding of grants.

What are the categories of community services?

Preventive, Supportive, and Rehabilitative Services

Community services, whether publicly or privately funded, can be categorized according to their primary function as *preventive*, *supportive*, or *rehabilitative*.

- **Preventive services** attempt to lessen the stresses and strains of life resulting from social and technological changes and to avert problems. For example, parks and recreation programs set up in rapidly developing urban areas are meant to be used by children in their free time to keep them from engaging in delinquent behavior.
- **Supportive services** include educational programs, counseling services, health services, policies related to demographic changes, employment training, and community development projects. These services maintain the health, education, and welfare of the community.
- **Rehabilitative services** enable or restore people's ability to participate in the community effectively.

preventive services programs that seek to lessen the stresses and strains of life resulting from social and technological changes and to avert problems

supportive services programs that maintain the health, education, and welfare of the community

rehabilitative services programs that enable or restore people's ability to participate in the community

Preventive Services: Parks, Recreation, and Education

The purpose of preventive services is to provide for people's needs for space, socializing, physical activity, and mental stimulation. Children need room to play and explore. Families need places to go to relax and enjoy each other's company. Everyone needs space to exercise and be physically fit. Many community members enjoy taking classes to learn new skills or to broaden their perspectives on life (cultural, historical, technological, linguistic).

Open spaces have been set aside for public enjoyment as far back in history as early Greek and Roman civilization. As Western European cities grew, parks or plazas were established. The first parkland in America designated for the public was purchased in 1660. As the colonies grew, so did the number of parks. One of the best-known parks, established in about 1853, is Central Park in New York City. The 843 acres of land were reserved for the purpose of recreation and relief from urban conditions. Other large cities followed New York's example (Rivkin, 1995).

In the 1890s and early 1900s, the public began to pressure government to assume responsibility for community recreation. This pressure was probably due to the growth of large cities and resultant lack of play space for children. Local governments responded by setting up agencies and organizations to provide recreation for children. By 1900, some 14 cities had made provision for supervised play, and in 1906, the Playground and Recreation Association of America (now called the National Recreation Association) was set up. Its purpose was to promote community recreational facilities and programs.

A park in the middle of the city allows all residents to enjoy outdoor activities.

Rafael Macia/PhotoLibrary

Some of the services that community parks and recreation programs supply are providing and maintaining natural or designed environments, promoting physical fitness, and offering classes to enable people to develop interests and skills for use of their leisure time or to enhance their employability.

Some of the private and voluntary groups providing recreational services to children in the community are the Boy Scouts of America, Girl Scouts of America, Boys' and Girls' Clubs of America, American Red Cross, Young Men's Christian Association (YMCA), and Young Women's Christian Association (YWCA). These agencies promote certain values, emphasize learning by doing, and are concerned with personal development; their leaders come from the community and serve as role models. For example, the Boy Scouts of America promotes the ability of young people to do things for themselves and others. Leaders train the boys in self-reliance, courage, and good citizenship. In addition, patriotism is emphasized. For another example, the Boys' and Girls' Clubs of America, which includes boys and girls ages 6 to 18 who are at risk for behavioral, social, or academic problems, provide programs and services to enhance children's lives and enable youth to develop skills to become employable. The clubs also build knowledge to engage in positive behaviors and safe health practices, as well as to become responsible citizens.

Supportive Services: Family and Child

The purpose of family services is to preserve a healthy family life by helping family members achieve harmonious relationships. In helping families, family services consider the influence of culture, religion, and family composition (Burger, 2010; Schorr, Both, & Copple, 1991).

Referrals

Problems that threaten the stability of family life include discord between husband and wife, discord between parent and child, illness, accidents, economic problems, desertion, delinquency, teen pregnancy, and alcohol or drug abuse. Family service agencies provide referrals to specific agencies dealing with these specific problems. They also give counseling, which may include advice on budgeting and home management, vocational opportunities, and family relationships.

Economic Assistance

Both public and private social agencies offer family services. Generally, public agencies offer services based on the family's economic need (families must meet legal eligibility requirements to qualify for assistance)—for example, in arranging financial assistance, finding a job, and locating affordable and suitable housing. Assistance may also include the distribution of food and medicine, as well as child-care services. Private family service agencies are concerned primarily with personal problems and emotional maladjustment of family members rather than with economic problems. Private agencies do, however, provide financial help in emergencies (especially when the family is waiting to see if it qualifies for public assistance or when the family has recently immigrated to the United States and does not qualify for public assistance). Family agencies may deal with personal problems involving an economic commitment such as placement of children in special schools or camps, or placement of adults in mental institutions or homes for the aged.

Counseling

Family services include marriage counseling, prenatal and family planning, family life education, homemaker services, and senior citizen services. Counseling services help marriage partners meet their marital responsibilities and resolve marital conflicts. They may also help in emotional maladjustment problems such as lack of communication between parents and teenagers, in premarital counseling, or in problems involved in adjusting to divorce. Prenatal care and family planning services promote the mental and physical health of children (and mothers) from the prenatal stage onward. Family planning includes birth control education. Child guidance services include family therapy and parenting training.

Family Preservation

The federal Family Preservation and Support Services Program (FPSSP) was officially enacted in 1993. States receive money to develop family preservation and support services, thereby providing incentives to change the way services have traditionally been delivered to families (see Table 10.2).

The purpose of family preservation services is (1) to keep the family safe, (2) to avoid unnecessary placement of children in substitute care and the consequent high human and financial cost, and (3) to improve family functioning so that the behavior that led to the crisis will be less likely to recur (Child Welfare Information Gateway, 2008). Family preservation services offer a mix of counseling, education, referrals, concrete assistance, and advocacy. An example is family life education, which includes education in home economics and management, parenting, and family relationships. Homemaker services send a trained person to the home when the mother is temporarily unable to care for the family. The services enable the family to stay together and carry on in crises such as hospitalization, chronic illness, and impairment due to a disabling condition.

Keeping families together involves protecting children's safety in the home and strengthening families' abilities to deal with their problems. Family preservation programs may include intensive family-based crisis intervention services. For example, when a child is at risk for abuse, rather than remove the child from the family, a trained professional goes to the home to give practical assistance on immediate problems and parenting training, and helps to link the family with other support services in the community.

Table 10.2 How Are Services to Families Delivered in the Community?

Family Preservation Support Services	Traditional Family Support Services
Build on family strengths	Emphasize family deficits
Focus on families	Focus on individuals
Respond flexibly to family needs	Program and funding source dictate services
Reach out to families	Have strict eligibility requirements
Treat families as partners in goal setting	Workers set goals and solutions
Offer services in home or homelike setting	Services are office-based
Respond quickly to needs	Often have waiting lists

The Administration for Children and Families under the USDHHS has published a guide for child welfare workers to help nonresident fathers have a positive impact on their children's lives. It focuses on how professionals can more effectively engage fathers whose children come to the attention of the child welfare system (Rosenberg & Bradford, 2006).

Senior Citizens

Senior citizen services may include economic assistance, in-home care, day care, institutionalization, recreation, Meals on Wheels (a program that delivers meals to the homes of the housebound), friendly visiting, and arranging for other community services to "adopt a grandparent" (for example, a child-care center might welcome the experience and extra help a senior citizen could provide for the children).

Child Health and Welfare

The term *child welfare* encompasses care for individuals who may be indigent, neglected, abused, deserted, sick, disabled, maladjusted, or delinquent. The purpose of child welfare agencies is to protect the physical, intellectual, and emotional well-being of children (Zaslow et al., 1998). Child welfare services provide

- economic and personal aid to children living in their own homes,
- foster care for children who have no home or cannot remain with their own families, and
- institutional care when children cannot be placed in a foster home or cannot remain with their own families (CWLA, 2002).

Traditionally, children whose families could not care for them because of death, illness, or poverty were placed in institutions. Private agencies and charitable organizations took the major responsibility for child welfare. Today, however, children are enabled to remain with their families; they are removed only as an emergency measure—for example, in cases of abuse.

The need for financial assistance to mothers in order to preserve the family was first emphasized at the White House Conference on the Care of Dependent Children in 1910. The first national welfare legislation was passed as part of the Social Security Act of 1935 (Zaslow et al., 1998). Public funds are available under the Temporary Assistance for Needy Families (TANF) Program, enabling families to provide a minimum of shelter, food, clothing, and medical care for their children. In 1996, the Family Support Act (amended in 2001) implemented the Job Opportunities and Basic Skills Training (JOBS) Program, which provided education and job training, as well as child care, for mothers with young children to enable them to make the transition from government assistance to independence. Today, the Personal Responsibility and Work Opportunity Reconciliation Act of 1996 sets time limits for the transition from government aid to the achievement of financial independence resulting from being trained for the workforce.

The states carry out maternal and child health programs with the financial support of the federal government. These programs include family planning services, prenatal clinics, well-baby clinics for regular medical examinations of young children, hearing and vision screening, birthing, nursing, dental services, and mental health services.

The state governments also administer programs that provide services for children with disabilities, partially financed by matching funds from the federal government. Services include locating children with disabilities (physicians, nurses, and teachers do the referrals); providing medical, surgical, and corrective services for them; providing facilities for diagnosis, hospitalization, and rehabilitative care; and providing aids and prosthetic appliances, physiotherapy, and medical social services.

Protective

There is a need for services that provide protection for children against abuse and neglect. Protective services are usually invoked upon a report from a teacher, doctor, or neighbor.

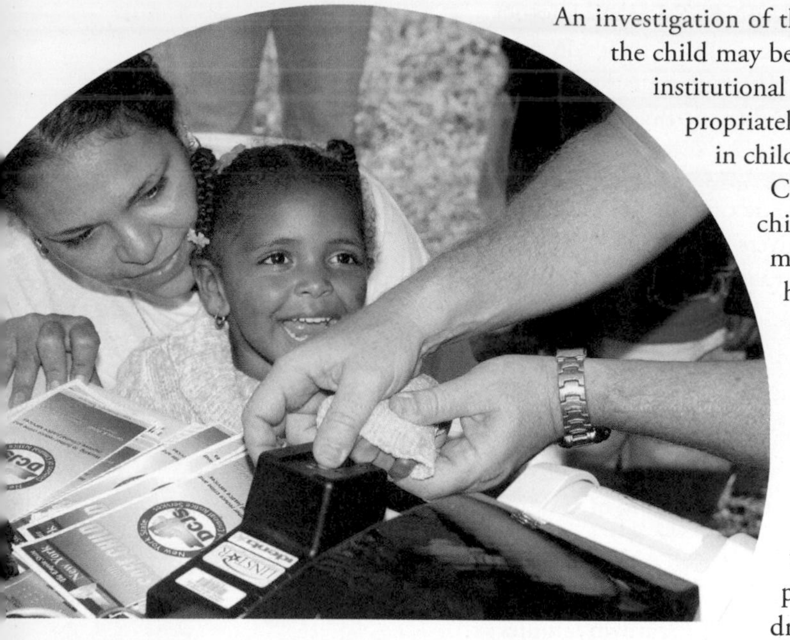

This child is being photographed and fingerprinted by police as a service to identify children should they be kidnapped.

Cengage Learning

An investigation of the family takes place and, depending on the circumstances, the child may be removed from the home and temporarily placed in foster or institutional care until the parents can prove they can care for the child appropriately. Often the parents must receive counseling and take classes in child development and parenting.

Children's services also include the care and protection of children born to unmarried mothers. Typical services for unmarried mothers include financial assistance, prenatal care, hospitalization, and counseling. Educational programs (child development, parenting, health and nutrition, vocational, and academic education) are often included.

Child Care

Child-care centers serve preschool children whose parents are employed. Most care is for children age 2 to 5, but more and more centers are serving infants and toddlers. Some centers include health and educational services as part of their programs. Extended day-care programs serve school-age children whose parents are employed. Children come to the center before and after school, as necessitated by their parents' work schedules. Extended day-care programs are sometimes located in elementary schools and sometimes in community centers. When necessary, the extended day-care program provides transportation between school and center.

Foster Care

Foster care services are provided for children who are neglected or abused and, therefore, need protection, as well as for children whose parents are temporarily unable to care for them. Foster homes are carefully selected by the community social service agency. Children placed in these homes are closely supervised by the agency, which provides money for room and board, clothing, medical and dental care, and often an allowance for the children. Counseling services are provided for the foster parents.

Adoption

In contrast to foster care, adoption is a social and legal process by which a child becomes a permanent member of the adopting family, with the same legal rights as a child born into the family. The social process of adoption seeks to provide children of incapacitated or deceased natural parents with a healthy home environment. The legal process seeks to ensure that separation from natural parents is resorted to only when absolutely necessary and only with consent, if the parents are alive. Social agencies arranging for adoption conduct investigations to match the child and the adoptive family. Character, motivation, age, finances, and sometimes cultural and religious background of the family are examined.

Rehabilitative Services: Correction, Mental Health, Special Needs

The purpose of rehabilitative agencies is to enable or restore an individual's capacity to participate effectively in the community by correcting behavior, addressing mental health, and/or providing needed services to those who have recently immigrated to this country as well as to those who have a disability.

Correction

Correctional services are provided for children, youths, and adults who have difficulties abiding by the legal rules of community life. What constitutes deviant behavior varies among different social groups. Some children may be encouraged by their friends and neighbors to behave delinquently; for example, stealing may be a prerequisite to being accepted by the neighborhood gang. Another child in another neighborhood who behaves similarly may be brought to a social agency, such as a child guidance clinic. Still another child may be arrested and cited before the juvenile court.

An explanation for variations in aggressive behavior may be one's attitudes toward fighting. Societal mores, as expressed by the U.S. legal system, punish aggressive acts, especially if the aggression harms someone or someone's property. An individual or group may feel that aggression is the only acceptable way to avenge an insult. Another explanation for variations in attitudes toward aggression is a reactive strategy to neighborhood dangers, disrespect, a social cognitive awareness of stereotypes, a lack of social supports, and/or a distorted personal orientation (a feeling of "superiority") (Spencer, 2001).

Children under age 18 who are deemed neglected or delinquent are under the jurisdiction of the juvenile court. The juvenile court is not a criminal court; it does not file charges against the child. Therefore, there is no jury to determine guilt or innocence. Rather, the court attempts to understand the causes for the particular maladjustment and determines what steps must be taken for rehabilitation. In order to understand the causes for the maladjusted or deviant behavior, the child and his or her family background are examined. Also, the physical, socioeconomic, and cultural conditions under which the child is living are explored.

IN CONTEXT Sometimes, to join a gang, middle and high school students will get tattoos, even though it is illegal for anyone under age 18 to get one. If these kids want to leave the gang, they have to either move out of town or get the tattoo removed so they won't be identified by rivals and possibly even killed.

A juvenile officer in Monrovia, California, established a corrective program in which, using funds from private donations, he helps a remorseful gang member get the tattoo removed in a medical facility with a ruby laser. The youth must write an essay on the reasons he/she got the tattoo, problems regarding it, and why he/she wants it removed. The officer then interviews the youth and tells him/her the requirements of the program: parental involvement, periodic contact for three years, and acceptable grades.

Juvenile court judges may place children under the supervision of their parents in their home, with the stipulation that the family receive counseling. Or children may be removed from their homes and placed in foster care or institutions. Judges may also require children (or their parents) to pay for damages caused by the delinquent behavior.

Mental Health

Children are usually referred to local child guidance clinics by teachers, medical personnel, or the court. Behavioral problems indicating the need for referral include truancy, running away, lying, stealing, vandalism, setting fires, and extreme aggressiveness. Other behaviors may include excessive shyness, apathy, daydreaming, withdrawal, excessive fearfulness, enuresis, eating disorders, and nightmares. Child guidance clinics provide medical and psychological examinations for the child. The parents and often the siblings, as well as the child, may come for treatment. Services are coordinated with the school.

Special Needs

Services for recent immigrants to the United States encompass education (English language, American history, government, and culture), financial assistance, housing assistance, and vocational counseling, as well as referrals to other agencies providing specific services.

Services for people with disabilities emphasize inclusion. Self-help and productive work are the goals of rehabilitation. These services encompass evaluation, special education, financial assistance, counseling, vocational training, recreation, and referrals for treatment (Epps & Jackson, 2000).

Table 10.3 summarizes the main categories of community services.

Table 10.3 Categories of Community Services

Preventive Agencies	Supportive Agencies	Rehabilitative Agencies
Parks	Family and child services	Correction
Recreation	Referrals	Mental health
Education	Economic assistance	Special needs
	Counseling	
	Family preservation	
	Senior citizens	
	Child health and welfare	
	Protective care	
	Child care	
	Foster care	
	Adoption	

How can communities be enabled to meet the needs of families and children?

Creating Caring Communities

Even though different communities can provide a variety of services, some of which were described earlier, many do not provide enough to adequately meet the needs of children and families. Sensitizing individuals, especially those on decision-making bodies, to the unmet needs of children and to society's obligation to respond to those needs is known as *child advocacy*. In general, *advocacy*, introduced in Chapter 2, refers to the process of supporting a person, group, or cause. *Society* can mean public agencies, such as the government or the school; private agencies, such as religious groups or businesses; or concerned members of the community.

The National Commission on Children (NCC) was created by Congress and the president "to serve as a forum on behalf of children of the Nation." The commission, comprised of parents, grandparents, teachers, health and child development experts, business leaders, professionals, elected officials, and others, became official in 1989. Its mandated task was to assess the status of children and families in the United States and to propose new directions for policy and program development in order to improve the opportunities for every young person, regardless of circumstances, to become a healthy, secure, educated, economically self-sufficient, and productive adult. The commission's final report, *Beyond Rhetoric: A New American Agenda for Children and Families* (NCC, 1991), made recommendations in nine general areas:

1. Ensuring income security
2. Improving health
3. Increasing educational achievement
4. Preparing adolescents for adulthood
5. Strengthening and supporting families
6. Protecting vulnerable children and their families
7. Making policies and programs work
8. Creating a moral climate for children
9. Providing financing for programs

Specific issues addressed were a yearly refundable tax credit for children; a government-guaranteed minimum child support payment, as well as tough enforcement; continuation of the job training program, as well as child care and health insurance, to help low-income families make the transition from welfare to work; and community responsibility for health care and education programs.

One of the NCC's recommendations was that the allocation of financial resources be shared by the private and public sectors. When George W. Bush became president of the United States, one of his first official acts was to create the White House Office of Faith-Based and Community Initiatives in 2001. This office was tasked with leading "a determined attack on need" by strengthening and expanding the role of faith-based and community organizations in addressing the nation's social problems. The president's goal was to allow faith-based organizations to compete equally with other, nonsectarian groups for government or private funds.

President Bush also created Centers for Faith-Based and Community Initiatives in the U.S. Departments of Justice, Agriculture, Labor, Health and Human Services, Housing and Urban Development, and Education, as well as the Agency for International Development. The mission of the White House office and these centers is to empower faith-based and other community organizations to apply for federal social service grants. The White House office and the centers strive to support organizations that serve people in need, particularly those that serve the following populations:

- At-risk youth
- Ex-offenders
- Homeless and hungry
- Substance abusers
- Those with HIV/AIDS
- Welfare-to-work families

Major disasters, such as Hurricane Katrina, revealed national gaps in emergency planning for children (such as evacuation plans, stockpiled supplies, and health services). Congress passed the Kids in Disasters Well-Being, Safety and Health Act of 2007, creating the National Commission on Children and Disasters. In 2010, a panel of experts recommended changes that federal, state, and local governments need to make to meet the needs of children in emergency planning, response, and recovery efforts when a disaster occurs. Relevant agencies must coordinate their services to prioritize children's needs in regard to

1. mental health,
2. physical health,
3. trauma,
4. emergency medical services and transport,
5. disaster case management,
6. disaster preparedness for child care/early education, elementary, secondary education, child welfare, and juvenile justice,
7. sheltering standards, services, and supplies,
8. housing, and
9. evacuation and reunification.

Economic Assistance to Families

What is being done to alleviate poverty in the community?

One in six children in the United States lives in poverty—these families have incomes below the federally designated poverty guideline ($22,050 for a family of four in 2009).

Many families are poor even though one or both parents are employed. Such families are often large and represent all cultural groups, although the largest recent increase in families that are poor has been among European Americans under age 30 (FIFCFS, 2010). Both family structure and the labor market affect the duration of childhood poverty (Haskins & Sawhill, 2007). Commonly, the head of household in poor families is less educated than heads of households in families that are not poor. A large proportion of families that are poor are headed by single women. Families headed by single mothers are more likely to be poor because of the cost of child care and the lower average wage paid to women than to men (FIFCFS, 2010).

IN CONTEXT Rafael Gomez works as a gardener for a landscape company. He earns $450 per week. He and his wife have five children, ranging in age from 6 months to 12 years. Mrs. Gomez stays home to care for the family. The rent for a three-bedroom apartment in a dilapidated building is $1,000 per month. The Gomez children wear hand-me-down clothes from each other and from relatives. The family does not own a car or have medical insurance.

Joan Thomas is age 20; she has three children, ages 1 month, 2 years, and 4 years. She gets temporary government assistance for welfare, food, and medical services. Her husband recently deserted her. Because she first became pregnant while in high school, she never completed her education. Her lack of education limits her job opportunities. She will have to work when her government assistance ends. She can enroll in a training program while on welfare and get financial help with child-care expenses. She worries about her ability to juggle all the responsibilities.

Federal programs that attempt to alleviate some of the conditions of poverty include the following:

- **Temporary Assistance for Needy Families (TANF)** is a federal and state matching program that provides temporary financial support for families with children. Eligibility, work requirements, and time limits for benefits are established by individual states. This welfare reform program replaced Aid to Families with Dependent Children (AFDC).
- **Unemployment compensation** covers all workers in the labor force. Financed by employers' contributions, it is intended to maintain about 50 percent of a worker's income for a temporary period of involuntary unemployment. The program is administered by federal and state governments.
- **Social Security survivor or disability benefits** are administered by the federal government; payments come from the Social Security Trust Fund, through taxes on employer and employee. Social Security benefits earned by those who die or become disabled are paid to their survivors or dependents.
- **Supplemental Security Income (SSI)** provides a guaranteed minimum income for the aged and disabled.
- **Veterans' benefits** are paid by the federal government to survivors or dependents of veterans who die or are disabled in the service.
- **Child nutrition services** are federally funded programs administered by the states. They are intended to improve the nutritional standards of low-income families. Included are the food stamp program, in which participants buy food stamps, according to a formula based on income and family size, at a subsidized cost and then use the stamps to buy food; the National School Lunch Program; the Special Supplemental Food Program for Women, Infants, and Children (WIC); and the National School Breakfast Program.
- **Other services** include a variety of social services funded through state grants under Title IV and Title XX of the Social Security Act. Large proportions of these funds provide day care for children of employed mothers and other child welfare services. Title I of the Elementary and Secondary Education Act and Head Start provide educational and related services to low-income children. Child health programs and Medicaid also provide services to poor families.

According to Haskins and Sawhill (2007), the following five major factors have been pushing more and more children and families into poverty, exemplifying the effects of exosystems and macrosystems:

Why have the federal programs not succeeded in alleviating poverty?

1. The persistently high rate of unemployment among parents
2. The inability of parents to earn high enough wages to escape poverty
3. The growth in the number of female-headed households because of divorce and out-of-wedlock births
4. Inadequate preschool education, public education, and job training
5. Inadequate budgets in government programs

Unemployment and low-wage employment have outcomes beyond poverty, including loss of self-worth, increased family tensions, desertions, alcoholism, abuse, and lower academic achievement of children. Often, when a family's economic support system breaks down, so does its ability to provide emotional support (Behrman, 2002; McLoyd, Aikens, & Burton, 2006).

In addition to unemployment compensation, the federal government creates certain jobs and provides certain tax exemptions. To create jobs, local units of government (cities, towns, counties) can submit applications for federal money to pay for local public construction—for example, road and street improvements or building additions. The local community thus both relieves unemployment and gets some funds for public works. The federal government also creates certain jobs by giving money to local units of government to hire unemployed individuals. Thus, needed public services are provided (clerks, park attendants), and jobs are created for those in need.

Which public policies are designed to overcome the effects of economic problems, especially unemployment?

Tax exemptions are provided for those receiving unemployment compensation; they are granted to businesses hiring certain individuals, such as those with disabilities or those in government work-training programs; and they are granted for child care required by the mother's employment.

Although welfare reform has contributed to declining poverty rates, problems regarding government support for poor families with children remain. Among the ongoing issues are the income level at which the government considers a family poor enough to receive assistance, the funding levels for welfare-to-work programs, implementation of job training, employment prospects, child care, housing, and adequate health care coverage (Haskins & Sawhill, 2007).

What is being done to address the needs of families who are homeless in the community?

According to the National Alliance to End Homelessness (NAEH, 2010), while circumstantial factors vary, homelessness occurs when people or households are unable to acquire and/or maintain housing they can afford. Homelessness is the result of many simultaneous trends: shrinking incomes for many young families, rising housing costs, a decreasing supply of low-cost housing, a decline in government housing assistance, and deinstitutionalization of those with mental disorders. A significant number of youths who are homeless have run away or been kicked out of their homes (U.S. Interagency Council on Homelessness [USICH], 2010).

- There are about 675,000 people experiencing homelessness on any given night in the United States—roughly 22 of every 10,000 people are homeless.
- Of that number, 37 percent are people in families and 63 percent are individuals, 18 percent of the homeless population is considered "chronic," and 20 percent of the homeless population is made up of veterans (NAEH, 2010).

The threat of homelessness is even graver than the statistics suggest because millions of families are just one crisis

The incidence of families that are homeless has increased greatly.

Tony Freeman/PhotoEdit

away from losing their homes. A crisis could be an unexpected expense, illness, disability, or job loss. Other families are at risk for homelessness because they spend most of their income on housing and have no financial cushion if their rent goes up or their income falls even slightly. The mortgage foreclosure crisis has forced homeowners into renting, living with relatives or friends, or becoming homeless. Other problems associated with those who are homeless are poverty, poor health, inadequate education, poor employment prospects, and social isolation (NAEH, 2010).

IN CONTEXT Thomas Green, age 6, took his stuffed dog and lay down on the mattress with his sister, Eva, age 3, who was already asleep. The mattress was a piece of foam rubber donated to the church that was to be Thomas's home for the next few months (the town had no public shelter for the homeless). Thomas's mother, Vicki, had been living in motel rooms with the children and whoever was her current boyfriend until he left or was arrested. Vicki took odd jobs in between boyfriends to support herself and the children, but being a high school dropout, she had limited skills and, consequently, limited work opportunities.

In the morning, Vicki took Thomas to the nearby school to enroll him in kindergarten. He had to repeat kindergarten because he had moved so many times the previous year that his school attendance hadn't enabled him to be ready for first grade. Eva was invited to go to the church preschool while Vicki spent the day looking for work.

Children who are homeless suffer psychological, as well as behavioral and educational, consequences. Homeless youth are those who leave home as a result of a severe family conflict which might include physical and/or sexual abuse. One-quarter of former foster youth experience homelessness within four years of exiting foster care. Nearly all state child protective services stop foster care payments when children reach age 18; few young people have the skills at this age to be self-supporting (USICH, 2010).

Research shows a high prevalence of depression, suicide initiation, and other mental health disorders among youth who are homeless. Chronic physical health conditions are common, as are high rates of substance abuse disorders. Many youth who become homeless have histories of academic difficulties including suspension and expulsion. Homeless youth often engage in risky behaviors and have high rates of prior arrests and convictions (NAEH, 2010; USICH, 2010).

The federal government has a strategic plan to end homelessness. It provides funding for various state and local programs for such things as temporary shelters, health and social services, and money to schools to assure that children who are homeless have access to free public education (USICH, 2010).

Teachers need to be sensitive to characteristics that may be observed in children who are homeless, including depression, anxiety, severe separation problems, poor-quality relationships, shyness, aggressiveness, sleep disorders, temper tantrums, and short attention spans (NAEH, 2010; USICH, 2010).

What is being done regarding preventing disease and increasing public access to health care in the community?

Health Care for Families

In general, children from economically advantaged homes (about 55 percent of all children) are most likely to have private health insurance, which is largely employment based, while children from economically disadvantaged homes (about 27 percent of all children) are most likely to have government health insurance, such as Medicaid. Children who are not covered by any health insurance program (about 12 percent of all children) are less likely to have a regular source of health care and more likely to receive late, or no, care for health problems, putting them at greater risk for hospitalization (FIFCFS, 2010; Kaiser Family Foundation, 2007).

IN CONTEXT Thu Truong, 7 years old, developed a high fever and a cough one Saturday night. His mother gave him aspirin and some cough syrup, but by Sunday the fever was still high and the cough was worse. Mrs. Truong decided to take him to the emergency room because she has no regular doctor (she relies on health clinics for medical care). It took her an hour and a half by bus to reach the hospital. Because Thu was not "critical" (not bleeding profusely or unable to breathe, for instance), he had to wait an hour before a doctor was available to examine him.

Lara Michaels had her third baby several weeks prematurely. The baby remained in intensive care for two months. Al Michaels' insurance policy did not cover newborn health care, so the Michaels face an enormous hospital bill that will keep them in debt for years.

The most important factors influencing child health occur before birth. A baby is likely to grow into a healthy child when the mother had good nutrition during childhood and during pregnancy, received prenatal care early in pregnancy, is between the ages of 20 and 35, is in good health, has not been pregnant recently, and does not abuse drugs or alcohol. A baby is more likely to have a low birth weight (under 5.5 lb.) and/or birth defects or die when its mother is poorly nourished, has no prenatal care, is under 18, is in poor health (has a sexually transmitted disease, for example), has just been pregnant, smokes, or abuses drugs or alcohol (FIFCFS, 2010; Logan, Moore, Manlove, Mincieli, & Cunningham, 2007).

Early and continuous health care for children after birth saves lives and helps minimize long-term health problems. High-quality preventive, primary, and remedial pediatric health care can ensure that problems that can develop during infancy, such as respiratory, neurologic, or orthopedic impairments, are detected and treated. Untreated problems such as vision, hearing, and dental, as well as anemia, mental health, developmental conditions, and obesity can impair a child's ability to benefit from school, thereby affecting that child's later life (FIFCFS, 2010).

Human-made environmental hazards increasingly threaten the health of all children. For example, absorption or inhalation of lead causes damage to the central nervous system, mental retardation, and blood and urinary tract infection. Thus, technological advances must continually be monitored for their environmental impact on health and safety.

Government programs promoting children's health include the following:

- **Medicaid** provides matching money to the states to pay for medical services for the indigent and medically needy. Children who are eligible for Medicaid receive early and periodic screening, diagnosis, and treatment.
- **Maternal and child health services** provide federal money to states for projects to reduce infant mortality and improve the health of low-income mothers and children; to provide comprehensive health care to low-income children up to age 21; to provide dental care for low-income children; and to provide outreach, diagnosis, and medical and related services for low-income and medically indigent children with physical disabilities. Also included are neighborhood health centers, migrant health centers, and Native American health services.
- **Centers for Disease Control** provide federal funds to the states for the purchase of vaccines.
- **Child nutrition programs** include school lunch programs, school breakfast programs, and special food programs for low-income children and children with disabilities in day care or other nonresidential settings. Also included is the Women, Infants and Children Program (WIC), which provides nutritious food to low-income pregnant and lactating women and children under age 4 who are at nutritional risk.

What social services exist in the community for families in need?

Social Support for Families

Traditionally, many U.S. family services have been provided by private voluntary organizations on a charitable basis. In recent years, more and more public agencies have begun to play a part in services to families. The combination of public and private social services is often fragmented and uncoordinated, but there are successful collaborative examples across the country (Burger, 2010).

Government programs providing some support to families include the following:

- **Child welfare services** fund state efforts to preserve families by strengthening their ability to address their problems and avoid unnecessary foster care, and to reunite with their parents children who have been placed in foster care.
- **Social services block grants (Title XX)** provide various preventive, counseling, and other support services for low-income children and families as well as for vulnerable, abused, and neglected children and their families.
- **Child and adolescent service system program** helps ensure that youths with serious emotional problems receive needed mental health services by improving coordination among the numerous agencies responsible for them.

IN CONTEXT Jill Sanger, age 15, lives in a suburban town. Her father is an engineer for an aerospace company and often works late. Her mother is not employed but is involved in school and community activities, as well as caring for her 10-year-old twin brothers and 6-year-old sister. Jill has been reported truant from school on several occasions. She refuses to communicate with her parents and has become involved with drugs. Her parents want to get help.

Helen Black, recently divorced, has two young children. Her ex-husband is lax in sending child support payments. Helen wants to become a computer programmer and feels confident she can get a job. Someday, she would like to buy a computer and work at home. Meanwhile, however, she must go to school, and needs child care.

Jack (age 13) and Sally (age 12) Baker have been cared for and supported by their mother since their father deserted them when Sally was a year old. When Jack was 6 and Sally was 5, however, their mother became very ill. She had to be hospitalized for three months and then recuperate for six months. Having no relatives, the children were placed in foster care. When their mother could again care for them, they were returned to her. A year later, however, their mother had a relapse and the children were placed in another foster home. This time they were separated because a home was not available that would take both of them.

Two changes in family structure have accelerated tremendously—the increase in the number of women employed, especially mothers of young children under age 6, and the growth in the number of children living in families headed by one parent, usually the mother. Among the family supports that can respond to the needs of mothers who are poor, employed, and/or single, as well as to the needs of the children, is a system of quality child-care services, in home or center settings.

Mothers who are employed outside the home and have school-age children often do not or cannot make provision for after-school care. These children are sometimes referred to as "latchkey children" because they have to let themselves into their homes with a key. Sometimes older children are given the responsibility for caring for younger siblings.

Research shows mixed findings regarding relations between type of after-school care and child outcome. The use of self-care is not associated with negative child outcomes for predominantly Euro-American children within rural and suburban populations. However, different outcomes for self-care are found within urban and minority communities (Sarampote, Bassett, &Winsler, 2004). Unsupervised by adults, such children who care for themselves tend to be vulnerable to delinquency, vandalism, injury, rape, and drug use (Collins, Harris, & Susman, 1995).

There are other problems, as well, for children in self-care. Studies comparing self-care children, ranging in age from 5 to 12, with their supervised counterparts have found that children who are left alone to care for themselves and/or siblings often feel afraid regardless of their age, capabilities, or parents' assurances (Behrman, 1999; Belle, 1999). Their fearfulness may stem from warnings and cautions about people coming to the door, about cooking, and about various household problems that might occur.

Government programs assisting families with child-care issues include the following:

- **Income tax deductions** are provided for child-care expenses of employed mothers.
- **Subsidized day care** (such as Head Start and Title XX) is among the social services supported by federal and state matching funds.

Special Services for Children with Special Needs

What is being done to support children in the community who have disabilities, been maltreated, or abandoned?

Some children have special needs—they have disabilities, are maltreated, or have been abandoned by their families; they are orphans, or have run away from desperate situations.

IN CONTEXT Julie was born prematurely and required special care when her mother brought her home from the hospital one month after she was born. After a week at home, Julie had lost a significant amount of weight and was listless. She was diagnosed as suffering from "failure to thrive" resulting from neglect and was placed in foster care. Her mother, just 18 years old, had a history of drug abuse. She had trouble keeping track of medical appointments, filling prescriptions, and meeting Julie's needs. In one year, Julie was shifted three times from her mother's care to foster care. Julie's current foster mother wants to adopt her, but the biological mother will not sign the papers.

Kenny, age 13, is the oldest of four children. Both his parents are alcoholics. Kenny has been involved in some stealing incidents in the neighborhood, but he was never reported to the police because the shopkeepers felt sorry for him. Kenny stole when his father spent his paycheck on booze and there was no food in the house. Recently, however, Kenny has been hanging around with some older kids who deal in drugs. Kenny sees this as an easy way to make money and get out of the house. The first time he tries to make a sale, though, he gets caught.

Mike was born without hip sockets. In order for him to use his legs and walk normally, he needs several surgeries. In addition to the surgeries, he will need special equipment such as a walker to keep mobile until he heals. He will also need daily physical therapy to strengthen his muscles. Mike's father deserted the family after Mike's birth; he couldn't deal with having a disabled son. Mike's mother has to work to support Mike and his two older sisters. She has no medical insurance, nor does she have the time or energy to give Mike the special care he needs.

Children who are abused and neglected have recently received more national attention, due in part to the establishment in 1974 of a National Center on Child Abuse and Neglect. Children who are abused, neglected, or abandoned, as well as those who are orphaned and sometimes those who run away, are often placed in foster homes. Foster care is funded by federal, state, and local sources. Foster care provides temporary care when children cannot be cared for in their own homes for any of the following reasons: death or illness of a parent, divorce or desertion, inadequate financial support, abuse or neglect, and behavioral problems with which the parent cannot cope. Many challenges regarding foster care placement exist—dealing with the emotional, physical, and behavioral needs of the child, working with sponsoring social service agencies, finding support services in the community, and dealing with one's own feelings about letting the foster child return to the birth parents (AACAP, 2005).

About 54 percent of children placed in foster care are adopted by their foster parents and about 30 percent are adopted by a relative (U.S. Children's Bureau, 2010). In certain

Table 10.4 Key Federal Assistance Programs for Children and Families

Poverty	Child Health	Support for Families	Special Child-Care Needs
Temporary Assistance for Needy Families	Medicaid	Child welfare services	Foster care
Unemployment compensation	Maternal and child health services	Social services block grant (Title XX)	Adoption Assistance Program
Social Security survivor or disability benefits	Children's health insurance programs	Child and adolescent service system program	Child abuse prevention and treatment
Supplemental Security Income	Centers for Disease Control	Income tax deduction for child-care expenses	Family violence prevention and services
Veteran's benefits			
Child nutrition services programs	Child nutrition		
Other services: child care, educational, health	Head Start	Subsidized child care	Head Start
Homeless assistance			

cases, support (financial, medical, dental) continues for foster children if they are adopted by the family with which they reside. In addition, the federal government Adoption Assistance Program provides financial grants to families adopting "hard to place" children, including those with health problems (physical or emotional) or disabling conditions and children from diverse cultural backgrounds.

In addition to foster care funding and adoption assistance, other government programs for children with special needs include the following (see also Table 10.4):

- **The Child Abuse Prevention and Treatment Act** authorizes grants to states to assist them in developing and strengthening programs designed to prevent child abuse and neglect while providing treatment for its victims.
- **The Family Violence Prevention and Services Program** supports local programs that provide immediate shelter and related services to victims of family violence and their children.

How can mesosystems collaborate to support children's development?

Mesosystem Influences: Linking Community Services to Families and Schools

To be effective in supporting children's development, community child-care services should be comprehensive in that they link with health, nutrition, social services, and education for children and their parents (Decker & Decker, 2001). Such collaboration strengthens the immediate environment of vulnerable children, making them more resilient to stress (Hurd, Lerner, & Barton, 1999; Walsh, 2006).

Examples of comprehensive service linkages between children, families, and schools are the Head Start preschool program (discussed in Chapter 5), Brookline Early Education Program (BEEP) for prekindergarten children in the public schools, and the Better Beginnings, Better Futures (BBBF) project for primary school children (age 4 to 8) in Canada, with follow-ups in grades 3, 6, and 9. Head Start addresses the physical, emotional, cognitive, and family support needs of the child. BEEP focuses on family involvement and empowerment in children's education. The BBBF addresses the ecological contexts in which a child develops, providing supportive links between child and family to school and community over time.

Examples of service linkages between children, families, and communities are child-care resource and referral agencies providing information to parents regarding child-care arrangements; health and social services; parent education; family-friendly businesses; and

IN PRACTICE

How Can Communities Help to Optimize Children's Development?

1. **Establish a local commission for children and families.** This commission should find out what is being done in the community and what needs to be done for children and families. More specifically, it should examine the adequacy of existing programs, such as maternal and child health services, social services, day-care facilities, and recreational opportunities. The commission should include representatives of the major institutions dealing with children and families, as well as business, industry, and labor representatives. Older children, who can speak from their own experience, should also be included.
2. **Establish a neighborhood family center.** A place that provides a focal point for leisure, learning, sharing, and problem solving should be established in a school, church, or community building. To eliminate the fragmentation of human services, the center should be the place where community members receive information on family health, social services, child care, legal aid, and welfare. The center should emphasize cross-age rather than age-segregated activities.
3. **Foster community projects.** Projects involving cleaning up the environment; caring for the aged, sick, or lonely; and planning parades, fairs, and picnics are excellent ways for community members of all ages to learn to work together and appreciate each other's talents and skills. These projects should provide an opportunity for young people to act as collaborators rather than subordinates.
4. **Combat alcohol, drugs, and violence.** Provide successful community role models for children. Work with families and schools to give children skills to solve problems without having to resort to substance abuse or violence. Work with families and schools on strong sanctions against substance abuse and violence.
5. **Foster youth participation in local policy bodies.** Every community organization affecting children and youth should include teenagers and older children as voting members. These would include such organizations as school boards, recreation commissions, health boards, and welfare commissions.
6. **Plan communities to consider the children who will be growing up in them.** When planning and designing new communities, some of the factors that should be considered are the location of shops and businesses where children can have contact with adults at work, recreational and day-care facilities that are readily accessible to parents as well as children, provision for a family neighborhood center and family-oriented facilities and services, availability of public transportation, and "places to walk, sit, and talk in common company" (Garbarino, 1995a; Maushard et al., 2007).

A neighborhood family center provides social and recreational services for a variety of age groups.

John T. Barr/Liason/Getty Images

university programs providing model schools, teacher training, and collaboration with schools in the community (Decker & Decker, 2001; Hurd, Lerner, & Barton, 1999). The BBBF provides an opportunity for community members to identify the needs of children and families in their communities, request funding from appropriate government agencies, and serve as advisors in implementing programs (Collins, 2010).

Community Involvement: Volunteerism and Advocacy

Why become involved in your community?

Being a citizen in your community means participating in community issues and providing help where needed. The following are some reasons for becoming involved:

- Learn about the needs in your community.
- Conserve funds for charities, nonprofit, faith-based, and other community organizations by contributing your time.

- Share your skills and gain new ones.
- Develop self-esteem and self-confidence by feeling needed and valued.
- Meet new people from all walks of life.
- Enhance your resume and make important networking contacts.

How do you become a volunteer?

Volunteer Groups

To learn how to become a volunteer and serve your community, see http://www.nationalservice.gov. Various national, state, and local programs are available for service.

The Corporation for National and Community Service was established in 1993 by the U.S. government, The corporation was created to connect Americans of all ages and backgrounds with opportunities to give back to their communities and their nation—the Senior Corps, AmeriCorps, and Learn and Serve America programs are examples. The corporation represents our nation's philosophy of commitment to building a culture of citizenship, service, and responsibility. The corporation gives out grants to support service and volunteering in community organizations by collaborating with nonprofit organizations, corporations, and foundations to determine their needs.

The members and volunteers who serve in corporation programs provide vital assistance to institutions and organizations that serve the public. Drawing on their skills, experience, and concern for others, they provide a wide range of services. These include

TeachSource Video Activity

Go to the Education CourseMate website to watch the video entitled "Volunteerism." What volunteer experience(s) have you had? How did you feel? If you haven't volunteered, what might you like to do?

- tutoring at-risk youth,
- building homes for low-income people,
- caring for homebound seniors,
- working at food banks,
- donating food, clothing, and household items,
- helping maintain parks by cleaning the environment,
- responding to natural disasters.

How do you become an advocate?

Advocacy Groups

Child advocacy is the process of sensitizing individuals and groups to the unmet needs of children and to society's obligation to provide a positive response to those needs. In addition to the unmet needs of children examined earlier in the chapter, there are still many others, such as child maltreatment, a more humane system of juvenile justice, and transition programs for young people leaving protective community services to become independent functioning adults. If these things bother you and you want to become an advocate, see http://www.savethechildren.org.

child advocacy the process of sensitizing individuals and groups to the unmet needs of children and to society's obligation to provide a positive response to those needs

Advocacy groups can form to solve and monitor a particular problem (for example, Action for Children's Television was instrumental in getting the Children's Television Act passed in 1990); they can be a source of ongoing support for children's problems in general (such as raising money); or they can be an official government lobby (pressuring members of Congress to pass appropriate legislation). Examples of ongoing children's advocacy groups follow:

- **Children's Defense Fund (CDF)**—provides a strong and effective voice for all the children in America who cannot vote, lobby, or speak for themselves. Particular attention is paid to the needs of poor, cultural minority children, and those with disabilities .The CDF's goal is to educate the nation about the needs of children and encourage preventive investment in children before they become ill, drop out of school, suffer family breakdown, or get into trouble. CDF monitors the development and implementation of federal and state policies (Children's Defense Fund, 2010).
- **Child Welfare League of America (CWLA)**—agencies that belong are grounded in knowledge and understanding of the needs of children and their families. The league takes the position that advocacy is an important aspect of the total responsibility of

contemporary child welfare agencies. According to the league's philosophy, a contemporary social agency cannot merely be a provider of services; it must also be concerned with the general welfare policies of the community. It must take into account the external forces and conditions that affect people's ability to function. Child welfare agencies are expected to help change unfavorable community conditions that affect children and their families adversely (Goffin & Lombardi, 1988). In this respect, CWLA employs an ecological approach to human development.

- **National Congress of Parents and Teachers (NCPT)**—a national coalition of local groups, called Parent–Teacher Associations (PTAs), which are devoted to improving relations between home and school on behalf of children.

Advocating for Child Protection

Inappropriate parenting practices resulting in child abuse or neglect were discussed in Chapter 4, and the role of the caregiver in protecting children who might be maltreated was discussed in Chapter 5. Here, advocacy for children is exemplified in the law (macrosystem influence) and in the community services provided to help families (mesosystem influence). The National Clearinghouse on Child Abuse and Neglect (2002) recommends the following:

1. **Know your state's child abuse/neglect laws.** All states require that suspected child abuse be reported, but each state defines abuse differently and has different reporting procedures. You can get a copy of your state's law from a department of social services; a law enforcement agency; a state, district, city, or county attorney's office; or a regional office of child development.

What can you do to help protect children?

2. **Know who must report abuse and neglect.** Injury, sexual molestation, death, abuse, or physical neglect that is suspected of having been inflicted upon any child under age 18 by other than accidental means *must* be reported by the following persons:
   - physician
   - surgeon
   - teacher
   - child caregiver
   - dental hygienist
   - ophthalmologist
   - pharmacist
   - commercial film and photographic print processor
   - dentist
   - chiropractor
   - osteopath
   - podiatrist
   - nurse
   - hospital intern or resident
   - foster parent
   - group home personnel
   - marriage, family, child counselor
   - school personnel
   - social worker
   - county medical examiner
   - psychologist
   - law enforcement officer
   - audiologist
   - clinical laboratory technician
   - speech pathologist
   - others having responsibility for child care
3. **Know how to report abuse and neglect according to the law.** Table 5.6 in Chapter 5, titled "Indications of Possible Maltreatment," describes physical and behavioral indicators of possible abuse. If you consistently notice several of the indicators over a period of time, you have a valid reason to report your observations.

Every state requires that a report of suspected child abuse be made "immediately" or "promptly." This means that as soon as you suspect abuse, you must inform the appropriate agency. The person taking the call is trained to determine whether it is an emergency situation and an immediate response is required or whether it can wait a few days. The response depends on the age of the child, the severity of the abuse, and how accessible the child is to the perpetrator. In a typical protective service investigation of alleged maltreatment, the professional must decide not "Has this child been maltreated?" but rather "Is this maltreatment extreme enough to justify community intervention?"

What treatment or intervention programs are available in the community for child maltreatment?

Beyond identifying and assessing maltreatment, agencies and practitioners confront the challenge of providing effective treatment or intervention programs. In order to protect children, *legal intervention* is the first requirement (CAPTA, 1974). Once suspected abuse or neglect is reported to the appropriate authorities, a social worker and/or a police officer is sent to the home or school to investigate. If it is determined that the child is endangered, the child is placed in protective custody—which usually means the child is taken away from the parents or guardians and is brought to a state, county, or city institution until the case is heard in court (usually within 72 hours). Some communities assign a child advocate to the child, usually a trained volunteer with an interest in helping children. The child advocate supports the child through interviews with police and lawyers as well as going to court with the child, if necessary. If, on the other hand, it is legally determined that the child is not in immediate danger but there may be some risk of future abuse or neglect, the social services agency, as directed by the court, may provide a variety of support services to the family. Such services may also be required if and when the child is returned home after being in protective custody.

The following are various types of *therapeutic intervention* or *treatment* used with families that are abusive, depending on the particular case (Paxton & Haskins, 2009):

- **Family preservation.** The child remains at home under the supervision of the protective agency. The child protective worker visits the home on a scheduled basis. The worker can teach child development and child management to the parents.
- **Parent education.** The parents take a formal course given in their community. Some programs are based on parent effectiveness training, which concentrates on developing good communication between parents and their children. These programs theorize that abuse often occurs because parents do not understand or know how to react to their children's expressions of need and affection. Other programs teach behavior modification techniques. The aim of these programs is to provide alternatives to physical punishment when disciplining children. Parents are trained to notice their children behaving appropriately and to reward them accordingly. In some communities, hotlines provide counseling advice, available any time of the day.
- **Child care.** The child is cared for during the day at a center or in a family day-care home.
- **Family therapy.** A therapist addresses the whole family's interaction patterns.
- **Kinship care.** The child is temporarily (or permanently) placed in the care of grandparents or other close relatives.
- **Foster care.** The child is temporarily placed in another home until his or her family can provide adequate care.
- **Parent support groups.** The parents are required to join a support group, such as Parents Anonymous (a voluntary organization of child abusers), and/or become involved in their child's school. Parents, on their own, can join Parents Anonymous or they can be ordered to join by the court. When parents join, they are taught how to handle anger or frustration—for example, going into a room alone and then screaming, kicking, or pounding. The point is to get the aggression out on objects so that no one gets hurt. Members share their difficulties and try to work them out at meetings, with the help of other members. They try to develop solutions to their problems and to learn to feel better about themselves. The members maintain a network of telephone numbers so that they can call one another for support when they feel a crisis coming on.
- **Institutionalization.** The child is temporarily placed in an institution for abused/neglected children until his or her family can provide adequate care.

- **Adoption.** When returning the child to his or her home is unwise or impossible, the child is put up for adoption. This avoids interminable foster care.

In sum, the goals of treating the family that is abusive are to help the parents with their problems, help the children with their problems, and improve the relationship between parents and children in order to prevent further abuse (Child Welfare Information Gateway, 2008).

Summary

- The community comprises a group of people living in the same district under common laws who have a sense of fellowship among themselves.
- The community is structured to have five functions: production/distribution/consumption, socialization, social control, social participation, and mutual support.
- The community influences socialization through available adult role models, by the way the people in it instill their norms and values in children, by the way it enforces its rules, and by serving as a context wherein children can "try themselves out" and learn the consequences of their behavior.
- Physical factors in the community that have an impact on socialization are population density and characteristics, noise, arrangement and types of houses, and play settings.
- Economic factors in a community play a central role in shaping the daily lives of families who live and work there.
- Certain social and personal factors, such as the neighborhood setting and patterns of community interaction, influence socialization. Community relationships can be classified as informal, mutually dependent, and caring (gemeinschaft) or formal, independent, and contractual (gesellschaft).
- Children can be involved in the community when the school uses the community as a learning environment and when the community opens itself to children.
- The community represents a formal support system through its community services. Community agencies may be public, private, or a combination. Some community services are preventive; some are supportive; and some are rehabilitative.
- Mesosystem influences involve linking community services to families.
- Community involvement includes volunteerism and advocacy.

Activity

PURPOSE To learn about the services in your community.

Following are 10 hypothetical case studies involving families and children in a community. Read each of these case studies and select one family (or make up your own hypothetical one*) that you would like to help. Then complete the following steps:

1. Provide the family with a list of three agencies that may be helpful to them in their particular situation. Your list should include the following information about each agency (share with your class):
   a. Name of agency
   b. Address
   c. Telephone
   d. Hours
   e. Services provided
   f. Eligibility
   g. Fees
   h. Area served
2. Choose one of the three agencies on the list, call to make an appointment to visit the agency, and interview one person employed there (for example, director, counselor, teacher, therapist, or case worker). In this section of your report, be sure to include the following information:
   a. What steps would the agency take to help this hypothetical family (person)? Explain the services provided by this agency.
   b. For the person interviewed, describe job requirements, educational background, previous experience, job satisfactions/dissatisfactions, and other pertinent information.
   c. For the agency, give the number of employees, physical layout, number of people served, and other information regarding its scope and mission.

* *Ideas*: at-risk infant (premature, drug- or alcohol-exposed); relative with a terminal disease; transition programs for 18-year-olds no longer eligible for special or protective services; disaster (tornado, fire, hurricane, earthquake) assistance.

Case Study 1: The Wilson Family

Matt Wilson is 67 years old. His wife has recently died. His daughter and her family, who live in another state, have persuaded Matt to sell his home and move close to them.

After he finds an apartment and gets somewhat settled, Matt's family notices that he is having a difficult time adjusting. He seems continually depressed and sometimes confused. He does not leave his apartment often (although he has a car and drives), spends his days watching television, and doesn't seem to seek out other people. He is also not eating properly, and his family is afraid that his physical, as well as mental, health will begin to decline rapidly.

Is there help available for Matt in your community? What would you recommend to Matt's family in order to help him?

Case Study 2: The Johnson Family

You are a first-grade teacher at an elementary school. You are especially worried about one of the students in your class, Michael Johnson. He always seems to arrive at school extra early (usually about 30 minutes). He is never dressed appropriately for the weather, and his general appearance is sloppy. His schoolwork is on grade level. However, at times his behavior is aggressive and hostile (especially toward classmates). On several occasions you have noticed bruises on Michael, and when you ask him about these, he is evasive. During your first parent–teacher conference, you share your concerns with Mrs. Johnson. She breaks down and tells you that her husband, Michael's stepfather, is very hard on him. He is sarcastic, always belittling Michael, and at times gets physically violent with him. Mrs. Johnson asks you for help. What is your role as a teacher? What assistance is available to Michael and to his family in your community?

Case Study 3: The Peterson Family

Mary Peterson is a single parent living in your community. She has three children, Pam (16), Brian (14), and Lynn (12). Mary works full-time, and the three children all attend school. Mary's oldest daughter, Pam, has always been a good student and has had a nice group of friends. Pam has rarely had any problems that could not be worked out easily. Recently, however, Pam has been very withdrawn and moody. She spends a lot of time in her room, and Mary suspects that she is crying a lot. When confronted, Pam gets emotional and shouts at Mary, "Mind your own business and leave me alone!" Mary questions her other children about Pam's behavior. Finally, Lynn tells her Mom that Pam thinks she is pregnant. Where would you suggest that Pam and Mary Peterson go for help in this situation? What kind of assistance is available to them in your community? Who can help Pam explore her options and make a decision about this pregnancy?

Case Study 4: The Meyers Family

Paula and Larry Meyers live in your community with their two children, Kelly (4) and Lisa (18 months). Lisa is not showing the normal development that Kelly did at this age, and Paula is very concerned. Lisa is not yet standing or walking. She does not respond to the family with love and affection and often seems to be in her own little world. Their pediatrician has suggested that the Meyers take Lisa to a neurologist for some testing. After extensive tests, it is determined that Lisa has cerebral palsy. Paula and Larry want to provide Lisa with every possible opportunity for a normal life. What services are available to Lisa and her family in your community? Where would you recommend the Meyers go to get assistance?

Case Study 5: The Simmons Family

Martin Simmons lives in your community with his wife, Sue, and their 14-year-old son, Steve. Martin has worked for a large engineering firm in the area for the past 12 years. Recently, due to cutbacks, Martin lost his job. He has been unemployed for the past eight months, and his family is really feeling the pressure of his job loss. Martin was actively looking for a job for the first month of his unemployment. Lately, however, he has begun drinking more and more and looking for work less and less. Since he began drinking, his relationship with his wife, and especially with his son, has suffered a tremendous strain. Sue is convinced that Martin is becoming addicted to alcohol and feels he is settling deeper and deeper into a depressed state. Steve is angry with his dad, and they are continually fighting with one another. Sue has asked you to help her find assistance for herself and her family. What agencies would you suggest the Simmons family contact for assistance?

Case Study 6: The Hernandez Family

During lunch break on the junior high school playground, you notice a group of boys in a small circle intently examining something. As you approach the group, Roberto hastily shoves something in his pocket. In the haste, a joint drops on the ground. You pick it up and escort the group to the principal's office. You learn that Roberto got the marijuana from his older brother, who is in a gang, and brought it to show his friends. Mr. and Mrs. Hernandez are called, and a conference is scheduled. After explaining the situation to the parents, where do you refer this family for help?

Case Study 7: The Lambert Family

Mrs. Lambert waits to speak to you after picking up her daughter at the day-care center. She tells you that her husband has been laid off and his unemployment checks will stop next week. She can't pay the tuition at the center, and she has no other place to leave her daughter while she works. She must work to pay the rent and buy food. She hopes her husband will find work soon (he spends all day looking), because unpaid bills are piling up. The family no longer has medical insurance since the father lost his job. They have several doctor bills to pay for a severe ear infection their daughter had last month. The family car's tire treads are so worn that driving is unsafe, yet the car is the family's only means of transportation to work, the day-care center, and the store. Mrs. Lambert is terrified of having her family become homeless. Where would you refer Mrs. Lambert for help?

Case Study 8: The Sullivan Family

You are a prekindergarten teacher at a local preschool. Brian is a student who turned 5 in November. Brian's behavior in class is causing problems for you and for the other students. He has difficulty sitting still, paying attention for extended periods, completing any activities, and keeping his hands to himself. Brian is easily frustrated and is prone to temper tantrums and outbursts of aggression. Mrs. Sullivan, a single parent, has experienced the same problems with Brian at home. What could be the cause of Brian's behavior, and where would you refer this family for help?

Case Study 9: The Nguyen Family

A child enters your public school preschool class the first day and speaks no English. You wait for his mother to pick him up so you can get some information about the child. The mother's English is very limited. You resort to communicating in simple words combined with gestures. You even draw pictures in order to communicate. You learn that the family has recently arrived from Vietnam and is staying with relatives who were sponsored to come to the United States the previous year. The father works in a local electronics factory, and the mother is expecting another child in three months. The mother is most anxious that her son, as well as she and her husband, learn English and the "American way" as quickly as possible. Where do you refer this family for help with American culture?

Case Study 10: The Horvath Family

For the past two years, Mr. Horvath has brought and picked up two of his children, now 4½ and 5½, to the children's center. You have never met the mother. One day a woman comes to the center claiming she is the Horvath children's mother. She asks to have them released to her. You refuse because her name is not on their information form. She produces a court document stating she has legal custody of the children and demands they be released to her. You assign someone to watch the children while you call the police and the father. The father admits the mother was granted legal custody, but says she was continually drunk, so he took them. He has had them for two years, and she has never even visited them once. What do you advise him to do?

Related Readings

Alderson, P. (2008). *Young children's rights: Exploring beliefs, principles, and practice (children in charge).* Philadelphia: Jessica Kingsley.

Barnes, J., Katz, I. B., Korbin, J. E., & O'Brien, M. (2006). *Children and families in communities: Theory, research, policy, and practice.* New York: Wiley.

Burger, W. R. (2010). *Human services in contemporary America* (8th ed.). Pacific Grove, CA: Brooks Cole.

Block, P. (2009). *Community: The structure of belonging.* San Francisco: Berrett-Koehler Publishers.

Decker, L. E., & Decker, V. A. (2001). *Engaging families and communities: Pathways to educational success* (2nd ed.). Fairfax, VA: National Community Education Association.

Garbarino, J. (1995). *Building a socially nourishing environment with children.* San Francisco: Jossey-Bass.

Putnam, R. D. (2000). *Bowling alone: The collapse and revival of American community.* New York: Simon & Schuster.

Robinson, A., & Stark, D. (2005). *Advocates in action: Making a difference for young children* (2nd ed.). Washington, DC: National Association for Young Children.

Resources

Child Trends—social science research for those who serve children
http://www.childtrends.org

Child Welfare Information Gateway—protecting children, strengthening families
http://www.childwelfare.gov

Save the Children—creating lasting changes for children in need in the United States and the world
http://www.savethechildren.org

PART 3

What Are the Developmental Consequences of Socialization Processes?

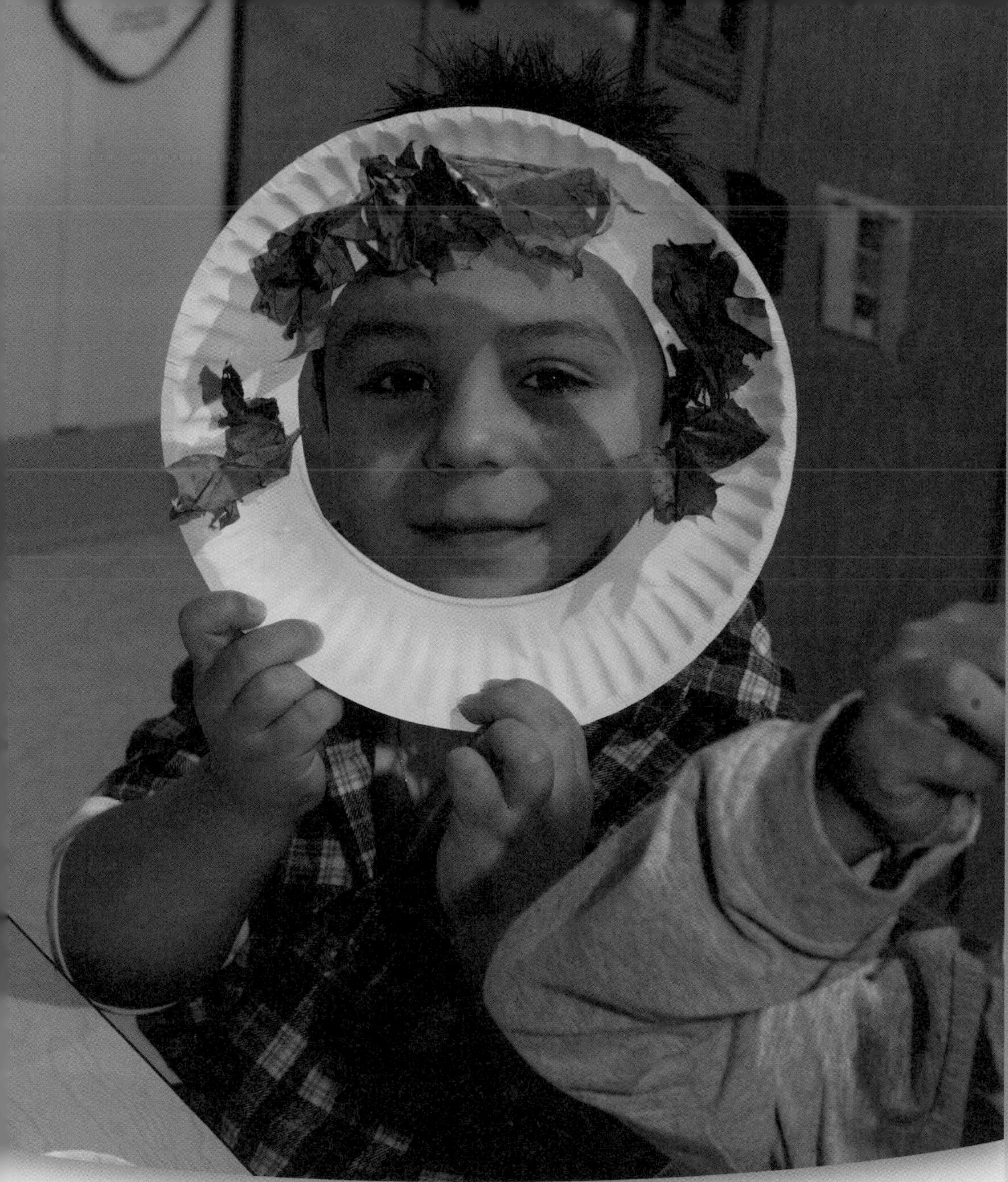

Cengage Learning

11

Emotional and Cognitive Socialization Outcomes

"The value of achieving lies in the achievement."

—ALBERT EINSTEIN

SOCIALIZATION SKETCHES

Martin Luther King Jr.

(1929–1968)

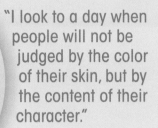

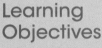

AP Photo

"I look to a day when people will not be judged by the color of their skin, but by the content of their character."

– MARTIN LUTHER KING JR.

This quote describes Dr. Martin Luther King Jr.'s values and why he became a civil rights advocate and activist. The socialization sketch relates to the chapter in that it describes influences on King's belief in the Declaration of Independence—"... all men are created equal and they are endowed by their Creator with certain unalienable rights" and his consequent actions to change people's attitudes in that regard.

Family

Martin Luther King Jr. was born in 1929 in Atlanta, Georgia. He was the son of Reverend Martin Luther King Sr. and Alberta Williams King. He had an older sister and a younger brother. His grandfather began the family's long tenure as pastors of the Ebenezer Baptist Church in Atlanta. His father served after his grandfather and Martin Jr. acted as co-pastor with his father from 1960 until his death.

School

Young King grew up in the segregated South. He attended David T. Howard Elementary School and Atlanta University Laboratory School, both of which had all-Black student populations. At that time, Blacks could not attend the same schools as Whites. King graduated from Booker T. Washington High School when he was 15 and went right on to college. Following in his grandfather's and father's footsteps, he attended Atlanta's Morehouse College, graduating with a degree in sociology. He then moved to Pennsylvania to study religion at the Crozer Theological Seminary. There he studied the teachings of Indian spiritual leader, Mohandas Gandhi. King experienced racial integration at the seminary, as the classes had diverse students. King continued his theology studies at Boston University, where he received a Doctor of Philosophy degree in 1955.

King married Coretta Scott before completing his Ph.D. He took on the job of pastor for the Dexter Avenue Baptist Church in Montgomery, Alabama, at that time. Together they had four children.

Community

King was instrumental in the founding of the Southern Christian Leadership Conference in 1957. The purpose was to unite Black churches in order to conduct nonviolent protests for civil rights reform.

King was so inspired by Gandhi's success with nonviolent activism that he visited Gandhi's family in India in 1959. He became convinced that nonviolent resistance was the most potent weapon available to oppressed people in their struggle for justice.

King organized and led marches for Blacks' right to vote, desegregation, labor rights, and other basic rights. Most of these rights were successfully enacted into U.S. law with the passage of the Civil Rights Act of 1964 and the Voting Rights Act of 1965.

In 1964, Martin Luther King Jr. became the youngest person to receive the Nobel Peace Prize for his work to end segregation and racial discrimination through civil disobedience and other nonviolent means. For example, in 1955, King led the Montgomery Bus Boycott, which lasted for over a year. For another, King was instrumental in the March on Washington in 1963, where he gave his famous speech, "I Have a Dream," raising public consciousness of the civil rights movement. As a result of his activism, King was arrested several times and became a target for threats on his life. As laws were passed to recognize the equal rights of all, King refocused his advocacy efforts on ending poverty and opposing the Vietnam War. On April 4, 1968, King was assassinated in Memphis, Tennessee.

- Have you ever experienced prejudice directly or indirectly?
- Have you ever tried to right a wrong?

Learning Objectives

After completing this chapter, you will be able to:

1. Define and explain values giving examples of society, family, personal values.
2. Define and explain what is meant by attitudes.
3. Describe influences on the development of attitudes, including how to change them.
4. Define and discuss influences on achievement motivation, or mastery orientation.
5. Define and explain locus of control.
6. Define and explain learned-helpless orientation. Give examples.
7. Define and explain how self-esteem develops.
8. Discuss the various influences on self-esteem.

The outcomes of socialization that are examined in this chapter and the next can be categorized as primarily emotional and cognitive (such as values, attitudes, motives, attributions, and self-esteem) or primarily social and behavioral (such as self-regulation, morals, and gender roles). These outcomes are the result of child, family, school, peer, and community interaction (mesosystems). Also influencing the development of these outcomes are exosystems (such as parents' work or school board policies), factors in individuals' macrosystems (such as religion, ethnicity, or economics), and the chronosystem (changes in society or in individuals themselves, such as today's sexual norms compared to those of one's grandparents). Figure 11.1 provides an ecological model of the systems involved in the process.

Values

What is important to you in life?

Values, as introduced in Chapter 2, are qualities or beliefs that are viewed as desirable or important. Certain basic *human* values are enshrined in the laws of most civilized societies. The Ten Commandments are an example of basic human values, some of

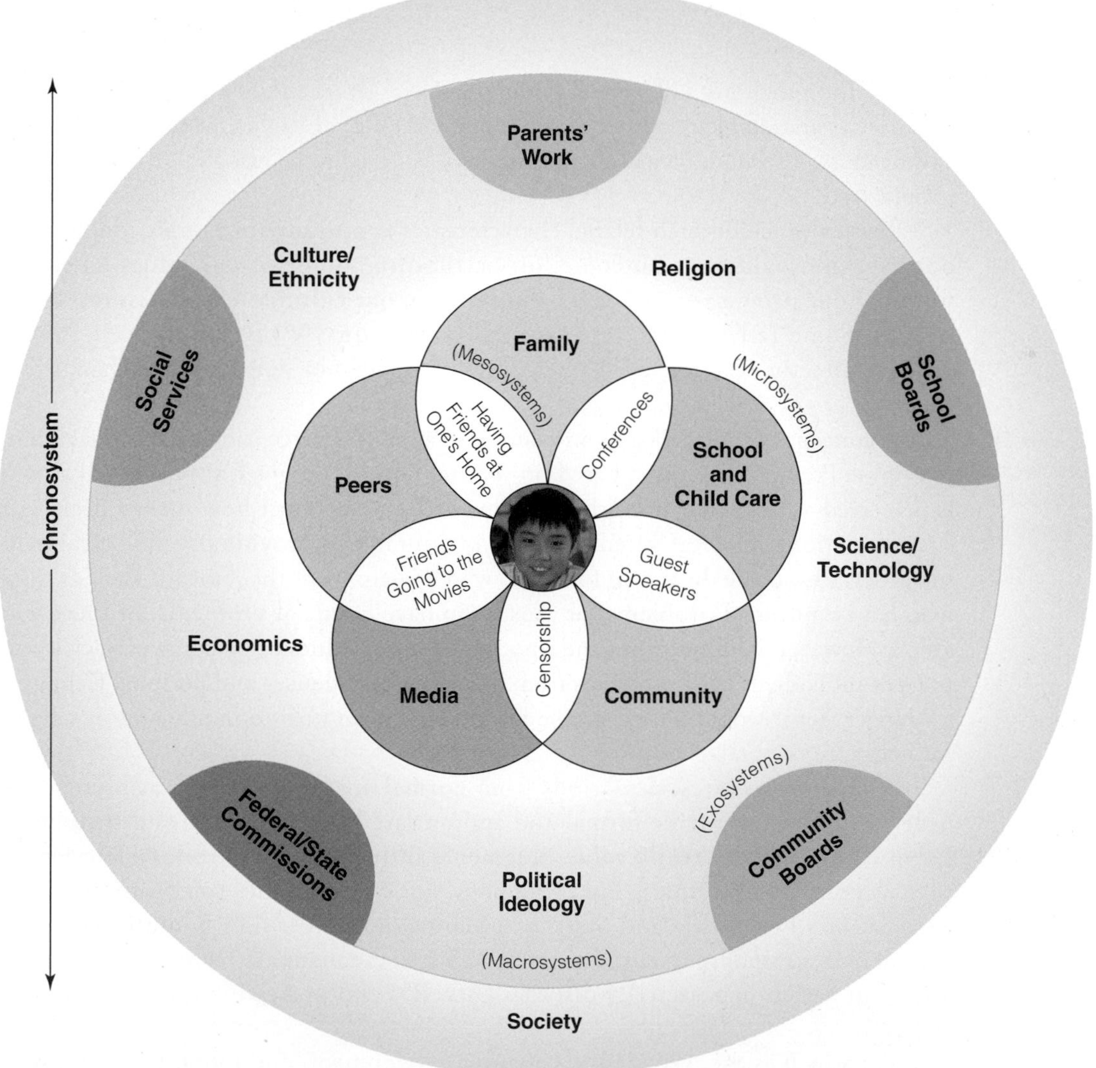

FIGURE 11.1 A Bioecological Model of Human Development
The child's values, attitudes, motives, attributions, and self-esteem are outcomes of his or her socialization.

Cengage Learning

IN PRACTICE

What Are Some Basic Societal Values?

- **Equal justice for all.** "Do unto others as you would have them do unto you." —The Golden Rule
- **Compassion for those in need.** "With malice toward none, with charity for all." —Abraham Lincoln
- **Equality of opportunity.** "We hold these truths to be self-evident: that all men are created equal, that they are endowed by their Creator with certain inalienable rights; that among these are life, liberty, and the pursuit of happiness."—Thomas Jefferson

What Are Some Basic Personal Values?

- **Truth.** "The truth shall make you free."—John
- **Love.** "To love and be loved."—Edgar Allan Poe
- **Knowledge.** "Knowledge is power."—Meditationes Sacrae

which ("Thou shalt not kill") are also found in laws. Other values are basic to a particular society. An example of a basic *societal* value is the Bill of Rights, which lists the rights and freedoms (freedom of speech, for instance) assumed to be essential to people in our society.

Values can include such related characteristics as attitudes or morals, which affect our behavior. Values are outcomes of socialization. Some of our values reflect the values of our parents, our teachers, our religion, our culture, our profession, or our friends. Some reflect what we have read or seen on TV or film, as well as what we have directly experienced. Values, whether societal or personal, can change over time.

How are values affected by societal perceptions?

The concept of "normality" is an example of a societal perception because, according to Sophie Freud (1999), it is based on societal norms at a given time, as well as who is perceived as deviating from those norms. Values also affect how society deals with such deviations. In the United States, it is common to provide psychological help, social services, or medical care for those who deviate from the "norm," such as those who have emotional problems, or those who have financial problems, or those who are ill. However, in other times and in other cultures, values of personal privacy would prevent individuals with problems from divulging confidences and personal feelings to a stranger. Yet it would be acceptable for individuals to turn to family and/or religion for help.

In the United States, deviations from normal are labeled (such as bipolar disorder) in order to provide formal and appropriate help (diagnosis and treatment). Labels, however, are really value judgments influenced by chronosystem factors such as politics, economics, and technology. For example, the American Psychiatric Association's Diagnostic and Statistical Manual no longer lists homosexuality as a disorder. As a response to current times, added to the manual's list of pathologies are attention deficit hyperactivity disorder (ADHD) and posttraumatic stress disorder (PTSD).

How are values affected by personal perceptions?

Factors such as age, experience, cognitive development, and moral reasoning affect values. The following story illustrates diverse personal perceptions, reflecting the perspectives of different generations.

IN CONTEXT

Tamra wanted to have a party for her graduation from high school. The neighborhood where she lived with her family had a recreation room, which was rented out for a nominal fee to various groups for meetings, club functions, and parties. Tamra's parents, Bill and Joy, agreed to let Tamra have the party provided the rules for rental were followed. One rule was that parties for minors had to be chaperoned; another was that there could be no more than 50 people; another was that the room had to be cleaned after the party; and the last was that no alcohol could be served to minors. Tamra agreed to all but the last: "How can you have a graduation party without beer? C'mon, get real . . . no one will come!" "Sorry," said Bill, "you want a party, you have to abide by the rules." "OK, OK, but we better have great food," Tamra grumbled.

One week before the party, Joy got a phone call from a parent of a girl she did not know. The parent wanted to confirm that there was in fact a party, that beer would be served, and that the cost of a formal invitation was $10. Joy could hardly contain her shock and anger. Apparently, a flyer had been distributed at school "advertising" the party. Joy thanked the parent and said there would be no such party.

Joy told Bill what happened and together they confronted Tamra. Tamra said it was one of her friends who had distributed the flyer (Tamra would not tell who). Bill said he was extremely disappointed that she hadn't stopped her friend, as they had agreed to the rules for the party—especially no alcohol—in advance; as a result, there would be no party. Bill explained that advertising the party, especially one in which beer would be served, was setting up her parents for trouble—uninvited kids having to be denied entrance to the party and leaving, angry neighbors calling the police, and he and Joy being responsible for any alcohol-related accidents. Tamra listened and said she understood her father's position but that he and Joy were out of touch with reality: All graduation parties have booze; they didn't understand her position; she couldn't have a party and not do what was expected. "Well, then, I guess the party is off," said Bill, "because we had expectations, too."

The next evening several of Tamra's friends came over to beg Bill and Joy to reconsider. They claimed drinking was going to occur on graduation night whether or not Tamra had the party; Tamra's having the party would at least keep the kids from driving around drunk. The best way to prevent alcohol-related accidents was to let Tamra have the party, take everyone's car keys, and have all the kids spend the night.

Joy said, "That's an interesting argument, but first, I feel morally wrong serving kids alcohol; second, the recreation room belongs to the community, and the rules cannot be broken; and third, it is illegal for kids under 21 to drink in this state."

Bill shook his head and said to Joy, "The values of this generation are so different from those of ours. Why does booze have to be the essential ingredient for having a good time?"

Tamra placed more value on what her friends thought than what her parents thought. Her parents, on the other hand, placed more value on obeying the law and following the community policy in regard to minors drinking alcohol than on Tamra's saving face with her friends.

In the pop culture, as portrayed by the media, much value is placed on drinking alcohol as a means of having fun, whereas in certain religious and cultural groups, drinking alcohol is considered sinful. Thus, some people might experience conflict in social situations.

As soon as children can understand language, they have access to their parents', as well as their culture's, values. As children develop cognitively and can interpret the meaning of their social interactions and real experiences, they begin to construct their own values, which will change and be redefined as they get older.

Many adolescents in this culture equate alcohol with having a good time.

Mandy Godbehear

How do individuals come to know what is personally important?

Values Clarification

values clarification the process of discovering what is personally worthwhile or desirable in life

One technique is known as **values clarification**—the process of discovering what is personally worthwhile or desirable in life. This process can help individuals understand their own moral codes, their attitudes and motives, their prosocial or antisocial behavior, their gender roles, and themselves. For example, in teaching about the founding of the United States, a *factual* discussion might explore dates and events; a *conceptual* discussion might discuss emigration and freedom of religion; a *values* discussion might address questions like these: What is so important to you that if it were taken away, you would leave your country? If you left, what would you take with you? A values clarification exercise can be found in the chapter activity.

Values clarification involves making decisions—choosing among alternatives. Sometimes the process is difficult because values may conflict. For example, Bill and Joy had to choose between their values of respect for the law and family harmony; Tamra had to weigh her value of preserving friendship as opposed to that of respecting the law.

How are values, attitudes, and behavior related?

Attitudes

Values are really the basis for attitudes. An *attitude*, as introduced in Chapter 2, is a tendency to respond positively (favorably) or negatively (unfavorably) to certain persons, objects, or situations. Attitudes are composed of beliefs, feelings, and behavior tendencies. Most psychologists agree that attitudes determine what we attend to in our environment, how we perceive the information about the object of our attention, and how we respond to that object. Thus, attitudes guide behavior. The In Context box exemplifies the diversity of attitudes regarding sports team mascots.

IN CONTEXT Core values of the National Collegiate Athletic Association (NCAA) include cultural diversity, ethical sportsmanship, and nondiscrimination. In 2005, the NCAA voted to ban the use of nicknames and mascots it considers "hostile or abusive" in terms of race, ethnicity, or national origin during its postseason college sports events. Most often cited were Native American images or references. The rationale behind the decision is the belief that stereotypes and caricatures embodied in logos or mascots are harmful to children. Some people argue that sports teams differ from street or city names because of the competition involved—a sports team creates a division because one team wins and one loses. Others disagree, saying that a school's use of a nickname and symbol shows honor and respect. For example, the Tribal Council of the Seminole Tribe of Florida supports Florida State University's use of Chief Osceola, who gallops onto the football field on horseback and plants a burning spear in the turf before home games. The new rules would "have us cover the Seminole name and symbol as if we were embarrassed," said the university president (Norwood, 2005, p. 20).

After many consultations with members of the community and experts in Aztec culture, San Diego State University replaced its Monty Montezuma mascot to make its depiction of Aztecs historically accurate and culturally appropriate. SDSU was successful in being excluded from the ban. Some people, often alumni, who have no ties to Native American heritage, develop strong identity ties to their team's mascot. One Caucasian woman told a reporter, "I'm a third generation Redskin!"

Generally, colleges and universities may adopt any logo or mascot they wish, as that is an institutional decision. However, the NCAA is a national organization that must be sensitive to the attitudes of people in the communities where postseason games or championships are held.

prejudice an attitude involving prejudgment; the application of a previously formed judgment to some person, object, or situation

Prejudice is an attitude. The word means "prejudgment." It generally refers to the application of a previously formed judgment to some person, object, or situation. It can be favorable or unfavorable. Usually, prejudice comes from categorizing or stereotyping.

The Seminole Tribal Council believes the NCAA is being prejudiced in deciding which mascots are inappropriate.

A *stereotype*, as introduced in Chapter 9, is an oversimplified, fixed attitude or set of beliefs that is held about members of a group. Stereotypical attitudes usually do not allow for individual exceptions. The reason for the NCAA ban is to minimize stereotyping of ethnic groups.

Development of Attitudes

How do attitudes develop?

The development of attitudes is influenced by age, cognitive development, and social experiences (Van Ausdale & Feagin, 2001). Researchers (Brown & Bigler, 2005; Van Ausdale & Feagin, 2001) suggest that attitudes about diverse cultural groups develop in the following sequence:

- Phase I—awareness of cultural differences, beginning at about age 2½ to 3
- Phase II—orientation toward specific culturally related words and concepts, beginning at about age 4
- Phase III—attitudes toward various cultural groups, beginning at about age 7

As children develop cognitively, they begin to categorize (assimilate and accommodate) similarities and differences. Reviewing many studies of European American children's attitudes toward other groups, Aboud (1988) and colleagues (Aboud & Amato, 2001) reported that 4- to 7-year-old European American children were already aware that "White" was the cultural identity favored by their society. They referred to other groups as "bad" or with negative characteristics. Children of color were reported to have ambivalent feelings about their cultural identity. Young children understand the hierarchy of status and privilege in the United States (Van Ausdale & Feagin, 2001). However, Aboud (1988) and colleagues (Aboud & Amato, 2001) found that after age 7, children of all cultural groups were less prejudiced toward other groups and had more positive attitudes toward their own group. Aboud explained young children's prejudicial attitudes as due to cognitive immaturity rather than malice.

Social experiences, including observation and interaction, provide children with a perspective of the macrosystem in which they live (Brown, 2010; Brown & Bigler, 2005). Children come to know attitudes about culture, religion, socioeconomic status, gender, disability, and age by watching TV, by hearing significant adults talk and seeing how they behave, and by noticing differences in neighborhood facilities (schools, theaters, sidewalks) and practices (employment, discrimination, violence).

Influences on Attitude Development

What role do significant socializing agents play in influencing children's attitudes toward those who are similar and those who are different?

The family, peers, media, community, and school all play a role in the development of attitudes.

Family

Parents have a large impact on children's attitudes and values. For example, a study of fourth- and fifth-grade children and their parents confirmed that children identify with their parents' attitudes (Sinclair, Dunn, & Lowery, 2005). Cultural prejudice also follows this general pattern. The cultural prejudices of elementary school children representing diverse groups tend to resemble those of their parents. Studies of young children show that those with the most prejudicial attitudes have parents who are authoritarian, who use strict disciplinary techniques, and who are inflexible in their attitudes toward right and wrong (Aboud, 1988; Aboud & Amato, 2001). Thus, rigid parental attitudes foster similar attitudes in their children.

Modeling

One explanation for the resemblance of children's and parents' cultural attitudes is that children develop attitudes through role modeling. Children identify with models who are powerful and admirable. Through the process of identification, they begin to assume the attitudes of the people they would like to emulate (parents, relatives, friends, fictional heroes or heroines, television and movie characters, rock stars).

Instruction

One way children learn attitudes is by instruction. Young children accept as true the statements of their parents and others they admire because, with their limited experience, they are not apt to have heard anything different.

According to Ramsey (2004), children assimilate culturally related attitudes, preferences, and social expectations at an early age. They understand the world in terms of absolutes and believe overgeneralizations. Therefore, because of their cognitive level of development, they are receptive to global stereotypical and prejudicial comments of adults. For example, in an experiment (Bigler, Brown, & Markell, 2001), 7- to 12-year-olds attending a summer school program were randomly assigned to groups denoted by yellow or blue T-shirts. The status of each group was artificially manipulated by the teachers; posters depicted members of the yellow group as having won more spelling and athletic competitions, giving their group higher status than the blue group. Teachers called attention to the different statuses, using them as a basis for seating arrangements, task assignments, and certain class privileges. When the children were asked to evaluate each other, those in the yellow group rated each other higher than the blue group, and the blue group rated each other lower. Those children not exposed to the artificial evaluative judgment of adults did not express prejudice toward each other.

Reinforcement and Punishment

The socializing techniques of reinforcement and punishment are also involved in the way children learn attitudes. For example, it has been demonstrated that attitudes

IN PRACTICE

How Does Prejudice Develop?

The following is a typical developmental sequence of how children become prejudiced.

- **Awareness**—being alert to, seeing, noticing, and understanding differences among people even though they may never have been described or talked about. Children model behavior they observe in adults they look up to.
- **Identification**—naming, labeling, and classifying people based on physical characteristics that children notice. Verbal identification relieves the stress that comes from being aware of or confused by something that you can't describe or no one else is talking about. Identification is the child's attempt to break the adult silence and make sense of the world. Children mimic what they see, hear, and read about.
- **Attitude**—having thoughts and feelings that become an inclination or opinion toward another person and their way of living in the world. Children may displace their feelings onto others who are less powerful.
- **Preference**—valuing, favoring, and giving priority to one physical attribute, person, or lifestyle over another, usually based on similarities and differences. Children understand the world from the perspective of their own experience.
- **Prejudice**—holding a preconceived hostile attitude, opinion, feeling, or action against a person, ethnic group, or their lifestyle without knowing them. Children generalize their personal experiences to the world.

Source: S. York (1991). *Roots and wings: Affirming culture in early childhood programs.* St. Paul, MN: Toys 'n' Things Press, pp. 169–170.

toward cultural groups can be influenced simply by associating them with positive words (reinforcement), such as *happy* or *successful*, or negative words (punishment), such as *ugly* or *failure* (Aboud, 1988; Aboud & Amato, 2001). Also, positive and negative remarks by friends influence prejudicial attitudes (Aboud & Fenwick, 1999). For another example, negative attitudes about individuals with disabilities, such as those who are vocationally limited or socially inept, are reinforced when such individuals are excluded from the mainstream of society (Gollnick & Chinn, 2008).

Peers

Peers influence attitudes and behavior. Children compare the acceptability of their beliefs with those of their friends. Children compare their characteristics with those of the in-group and the out-group; they are more likely to be prejudiced against the out-group (Brown, 2010). Because preadolescent children have a great need to identify with the peer group, someone who is culturally different or who has a disability is often excluded (Brown, 2010; Gollnick & Chinn, 2008). However, studies have shown that prejudice may be reduced by equal status contact between majority and minority groups in the pursuit of common goals (Oskamp, 2000).

Other attitudes influenced by peers involve dress, dating, personal problems, and sex (Sebald, 1986, 1989).

Mass Media

Television and Movies

Children and adolescents frequently cite television as a source of information that influences their attitudes about people and things (Comstock & Scharrer, 2007; Perse, 2001). "You see so much violence that it's meaningless. If I saw someone really get killed, it wouldn't be a big deal. I guess I'm turning into a hard rock," said an 11-year-old. "When I see a beautiful girl using shampoo or a cosmetic on TV, I buy them because I'll look like her. I have a ton of cosmetics," said a 13-year-old. Several studies have reported that middle and high school students rate the mass media as their most important source of information and opinions, even more important than their parents, teachers, and friends (Perse, 2001). Television, discussed in Chapter 9, is a source of social stereotypes. To illustrate, Middle Eastern Americans have experienced negative stereotyping in movies. They are often portrayed as villains, criminals, or terrorists, as well as polygamists (Bennett, 2010).

Although television and movies have generally had the reputation of perpetuating negative attitudes, they also have the potential for bringing people to new levels of empathetic understanding. TV documentaries and biographies of culturally diverse historical and sports figures, such as *The Jackie Robinson Story*, have given viewers insight, as have movies such as *Schindler's List*, which brought awareness to the plight of Jews during World War II; *The King's Speech*, which exposed the speech disability of King George VI and his struggles to overcome it in order to give an inspiring radio address to the British people about going to war; and *Precious,* about an overweight, illiterate African American teen from Harlem who discovers an alternate path in life after she begins attending a new school.

Books

Books are influential in attitude formation. Consider the controversy some books stir up, resulting in their removal from library shelves (Norton & Norton, 2006). For example, in the 1960s, Garth Williams' *The Rabbit's Wedding* (1982) was criticized because the illustrations showed the marriage of a black rabbit and a white rabbit. In the 1970s, Maurice Sendak's (1970) *In the Night Kitchen* was taken off some library shelves because the child in the story was nude. In the 1980s, Helen Bannerman's *The Story of Little Black Sambo*, which was first published in 1899 and had enjoyed much popularity over the years, was attacked for being offensive to African Americans because of the story line and crudely drawn figures of characters with stereotypical features.

Exemplifying how attitudes regarding people of color can be transmitted subtly, a 1993 Caldecott Honor Book (recognition given for pictures), *Seven Blind Mice* by Ed Young (1992), is about seven blind mice, each a different and brilliant color, whose task is to identify an object. The white mouse solves the riddle and correctly identifies the object as an elephant. Many have criticized the book, complaining that the white mouse is portrayed as the "savior," thereby perpetuating prejudicial attitudes of "white supremacy" (Jacobs & Tunnell, 1996). Children will abstract attitudinal concepts from their social experiences and try them out. For example, in wanting to control the space in the sandbox, 4-year-old Carla says only people who speak Spanish are allowed; experimenting with a racial epithet, Jimmy discovers he can be dominant by hurting others' feelings (Van Ausdale & Feagin, 2001).

A classic book defying gender stereotypes is *The Story of Ferdinand* by Munro Leaf (1936). Ferdinand is a bull who would rather smell the flowers than fight; the attitude portrayed is that it is OK to be yourself rather than conform to cultural role prescriptions.

Mike Lupica reading from a classic children's book, The Story of Ferdinand.

Joe Kohen/WireImage/Getty Images

Community

Community customs and traditions influence attitudes. For example, an American custom regarding privacy is to designate public restrooms "Men" or "Women"; other countries do not have such designations. This is an example of gender discrimination. (Why is the line to the ladies' room always much longer than the line to the men's?) Before the U.S. civil rights movement, it was customary in southern communities to have signs designating racially segregated bathrooms ("White," "Colored"). This is an example of race discrimination. Today, many community facilities are age-segregated. Signs that say "Adults Only" or charging different prices at the movies based on age are examples of discrimination. Children thus acquire attitudes that represent the status quo in their environment.

Is the community population diverse (age, SES, cultural background)? Or is it homogeneous? Do the people who live there have similar backgrounds? How do different people in the community interact? As has been discussed, research shows that positive interactions with people different from oneself foster positive attitudes toward them.

School

Schools influence attitude formation. A review of various studies (Sadker & Sadker, 1994; Sadker & Zittleman, 2009) illustrated how gender-role stereotyping is perpetuated in schools. Schools that separate male and female activities and encourage boys to play in the "block corner" or take science classes and girls to go to the "housekeeping" area or take English classes, for example, are teaching children which activities are gender appropriate. Teachers who project their gender-typed expectations on boys and girls reinforce traditional gender-role behavior (Good & Brophy, 2007). In other words, if a teacher *expects* boys to be more active and aggressive than girls, the teacher will tend to allow this behavior. Likewise, a teacher who *expects* girls to be passive and docile will likely encourage girls to conform to this pattern.

Friendship between these children is more important than societal attitudes about culturally diverse groups.

Cengage Learning

Classroom organization can be very effective in influencing attitudes toward others. For example, researchers (Johnson & Johnson, 1999; Johnson, Johnson, & Maruyama, 1983) tried to identify conditions in schools that led to positive attitudes regarding culturally diverse students as well as students with disabilities. They found that when members of both heterogeneous and homogeneous groups cooperated instead of competed to achieve a common goal, greater positive attitudes emerged among the group members. These positive attitudes included more realistic views of self and group members, greater expectations of success, and increased expectations of favorable future interactions with group members.

Changing Attitudes about Diversity

Can prejudicial attitudes be changed?

Several studies have explored educational ways to change children's attitudes, especially regarding diversity (Aboud & Fenwick, 1999; Jones & Foley, 2003). An example of classic techniques used to counter the culturally biased attitudes of second- and fifth-graders (as determined by a test) follow (Katz & Zalk, 1978).

1. *Increased positive intercultural contact.* Children worked in interethnic teams at an interesting puzzle and were all praised for their work.
2. *Vicarious intercultural contact.* Children heard an interesting story about a sympathetic and resourceful African American child.
3. *Perceptual differentiation.* Children were shown slides of a culturally diverse woman whose appearance varied depending on whether or not she was wearing glasses, which of two different hairdos she was wearing, and whether she was smiling or frowning. Each different-appearing face had a name, and the children were tested to see how well they remembered the names.

After two weeks, the children's levels of prejudice were measured again. All the groups that had been exposed to any of these techniques showed less prejudice than did children in the control groups. Four to six months after the experiment, a second posttest showed that the children who had learned to perceive differences in the culturally diverse faces, and those who had heard the stories about culturally diverse children had more positive attitudes than those in the other two groups. Younger children showed more gains than older children.

Apparently, prejudicial attitudes can be changed by enabling children to have positive experiences (both real and vicarious) with cultural minorities. When an adult mediates the experience by pointing out individual differences, it is especially effective. Thus, children learn to view people as individuals rather than as representatives of a certain group with certain fixed characteristics.

One of the purposes of the Individuals with Disabilities Education Act of 1990 (amended in 2004) was to include children with disabilities in public school. Teachers had to revise prior stereotypical attitudes; they might have had to emphasize *abilities* rather than *disabilities* (Heward, 2008)—for example, "Kevin is a third-grader who reads in a fourth-grade book and who needs assistance with physical tasks" rather than "Kevin is wheelchair-bound and requires an aide."

Participation of individuals with disabilities in athletic events has helped communicate positive attitudes regarding their abilities.

Cengage Learning

IN PRACTICE

How do you create an antibias classroom environment?

Some basics involve including:

- pictures in the room of diverse (by culture, gender, age, disability) individuals in their daily lives—interacting with others and doing work in the community
- stories about the contributions of diverse individuals in the curriculum
- fostering cooperative activities among the children so they can experience others' qualities, hence going beyond appearances

See http://www.ericdigests.org for more specifics on an antibias classroom.

TeachSource Video Activity

Go to the Education CourseMate website to watch the video entitled "Reducing Racial Prejudice." Have you experienced prejudice—racial, ethnic, gender, disability, or other—and how did you feel? Have you had an experience whereby you were prejudiced about someone or something and then changed your attitude? Explain.

How do you explain what drives you toward a goal?

Motives and Attributions

A *motive*, as introduced in Chapter 2, is a need or emotion that causes a person to act. To be *motivated* is to be *moved* to do something. An *attribution*, as introduced in Chapter 2, is an explanation for one's performance. "Do you *attribute* an Olympian's athletic ability to training, genetics, or both?"

According to Robert White (1959), people are motivated to act by the urge to be competent or to achieve. People of all ages strive to develop skills that will help them understand and control their environment, whether or not they receive external reinforcement. The inborn motive to explore, understand, and control one's environment is referred to as *mastery motivation*, as introduced in Chapter 2. This is illustrated when infants and toddlers open cabinets, empty out drawers, drop things in the toilet. Whereas mastery motivation is believed to be inborn, *achievement motivation* is thought to be learned. Children learn via socialization what is considered acceptable and unacceptable performance standards in their culture, as well as how to evaluate their behavior accordingly. Introduced in Chapter 2, *achievement motivation*, the motivation to be competent, expresses itself in behavior aimed at approaching challenging tasks with the confidence of accomplishment—for example, the child who tries out for the choir saying, "Oh, I know I'll make it."

Ryan and Deci (2000) distinguish between achievement motivation that is *intrinsic* (doing an activity for inherent satisfaction or enjoyment) and *extrinsic* (doing an activity to attain some separable outcome, to get a reward or avoid punishment). As people act to pursue different goals, why are some driven primarily intrinsically and others extrinsically? Explanations can be categorized as:

- within-person (intrinsic) changes resulting from cognitive or emotional maturation, such as becoming more curious as one is able to learn more and becoming more competent as one is able to master more, and
- socially mediated (extrinsic) changes resulting from contexts children experience as they grow, such as family, school, or peer group, and the accompanying feelings of autonomy or control (Wigfield et al., 2006).

According to Ryan and Deci (2000), home and classroom environments can "facilitate or forestall" intrinsic motivation by "supporting or thwarting" a child's psychological needs for competence and autonomy. Studies have shown that parents who respond to children's psychological needs bidirectionally (modifying their rules and incentives according to child's behavior), enhance intrinsic motivation (Pomerantz, Grolnick, & Price, 2007). Other studies (Ryan & Deci, 2000) have shown that tangible rewards (money, candy, toys), threats, deadlines, directives, and competition pressure related to task performance tend to diminish intrinsic motivation because they are experienced as controllers of behavior, whereas choice and the opportunity for self-direction appear to enhance intrinsic motivation because they enable a sense of autonomy. (See Figure 11.2.)

locus of control one's attribution of performance, or perception of responsibility for success or failure; may be internal or external

Attributions, or explanations for performance, are related to motives in that achievement motivation has been linked to **locus of control**—how one *attributes* his or her performance, or where one places responsibility for successes or failure. Locus of control is *internal* if one attributes responsibility inside the self; it is *external* if one attributes responsibility to forces outside the self. "Am I responsible for my grade, or is the teacher?" When individuals feel they have no control over events and, therefore, no responsibility, they are no longer motivated to achieve. *Learned helplessness*, as introduced in Chapter 7, is a phenomenon exhibited by people who no longer perform effectively in a number of situations; they have learned to be helpless as opposed to competent. The relationship of motives and attributions to actual performance is outlined in Figure 11.3.

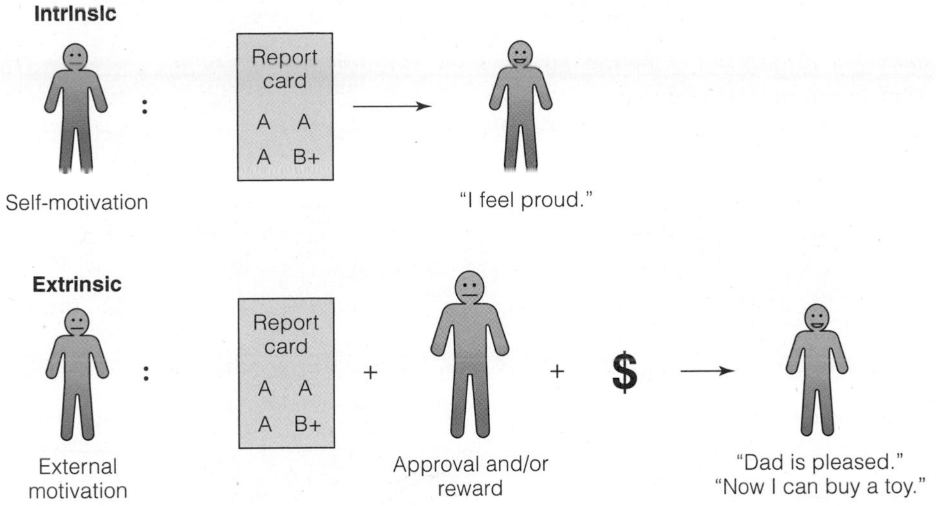

FIGURE 11.2 Intrinsic and Extrinsic Motivation

Achievement Motivation (Mastery Orientation)

How is achievement motivation assessed?

In a classic study to assess the differences in strengths of people's achievement motives, David McClelland and his colleagues (1953) developed a projection technique using selected picture cards from the Thematic Apperception Test (TAT). The technique assumes that when asked to write stories about the pictures, people will project their feelings about themselves onto the characters in the pictures shown to them.

achievement motivation refers to the motivation to achieve mastery of challenging tasks; hence it is sometimes called "mastery orientation" in research studies

The pictures show such scenes as two men ("inventors") in a shop working on a machine, a young boy and a violin, or a boy sitting at a desk with an open book in front of him. Participants are asked to answer the following questions about the pictures:

1. What is happening? Who are the persons?
2. What were the circumstances leading up to the situation in the pictures?
3. What are the characters thinking? What do they want?
4. What will happen? What will be done?

The assessment of the stories involves noting references to achievement goals (concern over reaching a standard of excellence). Subjects who refer often to achievement goals are rated high in achievement motivation; subjects who rarely or never refer to achievement goals are rated low.

Achievement motivation, or mastery orientation, is often correlated with actual achievement behavior (Bandura, 1997; Wigfield et al., 2006). The motivation to achieve, however, may manifest itself only in behavior that the child values. For example, a child's high motivation to achieve may be exhibited in athletics, but not in schoolwork. Thus, different situations have different achievement-attaining values for children (Harter & Connell, 1984; Wigfield et al., 2006).

What influence does parenting have on achievement motivation?

Parenting practices influence achievement motivation in that if standards set are unrealistic (too high or too low), then motivation tends to be low, whereas if standards set optimally challenge the child by providing tasks that can be done with effort (not too easy) so that the accomplishment is meaningful, then motivation tends to be high (Burhans & Dweck, 1995; Pomerantz, Grolnick, & Price, 2007). Such tasks are referred to as developmentally appropriate.

According to Wigfield and colleagues (Wigfield, et al., 2006), the child-rearing environment of children who show high achievement motivation includes developmentally appropriate timing of achievement demands (early, but not too early, and continuing encouragement), high confidence in the child's abilities, a supportive affective family

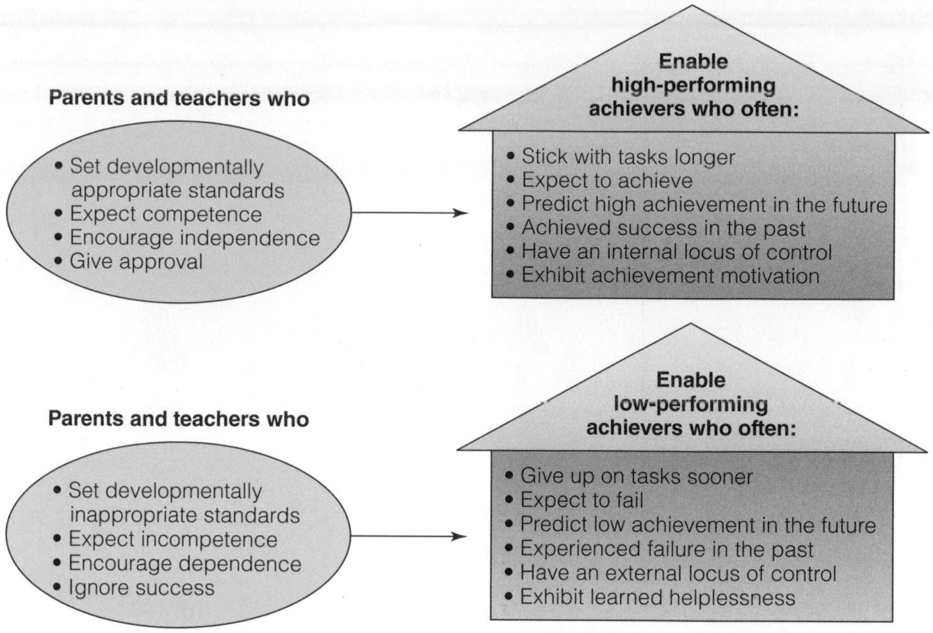

FIGURE 11.3 Relationship of Motives and Attributions to Actual Performance

environment (orientation toward exploration and investigation as well as positive feedback), and highly motivated role models.

What is the relationship between *child* performance/expectations and achievement motivation?

Children with high expectations for success on a task usually persist at it longer and perform better than children with low expectations. Studies have found that children with high IQs and high expectations of success in school did, in fact, get the highest grades, whereas children with high IQs and low expectations received lower grades than children with low IQs and high expectations (Eccles, 1983; Wigfield et al., 2006). In addition to child-rearing practices, discussed previously, teaching styles and communication affect children's attributions. When teachers are caring, supportive, and emphasize the learning process over performance outcomes, as well as give feedback, children tend to be motivated to achieve and expect success (Daniels, Kalkman, & McCombs, 2001).

One's expectation of success is related to:

- one's history of success or failure,
- one's perception of how difficult the task is, and
- the attributions for one's performance.

Generally, someone who has mostly been successful in the past expects to succeed in the present and future; someone who has mostly failed in the past expects to fail in the present and future. According to Skinner and Greene (2008), the perception of control over outcomes of one's actions

> is one of the most robust predictors of student resilience and academic success all across the elementary, middle, and high school years. Children and adolescents who are confident and optimistic are more likely to select challenging tasks, set high and concrete goals, initiate and maintain constructive engagement, deal productively with obstacles and setbacks, maintain access to their highest quality problem-solving, concentration, and focus even under stress, seek help as needed, rebound from failure, and eventually to develop more adaptive strategies of self-regulated learning. (p. 122)

This girl's achievement is influenced by her personal responsibility to perform and her confidence of success.

Cengage Learning

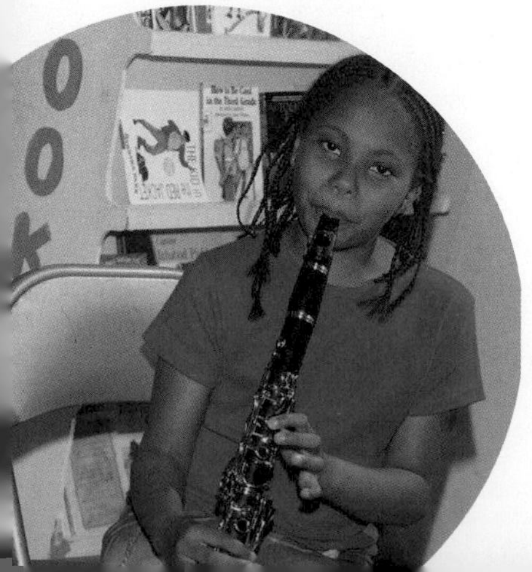

Locus of Control

Recall that *locus of control* relates to one's attribution of performance, or sense of personal responsibility for success or failure; it may be internal or external. Individuals who have strong beliefs that they are in control of their world, that they can cause things to happen if they choose, and that they can command their own rewards have an **internal locus of control**. These people attribute their success (or failure) to themselves. Individuals who perceive that others or outside forces have more control over them than they do over themselves have an **external locus of control**. These people attribute their success (or failure) to factors outside themselves.

Do you attribute responsibility for the consequences of your actions to your ability, to your effort, to others, to the task difficulty, to fate, or to luck?

internal locus of control perception that one is responsible for one's own fate

One factor influencing one's control beliefs is the perceived relationship between a person's actions and his or her success or failure (Skinner, 1995; Skinner & Greene, 2008). The more successful a person is at accomplishing tasks, the more likely it is that the person will feel "in control"; feeling "out of control" is more likely when failures outnumber successes. Achievement is related to whether the person believes he or she controls the outcome. Another factor related to control beliefs is age. As children get older, their understanding of causality and explanations for outcomes becomes more differentiated. Whereas 7- and 8-year-olds tend to consider all possible factors—luck, effort, ability, task difficulty—in explaining performance, 11- and 12-year-olds tend to put more emphasis on external factors, such as luck and task difficulty, than on internal factors, such as ability and effort, in attributing locus of control. (See Figure 11.4.) Moreover, 7- and 8-year-olds think that ability can change with effort, whereas 11- and 12-year-olds perceive ability as relatively stable (Skinner, 1995).

What factors influence an individual's belief that control lies inside or outside the self?

external locus of control perception that others or outside forces are responsible for one's fate

Julian Rotter (1966, 1971) developed a locus of control scale that is used to study the internal–external dimension of personal responsibility. The Internal–External Scale is constructed so that each item can be scored as *internal* or *external*. Some sample items are given in the In Practice box, "Measuring Locus of Control." Subjects are to indicate, in each pair of statements, the more appropriate of the two.

How is locus of control measured?

Locus of control is an aspect of personality that interests educators because children with an internal locus of control generally do better academically and are more competent and effective than those with an external locus of control (Patrick, Skinner, & Connell. 1993; Skinner & Greene, 2008). One explanation for the relationship between locus of control and academic achievement is that internals view outcomes as within their control. Therefore, if they succeed, they can figure out what they did correctly and do

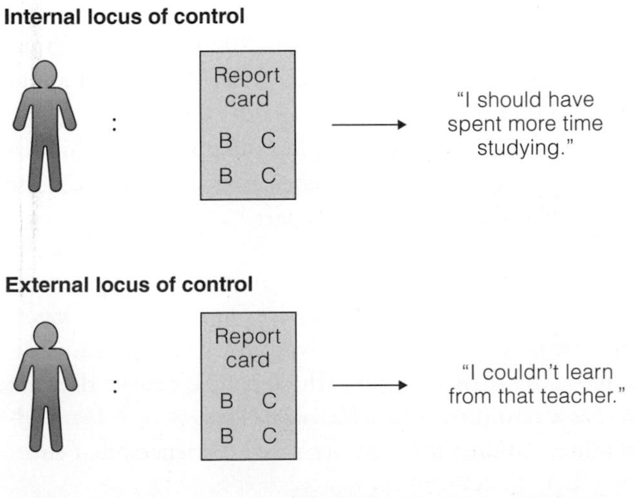

FIGURE 11.4 **Internal and External Locus of Control**

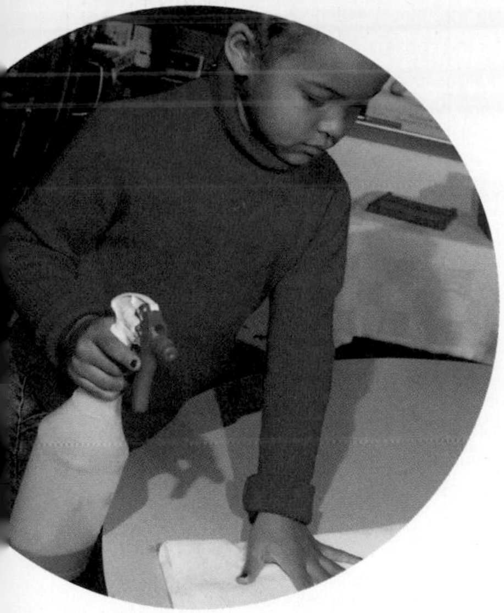

This child is given the opportunity to correct a mistake, thereby gaining a sense of autonomy.

Cengage Learning

IN PRACTICE

Measuring Locus of Control

I more strongly believe that:

1. a. Promotions are earned through hard work and persistence.
   b. Making a lot of money is largely a matter of getting the "right breaks."
2. a. There is usually a direct connection between how hard I study and the grades I get.
   b. Many times, the grades teachers give seem haphazard to me.
3. a. The number of divorces in our society indicates that more and more people are not trying to make their marriages work.
   b. Marriage is largely a gamble; it's no one's fault if it doesn't work.
4. a. When I am right, I can usually convince others that I am.
   b. It is silly to think that one can really change another person's basic attitudes.
5. a. In our society, earning power is dependent upon ability.
   b. Getting promoted is really a matter of being a little luckier than the next person.
6. a. If one knows how to deal with people, they are really quite easily led.
   b. I have little influence over the way other people behave.
7. a. People can change the course of world affairs if they make themselves heard.
   b. It is only wishful thinking to believe that one can really influence what happens in society at large.
8. a. I am the master of my fate.
   b. A great deal that happens to me is probably a matter of chance.
9. a. Getting along with people is a skill that must be practiced.
   b. It is impossible to figure out how to please some people.

Source: J. B. Rotter (1971). "Who Rules You? External Control and Internal Control." *Psychology Today,* 5, 37–42. Reprinted with permission from Psychology Today Magazine, copyright © 1971 Sussex Publishers, LLC.

it again. If they fail, they believe they can change the outcome in the future by exerting more effort to correct their mistakes (for example, study harder or differently). They develop a *mastery-oriented attribution*. Externals, on the other hand, view outcomes as outside their control. Therefore, if they succeed, they attribute it to good luck, and if they fail, they attribute it to bad luck or lack of ability. Since they don't attribute the outcomes of their performance to their own efforts or strategies, they give up quickly. They develop a *learned-helpless orientation* (Dweck & Leggett, 1988; Dweck, 2006).

Reviews of the literature on locus of control (Wigfield et al., 2006; Young & Shorr, 1986) confirmed that internal locus of control was significantly related to age (at about age 9, there is an increase in perceptions of internal control), gender (elementary school girls are more internal than boys), socioeconomic status (middle- and upper-class children are more internal than lower-class children), and achievement. In each case, the diverse socialization experiences of the group likely play a prominent part.

learned-helpless orientation is the perception, acquired through negative experiences, that effort has no affect on outcomes.

Why do some individuals "give up" easily?

Learned-Helpless Orientation

Martin Seligman presented evidence in his books *Helplessness* (1975) and *Learned Optimism* (1990) that people become passive and lose motivation when placed in situations where outcomes are unaffected by their behavior. These people believe they are pawns of external circumstances; as a result, they have *learned helplessness.* A **learned-helpless orientation** is the perception, acquired through negative experiences, that effort has no affect on outcomes.

When does helplessness first appear? Research on infants shows that infants exposed to mobiles that spin independently of their actions do not learn to control new mobiles presented to them that can be activated by turning their heads. In contrast, infants exposed to stationary mobiles and to mobiles that spin contingent upon their actions (head or arm moving) evidence no difficulty in learning to control the new mobiles. These differences in performance are still present after six weeks without any exposure to a mobile (Fincham & Cain, 1986). So certain experiences involving the ability to control outcomes can affect even infants (Fincham, 2008).

As children get older and the number of their experiences with objects and people increases, their perceptions of being able to control outcomes and their ability to understand cause and effect influence when, and if, they manifest a learned-helpless orientation as opposed to a mastery orientation (Fincham, 2008; Wigfield et al., 2006). Figure 11.3, earlier in this chapter, summarizes the factors involved in attributions for performance and their relation to actual performance.

By age 4, some children give up on even developmentally or age-appropriate tasks, such as building a tall tower out of blocks (Cain & Dweck, 1995). These children who are nonpersistent tend to believe they can't do the task and report feeling bad after failures. Children who are persistent, on the other hand, tend to believe they can succeed in challenging tasks if given more time and if they try harder. Children who are nonpersistent describe their parents as critical or punitive ("Daddy's going to get mad"). Children who are persistent describe their parents as supportive and encouraging ("Try it again, you'll do better next time").

In a series of classic studies on learned-helpless orientation, Dweck and colleagues found that when children believe their failures are due to uncontrollable factors in themselves, such as *lack of ability* ("I failed the math test because I'm dumb in math"), their subsequent task performance deteriorates after failure (Dweck, 1975; Dweck & Bush, 1976; Dweck & Gillard, 1975; Dweck & Reppucci, 1973; Elliot & Dweck, 1988).

In a different study of learned-helpless orientation in fourth- to sixth-grade children who had self-critical attributions, it was found that they had little knowledge about effective study techniques to help them succeed at academic tasks (Pomerantz & Saxon, 2001). In other words, they were unable to connect effort or persistence with success. In conclusion, if children are enabled to believe their failure was due to *lack of effort*, they tend to try harder on subsequent tasks and often show improved performance.

Do girls and boys get different messages in school about ability and effort?

In several classic studies, Dweck and colleagues (Dweck & Bush, 1976; Dweck & Gillard, 1975) found that girls are more likely than boys to demonstrate learned helplessness that comes from attributing *lack of ability* to themselves. Boys more often tend to believe that when they do not do well, it is because they have not worked hard enough. Since the boys and girls scored similarly on achievement tests, it can be inferred that ability was similar, but that the attributions for failure were different. Dweck and colleagues looked to the teachers to see if there was differential feedback to boys and girls relating to failure. They found that when boys submitted poor work, they were generally reprimanded for sloppiness, not paying attention, or *lack of effort*. Girls who submitted poor work were generally told, "You didn't do it right even though you tried."

In sum, if parents and teachers praise children for their effort when they succeed but question their ability when they fail, the children are less likely to persist at challenging tasks, thereby developing a learned-helpless orientation. If parents and teachers praise children's abilities when they succeed and emphasize *lack of effort* when they fail, the children are more likely to persist at challenging tasks, thereby developing a mastery orientation. Thus, if adults treat children as if their mistakes can be remedied by their own actions, the children are likely to reflect this opinion of themselves and behave accordingly.

What contributes to the feeling of being "in control"?

Self-Efficacy

self-efficacy the belief that one can master a situation and produce positive outcomes

As introduced in Chapter 2, **self-efficacy** is the belief that one can master a situation and produce positive outcomes. It is related to *empowerment* (enabling individuals to have control over resources affecting them), as well as to concepts discussed earlier in this chapter, such as achievement motivation, internal locus of control, history of and attributions of success/failure, and learned helplessness. Whereas helplessness is the belief that "I can't," self-efficacy is the belief that "I can" (Maddux & Volkmann, 2010).

Albert Bandura, known for his social cognitive theory (involving learning via observation and modeling), has elaborated on these concepts (achievement motivation, locus of control, and learned helplessness) to formulate a performance-based valid predictor of students' learning—namely, their perceived capability on specific tasks (Bandura, 1997, 2000). Self-efficacy differs from the aforementioned concepts in that it can not only explain present performance but also predict future performance.

personal agency the realization that one's actions cause outcomes

Self-efficacy beliefs provide students with a sense of **personal agency**—the realization that one's actions cause outcomes. Self-efficacy beliefs motivate learning because they enable students to use such self-regulatory processes as goal setting, self-monitoring, self-evaluation, and strategy use (Maddux & Volkmann, 2010; Zimmerman, 2000). Efficacious students embrace challenging goals. They are better at monitoring their working time, more persistent, less likely to reject correct hypotheses prematurely, and better at solving conceptual problems than inefficacious students of equal ability.

What are some influences on self-efficacy beliefs?

The most significant influence on self-efficacy beliefs is actual experience—successfully performing tasks, solving problems, making things happen. Next is vicarious experience—observing others execute competent behavior. Also influential are verbal instruction, encouragement, and feedback on performance. Finally, physiological reactions, such as fatigue, stress, or anxiety, may distort an individual's perception of his or her capability at a particular time or while engaged in a certain activity; some examples are "writer's block," an athletic "slump," and math anxiety (Maddux & Volkmann, 2010).

What can be done to support self-efficacious behavior?

Self-efficacy measures can be used diagnostically to improve academic motivation (Zimmerman, 2000). Following are some teaching strategies to improve children's self-efficacy (Schunk, 2000; Stipek, 1996).

1. Provide instruction in specific learning strategies, such as highlighting, summarizing, and outlining, to enable students to focus on a task.
2. Help students make short-term, as well as long-term, goals, guiding them to evaluate their progress by regularly providing feedback.
3. Make reinforcement contingent on performance of specific tasks; reward students for mastery of a task rather than mere engagement in one.
4. Give encouragement: "I know you can do this."
5. Provide positive adult and peer role models who demonstrate efficacious behavior—coping with challenging tasks, setting goals, using strategies, monitoring their effectiveness, and evaluating performance.

How do you feel about yourself?

Self-Esteem

self-esteem the value one places on his/her identity

Self-esteem is the value one places on one's identity. It is related to self-efficacy in that one's identity, or self-concept, incorporates many forms of self-knowledge and self-evaluative feelings (Zimmerman, 2000). It must be kept in mind that most of the research on self-esteem is in the context of Euro-American society, which is individualistic. Recently, however, cross-cultural research has provided an understanding of how self-esteem is conceptualized in collectivistic cultures, namely that it is viewed in terms of worthiness to the group, rather than in achievement competencies (Mruk, 2006).

Self-esteem can be described as high or low. Some view self-esteem as a global perception of the self, whereas others view it as multidimensional, consisting of (1) scholastic competence, (2) athletic competence, (3) social competence, (4) physical appearance, and (5) behavioral conduct, in addition to global self-worth (Harter, 1999, 2006). Occasionally, the terms *positive self-concept* or *negative self-concept* are used to describe self-esteem.

To exemplify these opposites, consider the following descriptions of two young girls, Alice and Zelda. Alice displays the characteristics of *competent* children (discussed in Chapter 4 in connection with parenting styles) (Baumrind, 1967; White, 1995). She uses adults as resources after first determining that a job is too difficult. She is capable of expressing affection and mild annoyance to peers as well as adults. She can lead and follow peers. She can compete with peers and shows pride in personal accomplishments. She is able to communicate well. She has the ability to anticipate consequences, can deal with abstractions, and can understand other points of view. She can plan and carry out complicated activities. Finally, she is aware of others, even while working on her own projects. Zelda, on the other hand, displays the characteristics of *incompetent* children; she is deficient in the aforementioned competencies.

This child has a sense of self-efficacy, feeling that any situation can be mastered.

lofoto/iStockphoto.com

IN CONTEXT

Alice is in kindergarten this year. You notice her immediately because she is so enthusiastic. She is almost always the first to raise her hand when the teacher asks a question. Sometimes she just calls out excitedly, "I know, I know." She doesn't always know, however. Sometimes she makes mistakes and answers incorrectly. When that happens, she shrugs her shoulders and giggles along with her classmates. She approaches her assignments with equal enthusiasm. When one approach fails, she tries another. If her persistence doesn't work, she asks the teacher for help. The other children like her. She is often the leader of the group, but also doesn't seem to mind following. At home she is responsible for dressing herself and keeping her room tidy. She is proud she can tie her shoelaces and make her bed.

Zelda is in first grade this year. Her progress last year in kindergarten was below average. This year it's no better. Zelda's IQ is similar to Alice's, yet Zelda answers most questions with "I don't know." She never raises her hand or volunteers information. She approaches her assignments unenthusiastically and gives up at the first sign of difficulty. She never asks for help, and when the teacher approaches her, she says, "I can't do it." Zelda has few friends and rarely participates in group activities. At home, Zelda is more talkative. She has no responsibilities, and her mother still helps her to dress. She waits for others to do things for her because she "can't" do them for herself (Chance, 1982, p. 54).

Alice and Zelda, even though alike in natural intelligence, are as far apart as A and Z in competence. Alice likes herself and feels comfortable in her environment. She takes control of her actions and takes responsibility for them. In other words, she decides what she is going to do, does it, and takes pride in doing it. If she makes a mistake, she owns up to it and tries again. Zelda, on the other hand, is full of self-doubt. She thinks her environment is harsh and unfriendly. She feels helpless in controlling what happens to her, so she does not even try. Alice has high self-esteem. She has a sense of trust, autonomy, and initiative. Zelda has low self-esteem. She has a sense of mistrust, self-doubt, and inferiority. The two represent opposite poles in Erikson's (1963) psychosocial stages of development, discussed in Chapter 2. Why have these two young children developed such differing levels of self-esteem?

IN CONTEXT When Alice was an infant, her mother most likely responded warmly and affectionately to her needs. When she fed Alice, her attention would be focused totally on her. After feeding, Alice's mother cuddled her and talked to her before putting her to bed. Zelda's mother probably was a bit cold and indifferent. She would use Zelda's feeding as a chance to catch up on her reading (she fed Zelda from a bottle). After feeding, Zelda's mother would bathe her and make sure her crib was immaculate before putting her to bed.

By age 2, Alice was securely attached to her mother. She could be left with a babysitter without too much fuss, yet she was very happy when her mother returned. Zelda, at age 2, was insecurely attached. She would cling to her mother, screaming, when the babysitter came, yet when her mother returned, Zelda would ignore her.

When Alice entered school, she made friends easily. Her eager smile seemed to welcome other children. Even when she put her sweater on inside out and a few children laughed, she just laughed with them. When Zelda entered school, she approached no one. The only friends she made were the two children who sat on either side of her at her table. When Zelda had trouble using her scissors, she just gave up (Chance, 1982, p. 54).

How do children's evaluations of themselves change through time?

Development of Self-Esteem

As children grow, they accumulate a personal, complex set of evaluations about themselves. They know how they look; they know what they are good at doing and what they are poor at doing. They also know what they would like to look like ("I hope I grow taller than my dad") and what they would like to be doing ("I'm going to be a dancer when I grow up"). As children grow, they begin to understand how they are viewed by others. During the process of socialization, people internalize the values and attitudes expressed by their significant others and, as a result, express them as their own. This holds true for values and attitudes about oneself as well as about other people, objects, and experiences. Thus, individuals come to respond to themselves in a way consistent with the way others have responded to them, thereby developing a concept of self. Alice's and Zelda's differing levels of self-esteem have emerged as a result of cumulative experiences in their young lives with other people, places, and things.

In a classic investigation of the level of self-esteem of hundreds of fifth- and sixth-grade Euro-American, middle-class boys (see Table 11.1), Coopersmith (1967) concluded that the following factors contribute to the development of self-esteem:

1. Significance—the way one perceives he or she is loved and cared about by significant others. Alice feels significant; Zelda does not.
2. Competence—the way one performs tasks one considers important. Alice usually succeeds at tasks and is popular; Zelda rarely succeeds and has few friends.
3. Virtue—how well one attains moral and ethical standards. Alice tells the truth; Zelda often lies to cover up her mistakes.
4. Power—the extent to which one has control or influence over one's life and that of others. Alice is able to minimize or discount the teasing of others; Zelda is sensitive to others' judgments. She takes them as confirmation of her self-image of helplessness.

More recent research concurs with Coopersmith's conclusions (Harter, 1999, 2006).

Whereas Coopersmith measured overall self-esteem, Susan Harter (1990, 1999, 2006) measured the five specific areas of competence listed earlier, as well as general feelings of self-worth ("I am happy with myself") in the Self-Perception Profile for Children. Harter found that self-esteem is well established by middle childhood. Children can make global judgments of their worth as well as distinguish their competencies. For example, a child may perceive himself or herself as a poor athlete but good scholastically. Finally, children's perceptions of themselves accurately reflect how others perceive them. Thus, Cooley's "looking-glass self" and Mead's "generalized other," described in Chapter 2, have found their way into contemporary conceptions of the self.

This child's smile reflects his sense of self.

Cengage Learning

Table 11.1 Level of Self-Esteem Inventory

	Like me	Unlike me
I'm pretty sure of myself.	—	—
I often wish I were someone else.	—	—
I never worry about anything.	—	—
There are lots of things about myself I'd change if I could.	—	—
I can make up my mind without too much trouble.	—	—
I'm doing the best work that I can.		
I give in very easily.		
My parents expect too much of me.		
Kids usually follow my ideas.		

Influences on the Development of Self-Esteem

How do significant socializing agents influence the development of self-esteem?

Family

Many research studies confirm that parental approval is particularly critical in determining the self-esteem of children (Harter, 2006).

Coopersmith (1967) investigated children's treatment by significant others—those whose attitudes matter most when children are forming their self-concepts. He did this by examining the parenting practices employed by his subjects' fathers and mothers. He focused on acceptance of the child and affection exhibited, the kind and amount of punishment used, the level of achievement demands placed on the child, the strictness and consistency with which rules were enforced, the extent to which the child was allowed to participate in family decision making, the extent to which the child was listened to and consulted when rules were being set and enforced, and the extent to which the child was allowed independence.

Coopersmith found some clear relationships between the parenting practices and self-esteem of sons. Parents of boys with high self-esteem were more often characterized as follows.

- *Warm* (accepting and affectionate). They frequently showed affection to their children, took an interest in their affairs, and became acquainted with their friends.
- *Strict*, but used noncoercive discipline. They enforced rules carefully and consistently. They believed it was important for children to meet high standards. They were firm and decisive in telling the child what he might or might not do. They disciplined their children by withdrawing privileges and by isolation. They tended to discuss the reasons behind the discipline with the children.
- *Democratic*. They allowed the children to participate in making family plans. The children were permitted to express their own opinions, even if it involved questioning the parents' point of view.

As discussed in Chapter 4, Baumrind (1967) found a similar relationship between an authoritative parenting style (high acceptance and high demandingness) and competent Euro-American children. Similar connections were found in studies of competent Euro-American adolescents (Steinberg, 2010). However, these findings don't always apply cross-culturally. For example, research on over 1,200 adolescents in Brazil, a collectivistic culture that is democratic, showed that those who scored the highest on self-esteem measures had parents who were indulgent, or permissive, exhibiting high responsiveness and low demandingness (Martinez, Garcia, & Yubero, 2007). For another example, Chao (1994, 2001) found that Chinese children, whose cultural heritage is hierarchal and collectivistic, benefited the most from an authoritarian parenting style (low responsiveness and high demandingness). An explanation for such cross-cultural differences is that parenting

IN PRACTICE

How Can Parents and Teachers Enhance Children's Self-Esteem?

1. *Enable children to feel accepted.* Understand and attend to their needs; be warm; accept their individuality; talk to them and listen to them.
2. *Enable children to be autonomous.* Provide opportunities for them to do things themselves; give them choices; encourage curiosity; encourage pride in achievement; provide challenges.
3. *Enable children to be successful.* Be an appropriate model; set clear limits; praise accomplishments and efforts; explain consequences and how to learn from mistakes.
4. *Enable children to interact with others positively.* Provide opportunities to cooperate with others; enable them to work out differences dealing with feelings and others' perspectives.
5. *Enable children to be responsible.* Encourage participation; provide opportunities for them to care for belongings, help with chores, and help others.

practices have different meanings and different outcomes in different cultures. In other words, parents who reflect the culture in their child-rearing practices are likely to have children with high self-esteem because the children have been socialized to "fit in."

School

Keep in mind that the valued personality type in American culture is a responsible, self-reliant, autonomous, competent individual; the child who is reared to conform to these traits is likely to have high self-esteem. It has been found that students with higher self-esteem are more likely to be successful in school and achieve more than children with low self-esteem (Cole, 1991; Harter, 1999, 2006). This relationship shows up as early as the primary grades and becomes even stronger as the student gets older.

Children who are raised in diverse cultural groups and experience different socialization from that of Euro-American children do not necessarily follow this pattern. For example, in a study of adolescents representing major cultural groups in the United States, Bankston and Zhou (2002) found that children of Asian immigrants do have the lowest self-reported level of self-esteem, yet have the highest grade-point averages. On the other hand, nonimmigrant African American children report the highest level of self-esteem, yet show low grade-point averages. Despite this apparent inconsistency, there is a positive relationship between school performance and self-esteem. The researchers explain that the parental immigrant status may influence self-reported low self-esteem (collectivistic versus individualistic orientations), but the adolescent's actual high achievement contributes to high self-esteem (in collectivistic cultures, it is viewed as making the family proud; in individualistic cultures, it is viewed as being competitive).

Peers

Children can be quite cruel to one another, as was discussed in Chapter 8. They tease and ostracize children who are different physically, intellectually, linguistically, or socially. Peer attitudes about "ideal" size, physique, and physical capabilities can influence children's self-esteem. Harter (1999, 2006) found that perceived physical appearance is consistently the domain most highly correlated with self-esteem from early childhood through adulthood, with no gender differences.

It is generally agreed that there are three basic human body types: *endomorphy* (short, heavy build), *mesomorphy* (medium, muscular build), and *ectomorphy* (tall, lean build).

Of course, in reality, most people are variations of these basic body types. Body type plays a role in self-esteem in cultures that emphasize a certain ideal type. In the United States, the ideal type for females is slim, well proportioned, and well toned; for males, it is the muscular type. Thus, short, fat adolescent girls (Clay, Vignoles, & Dittmar, 2005) and boys as well as tall, skinny adolescent boys (Cohane & Pope, 2001) are unhappy with their bodies. In general, children whose appearance differs from that of their peers tend to have lower self-esteem than those who are like their peers and who conform to their peers' ideal.

Not only does one's appearance compared to the perceived ideal of one's peers affect self-esteem, so does one's perceived status in relation to the rest of the group. Studies have found children's and adolescents' self-esteem to be dependent on their perceived popularity among their friends (DeBruyn & Van Den Boom, 2005; Harter, 1999, 2006). In addition, studies report that the self-esteem of adolescents is related to the status of the peer group to which they belong at school. Generally, those who belong to the "in" clique exhibit higher self-esteem than outsiders (Newman & Newman, 2011).

Mass Media

Where do children get their attitudes about ideal body and personality types? Advertising strategies on television and in magazines portray ideal physical stereotypes—handsome, mesomorphic, well-dressed men; beautiful, trim, well-dressed women. Advertising techniques often lead the viewer or reader to believe that the product advertised will produce or perpetuate ideal characteristics. For men, the TV emphasis is on strength, performance, and skill; for women, it is on attractiveness and desirability (Crawford & Unger, 2000; Pipher, 1994; Wolf, 1991). According to psychiatrists Derenne and Beresin (2006, p. 257), who traced the portrayal of body images in the media throughout history, the ideal of beauty has been difficult to achieve and has been shaped by social context. "Current mass media is ubiquitous and powerful, leading to increased body dissatisfaction among both men and women." According to Naomi Wolf, author of *The Beauty Myth* (1991), children's heroes and heroines in the media serve as models for the ideal type, and the self-serving interests of advertisers make the ideal unattainable, thereby promoting low self-esteem in order to motivate purchase of their products.

Community

The community, especially the business community, may contribute to the differences found in the self-esteem of males and females. Even though there are wider occupational choices for women today, they still earn less than men and there still is sexism present in the workplace (Bennett, Ellison, & Ball, 2010). This means that women don't advance as quickly as men and that attitudes about women's capabilities are still generally stereotyped. Thus, for women entering the business community, there is often a drop in self-esteem (Basow, 2010).

The relation between an individual's social identity (culture, religion, social class) and that of the majority of the people in the neighborhood affects one's self-esteem (Harter, 1999, 2006; Martinez & Dukes, 1991; Rosenberg, 1975). For example, Rosenberg (1975) found that the Jewish children raised in Jewish neighborhoods were likely to have higher self-esteem than Jewish children raised in Catholic neighborhoods. He and others (Martinez & Dukes, 1991) also found that African American students in integrated schools were likely to have lower self-esteem than those in all–African American schools. Children of lower socioeconomic status attending a school where the majority of children were of higher socioeconomic status also had lower self-esteem than those attending a school where the majority of children were from lower-socioeconomic status environments. The same was true of children of upper socioeconomic status who were in the minority. Apparently, being socially different affects one's self-esteem, as has already been discussed in regard to appearance.

Summary

- Values are qualities or beliefs that are viewed as desirable or important. They are outcomes of socialization, and provide the framework in which we think, feel, and act.
- Certain values are basic to all civilized societies; others are basic to a particular society; still others are personal.
- An attitude is a tendency to respond positively or negatively to certain persons, objects, or situations. Attitudes are composed of beliefs, feelings, and action tendencies.
- The development of attitudes is influenced by age, cognitive development, and social experiences. Parents and peers have a large impact on children's attitudes through instruction, modeling, reinforcement, and punishment.
- The media, the community, and the school have the potential to change prejudicial and stereotypical attitudes toward diversity.
- A motive causes a person to act. An attribution is an explanation of one's performance when one does act.
- Individuals are motivated to control the outcomes of their efforts. This motivation is exhibited in the need to achieve, or be competent. When one's efforts no longer produce desired outcomes, the motivation exhibited is learned helplessness.
- The development of achievement motivation, or mastery orientation, has been linked most often to parenting styles. Parenting styles in diverse cultures have varying affects on mastery orientation.
- Mastery orientation is also related to one's expectation of success and one's fear of failure, as well as one's history of success and failure.
- Locus of control relates to one's sense of personal responsibility. Individuals who believe they are in control of their world have an internal locus of control. Individuals who perceive that others or outside events have more control over them than they have over themselves have an external locus of control.
- Locus of control is related to age, gender, socioeconomic status, and performance attributes and outcomes.
- Self-efficacy refers to the belief that one can master a situation and produce positive outcomes. It is a performance-based measure of perceived capability. It is related to achievement motivation, locus of control, and learned helplessness.
- Self-esteem, the value one places on one's self-concept, is derived from the reflected appraisal of others. Specific dimensions of self-esteem in Euro-American society include scholastic competence, athletic competence, social competence, physical appearance, and behavioral conduct, as well as global self-worth. Diverse cultures differ in the emphasis put on these dimensions.
- The factors contributing to self-esteem are the amount of respectful, accepting, and concerned treatment an individual receives from significant others; an individual's history of successes and failures; his or her status among peers; and his or her manner of responding to devaluation or failure.
- Parenting practices contribute to the development of self-esteem. Children with high self-esteem are more likely to be successful in school and are likely to achieve more than children with low self-esteem.
- Peers influence self-esteem by their reinforcement of "ideal" types. Children who differ from the ideal tend to have lower self-esteem. Peers get their attitudes about ideal types from the media.
- The community influences self-esteem by providing equal opportunities for all groups of people to achieve and feel worthy.

Activity

PURPOSE To gain insight into personal values.

1. The 18 values listed in the form "What Values Are Important to You?" are in alphabetical order. Select the value that is most important to you and write a 1 next to it in column I. Then choose your next most important value and write a 2 beside it in the same column. Continue until you have ranked all 18 values in column I.
2. Now rank the 18 values as you believe your parents, your spouse, or a very close friend would have ranked them. Put these numbers in column II.
3. Finally, rank the 18 values as you believe a person with whom you have not been able to get along would have ranked them. Put these numbers in column III.
4. Compare the rankings of the values in the three columns. How do your values compare to those of the person you are close to? How do they compare to those of the person who is your adversary? Compare your rankings with others. What is your relationship with them? Is there any correlation between similarity in values and closeness of relationship?
5. What values are important to you? Because values and morals involve making choices, complete the forced choice exercise that follows.

What Values Are Important to You?

	I	II	III
A COMFORTABLE LIFE a prosperous life			
EQUALITY brotherhood, equal opportunity for all			
AN EXCITING LIFE a stimulating, active life			
FAMILY SECURITY taking care of loved ones			
FREEDOM independence, free choice			
HAPPINESS Contentedness			
INNER HARMONY freedom from inner conflict			
MATURE LOVE sexual and spiritual intimacy			
NATIONAL SECURITY protection from attack			
PLEASURE an enjoyable, leisurely life			
SALVATION saved, eternal life			
SELF-RESPECT self-esteem			
A SENSE OF ACCOMPLISHMENT lasting contribution			
SOCIAL RECOGNITION respect, admiration			
TRUE FRIENDSHIP close companionship			
WISDOM a mature understanding of life			
A WORLD AT PEACE free of war and conflict			
A WORLD OF BEAUTY beauty of nature and the arts			

Source: Copyright 1967, 1982 by Milton Rokeach. Permission to reprint Halgren Tests, 873 Persimmon Avenue, Sunnyvale, California 94087.

Forced Choice Exercise

Instructions: Write your top 10 values from the list in any order. If you had to choose between #1 and #2, which would you choose? Circle your choice. Make the same decision for #1 and #3; #1 and #4; and so on. If you had to choose between #2 and #3, which would you choose? Make the same decision for #2 and #4, and so on. Continue making forced choices until you've completed the list. Now rank your values in order.

		1 1 1 1 1 1 1 1 1
1.	___	2 3 4 5 6 7 8 9 10
		2 2 2 2 2 2 2 2
2.	___	3 4 5 6 7 8 9 10
		3 3 3 3 3 3 3
3.	___	4 5 6 7 8 9 10
		4 4 4 4 4 4
4.	___	5 6 7 8 9 10
		5 5 5 5 5
5.	___	6 7 8 9 10
		6 6 6 6
6.	___	7 8 9 10
		7 7 7
7.	___	8 9 10
		8 8
8.	___	9 10
		9
9.	___	10
10.	___	

Related Readings

Bandura, A. (2000). *Self-efficacy: The exercise of control.* New York: Freeman.

Brown, R. (2010). *Prejudice: Its social psychology* (2nd ed.). Malden, MA: Wiley-Blackwell.

Dweck, C. S. (2006). *Mindset: The new psychology of success.* New York: Random House.

Harter, S. (1999). *The construction of the self: A developmental perspective.* New York: Guilford.

Lawrence-Lightfoot, S. (1999). *Respect: An exploration.* Boulder, CO: Perseus.

McInerney, P. K., & Rainbolt, G. W. (1994). *Ethics.* New York: HarperCollins.

Mruk, C. J. (2006). *Self-esteem research, theory, and practice: Toward a positive psychology of self-esteem* (3rd ed.). New York: Springer Publishing.

Seligman, M. E. P. (1975). *Helplessness.* San Francisco: Freeman.

Seligman, M. E. P. (1990). *Learned optimism.* New York: Pocket Books.

Van Ausdale, D., & Feagin, J. R. (2001). *The first R: How children learn race and racism.* Lanham, MD: Rowman & Littlefield.

Resources

American Civil Liberties Union—protects individual rights under the Constitution and Bill of Rights

http://www.aclu.org

National Science Foundation—increasing knowledge of people and society

http://www.nsf.gov

The Prejudice Institute—policy research and education on all dimensions of prejudice, discrimination, and ethnoviolence

http://www.prejudiceinstitute.org

12

J. McPhail/Shutterstock.com

Social and Behavioral Socialization Outcomes

"Conscience is the guardian in the individual of the rules which the community has evolved for its own preservation."

—WILLIAM SOMERSET MAUGHAM

The National Archives

Learning Objectives

After completing this chapter, you will be able to:

1. Define antisocial behavior and describe how it is studied.
2. Discuss the theories explaining the causes of aggressive behavior.
3. Define prosocial behavior and describe how it is studied.
4. Discuss the theories explaining the development of altruistic behavior.
5. Discuss established methods of reducing antisocial behavior and increasing prosocial behavior.
6. Describe how one's moral code develops and the influences on moral development.
7. Define gender role and discuss sex stereotyping.
8. Discuss the theories explaining gender-role acquisition.
9. Discuss socializing influences on gender-role development.

SOCIALIZATION SKETCHES

Sally Ride

(b. 1951)

"I have been a bit of a risk taker all my life."

— SALLY RIDE

Sally Ride was the first American woman in space. This quote represents Sally Ride's desire to be a trailblazer in science. This socialization sketch illustrates concepts in the chapter related to cultural expectations of gender roles. Sally has not only been a role model for young girls; she has been a creator of school programs to keep girls engaged in science. She is president and CEO of Sally Ride Science, a company she founded to create entertaining science programs and publications for students in middle school and the upper grades of elementary school. An important element of the company's mission is to support girls whose interests lie in science, math, and technology. It sponsors Sally Ride Clubs for girls at schools across the country and Sally Ride Science Camps at a number of college campuses.

Family

Sally Ride was born in a suburb of Los Angeles, California. She describes her childhood as "probably the typical childhood for a kid growing up in Southern California in the '50s and early '60s." She loved being outside and being active. She loved sports, especially playing tennis. She also liked science and math, she says. "I was probably fortunate in that both of my parents really valued education and they didn't have any sort of preconception on what sort of field I should go into."

As a child, Sally liked to read. She read the Danny Dunn series of science books, the Nancy Drew mystery series, and *Scientific American* magazine (a subscription given to her by her parents). She also watched some of the early space launches on TV, wondering what it would be like to be on a rocket.

School

As a young girl, Sally was a nationally ranked junior tennis player, which enabled her to get a scholarship to Westlake School for Girls. In high school, she said there were two influential teachers; one taught physiology and the other taught chemistry. In addition to being good teachers, they encouraged her to go on in math and science, while boosting her confidence.

After graduation from high school, Sally enrolled at Swarthmore University in Pennsylvania but soon began wondering if she was missing the opportunity for a professional tennis career. Determined to find out, she left Swarthmore after her first year to see how far her tennis game would take her. After three months of intense training, she concluded that she would not have a professional athletic career.

Sally enrolled at Stanford University in Palo Alto, California. She graduated with bachelor's degrees in both English and physics, and remained at Stanford to earn a master's and a Ph.D. in physics. As a graduate student, she carried out research in astrophysics and free-electron laser physics.

Community

At age 27, just short of getting her Ph.D., she began looking for postdoctoral work in astrophysics. She saw an ad in the Stanford University newspaper that caught her eye. NASA was looking for astronauts. She applied and was one of only six women to be accepted, out of 8,000 applicants. She joined NASA in 1977 to undergo years of rigorous physical and scientific training. In 1983 she became the first American woman in space, flying a six-day mission on the space shuttle *Challenger*.

Her second mission lasted eight days, contributing to her career total of 343 hours in space. She was scheduled for a third mission, but in 1986 the *Challenger* exploded, killing some of her colleagues and putting the U.S. space program in jeopardy. She served on the presidential commission investigating the accident, and participated in long-term planning at the space agency's headquarters in Washington until her retirement from NASA.

Since 1989, she has been professor of physics at the University of California, San Diego, where her research interests center on the theory of nonlinear beam-wave interactions. She has also served as a science fellow of the Center for International Security and Arms Control at Stanford University and as director of the California Space Institute. A passionate advocate for science education, she has created science programs to encourage young girls interested in mathematics, science, and technology. She was inducted into the Astronaut Hall of Fame in 2003, exactly 20 years after her historic first flight.

- Have you ever taken a risk during your life? Describe.
- Have you experienced gender stereotyping growing up?

How do children learn to regulate their behavior appropriately?

self-regulation (or self-control) refers to the ability to regulate or control one's impulses, behavior, and/or emotions until an appropriate time, place, or object is available for expression

Self-Regulation/Behavior

Self-regulation (or *self-control*), as introduced in Chapter 2, refers to the ability to regulate or control one's impulses, behavior, and/or emotions until an appropriate time, place, or object is available for expression. Recall that self-regulation is one of the aims of socialization. Self-regulatory behavior involves the ability to delay gratification, the ability to sustain attention to a task, and the ability to plan and self monitor a goal-directed activity, whether social or moral conduct or academic or athletic achievement (similar to self-efficacy).

Self-regulatory skills are significantly related to inhibiting antisocial or aggressive behaviors and exhibiting prosocial or altruistic ones (Lengua, 2002). Self-regulatory difficulties may be symptomatic of conduct disorders, attention deficit hyperactivity disorder (ADHD), or depression (Winsler & Wallace, 2002). Figure 12.1 is an ecological model showing the relationships between microsystems and mesosystems, influenced by exosystems and macrosystems, as they affect social and behavioral outcomes of socialization.

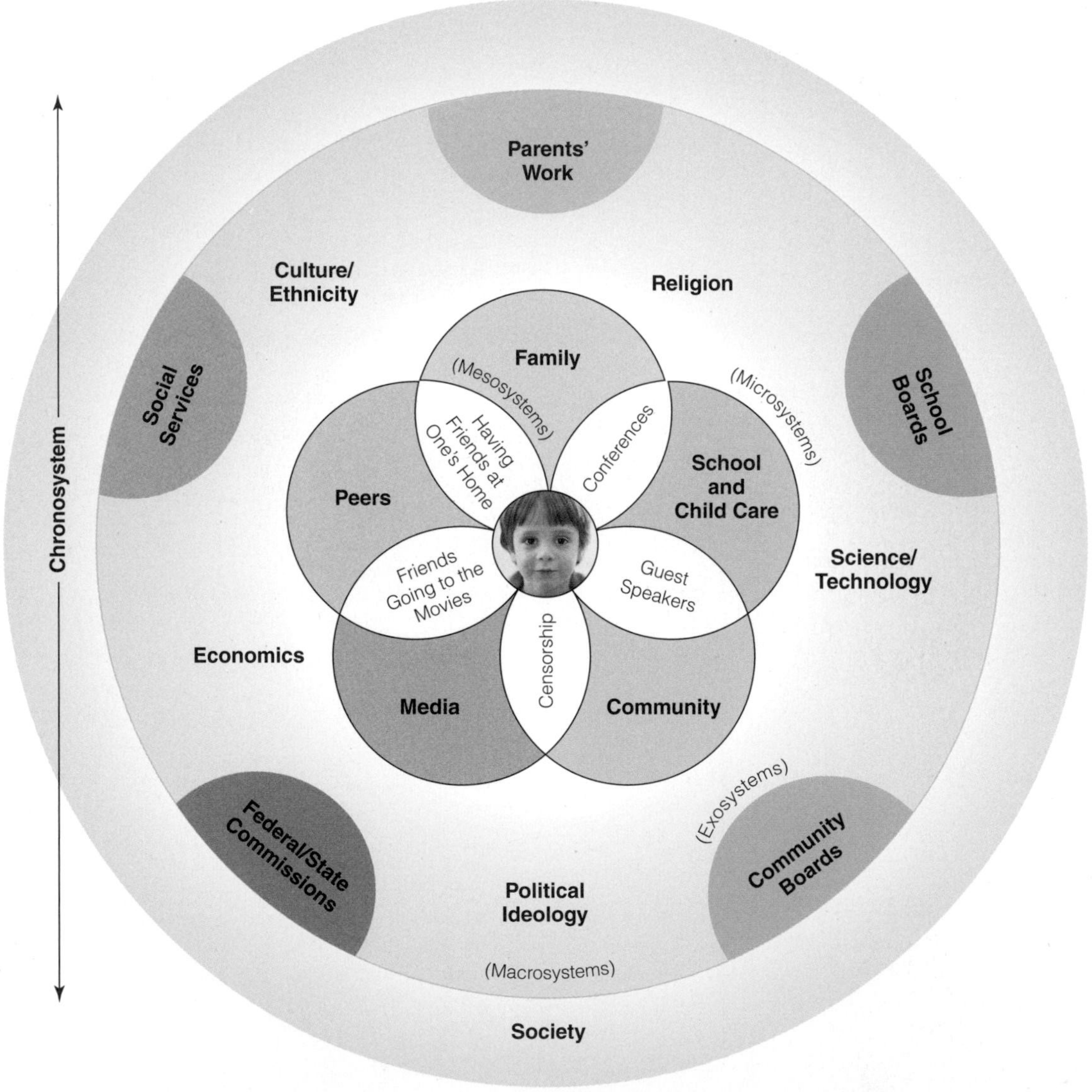

FIGURE 12.1 A Bioecological Model of Human Development
The child's antisocial or prosocial behavior, gender role, and self-esteem are outcomes of his or her socialization.

Nikolay Stefanov Dimitrov/Shutterstock.com

Self-regulation, or self-control, can be observed in children beginning about age 2 and increasing with age (Hofer & Eisenberg, 2008; Logue, 1995). To behave appropriately, children have to have the cognitive maturity to understand that they are separate, autonomous beings with the ability to control their own actions. They also have to have the language development to understand directives, the memory capabilities to store and retrieve a caregiver's instructions, and the information-processing strategies to apply them to a particular situation. In addition, children need to have some concept of the future, which expands as they get older ("If I don't tease my brother, Mommy said she would take me skating"). The development of self-regulatory ability depends partly on biological factors, such as the child's temperament, and partly on contextual factors, such as parenting practices (Hofer & Eisenberg, 2008).

Temperament (easy, slow-to-warm-up, difficult), discussed in Chapter 4, consists of genetically based characteristics that determine an individual's sensitivity to various experiences and responsiveness to patterns of social interaction. *Easy* children are more likely to comply with adult standards because, physiologically, they are more "relaxed." *Slow-to-warm-up* children may need time, reasoning, repetition, and patience to comply. *Difficult* children need even more of the same because they are more "tense" and, therefore, resistant to change.

Parenting practices influence the development of self-regulation in that the motive for children to internalize adult standards, as discussed in Chapter 2, is attachment. Children are willing to comply with parental demands because they want to please the individuals who love them; they try not to displease because they fear loss of that love. According to Damon (1988), this is the foundation of respect for authority and social order in society. Parenting practices in which there is extensive verbal give and take, reasoning, and nonpunitive adult control foster the development of self-control in Euro-American children.

Self-regulation, or control, is a continuous process, an outcome of affective, cognitive, and social forces. In the beginning, the child responds emotionally and instinctively to situations. These biological reactions are responded to by adults and redefined through social experience. Through continuous instruction, observation, participation, feedback, and interpretation, various levels of self-control are established (Damon, 1988). Children who are maltreated by parents and exposed to domestic violence are less likely to develop self-control and emotional regulatory abilities (Maughan & Cicchetti, 2002).

A component of self-regulation is emotional regulation, including the ability to control anger and exhibit empathy (Hofer & Eisenberg, 2008). These emotions are translated into antisocial behavior and prosocial behavior. **Antisocial behavior** includes any behavior that harms other people, such as aggression, violence, and crime. **Prosocial behavior** includes any behavior that benefits other people, such as altruism, sharing, and cooperation.

How do children learn behavior that is pro- rather than antisocial? Whereas antisocial behavior—aggression—has been studied for many years, it is only relatively recently that attention has been given to prosocial behavior—altruism. **Aggression** includes an unprovoked attack, fight, or quarrel. Types of aggression include *instrumental*, whose goal is to obtain an object, a privilege, or a space, and *hostile*, whose goal is to harm another person. (We focus on hostile aggression, because instrumental aggression usually declines as children develop language skills to express desires and self-regulatory skills to delay gratification.) **Altruism** encompasses voluntary actions that are intended to help or benefit another person or group of people without the actor's anticipation of external rewards. Such actions often entail some cost, self-sacrifice, or risk on the part of the actor (Eisenberg, Fabes, & Spinrad, 2006).

TeachSource Video Activity

Go to the Education CourseMate website to watch the video entitled "Self-Control."

How would you enable self-control in a 2-year-old? Give an example.

How would you enable self-control in a 6-year-old? Give an example.

How about a 12-year-old? Give an example.

What role do emotions play in self-regulatory behavior?

antisocial behavior any behavior that harms other people, such as aggression, violence, and crime

prosocial behavior any behavior that benefits other people, such as altruism, sharing, and cooperation

aggression unprovoked attack, fight, or quarrel

altruism voluntary actions that are intended to help or benefit another person or group of people without the actor's anticipation of external rewards

How does aggressive behavior develop?

Antisocial Behavior: Aggression

Researchers are interested in studying causes and correlates of aggressive behavior because childhood aggression, especially hostile aggression, often forecasts later maladaptive outcomes, such as delinquency and criminality (Bartol & Bartol, 2008; Dodge, Coie, & Lynam, 2006). Antecedents of aggressive behavior in children may be noncompliance with adults, oppositional behavior, lying, stealing, and destruction of property.

What theories explain the development of aggressive behavior?

Existing theories explaining the causes of aggression fall into the following general categories: (1) biological; (2) social cognitive; (3) sociocultural; and (4) ecological.

Biological Theories

Biologic influences on aggressive behavior include evolution, genetics, and neuroscience. *Evolution* encompasses passing on the survival and adaptive characteristics of the species from one generation to the next; *genetics* refers to the individual characteristics of the parents that are passed on to their children; *neuroscience* involves the brain and nervous system.

Evolution

Sigmund Freud (Freud, 1925; Hall, 1954) believed that humans are born with two opposing biological instincts that evolved to enable adaptation: a life instinct (*Eros*), which causes the person to grow and survive, and a death instinct (*Thanatos*), which works toward the individual's self-destruction. According to him, the death instinct is often redirected outward against the external world in the form of aggression toward others. Freud believed that the energy for the death instinct is constantly generated. If it cannot be released in small amounts in socially acceptable ways, it will eventually be released in an extreme and socially unacceptable form, such as violence against others or violence against the self. So if the aggressive instinct can be redirected (crying, punching a doll, hammering nails), then it can be defused.

While Freud's theory explains aggression as an evolved adaptive characteristic of humans in general, it does not explain individual differences in levels of aggressiveness within a society and situations.

Genetics

There is evidence supporting a genetic basis for individual levels of aggressiveness. Behavioral tendencies that might be influenced genetically include impulse control, frustration tolerance, and activity level (Bushman & Huesmann, 2010). Aggressive and antisocial behavior shows stability over the life course (Dodge, Coie, & Lynam, 2006). A large-scale study of adopted persons found that an individual was more likely to exhibit deviant

IN PRACTICE

Does Zero Tolerance Inhibit or Enhance Self-Control?

In order to provide a safe environment for learning, schools across the nation are exerting their punitive power to suspend or expel students who violate the rules, which vary by state, and even by school district. Generally, school rules for appropriate conduct involve truancy, weapons, drugs, aggressive behavior, sexual misconduct, and insubordination.

- Is a "one-size-fits-all" policy best for dealing with misbehavior, or are there others?
- Does suspension or expulsion from school lead to increased alienation or dropout rates?
- How can children who are punished learn to improve their behavior?
- How can the families of children who are punished be engaged to collaborate with schools over rules that could provide more optimal socialization outcomes?

criminal behavior if a biological parent was a criminal, regardless of the environment in the adoptive family (Mednick et al., 1986). In addition, the level of certain hormones present in a person has been shown to be related to aggressive behavior (Olweus, 1986). Finally, males are more aggressive than females, not only physically but also verbally (Bushman & Huesmann, 2010; Eley, Lichtenstein, & Stevenson, 1999).

Neuroscience

Neuroimaging—for example, positive emission tomography (PET) and magnetic resonance imaging (MRI)—has emerged as a means of locating brain irregularities in aggressive individuals. A PET study of 41 convicted murderers suggests that abnormal activity in specific regions of the brain, including the amygdala and medial temporal lobe, may contribute to a predisposition to violence in some individuals (Society for Neuroscience, 2007).

According to the Society for Neuroscience (2007), many people with pathological aggression go undiagnosed. Currently, no drugs for aggression have been approved by the Food and Drug Administration, and social programs are often underfunded or under pressure to serve all who need help. However, researchers have uncovered specific brain chemicals that can be manipulated to control different kinds of aggression in humans. For example, alcohol has been implicated in aggression. While most people who drink alcohol do not become aggressive, some who drink low to moderate amounts can become very aggressive. This suggests that individual responses to alcohol consumption may be linked to aggression-related personality traits, which are inherited. Alcohol's action on a specific inhibitory amino acid that influences, and possibly intensifies, aggressive behavior is a subject of ongoing research.

Scientists suspect that both genetic and environmental factors contribute to the complexity of aggressive behavior. Studies have shown that the amygdala, one of the brain structures responsible for controlling emotions, has an important role in mediating violence. Other advances include:

- Identifying a host of specific genes and chemical reactions in the brain that are linked to violent behavior.
- Discovering that dysfunctional regulation of the brain chemical serotonin, which affects mood, affects impulsiveness in humans.

Recent advances involving the mood-influencing brain chemical serotonin identified specific abnormal genes responsible for weakening the brain's ability to control impulsive behavior. Although not directly responsible for violent behavior, a variant of one of these genes breaks down serotonin and biases the brain toward impulsive, aggressive behavior. The gene variant was found mostly in men who tended to have smaller brain structures related to emotion and less activity in brain circuits that control impulsiveness. Less control over emotions may reduce one's ability to control stressful situations and increase the chances of violent behavior.

In sum, research analyses of the relationship of biological factors to aggressive behavior conclude that aggression occurs indirectly through the interaction of biological processes and environmental events (Bushman & Huesmann, 2010; Dodge, Coie, & Lynam, 2006; Gifford-Smith & Rabiner, 2004).

Social Cognitive Theories

Social cognitive theories explaining aggressive behavior include *learning* and *information-processing* theories.

Learning Theory

The basic principle of learning theory is that actions are contingent on consequences—behavior that is reinforced (rewarded) will be repeated; behavior that is not reinforced (ignored or punished) will cease (but may be suppressed). According to Bandura (1973, 1991),

This parent's harsh and punitive child-rearing methods will likely influence this child to have an externally oriented conscience, behaving out of fear of punishment.

Tony Freeman/PhotoEdit

children learn through a series of reinforcing and non-reinforcing experiences when it is appropriate to act aggressively, what forms of aggression are permissible, and to whom they can express aggression without disapproval or punishment. For example, children cannot hit their mothers when mothers take a toy away because severe socialization consequences ensue. However, children can hit their peers when peers take a toy away without experiencing such consequences.

Children not only learn from consequences of their own actions, they learn by observing the consequences of the actions of significant others. Children identify with role models (whom they admire and who are perceived to be similar to them) and imitate their behavior. The role models can be peers. For example, a child who has been attending school for a while may come home and display some new behavior never displayed before (such as biting when angry). The role models can be parents as well. For example, parents sometimes respond to aggressive acts by spanking. Punishing aggression with aggression is providing model behavior for the child to imitate.

Do children learn from the behavior of others?

IN CONTEXT There is much documentation on the relationship between authoritarian parenting practices (cold or hostile, demanding, and punitive or coercive) and childhood aggression in Euro-American children (Dodge, Coie, & Lynam, 2006; Kim, Hetherington, & Reiss, 1999; Patterson, 1982; Rubin, Stewart, & Chen, 1995). Thus, if parents want to discourage aggressive behavior in their children, they must not model it (spanking is aggressive behavior). They must also not reward it (let it succeed or go unnoticed). And they must teach alternative acceptable behaviors, such as talking about one's feelings.

In other cultures, those where punishment (moderate, not harsh) is considered to be part of normal childrearing, such as African American or Asian American (who use shame as a punishment), it is the authoritarian parenting style that has been found to reduce childhood aggression (Bushman & Huesmann, 2010; Chao, 2001).

Do children learn aggressive behavior from the media?

Whether or not aggressive acts will be imitated by the observer also depends on whether the aggressive model was rewarded or punished (Bushman & Huesmann, 2010). In a classic experiment by Bandura (1973), children were exposed to one of three conditions: They viewed a film showing a successful aggressive model enjoying a victory; they viewed a film showing an aggressive model being severely punished by the intended victim; or they did not see any film (the control condition). The children who saw the aggressive model rewarded for aggressive behavior exhibited more aggression on subsequent observation than did children who either saw the model punished or saw no model.

However, responses that are rewarded intermittently resist extinction or elimination. In other words, responses that are not rewarded every time they occur, but only sometimes, are very difficult to "unlearn." Aggressive acts are highly likely to be rewarded intermittently. For instance, they may be allowed to occur successfully by some children and not by others, and they may be punished by adults when noticed, which may not be every single occurrence.

As has been discussed, a number of studies (Comstock & Scharrer, 2006; Murray, 2007; Perse, 2001) report that both children and adults are exposed to a lot of television violence. Many people believe that watching a lot of aggression on television increases the tendency of the viewers, especially children, to behave aggressively. By watching, children may learn that aggression is acceptable, and they may even learn aggressive techniques. Children whose parents mediate TV viewing are less likely to imitate aggression.

When aggressive models are successful, they are likely to be imitated.

Tony Freeman/PhotoEdit

Information Processing Theory

Information processing refers to the way an individual attends to, perceives, interprets, remembers, and acts on events or situations. Regarding aggressive behavior, information processing theorists study impulsivity and frustration. People who behave impulsively act without thinking ahead regarding the consequences. People who are frustrated view interfering factors as preventing them from achieving a goal. Impulsivity is one of the characteristics of attention deficit hyperactivity disorder (ADHD). Children diagnosed with ADHD are more prone to aggressive behavior than are normal children, but improve when they are on medication (Bushman & Huesmann, 2010).

information processing the way an individual attends to, perceives, interprets, remembers, and acts on events or situations

Some believe impulsivity is a genetic temperamental trait that affects behavior (Buss & Plomin, 1984; Dodge, Coie, & Lynam, 2006; Kagan, 1994). Thus, aggressive behavior can be a response to frustrating experiences, especially in impulsive individuals (Staub, 1996). An example would be "road rage," in which people get involved in verbal or physical fights—or even shoot one another—when cut off in traffic. The strength of the frustrated motive, the degree of interference, and the number of goals blocked determine the intensity of the aggression exhibited (Grusec & Lytton, 1988).

Others (Bushman & Huesmann, 2010; Dodge & Pettit, 2003; Dodge, Coie, & Lynam, 2006) believe that people's reactions to frustration depend not so much on the social cues (what happens) as on how they process the information (their *interpretation* of what happens). Dodge (1986) assumes that children enter each social situation with a memory of past experiences and a goal (making friends, for example). When an event occurs, such as being bumped into, the child must interpret its meaning. A child's past experiences with social interaction as well as his or her skills in processing information will influence whether the event will be interpreted as "accidental" or "purposeful." Aggressive children tend to interpret ambiguous events as hostile, whereas nonaggressive children tend to interpret such events as benign. See Figure 12.2.

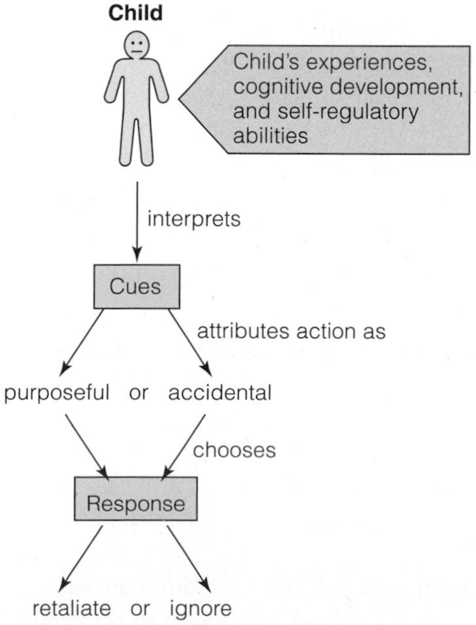

FIGURE 12.2 Information Processing and Aggressive Behavior

Sociocultural Theories

Sociocultural theories explain how people are influenced by the attitudes, values, and behavior patterns of those around them, particularly significant others.

Peers

Aggression can be a result of peer group pressure (Dodge, Coie, & Lynam, 2006; Wall, Power, & Arbona, 1993). Peers are thought to supply the individual with the attitudes, motivations, and rationalizations to support antisocial behavior, such as bullying, as well as providing opportunities to engage in specific delinquent acts (Dodge, Coie, & Lynam, 2006; Espeldge, Holt, & Henkel, 2003; Patterson, DeBaryshe, & Ramsey, 1989). A study of children from first to sixth grade found the classroom context to be influential in increasing or reducing aggressive behavior (Kellam et al., 1999). Aggressive first-graders in classrooms with aggressive peers showed an increase in aggressive behavior by sixth grade, whereas aggressive first-graders in classrooms using preventive intervention strategies showed a decrease in aggressive behavior by sixth grade.

Whether or not individuals succumb to group pressure depends on their personalities, the situation, and also the number of reference groups to which they belong. If they belong to several groups that use aggression as an acceptable means of revenge, then the tendency to behave aggressively increases. On the other hand, if they belong to one group that subscribes to this norm but also to other groups that do not, the likelihood of conforming to the aggressive behavior of the one group decreases. Thus, if one's peer group sanctions aggression, one is more likely to exhibit aggressive behavior.

Community

Individual aggressive tendencies are magnified through social contagion (Staub, 1996). Examples are gangs, urban rioters, rapacious soldiers, and mobs (groups of bullies) (Lagerspetz et al., 1982). Researchers (Staub, 1989; Zelli et al., 1999) have found that when restraining socialization forces are reduced, aggression is more likely. Restraining socialization forces can be external pressures, such as fear of consequences (punishment, criticism, opinion of others) or internal pressures (guilt, shame, moral development level).

"Sanctions for evil" (Sanford & Comstock, 1971) provided by a group may reduce internal restraining pressures such as guilt. Members of the group may feel that what they are doing is morally required, as in war. Soldiers are trained to do as they are ordered. Sanctions for evil were demonstrated in a famous experiment by Stanley Milgram carried out in 1963, which focused on the conflict between obedience to authority and personal conscience (Milgram, 1963, 2004). Subjects (in the role of teacher) were told to inflict electric shocks on other subjects (in the role of learner) when they gave a wrong answer. Shocks were not actually given, although the "learners" acted as if they were. Some "teachers" refused immediately, and some "teachers" quit the experiment after they heard the other "learners" scream. However, 65 percent of the "teachers" obeyed orders to punish the "learners" and actually inflicted (or believed they inflicted) the maximum level of shock possible (450 volts!).

The community usually provides the restraining socialization forces for aggression through its members, its laws, and its police. Community members are a restraining force when they are socially cohesive and willing to intervene in aggressive acts. Communities lacking social cohesiveness and exhibiting alienation have more violence and crime (Bushman & Huesmann, 2010). Also, communities who subscribe to the "culture of honor," believing that aggression is the acceptable reaction to personal affronts, have more incidence of violence (Nisbett & Cohen, 1996).

Members of individualistic cultures and collectivistic cultures have different perspectives on aggressive revenge. According to Shteynberg, Gelfand, and Kim (2009), American students report they feel more offended when their rights are violated, whereas Korean students report they feel more offended when their sense of duty and obligation is threatened. Collectivists are more likely than individualists to avenge another's shame. To collectivists, shame to someone is considered an injury to one's self.

Ecological Theories

The development of aggression must also be viewed in an ecological context. According to researchers (Beyers et al., 2003; Dodge, Coie, & Lynam, 2006; Parke, 1982), the complex variables operating in aggressive behavior involve the:

- *child* (personality, cognitive level, social skills),
- *family* (parenting, interaction),
- *school* (attitudes on handling aggressive behavior),
- *peer group* (modeling, norms, acceptance/rejection),
- *media* (modeling), and
- *community* (socioeconomic stressors, attitudes about what constitutes aggressive behavior, availability of support systems).

In reviews of the literature, Patterson and his colleagues (Patterson, DeBaryshe, & Ramsey, 1989; Reid, Patterson, & Snyder, 2002) have synthesized the findings on aggression in the hypothesis that the route to chronic delinquency is marked by a reliable developmental sequence of ecological experiences: The first experience is ineffective parenting (influenced by such variables as the way the parents were parented, socioeconomic status, ethnicity, neighborhood, and education); the second is behavioral conduct disorders that lead to academic failure and peer rejection, which, in turn, lead to increased risk of involvement in a deviant peer group; and the third, occurring in early adolescence, is chronic delinquent behavior.

Thus, antisocial behavior appears to be a developmental trait that begins early in life (observable by age 4 to 5) and often continues into adolescence and adulthood. The socialization for aggression is bidirectional and interactional in several ecological contexts; it includes poor parenting skills, which affect child behavior, and child behavior, which affects not only parenting but school performance and peer relationships as well (Snyder & Patterson, 1995). The unintentional coercive training might begin with a parental demand that the child go to bed. The child refuses, and the parent yells. The child whines, complaining about always being picked on. The parent gives in, hence reinforcing in the child a coercive method of getting his or her way.

How can children at risk for conduct disorders be identified?

A study by Dodge, Pettit, and Bates (1994) identified the following socialization mediators contributing to risky developmental outcomes:

- harsh parental discipline,
- lack of maternal warmth,
- exposure to aggressive adult models,
- maternal aggressive values,
- family life stressors,
- mother's lack of social support,
- peer group instability, and
- lack of cognitive stimulation.

The children, who were from the lowest socioeconomic status, were followed from preschool to third grade. The significance of these mediators as predictors of conduct disorders is that they often accompany socioeconomic stress found in families of low socioeconomic status or in those who were poor. Thus, it is not low socioeconomic status or poverty *per se* that influences aggressive behavior, but the *socialization mediators* that often accompany such socioeconomic stress (Dodge, Coie, & Lynam, 2006; Beyers et al., 2003; Huston, McLoyd, & Coll, 1994). Table 12.1 provides a summary of variables contributing to antisocial behavior.

Table 12.1 Summary of Variables Contributing to Antisocial Behavior

Child	Family	School	Peers	Media	Community
Biological influences (evolution, genetics)	Parenting style (authoritarian, coercive)	Teaching style (authoritarian)	Peer group pressure	Modeling	Modeling
Gender	Interaction	Modeling	Situation	Reinforcement/punishment of model	Acceptance of and/or sanctions for violence
Hormones	Modeling	Reinforcement/punishment for behavior	Aggressive norms	Mediation by adults	Degree of social cohesiveness/alienation
	Reinforcement/punishment for behavior	Expectations	Modeling		Degree of safety
Temperament (impulsivity, frustration tolerance, activity level)	Attitudes and values		Acceptance/rejection		Socioeconomic stressors
Ability to delay gratification					Availability of informal/formal support systems
Information-processing ability					
Internally/externally oriented conscience (guilt vs. fear of punishment)					
Cognitive maturity					
Social skills					
Moral reasoning/judgment					

How does altruistic behavior develop?

Prosocial Behavior: Altruism

One of the aims of socialization, as stated previously, is to teach developmental skills, which include getting along with others. To participate in a group, one must cooperate, share, and help others when needed. As we all know, some people exhibit more of these behaviors than others. What is it that motivates someone to rescue a total stranger from a fire, to send money to someone whose story has been told in the newspaper, or to volunteer to work in a senior citizen center?

Recall that altruism refers to behavior that is kind, considerate, generous, and helpful to others. Like aggression, it is biologically influenced and it shows some consistency over time. Some researchers believe the brain may be "prewired" to be empathetic and to cooperate with others (Hein & Singer, 2009). Altruistic behavior begins to appear during the preschool years (in some children, it appears by age 2). Children's ability to take the perspective of others increases as they get older, so they become more aware that others' feelings may differ from theirs and, thus, are more capable of experiencing empathy (Eisenberg, Fabes, & Spinrad, 2006). For example, Radke-Yarrow and Zahn-Waxler (1986) observed consistent patterns of sharing, helping, and comforting behaviors among 3- to 7-year-olds at play.

Prosocial responses, such as cooperating, sharing, giving comfort, and offering to help, become increasingly apparent throughout childhood as children develop cognitively and have more social interactions (Eisenberg, Fabes, & Spinrad, 2006). For example, toddlers, ages 2 to 3, exhibit some sharing and demonstrations of sympathy. They often react to others' distress by becoming distressed themselves (Zahn-Waxler, Radke-Yarrow et al., 1992). Preschoolers, age 3 to 6, begin to become less egocentric and exhibit altruistic acts if they also benefit the self ("I'll share so you'll be my friend"). School-agers, age 6 to 12, who can take the role of others, understand the legitimate needs of others ("I'll help because he can't

IN PRACTICE

What Can Be Done to Inhibit Aggressiveness in Young Children?

1. *Organize the environment to minimize conflicts.* Minimize crowding. Have plenty of stimulating and engaging developmentally appropriate materials. Have enough so children can play together with similar materials (bicycles, paint, toys, and so on).
2. *Set standards, stick to them, and provide consequences for noncompliance.* Let children know aggression is not sanctioned: "You hit Bobby on the playground; you must sit on the bench now for 10 minutes." "You did not control your temper today. Since you disappointed me, I will have to disappoint you; you cannot stay up late, as you had wanted, to watch that program on television."
3. *Stop aggression immediately.* If possible, try not to let it carry to a successful completion. For example, if you see two children struggling over a toy, take the toy and ask both children to tell you their versions of the incident. Then ask them how you should resolve it. If they don't come up with a solution, say, "Well, you both think about it, and meanwhile I'll hold the toy."
4. *Give children alternative ways of solving problems.* Teach them how to verbalize their feelings and how to listen to others.
5. *Anticipate possible situations in which aggressive behavior may occur.* For example, if children are playing together roughly or children are complaining they have nothing to do, redirect the children into an activity that interests them.
6. *Provide opportunities for cooperative activities.* Enable children to learn to listen to each other's ideas, to solve problems democratically, to compromise, and to respect each other.
7. *Foster helpfulness and cooperation.* "Could you help Daniel with that tower he's building?" "Could you help your sister put on her shoes while I make your lunch?"
8. *Be a positive role model.* Don't punish aggression with aggression; use alternative disciplinary methods.
9. *Discuss rules and the reasons for them.* Also discuss violence that children may be exposed to in the media or in their communities. Let children talk about their fears and feelings. Help children develop strategies for feeling protected by adults: "When you are scared, you can tell me." "Policeman Wilson is our friend."
10. *Reward prosocial behavior.* Give children attention when they share, are helpful or cooperative, or solve problems by discussion; don't allow them to get your attention only by being aggressive.

Sources: Caldwell and Crary, 1981; Slaby et al., 1995.

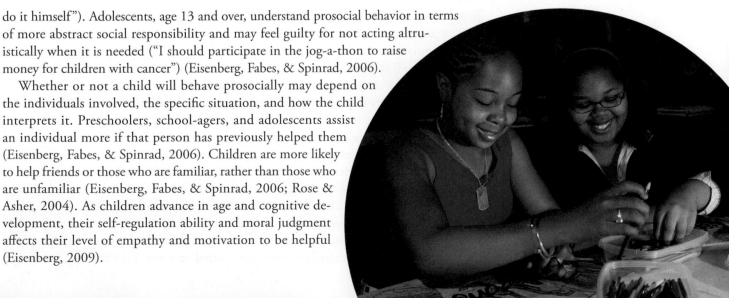

An example of prosocial behavior: cooperation.

Cengage Learning

do it himself"). Adolescents, age 13 and over, understand prosocial behavior in terms of more abstract social responsibility and may feel guilty for not acting altruistically when it is needed ("I should participate in the jog-a-thon to raise money for children with cancer") (Eisenberg, Fabes, & Spinrad, 2006).

Whether or not a child will behave prosocially may depend on the individuals involved, the specific situation, and how the child interprets it. Preschoolers, school-agers, and adolescents assist an individual more if that person has previously helped them (Eisenberg, Fabes, & Spinrad, 2006). Children are more likely to help friends or those who are familiar, rather than those who are unfamiliar (Eisenberg, Fabes, & Spinrad, 2006; Rose & Asher, 2004). As children advance in age and cognitive development, their self-regulation ability and moral judgment affects their level of empathy and motivation to be helpful (Eisenberg, 2009).

What theories explain the development of altruistic behavior?

Biological Theories

Biological drives such as reproduction and survival are inborn. According to Freud (1938), altruistic behavior is an indication of the ability to regulate biological drives. He explains that biological drives, such as reproduction (expressed in sexual desire) and survival (expressed in aggression), are seated in the part of the personality that seeks self-gratification. Freud labeled that part of the personality the *id*. Children's experiences with reality cause them to assess the feasibility of satisfying their biological drives. Freud labeled the rational part of the personality the *ego*, which helps one to delay gratification. Children also experience pleasant feelings when they comply with parental standards and unpleasant feelings when they don't. Out of fear of parental hostility or loss of parental love, they develop a *superego*, or conscience, to regulate their impulses and behave according to internalized parental standards. They may behave prosocially to avoid a feeling of guilt. Thus, children's adoption of prosocial values, according to Freud, results from identification with parents.

According to theorists interested in the biological basis for behavior (Simpson & Beckes, 2009; Sober & Wilson, 1998), altruistic behavior is an adaptive survival trait. Certain complex human social behaviors, such as altruism, are influenced by evolution and genes. They explain that children are genetically programmed to be kind and considerate as part of human nature. Altruism is regarded as behavior that promotes the genetic fitness of another at the expense of one's own fitness. Since altruism benefits the group's survival, natural selection favors those members of the species who have this characteristic (even though the altruistic member may die in performing the altruistic act). For example, protecting others is considered to be altruistic behavior. In the animal kingdom, the bee that protects the members of its species by stinging an intruder dies. Even though one member of the species dies, it is the altruistic action that enables the other members to live and reproduce. In the human species, the relationship of biology to sociology is explained by Richard Nalley (1973, p. 5) as follows.

> As early human beings bonded together in social groups, perhaps for the purpose of cooperative hunting, selection pressures began to build for those traits that allowed them to adapt to community life. Genes promoting flexibility and conformity, for example, were probably passed on. Aggression had to be harnessed, social structure improvised and forms of communication developed. This acted as a kind of positive feedback loop: better communication led to reduced aggression, and vice versa.

According to Hoffman (1981, 1991, 2000), empathy—vicariously experiencing another's emotions—is part of human nature in that it is an inherited biological predisposition. Empathy, along with the internalization of society's moral norms and values, is the motive for altruism. One study (Martin & Clark, 1982) found that newborns became distressed by the cries of other newborns, thus indicating that humans are designed from birth to respond to the distress of their peers. Twin children (14 months old) were found to react similarly to simulation of distress in others at home and in the laboratory settings (Zahn-Waxler, Robinson, & Emde, 1992). Other studies (Eisenberg, Fabes, & Spinrad, 2006; Rushton et al., 1986) found that identical twins (who have the same genes) were more similar to each other on questionnaires designed to assess altruism, empathy, and nurturance than were fraternal twins, who share about half of their genes. Thus, differences in genetic composition among people have a considerable influence on differences in their tendencies to behave both prosocially and antisocially.

According to neuroscientific studies (Hein & Singer, 2009), there is an area in the front of the brain's cerebral cortex, called the ventromedial area (located behind the bridge of the nose), that processes information regarding other people's suffering and one's own misdeeds. Apparently, the proper functioning of this area is vital to emotional responsiveness. Adults whose ventromedial areas were damaged were found not to react negatively to images of extreme human harm and were found to show less concern than others about not conforming to social norms for behavior (Damasio, 1994). Neuroimaging techniques, such as positron emission tomography (PET scanning) were used to demonstrate that brain neural structures known to be involved in emotional responding, such as the amygdala, were activated when subjects listened to sad stories designed to elicit sympathy, whereas they were not active when subjects listened to neutral, or unemotional, stories (Decety & Chaminade, 2003).

Magnetic resonance imaging (MRI), another neuroimaging technique, was used to demonstrate activated areas of the brain while subjects played a strategic cooperative/competitive game based on the classic Prisoner's Dilemma: Two suspects are taken into custody by the police, who do not have enough evidence to convict them. They are put in separate rooms to get them to confess. The one doing so first is promised freedom as a witness for the state. If both confess, both get sent to jail for a long time. If neither confesses, then the police can only jail them briefly for a minor offense. Thus, the motive for the prisoners to cooperate (remain silent) is a small consequence rather than a large one for competing to be the one to confess and losing. The researchers found that two areas of the brain significant in dopamine production (pleasure) were activated when the subjects worked together to share a reward rather than compete with one getting a reward and the other getting nothing (Rilling et al., 2002). Apparently, the human brain is "wired" to cooperate and rewards itself for doing so with pleasurable feelings.

Social Cognitive Theories

Children learn altruistic behavior from the actions of others via learning theory (consequences and modeling), instruction, and learning by doing.

Learning Theory

Despite the current uncertainty about how and when altruism begins, it is known that *direct reinforcement* (reward for an altruistic act) or *vicarious reinforcement* (observing someone else engaging in the act and getting reinforced for it) encourages altruism (Eisenberg, Fabes, & Spinrad, 2006). One investigator, for example, found that children age 4 were more likely to share marbles with other children if, after sharing, they were rewarded with bubble gum (Fischer, 1963). However, the effect of giving tangible rewards for prosocial behavior lasts only briefly. Social reinforcement, or praise, has been shown to increase altruism in children for longer periods. For example, after having been prompted to share and then praised for doing so, children were found to give more to others (Bar-Tal, Raviv, & Lesser, 1980; Gelfand et al., 1975).

Reciprocal behavior, mutual give and take, is relatively well established among adults. Dahlman, Ljunggvist, and Johanneson (2007) tested the existence of reciprocal behavior among children 3–8 years old. Three simple anonymous allocation games were conducted with 242 children. In the first stage, half of the children decided whether to give a bag of raisins to another anonymous child or not. The three games differed in terms of the cost of giving and the relative difference in payoffs. In the second stage, the roles were reversed between the two children. Reciprocal behavior was found in all three games, with the degree of reciprocity tending to increase with age. The effect of reciprocity was not found to be significant among 3–5-year-old children, whereas the effect was highly significant in all three games for 6–8-year-olds.

Although concrete rewards may induce altruism in the given context, the long-term effect of concrete rewards may be negative because it undermines intrinsic motivation (Zimmerman, 2000). Social rewards (praise) may induce altruism in the given context, but not in other contexts (Eisenberg, Fabes, & Spinrad, 2006).

Observing and imitating a model has been shown repeatedly to encourage observers to behave similarly. Helpful models encourage helpful behavior (Bandura, 1986; Eisenberg, Fabes, & Spinrad, 2006). This modeling effect is found whether the model is another child or an adult, and whether the model is live or on film. Media models, as shown on

A child modeling empathy—a prosocial behavior.

ECE Collection, Unity 1, GFOW 2867/Cengage Learning

Mister Rogers' Neighborhood or *Sesame Street*, who exhibit prosocial behavior are likely to be imitated by their viewers, especially when an adult reinforces the show's message by discussion (Perse, 2001).

Modeling altruism has generalizable effects. It has been shown that children who are taught to act helpfully in one situation will also act helpfully in others (Radke-Yarrow & Zahn-Waxler, 1986). And after having observed an altruistic model, children were still acting generously four months later (Radke-Yarrow & Zahn-Waxler, 1986).

Children learn from each other. They imitate behaviors of admired peers. For example, children who witness the charitable acts of an altruistic model are more likely to donate toys or money, even anonymously (Radke-Yarrow, Zahn-Waxler, & Chapman, 1983). Thus, if a child has a group of friends who consistently exhibit prosocial behavior, it is likely that child will exhibit it also (Eisenberg, Fabes, & Spinrad, 2006).

Instruction

Since a good altruistic example is so effective, what about just instructing children to be kind, considerate, and helpful? Generally, observing an adult sharing is more effective than just telling a child to share (Eisenberg, Fabes, & Spinrad, 2006).

Teaching altruism can be as effective as modeling it, especially if the instructions are strongly stated and reasons are given for sharing (Grusec, Saas-Korlsaak, & Simutis, 1978). In sum, children's altruistic behavior is linked to their repertoire of behaviors learned at home and school (Robinson & Curry, 2006).

Learning by Doing

The school can train children to be prosocial by using the technique of role playing (Eisenberg, Fabes, & Spinrad, 2006). For example, Staub (1971) worked with pairs of kindergarten children, asking one child to act the part of someone who needed help (carrying something too heavy) and the other child to act the part of a helping person (to think of actions to help). The children were then asked to change roles. A week after training, helpfulness was tested by giving the children the chance to help a crying child in the next room and the chance to share candy with another child. The trained children were compared to those who had not received training. The children who had undergone the reciprocal role training were more likely to be helpful to another child than the children who had not received this training.

Schools can also assign children the responsibility of teaching others to be helpful or to share (Eisenberg, Fabes, & Spinrad, 2006; Robinson & Curry, 2006). For example, Staub (1970) explicitly assigned responsibility to kindergarten and first-grade children. When the children were told they were "in charge" by a departing adult, there was an increase in the probability, especially among the first-graders, that they would go to the aid of another child who was heard crying in the next room. Thus, prosocial behavior can be increased in children via real-life experiences.

Prosocial behavior can also be increased by virtual experiences. Previous research has documented that playing violent video games has various negative effects on social behavior in that it causes an increase in aggressive behavior and a decrease in prosocial behavior. In contrast, there has been much less evidence on the effects of prosocial video games. Greitemeyer and Osswald (2010) examined the hypothesis that playing a prosocial (relative to a neutral) video game increases helping behavior. In fact, participants who had played a prosocial video game were more likely to help after a mishap, were more willing (and devoted more time) to assist in further experiments, and intervened more often in a harassment situation. Results further showed that exposure to prosocial video games activated the accessibility of prosocial thoughts, which in turn promoted prosocial behavior. Thus, depending on the content of the video game, playing video games not only has negative effects on social behavior but has positive effects as well.

Cognitive Developmental Theories

Perspective-Taking

Numerous theorists have hypothesized that as children develop cognitively, their ability to think about others increases. Their enhanced sociocognitive skills, particularly perspective taking and moral reasoning, foster prosocial behavior (Bengtsson, 2003; Eisenberg, Fabes, & Spinrad, 2006). When individuals can put themselves in another's place, they are more likely to empathize and give comfort and help.

Moral Reasoning

Lawrence Kohlberg (1976) believed prosocial behavior to be a component of moral reasoning, which is a function of cognitive development. Kohlberg emphasized the contributions of social interactions and cognitions regarding the ability to take others' perspectives and understand consequences of behavior. Whether an individual is self-oriented or other-oriented influences moral reasoning and consequent selfish or altruistic behavior. Emotions, such as empathy and guilt, may also play a role in moral judgment and behavior (Eisenberg, Fabes, & Spinrad, 2006; Hoffman, 2000).

Social Interactional Theories

Communication Style

The bidirectional interactions occurring in social groups, such as communication, influence prosocial behavior. The family provides such a context. For example, a team of researchers (Zahn-Waxler, Radke-Yarrow, & King, 1979) studied young children's altruism by asking mothers of a group of 15-month-olds and mothers of a group of 20-month-olds for careful reports of incidents occurring during the children's daily lives. The mothers were trained as observers, and the study lasted for nine months. The mothers tape-recorded descriptions of every incident in which someone in the child's presence expressed painful feelings (anger, fear, sorrow, pain, and/or fatigue). The mothers also described events preceding and following the incident, as well as both the child's and their own reactions.

When the researchers found that the number of altruistic reactions varied greatly from child to child, they examined the communication styles of the individual mothers' responses. They found that the way the mothers reprimanded their children was clearly related to the children's degree of altruism. The following comments and actions exemplify the various responses.

- Moralizing: "Look, you made Susie cry; it's not nice to pull hair."
- Prohibition with explanation or statement of principle: "You must never poke anyone's eyes! He won't be able to see!"
- Withdrawal of love, physical or verbal: "I can't hug you when you've been mean."
- Neutral: "Russell is crying because you hurt him."
- Prohibitions without explanation: "Don't ever do that!"
- Physical restraint
- Physical punishment

The mother's use of moralizing and prohibitions (with explanations or statements of principle) when the child exhibited antisocial behavior was related to a high proportion of altruistic behaviors. Unexplained verbal prohibitions and physical punishment were associated with low degrees of altruism. Neutral explanations had little effect either way.

Parenting Style

A warm, nurturant, affectionate relationship between children and parents seems to contribute to the development of prosocial tendencies, in contrast to a cold, indifferent, distant relationship (Eisenberg, Fabes, & Spinrad, 2006; Zhou et al., 2002).

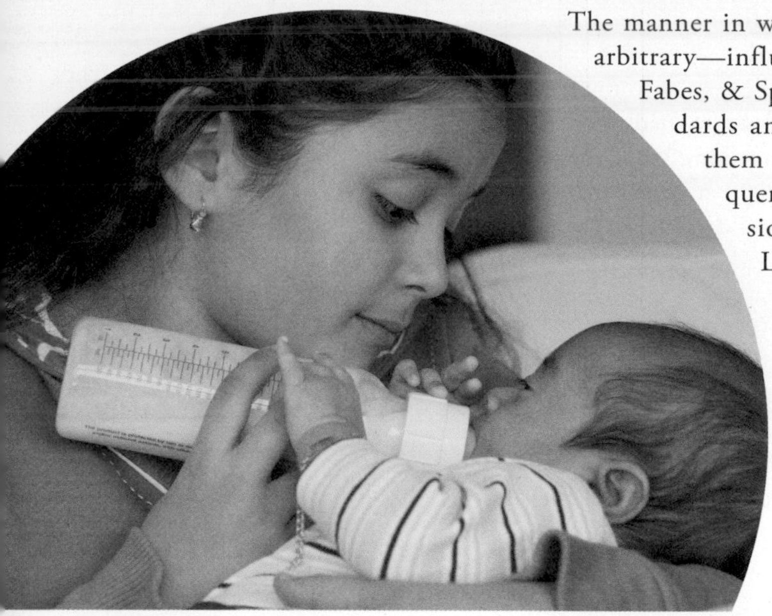

Children from cultures that give them early responsibility in family functioning tend to exhibit spontaneous altruism.

Ariel Skelley/Jupiter Images

The manner in which parents exert control—reasonable versus excessive or arbitrary—influences the development of prosocial behavior (Eisenberg, Fabes, & Spinrad, 2006). *Control* refers to the setting of certain standards and rules by parents and their insistence on adherence to them when deemed necessary. There is strong evidence that frequent use of physical punishment by parents results in aggression, hostility, and resistance in children (Dodge, Coie, & Lynam, 2006; Patterson, DeBaryshe, & Ramsey, 1989). On the other hand, nurturing persons who do not exert control seem to have no effect on prosocial behavior (Radke-Yarrow & Zahn-Waxler, 1986; Baumrind, 1967, 1971).

Sociocultural Theories

Anthropological and psychological studies in non-Western cultures show that societies vary greatly in the degree to which prosocial and cooperative behaviors are expected (Greenfield, Suzuki, & Rothstein-Fisch, 2006; Rogoff, 2003).

It has been documented that some societies provide more opportunities for learning to behave prosocially than do others, particularly by involving older children in the care of younger ones (Graves & Graves, 1983; Triandis, 1995; Whiting & Edwards, 1988). It has also been argued that the value a society puts on interdependence, cooperation, and social harmony (collectivistic orientation) versus independence, competition, and individual achievement (individualistic orientation) influences children accordingly (Greenfield, Suzuki, & Rothstein-Fisch, 2006). For example, Hindu Indian culture emphasizes more duty-based social responsibility than American culture, which emphasizes moral justice–based social responsibility (Miller & Bersoff, 1993). In other words, Hindus are more likely to respond prosocially out of duty or obligation, whereas Americans are more likely to do so because "it's the right or fair thing to do."

Cultural variations in children's tendencies to cooperate or compete have been investigated in a classic study by Madsen and Shapira (1970), using various games that can be played cooperatively or competitively. One of these games is diagrammed in Figure 12.3.

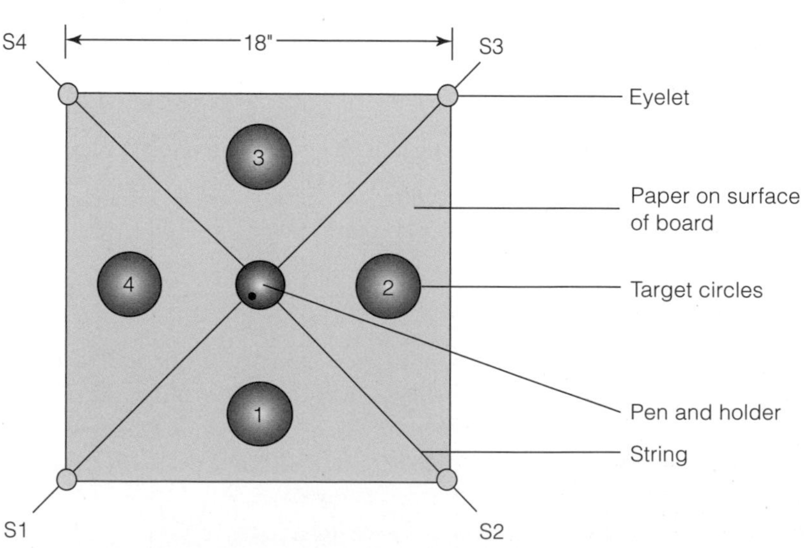

FIGURE 12.3 Cooperation Board Game

Source: M. C. Madsen and A. Shapira (1970). Cooperative and competitive behavior of urban Afro-American, Anglo-American, Mexican-American, and Mexican village children. *Developmental Psychology,* 3(1), p. 17. Copyright © 1970 by the American Psychological Association. Reprinted by permission of the publisher.

The game board is 18 square inches and has an eyelet at each corner. A string passes through each of the eyelets and is attached to a metal weight that serves as a holder for a ballpoint pen. A sheet of paper is placed on the game board for each trial so that the movement of the pen as the children pull their strings is recorded automatically.

In the *cooperative* condition, every time the pen crosses all four circles, all the players are rewarded. Thus, the more the children work together, the more they all win. In the *competitive* condition, each player is rewarded only when the pen crosses his or her circle. In this condition, if the children take turns helping one another, each child can win as often as any other. Some children never figure this out, however, and end up pulling the pen in their own direction, so no one wins.

Children reared in traditional rural subcultures and small, semi-agricultural communal settlements cooperated more readily than children reared in modern urban subcultures. For example, schoolchildren in Mexican villages and small towns were found to be more cooperative than their urban middle-class Mexican, Mexican American, African American, or European American peers (Madsen & Shapira, 1970). Similarly, Israeli children reared on a kibbutz and children from Arab villages were found to be more cooperative than Israeli urban children (Nadler, 1991; Shapira & Lomranz, 1972; Shapira & Madsen, 1974).

Cross-cultural comparisons by Beatrice and John Whiting (1973, 1975) illustrate in natural settings some of the laboratory findings. The Whitings found that the cultural variable most closely associated with altruistic behavior was the extent to which children in the various cultures were given the responsibility to perform household tasks or chores related to the family's economic security. Most of the children in Kenyan, Mexican, and Philippine cultures were high above the median of the total sample in altruism, whereas most of the children in the other three cultures (Okinawan, Indian, and American) scored low in altruism. Presumably,

> in simpler kin-oriented societies, with economies based upon subsistence gardening, altruistic behavior is highly valued and individual egoistic achievement frowned upon. Women must work in the fields, and the children must help in order for the family to subsist. To offer help, to support others, and to be responsible are taught both by precept and practice. Being helplessly dependent, showing off, boasting, and being egoistically dominant are incompatible with such a way of life.

IN PRACTICE

How Can Prosocial Behavior Be Fostered in Young Children?

1. *Be an example.* Exhibit helping, cooperating, and sharing behavior.
2. *Preach prosocial behavior, and give reasons.* Take advantage of specific situations to instruct children how to share, how to be helpful, and how to cooperate.
3. *Be warm and accepting.*
4. *Set firm standards of behavior.* Accompany with consequences for noncompliance.
5. *Provide role-playing opportunities.* Allow children to experience others' perspectives.
6. *Discuss how one's actions may affect another's feelings.*
7. *Provide activities that require cooperation,* such as group projects.
8. *Suggest specific ways in which children can be cooperative and helpful.*
9. *Provide meaningful responsibilities.* One's task is designed to help another person or the group.
10. *Praise prosocial behavior.*

Source: Eisenberg, Fabes, and Spinrad, 2006.

> On the other hand, in the more complex societies, where no child knows what he is going to be when he grows up, individual achievement and success must be positively valued. To help a friend sitting next to you in an examination is defined as cheating. To ask for help from specialists such as mechanics, dressmakers, shopkeepers, psychotherapists, priests, or servants is expected and paid for in cash rather than in reciprocal services. (Whiting & Whiting, 1973, p. 64)

Thus, "children who . . . perform more domestic chores, help more with economic tasks and spend more time caring for their infant brothers, sisters, and cousins, score high on the altruistic versus egoistic dimension" (1973, p. 63). Although children in Western industrialized societies are not usually routinely involved in many family-maintenance activities, those who are assigned tasks that benefit all family members (caring for younger members, animals) behave more prosocially than age-mates whose responsibilities consist mainly of self-care (cleaning one's own room) (Grusec, Goodenow, & Cohen, 1996).

Table 12.2 summarizes the variables contributing to prosocial behavior.

Table 12.2 Summary of Variables Contributing to Prosocial Behavior

Child	Family	School	Peers	Media	Community
Genetics	Parenting style (authoritative, warm)	Instruction/set standards	Peer group pressure	Mediated discussion by adults	Simple social organization
Temperament	Communication of prosocial/antisocial instructions	Positive/negative consequences	Learning by doing	Values of cooperation	Traditional, rural
Age	Reinforcement/ punishment	Reinforcement/ punishment	Collaborative activities	Modeling	Extended family ties
Cognitive maturity	Modeling	Modeling	Modeling		Early assignment of tasks and responsibility
Perspective and role-taking ability	Assignment of responsibility	Assignment of responsibility			Individualistic/collectivistic orientation
Empathy	Opportunities for role playing	Opportunities for role playing			Justice-based/duty-based social responsibility
Moral reasoning/ judgment	Discussion	Discussion			
Situation					

What is involved in a person's moral code?

Morals

Morals, as introduced in Chapter 2, encompass an individual's evaluation of what is right and wrong. They involve acceptance of rules and govern one's behavior toward others. Breaches of morals provoke consequences, as well as judgmental and emotional responses (Damon, 1990; Turiel, 2002, 2006).

Morality involves *feeling*, which includes empathy and guilt (Hoffman, 2000). Morality also involves *reasoning*, which includes the ability to understand rules, distinguish right from wrong, and take another person's perspective (Kohlberg, 1976; Piaget, 1965; Selman, 1980). Finally, morality involves *behaving*, which includes prosocial and antisocial acts (Eisenberg, Fabes, & Spinrad, 2006), as well as self-regulation of impulses.

Children develop the ability to self-regulate impulses from familial and cultural socialization—for example, being reinforced for obedience and being sanctioned for wrongdoing. Children construct moral concepts according to their cognitive and emotional development from social interactions, which provide experience in collaboration and conflict (Turiel, 2002, 2006).

Moral Development

How does one develop a moral code?

As children mature and develop, their morality changes. Infants and toddlers do not distinguish right from wrong. Thus, when they conform to parental demands it is usually because they are attached and fear loss of love. Preschoolers and school-agers consider right and wrong to be direct opposites, with nothing in between. They are not capable of factoring "on purpose" or "by mistake" into their judgments of wrongdoing. Adolescents begin to view right and wrong as a matter of degree. They take into account intention in judging an act.

Not only does children's maturation influence their moral codes, but so do intelligence, motivation, the need for approval, self-control, and the particular situation (Bandura, 1991). Most psychologists (Damon, 1990; Hoffman, 2000; Kohlberg, 1976; Piaget, 1965; Turiel, 2006) believe that one's moral code develops through social interaction in a societal context.

Piaget's Theory

What are the major theories of moral development?

Jean Piaget (1965) defined morality as "the understanding of and adherence to rules through one's own volition." Piaget analyzed morality from the perspective of how an individual's social experiences result in the formation of judgments about social relationships, rules, laws, and authority (Turiel, 2006).

Piaget worked with a group of Swiss schoolboys ranging in age from 4 to 13. He asked them questions about the rules of the game: What are the rules? Where did they come from? Could they be changed? Piaget found that for the youngest children (ages 4 and 5), the rules were poorly understood and were not binding. For the middle group of children (ages 6 to 9), rules were regarded as having been made by an authority ("morality of constraint") and were therefore sacred and unchangeable. Following rules is quite rigid; any bending of the rules results in "That isn't fair!" For the oldest group (ages 10 to 13), rules were regarded as law emanating from mutual consent ("morality of cooperation"); rules must be respected if you want to be loyal to the group, but rules can be changed if the majority of the group agrees.

heteronomous morality Piaget's stage of moral development in which children think of rules as moral absolutes that cannot be changed

autonomous morality Piaget's stage of moral development in which children realize that rules are arbitrary agreements that can be changed by those who have to follow them

Generally, children's moral reasoning shifts from the belief that one is subject to *external* laws (**heteronomous morality**—rules are moral absolutes that cannot be changed), to the belief that one is subject to *internal* laws (**autonomous morality**—rules are arbitrary agreements that can be changed by those who have to follow them). As children develop, they begin to understand that things are not totally right or totally wrong. They can also gradually see things from other perspectives and, therefore, can consider the intentionality of an act when deciding whether the act is right or wrong.

Piaget examined the idea that younger children reason about the wrongness of an act in terms of the amount of damage done, rather than whether the act was done purposefully or accidentally. Reading pairs of stories like the following to children of varying ages, he asked which character in the stories was naughtier.

1. A little boy who is called John is in his room. He is called to dinner. He goes into the dining room. But behind the door there was a chair, and on the chair there was a tray with 15 cups on it. John couldn't have known that there was all this behind the door. He goes in, the door knocks against the tray, bang go the 15 cups, and they all get broken!
2. Once there was a little boy whose name was Henry. One day, waiting for a time when his mother was out, he tried to get some jam out of the cupboard. He climbed up on a chair and stretched out his arm. But the jam was too high up and he couldn't reach it and have any. But while he was trying to get it, he knocked over a cup. The cup fell down and broke (Piaget, 1965, p. 122).

Parent explaining to child *why* lying is wrong; the goal being internalization of such moral behavior.

Cengage Learning

Piaget found that for the younger children interviewed, the goodness or badness of the actors in the story was related solely to the extent of the consequences. They judged John to be naughtier than Henry because John had broken more cups. Older children, however, recognized the role of intention behind the acts. They judged Henry to be naughtier than John because Henry had been purposefully sneaking something, whereas John had had an accident.

Contemporary researchers have corroborated Piaget's findings when his research methods are replicated (Jose, 1990; Lapsley, 1996). For example, young children in various cultures emphasize consequences more than intent in judging the wrongness of an act. Also, distinguishing between personal events (being hit by another child), social conventions (classroom rules about taking turns), and moral issues (lying) increased with age. Yau and Smetana (2003) interviewed 61 Chinese preschoolers from Hong Kong at ages 2, 4, and 6 years about familiar moral, social-conventional, and personal events. As the children got older, they viewed moral transgressions as more serious than breaking conventional rules about welfare and fairness, generalizably wrong, and wrong independent of authority and personal events.

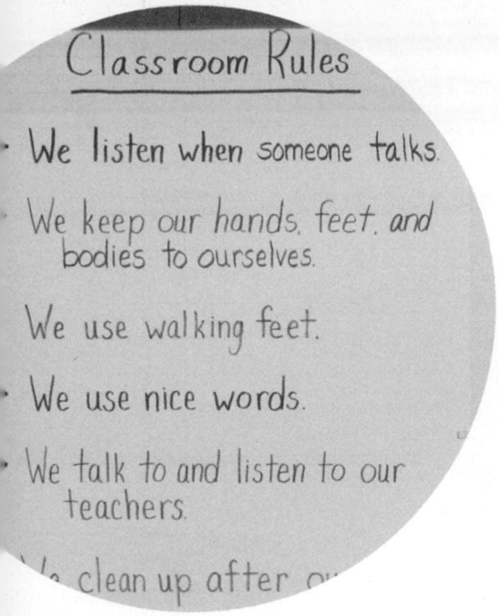

Classroom Rules
We listen when someone talks.
We keep our hands, feet, and bodies to ourselves.
We use walking feet.
We use nice words.
We talk to and listen to our teachers.

An example of social conventional rules.

ECE Collection, Unity 1, GFOW 3032/Cengage Learning

Kohlberg's Theory

Lawrence Kohlberg (1976), influenced by Piaget's work, developed a theory of moral development after 20 years of interviewing children, adolescents, and adults in different cultures (see Table 12.3). He proposed that there was no consistent relationship between parental conditions of child rearing and various measures of conscience or internalized values because morality cannot be imposed; it has to be constructed as a consequence of social experiences (Turiel, 2006). Kohlberg presented his subjects with stories involving moral dilemmas and questioned them about the stories. Probably the best known is the following:

> A woman in Europe was near death from cancer. One drug might save her, a form of radium that a druggist in the same town had recently discovered. The druggist was charging $2,000, 10 times what the drug cost him to make. The sick woman's husband, Heinz, went to everyone he knew to borrow money, but could get together only about half of what it cost. He told the druggist that his wife was dying and asked him to sell it cheaper or let him pay later. But the druggist said "no." The husband was desperate and broke into the man's store to steal the drug for his wife. Should the husband have done that? Why or why not? (Kohlberg, 1969, p. 379)

Clearly, there is no "right" answer to this story (or the others Kohlberg used). On the one hand, there are the husband's feelings; on the other, there are the legal rights of the druggist.

Based on the *reasoning* behind the responses to the stories (see Table 12.4), Kohlberg concluded that there are six distinct stages, or perspectives, of moral development, which are associated with changes in the individual's intellectual development; each perspective is broader, taking into account more variables or aspects of a moral problem. The stages begin at about age 6 and continue to adulthood. It is important to note that children and adults sometimes operate at several different stages simultaneously. According to Kohlberg (1976):

1. The stages of moral reasoning are the same for all persons, regardless of culture.
2. Individuals progress from one stage to the next.
3. Changing from stage to stage is gradual. The change results from many social experiences.
4. Some individuals move more rapidly than others through the sequence of stages. Some advance further than others; for example, only 25 percent of U.S. adults were found to reason at stage 5 (principled morality).
5. Although the particular stage of moral reasoning is not the only factor affecting people's moral conduct, the way they reason does influence how they actually behave in a moral situation.

Table 12.3 Stages of Moral Development

Level and Stage	What Is Right	Reasons for Doing Right	Social Perspective of Stage
Level I. Preconventional **Stage 1:** Heteronomous morality	To avoid breaking rules backed by punishment, obedience for its own sake, and avoiding physical damage to persons and property.	Avoidance of punishment and the superior power of authorities.	Egocentric point of view. Doesn't consider the interests of others or recognize that they differ from the actor's; doesn't relate two points of view. Actions are considered physically rather than in terms of psychological interests of others. Confusion of authority's perspective with one's own.
Stage 2: Individualism, instrumental purpose, and exchange	Following rules only when it is to someone's immediate interest; acting to meet one's own interests and needs and letting others do the same. Right is also what's fair, what's an equal exchange, a deal, an agreement.	To serve one's own needs or interests in a world where you have to recognize that other people have their interests, too.	Concrete individualistic perspective. Aware that everybody has his or her own exchange interest to pursue and that these interests conflict, so that right is relative (in the concrete individualistic sense).
Level II. Conventional **Stage 3:** Mutual interpersonal expectations, relationships, and interpersonal conformity	Living up to what is expected by people close to you or what people generally expect of your role as son, brother, friend, etc. "Being good" is important and means having good motives, showing concern about others. It also means keeping mutual relationships, such as trust, loyalty, respect, and gratitude.	The need to be a good person in your own eyes and those of others. Your caring for others. Belief in the Golden Rule. Desire to maintain rules and authority, which support stereotypical good behavior.	Individualistic perspective in relationships with other individuals. Aware of shared feelings, agreements, and expectations, which take primacy over individual interests. Relates points of view through the concrete Golden Rule, putting oneself in the other person's shoes. Does not yet consider generalized system perspective.
Stage 4: Social system and conscience	Fulfilling the actual duties to which you have agreed. Laws are to be upheld except in extreme cases where they conflict with other fixed social duties. Right is also contributing to society, the group, or institution.	To keep the institution going as a whole, to avoid the "if everyone did it," or the imperative of conscience to meet one's defined obligations (easily confused with stage 3 belief in rules and authority).	Differentiates societal point of view from interpersonal agreement or motives. Takes the point of view of the system that defines roles and rules. Considers individual relations in terms of place in the system.
Level III. Postconventional **Stage 5:** Social contract or utility and individual rights	Being aware that people hold a variety of values and opinions, that most values and rules are relative to your group. These relative rules should usually be upheld, however, in the interest of impartiality and because they are the social contract. Some nonrelative values and rights like *life* and *liberty*, however, must be upheld in any society and regardless of majority opinion.	A sense of obligation to law because of one's social contract to make and abide by laws for the welfare of all and for the protection of all people's rights. A feeling of contractual commitment, freely entered upon, to family, friendship, trust, and work obligations. Concern that laws and duties be based on rational calculation of overall utility, "the greatest good for the greatest number."	Perspective independent of formal rules. Perspective of a rational individual aware of values and rights (such as fairness) prior to social attachments and legal contracts. Integrates perspectives by formal mechanisms of agreement, legal contract, objective impartiality, and due process. Considers moral and legal points of view; recognizes that these sometimes conflict and finds it difficult to integrate them.
Stage 6: Universal ethical principles	Following self-chosen ethical principles. Particular laws or social agreements are usually valid because they rest upon such principles. When laws violate these principles, one acts in accordance with the principle. Principles are universal principles of justice: the equality of human rights and respect for the dignity of human beings as individual persons.	The belief as a rational person in the validity of universal moral principles, and a sense of personal commitment to them.	Perspective of a moral point of view from which social arrangements derive. Perspective is that of any rational individual recognizing the nature of morality or the fact that persons are ends in themselves and must be treated as such.

Source: Lawrence Kohlberg, "Moral Stages and Moralization," from *Moral Development and Behavior*, edited by T. Lickona, copyright © 1976 by Holt, Rinehart and Winston, Inc., reprinted by permission of the author.

Table 12.4 Types of Moral Judgments Made in Heinz's Dilemma

	Pro	Stage 1	Con
Level I. Preconventional (What Will Happen to Me?)	If you let your wife die, you will get in trouble. You'll be blamed for not spending the money to save her, and there'll be an investigation of you and the druggist for your wife's death.	Action is motivated by avoidance of punishment, and "conscience" is irrational fear of punishment.	You shouldn't steal the drug: You'll be caught and sent to jail. If you do get away, your conscience will bother you, thinking how the police will catch up with you at any minute.
	Pro	**Stage 2**	**Con**
	If you do happen to get caught, you could give the drug back, and wouldn't get much of a sentence. It wouldn't bother you much to serve a short jail term, if you have your wife when you get out.	Action motivated by desire for reward or benefit. Possible guilt reactions are ignored and punishment viewed in a pragmatic manner. (Differentiates own fear, pleasure, or pain from punishment/consequences.)	You may not get much of a jail term if you steal the drug, but your wife will probably die before you get out, so it won't do you much good. If your wife dies, you shouldn't blame yourself; it isn't your fault she has cancer.
	Pro	**Stage 3**	**Con**
Level II. Conventional (What Will Others Think of Me?)	No one will think you're bad if you steal the drug, but your family will think you're an inhuman husband if you don't. If you let your wife die, you'll never be able to look anybody in the face again.	Action motivated by anticipation of disapproval of others, actual or imagined/hypothetical (e.g., guilt). (Differentiation of disapproval from punishment, fear, and pain.)	It isn't just the druggist who will think you're a criminal; everyone else will, too. After you steal it, you'll feel bad thinking how you've brought dishonor on your family and yourself; you won't be able to face anyone again.
	Pro	**Stage 4**	**Con**
	If you have any sense of honor, you won't let your wife die because you're afraid to do the only thing that will save her. You'll always feel guilty that you caused her death if you don't do your duty to her.	Action motivated by anticipation of dishonor—that is, institutionalized blame for failure of duty—and by guilt over concrete harm done to others. (Differentiates formal dishonor from informal disapproval. Differentiates guilt for bad consequences from disapproval.)	You're desperate, and you may not know you're doing wrong when you steal the drug. But you'll know you did wrong after you're punished and sent to jail. You'll always feel guilty for your dishonesty and lawbreaking.
	Pro	**Stage 5**	**Con**
Level III. Postconventional (What Will I Think of Myself?)	You'd lose other people's respect, not gain it, if you don't steal. If you let your wife die, it would be out of fear, not out of reasoning. So you'd just lose self-respect and probably the respect of others, too.	Concern about maintaining respect of equals and of the community (assuming their respect is based on reason rather than emotions). Concern about own self-respect—that is, to avoid judging self as irrational, inconsistent, nonpurposive.	You'd lose your standing and respect in the community and violate the law. You'd lose respect for yourself if you're carried away by emotion and forget the long-range point of view.
	Pro	**Stage 6**	**Con**
	If you didn't steal the drug and you let your wife die, you'd always condemn yourself for it afterward. You wouldn't be blamed and you would have lived up to the outside rule of the law, but you wouldn't have lived up to your own standards of conscience.	Concern about self-condemnation for violating one's own principles. (Differentiates between community respect and self-respect. Differentiates between self-respect for generally achieving rationality and self-respect for maintaining moral principles.)	If you stole the drug, you wouldn't be blamed by other people, but you'd condemn yourself because you wouldn't have lived up to your own conscience and standards of honesty.

Source: Nicholas J. Anastasiow, *Educational Psychology: A Contemporary View*, p. 131. Copyright © 1979. CRM Books, Del Mar CA. Reprinted by permission of the publisher.

6. Experiences that provide opportunities for role-taking (assuming the viewpoints of others, putting oneself in another's place) foster progress through the stages. For example, children who participate in many peer relationships tend to be at more advanced moral stages than children whose peer interaction is low. Within the family, children whose parents encourage them to express their views and participate in family decisions reason at higher moral stages than children whose parents do not encourage these behaviors.

Basically, at the **preconventional level**, the individual considers and weighs the personal consequences of the behavior: "How will I be affected?" Preconventional moral reasoning focuses on individual results. At the **conventional level**, the individual can look beyond personal consequences and consider others' perspectives: "What will they think of me?" Conventional moral reasoning focuses on upholding the rules of society. At the **postconventional level**, the individual considers and weighs the values behind various consequences from various points of view: "How would I respect myself if I . . . ?" Postconventional moral reasoning considers principles that may be more important than upholding society's rules or laws.

preconventional level Kohlberg's stages of moral reasoning in which the individual considers and weighs the personal consequences of the behavior

conventional level Kohlberg's stages of moral reasoning in which the individual can look beyond personal consequences and consider others' perspectives

postconventional level Kohlberg's stages of moral reasoning in which the individual considers and weighs the values behind various consequences from various points of view

Postconventional reasoning can be illustrated by those who choose not to register with the U.S. Selective Service System, as is required of all 18-year-old men. Such an individual, who is generally a law-abiding citizen, may choose not to register because it violates his moral code, which says that only volunteers should be called for service; no one should be forced to fight.

Kohlberg (1976, 1986) believed that most children under age 9 are at the preconventional level of moral development (stages 1 and 2). Some preadolescents also score at this level. Most adolescents, and adults, reason at the conventional level (stages 3 and 4) when faced with moral dilemmas. A small percentage of older adolescents may reach the postconventional level (stages 5 and 6). Adults who are at the postconventional level are only a minority. Because of the idealistic nature of stage 6 reasoning, it was removed from the Kohlberg moral judgment scoring manual, but it is still considered to be theoretically important as a hypothetical construct (Colby & Kohlberg, 1987).

Views on Kohlberg's Theory

Kohlberg's stage theory has been criticized by some investigators even though his work has had significant influence on subsequent research (Turiel, 2006).

- **Moral reasoning and moral behavior.** The link is not as strong as Kohlberg's theory would predict (Blas, 1990; Rest et al., 2000). One's moral code consists of both moral reasoning (how one believes one should behave in a certain situation) and moral behavior (how one actually does behave in a certain situation). For some individuals, there is a difference between the two (Hartshorne & May, 1978; Kurtines & Gewirtz, 1991). When people think about real-life moral problems, they tend to rank at a lower stage than they do on hypothetical problems (Turiel, 2006).
- **Interviewing technique.** Subjects' answers to questions about Kohlberg's dilemmas, which cue further questions, don't really measure the inner processes that underlie moral behavior (Rest et al., 2000). Researchers in cognitive science and social cognition contend that self-reported explanations of one's own cognitive process have severe limitations. There is now a greater understanding of implicit processes and tacit knowledge regarding human decision making outside the awareness of the subject and beyond the subject's ability to verbally articulate them. The Defining Issues Test (DIT) takes a different approach to information collection. The DIT is a group-administered, multiple-choice, mechanically graded exam for activating moral schemas (to the extent that a person has developed them) and for assessing them in terms of importance judgments. The DIT uses Kohlberg's dilemmas and others; the subject's task is to rate and rank the items in terms of their moral importance, exemplified in the In Context Box.

IN CONTEXT

Should Heinz steal the drug? __Should Steal __Can't Decide __Should not steal

Please rate the following statements in terms of their importance. (1 = Great importance, 2 = Much importance, 3 = Some Importance, 4 = Little importance, 5 = No importance)

__1. Whether a community's laws are going to be upheld.
__2. Isn't it only natural for a loving husband to care so much for his wife that he'd steal?
__3. Is Heinz willing to risk getting shot as a burglar or going to jail for the chance that stealing the drug might help?

The DIT is regarded as neo-Kohlbergian in that the sequence of responses corresponds to Kohlberg's theory, but rather than 6 stages, individuals statistically fall into 3 groups beginning at age 12 (due to reading and cognitive ability, stage 1 is not considered):

1. Personal-interest schema (corresponds to stagse 2 and 3)
2. Maintaining norms schema (corresponds to stage 4)
3. Post-conventional schema (corresponds to stage 6)

■ **Cultural bias.** Kohlberg's theory favors a Western (individualistic) perspective on morality, involving justice or fairness to the individual. Studies comparing moral concepts in different cultures (Shweder, Mahapatra, & Miller, 1987; Turiel, 2006) have demonstrated that culture defines morality for a child; in collectivistic cultures, what is best or "right" may be putting one's family obligations or honor above what might be fairer to the individual. For example, Hindu children believed it was more "wrong" to get a haircut on the day of one's father's funeral than for a husband to beat his wife for going to the movies without permission. Family honor is regarded as morally superior to a person's painful consequence for disobedience.

■ **Gender bias.** Kohlberg's original sample was all male. According to Gilligan (1982), the difference in the responses of females compared to the responses of the original male sample sheds some doubt on the applicability of Kohlberg's delineated stages of moral reasoning to all human development. Others disagree, citing that in real-life dilemmas, as opposed to hypothetical ones, the moral reasoning of males and females is similar, even though females do cite relationship and caring issues more often (Jaffee & Hyde, 2000; Turiel, 2006; Walker, 1991).

justice moral perspective emphasizes the rights of the individual; when individual rights conflict, equitable rules of justice must prevail

care moral perspective views people in terms of their connectedness with others; others' welfare is intrinsically connected to one's own

Carol Gilligan (1982, 1985) argues that Kohlberg's theory views morality only from a perspective of *justice*. The **justice moral perspective** (individualistic) emphasizes the rights of the individual. When individual rights conflict, equitable rules of justice must prevail. Cultures with an individualistic orientation exhibit just such a moral perspective. According to Gilligan, a perspective of morality that is not given significance by Kohlberg is that of *care*. The **care moral perspective** (collectivistic) views people in terms of their connectedness with others. In other words, others' welfare is intrinsically connected to one's own. People share in each other's fortunes and misfortunes and must accept responsibility for one another's care. Various cultures around the world that have a collectivistic orientation socialize children to have such a care moral perspective. For example, children and adolescents growing up in India give priority to interpersonal relationships in moral conflict situations, whereas most children and adolescents growing up in the United States give priority to individual rights (Miller & Bersoff, 1993).

Gilligan related examples of boys' and girls' reasoning regarding the Heinz dilemma, such as the following (Gilligan, 1982, pp. 26–28);

Jake: For one thing, human life is worth more than money, and if the druggist only makes $1,000 he is still going to live; but if Heinz doesn't steal the drug, his wife is going to die. (Why is life worth more than money?) Because the druggist can get $1,000 later from rich people with cancer, but Heinz can't get his wife again.

Amy: Well, I don't think so. I think there might be other ways besides stealing it, like if he could borrow the money or get a loan or something, but he really shouldn't steal the drug—but his wife shouldn't die either. (Why shouldn't he steal the drug?) If he stole the drug, he might save his wife then, but if he did, he might have to go to jail, and then his wife might get sicker again, and he couldn't get more of the drug, and it might not be good. So, they should really just talk it out and find some other way to make the money.

In these examples, Jake's sense that people sometimes must act on their own, even in opposition to others, if they are to do the right thing is contrasted with Amy's assumption that people can work out their problems by "talking it out." Because Amy sees the social world as a network of relationships, she believes that the solution to the problem lies in making Heinz's wife's condition known to all concerned, especially the druggist. Surely, then, the people will work something out that will be responsive to the wife's needs. Jake, on the other hand, assumes no such consensus among those involved in the dilemma. So Jake believes Heinz may need to take the law into his own hands if he is to protect his rights. Jake concludes that Heinz's wife is a legitimate part of Heinz's rights by logically calculating the unique value of the wife's life as compared to the money the druggist can get for the drug from others (Damon, 1988).

In sum, despite the criticisms, Kohlberg's model of moral development has stood the test of time. Most psychologists agree that morality, no matter which perspective you take, is developmental; that is, children universally progress through stages of understanding, and even though the timing of the progression and the highest stage reached are individual, the sequence of the stages is the same. "Debates now center on the roles of emotions and judgments, on the individual and the collectivity, on the contributions of constructions of moral understandings and culturally based meanings, and on how to distinguish between universally applicable and locally based moralities" (Turiel, 2006, p. 794).

Influences on Moral Development

What significant factors influence moral development?

Contexts that have been shown to play a role in moral development are situational, individual, and socialization.

Situational Contexts

The situation an individual is in often influences actual moral behavior. Situational factors include the nature of the relationship between the individual and those involved in the problem, whether others are watching, previous experience in similar situations, and the value society places on various responses (Turiel, 2002, 2006). For example, killing in self-defense is condoned, whereas killing for revenge is not. Cognitive factors involve judgment of the situation, age of the child, and cultural orientation.

- **Judgment.** The relation between moral reasoning and moral behavior is not always clear. Turiel (1983, 2002, 2006) explains that the inconsistencies exhibited in people's moral reasoning are influenced by whether they judge the situation to be a "moral" or a "conventional," or social, situation. According to Turiel, a *moral situation* involves other people's rights or welfare (you cannot hit other children) whereas a *conventional situation* involves rules for appropriate behavior in a social group (you must not interrupt when someone else is talking).
- **Age.** Judith Smetana (1985, 1989, 2006) found that even 2½- to 3-year-olds distinguish between *moral* and *conventional* rules. Young children view *moral* transgressions, such as hitting, stealing, and refusing to share, as more serious and deserving of punishment than *conventional* transgressions, such as not saying "please" or forgetting

to put away a toy. Thus, young children seem to have a greater understanding of rules in different situations than Piaget originally assumed.

- **Cultural orientation.** Different cultures define *moral* and social *conventional* rules differently, depending on whether the culture has an individualistic or a collectivistic orientation (Rogoff, 2003; Shweder, Mahapatra, & Miller, 1987). According to Dien (1982), the Western system of morality (individualistic)—emphasizing individual autonomy and self-responsibility—is rooted in Judeo-Christian theology (humans were created with freedom of self-determination) and Greek philosophy (morality is based on rationality). In Western societies, morality emphasizes analytical thinking, individual choice, and responsibility. Means of resolving conflicts rely on laws that protect individual rights. In contrast, Eastern systems of morality (collectivistic), based on the doctrine of Confucianism, believe the universe was designed to be just and moral. Humans have a duty to act accordingly, subordinating their own identity to the interest of the group to ensure a harmonious social order. Judgments must be based on *conventional* norms of reciprocity, rules of exchange, available resources, and sensitivity to complex relationship networks in a given situation. The means for resolving conflicts is through reconciliation.

Individual Contexts

Individual contexts involve temperament, self-control, self-esteem, intelligence and education, social interaction, and emotions.

Temperament

Moral development may be affected by an individual's *temperament*—those innate characteristics that determine sensitivity to various experiences and responsiveness to patterns of social interaction. Kochanska's (1993, 1995, 1997) studies on children's temperament (inhibited or shy, impulsive or aggressive) and conscience development conclude that children's temperaments can affect parenting methods. For example, maternal reasoning, polite requests, suggestions, and distractions predicted internalized conscience development in inhibited, but not in impulsive, 2- and 3-year-olds. Impulsive children were more likely to comply with directives, but only when they had a secure attachment; power assertion resulted in anger and defiance. Such children internalize morals when the parent maintains an affectional relationship.

Self-Control

Moral development may also be related to *self-control*, or *self-regulation*—the ability to regulate impulses, behavior, and/or emotions, discussed earlier (Eisenberg, 2009). Some studies (Mischel, 1974; Mischel, Shoda, & Peake, 1988) have shown that preschool children who exhibit self-control, in that they are able to defer immediate gratification, are more successful than their more impulsive age-mates at resisting the temptation to cheat at experimental games. These self-controlled preschoolers were also rated as more self-competent and socially responsible ten years later in adolescence. Children who can delay gratification have time to assess social cues and thus enable positive peer group functioning (Gronau & Waas, 1997).

Self-Esteem

Another influence on moral development may be *self-esteem*—specifically, the extent to which an individual needs approval from others (Hogan & Emler, 1995). Approval from peers was found to be linked to adolescents who shoplifted, whereas approval from parents was linked to adolescents who did not shoplift (Forney, Crutsinger, & Forney, 2006). A longitudinal study (Dobkin et al., 1995) showed that the need to receive approval from others was related negatively to the level of moral behavior. Specifically, the greater the dependency on others for esteem, the more likely individuals were to abuse substances and engage in antisocial acts. On the other hand, the need for approval from oneself was positively related to the level of moral behavior and consequent avoidance of drugs.

Intelligence and Education

Kohlberg and his colleagues (Colby et al., 1983) reported data from a 20-year longitudinal study of moral judgment in boys who were 10, 13, and 16 when first assessed. The data supported the theory that moral reasoning is significantly linked with age, IQ, education, and socioeconomic status. It also showed that stage 4 did not emerge in a majority of individuals until early adulthood (20s).

Advanced education, particularly the critical thinking and discussion common in college classes, promotes advanced moral reasoning, probably because it provides an opportunity to be exposed to diverse views (Mason & Gibbs, 1993; Turiel, 2006). For example, health care professionals often encounter moral dilemmas in clinical practice that require increased responsibility and accountability for ethical decision making. In a study of health care professionals, Geddes, Salvatore, and Eva (2009) found improved scores of moral judgment on the DIT. Hence the value of moral or ethics education.

Social Interaction

Several researchers (Dunn, 2006; Walker & Taylor, 1991) believe that one's moral code develops through social interaction—discussion, debate, perspective-taking, and emergence of consensus. Social interaction begins in the family, where children's needs, parental control, issues of reciprocity, fairness, rights, obligations, and the welfare of others are experienced regularly and negotiated between children, siblings, and parents. The family is also the setting in which children begin to learn the conventional and moral rules of their society. Such learning continues via social interaction in the school, peer group, and community.

Emotions

Jerome Kagan (1984) believes the morality of most persons to be directed more by emotions than by reasoning. Avoidance of unpleasant feelings and achievement of pleasant feelings are the major motivations for morality. Unpleasant feelings include fear of punishment, social disapproval, and failure, as well as guilt and uncertainty. Pleasant feelings include affection, pride, sense of belonging, and contribution. Martin Hoffman (2000) believes the main source of moral motives to be the feeling of empathy for others; the feeling of guilt results from transgressions. Other researchers (Eisenberg, 2000; Malti & Latzko, 2010) have found it difficult to separate emotion from cognition when examining what drives moral development because to feel empathy, one must be able to take the perspective of another, and to feel guilty, one must understand one has done wrong.

Typically, to study emotions and morality, stories are told to children of different ages about a moral transgression, such as lying or stealing, to see what emotions they attribute to the victim and victimizer. Preschool children usually attribute "sadness" to the victim and "happiness" to the victimizer—because the victimizer gets what he/she wants; this is known as "the happy victimizer." By about age 7 or 8, children understand that the victimizer has done wrong and should feel bad even though he or she has gotten something desirable (Krettenauer, Malti, & Sokol, 2008).

Economic research has proposed that emotions related to morality might be important causes of strong reciprocal behavior and the willingness to sacrifice one's own resources for others. For example, a study by Gummerum and colleagues (2010) explored how 3–5-year-old children allocate resources in the "dictator game," and whether participants' understanding of moral emotions predicted allocations. The dictator game has been developed in experimental economics to measure people's altruism and fairness. In the simplest two-person, one-shot version of the game, one player, the proposer, is given a sum of money that he or she can—but does not have to—share with another anonymous person, the receiver. The receiver has no possibility to reject any offer by the proposer, nor can he or she reciprocate or punish the proposer's action. Keeping the money and being selfish has no negative consequences for the proposer, and sharing has no (evident) social gains.

A number of studies have examined developmental differences in children's decisions in dictator games and variables that might account for children's (fair) allocation behavior in dictator games such as age or gender. This study focused on the role that children's understanding of moral emotions plays for predicting allocations in this game. Understanding and anticipating others' emotions is a major developmental achievement that allows people to successfully engage in social interactions with others. The study found that the understanding of how one would feel after a moral violation is a strong predictor of preschool children's offers in dictator games, above and beyond the effects of age and gender.

In conclusion, moral development is socially constructed (Davidson & Youniss, 1995). It represents an individual's scheme of personal and societal values that include a coordination of emotions, thoughts, and actions (Turiel, 2006). If one acts exclusively on personal values, one may too often overlook the rights and privileges of others in the social environment. To illustrate, in the example discussed in Chapter 11, Tamra overlooked her parents' liability if they break the law and allow her to have a party with alcohol because she is more concerned with her peers. On the other hand, if one acts on societal values or social convention, contract, or laws, one may fail to see how they can unjustly affect a given individual. For example, Tamra's parents did not fully understand her position in feeling she had to fulfill the expectations of her peers because they were more concerned with their responsibilities.

Thus, mature moral development—which is influenced by one's capacity to anticipate the future, to predict consequences, and to put oneself in another's place, along with one's level of self-esteem—is the ability to make rational decisions that balance one's own personal value system with the value system of society.

IN PRACTICE

How Can Moral Growth Be Promoted in the Classroom?

1. Build a sense of community in the classroom where the students learn together in an atmosphere of respect and security.
2. Provide opportunities for the children to have a voice in establishing the rules of the classroom and the consequences for not following them.
3. Give reasons for consequences, stressing where possible the effect of the child's action on the group.
4. Discuss differences between rules for the good order of the school and rules affecting justice and human relations.
5. Provide opportunities for collaborative peer group work.
6. In stories and discussions of everyday experiences, help the children to consider the feelings of other persons, real or fictional.
7. Role-play experiences from daily life events that lead to disappointments, tensions, fights, and joys in order to provide opportunities for the students to see the events from perspectives other than their own.
8. Discuss concepts of fairness and unfairness.
9. Using stories, literature, history, current events, and/or films, stimulate discussions that will provoke higher-stage reasoning.
10. Be a role model and point out other role models as they occur in classroom activities.

Sources: Higgins, 1995; Nucci, 2008.

Gender Roles

How are gender differences perceived in society?

A *gender role*, or sex type, as discussed in Chapter 2, refers to the qualities an individual understands to characterize males and females in his or her culture. It is distinct from sex, which refers to the biological aspects of being male or female. Gender role is more of a psychological construct, whereas sex is more of a physical one.

The following English nursery rhyme from the early 1800s illustrates how gender differences are perceived in society. Verses like these, in turn, influence how children are socialized to acquire their appropriate gender roles (Gould & Gould, 1962).

What are little boys made of?
Frogs and snails
And puppy dogs' tails
That's what little boys are made of.
What are little girls made of?
Sugar and spice
And all things nice
That's what little girls are made of.

Development of Gender Roles

How do boys and girls learn how to act like males and females?

sex typing classification into gender roles based on biological sex

Sex typing, or classification into gender roles based on biological sex, begins at birth (Maccoby, 1998, 2000; Ruble, Martin, & Berenbaum, 2006). Parents and significant others apply gender stereotypes to children as soon as they are born (or even in utero, if the sex is known). As a result, girls and boys are channeled into sex-typed behaviors that do not necessarily reflect the potential of their individual abilities (Basow, 2008; Tennenbaum & Leaper, 2002; Leaper & Friedman, 2007). The child is given what society considers to be a girl's name or a boy's name (those children whose names are ambiguous—for example, Jordan, which could be a girl's or boy's name—are possible targets for teasing). The child is then dressed according to that classification. Certain colors are generally worn by girls and certain ones by boys. Even though in the United States most children of both sexes wear shirts and pants, those worn by girls are usually decorated differently. And throughout childhood, the child is given certain toys for play, also usually classified by sex. Girls' toys are generally related to nurturing or home activities (dolls, stuffed animals, dishes); boys' toys are generally related to action or work activities (cars, trucks, tools).

Although various cultures provide a "gender curriculum," children play a role in their gender socialization, perhaps driven by biological programming within each sex, as well as between them (Lippa, 2005; Maccoby, 2000). For example, my eldest granddaughter, whose mother rarely wears jewelry or makeup, has been fascinated with adorning herself ever since she saw such items in the store. Because of her interest, I polished her nails for her second birthday. Her sister, a year younger, has been attracted to climbing on everything and loves to take toys apart and throw and kick a ball. For her second birthday, I gave her a riding car. When the eldest was 7, she chose to take piano lessons. The younger granddaughter, who was then 6, chose to take jujitsu lessons.

Thus, biology and socialization practices interact to produce the variety of sex-typed behaviors observed within and between males and females (Lippa, 2005). It is generally accepted that socialization maximizes genetically determined sex differences (Leaper & Friedman, 2007; Ruble, Martin, & Berenbaum, 2006).

The following four main theories explain how children are socialized to assume the appropriate gender roles in their society (see Figure 12.4).

What are the major theories of gender-role development?

Psychoanalytic Theory

Psychoanalytic theory deals with how one comes to *feel* like a male or female. According to Sigmund Freud (cited in Hall, 1954; Freud, 1925), children identify with the same-sex parent out of sexual love for the opposite-sex parent and fear of punishment from the same-sex parent for that love. In other words, a boy identifies with his father because he loves his mother (*Oedipus complex*) and is fearful that his father, who also loves his mother, will punish him for that love. A girl identifies with her mother because she loves her father (*Electra complex*) and is fearful that her mother, who also loves her father, will punish her for that love. In identifying with the same-sex parent, children unconsciously take on the characteristics of that parent. A boy becomes like his father so that his mother will love him as she loves his father; and a girl becomes like her mother so that her father will love her as he loves her mother. The process of gender identification occurs sometime between the ages of 3 and 5, the phallic stage in Freud's sequence of personality development (where focus is on the genitals). After age 5 or 6, children enter Freud's latency stage, in which they engage in normal play activities with same-sex peers and sexuality is dormant. At puberty, children enter Freud's genital stage, in which they normally begin to be sexually attracted to the opposite gender.

Social Cognitive Theory

This theory deals with how one comes to *behave* as a male or female. According to theorists Walter Mischel (1970) and Albert Bandura (1989), children behave in what are considered to be gender-appropriate ways because they are reinforced or rewarded when they do so and punished when they do not by the various agents of socialization. Boys identify with male models (usually their fathers) because they are rewarded for doing so: "You are strong, just like your daddy." Girls identify with female models (usually their mothers) for the same reason: "You look pretty, just like your mommy." Children choose models with whom to identify on the basis of whether the model is perceived to be like themselves, is warm and affectionate, and has prestige in their eyes. When children identify with the same-sex parent, they incorporate that parent's behavior into their own.

These boys playing with cars and this girl playing with a doll exemplify gender stereotyping.

ECE Collection -a. Battery Park GFOW 3817, b. ECE2005 Astor, 274/Cengage Learning

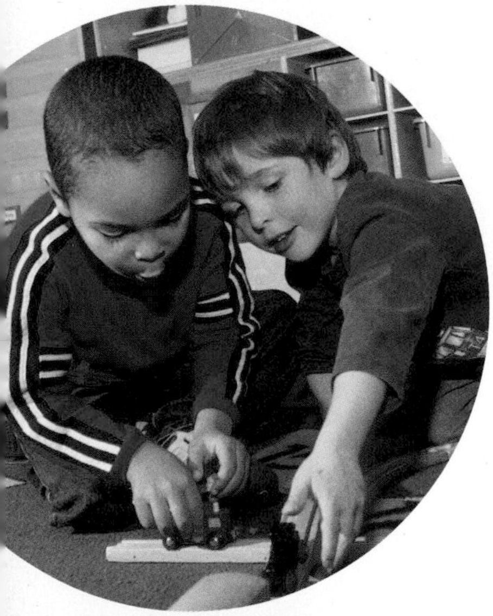

ECE Collection, Pough, IMG 9719/Cengage Learning

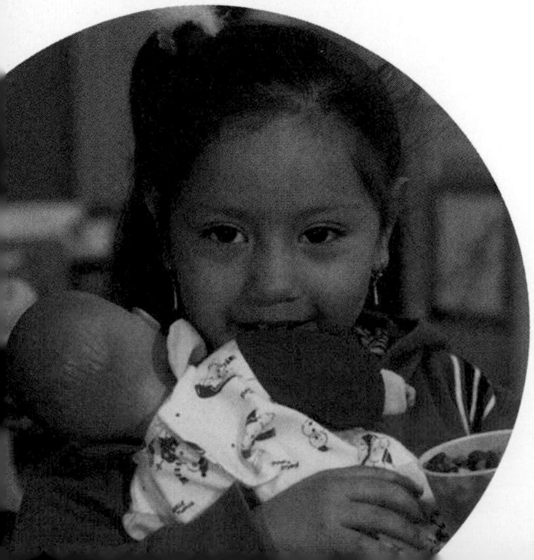

Cognitive Developmental Theory

This theory deals with how one comes to *reason* about oneself as a male or female. According to Lawrence Kohlberg (1966), the assumption of gender-role behavior is part of the child's total cognitive development. On the basis of their observations and interactions, children accommodate, or reconcile, the differences between the categories of male and female. Once children know and understand the concepts of maleness and femaleness (about age 5 or 6), they then assimilate the appropriate gender behavior that matches their biological sex. In other words, a boy thinks, "I am a boy; therefore, I do boy things," and a girl thinks, "I am a girl; therefore, I do girl things." What children consider to be appropriate gender behavior depends on their experiences in their family, peer group, school, and community, and what they observe in the media.

Gender Schema Theory

Gender schema theory, proposed by Sandra Bem (1981), as well as by Martin and Halverson (1981, 1987), deals with how one comes to *process information* about oneself as a male or female by perceiving and interpreting gender-linked information. A *schema* (plural *schemata*) is a conceptual framework of one's experiences and understandings. It explains how children code new information in terms of gender. The basis for coding information is first the recognition of males and females as distinct gender categories. Labeling occurs about age 2½. As children develop, they observe male and female behavior around them. Consequently, they form a schema for what males do in their society and another for what females do. These gender schemata influence how new information gets processed, guiding selective attention and imitation of same-sex models. For example, a girl observes her mother and her grandmother cooking. She also observes her father and other males doing repairs. About age 4 to 5, she can conceptualize that girls cook and boys fix things. Since she knows she is a girl, she chooses to engage in cooking activities rather than working with tools at preschool. Thus, she gains information about cooking and rejects information about building or doing repairs. By age 7 to 8, gender behavior is fairly rigid. Gender schema theory helps to explain why gender stereotypes are self-perpetuating and difficult to modify. It is as if one's earliest socialization experiences with gender set the path for later ones. This was demonstrated in a study of 5- to 10-year-olds, who were asked to predict feminine or masculine interests of target children with certain characteristics. For example, "I know a child who likes to play with tool kits. How much would this child want to wear a dress?" Older children's responses were more gender stereotypic ("No way!") than those of younger children (Martin, Wood, & Little, 1990).

Gender schema theory also proposes that self-concept is associated with the degree to which children perceive themselves as congruent with their schema of male or female. If their behavior matches what they interpret as appropriate to their gender, they feel positive about themselves; if they don't conform to the stereotype, they feel negative about themselves.

What does research say about gender roles?

Regardless of which theory or theories seem to best explain gender-role socialization, the fact remains that males and females behave differently. There is a consensus that biological, cognitive, and social factors interactively contribute to sex-typed behavior (Leaper & Bigler, 2011; Lippa, 2005; Ruble, Martin, & Berenbaum, 2006). Although genetics is a significant influence on sex-typed behavior, it is not wholly responsible, as documented by a large population study of 3- and 4-year-old twins and non-twin siblings (Iervolino et al., 2005). Although large differences in gender-role behavior are observed between the sexes, there is substantial variation within the sexes in typical male and female behavior. For example, in early childhood, boys generally prefer cars and trucks to dolls and jewelry and engage in more rough-and-tumble play than in caretaking role play. These sex-typed behaviors increase from early to middle childhood. However, twins who share the same environment, especially boys, exhibit more similar gender behavior than do non-twins who share the same environment (Iervolino et al., 2005).

In a classic review, researchers Eleanor Maccoby and Carol Jacklin (1974) analyzed more than 2,000 books and articles on possible psychological differences between males and females. They concluded that males are more aggressive than females, a difference that is apparent in infancy. They also concluded that girls have greater verbal ability than boys and that boys have greater visual–spatial ability than girls. These differences are more apparent in early adolescence. Maccoby and Jacklin discovered that some differences traditionally attributed to boys' and girls' behavior are myths. For example, girls are neither more "social" than boys, nor are they more suggestible. Boys do not have higher achievement motivation than girls, nor are they more "analytic." More recent reviews of research on gender differences have arrived at similar conclusions (Blakemore, Berenbaum, & Liben, 2009; Ruble, Martin, & Berenbaum, 2006).

By the time children reach preschool, they know which type of behavior is expected of their sex (Blakemore, Berenbaum, & Liben, 2009; Serbin, Powlishta, & Gulko, 1993). Several years ago, a little boy in my preschool class who was pretending to iron in the housekeeping corner was told by his friend, "Daddies don't iron!" As children enter elementary school, their gender roles become more restrictive (Ruble, Martin, & Berenbaum, 2006). They play with children of the same sex, thus learning "gender-appropriate" games (the boys tend to play games involving running or throwing a ball at recess; the girls tend to stay close to the teacher, talking or playing games such as jump rope or hopscotch). Because of their cognitive development, they are also becoming more aware of potential models of their sex with whom to identify. These models will be examined next to understand their influences on gender-role socialization.

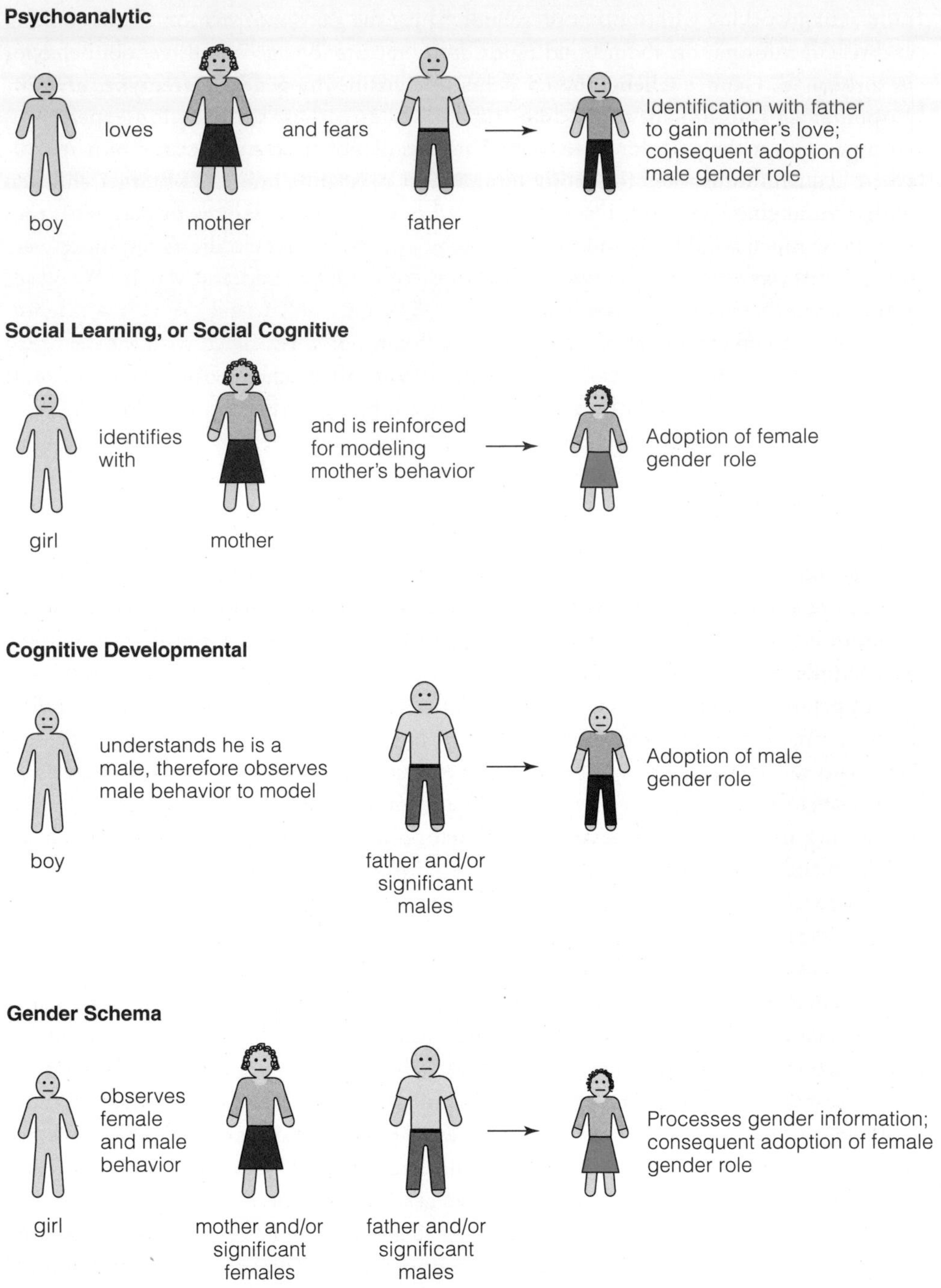

FIGURE 12.4 Theories of Gender Role Development

Influences on Gender-Role Development

Gender-role socialization takes place in the microsystems of family, peer group, school, community, and media.

Do mothers and fathers treat sons and daughters differently?

Family

According to researchers, mothers and fathers do treat sons and daughters differently (Blakemore, Berenbaum, & Liben, 2009; Leaper, 2000). Family dynamics and experiences are linked to individual differences in boys' and girls' gendered behavior (McHale, Crouter, & Whiteman, 2003). Studies show that parents describe their newborn sons as stronger, more coordinated, and more alert than daughters; and their newborn daughters as smaller, softer, and more fragile than sons (Huston, 1983; Sweeney & Bradbard, 1988).

Fathers, in particular, engage in more rough-and-tumble play with sons and more cuddly play with daughters (Leaper & Bigler, 2011; Lytton & Romney, 1991). Parents buy different toys for their sons and daughters (Blakemore, Berenbaum, & Liben, 2009; O'Brien & Huston, 1985; Ruble, Martin, & Berenbaum, 2006). For example, males are given trucks, war toys, and sports equipment; girls are given dolls, dollhouses, and books. Mothers and fathers even communicate differently to sons and daughters, using more directive and supportive language with girls than with boys (Ruble, Martin, & Berenbaum, 2006).

Throughout childhood, parents encourage males in active, gross motor, and manipulative play; females are encouraged in passive feminine role taking and fine motor play, with fathers being more stereotypical than mothers (Huston, 1983; Leaper, 2000). Males are also allowed to take risks (climb trees) and are left unsupervised more often and earlier than females (Basow, 2008; Blakemore, Berenbaum, & Liben, 2009). Finally, parents exert more achievement and independence demands on males while providing help more readily for females (Basow, 2008; Leaper, 2000).

Through observed interactions of fathers and mothers with sons and daughters, it has repeatedly been demonstrated that fathers are the more influential gender-role socialization agent (Caldera, Huston, & O'Brien, 1989; Lamb, 2004; Ruble, Martin, & Berenbaum, 2006). For example, fathers' and mothers' reactions to preschool children's choice of toys were observed. Toys available were traditionally feminine (doll furniture, pots and pans) and masculine (cars, trucks, trains). Studies (Blakemore, Berenbaum, & Liben, 2009; Langlois & Downs, 1980; Lytton & Romney, 1991) found that fathers, more than mothers, chose different kinds of toys for boys and girls and encouraged play that they considered gender appropriate and discouraged play they considered gender inappropriate. More specifically, the fathers rewarded their children by approving, helping, and joining in the play more often for play with gender-appropriate toys than for play with gender-inappropriate toys, and they discouraged play with gender-inappropriate toys more than play with gender-appropriate toys. Mothers encouraged both boys and girls to play with toys traditionally considered appropriate for girls. Mothers also tended to discourage both boys and girls from playing with "masculine" toys.

In addition, fathers engage in more physical play (tickling, chasing, playing ball) with both sons and daughters, whereas mothers spend more time in caretaking and nurturing activities (MacDonald & Parke, 1986). Apparently, this differential interaction with children enables mothers to become more, and fathers less, sensitive to individual needs of children (Lamb, 2004). Further, compared to mothers, fathers give more evaluative feedback of approval and disapproval (Fagot, 1995). Thus, fathers generally appear to be the more playful, less sensitive, more critical parent in terms of gender-role socialization.

When mothers are employed outside the home and fathers participate in child care, fathers' nontraditional activities influence their children's attitudes about gender-role stereotypes (Ruble, Martin, & Berenbaum, 2006). Although mothers employed outside the home still perform most child care and housekeeping chores, husbands of employed wives participate more than husbands of nonemployed wives (Hoffman, 2000). Thus, children whose mothers are employed have less stereotypical role models than those whose fathers are "breadwinners" and mothers are "breadbakers" (Gardner & LaBrecque, 1986).

The sibling sex constellation—presence of sisters and brothers, and their birth order—influences children's gender-role socialization, especially in traditional families (McHale, Crouter, & Whiteman, 1999; Rust et al., 2000). Boys with older brothers were found to be more masculine than boys with older sisters; boys without siblings scored in between the other two groups in masculine traits. The findings for girls were parallel. Not only do sisters and brothers model and reinforce gender-role behavior in their younger siblings, but their differential treatment according to sex by the parents has an impact on younger children's gender schemata.

What about families with same-sex parents? Research shows that children with gay or lesbian parents exhibit conventional gender norms (Patterson, 2006).

In sum, individual differences in sex typing are influenced by biology, culture, paternal involvement, maternal work status, sex typing of parental roles within the home, and sibling sex constellation (Blakemore, Berenbaum, & Liben, 2009; Lippa, 2005; Serbin, Powlishta, & Gulko, 1993).

How greatly do peers influence stereotyped gender behavior?

Peers

Peers become progressively more influential as gender-role socializing agents as children get older (Leaper & Bigler, 2011; Lippa, 2005). Peers begin to exert influence during preschool and become increasingly important during elementary school and high school. For example, peers encourage both boys and girls to play with gender-appropriate toys and actively punish (ridicule and tease) play with toys considered appropriate for the opposite gender, especially among boys (Blakemore, Berenbaum, & Liben, 2009; Fagot, 1984; Martin, 1989). Children and adolescents try to do what they perceive to be "cool" to gain acceptance and status among their peers. Preadolescent boys gain status on the basis of athletic ability and toughness, whereas girls' status relates to physical appearance and social skills (Basow & Rubin, 1999; Pollack, 1999; Ruble, Martin, & Berenbaum, 2006).

Sex segregation begins in the preschool years and intensifies during the school years. This can be observed cross-culturally in both boys and girls (Rogoff, 2003; Whiting & Edwards, 1988). Sex-segregated play groups value different behaviors for girls and boys (Blakemore, Berenbaum, & Liben, 2009; Liben & Bigler, 2002; Maccoby, 1998). Girls tend to enjoy mutual play and use conflict mitigation strategies, whereas boys tend to play more roughly and use physical assertion to resolve conflicts.

The result of sex segregation is that boys and girls tend to grow up in different peer environments—in other words, different subcultures (Leaper & Bigler, 2011; Maccoby, 1998). In separate studies, sociologists Janet Lever (1978) and Barrie Thorne (1993), found significant differences in the play of boys' and girls' peer groups. Lever observed fifth-grade children, mostly European American and middle class, in three schools. She discovered that boys' play was more complex than girls' play on all of the following dimensions and criteria.

- *Size of group.* Is it large or small?
- *Role differentiation.* Do the players have the same role, as in checkers, or different roles, as in baseball?
- *Player interdependence.* Does one player's move affect another's, as in chess or tennis, or not, as in darts or hopscotch?
- *Explicitness of goals.* Is playing merely a cooperative venture with no winners or end point, as in "playing house," or is the purpose playing for a goal, such as scoring the most points, or until a certain end point is reached (nine innings, for example)?
- *Number and specificity of rules.* Are there a few vague rules, as in tag, or many specific ones, as in baseball?
- *Team formation.* Does the play require teams?

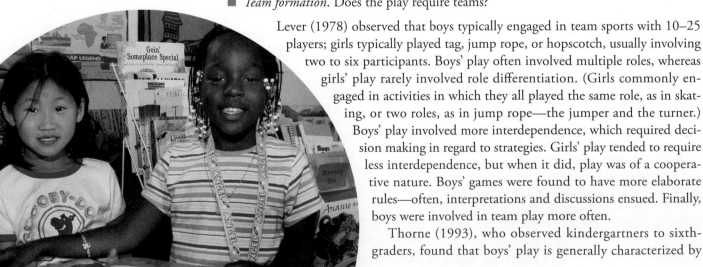

Peers influencing each other's behavior.

Cengage Learning

Lever (1978) observed that boys typically engaged in team sports with 10–25 players; girls typically played tag, jump rope, or hopscotch, usually involving two to six participants. Boys' play often involved multiple roles, whereas girls' play rarely involved role differentiation. (Girls commonly engaged in activities in which they all played the same role, as in skating, or two roles, as in jump rope—the jumper and the turner.) Boys' play involved more interdependence, which required decision making in regard to strategies. Girls' play tended to require less interdependence, but when it did, play was of a cooperative nature. Boys' games were found to have more elaborate rules—often, interpretations and discussions ensued. Finally, boys were involved in team play more often.

Thorne (1993), who observed kindergartners to sixth-graders, found that boys' play is generally characterized by larger groups, less proximity to adults, more public play, more fighting and physical contact, more dominance attempts, and the establishment of a hierarchical "pecking order." Girls' play is generally characterized by smaller, more intimate groups, closer proximity to adults, a strong convention of turn taking, and more mutuality in play and conversation.

The significance of peer group play is that it socializes individuals for adult roles in society, according to the particular skills that are reinforced. According to Lever (1978), boys' play tends to reinforce the ability to deal with diverse actions simultaneously, coordinate actions in order to foster group cohesiveness and work for collective goals, engage in competition, cope with impersonal rules, and engage in strategic thinking. Girls' play, on the other hand, tends to reinforce cooperation, spontaneity, imagination, flexibility, and empathy.

What socialization outcomes result from girls' participation in team sports? A study by Shaffer and Wittes (2006) found a positive relationship between girls' precollege sport participation and positive body image, physical competencies, and gender flexibility, which led to greater self-esteem. Another study (Miller et al., 1998) found that athletic participation influenced the status of girls and their relationships with boys. Specifically, athletic participation was associated with lower frequency of heterosexual intercourse, fewer partners, and later onset.

School

How does the school contribute to sex-typing?

Schools provide a number of gender-related messages to children, some intentional and some unintentional (Ruble, Martin, & Berenbaum, 2006; Sadker & Zittleman, 2009).

When I attended public school in the 1950s, there were two entrance doors, one marked "Girls" and one marked "Boys." At recess, the girls played jump rope, and the boys either ran around chasing and hitting each other or played ball. When the teacher blew the whistle, everyone lined up, the girls in one line, the boys in another; each line then entered the school building through the appropriate door. Why differentiate? We all knew which sex we were. Surprisingly, many school activities are still sex-segregated. Schools have traditionally treated males and females differently—through portrayals of gender roles in textbooks, through different course requirements (for example, boys took shop and girls took home economics), through treatment by teachers and counselors, and even, subtly, through the uneven sex distribution on the staff.

Men are disproportionately represented in positions of power and administration, whereas women are often teachers, particularly in the early grades. Only in older grades are children likely to have many male teachers, and these are often in male-typical classes such as mathematics and science (Ruble, Martin, & Berenbaum, 2006, pp. 902–903).

The passage of federal legislation (Title IX Education Amendment) in 1972 outlawed discrimination on the basis of sex. As a result, textbooks are reviewed for sexual bias, courses and extracurricular activities are open to males and females, and teachers and counselors must channel students into higher educational programs or occupations on the basis of individual competencies rather than what was traditionally acceptable for the sexes.

Despite Title IX and the greater awareness of how children develop gender-role attitudes, teachers respond differently to boys and girls at every level of schooling (Blakemore, Berenbaum, & Liben, 2009; Ruble, Martin, & Berenbaum, 2006). Research in preschools (Fagot, 1984) confirmed that more teacher attention was given to boys for achievement-related behaviors and to girls for compliance. Preschool teachers encourage gender-appropriate play and discourage gender inappropriate play. Serbin and her colleagues (Serbin et al., 1973; Serbin, Powlishta, & Gulko, 1993) found that teachers tend to respond negatively to the aggressive behavior of boys and positively to the proximity-seeking behavior of girls. Other studies (Sadker, Sadker, & Klein, 1991) revealed some differences in how elementary and high school teachers view male and female students.

"Good" male students were described by the teachers as active, adventurous, aggressive, assertive, curious, energetic, enterprising, frank, independent, and inventive. "Good" female students were described as appreciative, calm, conscientious, considerate, cooperative, mannerly, poised, sensitive, dependable, efficient, mature, obliging, and thorough. Such attitudes may influence the way teachers interact with students and may even influence the way the students view their own gender roles.

Sadker and colleagues (Sadker & Sadker, 1994; Sadker & Zittleman, 2009) report that from elementary to graduate school, boys are given not only more teacher attention, but more encouragement to learn. If a girl gave an incorrect answer when asked, the teacher called on someone else. If a boy gave an incorrect response, he was prompted to discover the right answer, then praised. When a girl gave a correct answer when asked, it was accepted with an "OK." If a girl called out a correct answer without being asked, she was likely to be reprimanded for talking out of turn; if a boy did the same, his answer was likely to be accepted. Thus, teachers tend to socialize boys to be active, assertive learners and girls to be quiet, passive learners.

What role does the community play in gender-role development?

Community

The community influences gender-role development through its attitudes regarding what is appropriate behavior for males and females and the gender-role models it provides with whom children can identify. The community's attitudes on gender roles affect what behaviors it reinforces and punishes in children. Comments like "That's unladylike" or "Go and stick up for yourself like a man" make a big impression on children. Sometimes community attitudes are expressed by the language used to describe males and females. Are females described by their appearance and men by their actions? Are occupational roles gender-free ("mail carrier," "salesperson")?

If the community has stereotypical attitudes—that women are nurturant and men are problem solvers, for example—the assignment of occupations to one or the other gender will be affected. Today, women still dominate occupations that involve service, nurturing, or teaching; men dominate such occupations as engineering, architecture, law, and medicine, which all involve problem solving (Watt, 2008). Such attitudes, together with the social visibility of men and women in their jobs, affect children's perceptions of and expectations for themselves.

The U.S. government has enforced equal opportunity laws, thereby opening up previously restricted fields to women. However, despite concentrated research and important legislative milestones on gender equality over the past quarter-century, gender-related disparities in science, technology, engineering, and math (referred to in studies as STEM) careers persist into the 21st century. Also, inequities remain in academics, salaries, leadership roles, and opportunities for advancement (Basow, 2008; U.S. Department of Commerce, 2011; Watt, 2008).

Culture and religious orientation influence children's perceptions and expectations for their gender. For example, in some families females are expected to marry, carry on domestic duties, and bear children even if they work (Sue, 1989). In some families women are traditionally subordinate to men (Uba, 1999). Cultural and religious orientation, as well as socioeconomic status, influences gender-role expectations, as exemplified in the career choices of high school seniors (Blustein, 2008).

In conclusion, to the extent that a child grows up in a *restrictive* gendered community world with strong pressures toward conformity, that child will likely place importance on behaving accordingly. In contrast, to the extent that a child grows up in a *flexible* gendered community emphasizing individual choice, that child is less likely to conform to stereotypical gender behavior (Eccles & Bryan, 1994; Lippa, 2005).

This adolescent boy exhibits nonstereotyped gender role behavior by reading to a group of preschool children.

Michelle Bridwell/PhotoEdit

IN PRACTICE

How Do You Determine the Type of Gender-Role Models Provided by the Community?

- In general, do mothers/fathers in the community stay home to raise their families, or are they employed outside the home?
- In what activities do most mothers/fathers in the community engage?
- Do children have an opportunity to observe people in their occupations?
- Do men and women who have various occupations come to school and talk to the children?
- Who occupies the positions of leadership in the community (government, church, service organizations, political organizations)?
- In what kinds of activities do boys and girls participate in the community outside of school?
- How are community jobs labeled?

How do the mass media contribute to sex typing?

Mass Media

Screen Media

The mass media affect gender-role development by the way the appearance and behavior of male and female characters are portrayed, as well as by the advertising messages. For example, not only do males appear with greater frequency on TV than females, they are also portrayed in a greater variety of occupations than are females and have higher-status jobs (Perse, 2001; Signorielli, 2007). Even though women in commercials are increasingly being shown as having diverse occupations, they are still portrayed as experts on food products, laundry soap, and beauty aids (Signorielli, 2007).

Children's programs are more gender-typed than adult programs. Males outnumber females in all types of programming, even educational (Signorielli, 2007). The personality characteristics of males and females, even though improved, continue to be stereotypic, with women presented as being emotional, romantic, and domestic, and men presented as being intelligent, technical, and aggressive (Comstock & Scharrer, 2007).

Although TV and movies have some influence on children's sex typing, children's prior attitudes about gender roles influence the impact of what they attend to. Children with highly stereotyped attitudes focus on traditional role portrayals, whereas children with more flexible attitudes attend equally well to both traditional and nontraditional role portrayals (Comstock & Scharrer, 2007).

While portrayals of male and female behavior in the screen media serve as role models for children, whether the messages about gender will actually be cultivated in children as they develop depends on the total media experience as well as the socialization influences of significant others regarding appropriate gender behavior. The American Psychological Association (APA, 2007b) is concerned that media messages are the predominating influence on female behavior. Their report on the sexualization of girls concluded that the proliferation of sexualized images of girls and young women in advertising, merchandising, and media is harming girls' self-image and healthy development; specifically, body dissatisfaction, depression, low self-esteem, and diminished perception of academic achievement and extracurricular activities as leading to later empowering life opportunities. Also of concern is the damaging effect of sexualization on relationships with other girls and with boys. When girls perceive their value is based on appearance and ability to attract boys, they tend to view other girls as competition, thereby interfering with potential friendships. When boys perceive girls' value to be based on appearance and sexually attractive behavior, they tend to expect a physical relationship.

Print Media

Books, magazines, and newspapers also influence gender-role socialization by the way in which males and females are stereotyped. Although improvements have occurred in children's literature regarding gender stereotyping, girls are still depicted as dependent and needing help more often than boys. Also, females are shown in relatively limited roles (Dickman & Murnen, 2004).

Males still dominate the world of picture books and are generally presented in more independent, varied, and exciting roles, using productive items; females are generally presented in more dependent, helping, and pleasing roles, using household objects (Blakemore, Berenbaum, & Liben, 2009; Gooden & Gooden, 2001).

Content analyses of many feature articles and advertisements in contemporary magazines, such as *Seventeen*, *Sports Illustrated*, *Teen*, *Time*, *Ebony*, *Newsweek*, and *Vogue*, have found that they contain sex-stereotyped messages, especially about appearance (Blakemore, Berenbaum, & Liben, 2009; Strasburger & Wilson, 2002). Articles for females deal with depending on someone else to solve personal problems, attracting guys, and being appearance-conscious shoppers. Articles for males deal with sports, hobbies, business/finance, and sex.

Audio Media

Do audio media contribute to stereotyped attitudes about male and female roles and sexual behavior because of their lyrics and videos, or are young people who already have those attitudes attracted to music genres that confirm their beliefs? Although the influence of popular music on gender-role socialization needs more research, we do know that stereotypes about men's and women's behavior are visible in rock music videos (Strasburger & Wilson, 2008). Males are depicted as sexually aggressive, rational, demanding, and adventuresome. Females are portrayed as emotional, deceitful, illogical, frivolous, dependent, and passive. One of the most popular themes in popular music is still romantic love (Roberts & Christenson, 2001). However, rock music videos also show violence against women and women as sex objects (Strasburger & Wilson, 2008). In an interview for *Newsweek* (October 9, 2000), rapper Ja Rule said, "What else can you rap about but money, sex, murder, or pimping? There isn't a whole lot else going on in our world."

A study of 12- to 14-year-olds regarding their exposure to sexual content in music, movies, television, and magazines over a two-year period showed an increase in their reported sexual activity, thereby increasing the risk of early sexual intercourse (Brown et al., 2006).

Interactive and Multimedia

A critical issue regarding the influence of the Internet on sex typing and behavior is the pervasiveness of sexual content in ads, e-mail messages, pop-ups, and the accessibility of pornographic websites (APA, 2007b; Strasburger & Wilson, 2008). Children may be exposed to information before they are mature enough to understand it and that it conflicts with family values.

Gender preferences in video games reinforce stereotypical behavior. Boys find games with action and violence, as well as sports and strategy, more appealing; girls like games of skill or luck, like puzzles or cards (Comstock & Scharrer, 2007). Video games are also a source of information for children and adolescents for what behaviors and attitudes are considered appropriately masculine or feminine. A study (Beasley & Standley, 2002) examined the way that males and females were clothed (or unclothed) in 47 randomly selected games from the Nintendo 64 and Sony PlayStation gaming systems. Only 13.74 percent of all the characters were females and the majority of the female characters wore clothing that exposed more skin than the male characters.

Summary

- Self-regulation, or self-control, refers to the ability to regulate one's impulses, behavior, and/or emotions until an appropriate time, place, or object is available for expression. Self-regulatory behavior includes the ability to delay gratification, sustain attention to a task, and plan and self-monitor a goal-directed activity.
- Antisocial behavior includes any behavior that harms other people, such as aggression, violence, and crime.
- The major theories explaining the causes of aggression are biological (evolution, genetics), social cognitive (learning, information processing), sociocultural, and ecological.
- Aggression can be inhibited by organizing the environment, establishing standards and consequences for behavior, providing alternative ways of solving problems, providing positive role models, and encouraging discussion and communication.
- Prosocial behavior includes any behavior that benefits other people, such as altruism, sharing, and cooperation.
- The theories explaining the causes of altruism are biological (evolution, genetics), learning (reinforcement, modeling, instruction, learning by doing), cognitive developmental (perspective-taking reasoning, parenting style), and sociocultural.
- Experiences in the contexts of family, school, peer group, community, and media influence the development of prosocial behavior.
- Morals encompass an individual's evaluation of what is right and wrong. They involve acceptance of rules that govern one's behavior toward others. Morality involves feeling, reasoning, and behavior.
- One's moral code develops through social interaction and reflects one's level of intellectual development, as well as one's attitudes. It involves awareness of alternatives, the ability to take another's perspective, and the ability to make judgments, as well as feelings about conformity and autonomy.
- As children develop, their morality changes. Infants and toddlers do not distinguish right from wrong. Preschoolers and school-agers consider only the act, not the intent. Adolescents consider intent as well as situation.
- Important theories of moral development are Piaget's (heteronomous and autonomous morality), Kohlberg's (preconventional, conventional, postconventional morality), and Gilligan's (morality of care versus morality of justice).
- At the lower moral development levels, people act out of concern for personal consequences; at the middle levels, they act out of concern for what others think; at the higher levels, they act to avoid self-condemnation.
- Influences on moral development are categorized as situational and individual contexts.
- Gender roles, or sex types, are the qualities that an individual understands as characterizing males and females in his or her culture.
- The four main theories of gender-role development are psychoanalytic (feelings), social learning or social cognitive (behaving), cognitive developmental (reasoning), and gender schema (information processing).
- Males and females behave differently. Males tend to be more aggressive and exhibit greater visual–spatial ability, and females tend to exhibit greater verbal ability. Socialization practices maximize gender differences; girls and boys are channeled into sex-typed behaviors valued by their culture.
- Parenting practices and sibling sex constellation influence the gender-role development of both boys and girls.
- Peers exert strong pressure to conform to traditionally stereotypical gender roles via modeling, reinforcement, punishment, and sex-segregated activities.
- The school, by its differential treatment of males and females, has maximized gender differences occurring through teachers' responses to boys and girls as well as through gender-role models in textbooks.
- The community's attitudes regarding gender roles and the models provided influence children's sex typing.
- The media (screen, print, audio, interactive, and multimedia) still tend toward stereotypical portrayals of gender roles.

Activity

PURPOSE To analyze changes in children's social behavior over time.

1. Separately observe a group (more than two) of preschoolers (ages 3–5) and a group of school-agers (ages 6–12) in a "free play" activity.
2. Record and compare incidents of prosocial (at least one) and antisocial (at least one) activity for the children in each group—antecedents, behavior, consequences.
   a. What event, item, or interaction preceded the prosocial or antisocial activity (antecedent)?

b. How did the children involved act (behavior)? Describe physical and verbal behavior.
c. What were the outcomes for all involved (consequences)?

3. Analyze similarities and differences in how preschoolers and school-agers interact with one another in a "free play" setting.
4. What factors, other than age, do you think were involved in influencing their behavior?

Related Readings

Damon, W. (2008). *The path to purpose: Helping our children find calling in life.* New York: Free Press.

Gilligan, C. (1982). *In a different voice: Psychological theory and women's development.* Cambridge, MA: Harvard University Press.

Lippa, R. A. (2005). *Gender, nature, and nurture* (2nd ed.). Mahwah, NJ: Lawrence Erlbaum.

Kimmell, M.S. (2000). *The gendered society.* New York: Oxford University Press.

Mussen, P. H., & Eisenberg-Berg, N. (1977). *Roots of caring, sharing, and helping: The development of prosocial behavior in children.* San Francisco: Freeman.

Nucci, L. P. (2008). *Nice is not enough: A teacher's guide to education in the moral domain.* Columbus, OH: Merrill.

Olweus, D. (1993). *Bullying at school: What we know and what we can do.* Cambridge, MA: Blackwell.

Slaby, R. G., et al. (1995). *Early violence prevention: Tools for teachers of young children.* Washington, DC: National Association for the Education of Young Children.

Staub, E. (2003). *The psychology of good and evil: Why children, adults, and groups help and harm others.* New York: Cambridge University Press.

Thorne, B. (1993). *Gender play: Girls and boys in school.* New Brunswick, NJ: Rutgers University Press.

Turiel, E. (2002). *The culture of morality: Social development, context, and conflict.* Cambridge, UK: Cambridge University Press.

Resources

Jigsaw Classroom—cooperative learning technique to reduce conflict among diverse children, promote better learning, and improve student motivation

http://www.jigsaw.org

Gender Public Advocacy Coalition—classroom communities and workplaces that are safe for everyone regardless of expectations of masculinity or femininity

http://www.sadker.org

Character Education Partnership—leading the nation in helping schools develop people of good character for a just and compassionate society

http://www.character.org

Glossary

abuse maltreatment that includes physical abuse, sexual abuse, and psychological or emotional abuse
accommodation a Piagetian term for mental adaptation to one's environment by reconciling differences of experiences
accountability making schools and teachers responsible for student learning or achievement outcomes
achieved status social class, rank, or position determined by education, occupation, income, and/or place of residence
achievement motivation, or mastery orientation the motivation to achieve mastery of challenging tasks
adaptation the modification of an organism or its behavior to make it more fit for existence under the conditions of its environment
advocacy speaking or writing in support of a person, a group, or a cause
affective having to do with feelings or emotions
aggression unprovoked attack, fight, or quarrel
alcoholism a chronic, progressive, and potentially fatal disease characterized by excessive tolerance for alcohol and by physical dependence and/or pathologic organ changes
altruism voluntary actions that are intended to help or benefit another person or group of people without the actor's anticipation of external rewards
antisocial behavior any behavior that harms other people, such as aggression, violence, and crime
apprenticeship a process in which a novice is guided by an expert to participate in and master tasks
ascribed status social class, rank, or position determined by family lineage, gender, birth order, or skin color
assimilation a Piagetian term for mental adaptation to one's environment by incorporating experiences
assumptive reality a theory about reality assumed to be true without examining or evaluating contradictory data
attachment an affectional tie that one person forms to another person, binding them together in space and enduring over time
attitude a tendency to respond positively (favorably) or negatively (unfavorably) to certain persons, objects, or situations
attributions explanations for one's performance
authentic assessment evaluation based on real performance, rather than test performance, showing mastery of a task
authoritarian parenting a style of parent-centered parenting characterized by unquestioning obedience to authority
authoritative parenting a style of democratic parenting in which authority is based on competence or expertise
autocracy a society in which one person has unlimited power over others
autonomous morality Piaget's stage of moral development in which children realize that rules are arbitrary agreements that can be changed by those who have to follow them
behavior what one does or how one acts in response to a stimulus
behaviorism the theory that observed behavior, rather than what exists in the mind, provides the only valid data for psychology
binuclear family family pattern in which children are part of two homes and two family groups
bioecological refers to the role organisms play in shaping their environment over time
bullying aggressive behavior intended to cause harm or distress that occurs repeatedly over time in an unbalanced relationship of power or strength
Caldecott Medal award given yearly for the most distinguished picture book for children
care moral perspective views people in terms of their connectedness with others; others' welfare is intrinsically connected to one's own
charter school a school, which is authorized and funded by a public school district, formed by a group of parents, teachers, or other community members with a shared educational philosophy
child advocacy the process of sensitizing individuals and groups to the unmet needs of children and to society's obligation to provide a positive response to those needs
chronosystem temporal changes in ecological systems producing new conditions that affect development
classism the differential treatment of people because of their class background and the reinforcing of those differences through values and practices of societal institutions
cliques friends who view themselves as mutually connected and do things together
cognitive conceit Elkind's term for children in Piaget's stage of concrete operations who put too much faith in their reasoning ability and cleverness
cognitively oriented curriculum a curriculum that attempts to blend the virtues of purposeful teaching with open-ended, child-initiated activities
collectivism emphasis on interdependent relations, social responsibilities, and the well-being of the group
community a group of people sharing fellowship and common interests; a group of people living in the same geographic area who are bound together politically and economically
community ecology the psychological and practical relationships between humans and their social, as well as physical, environment

competence refers to a pattern of effective adaptation to one's environment; it involves behavior that is socially responsible, independent, friendly, cooperative, dominant, achievement-oriented, and purposeful

competitive goal structure students working against each other to achieve goals that only a few students can attain

concrete operations the third stage in Piaget's theory of cognitive development (ages 7–11), in which the child can apply logical, systematic principles to specific experiences, but cannot distinguish between assumptions or hypotheses and facts or reality

contagion the phenomenon in which an individual exposed to a suggestion will act on it

conventional level Kohlberg's stages of moral reasoning in which the individual can look beyond personal consequences and consider others' perspectives

cooperative goal structure students working together to accomplish shared goals

crowds loosely organized reference groups of cliques

cultural assimilation the process whereby a minority (subordinate) cultural group takes on the characteristics of the majority (dominant) cultural group

cultural pluralism mutual appreciation and understanding of various cultures and coexistence in society of different languages, religious beliefs, and lifestyles

culture the learned, or acquired, behavior, including knowledge, beliefs, art, morals, law, customs, and traditions, that is characteristic of the social environment in which an individual grows up

curriculum the goals and objections of an educational program, the teacher's role, the equipment and materials, the space arrangement, the kinds of activities, and the way they are scheduled

deductive reasoning reasoning from a general principle to a specific case, or from a premise to a logical conclusion

democracy a society in which those ruled have equal power with those who rule

demographics statistical characteristics of human populations, such as age, income, race

desensitization the gradual reduction in response to a stimulus after repeated exposure

developmental appropriateness a curriculum that involves understanding children's normal growth patterns and individual differences

developmental interaction curriculum a curriculum that is individualized in relation to each child's stage of development while providing many opportunities for children to interact with peers and adults

developmental task a task that lies between an individual need and a societal demand

direct instruction curriculum a curriculum based on behaviorist principles

disability reduction in the functioning of a particular body part or organ, or its absence

discipline involves punishment, correction, and training to develop self-control

ecology the science of interrelationships between organisms and their environments

economics the production, distribution, and consumption of goods and services

egalitarian family family in which both sides of the extended family are regarded as equal

egocentrism the cognitive inability to look at the world from any point of view other than one's own

empowerment enabling individuals to have control over resources affecting them

equilibrium a Piagetian term for the state of balance between assimilation and accommodation, thereby allowing knowledge to be incorporated

ethnicity an ascribed attribute of membership in a group in which members identify themselves by national origin, culture, race, or religion

exosystem settings in which children do not actually participate, but which affect them in one of their microsystems (for example, parents' jobs, the school board, the city council)

experience-dependent the neural connections that develop in response to experience

experience-expectant the neural connections that develop under genetic influence, independent of experience, activity, or stimulation

extended day care nonparental care provided for children before or after school hours or during vacations

extended family relatives of the nuclear family who are economically and emotionally dependent on each other

external locus of control perception that others or outside forces are responsible for one's fate

extinction the gradual disappearance of a learned behavior following the removal of the reinforcement

family any two or more related people living in one household

family of orientation the family into which one is born

family of procreation the family that develops when one marries and has children

feedback evaluative information, both positive and negative, about one's behavior

fixation a Freudian term referring to arrested development

formal operations the fourth stage in Piaget's theory of cognitive development (ages 11 and up), in which the child can think logically about abstract ideas and hypotheses as well as concrete facts

gang a group of people who form an alliance for a common purpose and engage in unlawful or criminal activity

gemeinschaft communal, cooperative, close, intimate, and informal interpersonal relationships

gender role the qualities that an individual understands to characterize males and females in his or her culture

generativity interest in establishing and guiding the next generation

genotype the total composite of hereditary instructions coded in the genes at the moment of conception

gesellschaft associative, practical, objective, and formal interpersonal relationships

goodness-of-fit accommodation of parenting styles to children's temperaments

guidance involves direction, demonstration, supervision, and influence

handicap something that hampers a person; a disadvantage, a hindrance

handicapism assumptions and practices that promote the differential and unequal treatment of people because they are different physically, mentally, or behaviorally
heteronomous morality Piaget's stage of moral development in which children think of rules as moral absolutes that cannot be changed
high-context macrosystem culture generally characterized by intuitiveness, emotionality, cooperation, group identity, and tradition
humanism a system of beliefs concerned with the interests and ideals of humans rather than of the natural or spiritual world
ideology concepts about human life and behavior
imaginary audience the beliefs that others are as concerned with one's behavior and appearance as one is oneself
impairment physical damage or deterioration
incest sexual relations between persons closely related
inclusion the educational philosophy that all children are entitled to participate fully in their school and community
individualism emphasis on individual fulfillment and choice
individualized education program (IEP) a form of communication between school and family, developed by the group of people (teacher, parent, and other involved personnel) responsible for the education of a child with special needs
individualized goal structure one student's achievement of the goal is unrelated to other students' achievement of that goal
inductive reasoning reasoning from particular facts or individual cases to a general conclusion
information processing the way an individual attends to, perceives, interprets, remembers, and acts on events or situations
internal locus of control perception that one is responsible for one's own fate
justice moral perspective emphasizes the rights of the individual; when individual rights conflict, equitable rules of justice must prevail
laissez-faire a policy of letting people do as they please; permissive
latchkey children children who carry their own key and let themselves into their homes
learned helpless orientation the perception, acquired through negative experiences, that effort has no affect on outcomes
learner-directed curriculum a curriculum in which the learning activities emerge from individual interests and teacher guidance
learning style a consistent pattern of behavior and performance by which an individual approaches educational experiences
literacy the ability to communicate through reading and writing
locus of control one's attribution of performance, or perception of responsibility for success or failure; may be internal or external
low-context macrosystem culture generally characterized by rationality, practicality, competition, individuality, and progress
macrosystem the society and subculture to which the developing person belongs, with particular reference to the belief systems, lifestyles, patterns of social interaction, and life changes
magnet school a public school that offers special educational programs, such as science, music, or performing arts, and draws students from different neighborhoods by choice
maltreatment intentional harm to or endangerment of a child
marriage a legal contract with certain rights and obligations
mass media newspapers, magazines, books, radio, television, movies, videos, and other means of communication that reach large audiences via an impersonal medium between the sender and the receiver
mastery motivation the inborn motive to explore, understand, and control one's environment
matriarchal family family in which the mother has formal authority and dominance
maturation developmental changes associated with the biological process of aging
melting pot the idea that society should socialize diverse groups to blend into a common culture
mesosystem linkages and interrelationships between two or more of a person's microsystems (for example, home and school, school and community)
microsystem activities and relationships with significant others experienced by a developing person in a particular small setting such as family, school, peer group, or community
modeling a form of imitative learning that occurs by observing another person (the model) perform a behavior and experience its consequence
modern society a society that looks to the present for ways to behave and is thus responsive to change
Montessori curriculum a curriculum based on individual self-directed learning with the teacher as facilitator; materials provide exercises in daily living, sensory development, and academic development
morality of constraint behavior based on respect for persons in authority
morality of cooperation behavior based on mutual understanding between equals
morals an individual's evaluation of what is right and wrong
motives needs or emotions that cause a person to act
negative reinforcement the termination of an unpleasant condition following a desired response
neglect maltreatment involving abandonment, lack of supervision, improper feeding, lack of adequate medical or dental care, inappropriate dress, uncleanliness, and lack of safety
Newbery Medal award given yearly for the most distinguished contribution to American literature for children
nonparental child care (day care) the care given to children by persons other than parents during the parts of the day that parents are absent
norms rules, patterns, or standards that express cultural values and reflect how individuals are supposed to behave
nuclear family a family consisting of a husband and wife and their children
operant producing an effect
operational definition contains terms that are identifiable and can be researched
parenting the implementation of a series of decisions about the socialization of children
patriarchal family family in which the father has formal authority and dominance
peers individuals who are of approximately the same gender, age, and social status and who share interests
perception a biological construct that involves interpretation of stimuli from the brain

permissive parenting a style of child-centered parenting characterized by a lack of directives or authority
personal agency the realization that one's actions cause outcomes
physical abuse maltreatment involving deliberate harm to the child's body
play behavior enjoyed for its own sake
political ideology theories pertaining to government
positive reinforcement a reward, or pleasant consequence, given for desired behavior
postconventional level Kohlberg's stages of moral reasoning in which the individual considers and weighs the values behind various consequences from various points of view
preconventional level Kohlberg's stages of moral reasoning in which the individual considers and weighs the personal consequences of the behavior
prejudice an attitude involving prejudgment; the application of a previously formed judgment to some person, object, or situation
preoperational the second stage in Piaget's theory of cognitive development (ages 2–7), in which the child uses symbols to represent objects, makes judgments based on appearances, and believes that everyone has the same viewpoint as he or she
preventive services programs that seek to lessen the stresses and strains of life resulting from social and technological changes and to avert problems
prosocial behavior behavior that benefits other people, such as altruism, sharing, and cooperation
Protestant ethic belief in individualism, thrift, self-sacrifice, efficiency, personal responsibility, and productivity
psychological or emotional abuse maltreatment involving a destructive pattern of continual attack by an adult on a child's development of self and social competence, including rejecting, isolating, terrorizing, ignoring, and corrupting
punishment physically or psychologically painful stimuli or the temporary withdrawal of pleasant stimuli when undesirable behavior occurs
reality testing testing assumptions against facts
reasoning giving explanations or causes for an act
rehabilitative services programs that enable or restore people's ability to participate in the community
reinforcement an object or event that is presented following a behavior and that serves to increase the likelihood that the behavior will occur again
religion a unified system of beliefs and practices relative to sacred things
resilience the ability to withstand and rebound from crisis or persistent challenges
risk endangerment; vulnerability to negative developmental outcomes
rites of passage rituals that signify changes in individuals' status as they move through the cycle of life
ritual a ceremonial observation of a prescribed rule or custom
routines repetitive acts or established procedures
school voucher a certificate issued by the federal government in the amount the local school district would normally spend on that child's education at his or her assigned public school, which parents can apply toward tuition at a private school or use for reimbursement of home school expenses
selective attention choosing stimuli from one's environment to notice, observe, and consider
self-concept an individual's perception of his/her identity as distinct from others
self-efficacy the belief that one can master a situation and produce positive outcomes
self-esteem the value one places on his/her identity
self-regulation the ability to control one's impulses, behavior, and/or emotions until an appropriate time, place, or object is available for expression
sensorimotor the first stage of Piaget's theory of cognitive development (ages 1½–2), in which the child uses senses and motor abilities to interact with the environment and understands only the here and now
sex typing classification into gender roles based on biological sex
sexual abuse maltreatment in which a person forces, tricks, or threatens a child in order to have sexual contact with him or her
shaping the systematic immediate reinforcement of successive approximations of the desired behavior until the desired behavior occurs and is maintained
social capital term referring to individual and communal time and energy (human resources) available for such things as social networking, personal recreation, community improvement, civic engagement, and other activities that create social bonds between individuals and groups
social cognition conceptions and reasoning about people, the self, relations between people, social groups' roles and rules, and the relation of such conceptions to social behavior
social competence behavior informed by an understanding of others' feelings and intentions, the ability to respond appropriately, and knowledge of the consequences of one's actions
social support resources (tangible, intellectual, social, emotional) provided by others in times of need
socialization the process by which individuals acquire the knowledge, skills, and character traits that enable them to participate as effective members of groups and society
sociocentrism the ability to understand and relate to the views and perspectives of others
socioeconomic status rank or position within a society, based on social and economic factors
sociometry techniques used to measure patterns of acceptance, neglect, and rejection among members of a group
sociotherapy an intervention to help children who have trouble making and keeping friends learn to relate to others
standard a level or grade of excellence regarded as a goal or a measure of adequacy
standardized tests tests in which an individual is compared to a norm on scientifically selected items
stereotype an oversimplified representation of members of a particular group
stress any demand that exceeds a person's ability to cope
supportive services programs that maintain the health, education, and welfare of the community
symbols acts or objects that have come to be generally accepted as standing for something else

tabula rasa the mind before impressions are recorded on it by experience; a blank slate

teacher-directed curriculum a curriculum in which the learning activities are planned by the teacher for all the children

temperament the innate characteristics that determine an individual's sensitivity to various experiences and responsiveness to patterns of social interaction

theory an organized set of statements that explains observations, integrates different facts or events, and predicts future outcomes

tradition customs, stories, and beliefs handed down from generation to generation

traditional society a society that relies on customs handed down from past generations as ways to behave

transductive reasoning reasoning from one particular fact or case to another similar fact or case

uninvolved parenting a style of insensitive, indifferent parenting with few demands or rules

values qualities or beliefs that are viewed as desirable or important

values clarification the process of discovering what is personally worthwhile or desirable in life

violence behaviors that intentionally threaten, attempt, or inflict harm on others

zone of proximal development (ZPD) Vygotsky's term for the space between what a learner can do independently and what he or she can do while participating with more capable others

References

Aaronson, L. S., & MacNee, C. L. (1989). Tobacco, alcohol and caffeine use during pregnancy. *Journal of Obstetrics, Gynecology and Neonatal Nursing, 18,* 279–287.

Aber, J. L., Brown, J. L., & Jones, S. M. (2003). Developmental trajectories toward violence in middle childhood: Course, demographic differences, and response to school-based intervention. *Developmental Psychology, 39*(2), 324–348.

Aboud, F. (1988). *Children and prejudice.* Cambridge, MA: Basil Blackwell.

Aboud, F. E., & Amato, M. (2001). Developmental and socialization influences on intergroup bias. In R. Brown & S. L. Gaertner (Eds.), *Blackwell handbook of social psychology: Intergroup processes* (Vol. 4). Oxford, UK: Blackwell.

Aboud, F. E., & Fenwick, V. (1999). Exploring and evaluating school-based interventions to reduce prejudice. *Journal of Social Issues, 55,* 767–785.

Ackerman, B. P., Brown, E. D., & Izard, C. E. (2004). The relations between persistent poverty and contextual risk and children's behavior in elementary school. *Developmental Psychology, 40,* 367–377.

Adams, D. M., & Hamm, M. (2006). *Media and literacy: Learning in the information age—issues, ideas, and teaching strategies.* Springfield, IL: Charles C. Thomas.

Adams, G. R., & Crane, P. (1980). Assessment of parents' and teachers' expectations of preschool children's social preferences for attractive or unattractive children and adults. *Child Development, 51,* 224–231.

Adler, P. A., & Adler, P. (1998). *Peer power: Preadolescent culture and identity.* New Brunswick, NJ: Rutgers University Press.

Ahrons, C. R. (2007). Family ties after divorce: Long-term implications for children. *Family Process, 46*(1), 53–65.

Ainsworth, M. D. S. (1973). The development of infant–mother attachment. In B. M. Caldwell & H. N. Ricciuti (Eds.), *Review of child development research* (Vol. 3). Chicago: University of Chicago Press.

Ainsworth, M. D. S. (1979). Infant–mother attachment. *American Psychologist, 34,* 932–937.

Ainsworth, M. D. S. (1982). Attachment: Retrospect and prospect. In C. M. Parkes & J. Stevenson-Hinde (Eds.), *The place of attachment in human behavior.* New York: Basic Books.

Ainsworth, M. D. S., Blehar, M., Waters, E., & Wall, S. (1978). *Patterns of attachment: A psychological study of the strange situation.* Hillsdale, NJ: Erlbaum.

Albert, K. (2010, September 27). Never too young to help. KQED Radio: *Perspectives.*

Alexander, J. E., & Tate, M. A. (1999). *Web wisdom.* Mahwah, NJ: Erlbaum.

Amato, P. (1998). More than money? Men's contributions to their children's lives. In A. Booth & A. C. Crouter (Eds.), *Men in families. When do they get involved? What difference does it make?* Mahwah, NJ: Erlbaum.

Amato, P. R. (2000). The consequences of divorce for adults and children. *Journal of Marriage and the Family, 62,* 1269–1287.

American Academy of Child and Adolescent Psychiatry (AACAP). (2001). *Facts for families: Children online.* http://www.aacap.org/.

AACAP. (2002a). *Facts for families: Children of alcoholics.* http://www.aacap.org/.

AACAP. (2002b). *Facts for families: The adopted child.* http:// www.aacap.org/.

AACAP. (2002c). *Facts for families: Children and TV violence.* http://www.aacap.org/.

AACAP. (2004). *Facts for families: The influence of music and music videos.* http://www.aacap.org/.

AACAP. (2005). *Facts for families: Foster care.* http://www.aacap.org/.

AACAP. (2006a). *Facts for families: Children with lesbian, gay, bisexual and transgender parents.* http://www.aacap.org/.

AACAP. (2006b). *Facts for families: Drinking in pregnancy (fetal alcohol effects).* http://www.aacap.org/.

AACAP. (2006c). *Facts for families: Children and movies.* http://www.aacap.org/.

AACAP. (2006d). *Facts for families: Children and video games: Playing with violence.* http://www.aacap.org/.

American Academy of Pediatrics (AAP). (2002). *Peer groups and cliques.* http://www.aap.org/.

AAP. (2009). The built environment: Designing communities to promote physical activity in children. Policy statement. *Pediatrics, 123*(6), 1591–1598.

American Association of University Women. (1991). *How schools shortchange girls.* Washington, DC: American Association of University Women Educational Foundation.

American Library Association. (2008). http://www.ala.org.

American Psychological Association (APA). (2005). *Bullying.* http://www.apa.org.

APA. (2007a). *Stress in America.* http://www.apa.org.

APA. (2007b). *Report of the Task Force on the Sexualization of Girls.* Washington, DC: Author.

Anastasiow, N. J. (1979). *Educational psychology: A contemporary view.* Del Mar, CA: CRM Books.

Anderson, C. A., Carnagey, N. L. & Eubanks, J. (2003). Exposure to violent media: The effects of songs with violent lyrics on aggressive thoughts and feelings. *Journal of Personality and Social Psychology, 84*(5), 960–971.

Anderson, C. A., Funk, J. B., & Griffiths, M. D. (2004). Contemporary issues in adolescent game playing: Brief overview and introduction to the special issue. *Journal of Adolescence*, 27(1), 1–3.

Anderson, C. A., Gentile, D. A., & Buckley, K. E. (2006). *Violent video games effects on children and adolescents: Theory, research and public policy*. New York: Oxford University Press.

Anderson, C. A., Ihori, N., Bushman, B. J., Rothstein, H. R., Shibuya, A., Swing, E. L., Sakamoto, A., & Saleem, M. (2010). Violent video game effects on aggression, empathy, and prosocial behavior in Eastern and Western countries: A meta-analytic review. *Psychological Bulletin*, *136*(2), 151–173.

Anderson, D. R., & Evans, M. K. (2001). Peril and potential of media for infants and toddlers. *Zero-to-Three*, *22*(2), 10–16.

Anderson, D. R., Huston, A. C., Schmitt, K. L., Linebarger, D. L., & Wright, J. C. (2001). Early childhood television viewing and adolescent behavior: The recontact study. *Monographs of the Society for Research in Child Development*, *66*(1, Serial No. 264).

Andreasen, M. (2001). Evolution in the family's use of television: An overview. In J. Bryant & J. A. Bryant (Eds.), *Television and the American family* (2nd ed.). Mahwah, NJ: Erlbaum.

Applied Survey Research. (2007). Children's readiness for kindergarten in San Francisco: Comprehensive report. www.library.ca.gov.

Arensberg, C. M., & Niehoff, A. H. (1975). American cultural values. In J. P. Spradley & M. A. Rynkiewich (Eds.), *The Nacirema: Reading on American culture*. Boston: Little, Brown.

Aries, P. (1962). *Centuries of childhood: A social history of family life*. New York: Knopf.

Arnett, J. J. (1991). Adolescents and heavy metal music: From the mouths of metal heads. *Youth and Society*, *33*(1), 76–98.

Arnett, J. J. (2007). Socialization in emerging adulthood: From the family to the wider world, from socialization to self-socialization. In J. E. Grusec & P. D. Hastings (Eds.), *Handbook of socialization: Theory and research*. New York: Guilford.

Aronson, E., & Patenoe, S. (1996). *The jigsaw classroom: Building cooperation in the classroom*. Reading, MA: Addison-Wesley.

Asch, S. E. (1958). Effects of group pressure upon the modification and distortion of judgments. In E. E. Maccoby, T. M. Newcomb, & E. L. Hartley (Eds.), *Readings in social psychology*. New York: Holt, Rinehart & Winston.

Asher, S. R. (1982). Some kids are nobody's best friend. *Today's Education*, *71*(1), 23.

Asher, S. R., & McDonald, K. L. (2009). The behavioral basis of acceptance, rejection, and perceived popularity. In K. H. Rubin, W. M. Bukowski, & B. P. Laursen (Eds.), *Handbook of peer interactions, relationships, and groups*. New York: Guilford Press.

Asher, S. R., & Paquette, J. A. (2003). Loneliness and peer relations in childhood. *Current Directions in Psychological Science*, *12*(3), 75–78.

Aslin, R. N., Jusczyk, P. W., & Pisoni, D. B. (1998). Speech and auditory processing during infancy: Constraints on and precursors to language. In W. Damon (Ed.), *Handbook of child psychology* (5th ed., Vol. 2). New York: Wiley.

Ausubel, D. P. (1957). *Theory and problems of child development*. New York: Grune & Stratton.

Azar, S. T. (2002). Parenting and child maltreatment. In M. H. Bornstein (Ed.), *Handbook of parenting* (2nd ed., Vol. 4). Mahwah, NJ: Erlbaum.

Bagwell, C. L., Coie, J. D., Terry, R. A., & Lochman, J. E. (2000). Peer clique participation and social status in preadolescence. *Merrill-Palmer Quarterly*, *46*(2), 280–305.

Baker, A. K., Barthelemy, K. J., & Kurdek, L. A. (1993). The relation between fifth and sixth graders' peer-rated classroom social status and their perceptions of family and neighborhood factors. *Journal of Applied Developmental Psychology*, *14*, 547–556.

Baker, C. H., & Young, P. (1960). Feedback during training and retention of motor skills. *Canadian Journal of Psychology*, *14*, 257–264.

Ball, S. J., & Bogatz, G. (1970). *The first year of Sesame Street: An evaluation*. Princeton, NJ: Educational Testing Service.

Ballantine, J. H., & Spade, J. Z. (2004). *Schools and society: A sociological approach to education* (2nd ed.). Belmont, CA: Wadsworth.

Baltzell, A., Ginsberg, R. D., & Durant, S. (2006). *Whose game is it anyway? A guide to helping your child get the most from sports, organized by age and stage*. New York: Houghton Mifflin.

Bandura, A. (1965). Influence of models' reinforcement contingencies on the acquisition of imitative responses. *Journal of Personality and Social Psychology*, *1*, 589–595.

Bandura, A. (1973). *Aggression: A social learning analysis*. Englewood Cliffs, NJ: Prentice-Hall.

Bandura, A. (1974). Behavior theory and the models of man. *American Psychologist*, *29*, 859–869.

Bandura, A. (1986). *Social foundations of thought and action: A social cognitive theory*. Englewood Cliffs, NJ: Prentice-Hall.

Bandura, A. (1989). Social cognitive theory. In R. Vasta (Ed.), *Annals of child development*, Vol. 6: *Six theories of child development: Revised formulations and current issues*. Greenwich, CT: JAI Press.

Bandura, A. (1991). Social cognitive theory of moral thought and action. In W. M. Kurtines & J. L. Gewirtz (Eds.), *Handbook of moral behavior and development* (Vol. 1). Hillsdale, NJ: Erlbaum.

Bandura, A. (1997). *Self-efficacy: The exercise of control*. New York: Freeman.

Bandura, A. (2000). Self-efficacy. In A. Kazdin (Ed.), *Encyclopedia of mental health* (Vol. 3). San Diego: Academic Press.

Bandura, A. (2001). Social cognitive theory: An agentic perspective. *Annual Review of Psychology*, *52*, 1–26.

Bandura, A. (2009). Social cognitive theory of mass communication. In J. Bryant & M.B. Oliver (Eds.), *Media effects: Advances in theory and research* (3rd ed.). New York: Routledge.

Bandura, A., Ross, D., & Ross, S. (1963). Imitation of film-mediated aggressive models. *Journal of Abnormal and Social Psychology*, *66*, 3–11.

Bandura, A., & Walters, R. H. (1963). *Social learning and personality development*. New York: Holt, Rinehart & Winston.

Bangert-Drowns, R. L., Kulik, C. C., Kulik, J. A., & Morgan, M. (1991). The instructional effect of feedback in test-like events. *Review of Educational Research*, *61*, 213–238.

Banks, J. A. (2007). *Introduction to multicultural education* (4th ed.). Boston: Allyn and Bacon.

Bankston, C. L., III, & Zhou, M. (2002). Being well vs. doing well: Self esteem and school performance among immigrant and nonimmigrant racial and ethnic groups. *International Migration Review*, *36*(2), 389–415.

Barber, B. R. (1996). *Jihad vs. McWorld: How globalism and tribalism are reshaping the world*. New York: Ballantine Books.

Barclay, K., Benelli, C., & Curtis, A. (1995). Literacy begins at birth: What caregivers can learn from parents of children who read early. *Young Children, 50*(4), 24–28.

Barnett, R. C., & Hyde, J. S. (2001). Women, men, and family: An expansionist theory. *American Psychologist, 56*(10), 781–796.

Bar-Tal, D., Raviv, A., & Lesser, T. (1980). The development of altruistic behavior: Empirical evidence. *Developmental Psychology, 16*, 516–524.

Bartol, C. R., & Bartol, A. M. (2008). *Juvenile delinquency and antisocial behavior: A development of perspective* (3rd ed.). Englewood Cliffs, NJ: Prentice Hall.

Basow, S. A. (2008). Gender socialization or how long a way has baby come? In J. C. Chrisler, C. Golden, & P. D. Rozee (Eds.), *Lectures on the psychology of women* (4th ed.). New York: McGraw-Hill.

Basow, S. A., & Rubin, L. R. (1999). Gender influence on adolescent development. In N. G. Johnson, M. C. Roberts, & J. Worell (Eds.), *Beyond appearance: A new look at adolescent girls*. Washington, DC: American Psychological Association.

Baumrind, D. (1966). Effects of authoritative parental control on child behavior. *Child Development, 37*, 887–907.

Baumrind, D. (1967). Child care practices anteceding three patterns of preschool behavior. *Genetic Psychology Monographs, 74*, 43–88.

Baumrind, D. (1968). Authoritarian vs. authoritative parental control. *Adolescence, 3*(11), 255–272.

Baumrind, D. (1971). Current patterns of parental authority. *Developmental Psychology, 4*, 1–101.

Baumrind, D. (1973). The development of instrumental competence through socialization. In A. Pick (Ed.), *Minnesota symposium on child psychology* (Vol. 7). Minneapolis: University of Minnesota Press.

Baumrind, D. (1989). Rearing competent children. In W. Damon (Ed.), *Child development today and tomorrow*. San Francisco: Jossey-Bass.

Baumrind, D. (1991). Effective parenting during the early adolescent transition. In P. A. Cowan & E. M. Hetherington (Eds.), *Family transitions*. Hillsdale, NJ: Erlbaum.

Baumrind, D., & Thompson, R. A. (2002). The ethics of parenting. In M. H. Bornstein (Ed.), *Handbook of parenting* (2nd ed., Vol. 5). Mahwah, NJ: Erlbaum.

Bauserman, R. (2002). Child adjustment in joint custody versus sole custody arrangements. A meta-analytic review. *Journal of Family Psychology, 16*(1), 91–102.

Beasley, B., & Standley, T.C. (2002). Shirts vs. skins: Clothing as an indicator of gender role, stereotyping in video games. *Mass Communication and Society, 3*(3), 279–293.

Behrman, R. E. (Ed.). (1999). Executive summary: When school is out. *The Future of Children, 9*(2), 2–4.

Behrman, R. E. (Ed.). (2002). Children and welfare reform: Analysis and recommendations. *The Future of Children, 12*(1), 5–25.

Bell, P. A., Greene, T. C., Fisher, J. D., & Baum, A. (2005). *Environmental psychology* (6th ed.). Mahwah, NJ: Erlbaum.

Belle, D. (1999). *The after-school lives of children: Alone and with others while parents work*. Mahwah, NJ: Erlbaum.

Belsky, J. (1993). Etiology of child maltreatment: A developmental–ecological analysis. *Psychological Bulletin, 114*, 413–434.

Belsky, J. (2009). Classroom composition, childcare history and social development: Are childcare effects disappearing or spreading? *Social Development, 18*(1), 230–238.

Belsky, J., & Rovine, M. (1988). Nonmaternal care in the first year of life and infant–parent attachment security. *Child Development, 59*, 157–167.

Bem, S. L. (1981). Gender schema theory: A cognitive account of sex-typing. *Psychological Review, 88*, 354–364.

Bengston, V. L. (2001). Beyond the nuclear family: The increasing importance of multigenerational bonds. *Journal of Marriage and Family, 63*, 1–16.

Bengtsson, H. (2003). Children's cognitive appraisal of others' distressed and positive experiences. *International Journal of Behavioral Development, 27*, 457–466.

Benitez, M., Davidson, J., & Flaxman, L. (2009). *Small schools, big ideas: The essential guide to successful school transformation*. New York: Jossey-Bass.

Bennett, C. I. (2010). *Comprehensive multicultural education: Theory and practice* (7th ed.). Boston: Allyn and Bacon.

Bennett, J., Ellison, J., & Ball, S. (2010). Are we there yet? *Newsweek*, March 19. www.newsweek.com.

Bennett, W. J. (1993). *The book of virtues: A treasury of great moral stories*. New York: Simon & Schuster.

Bereiter, C., & Engelmann, S. (1966). *Teaching disadvantaged children in the preschool*. Englewood Cliffs, NJ: Prentice-Hall.

Berenda, R. (1950). *The influence of the group on the judgment of children*. New York: King's Crown Press.

Berg, M., & Medrich, E. A. (1980). Children in four neighborhoods: The physical environment and its effects on play and play patterns. *Environment and Behavior, 12*(3), 320–346.

Berger, E. H. (2007). *Parents as partners in education: Families and schools working together* (7th ed.). Upper Saddle River, NJ: Prentice-Hall.

Bergin, C., & McCullough, P. (2010). Attachment in substance-exposed toddlers: The role of caregiving and exposure. *Infant Mental Health Journal, 30*(4), 407–423.

Berk, L. E., & Winsler, A. (1995). *Scaffolding children's learning: Vygotsky and early childhood education*. Washington, DC: National Association for the Education of Young Children.

Berndt, T. J. (1979). Developmental changes in conformity to peers and parents. *Developmental Psychology, 15*, 608–616.

Berndt, T. J. (1983). Correlates and causes of sociometric status in childhood: A commentary on six current studies of popular, rejected and neglected children. *Merrill-Palmer Quarterly, 29*, 439–448.

Berndt, T. J., & Ladd, G. W. (1989). *Peer relationships in child development*. New York: Wiley.

Berndt, T. J., & McCandless, M. A. (2009). Methods for investigating children's relationships with friends. In K. H. Rubin, W. M. Bukowski, & B. P. Laursen (Eds.), *Handbook of peer interactions, relationships, and groups*. New York: Guilford Press.

Bernhard, J. K., Lefebvre, M. L., Kilbride, K. M., Chud, G., & Lange, R. (1998). Troubled relationships in early childhood education: Parent–teacher interactions in ethnoculturally diverse childcare settings. *Early Education and Development, 9*, 5–28.

Bernstein, B. (1961). Social class and linguistic development: A theory of social learning. In A. H. Halsey, J. Floud, & C. A. Anderson (Eds.), *Education, economy and society*. New York: Free Press.

Berry, G. L., & Asamen, J. K. (2001). Television, children, and multicultural awareness: Comprehending the medium in a complex multimedia society. In D. G. Singer & J. L. Singer (Eds.), *Handbook of children and the media*. Thousand Oaks, CA: Sage.

Best, R. (1983). *We've all got scars: What boys and girls learn in elementary school*. Bloomington: Indiana University Press.

Bettelheim, B. (1976). *The uses of enchantment: The meaning and importance of fairy tales*. New York: Random House.

Beyers, J. M., Bates, J. E., Pettit, G. S., & Dodge, K. A. (2003). Neighborhood structure, parenting processes, and the development of youths externalizing behaviors: A multilevel analysis. *American Journal of Community Psychology, 36*, 35–53.

Bhavnagri, N. P. (1997). The cultural context of caregiving. *Childhood Education, 74*(1), 2–7.

Bianchi, S., & Milkie, M. (2010). Work and family research in the first decade of the 21st century. *Journal of Marriage and Family, 72*(3), 705–725.

Bigler, R. S., Brown, C. S., & Markell, M. (2001). When groups are not created equal: Effects of group status on the formation of intergroup attitudes in children. *Child Development, 72*, 1151–1162.

Bigner, J. (1979). *Parent–child relations*. New York: Macmillan.

Biklen, D., & Bogdan, R. (1977). Media portrayals of disabled people: A study in stereotypes. *Interracial Books for Children Bulletin, 6*, 4–9.

Biskind, P. (1983). *Seeing is believing: How Hollywood taught us to stop worrying and love the fifties*. New York: Pantheon Books.

Blake, J. (1989). *Family size and achievement*. Berkeley: University of California Press.

Blake, K. (1994). Language development and socialization in young African-American children. In P. M. Greenfield & R. R. Cocking (Eds.), *Cross-cultural roots of minority child development*. Hillsdale, NJ: Erlbaum.

Blakemore, J. E., Berenbaum, S. A., & Liben, L. S. (2009). *Gender development*. New York: Taylor & Francis Group.

Blas, A. (1990). Kohlberg's theory and moral development. In D. Schrader (Ed.), *New directions for child development* (No. 47). San Francisco: Jossey-Bass.

Bloom, B. S. (1982). *Human characteristics and school learning*. New York: McGraw-Hill.

Blume, J. (1970). *Are you there, God? It's me, Margaret*. New York: Dell.

Blume, J. (1974). *Blubber*. New York: Dell.

Blumenfeld, P. C., Marx, R. W., & Harris, C. J. (2006). Learning environments. In W. Damon & R. M. Lerner (Eds.), *Handbook of child psychology* (6th ed., Vol. 4). New York: Wiley.

Blustein, D. L. (2008). The role of work in psychological health and well being: A conceptual, historical, and public policy perspective. *American Psychologist, 63*, 228–240.

Boggiano, A. K., & Pittman, T. S. (1993). *Achievement and motivation: A social-developmental perspective*. Cambridge: Cambridge University Press.

Bolger, K. E., & Patterson, C. J. (2001). Developmental pathways from child maltreatment to peer rejection. *Child Development, 72*, 549–568.

Bond, R., & Smith, P. B. (1996). Culture and conformity: A meta-analysis of studies using Asch's (1952b, 1956) line judgment task. *Psychological Bulletin, 119*, 111–137.

Bornstein, M. H. (2006). Parenting science and practice. In W. Damon & R. M. Lerner (Eds.), *Handbook of child psychology* (6th ed., Vol. 4). Hoboken, NJ: Wiley.

Bornstein, M. H., & Bradley, R. (Eds.). (2003). *Socioeconomic status, parenting, and child development*. Mahwah, NJ: Erlbaum.

Bossard, J. H. S., & Boll, E. S. (1956). *The large family system*. Philadelphia: University of Pennsylvania Press.

Bowlby, J. (1966). *Maternal care and mental health* (2nd ed.). New York: Schocken. (Original publication by U.N. World Health Organization, Geneva, 1952.)

Bowlby, J. (1969). *Attachment* (Vol. 1). New York: Basic Books.

Bowlby, J. (1973). *Loss* (Vol. 2). New York: Basic Books.

Boyer, E. L. (1991). *Ready to learn: A mandate for the nation*. Princeton, NJ: Carnegie Foundation for the Advancement of Technology.

Bradley, R. H. (2002). Environment and parenting. In M. H. Bornstein (Ed.), *Handbook of parenting* (2nd ed., Vol. 4). Mahwah, NJ: Erlbaum.

Bradley, R. H., Caldwell, B. M., & Rock, S. L. (1990). Home environment classification system: A model for assessing the home environments of developing children. *Early Education and Development, 1*, 237–265.

Bradley, R. H., Corwyn, R. F., Caldwell, B. M., Whiteside-Mansell, L., Wasserman, G. A., & Mink, I. T. (2000). Measuring the home environment of children in early adolescence. *Journal of Research on Adolescence, 10*(3), 247–288.

Bransford, J. D., Brown, A. L., & Cocking, R. R. (Eds.). (2000). *How people learn: Brain, mind, experience, and school* (expanded ed.). Washington, DC: National Academy Press.

Bray, J. H. (1999). Step families: The intersection of culture, context, and biology. *Monographs of the Society for Research in Child Development, 64*(4), 210–218.

Bray, S. H. (1988). Children's development during early remarriage. In E. M. Hetherington & J. D. Arasteh (Eds.), *Impact of divorce, single parenting and stepparenting on children*. Hillsdale, NJ: Erlbaum.

Brazelton, T. B., & Sparrow, J. D. (2003). *Discipline the Brazelton way*. Cambridge, MA: Perseus.

Bredekamp, S. (Ed.). (1986). *Developmentally appropriate practice*. Washington, DC: National Association for the Education of Young Children.

Bredekamp, S., & Copple, C. (Eds.). (1997). *Developmentally appropriate practice in early childhood programs* (rev. ed.). Washington, DC: National Association for the Education of Young Children.

Brenner, J., & Von Moschzisker, M. (1971). *The school without walls*. New York: Holt, Rinehart & Winston.

Bridges, K. B. (1933). A study of social development in early infancy. *Child Development, 4*, 36–49.

Bridges, L. J., & Grolnick, W. S. (1995). The development of emotional self-regulation in infancy and early childhood. In N. Eisenberg (Ed.), *Review of personality and psychology*. Newbury Park, CA: Sage.

Brim, O. G. (1966). Socialization through the life cycle. In O. G. Brim & S. Wheeler (Eds.), *Socialization after childhood: Two essays*. New York: Wiley.

Brody, G. H., & Flor, D. L. (1998). Maternal resources, parenting practices, and child competence in rural, single-parent African American families. *Child Development, 69*, 803–816.

Bromer, J. (1999). Cultural variations in child care: Values and action. *Young Children, 54*(6), 72–75.

Bronfenbrenner, U. (1979). *The ecology of human development.* Cambridge MA: Harvard University Press.

Bronfenbrenner, U. (1989). Ecological systems theory. In R. Vasta (Ed.), *Annals of child development* (Vol. 6). Greenwich, CT: JAI Press.

Bronfenbrenner, U. (1993). The ecology of cognitive development: Research models and fugitive findings. In R. H. Wozniak & K. W. Fisher (Eds.), *Development in context: Acting and thinking in specific environments.* Hillsdale, NJ: Erlbaum.

Bronfenbrenner, U. (1995). Developmental ecology through space and time: A future perspective. In P. Moen, G. H. Elder, Jr., & K. Luscher (Eds.), *Examining lives in context: Perspectives on the ecology of human development.* Washington, DC: American Psychological Association.

Bronfenbrenner, U. (Ed.). (2005). *Making human beings human: Bioecological perspectives on human development.* New York: Sage.

Bronfenbrenner, U., & Crouter, A. (1982). Work and family through time and space. In S. B. Kammerman & C. D. Hayes (Eds.), *Families that work: Children in a changing world.* Washington, DC: National Academy Press.

Bronfenbrenner, U., & Morris, P. A. (2006). The bioecological model of human development. In W. Damon & R. M. Lerner (Eds.), *Handbook of child psychology* (6th ed., Vol. 1). Hoboken, NJ: Wiley.

Bronson, M. B. (2000). *Self-regulation in early childhood: Nature and nurture.* New York: Guilford.

Brooks-Gunn, J. & Donahue, E. H. (2008). Introducing the issue. *The Future of Children: Children and Electronic Media, 18*(1), 3–9.

Brooks-Gunn, J., & Furstenberg, F. F., Jr. (1989). Adolescent sexual behavior. *American Psychologist, 44*(2), 249–257.

Brooks-Gunn, J., Han, W. J., & Waldfogel, J. (2010). First-year maternal employment and child development. *Monographs of the Society for Research in Child Development, 75*(2), Serial No. 296.

Brophy, B. (1989, August 7). Spock had it right: Studies suggest that kids thrive when parents set firm limits. *U.S. News & World Report*, 49–51.

Brophy, J., & Wentzel, K. (2010). *Motivating students to learn* (3rd ed.). New York: Routledge.

Brown, B. B., Clasen, D. R., & Eicher, S. A. (1986). Perceptions of peer pressure, peer conformity dispositions and self-reported behavior among adolescents. *Developmental Psychology, 22*, 521–530.

Brown, B. B., & Dietz, E. L. (2009). Informal peer groups in middle childhood and adolescence. In K. H. Rubin, W. M. Bukowski, & B. P. Laursen (Eds.), *Handbook of peer interactions, relationships, and groups.* New York: Guilford Press.

Brown, C. S., & Bigler, R. S. (2005). Children's perceptions of discrimination. A developmental model. *Child Development, 76*(3), 533–553.

Brown, J. D., L'Engle, K. L., Pardun, C. J., Guo, G., Kenneavy, K., & Jackson, C. (2006). Sexy media matter: Exposure to sexual content in music, movies, television, and magazines predicts black and white adolescents' sexual behavior. *Pediatrics, 117*(4), 1427–1431.

Brown, M. W. (1947). *Goodnight moon.* New York: Harper and Row.

Brown, R. (2010). *Prejudice: Its social psychology* (2nd ed.). Malden, MA: Wiley-Blackwell.

Brown, W. K., & Newman, T. A. (2010). *Children from alcoholic families (family matters)* (5th ed.). Tallahassee, FL: William Gladden Press.

Bruer, J. T., & Greenough, W. T. (2001). The subtle science of how experience affects the brain. In D. B. J. Bailey, J. T. Bruer, F. J. Symons, & J. W. Lichtman (Eds.), *Critical thinking about critical periods.* Baltimore, MD: Paul H. Brooks.

Bruner, J. (1981). The art of discovery. In M. Kaplan-Sangoff & R. Y. Magid (Eds.), *Exploring early childhood.* New York: Macmillan.

Buckingham, D. (2006). Is there a digital generation? In D. Buckingham & R. Willett (Eds.), *Digital generations.* Mahwah, NJ: Erlbaum.

Bugental, D. B. (2000). Acquisition of the algorithms of social life: A domain-based approach. *Psychological Bulletin, 126*(2), 187–219.

Bugental, D. B., & Grusec, J. F. (2006). Socialization processes. In W. Damon & R. M. Lerner (Eds.), *Handbook of child psychology* (6th ed., Vol. 3). Hoboken, NJ: Wiley.

Bukowski, W. M., Brendgen, M., & Vitaro, F. (2007). Peers and socialization: Effects on externalizing and internalizing problems. In J. E. Grusec & P. D. Hastings (Eds.), *Handbook of socialization: Theory and research.* New York: Guilford.

Bukowski, W. M., Newcomb, A. F., & Hartup, W. W. (1996). Friendships and their significance in childhood and adolescence: Introduction and comment. In W. M. Bukowski, A. F. Newcomb, & W. W. Hartup (Eds.), *The company they keep: Friendship in childhood and adolescence.* New York: Cambridge University Press.

Bullock, J. R. (1992, Winter). Children without friends: Who are they and how can teachers help? *Childhood Education*, 92–96.

Burchinal, M. R., Peisner-Feinberg, E., Bryant, D. M., & Clifford, R. (2000). Children's social and cognitive development and child-care quality: Testing for differential associations related to poverty, gender, or ethnicity. *Applied Developmental Science, 4*(3), 149–165.

Burger, W. R. (2010). *Human services in contemporary America* (8th ed.). Pacific Grove, CA: Brooks Cole.

Burgess, K. B., Marshall, P. J., Rubin, K. H., & Fox, N. A. (2003). Infant attachment and temperament as predictors of subsequent externalizing problems and cardiac physiology. *Journal of Child Psychology and Psychiatry, 44*(6), 819–831.

Burhans, K. K., & Dweck, C. S. (1995). Helplessness in early childhood: The role of contingent worth. *Child Development, 66*, 1719–1738.

Bushman, B. J., & Huesmann, R. (2010). Aggression. In S. T. Fiske, D. T., Gilbert, & G. Lindsey (Eds.), *Handbook of social psychology* (5th ed.). Hoboken, NJ: Wiley.

Buss, A. H., & Plomin, R. (1984). *Temperament: Early developing personality traits.* Hillsdale, NJ: Erlbaum.

Cain, K. M., & Dweck, C. J. (1995). The relation between motivational patterns and achievement cognitions through the elementary school years. *Merrill Palmer Quarterly, 41*, 25–52.

Caldera, Y. M., Huston, A. C., & O'Brien, M. (1989). Social interactions and play patterns of parents and toddlers with feminine, masculine, and neutral toys. *Child Development, 60*, 70–76.

Caldwell, B. M., & Bradley, R. H. (1984). *Manual for the home observation for measurement of the environment.* Little Rock: University of Arkansas Press.

Caldwell, B. M., & Crary, D. (1981). Why are kids so darned aggressive? *Parents, 56*(2), 52–56.

Calvert, S. L. (2008). Children as consumers. *The Future of Children: Children and Electronic Media, 18*(1), 205–234.

Campbell, J. (1968). *The hero with a thousand faces* (2nd ed.). Princeton, NJ: Princeton University Press.

Campbell, J. J., Lamb, M. E., & Hwang, C. P. (2000). Early childcare experiences and children's social competence between 1½ and 15 years of age. *Applied and Developmental Science, 4*(3), 166–175.

Cantor, J. (1998). *"Mommy, I'm scared": How TV and movies frighten children and what we can do to protect them.* San Diego, CA: Harcourt Brace.

Carle, E. (1986). *The very hungry caterpillar.* New York: Putnam.

Carpenter, C. J. (1983). Activity, structure, and play: Implications for socialization. In M. B. Liss (Ed.), *Social and cognitive skills: Sex roles and children's play.* New York: Academic Press.

Carpenter, C. J., Huston, A. C., & Hart, W. (1986). Modification of preschool sex-typed behaviors by participation in adult-structured activities, *Sex Roles, 4,* 603–615.

Cashdan, S. (1999). *The witch must die: How fairy tales shape our lives.* New York: Basic Books.

Cass, J. (2010). *"Held captive": Child poverty in America.* Washington, DC: Children's Defense Fund.

Cebello, R., & McLoyd, V. C. (2002). Social support and parenting in poor, dangerous neighborhoods. *Child Development, 73* (4), 1310–1321.

Center for Children and Families in the Justice System. (2002). http://www.lfcc.on.ca.

Center for Communication and Social Policy. (1998). *National television violence study* (Vol. 3). Thousand Oaks, CA: Sage.

Centers for Disease Control and Prevention (CDC). (2009a). National Center for Environmental Health. *Social capital.* http://www.cdc.gov/social_capital.

CDC. (2009b). *Understanding intimate partner violence: Fact sheet.* Washington, DC: U.S. Government Printing Office.

CDC. (2010). *Understanding school violence: Fact sheet.* Washington, DC: U.S. Government Printing Office.

CDC. (2011). *Healthy youth.* http://www.cdc.gov/healthy_youth.

Chall, J. (2000). *The academic achievement challenge: What really works in the classroom.* New York: Guilford.

Chance, P. (1982). Your child's self-esteem. *Parents, 57,* 54–59.

Chang, J. (2005). *Can't stop won't stop: A history of the hip-hop generation.* New York: St. Martin's Press.

Chao, R. (1994). Beyond parent control and authoritarian parenting style: Understanding Chinese parenting through the culture notion of training. *Child Development, 65,* 1111–1119.

Chao, R. (2001). Extending research on the consequences of parenting style for Chinese Americans and European Americans. *Child Development, 72,* 1832–1843.

Char, C. A., & Meringoff, L. K. (1981, January). The role of story illustrations: Children's story comprehension in three different media. *Harvard Project Zero Technical Report* (No. 22).

Chen, X., Chung, J., & Hsiao, C. (2008). Peer interactions and relationships from a cross-cultural perspective. In K. H. Rubin, W. M. Bukowski, & B. P. Laursen (Eds.), *Handbook of peer interactions, relationships, and groups.* New York: Guilford Press.

Cheng, H., & Furnham, A. (2004). Perceived parental rearing style, self-esteem, and self-criticism as predictors of happiness. *Journal of Happiness Studies, 5*(1), 1–21.

Chess, S., & Thomas, A. (1996). *Know your child: An authoritative guide for today's parents.* New York: Jason Aronson.

Child Welfare Information Gateway. (2008). *Family preservation services.* http://www.childwelfare.gov.

Child Welfare League of America (CWLA). (2002). *Fact sheet.* http://www.cwla.org/.

Children Now. (2003). *Fall colors 2003–04: Prime-time diversity report.* Oakland, CA: Author.

Children's Defense Fund (CDF). (2010). *The state of America's children, 2010.* Washington, DC: Author.

Chisholm, K. (1998). A three-year follow-up of attachment and indiscriminate friendliness in children adopted from Romanian orphanages. *Child Development, 69*(4), 1092–1106.

Christenson, P. G., & Roberts, D. F. (1998). *It's not only rock & roll: Popular music in the lives of adolescents.* Cresskill, NJ: Hampton Press.

Cicchetti, D., & Toth, S. L. (2005). Child maltreatment. *Annual Review of Clinical Psychology, 1,* 409–438.

Cillessen, A. N. (2009). Sociometric methods. In K. H. Rubin, W. M. Bukowski, & B. P. Laursen (Eds.), *Handbook of peer interactions, relationships, and groups.* New York: Guilford Press.

Cillessen, A. N., & Mayeux, L. (2004). From censure to reinforcement: Developmental changes in the association between aggression and social status. *Child Development, 75,* 147–163.

Clarke-Stewart, K. A. (1987). Predicting child development from day care forms and features: The Chicago study. In D. A. Phillips (Ed.), *Quality in childcare: What does research tell us? Research Monographs of the National Association for the Education of Young Children* (Vol. 1). Washington, DC: National Association for the Education of Young Children.

Clarke-Stewart, K. A. (1992). Consequences of child care for children's development. In A. Booth (Ed.), *Childcare in the 1990s: Trends and consequences.* Hillsdale, NJ: Erlbaum.

Clarke-Stewart, K. A. (1993). *Daycare* (rev. ed.). Cambridge, MA: Harvard University Press.

Clarke-Stewart, K. A., & Allhusen, V. D. (2002). Nonparental caregiving. In M. H. Bornstein (Ed.), *Handbook of parenting* (2nd ed., Vol. 3). Mahwah, NJ: Erlbaum.

Clarke-Stewart, K. A., & Allhusen, V. D. (2005). *What we know about child care (developing child).* Cambridge, MA: Harvard University Press.

Clay, D., Vignoles, V. L., & Dittmar, H. (2005). Body image and self-esteem among adolescent girls: Testing the influence of sociocultural factors. *Journal of Research on Adolescence, 15*(4), 451–477.

Clay, R. A. (2009). Mini-multitaskers. *Monitor on Psychology, 40*(2), 38–40.

Cochran, M. (1993). Parenting and personal social networks. In T. Luster & L. Okagaki (Eds.), *Parenting: An ecological perspective.* Hillsdale, NJ: Erlbaum.

Cochran, M., & Niego, S. (2002). Parenting and social networks. In M. H. Bornstein (Ed.), *Handbook of parenting* (2nd ed., Vol. 1). Mahwah, NJ: Erlbaum.

Cohane, G. H., & Pope, G. H. (2001). Body image in boys: A review of the literature. *International Journal of Eating Disorders, 29*(4), 373–379.

Cohen, R., Bornstein, R., & Sherman, R. C. (1973). Conformity behavior of children as a function of group make-up and task ambiguity. *Developmental Psychology, 9*, 124–131.

Coie, J. D., & Cillesen. A. (1993). Peer rejection: Origins and effects on children's development. *Current Directions in Psychological Science, 2*, 89–92.

Coie, J. D., Dodge, K. A., & Kupersmidt, J. B. (1990). Peer group behavior and social status. In S. R. Asher & J. D. Coie (Eds.), *Peer rejection in childhood*. New York: Cambridge University Press.

Coiro, J., & Dobler, E. (2007). Exploring the online reading comprehension strategies used by sixth-grade readers to search for and locate information on the Internet. *Reading Research Quarterly, 42*(2), 214–257.

Colby, A., & Kohlberg, L. (1987). *The measurement of moral judgement*, Vol. 1: *Theoretical foundations and research validation*. Cambridge, UK: Cambridge University Press.

Colby, A., Kohlberg, L., Gibbs, J., & Lieberman, M. A. (1983). A longitudinal study of moral judgment. *Monographs of the Society for Research in Child Development, 48*(1–2, Serial No. 200).

Cole, P. M., & Tan, P. Z. (2007). Emotion socialization from a cultural perspective. In J. E. Grusec & P. D. Hastings (Eds.), *Handbook of socialization: Theory and research*. New York: Guilford.

Coleman, J. (1961). *The adolescent society*. New York: Macmillan.

Collins, A., & Halverson, R. (2009). *Rethinking education in the age of technology: The digital revolution and schooling in America*. New York: Teachers College Press.

Collins, W. A. (Ed.). (2010). The better beginnings, better futures project: Findings from grade 3 to 9. *Monographs of the Society for Research in Child Development, 75*(No. 3, Serial No. 297).

Collins, W. A., Harris, M. L., & Susman, A. (1995). Parenting during middle childhood. In M. H. Bornstein (Ed.), *Handbook of parenting* (Vol. 1). Mahwah, NJ: Erlbaum.

Collins, W. A., & Laursen, B. (2004). Parent–adolescent relationships and influences. In R. Lerner & L. Steinberg (Eds.), *Handbook of adolescent psychology* (2nd ed.). New York: Wiley.

Collins, W. A., Maccoby, E. E., Steinberg, L., Hetherington, E. M., & Bornstein, M. H. (2000). Contemporary research on parenting: The case for nature and nurture. *American Psychologist, 55*(2), 218–232.

Coloroso, B. (2003). *The bully, the bullied, and the bystander*. New York: Harper Collins.

Comer, J. P. (2004). *Leave no child behind: Preparing today's youth for tomorrow's world*. New Haven, CT: Yale University Press.

Comstock, G., & Scharrer, E. (2007). *Media and the American child*. San Diego, CA: Academic Press.

Conger, R. D., & Conger, K. J. (2002). Resilience in midwestern families: Selected findings from the first decade of a prospective longitudinal study. *Journal of Marriage and Family, 64*, 361–373.

Conger, R. D., & Dogan, S. J. (2007). Social class and socialization in families. In J. E. Grusec & P. D. Hastings (Eds.), *Handbook of socialization: Theory and research*. New York: Guilford.

Conger, R. D., Xiaojia, G., Elder, G. H., Jr., Lorenz, F. O., Simons, R. L., & Whitebeck, L. B. (1994). Economic stress, coercive family process, and developmental problems of adolescents. *Child Development, 65*, 541–561.

Cooley, C. (1964). *Human nature and the social order*. New York: Schocken. (Original work published 1909.)

Coontz, S. (1997). *The way we really are: Coming to terms with America's changing families*. New York: Basic Books.

Coontz, S. (2007). The origins of modern divorce. *Family Process, 45*(1), 7–16.

Coopersmith, S. (1967). *The antecedents of self-esteem*. San Francisco: Freeman.

Coplan, R. J., & Arbeau, K. A. (2009). Peer interactions and play in early childhood. In K. H. Rubin, W. M. Bukowski, & B. P. Laursen (Eds.), *Handbook of peer interactions, relationships, and groups*. New York: Guilford Press.

Copple, C., & Bredenkamp, S. (Eds.). (2009). *Developmentally appropriate practice (in early childhood programs, serving children from birth through age 8)* (3rd ed.). Washington, DC: NAEYC.

Corporation for Public Broadcasting. (2004). *Television goes to school: The impact of video on student learning in formal education*. New York: Author.

Corsaro, W. A. (1981). Friendship in the nursery school: Social organization in a peer environment. In S. R. Asher & J. M. Gottman (Eds.), *The development of children's friendships*. Cambridge, UK: Cambridge University Press.

Cost, Quality, and Child Outcomes Study (CQO). (1995). *Cost, quality, and child outcomes in child care centers: Executive summary* (2nd ed.). Denver: University of Colorado, Economics Department.

CQO. (1999). *The children of the cost, quality, and outcomes study go to school*. Denver: University of Colorado, Economics Department.

Council of Better Business Bureaus. (2000). *The children's advertising review unit. Self-regulatory guidelines for children's advertising*. http://www.bbb.org/.

Cowan, P. A., Powell, D., & Cowan, C. P. (1998). Parenting interventions. Family interventions: A family systems perspective. In W. Damon (Ed.), *Handbook of child psychology* (5th ed., Vol. 4). New York: Wiley.

Cox, M. J., Owen, M. T., Henderson, V. K., & Margand, N. A. (1992). Prediction of infant–father and infant–mother attachment. *Developmental Psychology, 28*(3), 474–483.

Craig, L. (2006). Does father care mean fathers share? A comparison of how mothers and fathers in intact families spend time with children. *Gender & Society, 20*, 259–281.

Crawford, M. T., & Unger, R. (2000). *Women and gender: A feminist psychology* (3rd ed.). New York: McGraw-Hill.

Crespo, C. J., Smit, E., Troiano, R. P., Bartlett, S. J., Macera, C. A., & Anderson, R. E. (2001). Television watching, energy intake, and obesity in U.S. children. *Archives of Pediatric and Adolescent Medicine, 155*, 360–365.

Crick, N. R., Casas, J. F., & Ku, H.-C. (1999). Relation of physical forms of peer victimization in preschool. *Developmental Psychology, 35*, 376–385.

Crnic, K., & Acevedo, M. (1995). Everyday stress and parenting. In M. H. Bornstein (Ed.), *Handbook of parenting* (Vol. 4). Mahwah, NJ: Erlbaum.

Crocetti, E., Rubini, M., Luyckx, K., & Meeus, W. (2007). Identity formation in early and middle adolescents from various ethnic groups: From three dimensions to five statuses. *Journal of Youth and Adolescence*. http://www.SpringerLink.com

Crohn, J. (1995). *Mixed matches: How to create successful interracial, interethnic, and interfaith relationships*. New York: Ballantine.

Crouter, A. C., Bumpus, M. F., Maguire, M. C., & McHale, S. M. (1999). Linking parents' work pressure and adolescent's well-being: Insights into dynamics in dual-earner families. *Developmental Psychology, 35*, 1453–1461.

Crouter, A. C., & McHale, S. M. (2005). The long arm of the job revisited: Parenting in dual-earner families. In T. Luster & L. Okagaki (Eds.), *Parenting: An ecological perspective* (2nd ed.). Mahwah, NJ: Erlbaum.

Cummings, E. M., & Cummings, J. S. (2002). Parenting and attachment. In M. H. Bornstein (Ed.), *Handbook of parenting* (2nd ed., Vol. 5). Mahwah, NJ: Erlbaum.

Curran, D. (1985). *Stress and the healthy family*. Minneapolis, MN: Winston Press.

Dahlman, S., Ljunggvist, P., & Johannesson, M. (2007). *Reciprocity in young children*. http://en.scienticcommons.org.

Damasio, A. R. (1994). *Descartes' error: Emotion, reason, and the human brain*. New York: Putnam.

Damon, W. (1990). *The moral child: Nurturing children's natural moral growth*. New York: Free Press.

Damon, W. D. (1999). The moral development of children. *Scientific American, 281*(2), 72–78.

Daniels, D. H., Kalkman, D. L., & McCombs, B. L. (2001). Young children's perspectives on learning and teacher practices in different classroom contexts: Implications for motivation. *Early Education and Development, 12*, 253–273.

Daniels Fund. (2005). www.danielsfund.org.

Darling, S., & Westberg, L. (2004). Parent involvement in children's acquisition of reading. *The Reading Teacher, 57*(8), 774–776.

Davidson, P., & Youniss, J. (1995). Moral development and social construction. In W. M. Kurtines & J. L. Gewirtz (Eds.), *Moral development: An introduction*. Boston: Allyn and Bacon.

Dean, C. (1984). Parental empowerment through family resource programs. *Human Ecology Forum, 14*(1), 17–22.

DeBruyn, E. H., & Van Den Boom, D. C. (2005). Interpersonal behavior, peer popularity, and self-esteem in early adolescence. *Social Development, 14*(4), 555–573.

Decety, J., & Chaminade, T. (2003). Neural correlates of feeling sympathy. *Neuropsychologia, 41*, 127–138.

Decker, L. E., & Decker, V. A. (2001). *Engaging families and communities: Pathways to educational success*. Fairfax, VA: National Community Education Association.

De Garmo, D. S. (2010). Coercive and prosocial fathering, antisocial personality, and growth in children's postdivorce noncompliance. *Child Development, 81*(2), 503–516.

Dellman-Jenkins, M., Florjancic, L., & Swadener, E. B. (1993). Sex roles and cultural diversity in recent award-winning picture books for young children. *Journal of Research in Childhood Education, 7*(2), 74–82.

DeLoache, J. S. (1991). Symbolic functioning in very young children: Understanding of pictures and models. *Child Development, 62*(4), 736–752.

DeLoache, J. S., Chiang, C., Sherman, K., Islam, N., Vanderborght, M., Troseth, G. L., Strouse, G. A., & O'Doherty, K. (2010). Do babies learn from baby media? *Psychological Science, 21*(11), 1570–1574.

Dennison, B. A., Erb, T. A., & Jenkins, P. L. (2002). Television viewing and television in bedroom associated with overweight risk among low-income preschool children. *Pediatrics, 109*, 1028–1035.

DePanfilis, D. (2006). *Child neglect: A guide for prevention assessment and intervention*. Washington, DC: U.S. Department of Health and Human Services.

Derenne, J. L., & Beresin, E. V. (2006). Body image, media, and eating disorders. *Academic Psychiatry, 30*(3), 257–261.

Desmond, R. (2001). Free reading: Implication for child development. In D. G. Singer & J. L. Singer (Eds.), *Handbook of children and the media*. Thousand Oaks, Sage.

Desmond, R. J., Singer, J. L., & Singer, D. G. (1990). Family mediation: Parental communication patterns and the influences of television on children. In J. Bryant (Ed.), *Television and the American family*. Hillsdale, NJ: Erlbaum.

DeToledo, S., & Brown, D. E. (1995). *Grandparents as parents*. New York: Guilford.

Dewey, J. (1944). *Democracy and education*. New York: Macmillan.

DeWolff, M. S., & van IJzendoorn, M. H. (1997). Sensitivity and attachment: A meta-analysis on parental antecedents of infant attachment. *Child Development, 67*, 3071–3085.

Diamond, A., Barnett, W. S., Thomas, J., & Munro, S. (2007). Preschool program improves cognitive control. *Science, 318* (5855), 1387–1413.

Dickinson, D. K., & Smith, M. W. (1994). Long-term effects of preschool teachers' book readings on low-income children's vocabulary and story comprehension. *Reading Research Quarterly, 29*(2), 104–122.

Dickman, A. B., & Murnen, S. K. (2004). Learning to be little woman and little men: The inequitable gender equality of nonsexist children's literature. *New Roles, 50*(5/6), 373–385.

Dien, D. S. F. (1982). A Chinese perspective on Kohlberg's theory of moral development. *Developmental Review, 2*, 331–341.

Dill, K. E., & Thill, K. P. (2007). Video game characters and the socialization of gender roles: Young people's perceptions mirror sexist media depictions. *Sex Roles, 57*(Nos. 11–12), 851–864.

Dobkin, P. L., Tremblay, R. E., Masse, L. C., & Vitaro, F. (1995). Individual and peer characteristics in predicting boys' early onset of substance abuse: A seven-year longitudinal study. *Child Development, 66*, 1198–1214.

Dobson, J. (1996). *The new dare to discipline book*. Carol Stream, IL: Tyndale House.

Dodge, K. A. (1986). A social information processing model of social competence in children. In M. Perlmutter (Ed.), *Minnesota symposia on child psychology* (Vol. 18). Hillsdale, NJ: Erlbaum.

Dodge, K. A., Bates, J. E., & Pettit, G. S. (1990). Mechanisms in the cycle of violence. *Science, 250*, 1678–1683.

Dodge, K. A., Coie, J. D., & Lynam, D. (2006). Aggression and antisocial behavior in youth. In W. Damon & R. M. Lerner (Eds.), *Handbook of child psychology* (6th ed., Vol. 4). Hoboken, NJ: Wiley.

Dodge, K. A., & Pettit, G. S. (2003). A biopsychosocial model of the development of chronic conduct problems in adolescence. *Developmental Psychology, 39*, 349–371.

Dodge, K. A., Pettit, G. S., & Bates, J. E. (1994). Socialization mediators of the relation between socioeconomic status and child conduct problems. *Child Development, 65*, 649–665.

Doherty, W. J., Kouneski, E. F., & Erickson, M. F. (1998). Responsible fathering: An overview and conceptual framework. *Journal of Marriage and the Family, 60*, 277–292.

Dornbusch, S. M., Ritter, P. L., Leiderman, P. H., & Roberts, D. F. (1987). The relationship of parenting style to adolescent school performance. *Child Development, 58*(5), 1244–1257.

Dorr, A., & Rabin, B. E. (1995). Parents, children, and television. In M. H. Bornstein (Ed.), *Handbook of parenting* (Vol. 4). Mahwah, NJ: Erlbaum.

Dreikurs, R., & Grey, L. (1968). *A new approach to discipline: Logical consequences.* New York: Hawthorn.

Dresser, N. (1999). *Multicultural celebrations.* New York: Three Rivers Press.

Dresser, N. (2005). *Multicultural manners: New rules of etiquette for a changing society* (rev. ed.). New York: Wiley.

Dubow, E. F., Huesmann, L. R., & Greenwood, D. (2007). Media and youth socialization: Underlying processes and moderations of effects. In J. E. Grusec & P. D. Hastings (Eds.), *Handbook of socialization: Theory and research.* New York: Guilford.

Dubowitz, H., & DePanfilis, D. (Eds.). (2000). *Handbook for child protection practice.* Thousand Oaks, CA: Sage.

Duncan, G. J., & Magnuson, K. A. (2005). Can family socioeconomic resources account for racial and ethnic test score gaps? School readiness: Closing racial and ethnic gaps. *The Future of Children, 15*(1), 35–54.

Duncan, G. J., & Raudenbush, S. W. (2001). Neighborhoods and adolescent development: How can we determine the links? In A. Booth & A. C. Crouter (Eds.), *Does it take a village?* Mahwah, NJ: Erlbaum.

Dunn, J. (1988). *The beginnings of social understanding.* Cambridge, MA: Harvard University Press.

Dunn, J. (1992). Siblings and development. *Current Directions in Psychological Science, 1*(1), 6–9.

Dunn, J. (1993). *Young children's close relationship: Beyond attachment.* Newbury Park, CA: Sage.

Dunn, J. (2004). *Children's friendships: The beginnings of intimacy.* Malden, MA: Blackwell.

Dunn, J. (2006). Moral development in early childhood and social interaction in the family. In M. Killen and J. G. Smetana (Eds.), *Handbook of moral development.* Mahwah, NJ: Erlbaum.

Dunn, J. (2007). Siblings and socialization. In J. E. Grusec & P. D. Hastings (Eds.), *Handbook of socialization: Theory and research.* New York: Guilford.

Dunn, J., Davies, L. C., O'Connor, T. G., & Sturgess, W. (2000). Parents' and partners' life course and family experiences: Links with parent–child relationships in different family settings. *Journal of Child Psychology and Psychiatry and Allied Disciplines, 41*, 955–968.

Durkheim, E. (1947). *The elementary forms of the religious life.* Glencoe, IL: Free Press.

Dweck, C. S. (1975). The role of expectations and attributions in the alleviation of learned helplessness. *Journal of Personality and Social Psychology, 31*, 674–685.

Dweck, C. S. (1981). Social-cognitive processes in children's friendships. In S. R. Asher & J. M. Gottman (Eds.), *The development of children's friendships.* Cambridge, UK: Cambridge University Press.

Dweck, C. S. (2002). The development of ability conceptions. In A. Wigfield & J. S. Eccles (Eds.), *Development of achievement motivation.* San Diego, CA: Academic Press.

Dweck, C. S. (2006). *Mindset: The new psychology of success.* New York: Random House.

Dweck, C. S., & Bush, E. S. (1976). Sex differences in learned helplessness, I: Differential debilitation with peer and adult evaluators. *Journal of Personality and Social Psychology, 12*, 147–156.

Dweck, C. S., & Gillard, D. (1975). Expectancy statements as determinants of reactions to failure: Sex differences in persistence and expectancy change. *Journal of Personality and Social Psychology, 32*, 1077–1084.

Dweck, C. S., & Leggett, E. L. (1988). A social-cognitive approach to motivation and personality. *Psychological Review, 95*, 256–273.

Dweck, C. S., & Reppucci, N. D. (1973). Learned helplessness and reinforcement responsibility in children. *Journal of Personality and Social Psychology, 25*, 109–116.

Eccles, J. (1983). Expectancies, values, and academic behaviors. In J. T. Spence (Ed.), *Achievement and achievement motives: Psychological and sociological approaches.* San Francisco: Freeman.

Eccles, J. S., & Bryan, J. (1994). Adolescence and gender-role transcendence. In M. Stevenson (Ed.), *Gender roles across the life span.* Muncie, IN: Ball State University Press.

Eder, D. (1995). *School talk: Gender and adolescent school culture.* New Brunswick, NJ: Rutgers University Press.

Eisenberg, N. (2000). Emotion, regulation, and moral development. *Annual Review of Psychology, 51*, 665–697.

Eisenberg, N. (2002). Emotion-related regulation and its relation to quality of social functioning. In W. W. Hartup & R. A. Weinberg (Eds.), *Minnesota symposium on child psychology,* Vol. 32: *Child psychology in retrospect and prospect.* Mahwah, NJ: Erlbaum.

Eisenberg, N. (2006). Introduction. In W. Damon & R. M. Lerner (Eds.), *Handbook of child psychology* (6th ed., Vol. 3). Hoboken, NJ: Wiley.

Eisenberg, N. (2009). Empathy-related responding: Links with self-regulation, moral judgement, and moral behavior. In M. Mikulincer & P. R. Shaver (Eds.), *Prosocial motives, emotions, and behavior: To better angels of our nature.* Washington, DC: American Psychological Association.

Eisenberg, N., Fabes, R. A., & Spinrad, T. L. (2006). Prosocial development. In W. Damon & R. M. Lerner (Eds.), *Handbook of child psychology* (6th ed., Vol. 4). Hoboken, NJ: Wiley.

Eisenberg, N., Zhou, Q., Spinrad, T. L., Valiente, C., Fabes, R. A., & Liew, R. A. (2005). Relations among positive parenting, children's effortful control, and externalizing problems: A three-wave longitudinal study. *Child Development, 76*(5), 1055–1071.

Elder, G. H., Jr. (1963). Parental power legitimation and its effect on the adolescent. *Sociometry, 26*, 50–65.

Elder, G. H., Jr. (1974). *Children of the Great Depression: Social change in life experience.* Chicago: University of Chicago Press.

Elder, G. H., Jr. (1979). Historical change in life patterns and personality. In P. Baltes & O. Brim (Eds.), *Life-span development and behavior* (Vol. 2). New York: Academic Press.

Elder, G. H., Jr., & Bowerman, C. E. (1963). Family structure and child-rearing patterns: The effect of family size and sex composition. *American Sociological Review, 30*, 81–96.

Elder, G. H., Jr., & Hareven, T. K. (1993). Rising above life's disadvantage: From the Great Depression to war. In G. H. Elder, Jr., J. Modell, & R. D. Parke (Eds.), *Children in time and space: Development and historical insights*. New York: Cambridge University Press.

Elder, G. H., Jr., & Shanahan, M. J. (2006). The life course and human development. In W. Damon & R. M. Lerner (Eds.), *Handbook of child psychology* (6th ed., Vol. 1). Hoboken, NJ: Wiley.

Elder, G. H., Jr., Van Nguyen, T. V., & Casper, A. (1985). Linking family hardship to children's lives. *Child Development, 56*, 361–375.

Elders, J. (1994). Violence as a public health issue for children. *Childhood Education, 70*(5), 260–262.

Eldridge, S. (1999). *Twenty things adopted kids wish their adoptive parents knew*. New York: Dell.

Eley, T. C., Lichtenstein, P., & Stevenson, J. (1999). Sex differences in the etiology of aggressive and nonaggressive antisocial behavior: Results from two twin studies. *Child Development, 70*, 155–168.

Elkind, D. (1981a). Egocentrism in children and adolescents. In D. Elkind (Ed.), *Children and adolescents: Interpretive essays on Jean Piaget* (3rd ed.). New York: Oxford University Press.

Elkind, D. (1981b). How grown-ups help children learn. *Education Digest, 80*(3), 20–24.

Elkind, D. (1994). *Ties that stress: The new family imbalance*. Cambridge, MA: Harvard University Press.

Elkind, D. (2001). *The hurried child: Growing up too fast too soon* (25th anniv. ed.). Cambridge, MA: Da Capo Press/Perseus Books.

Elliot, E. S., & Dweck, C. S. (1988). Goals: An approach to motivation and achievement. *Journal of Personality and Social Psychology, 54*, 5–12.

Ellis, B. J., Bates, J. E., Dodge, K. A., Fergusson, D. M., Horwood, J. L., Pettit, G. S., et al. (2003). Does father absence place daughters at risk for early sexual activity and teenage pregnancy? *Child Development, 74*, 801–821.

Ellis, J. B. (1994). Children's sex-role development: Implications for working mothers. *Social Behavior and Personality, 22*, 131–136.

Ellis, S., Rogoff, B., & Cromer, C. C. (1981). Age segregation in children's social interactions. *Developmental Psychology, 17*, 399–407.

Emery, R. E. (1989). Family violence. *American Psychologist, 44*, 321–332.

Emery, R. E. (2004). *The truth about children and divorce: Dealing with emotions so you and your children can thrive*. New York: Viking.

Emmer, E., & Stough, L. (2001). Classroom management: A critical part of educational psychology with implications for teacher education. *Educational Psychologist, 36*, 103–112.

Epps, S., & Jackson, B. J. (2000). *Empowered families, successful children*. Washington, DC: American Psychological Association.

Epstein, J. L., & Sanders, M. G. (2002). Family, school and community partnerships. In M. H. Bornstein (Ed.), *Handbook of parenting* (2nd ed., Vol. 5). Mahwah, NJ: Erlbaum.

Epstein, J. L., & Sheldon, S. B. (2006). Moving forward: Ideas for research on school, family, and community partnerships. In C. F. Conrad & R. Sterling (Eds.), *SAGE handbook for research in education: Engaging ideas and enriching inquiry*. Thousand Oaks, CA: Sage.

Erikson, E. H. (1963). *Childhood and society*. New York: Norton.

Erikson, E. H. (1980). *Identity and the life cycle*. New York: Norton.

Escober-Chavez, S. L., & Anderson, C. A. (2008). Media and risky behaviors. *The Future of Children: Children and the Electronic Media, 18*(1), 147–184.

Espeldge, D. L., Holt, M. K., & Henkel, R. R. (2003). Examination of peer-group contextual effects on aggression during early adolescence. *Child Development, 74*, 205–220.

Etzioni, A. (1993). *The spirit of community: The reinvention of American society*. New York: Touchstone.

Evans, E. D., & McCandless, B. R. (1978). *Children and youth: Psychosocial development*. New York: Holt, Rinehart & Winston.

Evans, E. D., Rutberg, J., Sather, C., & Turner, C. (1991). Content analysis of contemporary teen magazines for adolescent females. *Youth Society, 23*(1), 99–120.

Evans, G. W. (2006). Child development and the physical environment. *Annual Review of Psychology, 57*, 423–451.

Evans, G. W., & English, K. (2002). The environment of poverty: Multiple stressor exposure, psychophysiological stress, and socioemotional adjustment. *Child Development, 73*, 1238–1248.

Evans, G. W., & Stecker, R. (2004). Motivational consequences of environmental stress. *Journal of Environmental Psychology, 24*(2), 143–165.

Evans, W. D. (2008). Social marketing campaigns and children's media use. *The Future of Children: Children and the Electronic Media, 18*(1), 181–207.

Fagot, B. I. (1984). Teacher and peer reactions to boys' and girls' play styles. *Sex Roles, 11*, 691–702.

Fagot, B. I. (1995). Parenting boys and girls. In M. H. Bornstein (Ed.), *Handbook of parenting* (Vol. 1). Mahwah, NJ: Erlbaum.

Falbo, T., & Polit, D. (1986). A quantitative review of the only child literature: Research evidence and theory development. *Psychological Bulletin, 100*, 176–189.

Farmer, S. (1989). *Adult children of abusive parents*. New York: Ballantine.

Farrington, D. P., & Loeber, R. (2000). Epidemiology of juvenile violence. *Juvenile Violence, 9*, 733–748.

Fearan, R. P., Bakermans-Kranenburg, M. J., van Jzendoorn, M. H., Lapsley, A. M., & Roisman, G. I. (2010). The significance of insecure attachment and disorganization in the development of children's externalizing behavior: A meta-analytic study. *Child Development, 81*(2), 435–456.

Federal Interagency Forum on Child and Family Statistics (FIFCFS). (2010). *America's children: Key national indicators of well-being, 2010*. Washington, DC: U.S. Government Printing Office.

Fedorak, S. (2009). *Pop culture: The culture of everyday life*. Toronto: University of Toronto Press.

Fiese, B. H. (2006). *Family routines and rituals*. New Haven: Yale University Press.

Fiese, B. H., Sameroff, A. J., Grotevant, H. D., Wamboldt, F. S., Dickenstein, S., & Fravel, D. H. (1999). The stories that families tell: Narrative coherence, narrative interaction, and relationship beliefs. *Monographs of the Society for Research in Child Development, 64*(2, Serial No. 257).

Fincham, F. D. (2008). Learned helplessness. In *Psychology of classroom learning: An encyclopedia.* Farmington Hills, MI: Gale.

Fincham, F. D., & Cain, K. (1986). Learned helplessness in humans: A developmental analysis. *Developmental Review, 6,* 301–333.

Fincham, F. D., & Hall, J. H. (2005). Parenting and the marital relationship. In T. Luster & L. Okagaki (Eds.), *Parenting: An ecological perspective* (2nd ed.). Mahwah, NJ: Erlbaum.

Finkelhor, D. (1984). *Child abuse: New theory and research.* New York: Free Press.

Fischer, W. (1963). Sharing in preschool children as a function of amount and type of reinforcements. *Genetic Psychological Monographs, 68,* 215–245.

Fiske, A. P. (1992). The four elementary forms of sociality: Framework for a unified theory of social relations. *Psychological Review, 99,* 689–723.

Fiske, E. B. (1992). *Smart schools, smart kids.* New York: Touchstone.

Fletcher, A. C., Darling, N. E., Steinberg, L., & Dornbusch, S. M. (1995). The company they keep: Relation of adolescents' adjustment and behavior to their friends' perceptions of authoritative parenting in the social network. *Developmental Psychology, 31,* 300–310.

Fontana, D. (2003). *Psychology, religion, and spirituality.* Malden, MA: Blackwell.

Forman, D. R., Aksan, N., & Kochanska, G. (2004). Toddlers' responsive imitation predicts preschool-age conscience. *Psychological Science, 15,* 699–704.

Forman, D. R., & Kochanska, G. (2001). Viewing imitation and child responsiveness: A link between teaching and discipline domains of socialization. *Developmental Psychology, 37,* 198–200.

Forney, W. S., Crutsinger, C., & Forney, J. C. (2006). Self-concepts and self-worth as predictors of self perception of morality: Implications for delinquent risk behavior associated with shoplifting. *Family and Consumer Sciences Research Journal, 35*(1), 24–43.

Foster-Clark, F. S., & Blyth, D. A. (1991). Peer relations and influences. In R. M. Lerner, A. C. Petersen, & J. Brooks-Gunn (Eds.), *Encyclopedia of adolescence* (Vol. 2). New York: Garland.

Fragin, S. (2000, November). Who cares for kids? *Working Mother,* 57–75.

Francke, L. B. (1983). *Growing up divorced.* New York: Fawcett/Crest.

Frawley, T. (2005). Gender bias in the classroom: Current controversies and implications for teachers. *Childhood Education, 81*(4), 221–227.

Frede, E. C. (1995). The role of program quality in producing early childhood program benefits. *The Future of Children, 5*(3), 115–132.

Freeman, N., & Brown, M. (2008). Authentic approach to assessing prekindergarten programs: Redefining readiness. *Childhood Education, 84*(5), 267–274.

Freud, A. (1968). *The psychoanalytical treatment of children.* New York: International Universities Press.

Freud, S. (1925). Some psychical consequences of the anatomical distinction between the sexes. In J. Strachey (Ed. and Trans.), *The standard edition of the complete psychological works of Sigmund Freud.* London: Hogarth Press.

Freud, S. (1938). *The basic writings of Sigmund Freud.* New York: Random House.

Freud, S. (1999). The social construction of normality. *Families in Society: The Journal of Contemporary Human Services, 80*(4), 333–337.

Friedrich, L. K., & Stein, S. H. (1973). Aggressive and prosocial television programs and the natural behavior of preschool children. *Monographs of the Society for Research in Child Development, 38*(Serial No. 151).

Fuligni, A. J., & Eccles, J. S. (1993). Perceived parent–child relationships and early adolescents' orientation toward peers. *Developmental Psychology, 29,* 622–632.

Furman, W. (1995). Parenting siblings. In M. H. Bornstein (Ed.), *Handbook of parenting* (Vol. 1). Mahwah, NJ: Erlbaum.

Furman, W., & Masters, J. C. (1980). Affective consequences of social reinforcement, punishment, and neutral behavior. *Developmental Psychology, 16,* 100–104.

Furrow, J. L., King, P. E., & White, K. (2004). Religion and positive youth development: Identity, meaning, and prosocial concerns. *Applied Developmental Science, 8*(1), 17–26.

Furstenburg, F. F., & Cherlin, A. J. (1991). *Divided families: What happens to children when parents part.* Cambridge, MA: Harvard University Press.

Galinsky, E. (1981). *Between generations: The six stages of parenthood.* New York: Times Books.

Galinsky, E. (1992). The impact of child care on parents. In A. Booth (Ed.), *Childcare in the 1990s: Trends and consequences.* Hillsdale, NJ: Erlbaum.

Gallay, L. S., & Flanagan, C. A. (2000). The well-being of children in a changing economy: Time for a new social contract in America. In R. D. Taylor & M. C. Wang (Eds.), *Resilience across contexts: Family, work, culture, and community.* Mahwah, NJ: Erlbaum.

Garbarino, J. (1977). The human ecology of child maltreatment: A conceptual model for research. *Journal of Marriage and the Family, 39,* 721–736.

Garbarino, J. (1992). *Children and families in the social environment* (2nd ed.). New York: Aldine de Gruyter.

Garbarino, J. (1995a). *Building a socially nourishing environment with children.* San Francisco: Jossey-Bass.

Garbarino, J. (1995b). *Raising children in a socially toxic society.* San Francisco: Jossey-Bass.

Garbarino, J., Bradshaw, C. P., & Kostelny, K. (2005). Neighborhood and community influences on parenting. In T. Luster & L. Okagaki (Eds.), *Parenting: An ecological perspective* (2nd ed.). Mahwah, NJ: Erlbaum.

Garbarino, J., & Gilliam, G. (1980). *Understanding abusive families.* Lexington, MA: Heath.

Garbarino, J., Guttman, E., & Seely, J. W. (1986). *The psychologically battered child: Strategies for identification, assessment and intervention.* San Francisco: Jossey-Bass.

Garbarino, J., & Sherman, D. (1980). High-risk neighborhoods and high-risk families. *Child Development, 51,* 188–198.

Garcia, R. L. (1998). *Teaching for diversity.* Bloomington, IN: Phi Delta Kappa Educational Foundation.

Garcia-Coll, C. T. (1990). Developmental outcome of minority infants: A process-oriented look into our beginnings. *Child Development, 61,* 270–289.

Garcia-Coll, C. T., Meyer, E. C., & Britton, L. (1995). Ethnic and minority parenting. In M. H. Bornstein (Ed.), *Handbook of parenting* (Vol. 2). Mahwah, NJ: Erlbaum.

Gardner, H. (1999). *Intelligence reframed: Multiple intelligences for the 21st century.* New York: Basic Books.

Gardner, H. (2006). *Five minds for the future.* Boston, MA: Harvard Business School Press.

Gartrell, N., & Bos, H. (2010). U.S. national longitudinal lesbian family study: Psychological adjustment of 17-year-old adolescents. *Pediatrics, 126*(1), 28–36.

Gauvain, M., & Perez, S. M. (2007). In J. E. Grusec & P. D. Hastings (Eds.), *Handbook of socialization: Theory and research.* New York: Guilford.

Geddes, E. L., Salvatori, P., & Eva, K. W. (2009). Does moral judgement improve in occupational therapy and physiotherapy students over the course of their pre-licensure training? *Learning in Health and Social Care, 8*(2), 92–102.

Gelfand, D., Hartman, D. P., Cromer, C. C., Smith, C. L., & Page, B. C. (1975). The effects of instructional prompts and praise on children's donation rates. *Child Development,* 46, 980–983.

Gellene, D. (1996, August 7). Scaring up lots of young readers. *Los Angeles Times,* pp. A1, 18–19.

Gerbner, G., Gross, L., Jackson-Beck, N., Jeffries-Fox, S., & Signorielli, N. (1978). *Violence profile* (No. 9). Philadelphia: University of Pennsylvania Press.

Gerbner, G., Gross, L., Morgan, M., & Signorielli, N. (2002). Growing up with television: Cultivation process. In J. Bryant & D. Zillman (Eds.), *Media effects: Advances in theory and research* (2nd ed.). Mahwah, NJ: Erlbaum.

Gesell, A., & Ilg, F. (1943). *Infant and child in the culture of today.* New York: Harper & Row.

Ghazvini, A., & Mullis, R. L. (2002). Center-based care for young children: Examining predictors of quality. *Journal of Genetic Psychology, 163,* 112–126.

Giannetti, C. C., & Sagarese, M. (2008). The newest breed of bully, the cyberbully. http://www.PTA.org.

Gifford-Smith, M. E., & Rabiner, D. L. (2004). Social information processing and children's social adjustment. In J. J. Kupersmidt & K. A. Dodge (Eds.), *Children's peer relations: From development to intervention to policy: A festsschrift to honor John D. Coie.* Washington, DC: American Psychological Association.

Gilbert, D. (2008). *The American class structure in an age of growing inequality* (7th ed.). Thousand Oaks, CA: Sage.

Gilkeson, E. C., & Bowman, G. W. (1976). *The focus is on children.* New York: Bank Street Publications.

Gilligan, C. (1982). *In a different voice.* Cambridge, MA: Harvard University Press.

Gilligan, C. (1985, April). *Response to critics.* Paper presented at the biennial meeting of the Society for Research in Child Development, Toronto.

Ginsburg, G. S., & Bronstein, D. (1993). Family factors related to children's intrinsic/extrinsic motivational orientation and academic performance. *Child Development, 64,* 1461–1474.

Goffin, S. G., & Lombardi, J. (1988). *Speaking out: Early childhood advocacy.* Washington, DC: National Association for the Education of Young Children.

Goldberg, A. E. (2009). *Lesbian and gay parents and their children: Research on the family life cycle.* Washington, DC: APA.

Golding, W. (1954). *Lord of the flies.* New York: Putnam.

Goldstein, A. P. (1991). *Delinquent gangs: A psychological perspective.* Champaign, IL: Research Press.

Goleman, D. (1995). *Emotional intelligence.* New York: Bantam.

Gollnick, D. M., & Chinn, P. C. (2008). *Multicultural education in a pluralistic society* (8th ed.). Upper Saddle River, NJ: Merrill/Prentice-Hall.

Good, T. L., & Brophy, J. E. (1986). *Educational psychology* (3rd ed.). New York: Longman.

Good, T. L., & Brophy, J. E. (2007). *Looking in classrooms* (10th ed.). New York: Allyn and Bacon.

Goode, W. J. (1982). *The family* (2nd ed.). Englewood Cliffs, NJ: Prentice-Hall.

Gooden, A. M., & Gooden, M. A. (2001). Gender representation in notable children's picture books: 1995–1999. *Sex Roles, 45*(1/2), 89–101.

Goodlad, J. I. (2004). *A place called school: Prospects for the future* (20th anniv. ed.). New York: McGraw-Hill.

Gorsuch, R. L. (1976). Religion as a major predictor of significant human behavior. In W. J. Donaldson, Jr. (Ed.), *Research in mental health and religious behavior.* Atlanta: Psychological Studies Institute.

Gottfried, A. E., Gottfried, A. W., & Buthurst, K. (2002). Maternal and dual earner employment status and parenting. In M. H. Bornstein (Ed.), *Handbook of parenting* (2nd ed., Vol. 2). Mahwah, NJ: Erlbaum.

Gottman, J., Gonso, J., & Rasmussen, B. (1975). Social interaction, social competence, and friendship in children. *Child Development, 46,* 709–718.

Gould, W. S., & Gould, C. B. (1962). *Annotated Mother Goose.* New York: Clarkson N. Potter.

Graves, N. B., & Graves, T. O. (1983). The cultural context of prosocial development: An ecological model. In D. L. Bridgeman (Ed.), *The nature of prosocial development: Interdisciplinary theories and strategies.* New York: Academic Press.

Greely, A. M. (2001, March/April). The future of religion in America. *Society,* 32–37.

Greenberger, E., & Chen, C. (1996). Perceived family relationships and depressed mood in early and late adolescence: A comparison of European and Asian Americans. *Developmental Psychology, 32,* 707–717.

Greenfield, P. M. (1984). *Mind and media: The effects of television, video games and computers.* Cambridge, MA: Harvard University Press.

Greenfield, P. M., & Juvonen, J. (1999). A developmental look at Columbine. *APA Monitor Online, 30*(7).

Greenfield, P. M., Keller, H., Fuligni, A., & Maynard, A. (2003). Cultural pathways through universal development. *Annual Review of Psychology, 54,* 461–490.

Greenfield, P. M., Suzuki, L. K., & Rothstein-Fisch, C. (2006). Cultural pathways through human development. In W. Damon & R. M. Lerner (Eds.), *Handbook of child psychology* (6th ed., Vol. 4). Hoboken, NJ: Wiley.

Greitemeyer, T., & Osswald, S. (2010). Effect of prosocial video games on prosocial behavior. *Journal of Personality and Social Behavior, 98*(20), 211–221.

Grolnick, W. S., & Ryan, R. M. (1989). Parents' styles associated with children's self-regulation and competence in school. *Journal of Educational Psychology, 81,* 143–154.

Gronau, R. C., & Waas, G. A. (1997). Delay of gratification and cue utilization: An examination of children's social information processing. *Merrill-Palmer Quarterly, 43,* 305–322.

Groos, K. (1901). *The play of man*. New York: Appleton.

Gross, E. F. (2004). Adolescent internet use: What we expect, what teens report. *Journal of Applied Developmental Psychology, 25*(6), 633–649.

Grotevant, H. D. (1998). Adolescent development in family contexts. In W. Damon (Ed.), *Handbook of child psychology* (5th ed., Vol. 3). New York: Wiley.

Grusec, J. E. (2002). Parental socialization and children's acquisition of values. In M. Bornstein (Ed.), *Handbook of parenting.* Mahwah, NJ: Erlbaum.

Grusec, J. E., & Abramovitch, R. (1982). Imitation of peers and adults in a natural setting: A functional analysis. *Child Development, 53*, 636–642.

Grusec, J. E., & Davidov, M. (2007). Socialization in the family: The roles of parents. In J. E. Grusec & P. D. Hastings (Eds.), *Handbook of socialization: Theory and research.* New York: Guilford Press.

Grusec, J. E., & Davidov, M. (2010). Integrating different perspectives on socialization theory and research: A domain-specific approach. *Child Development, 81*(3), 687–709.

Grusec, J. E., Goodenow, J. J., & Cohen, L. (1996). Household work and the development of concern for others. *Developmental Psychology, 32*, 999–1007.

Grusec, J. E., & Lytton, H. (1988). *Social development: History, theory, and research.* New York: Springer-Verlag.

Grusec, J. E., Saas-Korlsaak, P., & Simutis, Z. M. (1978). The role of example and moral exhortation in the training of altruism. *Child Development, 49*, 920–923.

Gummerum, M., Hanoch, Y., Keller, M., Parsons, K., & Hummel, A. (2010). Preschoolers allocations in the dictator game: The role of moral emotions. *Journal of Economic Psychology, 31*, 24–34.

Haefner, M. J., & Wartella, E. A. (1987). Effects of sibling coviewing on children's interpretations of television programs. *Journal of Broadcasting and Electronic Media, 31*, 153–168.

Hale, J. (1994). *Unbank the fire.* Baltimore, MD: Johns Hopkins University Press.

Hale, J. (2004). How schools shortchange African-American children. *Educational Leadership, 62*(3), 34–39.

Hale-Benson, J. E. (1986). *Black children: Their roots, culture, and learning styles* (rev. ed.). Baltimore, MD: Johns Hopkins University Press.

Hall, C. S. (1954). *A primer of Freudian psychology.* New York: New American Library.

Hall, E. T. (1964). *The silent language.* New York: Doubleday.

Hall, E. T. (1966). *The hidden dimension.* New York: Doubleday.

Hall, E. T. (1976). *Beyond culture.* New York: Doubleday.

Hall, E. T. (1983). *The dance of life.* New York: Doubleday.

Hallahan, D. P., Kauffman, J. M., & Pullen, P.C. (2009). *Exceptional children: Introduction to special education* (11th ed.). Columbus, OH: Merrill.

Hamm, R. H., & Hoving, K. L. (1969). Conformity of children in an ambiguous perceptual situation. *Child Development, 40*(3), 773–784.

Hamilton, M. C., Anderson, D., Broaddus, M., & Young, K. (2000). Gender stereotyping and under-representation of female characters in 200 popular children's picture books: A twenty-first century update. *Sex Roles, 55*(11–12), 757–765.

Hamre, B. K., & Pianta, R. C. (2001). Early teacher-child relationships and the trajectory of children's school outcomes through eighth grade. *Child Development, 72*(2), 625–638.

Handel, G., Cahill, S. E., & Elkin, F. (2007). *Children and society: The sociology of children and childhood socialization.* Los Angeles: Roxbury.

Haney, C., Banks, W. C., & Zimbardo, P. G. (1973). Interpersonal dynamics in a simulated prison. *International Journal of Criminology and Penology, 1*, 69–97.

Harris, J. R. (2009). *The nurture assumption: Why children turn out the way they do; revised and updated.* New York: Free Press.

Harris, R. (1999). *A cognitive psychology of mass communication* (3rd ed.). Mahwah, NJ: Erlbaum.

Harrison, A., Serafica, F., & McAdoo, H. (1984). Ethnic families of color. In R. D. Parke (Ed.), *Review of child development research*, Vol. 7: *The family.* Chicago: University of Chicago Press.

Hart, C. H., DeWolf, D. M., & Burts, D. C. (1992). Linkages among preschoolers' playground behavior, outcome expectations, and parental disciplinary strategies. *Early Education and Development, 3*, 265–283.

Harter, S. (1990). Issues in the assessment of the self-concept of children and adolescents. In A. M. LaGreco (Ed.), *Through the eyes of the child: Obtaining self-reports from children and adolescents.* Boston: Allyn and Bacon.

Harter, S. (1999). *The construction of the self: A developmental perspective.* New York: Guilford Press.

Harter, S. (2006). The self. In W. Damon & R. M. Lerner (Eds.), *Handbook of child psychology* (6th ed., Vol. 3). Hoboken, NJ: Wiley.

Harter, S., & Connell, J. P. (1984). A model of children's achievement and related self-perceptions of competence, control, and motivational orientations. In J. Nicholls (Ed.), *The development of achievement-related cognition and behavior.* Greenwich, CT: JAI Press.

Hartshorne, H., & May, M. (1978). *Studies in the nature of character*, Vol. 1: *Studies in deceit.* New York: Macmillan.

Hartup, W. W. (1983). Peer relations. In P. H. Mussen (Ed.), *Handbook of child psychology* (4th ed., Vol. 4). New York: Wiley.

Hartup, W. W. (1996). The company they keep: Friendships and their developmental significance. *Child Development, 67*, 1–13.

Hartup, W. W., & Coates, B. (1967). Imitation of a peer group and rewardingness of the model. *Child Development, 38*, 1003–1016.

Haskins, R., & Rouse, C. (2005). Closing achievement gaps: School readiness: Closing racial and ethnic gaps. *The Future of Children, 15*(1), 1–7.

Haskins, R., & Sawhill, I. (Eds.). (2007). Introducing the issue. *The Future of Children: The Next Generation of Antipoverty Policies, 17*(2), 1–9.

Hatcher, B., & Beck, S. S. (1997). *Learning opportunities beyond the school* (2nd ed.). Olney, MD: Association for Childhood Education International.

Havighurst, R. (1972). *Human development and education* (3rd ed.). New York: McKay.

Hay, D. F., Caplan, M., & Nash, A. (2009). Beginnings of peer relations. In K. H. Rubin, W. M. Bukowski, & B. P. Laursen (Eds.), *Handbook of peer interactions, relationships, and groups.* New York: Guilford Press.

Hayslip, B. J., & Kaminski, B. L. (2005). Grandparents raising grandchildren: A review of the literature and suggestions for practice. *The Gerontologist, 45*(2), 262–269.

Hayton, J. C., George, G., & Zahra, S. A. (2002). National culture and entrepreneurship: A review of behavioral research. *Entrepreneurship: Theory and Practice, 26*(4), 33–53.

Hayward, D. G., Rothenberg, M., & Beasley, R. R. (1974). Children's play in urban playground environments: A comparison of traditional, contemporary and adventure playground types. *Environment and Behavior, 6*(2), 131–168.

Healy, J. (1990). *Endangered minds: Why children don't think and what to do about it.* New York: Touchstone Books.

Heath, S. B. (1989). Oral and literate traditions among black Americans living in poverty. *American Psychologist, 44*(2), 367–373.

Hedley, A. A., Ogden, C. L., Johnson, C. L., Carroll, M. D., Curtin, L. R., & Flegal, K. M. (2004). Prevalence of overweight and obesity among U.S. children, adolescents, and adults, 1999–2002. *Journal of the American Medical Association, 291*(23), 2847–2850.

Hein, G., & Singer, T. (2009). Neuroscience meets social psychology: An integrative approach to human empathy and prosocial behavior. In M. Mikulincer & P. R. Shaver (Eds.), *Prosocial motives in emotions and behavior: The better angels of our nature.* Washington, DC: American Psychological Association.

Helburn, S. W., & Howes, C. (1996). Child care cost and quality. *The future of children, 6*(2), 62–82.

Helfer, M. E., Kempe, R. S., & Krugman, R. D. (Eds.). (1999). *The battered child* (5th ed.). Chicago: University of Chicago Press.

Hershkowitz, I., Lamb, M. E., Horowitz, D. (2007). Victimization of children with disabilities. *American Journal of Orthopsychiatry, 77*(4), 624–635.

Hetherington, E. M. (1988). Parents, children, and siblings six years after divorce. In R. A. Hinde & J. Stevenson-Hinde (Eds.), *Relationships within families.* Oxford: Oxford University Press.

Hetherington, E. M. (1989). Coping with family transitions: Winners, losers, and survivors. *Child Development, 60,* 1–4.

Hetherington, E. M. (1993). A review of the Virginia longitudinal study of divorce and remarriage: A focus on early adolescence. *Journal of Family Psychology, 7,* 39–56.

Hetherington, E. M., & Clingempeel, W. G. (1992). Coping with marital transitions. *Monographs of the Society for Research in Child Development, 57*(2–3, Serial No. 227).

Hetherington, E. M., & Kelly, J. (2002). *For better or for worse: Divorce reconsidered.* New York: Norton.

Hetherington, E. M., & Stanley-Hagen, N. (2002). Parenting in divorced and remarried families. In M. H. Bornstein (Ed.), *Handbook of parenting* (2nd ed.). Mahwah, NJ: Erlbaum.

Heward, W. L. (2008). *Exceptional children: An introduction to special education* (9th ed.). Englewood Cliffs, NJ: Prentice-Hall.

Hewitt, J. P. (2003). *Self and society: A symbolic interactionist social psychology* (9th ed.). Boston: Allyn and Bacon.

Hewlett, S. A., & West, C. (1998). *The war against parents.* Boston: Houghton Mifflin.

Heywood, C. (2001). *A history of childhood: Children and childhood.* Malden, MA: Blackwell.

Higgins, A. (1995). Educating for justice and community: Lawrence Kohlberg's vision of moral education. In W. M. Kurtines & J. L. Gewirtz (Eds.), *Moral development: An introduction.* Boston: Allyn and Bacon.

Hilgers, L. (2006). *Youth sports drawing more than ever.* www.CNN.com.

Hilliard, A. (1992, Summer). Behavioral style, culture, and teaching and learning. *Journal of Negro Education, 61*(3), 370–371.

Hilton, J. M., & DeVall, E. L. (1998). Comparison of parenting and children's behavior in single-mother, single-father, and intact families. *Journal of Divorce and Remarriage, 29,* 23–54.

Hitlin, S., Brown, J. S., Elder, G. H., Jr. (2006). Racial self-categorization in adolescence: Multiracial development and social pathways. *Child Development, 77*(57), 1298–1308.

Hochschild, A. R. (1989). *The second shift.* New York: Avon.

Hochschild, A. R. (1997). *The time bind.* New York: Metropolitan Books.

Hofer, C., & Eisenberg, N. (2008). Emotion-related regulation: Biological and cultural bases. In M. Vandekerckhove, C. von Scheve, S. Ismer, S. Jung, & S. Kronast (Eds.), *Regulating emotions: Culture, social necessity, and biological inheritance.* Oxford, UK: Blackwell Publishing.

Hoff, E., Laursen, B., & Tardiff, T. (2002). Status and parenting. In M. H. Bornstein (Ed.), *Handbook of parenting* (2nd ed., Vol. 3). Mahwah, NJ: Erlbaum.

Hofferth, S. L. (1996). Child care in the United States today. *The Future of Children, 6*(2), 41–61.

Hofferth, S. L. (2010). Home media and children's achievement and behavior. *Child Development, 81*(5), 1598–1619.

Hoffman, L. W. (2000). Maternal employment: Effects of social context. In R. D. Taylor & M. C. Wing (Eds.), *Resilience across contexts.* Mahwah, NJ: Erlbaum.

Hoffman, L. W., & Youngblade, L. H. (1999). *Mothers at work: Effects on children's well-being.* New York: Cambridge University Press.

Hoffman, M. L. (1983). Affective and cognitive processes in moral internalization. In E. T. Higgins, D. N. Ruble, & W. W. Hartup (Eds.), *Social cognition and social development.* Cambridge, UK: Cambridge University Press.

Hoffman, M. L. (1991). Empathy, social cognition, and moral actions. In W. M. Kurtines & J. L. Gewirtz (Eds.), *Handbook of moral behavior and development,* Vol. 1: *Theory.* Hillsdale, NJ: Erlbaum.

Hoffman, M. L. (2000). *Empathy and moral development.* New York: Cambridge University Press.

Hofstede, G. (1991). *Organizations and cultures: Software of the mind.* New York: McGraw-Hill.

Hogan, R., & Emler, N. (1995). Personality and moral development. In W. M. Kurtines & J. L. Gewirtz (Eds.), *Moral development: An introduction.* Boston: Allyn and Bacon.

Hohmann, M., & Weikart, D. P. (1995). *Educating young children: Active learning practices for preschool educators and child care programs.* Ypsilanti, MI: High/ScopePress.

Holmbeck, G. N., Paikoff, R. L., & Brooks-Gunn, J. (1995). Parenting adolescents. In M. H. Bornstein (Ed.), *Handbook of parenting* (Vol. 1). Mahwah, NJ: Erlbaum.

Honig, A. S. (1986). Stress and coping in children (Part I). *Young Children, 41*(4), 50–63.

Honig, A. S. (1993). Mental health for babies: What do theory and research teach us? *Young Children, 48*(3), 69–76.

Honig, A. S. (2002). Choosing child care for young children. In M. H. Bornstein (Ed.), *Handbook of parenting* (2nd ed., Vol. 4). Mahwah, NJ: Erlbaum.

Hopkins, H. R., & Klein, H. A. (1994). Multidimension self-perception: Linkages to parental nurturance. *Journal of Genetic Psychology, 154,* 465–473.

Horowitz, F. D., & Paden, L. Y. (1973). The effectiveness of environmental intervention programs. In B. M. Caldwell & H. N. Riccuiti (Eds.), *Review of child development research* (Vol. 3). Chicago: University of Chicago Press.

Howell, J. C., & Egley, A., Jr. (2005). Moving risk factors into developmental theories of gang membership. *Youth Violence and Juvenile Justice, 3*(4), 334–354.

Howes, C. (1988). Peer interaction of young children. *Monographs of the Society for Research in Child Development, 43*(1, Serial No. 217).

Howes, C. (2009). Friendship in early childhood. In K. H. Rubin, W. M. Bukowski, & B. P. Laursen (Eds.), *Handbook of peer relationships, interactions, and groups*. New York: Guilford Press.

Howes, C., & Matheson, C. C. (1992). Sequences in the development of competent play with peers: Social and social pretend play. *Developmental Psychology, 28*, 961–974.

Howes, C., Matheson, C. C., & Hamilton, C. E. (1994). Maternal, teacher, and child care history correlates of children's relationships with peers. *Child Development, 65*, 264–273.

Huck, C. S., Keifer, B. Z., Helper, S., & Hickman, J. (Eds.). (2004). *Children's literature in the elementary school* (8th ed.). New York: McGraw-Hill.

Huesmann, L. R., Eron, L. D., Klein, R., Brice, P., & Fisher, P. (1983). Mitigating the imitation of aggressive behavior by changing children's attitudes about media violence. *Journal of Personality and Social Psychology, 44*, 899–910.

Huesmann, L. R., Moise-Titus, J., Podolski, C., & Eron, L. D. (2003). Longitudinal relations between children's exposure to TV violence and their aggressive and violent behavior in young adulthood: 1977–1992. *Developmental Psychology, 39*(2), 201–221.

Hughes, F. P. (Ed.). (2010). *Children, play, and development* (4th ed.). Thousand Oaks: Sage.

Humphrey, J. H. (2003). *Child development through sports*. New York: Routledge.

Hurd, T. L., Lerner, R. M., & Barton, C. E. (1999). Integrated services: Expanding partnerships to meet the needs of today's children and families. *Young Children, 54*(2), 74–80.

Huston, A. C. (1983). Sex-typing. In P. H. Mussen (Ed.), *Handbook of child psychology* (4th ed., Vol. 4). New York: Wiley.

Huston, A. C., Bickham, D. S., Lee, J. M., & Wright, J. C. (2007). From attention to comprehension: How children watch and learn from television. In N. Pecora, J. P. Murray, & E. A. Wartella (Eds.), *Children and television: Fifty years of research*. Mahwah, NJ: Erlbaum.

Huston, A. C., Carpenter, C. J., Atwater, J. B., & Johnson, L. M. (1986). Gender, adult structuring of activities, and social behavior in middle childhood. *Child Development, 57*, 200–209.

Huston, A. C., Duncan, G. J., Granger, R., Bos, J., McLoyd, V., Mistry, R., et al. (2001). Work-based antipoverty programs for parents can enhance the school performance and social behavior of children. *Child Development, 72*, 318–336.

Huston, A. C., McLoyd, V. C., & Coll, C. G. (1994). Children and poverty: Issues in contemporary research. *Child Development, 65*, 275–282.

Huston, A. C., & Wright, J. C. (1998). Mass media and children's development. In W. Damon (Ed.), *Handbook of child psychology* (5th ed., Vol. 4). New York: Wiley.

Huston, A. C., Zillman, D., & Bryant, J. (1994). Media influence, public policy, and the family. In D. Zillman, J. Bryant, & A. C. Huston (Eds.), *Media, children, and the family: Social scientific, psychodynamic, and clinical perspectives*. Hillsdale, NJ: Erlbaum.

Hyde, J. S., Else-Quest, N. M., Goldsmith, H. H., & Biesanz, J. (2004). Children's temperament and behavior problems predict their employed mothers' work functioning. *Child Development, 75*(2), 580–594.

Hymel, S., Bowker, A., & Woody, E. (1993). Aggressive versus withdrawn unpopular children: Variations in peer and self-perceptions in multiple domains. *Child Development, 64*, 879–896.

Iervolino, A. C., Hines, M., Golombok, S. E., Rust, J., & Plomin, R. J. (2005). Genetics and environmental influences on sex-typed behavior during the preschool years. *Child Development, 76*, 826–840.

Ikramullah, E., Manlove, J., Cui, C., & Moore, K. A. (2009). Parents matter: The role of parents in teens' decisions about sex. *Child Trends* (www.childtrends.org).

Inhelder, B., & Piaget, J. (1958). *The growth of logical thinking from childhood to adolescence*. New York: Basic Books.

Inkeles, A. (1969). Social structure and socialization. In D. A. Goslin (Ed.), *Handbook of socialization theory and research*. Chicago: Rand McNally.

Institute of Education Sciences. (1999). *Service-learning and community service in K–12 public schools*. Washington, DC: U.S. Department of Education.

Jackson, L. A., von Eye, A., Biocca, F. A., Barbatsis, G., Zhao, K., & Fitzgerald, H. E. (2006). Does home Internet use influence the academic performance of low-income children? *Developmental Psychology, 42*(3), 429–435.

Jackson, R. K., & McBride, W. D. (2000). *Understanding street gangs*. Belmont, CA: Wadsworth.

Jackson, Y., & Warren, J. S. (2000). Appraisal, social support, and life events: Predicting outcome behavior in school-age children. *Child Development, 71*(5), 1441–1457.

Jacobs, J. A., & Gerson, K. (2004). *The time divide: Work, family, and gender inequality*. Cambridge, MA: Harvard University Press.

Jacobs, J. S., & Tunnell, M. O. (1996). *Children's literature, briefly*. Englewood Cliffs, NJ: Prentice-Hall.

Jacobson, J. L., & Wille, D. E. (1986). The influence of attachment pattern on developmental changes in peer interaction from the toddler to the preschool period. *Child Development, 57*, 338–347.

Jaffee, S., & Hyde, J. H. (2000). Gender differences in moral orientation: A meta-analysis. *Psychological Bulletin, 12*, 703–726.

Jaffee, S. R., Caspi, A., Moffitt, T. E., Polo-Thomas, M., Price, T. S., & Taylor, A. (2004). The limits of child effects: Evidence for genetically mediated child effects on corporal punishment, but not on physical maltreatment. *Developmental Psychology, 40*(6), 1047–1055.

James, M., & Jongeward, D. (1971). *Born to win*. Reading, MA: Addison-Wesley.

Johnson, D. W., & Johnson, R. T. (1999). *Learning together and alone: Cooperative, competitive, and individualistic learning* (5th ed.). Boston: Allyn and Bacon.

Johnson, D. W., Johnson, R. T., & Maruyama, G. (1983). Interdependence and interpersonal attraction among heterogeneous and homogeneous individuals: A theoretical formulation and a meta-analysis of the research. *Review of Education Research, 53*, 5–54.

Johnson, J. A., Musial, D. L., Hall, G. E., Gollnick, D. M., & Dupuis, V. L. (2004). *Introduction to the foundations of American education* (13th ed.). Needham Heights, MA: Allyn and Bacon.

Johnson, S., & O'Conner, E. (2002). *The gay baby boom: The psychology of gay parenthood*. New York: NYU Press.

Jones, K. L., Smith, D. W., Ulleland, C. L., & Streissguth, P. (1973). Patterns of malformation in offspring of chronic alcoholic mothers. *Lancet, 1*, 1267–1271.

Jones, L. M., & Foley, L. A. (2003). Educating children to decategorize racial groups. *Journal of Applied Social Psychology, 33* (3), 554–564.

Jose, P. E. (1990). Just world reasoning in children's immanent justice judgments. *Child Development, 61*, 1024–1033.

Joyce, B. R., Weil, M., & Calhoun, E. (2009). *Models of teaching* (8th ed.). Boston, MA: Allyn & Basor.

Jung, C. G. (1938). *Psychology and religion*. New Haven, CT: Yale University Press.

Jussim, L., & Eccles, J. (1995). Naturally occurring interpersonal expectancies. In N. Eisenberg (Ed.), *Social development: Review of personality and social psychology*. Thousand Oaks, CA: Sage.

Kacerguis, M. A., & Adams, G. R. (1980). Erikson stage resolution: The relationship between identity and intimacy. *Journal of Youth and Adolescence, 9*(2), 117–126.

Kagan, J. (1971). *Personality development*. New York: Harcourt Brace Jovanovich.

Kagan, J. (1984). *The nature of the child*. New York: Basic Books.

Kagan, J. (1994). *Galen's prophecy: Temperament in human nature*. New York: Basic Books.

Kagan, J. (1998). Biology and the child. In W. Damon (Ed.), *Handbook of child psychology* (5th ed., Vol. 3). New York: Wiley.

Kagicibasi, C. (1996). *Family and human development across cultures: A view from the other side*. Mahwah, NJ: Erlbaum.

Kaiser Family Foundation (KFF). (2003a). *Zero to six: Electronic media in the lives of infants, toddlers, and preschoolers*. Menlo Park, CA: Author.

KFF. (2003b, Spring). *Key facts: TV violence*. www.kff.org.

KFF. (2004). *Tweens, teens, and magazines*. Menlo Park, CA: Author.

KFF. (2005). *Sex-on-TV—4*. Menlo Park, CA: Author.

KFF. (2007). *The uninsured: A primer. Key facts about Americans without health insurance*. Menlo Park, CA: Author.

KFF. (2010). *Generation M^2: Media in the lives of 8- to 18-year olds*. Menlo Park, CA: Author.

Kalichman, S. C. (1999). *Mandated reporting of suspected child abuse: Ethics, law, and policy* (2nd ed.). Washington, DC: American Psychological Association.

Kallen, H. M. (1956). *Cultural pluralism and the American ideal*. Philadelphia: University of Pennsylvania Press.

Karoly, L. A. (Ed.). (1998). *Investing in our children: What we know and don't know about the costs and benefits of early childhood interventions*. Santa Monica, CA: Rand.

Kaslow, F. W. (2001). Families and family psychology at the millennium: Intersecting crossroads. *American Psychologist, 56*(1), 37–46.

Katchadourian, H. (1990). Sexuality. In S. S. Feldman & G. R. Elliot (Eds.), *At the threshold: The developing adolescent*. Cambridge, MA: Harvard University Press.

Katz, L. B. (1995). *Talks with teacher of young children: A collection*. Norwood, NJ: Ablex Publishing.

Katz, P., & Zalk, S. (1978). Modification of children's racial attitudes. *Developmental Psychology, 14*(5), 447–461.

Kearny, M. (1999). The role of teachers in helping children of domestic violence. *Childhood Education, 75*(5), 290–296.

Kellam, S. G., Ling, X., Merisca, R., Brown, C. H., & Ialongo, N. (1999). The effect of the level of aggression in the 1st grade classroom on the course and malleability of aggressive behavior into middle school. *Development and Psychopathology, 10*, 165–185.

Kelly, J. B. (2000). Children's adjustment in conflicted marriage and divorce: A decade's review of research. *Journal of the American Academy of Child and Adolescent Psychiatry, 39*, 963–973.

Kelly, J. B., & Emery, R. B. (2003). Children's adjustment following divorce: Risk and resilience perspectives. *Family Relations, 52*(4), 352–362.

Kemple, K. M. (1991). Research in review: Preschool children's peer acceptance and social interaction. *Young Children, 46*(5), 47–54.

Kerns, K. A., Contreras, J. M., & Neal-Barnett, A. M. (2000). *Family and peers: Linking two social worlds*. Westport, CT: Praeger.

Killen, M., Rutland, A., & Jampol, N. S. (2009). Social exclusion in childhood and adolescence. In K. H. Rubin, W. M. Bukowski, & B. P. Laursen (Eds.), *Handbook of peer interactions, relationships, and groups*. New York: Guilford Press.

Kim, J. E., Hetherington, E. M., & Reiss, D. (1999). Associations among family relationships, antisocial peers, and adolescents' externalizing behaviors: Gender and family type differences. *Child Development, 70*, 1209–1230.

Kindermann, T. (1998). Children's development within peer groups: Using composite social maps to identify peer networks and study their influences. In W. M. Bukowski & A. H. Cillesen (Eds.), *New directions for child development* (No. 80). San Francisco: Jossey-Bass.

Kindermann, T. A., & Gest, S. D. (2009). Assessment of the peer group: Identifying naturally occurring social networks and capturing their effects. In K. H. Rubin, W. M. Bukowski, & B. P. Laursen (Eds.), *Handbook of peer interactions, relationships, and groups*. New York: Guilford Press.

Kinney, D. A. (1993). From nerds to normals. *Sociology of Education, 66*(1), 21–40.

Kirkorian, H. L., Wartella, E. A., & Anderson, D. R. (2008). Media and young children's learning. *The Future of Children: Children and the Media, 18*(1), 39–65.

Kluckhohn, F. (1961). Dominant and variant value orientation. In C. Kluckhohn & H. Murray (Eds.), *Personality in nature and society*. New York: Knopf.

Kluckhohn, F., & Strodbeck, F. (1961). *Variations in value orientations*. Evanston, IL: Row Peterson.

Koblinsky, S., & Behana, N. (1984). Child sexual abuse: The educator's role in prevention, detection, and intervention. *Young Children, 39*(6), 3–15.

Kochanska, G. (1993). Toward a synthesis of parental socialization and child temperament in early development of conscience. *Child Development, 64*, 325–347.

Kochanska, G. (1995). Children's temperament, mothers' discipline, and security of attachment: Multiple pathways to emerging internalization. *Child Development, 66*, 597–615.

Kochanska, G. (1997). Multiple pathways to conscience for children with different temperaments: From toddlerhood to age 5. *Developmental Psychology, 33*, 228–240.

Kochanska, G., Askan, N., & Carlson, J. J. (2005). Temperament, relationships, and young children's receptive cooperation with their parents. *Developmental Psychology, 41*, 648–660.

Kohlberg, L. (1969). Stage and sequence: The cognitive developmental approach to socialization. In D. A. Goslin (Ed.), *Handbook of socialization theory and research.* Chicago: Rand McNally.

Kohlberg, L. (1976). Moral stages and moralization. In T. Lickona (Ed.), *Moral development and behavior.* New York: Holt, Rinehart & Winston.

Kohlberg, L. (1986). A current statement on some theoretical issues. In S. Modgil & C. Modgil (Eds.), *Lawrence Kohlberg.* Philadelphia: Folmer.

Kohn, M. (1977). *Class and conformity: A study in values* (2nd ed.). Chicago: University of Chicago University Press.

Kohn, M. (1995). Social structure and personality through time and space. In P. Moen, G. H. Elder, & K. Luscher (Eds.), *Examining lives in context: Perspectives on the ecology of human development.* Washington, DC: American Psychological Association.

Kohn, M. L. (2006). *Change and stability: A cross-national analysis of social structure and personality.* Boulder, CO: Paradigm.

Kostelnik, M. J., Whiren, A. P., & Stein, L. C. (1986). Living with He-Man. *Young Children, 41*(4), 3–9.

Kounin, J. (1970). *Discipline and group management in the classroom.* New York: Holt, Rinehart & Winston.

Kowaleski-Jones, L. (2000). Staying out of trouble: Community resources and problem behavior among high-risk adolescents. *Journal of Marriage and Family, 62*(2), 449–464.

Kozol, J. (1991). *Savage inequalities: Children in America's schools.* New York: Crown.

Krettenauer, T., Malti, T., & Sokol, B. (2008). The development of moral emotions and the happy victimizer phenomenom: A critical review of theory and applications. *European Journal of Developmental Science, 2*(3), 221–235.

Kristof, K. M. (2007, April 1). Venerable finance game abandons cash for credit. *Los Angeles Times*, p. C3.

Kuczen, B. (1987). *Childhood stress.* New York: Dell.

Kuczynski, L. (2003). Beyond bidirectionality: Bilateral conceptual frameworks for understanding dynamics in parent–child relations. In L. Kuczynski (Ed.), *Handbook of dynamics in parent–child relationships.* Thousand Oaks, CA: Sage.

Kunkel, D. (2001). Children and television advertising. In D. G. Singer & J. L. Singer (Eds.), *Handbook of children and the media.* Thousand Oaks, CA: Sage.

Kurtines, W. M., & Gewirtz, J. (Eds.). (1991). *Handbook of moral behavior and development.* Hillsdale, NJ: Erlbaum.

Ladd, G. W. (1990). Having friends, keeping friends, making friends, and being liked by peers in the classroom: Predictions of children's early school adjustment. *Child Development, 61*, 1081–1100.

Ladd, G. W. (2005). *Children's peer relations and social competence: A century of progress.* New Haven, CT: Yale University Press.

Ladd, G. W., & LeSieur, K. D. (1995). Parents and peer relationships. In M. H. Bornstein (Ed.), *Handbook of parenting* (Vol. 4). Mahwah, NJ: Erlbaum.

Ladd, G. W., & Pettit, G. S. (2002). Parenting and the development of children's peer relationships. In M. H. Bornstein (Ed.), *Handbook of parenting* (2nd ed.). Mahwah, NJ: Erlbaum.

Lagerspetz, K. M. J., Bjorkquist, K., Berts, M., & King, E. (1982). Group aggression among school children in three schools. *Scandinavian Journal of Psychology, 23*, 45 52.

Laible, D., & Thompson, R. A. (2007). Early socialization: A relationship perspective. In J. E. Grusec & P. D. Hastings (Eds.), *Handbook of socialization: Theory and research.* New York: Guilford.

Lamb, M. E. (2000). The effects of quality of care on child development. *Applied Developmental Science, 4*(3), 112–115.

Lamb, M. E. (Ed.). (2004). *The role of the father in child development* (4th ed.). New York: Wiley.

Lamb, M. E., & Ahnert, L. (2006). Nonparental child care: Context, concepts, correlates, and consequences. In W. Damon & R. M. Lerner (Eds.), *Handbook of child psychology* (6th ed., Vol. 4). Hoboken, NJ: Wiley.

Lamb, M. E., Hwang, C. P., Ketterlinus, R. D., & Fracasso, M. F. (1999). Parent–child relationships: Development in the context of the family. In M. H. Bornstein & M. E. Lamb (Eds.), *Developmental psychology: An advanced textbook* (4th ed.). Mahwah, NJ: Erlbaum.

Landre, R., Miller, M., & Porter, D. (1997). *Gangs: A handbook for community awareness.* New York: Facts on File.

Langlois, J. H. (1986). From the eye of the beholder to behavioral reality: Development of social behavior and social relations as a function of physical attractiveness. In C. P. Herman, M. P. Zanna, & E. T. Higgins (Eds.), *Physical behavior: The Ontario Symposium* (Vol. 3). Hillsdale, NJ: Erlbaum.

Langlois, J. H., & Downs, A. C. (1980). Mothers, fathers, and peers as socialization agents of sex-typed behaviors in young children. *Child Development, 51*, 1217–1247.

Langlois, J. H., & Liben, L. S. (2003). Child care research: An editorial perspective. *Child Development, 74*(4), 969–975.

Lansford, J. E. (2009). Parental divorce and children's adjustment. *Perspectives in Psychological Science, 4*(2), 140–152.

Lapsley, D. K. (1996). *Moral psychology.* Boulder, CO: Westview.

Lareau, A. (2002). Invisible inequality: Social class and child rearing in black and white families. *American Sociological Review, 67*(5), 747–776.

Larson, R. (1995). Secrets in the bedroom: Adolescents' private use of media. *Journal of Youth and Adolescence, 24*(5), 535–550.

Larson, R., Kubey, R., & Colletti, J. (1989). Changing channels: Early adolescent media choices and shifting investments in family and friends. *Journal of Youth and Adolescence, 18*(16), 583–599.

Lasker, J. (1972). *Mothers can do anything.* Chicago: Albert Whitman.

Leach, P. (1994). *Children first.* New York: Knopf.

Leaf, M. (1936). *The story of Ferdinand.* New York: Viking/Penguin.

Leaper, C. (2000). Gender, affiliation, assertion, and the interactive context of parent–child play. *Developmental Psychology, 36*, 381–393.

Leaper, C. (2002). Parenting girls and boys. In M. H. Bornstein (Ed.), *Handbook of parenting* (2nd ed., Vol. 1). Mahwah, NJ: Erlbaum.

Leaper, C., & Bigler, R. S. (2011). Gender as a context for social development. In M. Underwood & C. H. Rosen (Eds.), *Social development*. New York: Guilford Press.

Leaper, C., & Friedman, C. K. (2007). The socialization of gender. In J. E. Grusec & P. D. Hastings (Eds.), *Handbook of socialization: Theory and research*. New York: Guilford.

Lee, V. E. (2004). School size and the organization of secondary schools. In J. H. Ballantine & J. Z. Spade (Eds.), *Schools and society: A sociological approach to education* (2nd ed.). Belmont, CA: Wadsworth.

Leithwood, K., & Jantzi, D. (2009). A review of empirical evidence about school size effects: A policy perspective. *Review of Educational Research, 79*(1), 464–490.

Lengua, L. J. (2002). The contribution of emotionality and self-regulation to the understanding of children's response to multiple risk. *Child Development, 73*, 144–161.

Lerner, J. V. (1993). The influence of child temperamental characteristics on parent behaviors. In T. Luster & L. Okagaki (Eds.), *Parenting: An ecological perspective*. Hillsdale, NJ: Erlbaum.

Lerner, R. M. (2006). Developmental science, developmental systems and contemporary theories of human development. In W. Damon & R. M. Lerner (Eds.), *Handbook of child psychology* (6th ed., Vol. 1). Hoboken, NJ: Wiley.

Leu, D. J., Jr., Castek, J., Hartman, D., Coiro, J., Henry, L. A., Kulikowich, J., & Lyver, S. (2005). *Evaluating the development of scientific knowledge and new forms of reading comprehension during online learning*. Grant funded by the North Central Regional Educational Laboratory, subdivision of Learning Associates.

Leventhal, T., & Brooks-Gunn, J. (2000). The neighborhoods they live in: The effects of neighborhood residence on child and adolescent outcomes. *Psychological Bulletin, 126*(2), 309–337.

Lever, J. (1978). Sex differences in the complexity of children's play. *American Sociological Review, 43*, 471–482.

Levin, D. E. (1998). *Remote control childhood? Combating the hazards of media culture*. Washington, DC: National Association for the Education of Young Children.

Levin, D. E., & Carlsson-Paige, N. (1995). The Mightly Morphin Power Rangers: Teachers voice concern. *Young Children, 50*(6), 67–72.

Levin, D. E., & Kilbourne, J. (2009). So sexy so soon: The new sexualized childhood and what parents can do to protect their kids. New York: Ballantine Books.

LeVine, R. A. (1988). Human parental care: Universal goals, cultural strategies, individual behavior. In R. A. LeVine, P. M. Miller, & M. M. West (Eds.), *Parental behavior in diverse societies*. San Francisco: Jossey-Bass.

LeVine, R. A. (2003). *Childhood socialization: Comparative studies of parenting, learning and educational change*. Seattle, WA: University of Washington Press.

Lewin, K., Lippitt, R., & White, R. (1939). Patterns of aggressive behavior in experimentally created social climates. *Journal of Social Psychology, 10*, 271–299.

Leyendecker, B., Harwood, R. L., & Compacini, L. (2005). Socioeconomic status, ethnicity, and parenting. In T. Luster & L. Okagaki (Eds.), *Parenting: An ecological perspective* (2nd ed.). Mahwah, NJ: Erlbaum.

Liben, L. S., & Bigler, R. S. (2002). The developmental course of gender differentiation: Conceptualizing, measuring, and evaluating constructs and pathways. *Monographs of the Society for Research in Child Development, 67*(2, Serial No. 269).

Limber, S. P., & Nation, M. A. (1998). Violence within the neighborhood and community. In P. K. Trickett & C. J. Schellenbach (Eds.), *Violence against children in the family and the community*. Washington, DC: American Psychological Association.

Linney, J. A., & Seidman, E. (1989). The future of schooling. *American Psychologist, 44*(2), 336–340.

Lippa, R. A. (2005). *Gender, nature, and nurture* (2nd ed.). Mahwah, NJ: Erlbaum.

Lippitt, R., & White, R. K. (1943). The social climate of children's groups. In R. G. Barker, J. S. Korinen, & H. F. Wright (Eds.), *Child behavior and development*. New York: McGraw-Hill.

Livingston, G., & Parker, K. (2010). *Since the start of the Great Recession, more children raised by grandparents*. Washington, DC: Pew Research Center.

Livingstone, S. (2009). *Children and the Internet: Great expectations, challenging realities*. Cambridge, UK: Polity.

Logan, C., Moore, K., Manlove, J., Mincieli, L., & Cunningham, S. (2007). Conceptualizing a "strong start": Antecedents of positive child outcomes at birth and into early childhood. *Child Trends Research Brief* # 2007–10, 1–8.

Logue, A. W. (1995). *Self-control: Waiting until tomorrow for what you want today*. Englewood Cliffs, NJ: Prentice-Hall.

Long, C. (2008). Silencing the cyberbullies. *NEA Today, 26*(8), 28–29.

Longmore, M. A., Eng, A. L., Giordano, P. C., & Manning, W. D. (2009). Parenting and adolescents' sexual initiation. *Journal of Marriage and Family, 71*(4), 969–982.

Lonigan, C. J., Burgess, S. R., & Anthony, J. L. (2000). Development of emergent literacy and early reading skills in preschool children: Evidence from a latent-variable longitudinal study. *Developmental Psychology, 36*, 596–613.

Lorch, E. P. (2007). Health, drugs, and values. In N. Pecora, J. P. Murray, & E. A. Wartella (Eds.), *Children and television: Fifty years of research*. Mahwah, NJ: Erlbaum.

Lowenthal, B. (1999). Effects of maltreatment and ways to promote children's resiliency. *Childhood Education, 75*(4), 204–209.

Lull, J. (1980). The social uses of television. *Human Communication Research, 6*, 197–209.

Luster, T., & Okagaki, L. (1993). Multiple influences on parenting: Ecological and life-course perspectives. In T. Luster & L. Okagaki (Eds.), *Parenting: An ecological perspective*. Hillsdale, NJ: Erlbaum.

Lustig, M., & Koester, J. (1999). *Intercultural competence: Interpersonal communication across cultures*. New York: Longman Press.

Luthar, S. S., & Becker, B. E. (2002). Privileged but pressured? A study of affluent youth. *Child Development, 73*, 1593–1610.

Lytton, H., & Romney, D. M. (1991). Parents' differential socialization of boys and girls: A meta-analysis. *Psychological Bulletin, 109*, 267–296.

Maas, C., Herrenkohl, T. I., Sousa, C. (2008, January). Review of research on child maltreatment and violence in youth. *Trauma Violence Abuse, 9*(1), 56–67.

Maccoby, E. E. (1990). Gender and relationships: A developmental account. *American Psychologist, 45*, 513–520.

Maccoby, E. E. (1998). *The two sexes: Growing up apart, coming together*. Cambridge, MA: Harvard University Press.

Maccoby, E. E. (2000). Perspectives on gender development. *International Journal of Behavioral Development, 24*, 398–406.

Maccoby, E. E. (2007). Historical overview of socialization research and theory. In J. E. Grusec & P. D. Hastings (Eds.), *Handbook of socialization: Theory and research*. New York: Guilford.

Maccoby, E. E., & Jacklin, C. N. (1974). *The psychology of sex differences*. Stanford, CA: Stanford University Press.

Maccoby, E. E., & Martin, J. (1983). Socialization in the context of family: Parent–child interaction. In P. H. Mussen (Ed.), *Handbook of child psychology* (4th ed., Vol. 4). New York: Wiley.

Maccoby, E. E., & Mnooken, R. (Eds.). (1992). *Dividing the child*. Cambridge, MA: Harvard University Press.

MacDonald, K., & Parke, R. D. (1986). Parent–child physical play: The effects of sex and age of children and parents. *Sex Roles, 15*(7/8), 367–378.

Macionis, J. (2005). *Sociology* (10th ed.). Upper Saddle River, NJ: Prentice Hall.

MacLeod, A. S. (1994). *American childhood*. Athens: University of Georgia Press.

Macleod, J. (2008). *Ain't no makin' it* (3rd ed.). Boulder, CO: Westview Press.

Maddux, J. E., & Volkmann, J. (2010). Self-efficacy. In R. H. Hoyle (Ed.), *Handbook of personality and self-regulation*. Oxford, UK: Wiley-Blackwell.

Madon, S., Jussim, L., & Eccles, J. (1997). In search of the powerful self-fulfilling prophecy. *Journal of Personality and Social Psychology, 72*, 791–809.

Madsen, M. C., & Shapira, A. (1970). Cooperative and competitive behavior of urban Afro-American, Anglo-American, and Mexican-American and Mexican village children. *Developmental Psychology, 3*, 16–20.

Maehr, M. L. (1974). *Sociocultural origins of achievement*. Monterey, CA: Brooks/Cole.

Magno, C., Profugo, D., & Mendoza, S. (2008). Developing Asian values, self-construal and resiliency through family efficacy and parental closeness. *Journal of Research and Review, 1*(1), 1–17.

Mahoney, J. L., Larson, R. W., Eccles, J. S., & Lord, H. (2005). Organized activities as developmental contexts for children and adolescents. In J. L. Mahoney, R. W. Larson, & J. S. Eccles (Eds.), *Organized activities as contexts for development*. Mahwah, NJ: Lawrence Erlbaum.

Main, M., & Solomon, J. (1990). Procedures for identifying infants as disorganized/disoriented during the Ainsworth strange situation. In M. T. Greenberg, D. Cicchetti, & E. M. Cummings (Eds.), *Attachment in the preschool years: Theory, research, and intervention*. Chicago: University of Chicago Press.

Malamuth, N. M., & Impett, E. A. (2001). Research on sex in the media. In D. G. Singer & J. L. Singer (Eds.). *Handbook of children and the media*. Thousand Oaks, CA: Sage.

Malti, T., & Latzko, B. (2010). Children's moral emotions and moral cognition towards an integrative perspective. In B. Latzko & T. Malti (Eds.), *Children's moral emotions and moral cognition: Developmental and educational perspectives, new directions for child and adolescent development*. San Francisco, CA: Jossey Bass.

Marcia, J. E. (1966). Development and validation of ego-identity status. *Journal of Personality and Social Psychology, 3*, 551–558.

Margolin, G. (1998). Effects of domestic violence on children. In P. K. Trickett & C. J. Schellenbach (Eds.), *Violence against children in the family and the community*. Washington, DC: American Psychological Association.

Martin, C. L. (1989). Children's use of gender-related information in making social judgments. *Developmental Psychology, 25*, 80–88.

Martin, C. L., & Halverson, C. F. (1981). A schematic processing model of sex-typing and stereotyping in children. *Child Development, 52*, 1119–1134.

Martin, C. L., & Halverson, C. F., Jr. (1987). The roles of cognition in sex-roles and sex-typing. In D. B. Carter (Ed.), *Current conceptions of sex roles and sex-typing: Theory and research*. New York: Praeger.

Martin, C. L., Wood, C. H., & Little, J. K. (1990). The development of gender stereotype components. *Child Development, 61*, 1891–1904.

Martin, G., & Pear, J. (2010). *Behavior modification: What it is and how to do it* (9th ed.). Upper Saddle River, NJ: Prentice-Hall.

Martin, G. B., & Clark, R. D., III. (1982). Distress crying in neonates: Species and peer specificity. *Developmental Psychology, 18*, 3–9.

Martinez, I., Garcia, J. F., & Pubero, S. (2007). Parenting styles and adolescents' self-esteem in Brazil. *Psychological Reports, 100*, 731–745.

Martinez, R., & Dukes, R. L. (1991). Ethnic and gender differences and self-esteem. *Youth and Society, 3*, 318–338.

Martino, S. C., Ellickson, P. L., & McCaffrey, D. F. (2009). Multiple projectories of peer and parental influence and their association with the development of adolescent heavy drinking. *Addiction Behavior, 34*(8), 693–700.

Mason, K. O., & Duberstein, L. (1992). Consequences of child-care practices and arrangements for the well-being of parents and providers. In A. Booth (Ed.), *Child care in the 1990s: Trends and consequences*. Hillsdale, NJ: Erlbaum.

Mason, M. A. (1998). *The custody wars: Why children are losing the legal battle—and what we can do about it*. New York: Basic Books.

Mason, M. G., & Gibbs, J. C. (1993). Social perspective taking and moral judgement among college students. *Journal of Adolescent Research, 8*, 109–123.

Massoni, K. (2010). *Fashioning teenagers: A cultural history of Seventeen magazine*. Walnut Creek, CA: Left Coast Press.

Masten, A. S., & Coatsworth, J. D. (1998). The development of competence in favorable and unfavorable environments. *American Psychologist, 53*(2), 205–220.

Maughan, A., & Cicchetti, D. (2002). Impact of child maltreatment and interadult violence on children's emotion-regulation abilities and socioemotional adjustment. *Child Development, 73*, 1525–1542.

Maushard, M., Martin, C. S., Hutchins, D. J., Greenfield, M. D., Thomas, B. G., Founier, A., & Pickett, G. (Eds.). (2007). *Promising partnership practices 2007*. Baltimore, MD: National Network of Partnership Schools.

Mayer, S. (1997). *What money can't buy: Family income and children's life chances*. Cambridge, MA: Harvard University Press.

Mayes, L. C., & Zigler, E. (1992). An observational study of the affective concomitants of mastery in infants. *Journal of Psychology and Psychiatry, 4*, 659–667.

McClelland, D. C., Atkinson, J. W., Clark, R. A., & Lowell, E. L. (1953). *The achievement motive*. New York: Appleton-Century-Crofts.

McGoldrick, M., Giordano, J., Pearse, J. K., & Giordano, J. (1996). *Ethnicity and family therapy* (2nd ed.). New York: Guilford.

McHale, J. P. (1995). Coparenting and triadic interactions during infancy: The roles of marital distress and child gender. *Developmental Psychology, 31*, 985–996.

McHale, S. M., Crouter, A. C., & Tucker, C. J. (1999). Family context and gender-role socialization in middle childhood: Comparing girls to boys and sisters to brothers. *Child Development, 70*, 990–1004.

McHale, S. M., Crouter, A. C., & Whiteman, S. D. (2003). The family contexts of gender development in childhood and adolescence. *Social Development, 12*(1), 125–148.

McHale, S. M., Updegraff, K. A., Jackson-Newsom, J., Tucker, C. J., & Crouter, A. C. (2000). When does parents' differential treatment have negative implications for siblings? *Social Development, 9*, 149–172.

McLanahan, S., & Carlson, M. J. (2002). Welfare reform, fertility, and father involvement: Children and welfare reform. *The Future of Children, 12*(1), 147–165.

McLane, J. B., & McNamee, G. D. (1990). *Early literacy*. Cambridge, MA: Harvard University Press.

McLean, M. E., Wolery, M., & Bailey, D. B. (2003). *Assessing infants and preschoolers with special needs* (3rd ed.). Upper Saddle River, NJ: Prentice Hall.

McLoyd, V. C., Aikens, N. L., & Burton, L.M. (2006). Children in poverty: Development, public policy, and practice. In W. Damon & R. M. Lerner (Eds.), *Handbook of child psychology* (6th ed., Vol. 4). Hoboken, NJ: Wiley.

McLuhan, M. (1964). *Understanding media: The extension of man*. New York: McGraw-Hill.

McLuhan, M. (1989). A McLuhan mosaic. In G. Sanderson & F. Macdonald (Eds.), *Marshall McLuhan: The man and his message*. Golden, CO: Fulcrum.

McNally, L., Eisenberg, J., & Harris, J. D. (1991). Consistency and change in maternal child-rearing practices and values: A longitudinal study. *Child Development, 62*, 190–198.

McNeal, J. (1987). *Children as consumers*. Lexington, MA: Lexington Books.

McNeely, C. A., Nonnemaker, J. M., & Blum, R. (2002). Promoting student connectedness to school: Evidence from the National Longitudinal Study of Adolescent Health. *Journal of School Health, 72*(4), 138–146.

Mead, G. H. (1934). *Mind, self, and society*. Chicago: University of Chicago Press.

Meadow-Orlans, K. P. (1995). Parenting with a sensory or physical disability. In M. H. Bornstein (Ed.), *Handbook of parenting* (Vol. 4). Mahwah, NJ: Erlbaum.

Mednick, S. A., Moffit, M., Gabrielli, W., Jr., & Hutchings, B. (1986). Genetic factors in criminal behavior: A review. In D. Olweus, J. Block, & M. Radke-Yarrow (Eds.), *Development of antisocial and prosocial behavior: Research, theories, and issues*. Orlando, FL: Academic Press.

Medrich, E. A., Roizen, J., Rubin, V., & Buckley, S. (1981). *The serious business of growing up: A study of children's lives outside of school*. Berkeley: University of California Press.

Meisels, S. J., Jablou, J. R., Marsden, D. B., Dichtelmiller, M. L., & Dorfman, A. B. (2001). *The work sampling system*. New York: Pearson Early Learning.

Meisels, S. J., & Shonkoff, J. P. (Eds.). (2000), *Handbook of early childhood intervention* (2nd ed.). New York: Cambridge University Press.

Meringoff, L. K. (1980). Influence of the medium on children's story comprehension. *Journal of Educational Psychology, 72*, 240–249.

Meyers, J., & Kyle, J. E. (1998). The makings of a family-friendly city and municipal government's role. *Nation's Cities Weekly, 21*(28), 9–16.

Milgram, S. (1963). Behavioral study of obedience. *Journal of Abnormal and Social Psychology, 67*, 371–378.

Milgram, S. (1967). The small world problem. *Psychology Today, 61*(1), 60–67.

Milgram, S. (2004). *Obedience to authority: An experimental view*. New York: Harper Collins.

Miller, D. F. (1989). *First steps toward cultural differences: Socialization in infant/toddler day care*. Washington, DC: Child Welfare League of America.

Miller, E., & Almon, J. (2009). *Crisis in the kindergarten: Why children need play in school*. Alliance for Childhood, www.allianceforchildhood.org.

Miller, J. G., & Bersoff, D. M. (1993, March). *Culture and affective closeness in the morality of caring*. Paper presented at the biennial meeting of the Society for Research in Child Development, New Orleans.

Miller, K. E., Sabo, D. F., Farrell, M. P., Barnes, G. M., & Melnick, M. J. (1998). Athletic participation and sexual behavior in adolescents: The different worlds of boys and girls. *Journal of Health and Social Behavior, 39*, 108–123.

Miller, L. B., & Dyer, J. L. (1975). Four preschool programs: Their dimensions and effects. *Monographs of the Society for Research in Child Development, 40*(5–6, Serial No. 162).

Mintz, S. (1998). From patriarchy to androgeny and other myths: Placing men's family roles in historical perspectives. In A. Booth & A. C. Crouter (Eds.), *Men in families*. Mahwah, NJ: Erlbaum.

Mintz, S. (2006). *Huck's raft: A history of American childhood*. Cambridge, MA: Belknap, Harvard University Press.

Mischel, W. (1974). Processes in the delay of gratification. In L. Berkowitz (Ed.), *Advances in experimental social psychology* (Vol. 7). Orlando, FL: Academic Press.

Mischel, W., Shoda, Y., & Peake, P. K. (1988). The nature of adolescent competencies predicted by preschool delay of gratification. *Journal of Personality and Social Psychology, 54*, 687–696.

Mistry, R. S., Vandewater, E. A., Huston, A. C., & McLoyd, V. C. (2002). Economic well-being and children's social adjustment: The role of family process in an ethnically diverse low-income sample. *Child Development, 73*, 935–951.

Mize, J., & Ladd, G. W. (1990). A cognitive social learning approach to social skill training with low-status preschool children. *Developmental Psychology, 26*, 388–397.

Montessori, M. (1967). *The absorbent mind.* New York: Holt, Rinehart & Winston.

Montgomery, K. C. (2000). Children's media culture in the new millenium: Mapping the digital landscape. Children and computer technology. *The Future of Children, 10*(2), 145–167.

Moore, K. A., Redd, Z., Burkhauser, M., Mbwana, K., & Collins, A. (2009). Children in poverty: Trends, consequences, and policy options. *Child Trends Research Brief.* Washington, DC: Child Trends.

Moore, S., & Rosenthal, D. (2006). *Sexuality in adolescence: Current trends.* New York: Routledge.

Morrison, G. H. (1980). *Early childhood education today* (2nd ed.). Columbus, OH: Merrill.

Mounts, N. S. (2002). Parental management of adolescent peer relationships in context: The role of parenting style. *Journal of Family Psychology, 16*, 58–69.

Mruk, C. J. (2006). *Self-esteem research, theory, and practice: Toward a positive psychology of self-esteem* (3rd ed.). New York: Springer Publishing Company.

Murdock, G. P. (1962). Structures and functions of the family. In R. F. Winch, R. M. McGinnis, & H. R. Barringer (Eds.), *Selected studies in marriage and the family.* New York: Holt, Rinehart & Winston.

Murphy, S. (1999). *The cheers and the tears: A healthy alternative to the dark side of youth sports today.* San Francisco: Jossey-Bass.

Murray, J. P. (2007). TV violence: Research and controversy. In N. Pecora, J. P. Murray, & E. A. Wartella (Eds.), *Children and television: Fifty years of research.* Mahwah, NJ: Erlbaum.

Nader, R. (1965). *Unsafe at any speed: The designed-in dangers of the American automobile.* New York: Grossman.

Nadler, A. (1991). Help-seeking behavior: Psychological costs and instrumental benefits. In M. S. Clark (Ed.), *Prosocial behavior.* Newbury Park, CA: Sage.

Naisbitt, J. (2006). *Mind set! Reset your thinking and see the future.* New York: Harper Collins.

Naisbitt, J., & Auberdene, P. (1990). *Megatrends 2000.* New York: William Morrison.

Nalley, R. (1973). Sociobiology: A new view of human nature. In H. E. Fitzgerald & T. H. Carr (Eds.), *Human development 83/84.* Guilford, CT: Dushkin.

Nathanson, A. I. (2001). Parents versus peers: Exploring the significance of peer mediation of antisocial television. *Communication Research, 28*(3), 251–274.

National Alliance to End Homelessness. (2010). *Snapshot of homelessness.* Author (http://www.endhomelessness.org).

National Association for the Education of Young Children (NAEYC). (1984). *Accreditation criteria and procedures of the National Academy of Early Childhood Programs.* Washington, DC: Author.

NAEYC. (1988). NAEYC position statement on standardized testing of young children 3 through 8 years of age. *Young Children, 43*(3), 42–47.

NAEYC (1995). *Position statements on school readiness.* http://www.naeyc.org/resources/position.

NAEYC. (1996a). NAEYC position statement: Responding to linguistic and cultural diversity—Recommendations for effective early childhood education. *Young Children, 51*(2), 4–12.

NAEYC. (1996b). Public policy report: Be a children's champion. *Young Children, 51*(2), 58–60.

National Association of School Psychologists. (2001). *Helping children cope with loss, death, and grief: Response to a national tragedy.* Bethesda, MD: Author.

National Association of Social Workers. (2005). *NASW standards for social work practice in child welfare.* http://www.socialworkers.org.

National Association of State Boards of Education (NASBE). (2000). *Fit, healthy, and ready to learn,* Part 1: *Physical activity, healthy eating, and tobacco-use prevention.* Alexandria, VA: National Association of State Boards of Education.

National Center on Addiction and Substance Abuse. (1998). *No safe haven: Children of substance abusing parents.* New York: Columbia University.

National Center for Education Statistics (NCES), Institute of Education Science (IES). (2007). *Status and trends in the education of racial and ethnic minorities.* Washington, DC: U.S. Department of Education.

NCES, (IES) (2008). *Number, percentage, and percentage distribution of children ages 3 to 21 served under the Individuals with Disabilities Education Act (IDEA), by race and ethnicity.* Washington, DC: U.S. Department of Education.

National Clearinghouse on Child Abuse and Neglect. (2002). *http://*www.childwelfare.gov.

National Coalition Against Domestic Violence. (1999). *The Violence Against Women Act of 1999.* www.ncadv.org.

National Commission on Children (NCC). (1991). *Beyond rhetoric: A new American agenda for children and families.* Washington, DC: U.S. Government Printing Office.

National Commission on Excellence in Education. (1983). *A nation at risk: The imperative for educational reform.* Washington, DC: U.S. Government Printing Office.

National Conference of State Legislators. (2008). http://www.NCSL.org.

National Education Association. (2009). Hate crime prevention act. *Legislative Action Center.* http://www.nea.org/

National Education Goals Panel. (1999). *The national education goals report: Building a nation of learners 1999.* Washington, DC: U.S. Government Printing Office.

National Institute of Child Health and Development (NICHD). (2001). *Adventures in parenting.* Washington, DC: U.S. Government Printing Office.

NICHD Early Child Care Research Network. (1996). Characteristics of infant child care: Factors contributing to positive caregiving. *Early Childhood Research Quarterly, 11*, 269–306.

NICHD Early Child Care Research Network. (1997). The effects of infant child care on infant–mother attachment security: Results of the NICHD study of early child care. *Child Development, 68*, 860–879.

NICHD Early Child Care Research Network. (1998). Early child care and self-control, compliance, and problem behavior at twenty-four and thirty-six months. *Child Development, 69*, 1145–1170.

NICHD Early Child Care Research Network (Eds.). (2005). *Child care and child development.* New York: Guilford.

NICHD Early Childcare Research Network. (2007). Are there long-term effects of early child care? *Child Development, 78*(2), 681–701.

NICHD Early Childcare Research Network. (2010). Do effects of early childhood care extend to age 15? Results from the NICHD study of early child care and youth development. *Child Development, 81*(3), 731–756.

National Institute on Drug Abuse (NIDA). (2008). http://www.drugabuse.gov.

NIDA. (2010). *Drugs, brains, and behavior: The science of addiction.* Washington, DC: U.S. Government Printing Office.

National Institute on Media and the Family. (2001). *Fact sheet: Effects of video playing on children.* http://www.mediaandthefamily.org/.

National Institutes of Health. (2003). *Preventing drug use among children and adolescents: A research-based guide for parents, educators, and community leaders* (2nd ed.). Washington DC: U.S. Government Printing Office.

Neuman, S. G. (1995). *Literacy in the television age: The myth of the TV effect* (2nd ed.). Norwood, NJ: Ablex.

Newman, B. N., & Newman, P. R. (2011). *Development through life: A psychosocial approach* (11th ed.). Belmont, CA: Wadsworth.

Niles, F. S. (1981). The youth culture controversy: An evaluation. *Journal of Early Adolescence, 1*(3), 265–271.

Nisbett, R. E., & Cohen, D. (1996). *Culture of honor.* Boulder. CO: Westview Press.

Norton, D. E., & Norton, S. E. (2010). *Through the eyes of a child: An introduction to children's literature* (8th ed.). Upper Saddle River, NJ: Prentice-Hall.

Norwood, R. (2005, August 6). NCAA to crack down on "hostile" nicknames. *Los Angeles Times*, pp. A1, A20.

Novotney, A. (2009). The price of affluence. *Monitor on Psychology, 40*(1), 50–52.

Novotney, A. (2010). The recession's toll on children. *Monitor on Psychology, 41*(8), 43–45.

Nucci, L. P. (2008). *Nice is not enough: A teacher's guide to education in the moral domain.* Columbus, OH: Merrill.

Oakes, J. M., & Rossi, P. H. (2003). The measurement of SES in health research: Current practice and steps toward a new approach. *Social Science and Medicine, 56*, 769–784.

O'Brien, S. J. (1984). *Child abuse and neglect: Everyone's problem.* Wheaton, MD: Association for Childhood Education International.

Oden, S., & Asher, S. (1977). Coaching children in social skills for friendship making. *Child Development, 48*, 495–506.

Ogbu, J. U. (1994). From cultural differences to cultural frames of reference. In P. M. Greenfield & R. R. Cocking (Eds.), *Cross-cultural roots of minority child development.* Hillsdale, NJ: Erlbaum.

Ojalvo, H. E. (August 16, 2010). Resources on service learning and community service. *The New York Times*, http://learning.blogs.nytimes.com/2010/08/16.

Olsen, G., & Fuller, M. L. (2007). *Home–school relations: Working successfully with parents and families* (3rd ed.). Boston: Allyn and Bacon.

Olweus, D. (1986). Aggression and hormones: Behavioral relationship with testosterone and adrenaline. In D. Olweus, J. Block, & M. Radke-Yarrow (Eds.), *Development of antisocial and prosocial behavior: Research, theories, and issues.* Orlando, FL: Academic Press.

Olweus, D. (1993). *Bullying at school: What we know and what we can do.* Cambridge, MA: Blackwell.

Oppenheimer, T. (2003). *The flickering mind: The false promise of technology in the classroom and how learning can be saved.* New York: Random House.

Orellana, M. F., Dorner, L., & Pulido, L. (2003). Accessing assets: Immigrant youths work as family translators or "para-phrasers." *Social Problems, 50*, 505–524.

Oskamp, S. (Ed.). (2000). *Reducing prejudice and discrimination.* Mahwah, NJ: Erlbaum.

Pagano, A. I. (1997). Community service groups enhance learning. In B. Hatcher & S. S. Beck (Eds.), *Learning opportunities beyond the school* (2nd ed.). Olney, MD: Association for Childhood Education International.

Pagelow, M. D. (1982). Children in violent families: Direct and indirect victims. In S. B. Hill & B. J. Barnes (Eds.), *Young children and their families.* Lexington, MA: D. C. Heath.

Paik, H., & Comstock, G. (1994). The effects of television violence on antisocial behavior: A meta-analysis. *Communication Research, 21*, 516–546.

Papert, S. (1993). *The children's machine: Rethinking school in the age of the computer.* New York: Basic Books.

Parcel, T. L., & Menaghan, E. G. (1994). *Parents' jobs and children's lives.* New York: Aldine DeGruyter.

Park, C. C. (2001). Learning style preferences of Armenian, African, Hispanic, Hmong, Korean, Mexican, and Anglo students in American secondary schools. *Learning Environments Research, 94*(2), 175–191.

Park, K. A., & Waters, E. (1989). Security of attachment and preschool friendships. *Child Development, 60*, 1076–1080.

Park, L. S. (2001). *A single shard.* Boston: Clarion/Houghton Mifflin.

Parke, R. D. (1982). On prediction of child abuse: Theoretical considerations. In R. Starr (Ed.), *Prediction of abuse: Policy implications.* Philadelphia: Ballinger.

Parke, R. D. (1990, Fall). Family–peer systems: In search of a linking process. *Newsletter: Developmental Psychology.* Washington, DC: American Psychological Association (Division 7).

Parke, R. D. (2002). Fathers and families. In M. H. Bornstein (Ed.), *Handbook of parenting* (2nd ed., Vol. 3). Mahwah, NJ: Erlbaum.

Parke, R. D., & Buriel, R. (2006). Socialization in the family: Ethnic and ecological perspectives. In W. Damon & R. M. Lerner (Eds.), *Handbook of child psychology* (6th ed., Vol. 3). Hoboken, NJ: Wiley.

Parke, R. D., & Lewis, N. G. (1981). The family in context: A multilevel interactional analysis of child abuse. In R. Henderson (Ed.), *Parent–child interaction.* New York: Academic Press.

Parker, J. G., & Gottman, I. M. (1989). Social and emotional development in a relational context: Friendship interaction from early childhood to adolescence. In T. J. Berndt & G. W. Ladd (Eds.), *Peer relations in child development.* New York: Wiley.

Parker, S. T. (1984). Playing for keeps: An evolutionary perspective on human games. In P. K. Smith (Ed.), *Play in animals and humans.* Oxford: Basil Blackwell.

Parkhurst, J. T., & Asher, S. R. (1992). Peer rejection in middle school: Subgroup differences in behavior, loneliness, and interpersonal concerns. *Developmental Psychology, 28*, 231–241.

Parten, M. (1932). Social play among preschool children. *Journal of Abnormal and Social Psychology, 27*, 243–269.

Patchin, J. W., & Hinduja, S. (2006). Bullies move beyond the schoolyard: A preliminary look at cyberbullying. *Youth Violence and Juvenile Justice, 4*(2), 148–169.

Patrick, B. C., Skinner, E. A., & Connell, J. P. (1993). What motivates children's behavior and emotion? Joint effects of perceived control and autonomy in the academic domain. *Journal of Personality and Social Psychology, 65*(4), 781–791.

Patterson, C. J. (2002). Lesbian and gay parenthood. In M. H. Bornstein (Ed.), *Handbook of parenting* (2nd ed., Vol. 3). Mahwah, NJ: Erlbaum.

Patterson, C. J. (2006). Children of lesbian and gay parents. *Current Directions in Psychological Science, 15*(5), 241–244.

Patterson, C. J. (2009). Children of lesbian and gay parents: Psychology, law, and policy. *American Psychologist, 64*, 727–736.

Patterson, C. J., & Hastings, P. D. (2007). Socialization in the context of family diversity. In J. E. Grusec & P. D. Hastings (Eds.), *Handbook of socialization: Theory and research*. New York: Guilford.

Patterson, G. R. (1982). *Coercive family processes*. Eugene, OR: Castilia Press.

Patterson, G. R., DeBaryshe, D., & Ramsey, E. (1989). A developmental perspective on antisocial behavior. *American Psychologist, 44*(2), 329–335.

Patterson, G. R., & Dishion, T. J. (1988). Multilevel family process models: Traits, interactions, and relationships. In R. A. Hinde & J. Hinde-Stevenson (Eds.), *Relationships within families*. Oxford: Oxford University Press.

Pavao, J. M. (2005). *The family of adoption* (rev. ed.). Boston: Beacon Press.

Paxton, C., & Haskins, R. (2009). Introducing the issue: Preventing child maltreatment. *The Future of Children, 19*(2), 1–17.

Pecora, N. (2007). The changing nature of children's television: Fifty years of research. In N. Pecora, J. P. Murray, & E. A. Wartella (Eds.), *Children and television: Fifty years of research*. Mahwah, NJ: Erlbaum.

Perse, E. M. (2001). *Media effects and society*. Mahwah, NJ: Erlbaum.

Peterson, B. E. (2002). Longitudinal analysis of midlife generativity, intergenerational role, and caregiving. *Psychology of Aging, 17*(1), 161–168.

Peterson, G. W., Steinmetz, S. K., & Wilson, S. M. (2003). Introduction: Parenting styles in diverse perspectives. *Marriage and Family Review, 34*, 1–4.

Peterson, R. R. (1996). A re-evaluation of the economic consequences of divorce. *American Sociological Review, 61*, 528–536.

Pettit, G. S., & Mize, J. (1993). Substance and style: Understanding the ways in which parents teach children about social relationships. In S. Duck (Ed.), *Learning about relationships*. Newbury Park, CA: Sage.

Pew Research Reports. (2007). *The Pew Forum on religion and public life*. Washington, DC: Pew Research Center.

Pew Research Reports. (2010). *The return of the multigenerational family*. Washington, DC: Pew Research Center.

Phillips, D. A., & Howes, C. (1987). Indicators of quality in child care: Review of research. In D. A. Phillips (Ed.), *Quality in child care. What does research tell us?* Washington, DC: National Association for the Education of Young Children.

Piaget, J. (1952). *The origins of intelligence in children* (M. Cook, Trans.). New York: New American Library.

Piaget, J. (1962). *Play, dreams, and imitation in childhood* (C. Gattegno & F. M. Hodgson, Trans.). New York: Norton.

Piaget, J. (1965). *The moral judgment of the child* (M. Gabain, Trans.). New York: Free Press.

Piaget, J. (1974). *The language and thought of the child* (M. Gabain, Trans.). New York: New American Library.

Pipher, M. (1994). *Reviving Ophelia: Saving the selves of adolescent girls*. New York: Ballantine.

Pleck, E. H. (2000). *Celebrating the family: Ethnicity, consumer culture, and family rituals*. Cambridge, MA: Harvard University Press.

Plomin, R., & Asbury, K. (2002). Nature and nurture in the family. *Marriage and Family Review, 33*, 275–283.

Plowman, L., Stephen, C., & McPake, L. (2010). *Growing up with technology: Young children learning in a digital world*. New York: Routledge.

Poinsett, A. (1997, March). *The role of sports in youth development*. Report of Carnegie Corporation Meeting. New York: Carnegie Corporation.

Pollack, W. S. (1999). *Real boys: Rescuing our sons from the myths of boyhood*. New York: Henry Holt.

Pollock, L. (1984). *Forgotten children: Parent-child relations from 1500 to 1900*. New York: Cambridge University Press.

Pomerantz, E. M., Grolnick, W. S., & Price, C. E. (2007). The role of parents in how children approach achievement: A dynamic process perspective. In A. J. Elliot & C. S. Dweck (Eds.), *Handbook of competence and motivation*. New York: Guilford Press.

Pomerantz, E. M., & Saxon, J. L. (2001). Conceptions of ability as stable and self-evaluative processes: A longitudinal examination. *Child Development, 72*, 152–173.

Postman, N. (1986). *Amusing ourselves to death*. New York: Penguin Books.

Postman, N. (1992). *Technopoly: The surrender of culture to technology*. New York: Vintage.

Postman, N. (1994). *The disappearance of childhood*. New York: Vintage.

Power, T. G. (1987). Parents as socializers: Maternal and paternal views. *Journal of Youth and Adolescence, 18*, 203–220.

Powlishta, K. K., Serbin, L. A., & Moller, L. C. (1993). The stability of individual differences in gender typing: Implications for understanding gender segregation. *Sex Roles, 239*(11/12), 723–737.

Prensky, M. (2010). *Teaching digital natives: Partnering for real learning*. Thousand Oaks, CA: Corwin/Sage.

Prinsky, L. E., & Rosenbaum, J. L. (1987). Leerics or lyrics? *Youth and Society, 18*, 384–394.

Provenzo, E. F. (1991). *Video kids: Making sense of Nintendo*. Cambridge, MA: Harvard University Press.

Putnam, R. D. (2000). *Bowling alone: The collapse and revival of American community*. New York: Simon & Schuster.

Putnam, S. P., Sanson, A. V., & Rothbart, M. (2002). Child temperament and parenting. In M. H. Bornstein (Ed.), *Handbook of parenting* (2nd ed., Vol. 3). Mahwah, NJ: Erlbaum.

Quintana, S. M., Aboud, F. E., Chao, R. K., Contreras-Grau, J., Cross, W. E. Jr., Hudley, C., Hughes, D., Liben, L. S., Nelson-LeGall, S., & Vietze, D. L. (2006). Race, ethnicity, and culture in child development: Contemporary research and future directions. *Child Development, 77*(5), 1129–1141.

Radke-Yarrow, M., & Zahn-Waxler, C. (1986). The role of familial factors in the development of prosocial behavior: Research findings and questions. In D. Olweus, J. Block, & M. Radke-Yarrow (Eds.), *Development of antisocial and prosocial behavior: Research, theories, and issues.* Orlando, FL: Academic Press.

Radke-Yarrow, M., Zahn-Waxler, C., & Chapman, H. (1983). Prosocial dispositions and behavior. In P. H. Mussen (Ed.), *Handbook of child psychology* (4th ed., Vol. 4). New York: Wiley.

Raikes, H., Pan, B. A., Luza, G., Tamis-LeMonda, C. S., Brooks-Gunn, J., Constantine, J., Tarullo, L. B., Raikes, H. A., & Rodriguez, E. T. (2006). Mother–child book-reading in low-income families: Correlates and outcomes during the first three years of life. Child *Development, 77*(4), 924–953.

Ramsey, P. G. (2004). *Teaching and learning in a diverse world: Multicultural education for young children* (3rd ed.). New York: Teachers College Press.

Reid, J. B., Patterson, G. R., & Snyder, J. (2002). *Antisocial behavior in children and adolescents: A developmental analysis and model for intervention.* Washington, DC: American Psychological Association.

Rest, J. R., Narvaez, D., Thomas, S. J., & Bebeau, M. J. (2000). A neo-Kohlbergian approach to morality research. *Journal of Moral Education, 29*(4), 381–395.

Rice, M. L., Huston, A. C., Truglio, R., & Wright, J. C. (1990). Words from *Sesame Street*: Learning vocabulary while viewing. *Developmental Psychology, 26*, 421–428.

Rich, D. (1992). *Megaskills* (rev. ed.). Boston: Houghton Mifflin.

Rich, M., Woods, E. R., Goodman, E., Emans, S. J., & DuRant, R. H. (1998). Aggressors or victims: Gender and race in music video violence. *Pediatrics, 101*(4, Part 1), 669–674.

Richman, A. L., LeVine, R. A., New, R. S., & Howrigan, G. A. (1988). Maternal behavior to infants in five cultures. In R. A. Levine, P. M. Miller, & M. M. West (Eds.), *Parental behavior in diverse societies.* San Francisco: Jossey-Bass.

Rickel, A. U., & Becker, E. (1997). *Keeping children from harm's way: How national policy affects psychological development.* Washington. DC: American Psychological Association.

Rilling, J. K., Gutman, D. A., Zeh, T. R., Pagnoni, G., Berns, G. S., & Kilts, C. D. (2002). A neural basis for social cooperation. *Neuron, 35*, 377–405.

Ritts, V., Patterson, M. L., & Tubbs, M. E. (1992). Expectations, impressions, and judgments of physically attractive students: A review. *Review of Educational Research, 62*, 413–426.

Rivkin, M. S. (1995). *The great outdoors: Restoring children's right to play outside.* Washington, DC: National Association for the Education of Young Children.

Roberts, D. F., & Christenson, P. G. (2001). Popular music in childhood and adolescence. In D. G. Singer & J. L. Singer (Eds.), *Handbook of children and the media.* Thousand Oaks, CA: Sage.

Roberts, D. F., Christenson, P. G., & Gentile, D. A. (2003). The effects of violent music on children and adolescents. In D. A. Gentile (Ed.), *Media, violence and children: A complete guide for parents and professionals.* New York: Praeger Publishers.

Roberts, D. F., & Foehr, U. G. (2004). *Kids and the media in America.* New York: Cambridge University Press.

Roberts, D. F., & Foehr, U. G. (2008). Trends in media use. *The Future of Children: Children and Electronic Media, 18*(1), 11–37.

Robinson, E. H., & Curry, J. R. (2006). Promoting altruism in the classroom. *Childhood Education, 82*(2), 68–73.

Rogers, C. (1969). *Freedom to learn.* Columbus, OH: Merrill.

Rogoff, B. (1990). *Apprenticeship in thinking: Cognitive development in social context.* New York: Oxford University Press.

Rogoff, B. (2003). *The cultural nature of human development.* New York: Oxford University Press.

Rogosch, F. A., Cicchetti, D., Shields, A., & Toth, S. L. (1995). Parenting dysfunction in child maltreatment. In M. H. Bornstein (Ed.), *Handbook of parenting* (Vol. 4). Mahwah, NJ: Erlbaum.

Rose, A. J., & Asher, S. R. (2004). Children's strategies and goals in response to help-giving and help-seeking tasks within a friendship. *Child Development, 73*, 749–780.

Rose, A. J., & Smith, A. J. (2009). Sex differences in peer relationships. In K. H. Rubin, W. M. Bukowski, & B. P. Laursen (Eds.), *Handbook of peer interactions, relationships, and groups.* New York: Guilford Press.

Rosen, L. D. (2007). *Me, my space and I: Parenting the Net generation.* New York: Palgrave Macmillan.

Rosenberg, J., & Bradford, W. W. (2006). *The importance of fathers in the healthy development of children.* Administration for Children and Families, USDHHS. Washington, DC: U.S. Government Printing Office.

Rosenberg, M. (1975). The dissonant context and the adolescent self-concept. In S. E. Dragastin & G. H. Elder, Jr. (Eds.), *Adolescence in the life cycle: Psychological change and social context.* New York: Wiley.

Rosenthal, M. K. (2003). Quality in early childhood education and care: A cultural context. *European Early Childhood Education Research Journal, 11*(2), 101–116.

Rosenthal, R., & Jacobson, L. (1968). *Pygmalion in the classroom.* New York: Holt, Rinehart & Winston.

Ross, H., & Howe, N. (2009). Family influences on children's peer relationships. In K. H. Rubin, W. M. Bukowski, & B. P. Laursen (Eds.), *Handbook of peer interactions, relationships, and groups.* New York: Guilford Press.

Ross, R. P., Campbell, T., Wright, J. C., Huston, A. C., Rice, M. L., & Turk, P. (1984). When celebrities talk, children listen: An experimental analysis of children's responses to TV ads with celebrity endorsement. *Journal of Applied Developmental Psychology, 5*, 185–202.

Rothbart, M. K., & Bates, J. E. (2006). Temperament. In W. Damon & R. M. Lerner (Eds.), *Handbook of child psychology* (6th ed., Vol. 3). Hoboken, NJ: Wiley.

Rotter, J. B. (1966). Generalized expectancies for internal versus external control of reinforcement. *Psychological Monographs, 80* (Whole No. 609).

Rotter, J. B. (1971). Who rules you? External control and internal control. *Psychology Today, 5*, 37–42.

Rovenger, J. (2000). Fostering emotional intelligence. *School Library Journal, 46*(2), 40–43.

Rubin, A. (2002). The uses-and-gratifications perspective of media effects. In J. Bryant & D. Zillman (Eds.), *Media effects: Advances in theory and research* (2nd ed.). Mahwah, NJ: Erlbaum.

Rubin, K. H., Bukowski, W., & Parker, J. G. (2006). Peer interactions, relationships, and groups. In W. Damon & R. M. Lerner (Eds.), *Handbook of child psychology* (6th ed., Vol. 3). Hoboken, NJ: Wiley.

Rubin, K. H., & Burgess, K. (2002). Parents of aggressive and withdrawn children. In M. Bornstein (Ed.), *Handbook of parenting* (2nd ed., Vol. 1), Hillsdale, NJ: Erlbaum.

Rubin, K. H., & Coplan, R. J. (1992). Peer relationships in childhood. In M. H. Bornstein & M. E. Lamb (Eds.), *Developmental psychology: An advanced textbook* (3rd ed.). Hillsdale, NJ: Erlbaum.

Rubin, K. H., Stewart, S. L., & Chen, X. (1995). Parents of aggressive and withdrawn children. In M. H. Bornstein (Ed.), *Handbook of parenting* (Vol. 1). Mahwah, NJ: Erlbaum.

Rubin, K. H., & Thompson, A. (2003). *The friendship factor*. New York: Penguin.

Ruble, D., Martin, C. L., & Berenbaum, S. A. (2006). Gender development. In W. Damon & R. M. Lerner (Eds.), *Handbook of child psychology* (6th ed., Vol. 3). Hoboken, NJ: Wiley.

Ruopp, R., Travers, J., Glantz, F., & Coelen, G. (1979). *Children at the center: Final results of the national day care study*. Cambridge, MA: Abt Associates.

Rushton, J. P., Fulker, D. W., Neal, M. C., Nias, D. K. B., & Eysenck, H. J. (1986). Altruism and aggression: The heritability of individual differences. *Journal of Personality and Social Psychology, 50*, 1192–1198.

Rust, J., Golombok, S., Hines, M., Johnson, K., & Golding, J. (2000). The role of brothers and sisters in the gender development of preschool children. *Journal of Experimental Child Psychology, 77*, 292–303.

Rutter, M. (2006). *Genes and behavior: Nature-nurture interplay explained*. Hoboken, NJ: Wiley-Blackwell.

Rutter, M., Giller, H., & Hagell, A. (1998). *Antisocial behavior by young people*. Cambridge, UK: Cambridge University Press.

Rutter, M. & O'Connor, T. G. (2004). Are there biological programming effects for psychological development? Findings from a study of Romanian adoptees. *Developmental Psychology, 40*(1), 81–90.

Rutter, V. (1994, May/June). Lessons from step families. *Psychology Today, 27*, 30–33, 60, 62, 64, 66, 68–69.

Ryan, R. M., & Deci, E. L. (2000). Intrinsic and extrinsic motivations: Classic definitions and new directions. *Contemporary Educational Psychology, 1*, 54–67.

Rylands, K. J., & Rickwood, D. J. (2001). Ego-integrity versus ego-despair: The effect of accepting the past on depression in older women. *The International Journal of Aging and Human Development, 53*(1), 75–89.

Saarni, C., Mumme, D. L., & Campos, J. J. (1998). Emotional development: Action, communication, and understanding. In W. Damon (Ed.), *Handbook of child psychology* (5th ed., Vol. 3). New York: Wiley.

Sadker, D., & Zittleman, K. (2009). *Teachers, schools, and society* (9th ed.). New York: McGraw-Hill.

Sadker, M., & Sadker, D. (1994). *Failing at fairness: How America's schools cheat girls*. New York: Scribner's.

Sadker, M., Sadker, D., & Klein, S. (1991). The issue of gender in elementary and secondary education. *Review of Research in Education, 17*, 269–334.

Salmivalli, C., & Peets, K. (2009). Bullies, victims, and bully-victim relationships in middle childhood and early adolescence. In K. H. Rubin, W. M. Bukowski, & B. P. Laursen (Eds.), *Handbook of peer interactions, relationships, and groups*. New York: Guilford Press.

Sameroff, A. J. (1994). Developmental systems and family functioning. In R. D. Parke & S. G. Kellan (Eds.), *Exploring family relationships with other social contexts*. Hillsdale, NJ: Erlbaum.

Sameroff, A. J. (2006). Identifying risk and protective factors for healthy child development. In A. C. Clarke-Stewart & J. Dunn (Eds.), *Families count: Effects on child and adolescent development*. Cambridge, UK: Cambridge University Press.

Sameroff, A. J. (2009). The transactional model. In A. J. Sameroff (Ed.), *The transactional model of development: How children and contexts shape each other*. Washington, DC: American Psychological Association.

Sampson, R. J. (2001). How do communities undergird or undermine human development? Relevant contexts and social mechanisms. In A. Booth & A. C. Crouter (Eds.), *Does it take a village? Community effects on children, adolescents, and families*. Mahwah, NJ: Erlbaum.

Sandstrom, M. J., & Coie, J. D. (1999). A developmental perspective on peer rejection: Mechanisms of stability and change. *Child Development, 70*, 955–966.

Sanford, N., & Comstock, C. (Eds.). (1971). *Sanctions for evil*. San Francisco: Jossey-Bass.

Sarampote, N. C., Bassetl, H. H., & Winsler, A. (2004). After-school care: Child outcomes and recommendations for research and policy. *Child and Youth Care Forum, 33*(5), 329–348.

Savage, D. G. (1983, February 15). Freeway noise linked to poorer test scores. *Los Angeles Times*, Part I, p. 1.

Sayer, L. C. (2005). Gender, time, and inequality: Trends in women's and men's paid work, unpaid work, and free time. *Social Forces, 84*, 285–303.

Scarlett, W. G., Naudeau, S. C., Salonius-Pasternak, D., & Ponte, I. C. (2005). *Children's play*. Thousand Oaks, CA: Sage.

Scarr, S. (1992). Theories for the 1990s: Developmental and individual differences. *Child Development, 63*, 1–19.

Scarr, S., & McCartney, K. (1983). How people make their own environments: A theory of genotype–environment effects. *Child Development, 54*, 424–435.

Schank, R. C. (2004). *Making minds less well-educated than our own*. Mahwah, NJ: Erlbaum.

Schmidt, M. E., & Vandewater, E. A. (2008). Media and attention, cognition, and school achievement. *The Future of Children: Children and Electronic Media, 18*(1), 63–89.

Schneider, B. H. (2000). *Friends and enemies: Peer relations in childhood*. New York: Oxford University Press.

Schneider, B. H., Atkinson, L., & Tardif, C. (2001). Child–parent attachment and children's peer relations: A quantitative review. *Developmental Psychology, 37*, 86–100.

Schorr, L. B. (1997). *Common purpose: Strengthening families and neighborhoods to rebuild America*. New York: Anchor Books.

Schorr, L. B., Both, D., & Copple, C. (Eds.). (1991). *Effective services for young children: Report of a workshop*. Washington, DC: National Academy Press.

Schramm, W., Lyle, J., & Parker, E. (1961). *Television in the lives of our children*. Stanford, CA: Stanford University Press.

Schunk, D. H. (2000). *Theories of learning* (3rd ed.). Upper Saddle River, NJ: Prentice-Hall.

Schweinhart, L. J., Montie, J., Xiang, Z., Barnett, W. S., Belfield, C. R., & Nores, M. (2005). *Lifetime effects: The High/Scope Perry Preschool Study through age 40*. Ypsilanti, MI: High/Scope.

Schweinhart, L. J., & Weikart, D. P. (1993). Success by empowerment: The High/Scope Perry Preschool Study through age 27. *Young Children, 49*(1), 54–58.

Schweinhart, L. J., Weikart, D. P., & Larner, M. B. (1986). Child-initiated activities in early childhood programs may help prevent delinquency. *Early Childhood Research Quarterly, 1*(3), 303–312.

Sealander, J. (2003). *The failed century of the child: Governing America's young in the twentieth century*. Cambridge, UK: Cambridge University Press.

Sears, W., Sears, M., & Pantley, E. (2002). *The successful child: What parents can do to help kids turn out well*. New York: Little Brown & Co.

Seaver, W. B. (1973). Effects of naturally induced teacher expectancies. *Journal of Personality and Social Psychology, 28*, 333–342.

Sebald, H. (1986). Adolescents' shifting orientation toward parents and peers: A curvilinear trend over recent decades. *Journal of Marriage and the Family, 48*, 5–13.

Sebald, H. (1989). Adolescent peer orientation: Changes in the support system during the last three decades. *Adolescence, 24*, 937–945.

Sebald, H. (1992). *Adolescence: A social psychological analysis* (4th ed.). Englewood Cliffs, NJ: Prentice-Hall.

Seligman, M. E. P. (1975). *Helplessness*. San Francisco: Freeman.

Seligman, M. E. P. (1990). *Learned optimism*. New York: Pocket Books.

Selman, R. L. (1980). *The growth of interpersonal understanding*. New York: Academic Press.

Selman, R. L., & Selman, A. P. (1979). Children's ideas about friendship: A new theory. *Psychology Today, 12*(4), 71–80.

Selye, H. (1956). *The stress of life*. New York: McGraw-Hill.

Senechal, M., & LeFevre, J. (2002). Parental involvement in the development of children's reading skill: A five-year longitudinal study. *Child Development, 73*(2), 443–460.

Sendak, M. (1963). *Where the wild things are*. New York: HarperCollins.

Sendak, M. (1970). *In the night kitchen*. New York: Harper & Row.

Serbin, L. A., Powlishta, K. K., & Gulko, J. (1993). The development of sex typing in middle childhood. *Monographs of the Society for Research in Child Development, 58*(2, Serial No. 232).

Shaffer, D. R., & Wittes, E. (2006). Women's precollege sports participation, enjoyment of sports, and self-esteem. *Sex Roles, 55*(3–4), 225–232.

Shantz, C. U. (1983). Social cognition. In P. H. Mussen (Eds.), *Handbook of child psychology* (4th ed., Vol. 3). New York: Wiley.

Shapira, A., & Lomranz, J. (1972). Cooperative and competitive behavior of rural Arab children in Israel. *Journal of Cross-Cultural Psychology, 3*, 353–359.

Shapira, A., & Madsen, M. C. (1974). Between- and within-group cooperation and competition among kibbutz and non-kibbutz children. *Developmental Psychology, 10*, 140–145.

Sheldon, R. G., Tracy, S. K., & Brown, W. B. (2000). *Youth gangs in American society* (2nd ed.). Belmont, CA: Wadsworth.

Sherif, M. (1956). Experiments in group conflict. *Scientific American, 195*(2), 54–58.

Sherif, M., Harvey, O. J., White, B. J., Hood, W. R., & Sherif, C. W. (1961). *Intergroup conflict and cooperation: The robber's cave experiment*. Norman: University of Oklahoma, Institute of Group Relations.

Shibusawa, T. (2001). Parenting in Japanese American families. In N. B. Webb (Ed.), *Culturally diverse parent-child and family relationships: A guide for social workers and other practitioners*. New York: Columbia University Press.

Shonk, S. M., & Cicchetti, D. (2001). Maltreatment, competency, deficits, and risk for academic and behavioral maladjustment. *Developmental Psychology, 37*, 3–17.

Shonkoff, J. P., & Phillips, D. A. (Eds.). (2000). *From neurons to neighborhoods: The science of early childhood development*. Washington, DC: National Academy Press.

Shteynberg, G., Gelfand, M., & Kim, K. (2009). Peering into the "magnum mysterium" of culture: The explanatory power of descriptive norms. *Journal of Cross-Cultural Psychology, 40*(1), 46–49.

Shweder, R. A., Mahapatra, M., & Miller, J. G. (1987). Culture and moral development. In J. Kagan & S. Lamb (Eds.), *The emergence of morality in young children*. Chicago: University of Chicago Press.

Signorielli, N. (1989). Television and conceptions about sex roles: Maintaining conventionality and the status quo. *Sex Roles, 21* (5/6), 341–360.

Signorielli, N. (2007). Occupational portrayals on television, gender roles on television, media images of African Americans, historical trends of television violence. In J. J. Arnett (Ed.), *Encyclopedia of children, adolescents and the media*. Thousand Oaks, CA: Sage.

Simpson, J. A., & Beckes, L. (2009). Evolutionary perspectives on prosocial behavior. In M. Mikulincer & P. R. Shaver (Eds.), *Prosocial motives, emotions, and behavior: The better angels of our nature*. Washington, DC: APA.

Sinclair, S., Dunn, E., & Lowery, B. (2005). The relationship between parental racial attitudes and children's implicit prejudice. *Journal of Experimental Social Psychology, 41*(3), 283–289.

Singer, D. G., & Singer, J. L. (1980). Television viewing and aggressive behavior in preschool children: A field study. *Forensic Psychology and Psychiatry, Annals of the New York Academy of Science, 347*, 289–303.

Singer, D. G., & Singer, J. L. (2001). The popular media as educators and socializers of growing children. In D. G. Singer & J. L. Singer (Eds.), *Children and the media*. Thousand Oaks, CA: Sage.

Sirin, S. R. (2005). Socioeconomic status and achievement: A meta-analytic review of research. *Review of Educational Research, 75*(3), 417–453.

Skeels, H. M. (1966). Adult status of children with contrasting early life experiences. *Monographs of the Society for Research in Child Development, 31*(3, Whole No. 105).

Skinner, B. F. (1948). *Walden two*. New York: Macmillan.

Skinner, B. F. (1968). *The technology of teaching*. Englewood Cliffs, NJ: Prentice-Hall.

Skinner, E. A. (1995). *Perceived control, motivation, and coping*. Thousand Oaks, CA: Sage.

Skinner, E. A., & Belmont, M. J. (1993). Motivation in the classroom: Reciprocal effects of teacher behavior and student engagement across the school year. *Journal of Educational Psychology, 85*(4), 571–581.

Skinner, E. A., & Greene, T. (2008). Perceived control: Engagement, coping, and development. In T. L. Good (Ed.), *21st century education: A reference handbook* (Vol. 1). Newbury Park, CA: Sage.

Sklaroff, S. (2002). One nation under a groove. *U.S. News & World Report, 133*(2), 20–21.

Skolnick, A. (1987). *The intimate environment: Exploring marriage and the family* (4th ed.). Boston: Little, Brown.

Slaby, R. G., Roedell, W. C., Arezzo, D., & Hendrix, K. (1995). *Early violence prevention: Tools for teachers of young children.* Washington, DC: National Association for the Education of Young Children.

Slavin, R. E. (2006). *Educational psychology: Theory and practice* (8th ed.). Saddle River, NJ: Prentice-Hall.

Sleek, S. (1998). Isolation increases with Internet use. *APA Monitor, 29*(9), 1, 30–31.

Small, J. (Ed.). (1987). *Children of alcoholics: A special report.* Washington, DC: National Institute on Alcohol Abuse and Alcoholism.

Small, S., & Luster, T. (1994). Adolescent sexual activity: An ecological risk-factor approach. *Journal of Marriage and the Family, 56*, 181–192.

Small, S., & Supple, A. (2001). Communities as systems: Is a community more than the sum of its parts? In A. Booth & A. C. Crouter (Eds.), *Does it take a village?* Mahwah, NJ: Erlbaum.

Smerdon, B. A., & Borman, K. M. (2009). *Saving America's high schools.* Washington, DC: Urban Institute Press.

Smetana, J. G. (1985). Preschool children's conceptions of transgressions: Effects of varying moral and conventional domain-related attributes. *Developmental Psychology, 21*, 18–29.

Smetana, J. G. (1989). Toddlers' social interactions in the context of moral and conventional transgressions in the home. *Developmental Psychology, 25*, 499–508.

Smetana, J. G. (2006). Social domain theory: Consistencies and variations in children's moral and social judgements. In M. Killen & J. G. Smetana (Eds.), *Handbook of moral development.* Mahwah, NJ: Erlbaum.

Smith, M. W. (2001). Children's experiences in preschool. In D. K. Dickinson & P. O. Tabors (Eds.), *Beginning literacy with language: Young children learning at home and school.* Baltimore, MD: Brookes Publishing.

Smith, P. K., & Drew, L. M. (2002). Grandparenthood. In M. H. Bornstein (Ed.), *Handbook of parenting* (2nd ed., Vol. 3). Mahwah, NJ: Erlbaum.

Smith, P. K., & Dutton, S. (1979). Play and training indirect and innovative problem solving. *Child Development, 60*, 830–836.

Smolensky, E., & Gootman, J. A. (Eds.). (2003). *Working families and growing kids: Caring for children and adolescents.* Washington, DC: National Academies Press.

Snow, M. E., Jacklin, C. N., & Maccoby, E. E. (1981). Birth order differences in peer sociability at thirty-three months. *Child Development, 52*, 589–596.

Snyder, J. J., & Patterson, G. R. (1995). Individual differences in social aggression: A test of a reinforcement model of socialization in the natural environment. *Behavior Therapy, 26*, 371–391.

Sober, E., & Wilson, D. (1998). *Unto others: The evolution and psychology of unselfish behavior.* Cambridge, MA: Harvard University Press.

Sobolewski, J. M., & Amato, P. R. (2005). Economic hardship in the family of origin and children's psychological well-being. *Journal of Marriage and Family, 67*, 141–156.

Society for Neuroscience. (2007). *Brain briefings.* http://www.sfn.org.

Soldier, L. L. (1985). To soar with the eagles: Enculturation and acculturation of Indian children. *Childhood Education, 61*(3), 185–191.

Somers, C. L., & Surmann, A. T. (2004). Adolescents' preference for source of sex education. *Child Study Journal, 34*, 47–50.

Spencer, M. B. (2001). Resiliency and fragility factors associated with the contextual experiences of low resource urban African American male youth and families. In A. Booth & A. C. Crouter (Eds.), *Does it take a village?* Mahwah, NJ: Erlbaum.

Spitz, E. H. (1999). *Inside picture books.* New Haven, CT: Yale University Press.

Spitz, R. (1946). Hospitalism: An inquiry into the genesis of psychiatric conditioning in early childhood. In A. Freud (Ed.), *Psychoanalytic studies of the child* (Vol. 1). New York: International Universities Press.

Spock, B. (1946). *The common sense book of baby and child care.* New York: Duell Sloan Pearce.

Spock, B. (1957). *The pocket book of baby and child care.* New York: Pocket Books.

Sprafkin, J. M., Liebert, R. M., & Poulos, R. W. (1975). Effects of a prosocial example on children's helping. *Journal of Experimental Child Psychology, 20*, 119–126.

Sroufe, L. A. (1996). *Emotional development.* Cambridge, UK: Cambridge University Press.

Sroufe, L. A., Egeland, B., Carlson, E., & Collins, W. A. (2005). Placing early attachment experiences in developmental context: The Minnesota longitudinal study. In K. E. Grossmann & E. Waters (Eds.), *Attachment from infancy to adulthood: The major longitudinal studies.* New York: Guilford Press.

St. Peters, M., Marguerite, F., Huston, A. C., Wright, J. C., & Eakins, D. J. (1991). Television and families: What do young children watch with their parents? *Child Development, 62*, 1409–1413.

Stabiner, K. (1993, August 15). Get 'em while they're young. *Los Angeles Times Magazine*, pp. 12, 14, 15, 16, 38.

Stallings, J. (1974). *Follow through classroom observation evaluation, 1972–1973: Executive summary.* Menlo Park, CA: Stanford Research Institute.

Starr, R. H., Jr. (1990, June). The lasting effects of child maltreatment. *The Word and I*, 484–499.

Staub, E. (1970). A child in distress: The effect of focusing responsibility on children on their attempts to help. *Developmental Psychology, 2*, 152–153.

Staub, E. (1971). The use of role playing and induction in children's learning of helping and sharing behavior. *Child Development, 42*, 805–816.

Staub, E. (1989). *The roots of evil: The origins of genocide and other group violence.* Cambridge, UK: Cambridge University Press.

Staub, E. (1996). Altruism and aggression in children and youth: Origins and cures. In R. Feldman (Ed.), *The psychology of adversity.* Amherst, MA: University of Massachusetts Press.

Stead, R. (2009). *When you reach me.* New York: Wendy Lamb Books.

Steinberg, L. (1987). Single parents, step parents, and the susceptibility of adolescents to antisocial peer pressure. *Child Development, 58,* 269–275.

Steinberg, L. (2001). We know some things: Adolescent parent relationships in retrospect and prospect. *Journal of Research on Adolescence, 11*(1), 1–19.

Steinberg, L. (2010). *Adolescence.* New York: McGraw-Hill.

Steinberg, L., Elmen, J. D., & Mounts, N. S. (1989). Authoritative parenting, psychosocial maturity, and academic success among adolescents. *Child Development, 60,* 1424–1436.

Steinberg, L., Lamborn, S. D., Darling, N., Mounts, N., & Dornbusch, S. M. (1994). Over-time changes in adjustment and competence among adolescents from authoritative, authoritarian, indulgent, and neglectful families. *Child Development, 65,* 754–770.

Steinberg, L., & Morris, A. S. (2001). Adolescent development. *Annual Review of Psychology, 52,* 83–110.

Steinberg, L., Mounts, N. S., Lamborn, S. D., & Dornbusch, S. M. (1991). Authoritative parenting and adolescent adjustment across various ecological niches. *Journal of Research on Adolescence, 1,* 19–36.

Stendler, C. B. (1950). Sixty years of child training practices. *Journal of Pediatrics, 36,* 122–134.

Stepfamily Association of America. (2000). www.saafamilies.org.

Stevenson, H. W., & Lee, S. Y. (1990). Contents of achievement: A study of American, Chinese, and Japanese children. *Monographs of the Society for Research in Child Development, 55*(1–2, Serial No. 221).

Stewart, E. C., & Bennett, M. J. (1991). *American cultural patterns: A cross-cultural perspective* (rev. ed.). Yarmouth, ME: Intercultural Press.

Stewart, S. D. (2007). *Brave new stepfamilies: Diverse paths toward stepfamily living.* Thousand Oaks, CA: Sage.

Stinnett, N., & Defrain, J. (1985). *Secrets of strong families.* Boston: Little, Brown.

Stipek, D. (1996). Motivation and instruction. In D. C. Berliner & R. C. Calfee (Eds.), *Handbook of educational psychology.* New York: Macmillan.

Strasburger, V. C., Wilson, B. J., & Jordan, A. B. (2008). *Children, adolescents, and the media* (2nd ed.). Thousand Oaks, CA: Sage.

Streitmatter, J. (1994). *Toward gender equity in the classroom: Everyday teachers' beliefs and practices.* New York: State University of New York Press.

Strouse, J. S., Buerkel-Rothfuss, N., & Long, E. C. J. (1995). Gender and family as moderators of the relationship between music video exposure and adolescent sexual permissiveness. *Adolescence, 30*(119), 505–522.

Subrahmanyam, K., Kraut, R. E., Greenfield, P. M., & Gross, E. F. (2001). New forms of electronic media. In D. G. Singer & J. L. Singer (Eds.), *Handbook of children and the media.* Thousand Oaks, CA: Sage.

Sue, D. W. (1989). Ethnic identity: The impact of two cultures on the psychological development of Asians in America. In D. R. Atkinson, G. Morten, & D. W. Sue (Eds.), *Counseling American minorities* (3rd ed.). Dubuque, IA: Wm. C. Brown.

Sunley, R. (1955). Early nineteenth-century American literature on child rearing. In M. Mead & M. Wolfenstein (Eds.), *Childhood in contemporary cultures.* Chicago: University of Chicago Press.

Sutton-Smith, B. (1971). Children at play. *Natural History, 80,* 54–59.

Sutton-Smith, B. (1972). *The folkgames of children.* Austin: University of Texas Press.

Sutton-Smith, B. (1982). Birth order and sibling status effects. In M. E. Lamb (Ed.), *Sibling relationships: Their nature and significance over the lifespan.* Hillsdale, NJ: Erlbaum.

Sweeney, J., & Bradbard, M. R. (1988). Mothers' and fathers' changing perceptions of their male and female infants over the course of pregnancy. *Journal of Genetic Psychology, 149*(3), 393–404.

Sylvie, M., & Windle, M. (2010). Prospective effects of violence exposure across multiple contexts on early adolescents' internalizing and externalizing problems. *Journal of Child Psychology and Psychiatry, 51*(8), 953–961.

Tamis-LeMonda, C. S., & Cabrera, N. J. (1999). Perspectives on father involvement: Research and policy. *Social Policy Report, Society for Research in Child Development, 12*(2).

Teasley, S. D., & Parker, J. G. (1995, March). *The effects of gender, friendship, and popularity on the targets and topics of adolescent gossip.* Paper presented at the Biennial Meeting of the Society for Research in Child Development, Indianapolis, IN.

Tennenbaum, H. R., & Leaper, C. (2002). Are parents' gender schemas related to their childrens' gender-related cognitions? *Developmental Psychology, 38,* 615–630.

Tharp, R. G. (1989). Psychocultural variables and constraints: Effects on teaching and learning in schools. *American Psychologist, 44*(2), 349–359.

Thiederman, S. (1991). *Bridging cultural barriers for success: How to manage the cultural work force.* New York: Lexington Books.

Thomas, A., & Chess, S. (1977). *Temperament and development.* New York: Brunner/Mazel.

Thomas, A., & Chess, S. (1980). *The dynamics of psychological development.* New York: Brunner/Mazel.

Thomas, A., Chess, S., & Birch, H. S. (1970). The origin of personality. *Scientific American, 223,* 102–109.

Thompson, K. P. (1993). Media, music, and adolescents. In R. M. Lerner (Ed.), *Early adolescents: Perspectives on research, policy, and intervention.* Hillsdale, NJ: Erlbaum.

Thompson, M., Cohen, L. J., & Grace, C. O. (2002). *Best friends, worst enemies: Understanding the social lives of children.* New York: Ballantine Books.

Thompson, R. A. (1994). Social support and the prevention of child maltreatment. In G. B. Melton & F. Barry (Eds.), *Safe neighborhoods: Foundations for a new national strategy on child abuse and neglect.* New York: Guilford.

Thompson, R. L., & Larson, R. (1995). Social context and the subjective experience of different types of rock music. *Journal of Youth and Adolescence, 24*(6), 731–744.

Thorne, B. (1993). *Gender play: Girls and boys in school.* New Brunswick, NJ: Rutgers University Press.

Tobin, J. J., Wu, D. Y. H., & Davidson, D. H. (1989, April). How three key countries shape their children. *World Monitor,* 36–45.

Toffler, A., & Toffler, H. (2006). *Revolutionary wealth.* New York: Knopf.

Tonnies, F. (1957). *Community and society* (Gemeinschaft und Gesellschaft) (C. P. Loomis, Trans.). East Lansing: Michigan State University.

Tozer, S. E., Violas, P. C., & Senese, G. (2008). *School and society: Historical and contemporary perspectives* (6th ed.). New York: McGraw-Hill.

Trelease, J. (2006). *The read-aloud handbook* (5th ed.). New York: Penguin Group.

Triandis, H. C. (1995). *Individualism and collectivism*. Boulder, CO: Westview Press.

Troy, M., & Sroufe, L. A. (1987). Victimization among preschoolers: Role of attachment relationship history. *Journal of the American Academy of Child and Adolescent Psychiatry, 26*, 166–172.

Trumbull, E., Rothstein-Fisch, C., Greenfield, P. M., & Quiroz, B. (2001). *Bridging cultures between home and school*. Mahwah, NJ: Erlbaum.

Tubman, J. G. (1993). Family risk factors, parental alcohol use, and problem behaviors among school-age children. *Family Relations, 42*, 81–86.

Tudge, J. R. H., Odero, D. A., Hogan, D. M., & Etz, K. E. (2003). Relations between the everyday activities of preschoolers and their teachers' perceptions of their competence in the first years of school. *Early Childhood Research Quarterly, 18*(1), 42–64.

Turiel, E. (1983). *The development of social knowledge: Morality and convention*. Cambridge, UK: Cambridge University Press.

Turiel, E. (2002). *The culture of morality: Social development, context, and conflict*. Cambridge, UK: Cambridge University Press.

Turiel, E. (2006). The development of morality. In W. Damon & R. M. Lerner (Eds.), *Handbook of child psychology* (6th ed., Vol. 3). Hoboken, NJ: Wiley.

Turkle, S. (2011). Alone together: Why we expect more from technology and less from each other. New York: Basic Books.

Turnbull, A. P., & Turnbull, H. R. (2001). *Families, professionals, and exceptionality: Collaborating for empowerment* (4th ed.). Upper Saddle River, NJ: Prentice-Hall.

Tyler, R. (1992, May). Prenatal drug exposure: An overview of associated problems and intervention strategies. *Phi Delta Kappan*, 705–708.

Uba, L. (1999). *Asian Americans: Personality patterns, identity, and mental health*. New York: Guilford Press.

Ungar, M. T. (2000). The myth of peer pressure. *Adolescence, 35* (137), 167–171.

U.S. Bureau of the Census. (2007). *Language use in the United States: 2007*. Washington, DC: U.S. Government Printing Office.

U.S. Bureau of the Census. (2009a). *Statistical abstract of the United States*. Washington, DC: U.S. Government Printing Office.

U.S. Bureau of the Census. (2009b). *Population division, population estimates, county characteristics*. Washington, DC: U.S. Government Printing Office.

U.S. Children's Bureau. (2010). *Trends in foster care and adoption: Adoption and foster care analysis and reporting system (AFCARS)*. www.acf.hhs.gov.

U.S. Department of Commerce, Economics and Statistics Administration. (2011). *Women in STEM. A gender gap to innovation*. http://www.esa.doc.gov

U.S. Department of Education. (2000). *The class-size reduction program*. Washington, DC: U.S. Government Printing Office.

U.S. Department of Education Office of Safe and Drug-Free Schools. (2007). *Practical information on crisis planning: A guide for schools and communities*. Washington, DC: U.S. Government Printing Office.

U.S. Department of Health and Human Services (USDHHS). (2002). *HHS invests in America's children*. Washington, DC: Author.

USDHHS. (2008). *Proceeding from a working meeting on recent school readiness research: Guiding the synthesis of early childhood research*. Washington, DC: U.S. Government Printing Office.

U.S. Department of Justice. (August 2000). Youth gangs in school. *Juvenile Justice Bulletin*. Washington, DC: U.S. Government Printing Office.

U.S. Interagency Council on Homelessness. (2010). *Opening doors: The federal strategic plan to prevent and end homelessness*. Washington, DC: U.S. Government Printing Office.

Valkenburg, P. M., & Peter, J. (2007). Internet communication and its relation to well-being: Identifying some underlying mechanisms. *Media Psychology, 9*(1), 43–58.

Van Ausdale, D., & Feagin, J. R. (2001). *The first R: How children learn race and racism*. Lanham, MD: Rowman and Littlefield.

Vandell, D. L., Belsky, J., Burchinal, M., Steinberg, L, Vandergrift, N., & NICHD Early Child Care Research Network. (2010). Do effects of early child care extend to age 15 years? Results from the NICHD study of early child care and youth development. *Child Development, 81*(3), 737–756.

Vandell, D. L., & Su, H.-C. (1999). Child care and school-age children. *Young Children, 54*(6), 62–71.

Vanderslice, V. J. (1984). Empowerment: A definition of process. *Human Ecology Forum, 14*(1), 2–3.

Vander Zanden, J. W. (1995). *Sociology: The core* (3rd ed.). New York: McGraw-Hill.

Vaughn, S., Bos, C. S., & Schumm, J. S. (1997). *Teaching mainstreamed, diverse, and at-risk students in the general education classroom*. Boston: Allyn and Bacon.

Verdugo, R.R. (2008). *School safety: What works*. Washington, DC: National Education Association.

Villani, S. D. (2001). Impact of media on children and adolescents: A 10-year review of the research. *Journal of the American Academy of Child and Adolescent Psychiatry, 40*(4), 392–401.

Vorrath, H. H., & Brendtro, L. K. (1985). *Positive peer culture* (2nd ed.). New York: Aldine.

Vygotsky, L. S. (1978). *Mind and society: The development of higher psychological processes* (M. Cole, V. John-Steiner, S. Scribner, & E. Souberman, Eds.). Cambridge, MA: Harvard University Press.

Wachs, T. D., & Bates, J. E. (2001). Temperament. In G. Bremmer & A. Fogel (Eds.), *Blackwell handbook of infant developmental psychology*. Madden, MA: Blackwell.

Walberg, R., & Mrozek, A. (2010). *Canada's top family-friendly cities*. Institute of Marriage and Family Canada (www.imfcanada.org).

Walker, L. J. (1991). Sex differences in moral development. In W. M. Kurtines & J. Gewirtz (Eds.), *Handbook of moral behavior and development* (Vol. 2). Hillsdale, NJ: Erlbaum.

Walker, L. J., Hennig, K. H., & Krettenauer, T. (2000). Parent and peer contexts for children's moral reasoning development. *Child Development, 71*(4), 1033–1048.

Walker, L. J., & Taylor, J. H. (1991). Family interaction and the development of moral reasoning. *Child Development, 62*, 264–283.

Wall, J. A., Power, T. G., & Arbona, C. (1993). Susceptibility to antisocial peer pressure and its relation to acculturation in Mexican-American adolescents. *Journal of Adolescent Research, 8*, 403–418.

Wallerstein, J. S., Corbin, S. B., & Lewis, J. H. (1988). Children of divorce: A ten-year study. In E. M. Hetherington & J. D. Arasteh (Eds.), *Impact of divorce, single parenting and stepparenting on children*. Hillsdale, NJ: Erlbaum.

Wallerstein, J. S., & Kelly, J. B. (1996). *Surviving the breakup: How parents and children cope with divorce*. New York: Basic Books.

Walsh, F. (2006). *Strengthening family resilience* (2nd ed.). New York: Guilford.

Wang, J., & Wildman, L. (1995). The effects of family commitment in education on student achievement in seventh grade mathematics. *Education, 115*, 317–319.

Wang, M. C. (2000). Preface. In R. D. Taylor & M. C. Wang (Eds.), *Resilience across contexts: Family, work, culture, and community*. Mahwah, NJ: Erlbaum.

Warren, R. (1988). The community in America. In R. L. Warren & L. Lyon (Eds.), *New perspectives on the American community*. Belmont, CA: Wadsworth.

Warren, R. (2005). Parental mediation of children's television viewing in low-income families. *Journal of Communication, 55*(4), 847–863.

Wartella, E. A., & Jennings, N. (2000). Children and computers: New technology—old concerns. *The Future of Children, 10*(2), 31–43.

Waters, E., Posada, G., Crowell, J., & Kengling, L. (1993). Is attachment theory ready to contribute to our understanding of disruptive behavior problems? *Development and Psychopathology, 5*, 215–224.

Watkins, S. C. (2005). *Hip-hop matters: Politics, pop culture and the struggle for the soul of a movement*. Boston: Beacon Press.

Watt, H. M. (2008). Gender and occupational outcomes: An introduction. In H. M. Watt & J. S. Eccles (Eds.), *Gender and occupational outcomes: Longitudinal assessment of individual, social, and cultural influences*. Washington, DC: American Psychological Association.

Wayne, A. J., & Youngs, P. (2003). Teacher characteristics and student achievement gains: A review. *Review of Educational Research, 73*(1), 89–122.

Weber, M. (1930). *The Protestant ethic and the spirit of capitalism*. London: Allen.

Wechsler, H., McKenna, M. L., Lee, S. M., & Dietz, W. H. (December 2004). The role of schools in preventing childhood obesity. *The State Education Standard, 5*, 4–12.

Wells, G. (2001). *Action, talk, and text: Learning and teaching through inquiry*. New York: Teachers College Press.

Wen-Jui, H., Leventhal, T., & Linver, M. R. (2004). The Home Observation for Measurement of the Environment (HOME) in middle childhood: A study of three large-scale data sets. *Parenting, 4*(2–3), 189–210.

Werner, E. E. (1993). Risk, resilience, and recovery: Perspectives from Kauai longitudinal study. *Development and Psychopathology, 5*, 503–515.

Werner, E. E., & Smith, R. S. (1992). *Overcoming the odds: High risk children from birth to adulthood*. Ithaca, NY: Cornell University Press.

West, M. M. (1988). Parental values and behavior in the outer Fiji Islands. In R. A. Levine, P. M. Miller, & M. M. West (Eds.), *Parental behavior in diverse societies*. San Francisco: Jossey-Bass.

White, B. L. (1971, October). *Fundamental early environmental influences on the development of competence*. Paper presented at Third Western Symposium on Learning: Cognitive Learning, Western Washington State College, Bellingham.

White, B. L. (1995). *The new first three years of life*. New York: Simon & Schuster.

White, B. L., & Watts, J. C. (1973). *Experience and environment: Major influences on the development of the young child* (Vol. 1). Englewood Cliffs, NJ: Prentice-Hall.

White, L. (1960). Symbol, the basis of language and culture. In W. Goldschmidt (Ed.), *Exploring the ways of mankind*. New York: Holt, Rinehart & Winston.

White, R. W. (1959). Motivation reconsidered: The concept of competence. *Psychology Review, 66*, 297–333.

White, S., & Tharp, R. G. (1988, April). *Questioning and wait-time: A cross-cultural analysis*. Paper presented at the annual meeting of the American Educational Research Association, New Orleans.

Whitebook, M., Howes, C., & Phillips, D. (1989). *Who cares? Child care teachers and the quality of care in America: Final report, National Child Care Staffing Study*. Oakland, CA: Child Care Employee Project.

Whitehurst, G. J., & Lonigan, C. J. (1998). Child development and emergent literacy. *Child Development, 69*, 848–872.

Whiting, B. B., & Edwards, C. P. (1988). *Children of different worlds: The formation of social behavior*. Cambridge, MA: Harvard University Press.

Whiting, B. B., & Whiting, J. W. M. (1973). Altruistic and egoistic behavior in six cultures. In L. Nader & T. W. Maretski (Eds.), *Cultural illness and health: Essays in human adaptation*. Washington, DC: American Anthropological Association.

Whiting, B. B., & Whiting, J. W. M. (1975). *Children of six cultures: A psychoanalysis*. Cambridge, MA: Harvard University Press.

Whitmire, R. (2010). *Why boys fail: Saving our sons from an educational system that's leaving them behind*. New York: AMACOM.

Wiesner, D. (2001). *The three pigs*. Boston: Clarion/Houghton Mifflin.

Wigfield, A., & Eccles, J. S. (2002). The development of competence beliefs and values from childhood through adolescence. In A. Wigfield & J. S. Eccles (Eds.), *Development of achievement motivation*. San Diego, CA: Academic Press.

Wigfield, A., Eccles, J. S., Schiefele, U., Rosser, R. W., & Davis-Kean, P. (2006). Development of achievement motivation. In W. Damon & R. M. Lerner (Eds.), *Handbook of child psychology* (6th ed., Vol. 3). Hoboken, NJ: Wiley.

Williams, G. (1982). *The rabbit's wedding*. New York: HarperCollins.

Williams, R. M. (1960). Generic American values. In W. Goldschmidt (Ed.), *Exploring the ways of mankind*. New York: Holt, Rinehart & Winston.

Wilson, B. J., & Weiss, A. J. (1993). The effects of sibling coviewing on preschoolers' reactions to a suspenseful movie scene. *Communication Research, 20*, 214–248.

Wilson, S., & Mishra, R. (1999, April 28). In high school, groups provide identity. *Washington Post*, p. A1.

Winsler, A., & Wallace, G. L. (2002). Behavior problems and social skills in preschool children: Parent–teacher agreement and relations with classroom observations. *Early Education and Development, 13*, 41–58.

Wiseman, R. (2009). *Queen bees and wannabes: Helping your daughter survive cliques, gossip, boyfriends, and the new realities of girl world.* New York: Three Rivers Press.

Woititz, J. G. (1990). *Adult children of alcoholics: Common characteristics* (expanded ed.). Hollywood, FL: Heath Communications.

Wolak, J., Mitchell, K. J., & Finkelhor, D. (2003). Escaping or connecting? Characteristics of youth who form close online relationships. *Journal of Adolescence, 26*(1), 105–119.

Wolak, J., Mitchell, K. J., & Finkelhor, D. (2007). Unwanted and wanted exposure to online pornography in a national sample of youth internet users. *Pediatrics, 119*(2), 247–257.

Wolf, N. (1991). *The beauty myth: How images of beauty are used against women.* New York: Anchor.

Wolfenstein, M. (1953). Trends in infant care. *American Journal of Orthopsychiatry, 23*, 120–130.

Women Employed. http://www.womenemployed.org.

Woodward, K. (1975). The parent gap. *Newsweek*, 86(12), 48–56.

Wrigley, J. (1995). *Other people's children.* New York: Basic Books.

Yau, J., & Smetana, J. G. (2003). Conceptions of moral, social-conventional, and personal events among Chinese preschoolers in Hong Kong. *Child Development, 74*(3), 647–658.

Yogman, M. W., & Brazelton, T. B. (1986). The family: Stressed yet protected. In M. W. Yogman & T. B. Brazelton (Eds.), *In support of families.* Cambridge, MA: Harvard University Press.

York, S. (1991). *Roots and wings: Affirming culture in early childhood programs.* St. Paul, MN: Toys 'n' Things Press

Young, E. (1992). *Seven blind mice.* New York: Putnam.

Young, T. W., & Shorr, D. N. (1986). Factors affecting locus of control in school children. *Genetic, Social, and General Psychology Monographs, 112*(4).

Youniss, J., & Volpe, J. (1978). A relational analysis of children's friendship. In W. Damon (Ed.), *Social cognition.* San Francisco: Jossey-Bass.

Zahn-Waxler, C., & Radke-Yarrow, M. (1990). The origin of empathetic concern. *Motivation and Emotion, 14*, 107–130.

Zahn-Waxler, C., Radke-Yarrow, M., & King, R. A. (1979). Child-rearing and children's prosocial initiations toward victims of distress. *Child Development, 50*, 319–330.

Zahn-Waxler, C., Radke-Yarrow, M., Wagner, E., & Chapman, M. (1992). Development of concern for others. *Developmental Psychology, 28*, 126–136.

Zahn-Waxler, C., Robinson, J., & Emde, R. (1992). The development of empathy in twins. *Developmental Psychology, 28*, 1038–1047.

Zajonc, R. B. (1976). Family configuration and intelligence. *Science, 912*, 227–236.

Zarbatany, L., Hartmann, D. P., & Rankin, D. B. (1990). The psychological functions of preadolescent peer activities. *Child Development, 61*, 1067–1080.

Zaslow, M., Tout, K., Smith, S., & Moore, K. (1998). Implications of the 1996 welfare legislation for children: A research perspective. *Social Policy Report, 12*(3), 1–34.

Zelli, A., Dodge, K., Lochman, J., Laird, R., & the Conduct Problems Prevention Research Group. (1999). The distinction between beliefs legitimizing aggression and deviant processing of social cues: Testing measurement validity and the hypothesis that biased processing mediates the effects of beliefs on aggression. *Journal of Personality and Social Psychology, 77*, 150–166.

Zhou, Q., Eisenberg, N., Losoya, S. H., Fabes, R. A., Reiser, M., Guthrie, I. K., Murphy, B.C., Cumberland, A. J., & Shepard, S. A. (2002). The relations of parental warmth and positive expressiveness to children's empathy-related responding and social functioning: A longitudinal study. *Child Development, 73*, 893–915.

Zimmerman, B. J. (2000). Self-efficacy: An essential motive to learn. *Contemporary Educational Psychology, 23*, 82–91.

Zimmerman, F. J., & Christakes, D. A. (2005). Children's television viewing and cognitive outcomes: A longitudinal analysis of national data. *Archives of Pediatrics and Adolescent Medicine, 159*, 619–625.

Zuckerman, B., & Khandekar, A. (2010). Reach out and read: Evidence based approach to promoting early child development. *Current Opinion in Pediatrics, 22*(4), 539–544.

Zussman, J. U. (1980). Situational determinants of parental behavior: Effects of competing cognitive activity. *Child Development, 51*, 792–800.

Index

Italic page numbers indicate material in tables or figures.

Q

R

National Association for The Education of Young Children (NAEYC) Professional Preparation Standards

The NAEYC Standards for Initial and Advanced Early Childhood Professional Preparation Programs provide the basis for accreditation from the NAEYC Commission on Early Childhood Associate Degree Accreditation or NAEYC recognition of baccalaureate and graduate programs as part of National Council for Accreditation of Teacher Education (NCATE) accreditation of schools, colleges, and departments of education. These core standards are used across both NCATE and NAEYC accreditation systems and across associate, baccalaureate, and graduate degree levels. The Initial Standards are used in programs preparing candidates for first-time early childhood licensure and for positions in early learning settings that do not currently require licensure. Note that Initial programs may be offered at both undergraduate and graduate levels. *Child, Family, School, Community* has been used as a text at two- and four-year institutions, as well as at graduate levels by varying the scope and depth of knowledge required and implementing assignments of varying degrees of difficulty. The Advanced Standards are used in graduate programs preparing candidates for leadership roles in the field as accomplished teachers, administrators, state early childhood specialists, child and family advocates, professional development specialists, teacher educators, and researchers.

Standard	Explanation	Related Concepts
1. Promoting Child Development and Learning	Candidates prepared in early childhood degree programs are grounded in a child development knowledge base. They use their understanding of young children's characteristics and needs, and of multiple interacting influences on children's development and learning, to create environments that are healthy, respectful, supportive, and challenging for each child.	Chapters 1, 2, 5, 6, 7, 8, 9
2. Building Family and Community Relationships	Candidates prepared in early childhood degree programs understand that successful early childhood education depends upon partnerships with children's families and communities. They know about, understand, and value the importance and complex characteristics of children's families and communities. They use this understanding to create respectful, reciprocal relationships that support and empower families, and to involve all families in their children's development and learning.	Chapters 3, 4, 5, 10
3. Observing, Documenting, and Assessing to Support Children and Families	Candidates prepared in early childhood degree programs understand that child observation, documentation, and other forms of assessment are central to the practice of all early childhood professionals. They know about and understand the goals, benefits, and uses of assessment. They know about and use systematic observations, documentation, and other effective assessment strategies in a responsible way, in partnership with families and other professionals, to positively influence the development of every child.	Chapters 5, 7
4. Using Developmentally Effective Approaches	Candidates prepared in early childhood degree programs understand that teaching and learning with young children is a complex enterprise, and its details vary depending on children's ages, characteristics, and the settings within which teaching and learning occur. They understand and use positive relationships and supportive interactions as the foundation for their work with young children and families. Candidates know, understand, and use a wide array of developmentally appropriate approaches, instructional strategies, and tools to connect with children and families and positively influence each child's development and learning.	Chapters 1, 2, 5, 7
5. Using Content Knowledge to Provide Meaningful Curriculum	Candidates prepared in early childhood degree programs use their knowledge of academic disciplines to design, implement, and evaluate experiences that promote positive development and learning for each and every young child. Candidates understand the importance of developmental domains and academic (or content) disciplines in early childhood curriculum. They know the essential concepts, inquiry tools, and structure of content areas, including academic subjects, and can identify resources to deepen their understanding. Candidates use their own knowledge and other resources to design, implement, and evaluate meaningful, challenging curriculum that promotes comprehensive developmental and learning outcomes for every young child.	Chapters 5, 7, 11, 12

Standard	Explanation	Related Concepts
6. Becoming a Professional	Candidates prepared in early childhood degree programs identify and conduct themselves as members of the early childhood profession. They know and use ethical guidelines and other professional standards related to early childhood practice. They are continuous, collaborative learners who demonstrate knowledgeable, reflective and critical perspectives on their work, making informed decisions that integrate knowledge from a variety of sources. They are informed advocates for sound educational practices and policies.	Chapters 5, 6, 7
7. Early Childhood Field Experiences	Field experiences and clinical practice are planned and sequenced so that candidates develop the knowledge, skills, and professional dispositions necessary to promote the development and learning of young children across the entire developmental period of early childhood in at least two of the three early childhood age groups (birth–age 3, 3 through 5, 5 through 8 years) and in the variety of settings that offer early education (early school grades, child care centers and homes, Head Start programs).	Chapters 5, 6, 10

Source: NAEYC Professional Preparation Standards, copyright © 2010 by the National Association for the Education of Young Children.

ADVANCED STANDARDS SUMMARY

The Advanced NAEYC Standards require depth, breadth, and specialization that expand upon and exceed the expectations of Initial early childhood licensure programs. Assessments and scoring guides for Advanced Programs should be different from and expect more advanced work than Initial Programs.

Beyond a common core of courses and experiences, each candidate needs the opportunity to gain significant depth and specialization in theory, research, and professional competence in an area relevant to the candidate's current work and future goals.

Strong advanced programs also offer candidates intensive internships, field experiences, research opportunities, or other contexts in which to apply theoretical and research-based knowledge in a systematic, scholarly way and to develop advanced skills.

Whatever the specialization or professional focus, advanced programs include a well-designed and well-assessed capstone experiences that promote synthesis and reflection, such as a thesis or portfolio.

The features just described are appropriate and relevant for all advanced master's and doctoral programs in professional education, including those that prepare early childhood candidates. But some special characteristics of the early childhood field are also important standards:

1. **Early childhood as a strongly interdisciplinary, collaborative, and systems-oriented profession**
   Early childhood leaders need to integrate knowledge of all aspects of child development, content knowledge in academic disciplines, early intervention programs and other language therapy, occupational therapy, special education, bilingual education, family dynamics, mental health, and multiple other approaches for the comprehensive well-being of young children and their families.
2. **Highly dynamic, developmental, and policy-relevant nature of the early childhood field**
   Whether leadership is exerted in a classroom role, at the program or agency level, or in two- or four-year institutions, advanced program candidates and advanced program faculty need a strong future orientation. While articulating the profession's traditions and core values, advanced program candidates must also be taught how to analyze trends, how to critically assess the field's emerging knowledge base, and how to use a variety of tools to find professional resources that will enable them to stay at the forefront of their field as lifelong learners. Finally, the nature of the early childhood field requires that all professionals, whatever their specific role, share a commitment to and skill in advocacy for young children, families, and their profession.
3. **Diversity and focus in early childhood professional settings and roles**
   Early childhood professionals work in a much greater variety of settings and professional roles than many other education professionals. Public school programs from state-funded pre-K to third grade, community child care programs, Head Start, resource-and-referral agencies, specialized infant/toddler programs, inclusive early childhood programs, state agencies, nonprofit organizations serving children and families, community colleges, university teacher education programs, and many other settings are typical of the diversity of the early childhood world. Within those settings, professionals holding advanced degrees may be master teachers, program directors, trainers, faculty, early education specialists, advocates, agency administrators—or other professionals. The NAEYC standards require programs to identify one or more areas of focus and to document how program candidates achieve depth while also gaining a broad understanding of the complexities of the early childhood field.

National Association of Social Workers (NASW) Standards for Social Work Practice in Child Welfare

The child welfare system serves some of our nation's most vulnerable and troubled children and families. The goal of child welfare services is to provide an array of prevention and intervention services to children and families, particularly children who have been or are at risk of abuse or neglect; children with special medical or mental health needs; delinquent children; and children who do not have adult caregivers. The child welfare system is designed to support families and to protect children from harm.

Historically, social workers have played a key role in the child welfare system by protecting children at risk and supporting families in need. The National Association of Social Workers (NASW) led the field in the development of best practices for social workers in child welfare. The NASW Standards for Social Work Practice in Child Welfare reflect and promote sound social work practice. They have been revised and expanded beyond child protection to reflect changing practices and policies for social work practice in a variety of child welfare settings. These standards can be regarded as a basic tool for social work practice in child welfare that might include family preservation and support, out-of-home care, family foster care, kinship care, residential group homes, adoption, independent living, child day care, adolescent pregnancy and parenting services, hospitals, and nontraditional settings such as faith-based facilities.

Child, Family, School, Community provides theories and applications to understand how the contexts in which a child develops affect socialization outcomes. It gives students who may want to enter the field of social work a research-oriented knowledge base, critical thinking skills, and opportunities to experience real life settings.

Standard	Explanation	Related Concepts
1. **Ethics and Values**	The NASW Code of Ethics establishes the ethical responsibilities of all social workers with respect to themselves, clients, colleagues, employees and employing organizations, the social work profession, and society. Acceptance of these responsibilities guides and fosters competent social work practice in all child welfare tasks and activities. As an integral component of the child welfare system, social workers have a responsibility to know and comply with local, state, and federal legislation, regulations, and policies. Legal and regulatory guidelines as well as administrative practices may conflict with the best interests of the child and/or family. In the event that conflicts arise, social workers are directed to the NASW Code of Ethics (1999) as a tool in their decision making.	Chapters 1, 3, 10, 12
2. **Qualifications**	All social workers practicing in child welfare should hold a BSW or MSW degree from an accredited school of social work.	Chapters 1–12
3. **Continuing Education**	Continuing education is an essential activity for ensuring quality social work services for consumers. By consistent participation in educational opportunities beyond the basic, entry-level professional degree, social workers empower children and their families in both urban and rural settings. System changes can be implemented by making changes in direct practice as well as by making changes in laws or policies.	Chapters 3, 4
4. **Advocacy**	The professional social worker in child welfare practice is expected to advocate for resources and system reforms that will improve services for children and their families, as appropriate, within the context of their job. Emphasis on system reforms should seek to make child welfare services more responsive to children and their families, communities, and diverse cultures. Such advocacy should emphasize the strengths and assets approach.	Chapters 2, 3, 10
5. **Knowledge Requirements**	Social workers in child welfare shall possess knowledge related to child development, parenting issues, family dynamics, and the community/local systems where the client resides.	Chapters 2, 3, 4, 5, 10

Standard	Explanation	Related Concepts
6. **Confidentiality of Client Information**	Social workers in child welfare shall maintain the appropriate safeguards for the privacy and confidentiality of client information.	Chapters 11, 12
7. **Supervision**	Social workers who act as supervisors should ensure quality service delivery, provide for the in-service training needs of their staff, and assess the needs of the persons served. They must also possess knowledge of the political, legislative, and economic factors that affect service delivery in their community and be able to mentor staff in learning to negotiate those systems.	Chapter 10
8. **Cultural Competence**	Social workers in child welfare should use social work methods and skills that include knowledge of the role of culture, race, and ethnicity in the helping process. Supervisors should develop training for social workers on culturally competent practice. When providing services, social workers may need to explore the role of spirituality, religion, sexual orientation, and age as factors affecting outcomes.	Chapters 1, 2, 3, 4
9. **Collaboration**	There is a collaborative relationship between child welfare professionals and other professionals whose mission includes child protection. The social worker should understand the roles and goals of other professionals in the field and work toward enhanced collaboration and understanding.	Chapters 5, 6, 7
10. **Focus on Prevention**	Social workers recognize families' and individuals' growth potential and ability to improve their functioning to protect and nurture their children. Social workers also have knowledge of personal, familial, and social factors that decrease or tax a family's resources to care for its members.	Chapters 1, 3, 4, 8
11. **Engagement**	Engagement requires social workers in child welfare to be clear about the reasons for the family intervention, whether it is an investigation, or services following an investigation. The social worker shall seek to understand and incorporate, as appropriate, the family's perspective and definition of the problem and potential solutions.	Chapters 3, 4, 10
12. **Comprehensive Service Plan**	The goal of the service plan is to ensure that the child's needs for safety and nurturance are met, with particular attention to child developmental stages and special needs. Implementation of the service plan needs to be flexible and adapted to the changing circumstances of the family, their response to the interventions, and the social worker's increased understanding of the family, the child welfare system, and the larger community. Technology should be used to facilitate the casework process.	Chapters 4, 7
13. **Child Protection**	The social worker must be able to assess imminent risk and ensure that arrangements are made to protect the child in accordance with state and federal laws, agency policies, and administrative directives governing child protection. The assessment must take into account the child's best interests.	Chapters 4, 5, 10
14. **Out-of-Home Care**	When a child's safety is at risk, the social worker in child welfare is required to report and document the risk to protective authorities. If the social worker's role involves child protection, the worker is required to use the legal process available to protect the child and to document evidence and concerns to guide the child protective intervention.	Chapters 4, 5, 10
15. **Permanency**	Permanence for children is achieved within a family relationship that offers safe, stable, and committed parenting, unconditional love and lifelong support, and legal family membership status. Permanence can be the result of preservation of the family, reunification with the birth family, or legal guardianship or adoption by kin or other caring and committed adults.	Chapters 4, 10

Source: National Association of Social Workers (2005). NASW standards for social work practice in child welfare (http://www.socialworkers.org).

The Bioecological Model of Human Development

Please use this bookmark as a study aid to continually visualize the whole picture of human development while you learn how its multiple contexts interact and influence one another. Also use it as a lens to expand your views of human behavior in your everyday experiences. And finally, use it as a reminder that "it takes a village to raise a child."

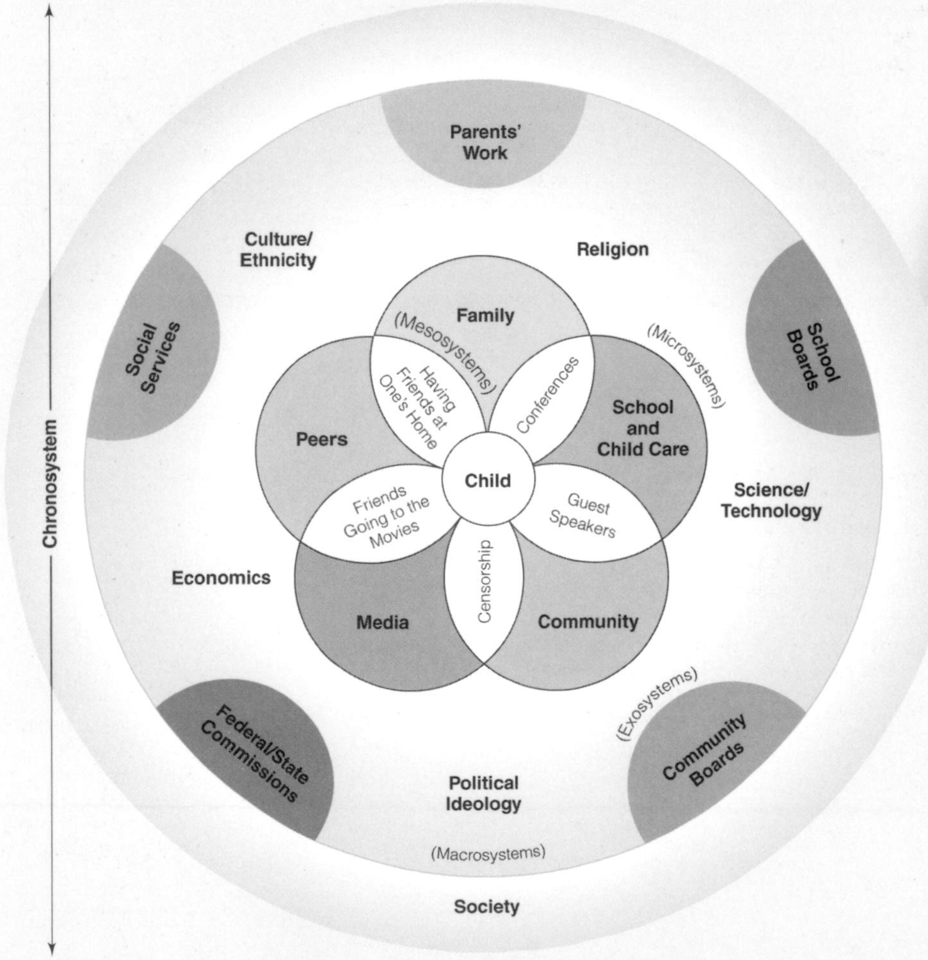

ISBN-13: 978-1-111-83096-0
ISBN-10: 1-111-83096-7

WADSWORTH
CENGAGE Learning™

To learn more about Wadsworth, visit **www.cengage.com/wadsworth**

Purchase any of our products at your local college store or at our preferred online store **www.cengagebrain.com**